MW00770859

BORN
IN THE
USA

BORN
IN THE
USA

The Story of Immigration
AND BELONGING

LAWRENCE GOLDSTONE
art by JAMES OTIS SMITH

First Second

NEW YORK

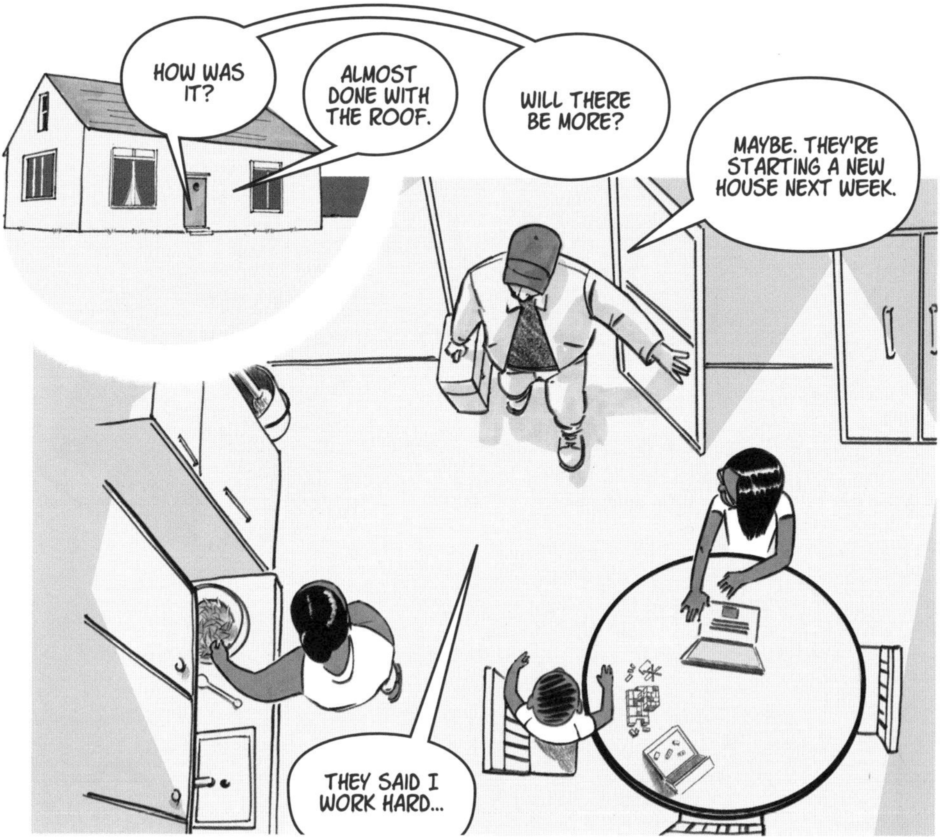
HOW WAS IT?
ALMOST DONE WITH THE ROOF.
WILL THERE BE MORE?
MAYBE. THEY'RE STARTING A NEW HOUSE NEXT WEEK.
THEY SAID I WORK HARD...

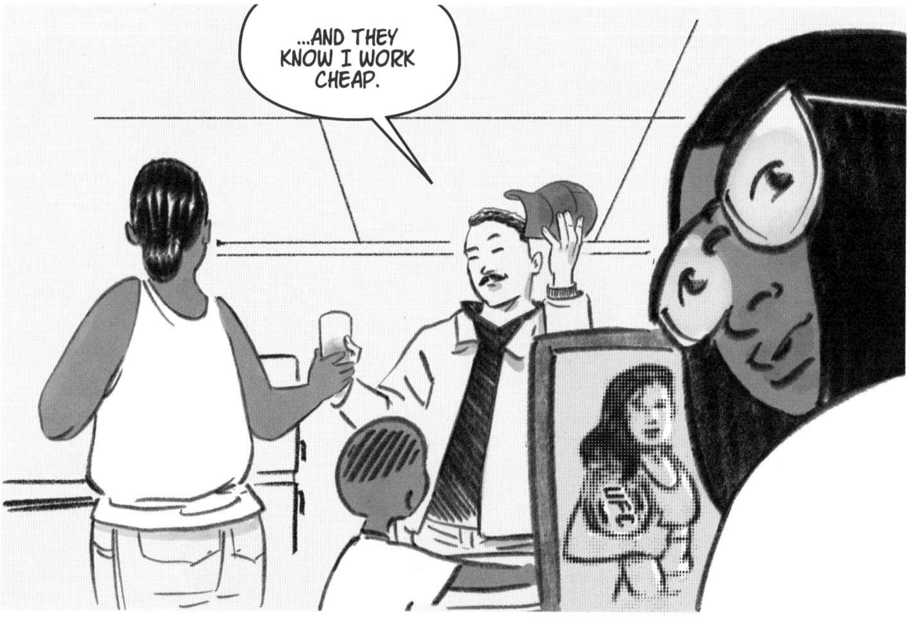
...AND THEY KNOW I WORK CHEAP.
UFC

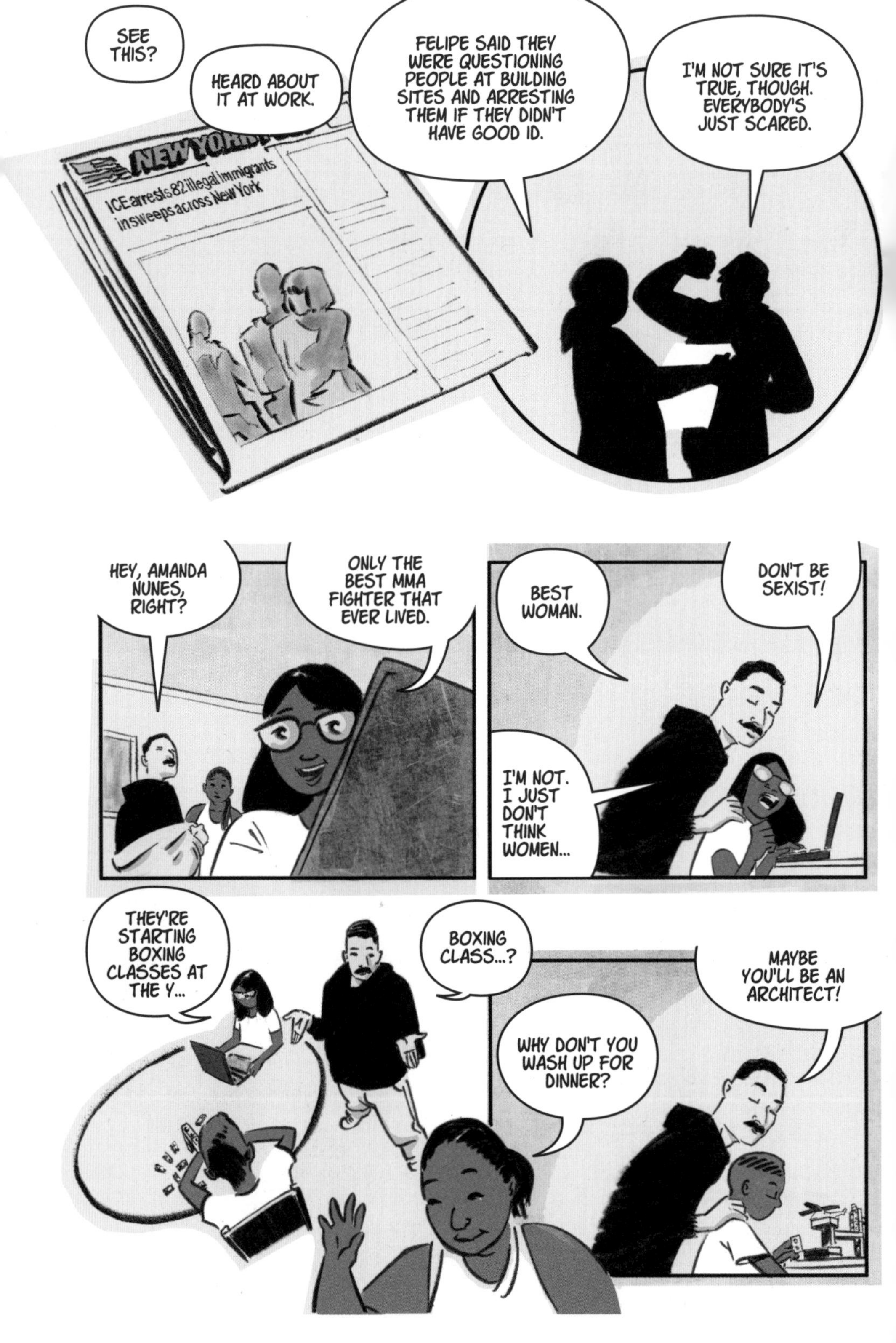
SEE THIS?
HEARD ABOUT IT AT WORK.
NEW YORK
ICE arrests 82 illegal immigrants in sweeps across New York
FELIPE SAID THEY WERE QUESTIONING PEOPLE AT BUILDING SITES AND ARRESTING THEM IF THEY DIDN'T HAVE GOOD ID.
I'M NOT SURE IT'S TRUE, THOUGH. EVERYBODY'S JUST SCARED.
HEY, AMANDA NUNES, RIGHT?
ONLY THE BEST MMA FIGHTER THAT EVER LIVED.
BEST WOMAN.
DON'T BE SEXIST!
I'M NOT. I JUST DON'T THINK WOMEN...
THEY'RE STARTING BOXING CLASSES AT THE Y...
BOXING CLASS...?
MAYBE YOU'LL BE AN ARCHITECT!
WHY DON'T YOU WASH UP FOR DINNER?

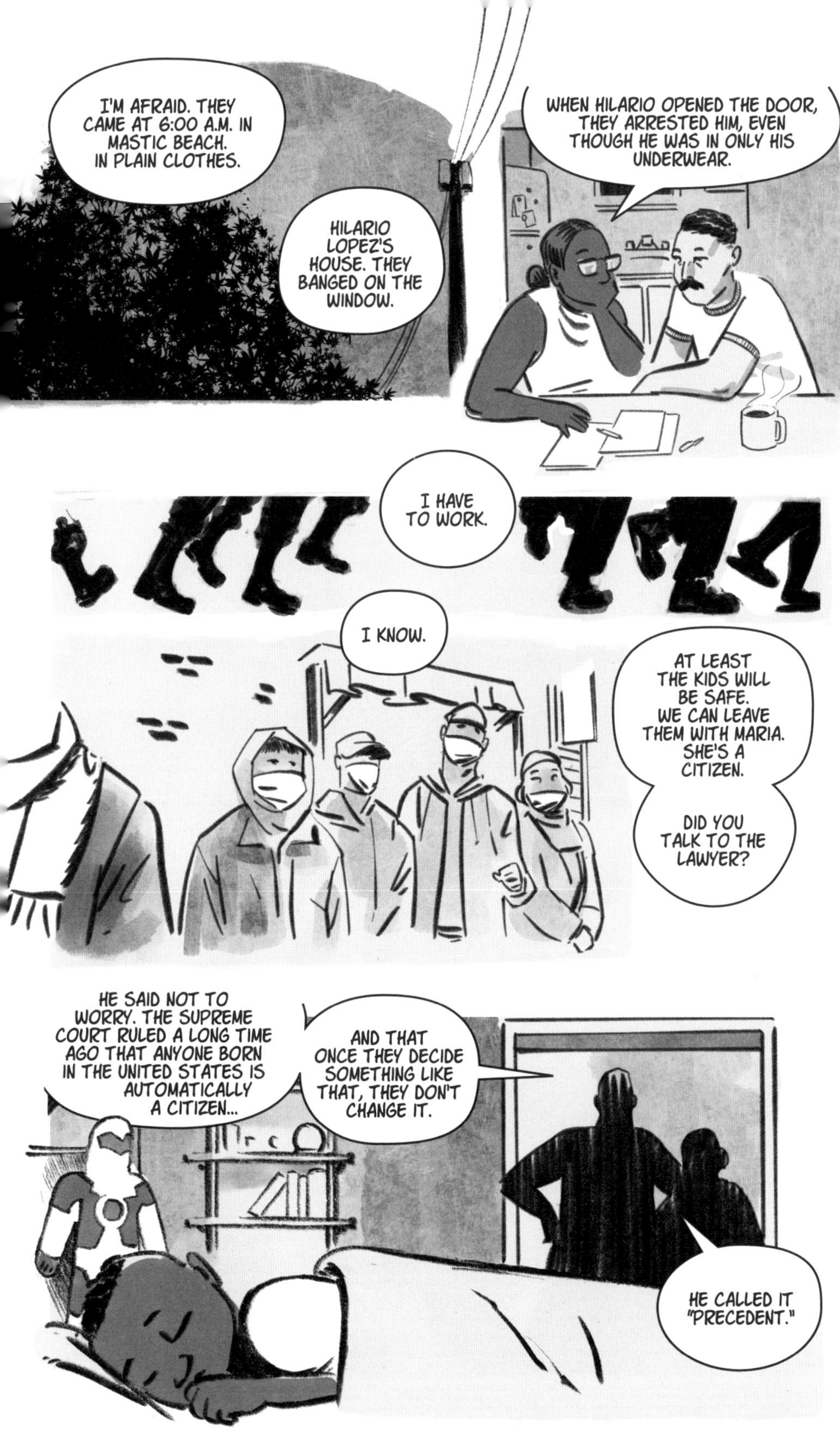
I'M AFRAID. THEY CAME AT 6:00 A.M. IN MASTIC BEACH. IN PLAIN CLOTHES.
HILARIO LOPEZ'S HOUSE. THEY BANGED ON THE WINDOW.
WHEN HILARIO OPENED THE DOOR, THEY ARRESTED HIM, EVEN THOUGH HE WAS IN ONLY HIS UNDERWEAR.
I HAVE TO WORK.
I KNOW.
AT LEAST THE KIDS WILL BE SAFE. WE CAN LEAVE THEM WITH MARIA. SHE'S A CITIZEN.
DID YOU TALK TO THE LAWYER?
HE SAID NOT TO WORRY. THE SUPREME COURT RULED A LONG TIME AGO THAT ANYONE BORN IN THE UNITED STATES IS AUTOMATICALLY A CITIZEN...
AND THAT ONCE THEY DECIDE SOMETHING LIKE THAT, THEY DON'T CHANGE IT.
HE CALLED IT "PRECEDENT."

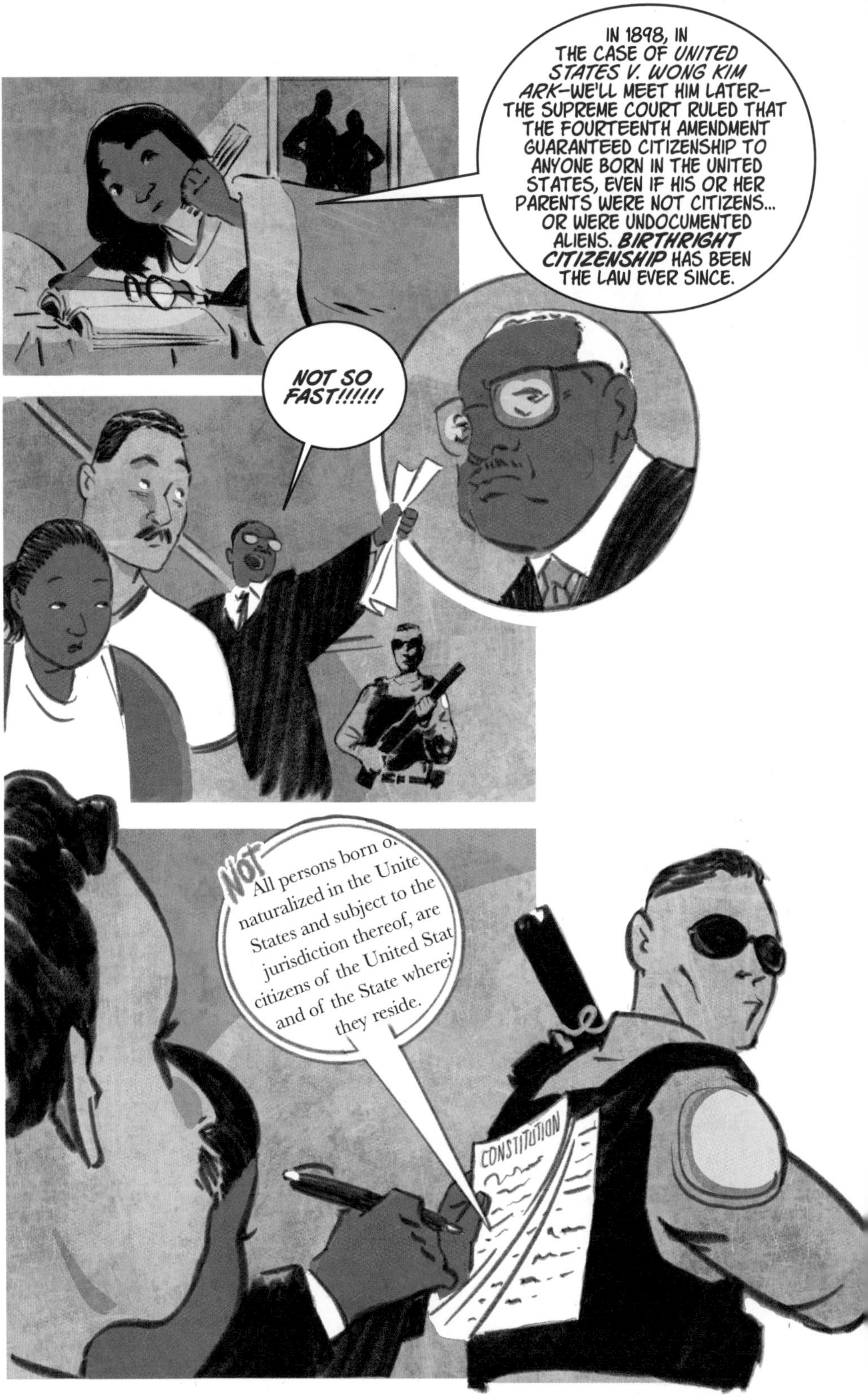
IN 1898, IN THE CASE OF *UNITED STATES V. WONG KIM ARK*—WE'LL MEET HIM LATER—THE SUPREME COURT RULED THAT THE FOURTEENTH AMENDMENT GUARANTEED CITIZENSHIP TO ANYONE BORN IN THE UNITED STATES, EVEN IF HIS OR HER PARENTS WERE NOT CITIZENS... OR WERE UNDOCUMENTED ALIENS. ***BIRTHRIGHT CITIZENSHIP*** HAS BEEN THE LAW EVER SINCE.
NOT SO FAST!!!!!!
NOT
All persons born or naturalized in the United States and subject to the jurisdiction thereof, are citizens of the United States and of the State wherein they reside.
CONSTITUTION

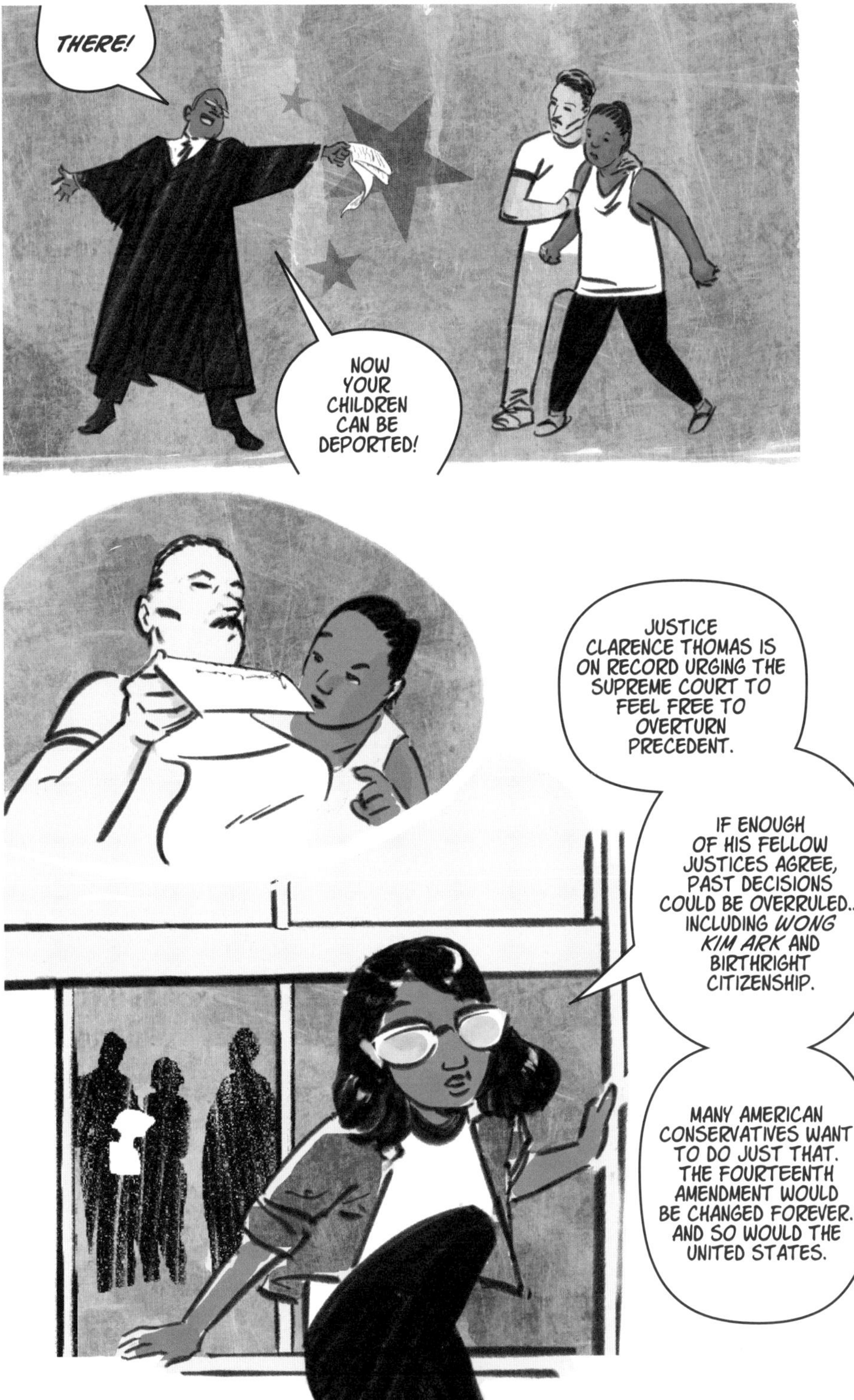
THERE!
NOW YOUR CHILDREN CAN BE DEPORTED!
JUSTICE CLARENCE THOMAS IS ON RECORD URGING THE SUPREME COURT TO FEEL FREE TO OVERTURN PRECEDENT.
IF ENOUGH OF HIS FELLOW JUSTICES AGREE, PAST DECISIONS COULD BE OVERRULED... INCLUDING *WONG KIM ARK* AND BIRTHRIGHT CITIZENSHIP.
MANY AMERICAN CONSERVATIVES WANT TO DO JUST THAT. THE FOURTEENTH AMENDMENT WOULD BE CHANGED FOREVER. AND SO WOULD THE UNITED STATES.

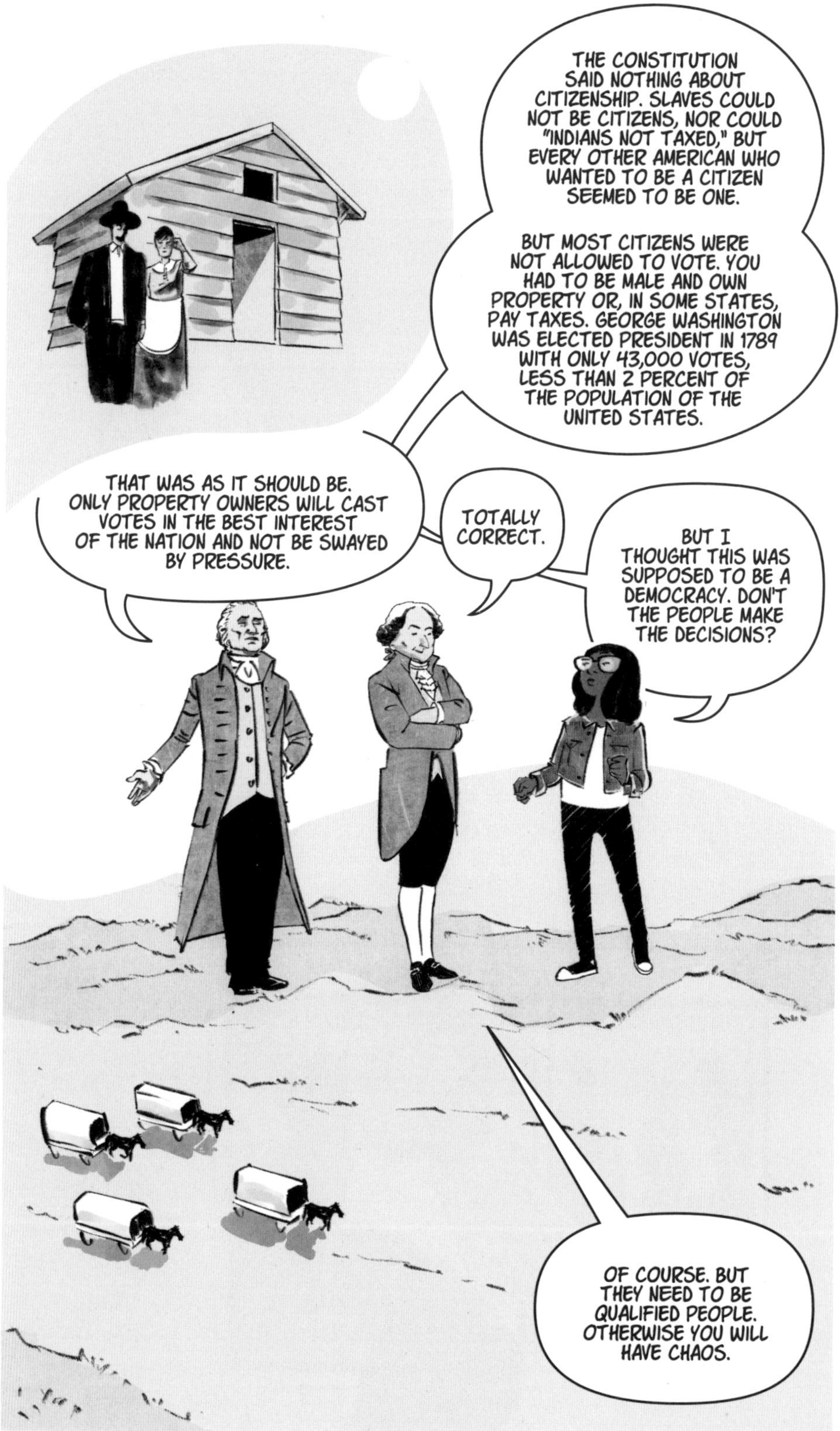
THE CONSTITUTION SAID NOTHING ABOUT CITIZENSHIP. SLAVES COULD NOT BE CITIZENS, NOR COULD "INDIANS NOT TAXED," BUT EVERY OTHER AMERICAN WHO WANTED TO BE A CITIZEN SEEMED TO BE ONE.
BUT MOST CITIZENS WERE NOT ALLOWED TO VOTE. YOU HAD TO BE MALE AND OWN PROPERTY OR, IN SOME STATES, PAY TAXES. GEORGE WASHINGTON WAS ELECTED PRESIDENT IN 1789 WITH ONLY 43,000 VOTES, LESS THAN 2 PERCENT OF THE POPULATION OF THE UNITED STATES.
THAT WAS AS IT SHOULD BE. ONLY PROPERTY OWNERS WILL CAST VOTES IN THE BEST INTEREST OF THE NATION AND NOT BE SWAYED BY PRESSURE.
TOTALLY CORRECT.
BUT I THOUGHT THIS WAS SUPPOSED TO BE A DEMOCRACY. DON'T THE PEOPLE MAKE THE DECISIONS?
OF COURSE. BUT THEY NEED TO BE QUALIFIED PEOPLE. OTHERWISE YOU WILL HAVE CHAOS.

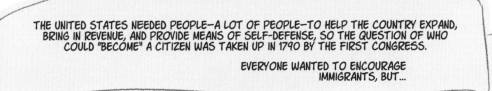

THE UNITED STATES NEEDED PEOPLE—A LOT OF PEOPLE—TO HELP THE COUNTRY EXPAND, BRING IN REVENUE, AND PROVIDE MEANS OF SELF-DEFENSE, SO THE QUESTION OF WHO COULD "BECOME" A CITIZEN WAS TAKEN UP IN 1790 BY THE FIRST CONGRESS.

EVERYONE WANTED TO ENCOURAGE IMMIGRANTS, BUT...

WHEN WE ARE CONSIDERING THE ADVANTAGES THAT MAY RESULT FROM AN EASY MODE OF NATURALIZATION—

—WE OUGHT ALSO TO CONSIDER THE CAUTION NECESSARY TO GUARD AGAINST ABUSES.

...THEY HAD TO BE THE RIGHT SORT OF IMMIGRANT.

Congressman James Madison, "Father of the Constitution."

I DO NOT WISH THAT ANY MAN SHOULD ACQUIRE THE PRIVILEGE, BUT WHO, IN FACT, IS A REAL ADDITION TO THE WEALTH OR STRENGTH OF THE UNITED STATES.

THEY ENDED UP OFFERING CITIZENSHIP ONLY TO ANY "FREE WHITE PERSON" OF "GOOD CHARACTER," WHO LIVED IN THE UNITED STATES FOR TWO YEARS STRAIGHT AND IN A SPECIFIC STATE FOR ONE YEAR.

We the WHITE People of the
insure domestic Tranquility, provide for the common defense and our Posterity, do ordain and establish this Constitution.
Article 1

NOT EVERYONE WAS PLEASED.

THE TRUTH OF THE MATTER IS THAT IT IS A VILE BILL, ILLIBERAL. VOID OF PHILANTHROPY AND NEEDED MENDING MUCH. WE PENNSYLVANIANS ACT AS IF WE BELIEVED THAT GOD MADE OF ONE BLOOD ALL FAMILIES OF THE EARTH.

Senator William Maclay, Pennsylvania

naturalization law residency of no less than 2 5 14 5

MACLAY'S MENDING NEVER HAPPENED.

A SERIES OF NEW LAWS CHANGED THE RESIDENCY REQUIREMENT, ENDING AT FIVE YEARS, WHERE IT REMAINS TODAY...

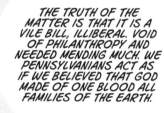

BUT THE OTHER MAIN PROVISIONS REMAINED UNCHANGED.

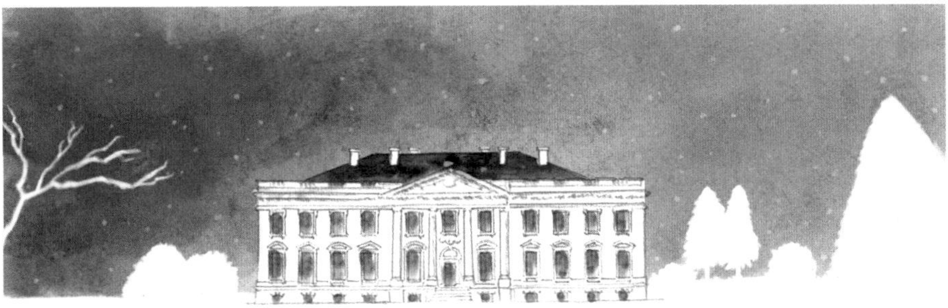

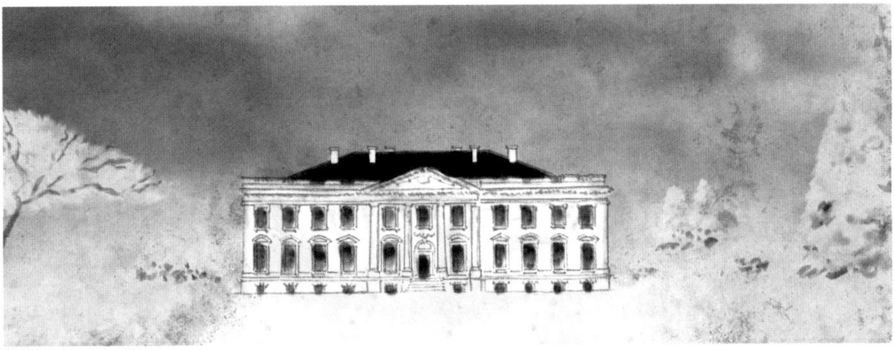

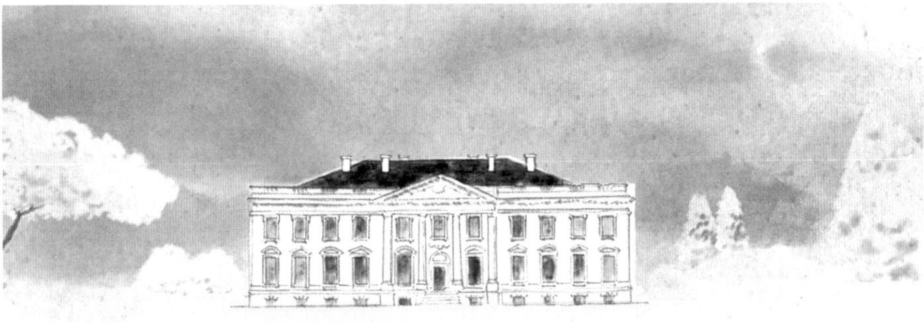

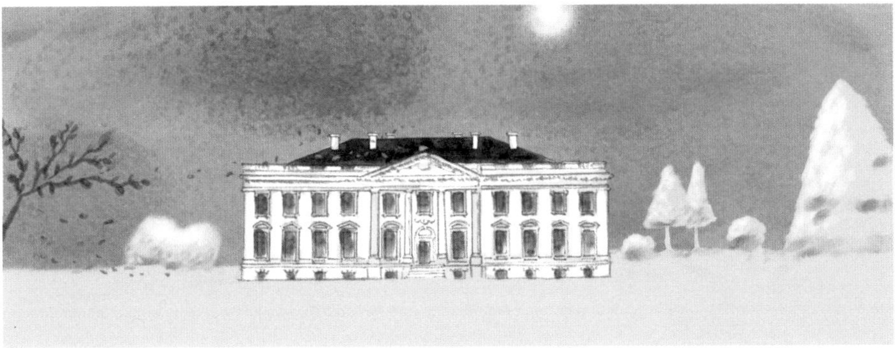

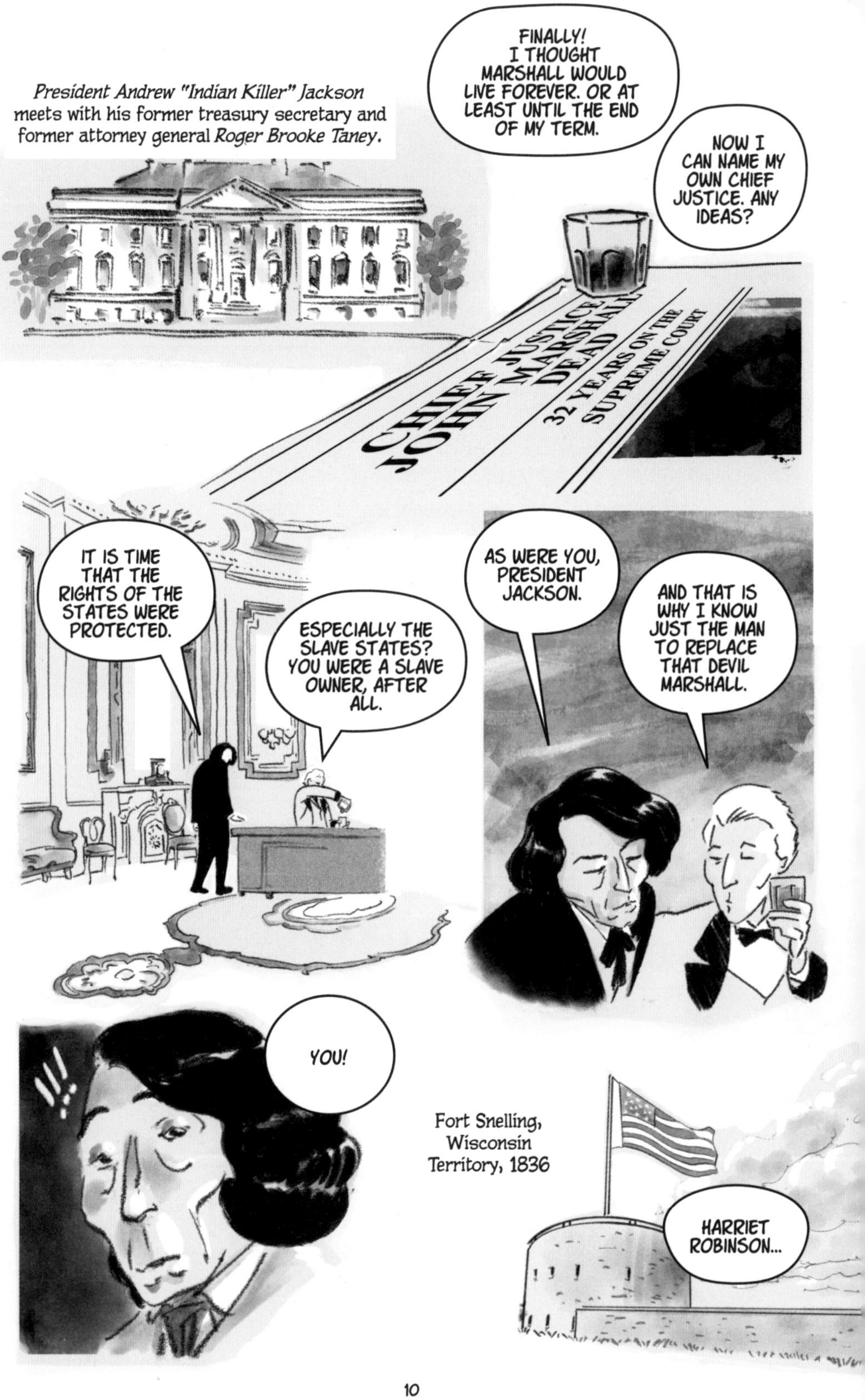
President Andrew "Indian Killer" Jackson meets with his former treasury secretary and former attorney general Roger Brooke Taney.
FINALLY! I THOUGHT MARSHALL WOULD LIVE FOREVER. OR AT LEAST UNTIL THE END OF MY TERM.
NOW I CAN NAME MY OWN CHIEF JUSTICE. ANY IDEAS?
CHIEF JUSTICE JOHN MARSHALL DEAD
32 YEARS ON THE SUPREME COURT
IT IS TIME THAT THE RIGHTS OF THE STATES WERE PROTECTED.
ESPECIALLY THE SLAVE STATES? YOU WERE A SLAVE OWNER, AFTER ALL.
AS WERE YOU, PRESIDENT JACKSON.
AND THAT IS WHY I KNOW JUST THE MAN TO REPLACE THAT DEVIL MARSHALL.
YOU!
Fort Snelling, Wisconsin Territory, 1836
HARRIET ROBINSON...

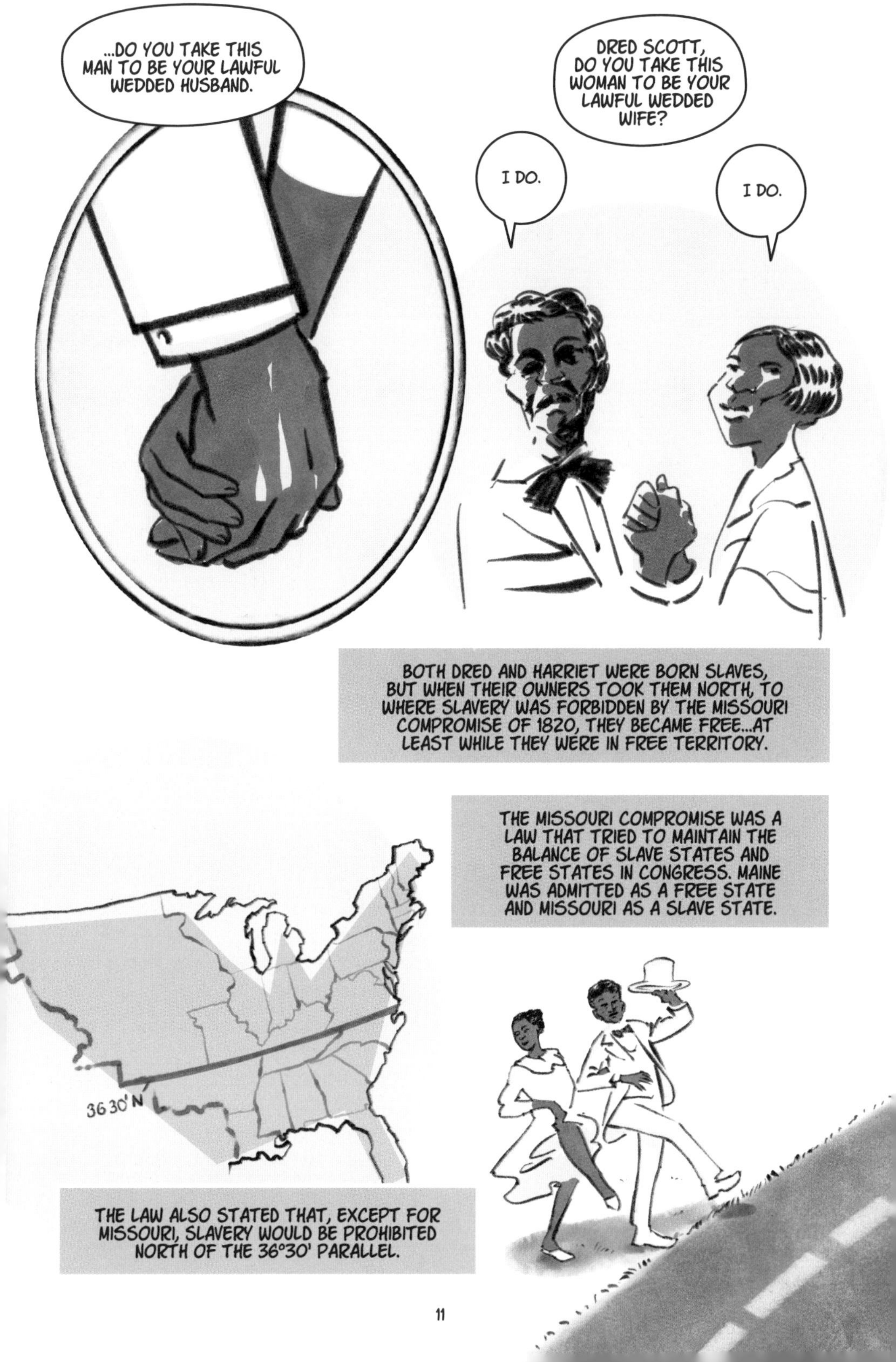
...DO YOU TAKE THIS MAN TO BE YOUR LAWFUL WEDDED HUSBAND.
DRED SCOTT, DO YOU TAKE THIS WOMAN TO BE YOUR LAWFUL WEDDED WIFE?
I DO.
I DO.
BOTH DRED AND HARRIET WERE BORN SLAVES, BUT WHEN THEIR OWNERS TOOK THEM NORTH, TO WHERE SLAVERY WAS FORBIDDEN BY THE MISSOURI COMPROMISE OF 1820, THEY BECAME FREE...AT LEAST WHILE THEY WERE IN FREE TERRITORY.
THE MISSOURI COMPROMISE WAS A LAW THAT TRIED TO MAINTAIN THE BALANCE OF SLAVE STATES AND FREE STATES IN CONGRESS. MAINE WAS ADMITTED AS A FREE STATE AND MISSOURI AS A SLAVE STATE.
36 30' N
THE LAW ALSO STATED THAT, EXCEPT FOR MISSOURI, SLAVERY WOULD BE PROHIBITED NORTH OF THE 36°30' PARALLEL.

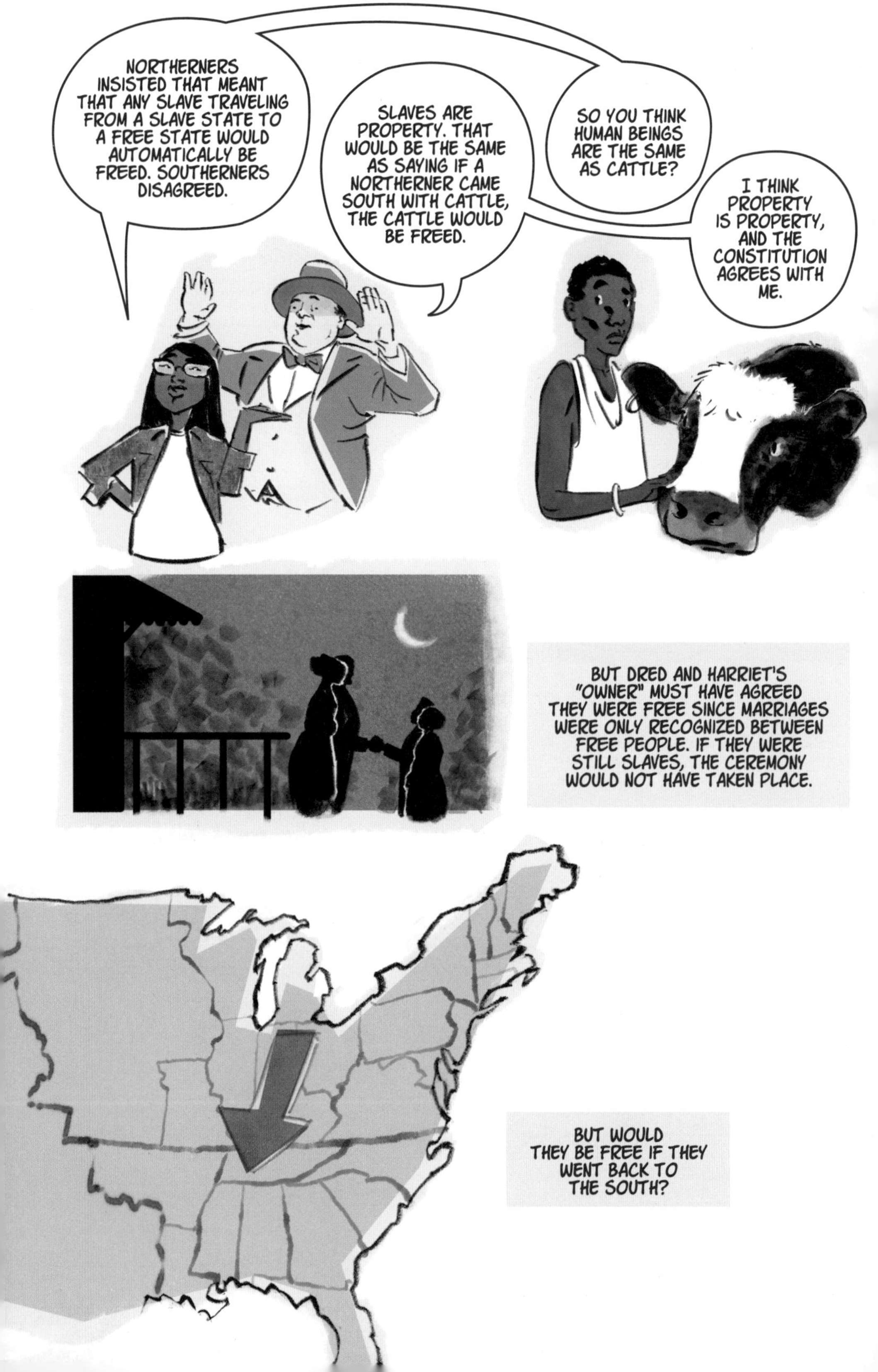
NORTHERNERS INSISTED THAT MEANT THAT ANY SLAVE TRAVELING FROM A SLAVE STATE TO A FREE STATE WOULD AUTOMATICALLY BE FREED. SOUTHERNERS DISAGREED.
SLAVES ARE PROPERTY. THAT WOULD BE THE SAME AS SAYING IF A NORTHERNER CAME SOUTH WITH CATTLE, THE CATTLE WOULD BE FREED.
SO YOU THINK HUMAN BEINGS ARE THE SAME AS CATTLE?
I THINK PROPERTY IS PROPERTY, AND THE CONSTITUTION AGREES WITH ME.
BUT DRED AND HARRIET'S "OWNER" MUST HAVE AGREED THEY WERE FREE SINCE MARRIAGES WERE ONLY RECOGNIZED BETWEEN FREE PEOPLE. IF THEY WERE STILL SLAVES, THE CEREMONY WOULD NOT HAVE TAKEN PLACE.
BUT WOULD THEY BE FREE IF THEY WENT BACK TO THE SOUTH?

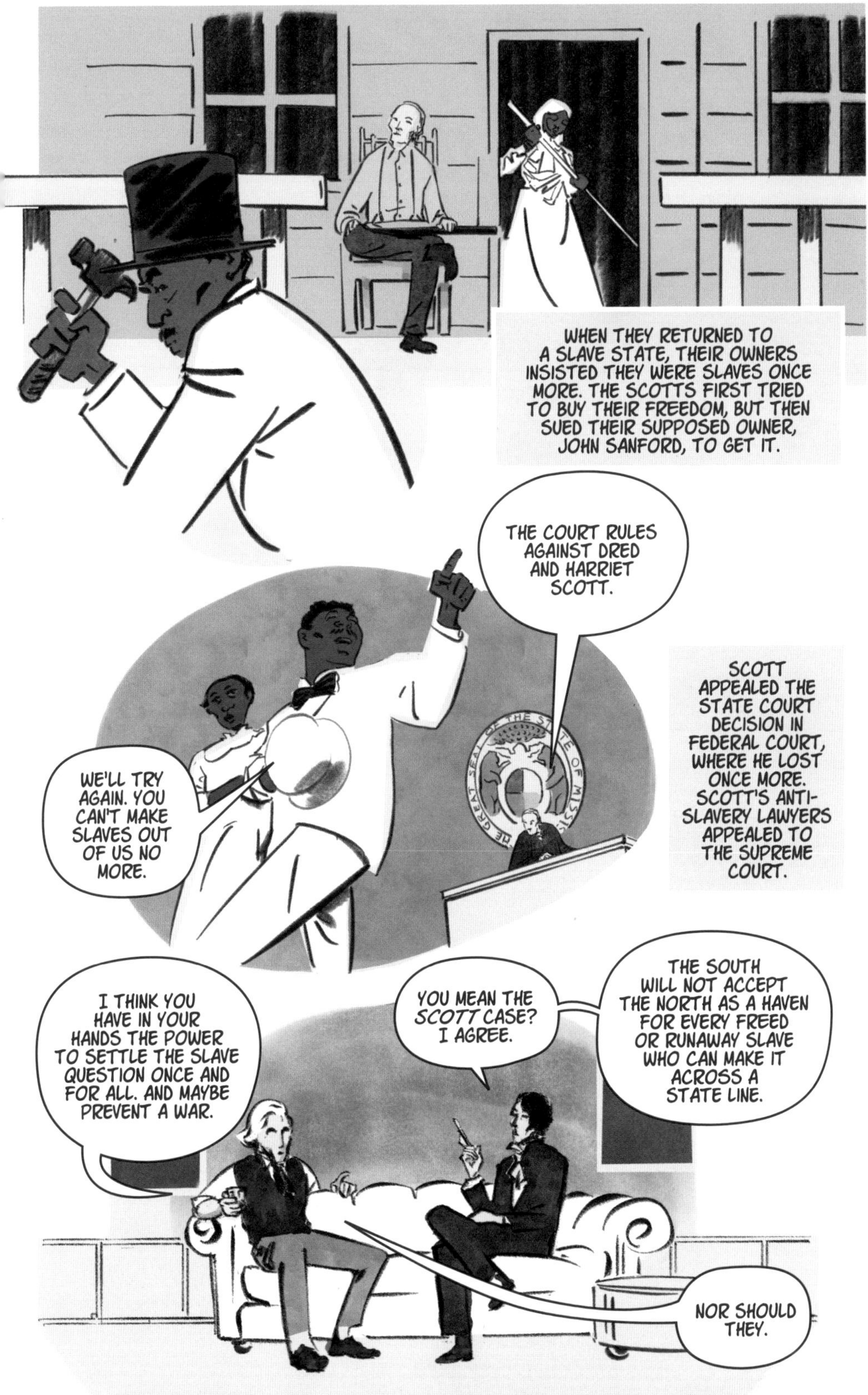
WHEN THEY RETURNED TO A SLAVE STATE, THEIR OWNERS INSISTED THEY WERE SLAVES ONCE MORE. THE SCOTTS FIRST TRIED TO BUY THEIR FREEDOM, BUT THEN SUED THEIR SUPPOSED OWNER, JOHN SANFORD, TO GET IT.
THE COURT RULES AGAINST DRED AND HARRIET SCOTT.
WE'LL TRY AGAIN. YOU CAN'T MAKE SLAVES OUT OF US NO MORE.
THE GREAT SEAL OF THE STATE OF MISSOURI
SCOTT APPEALED THE STATE COURT DECISION IN FEDERAL COURT, WHERE HE LOST ONCE MORE. SCOTT'S ANTI-SLAVERY LAWYERS APPEALED TO THE SUPREME COURT.
I THINK YOU HAVE IN YOUR HANDS THE POWER TO SETTLE THE SLAVE QUESTION ONCE AND FOR ALL. AND MAYBE PREVENT A WAR.
YOU MEAN THE *SCOTT* CASE? I AGREE.
THE SOUTH WILL NOT ACCEPT THE NORTH AS A HAVEN FOR EVERY FREED OR RUNAWAY SLAVE WHO CAN MAKE IT ACROSS A STATE LINE.
NOR SHOULD THEY.

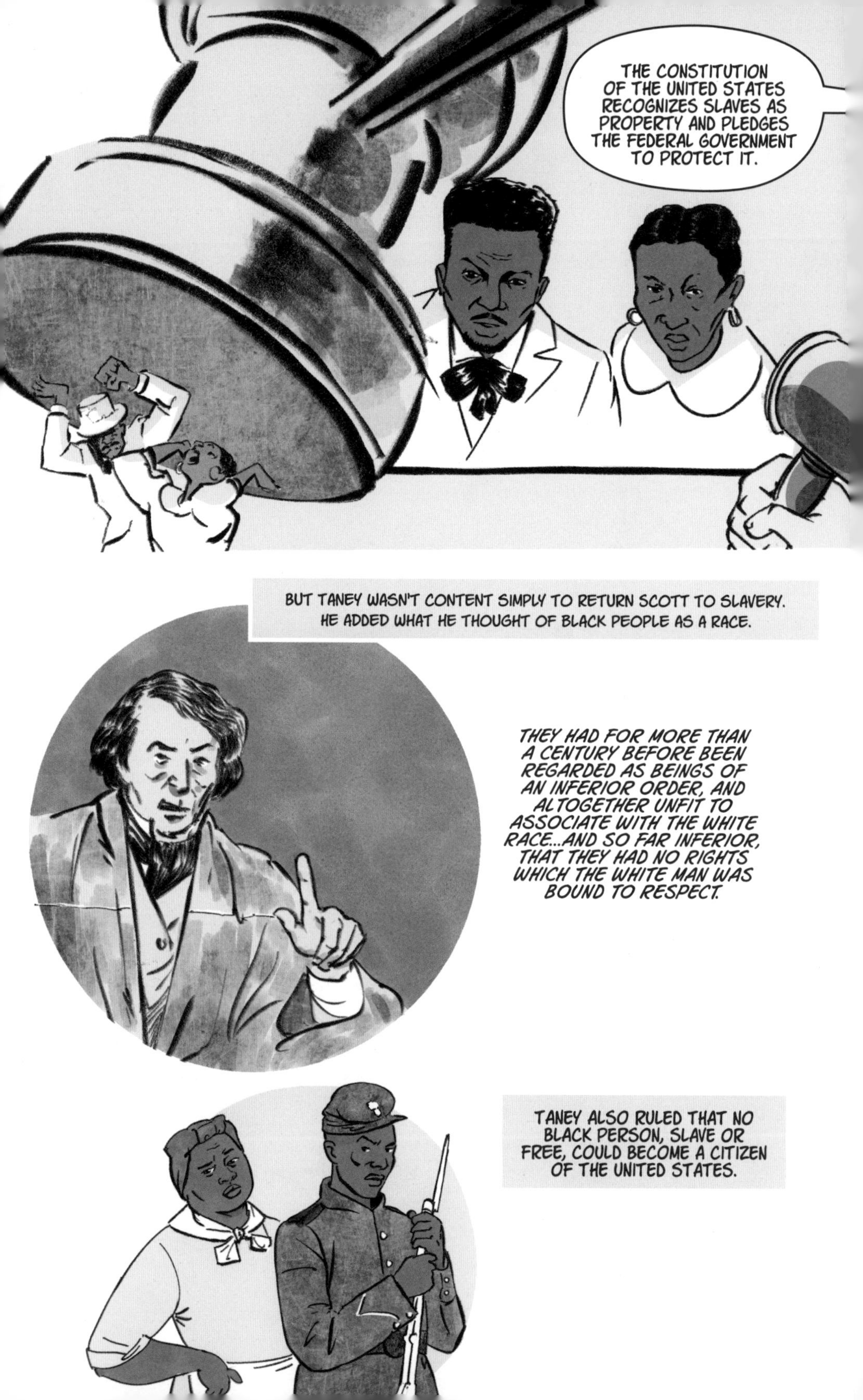
THE CONSTITUTION OF THE UNITED STATES RECOGNIZES SLAVES AS PROPERTY AND PLEDGES THE FEDERAL GOVERNMENT TO PROTECT IT.
BUT TANEY WASN'T CONTENT SIMPLY TO RETURN SCOTT TO SLAVERY. HE ADDED WHAT HE THOUGHT OF BLACK PEOPLE AS A RACE.
THEY HAD FOR MORE THAN A CENTURY BEFORE BEEN REGARDED AS BEINGS OF AN INFERIOR ORDER, AND ALTOGETHER UNFIT TO ASSOCIATE WITH THE WHITE RACE...AND SO FAR INFERIOR, THAT THEY HAD NO RIGHTS WHICH THE WHITE MAN WAS BOUND TO RESPECT.
TANEY ALSO RULED THAT NO BLACK PERSON, SLAVE OR FREE, COULD BECOME A CITIZEN OF THE UNITED STATES.

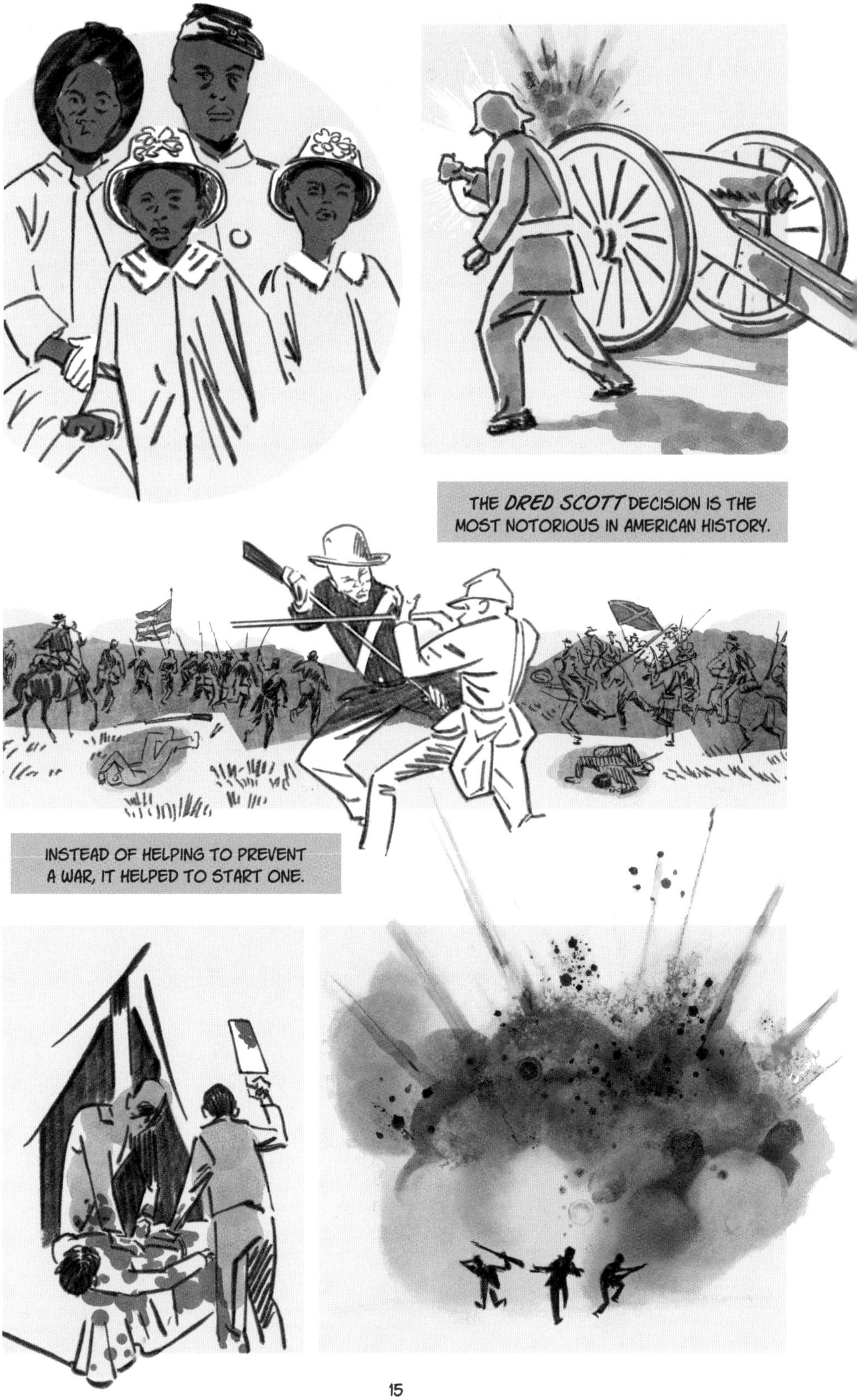
THE *DRED SCOTT* DECISION IS THE MOST NOTORIOUS IN AMERICAN HISTORY.
INSTEAD OF HELPING TO PREVENT A WAR, IT HELPED TO START ONE.

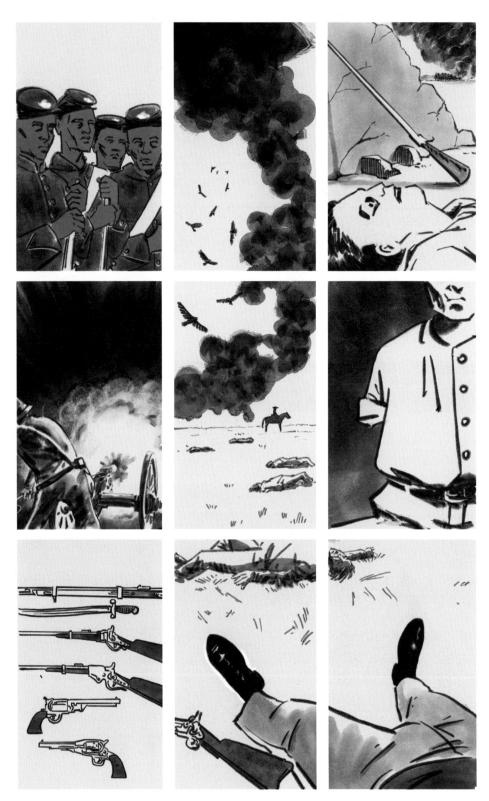

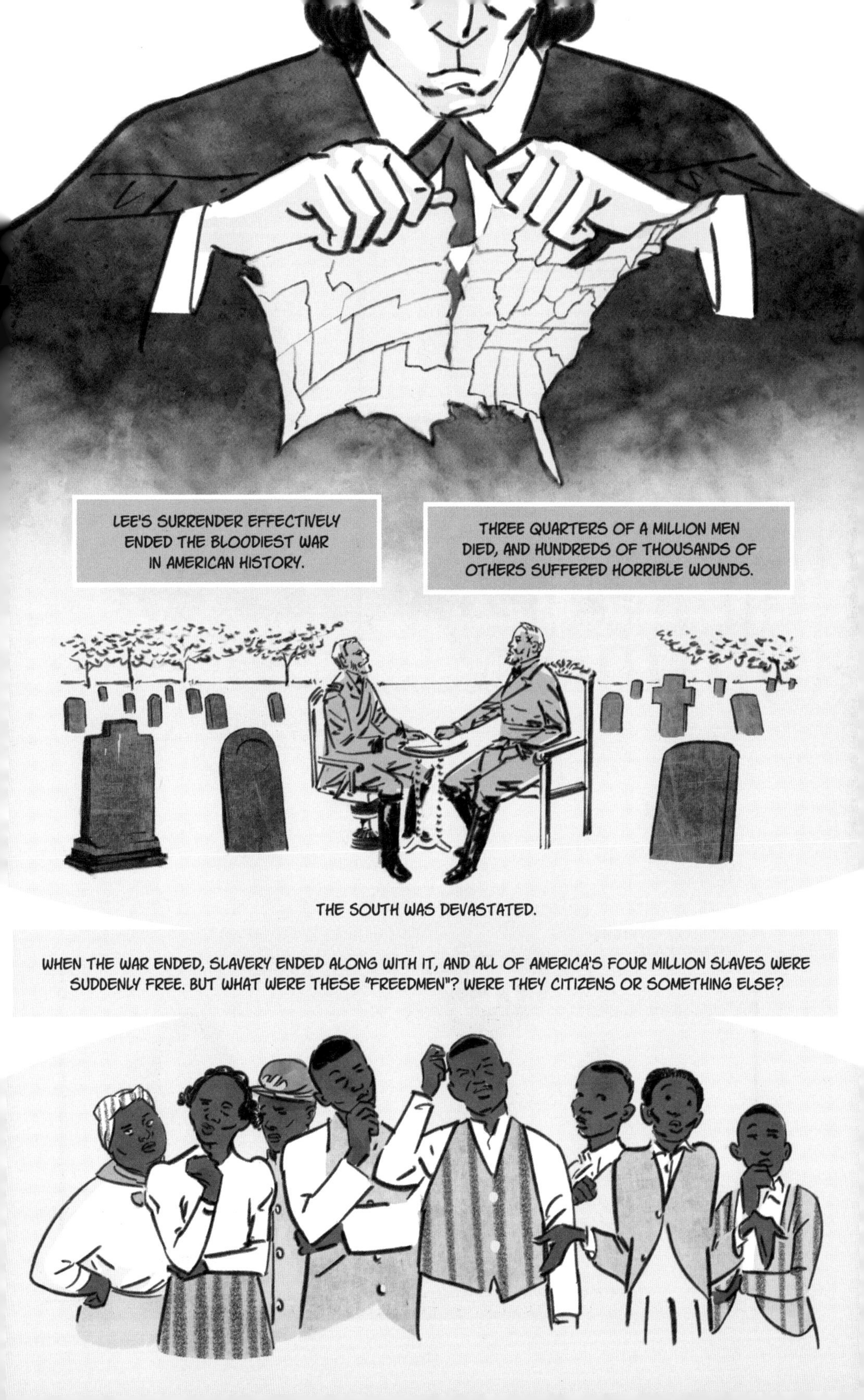
LEE'S SURRENDER EFFECTIVELY ENDED THE BLOODIEST WAR IN AMERICAN HISTORY.
THREE QUARTERS OF A MILLION MEN DIED, AND HUNDREDS OF THOUSANDS OF OTHERS SUFFERED HORRIBLE WOUNDS.
THE SOUTH WAS DEVASTATED.
WHEN THE WAR ENDED, SLAVERY ENDED ALONG WITH IT, AND ALL OF AMERICA'S FOUR MILLION SLAVES WERE SUDDENLY FREE. BUT WHAT WERE THESE "FREEDMEN"? WERE THEY CITIZENS OR SOMETHING ELSE?

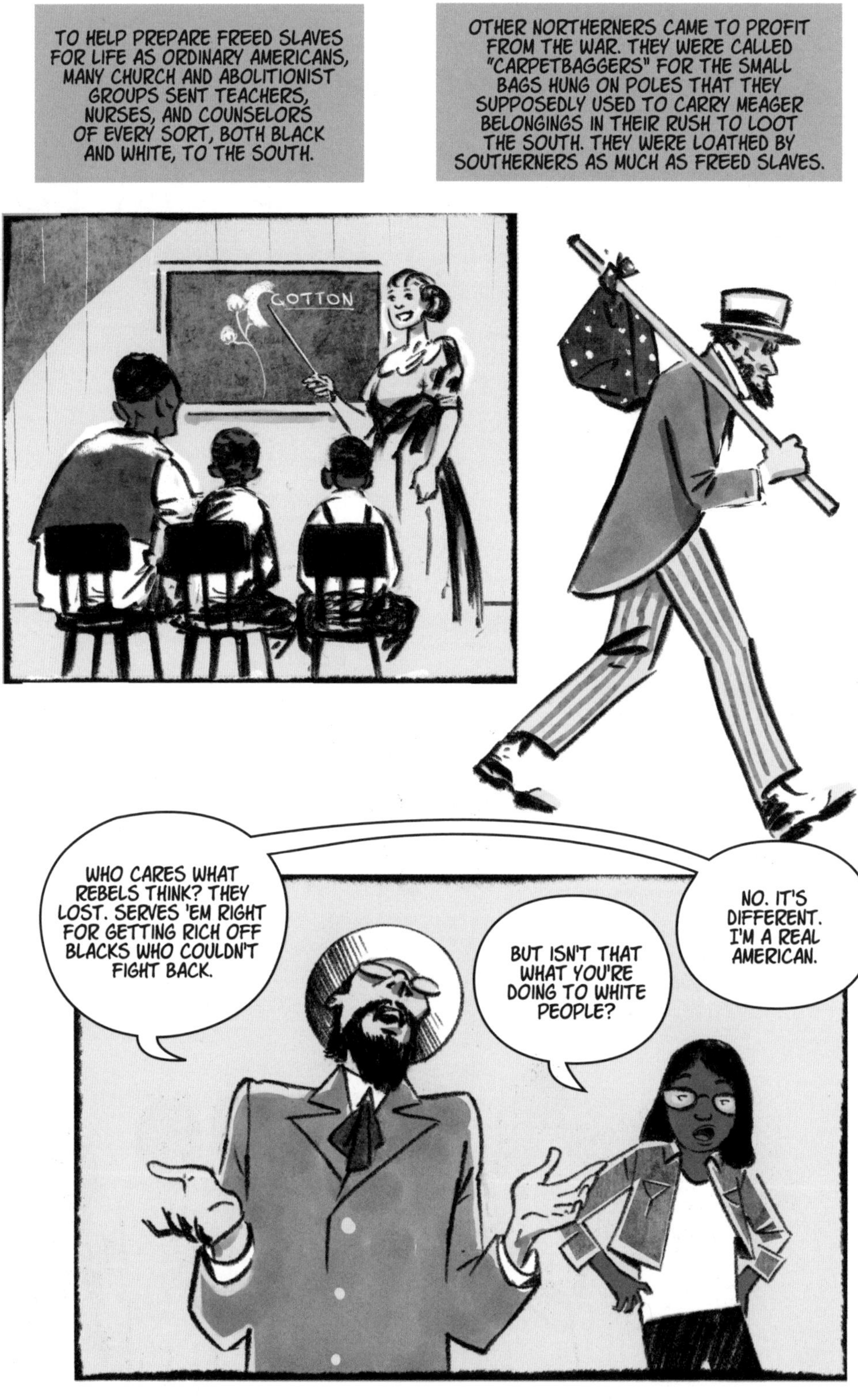
TO HELP PREPARE FREED SLAVES FOR LIFE AS ORDINARY AMERICANS, MANY CHURCH AND ABOLITIONIST GROUPS SENT TEACHERS, NURSES, AND COUNSELORS OF EVERY SORT, BOTH BLACK AND WHITE, TO THE SOUTH.
OTHER NORTHERNERS CAME TO PROFIT FROM THE WAR. THEY WERE CALLED "CARPETBAGGERS" FOR THE SMALL BAGS HUNG ON POLES THAT THEY SUPPOSEDLY USED TO CARRY MEAGER BELONGINGS IN THEIR RUSH TO LOOT THE SOUTH. THEY WERE LOATHED BY SOUTHERNERS AS MUCH AS FREED SLAVES.
COTTON
WHO CARES WHAT REBELS THINK? THEY LOST. SERVES 'EM RIGHT FOR GETTING RICH OFF BLACKS WHO COULDN'T FIGHT BACK.
BUT ISN'T THAT WHAT YOU'RE DOING TO WHITE PEOPLE?
NO. IT'S DIFFERENT. I'M A REAL AMERICAN.

ANDREW JOHNSON, A DEMOCRAT* FROM TENNESSEE, WAS DEEPLY RACIST AND DETERMINED TO ALLOW THE DEFEATED SOUTH TO RETURN TO WHITE RULE. SOUTHERN STATE GOVERNMENTS, DOMINATED BY FORMER CONFEDERATES, PASSED LAWS KNOWN AS ***BLACK CODES*** THAT REQUIRED AFRICAN AMERICANS TO WORK UNDER THE SAME HORRIBLE CONDITIONS AS BEFORE THE WAR.

*AT THE TIME, DEMOCRATS WERE THE PARTY OF WHITE SUPREMACY.

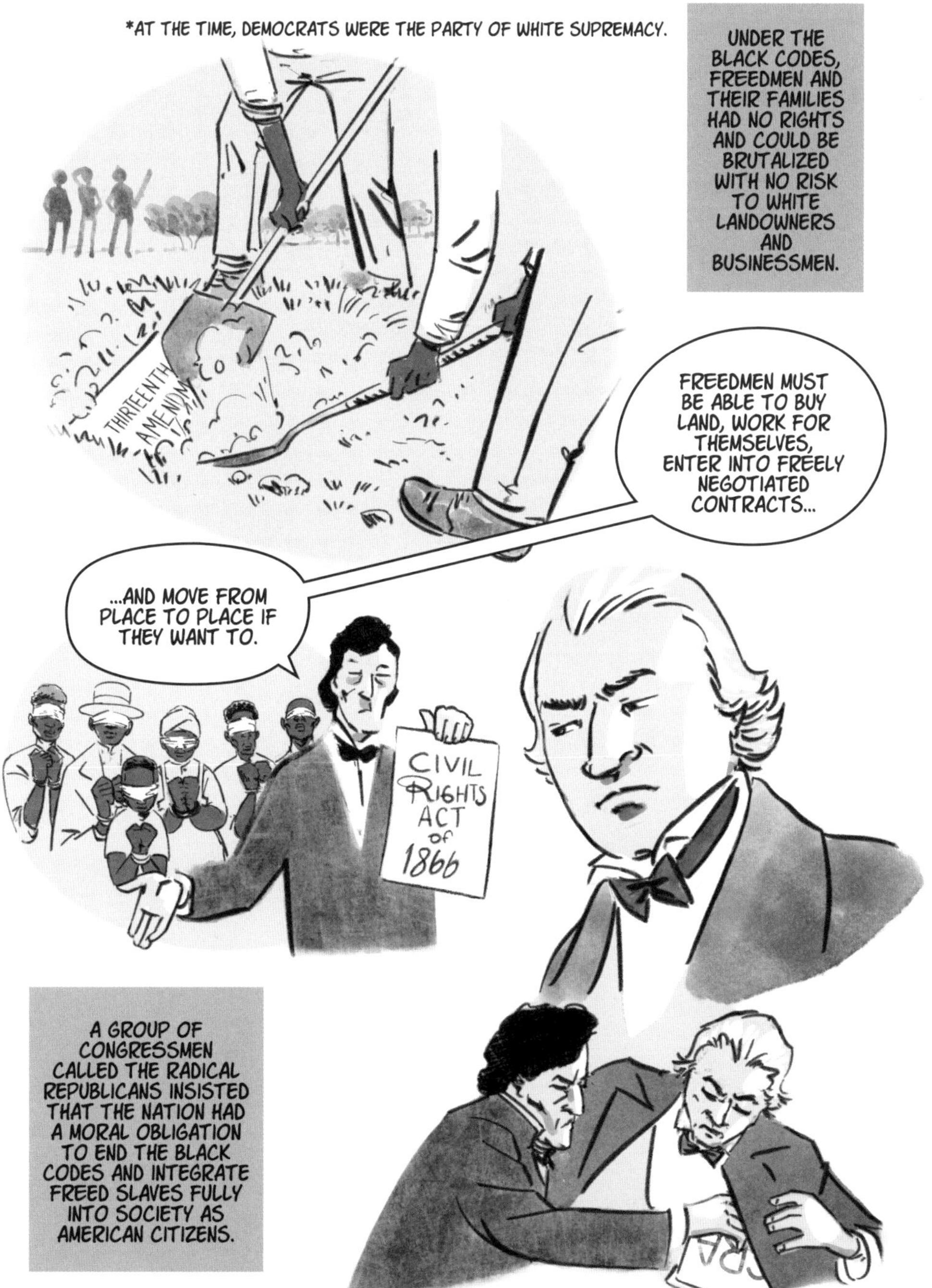
UNDER THE BLACK CODES, FREEDMEN AND THEIR FAMILIES HAD NO RIGHTS AND COULD BE BRUTALIZED WITH NO RISK TO WHITE LANDOWNERS AND BUSINESSMEN.
THIRTEENTH AMENDM
FREEDMEN MUST BE ABLE TO BUY LAND, WORK FOR THEMSELVES, ENTER INTO FREELY NEGOTIATED CONTRACTS...
...AND MOVE FROM PLACE TO PLACE IF THEY WANT TO.
CIVIL RIGHTS ACT of 1866
A GROUP OF CONGRESSMEN CALLED THE RADICAL REPUBLICANS INSISTED THAT THE NATION HAD A MORAL OBLIGATION TO END THE BLACK CODES AND INTEGRATE FREED SLAVES FULLY INTO SOCIETY AS AMERICAN CITIZENS.

AS PART OF THAT EFFORT, THE RADICALS FORCED THROUGH CONGRESS THE FIRST CIVIL RIGHTS ACT IN THE NATION'S HISTORY AND OVERRODE ANDREW JOHNSON'S VETO TO MAKE IT LAW. THE CIVIL RIGHTS ACT OF 1866 MADE "ALL PERSONS BORN IN THE UNITED STATES CITIZENS OF THE UNITED STATES."*

*EXCEPT NATIVE AMERICANS, WHO WERE STILL CONSIDERED SUBJECTS OF THEIR VARIOUS TRIBES AND NOT UNDER THE JURISDICTION OF THE UNITED STATES GOVERNMENT.

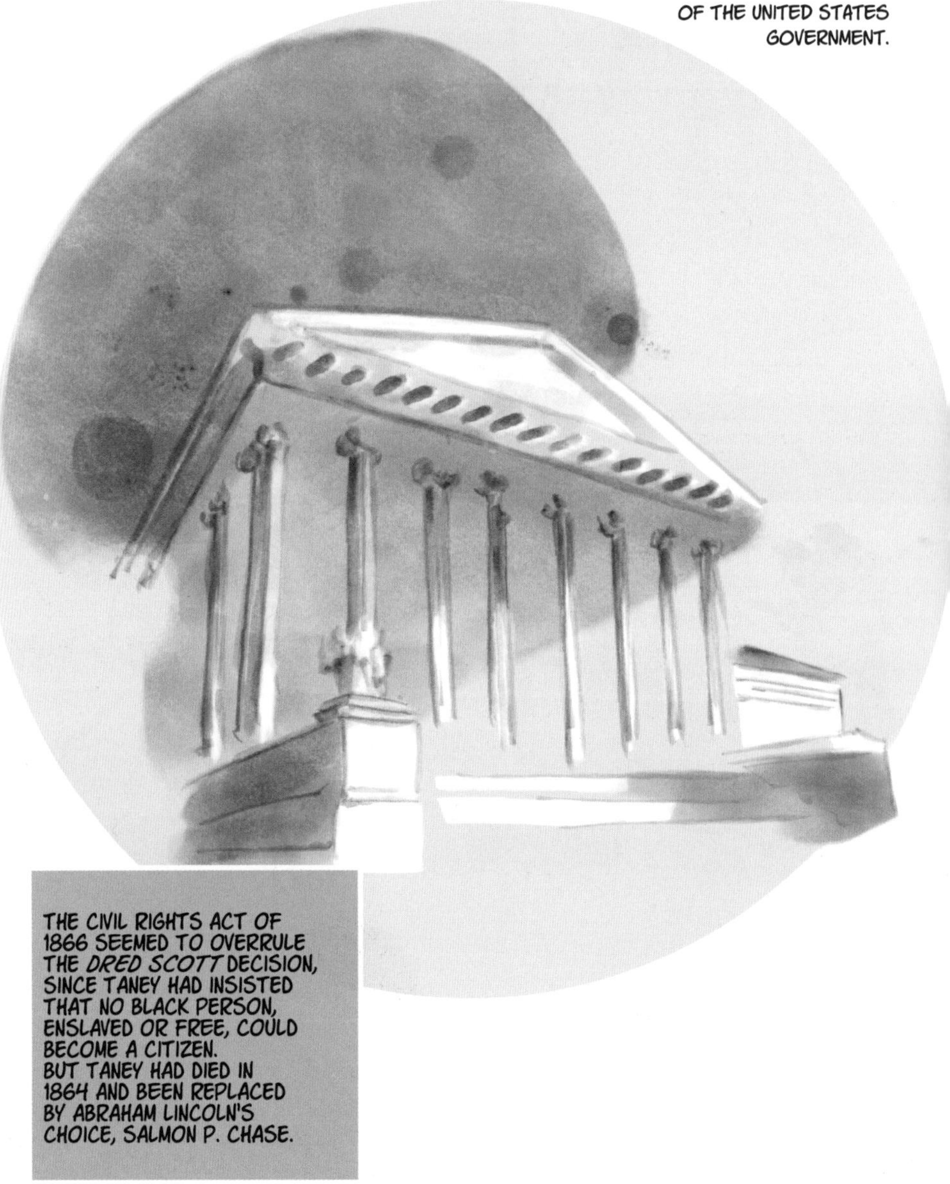

THE CIVIL RIGHTS ACT OF 1866 SEEMED TO OVERRULE THE *DRED SCOTT* DECISION, SINCE TANEY HAD INSISTED THAT NO BLACK PERSON, ENSLAVED OR FREE, COULD BECOME A CITIZEN.
BUT TANEY HAD DIED IN 1864 AND BEEN REPLACED BY ABRAHAM LINCOLN'S CHOICE, SALMON P. CHASE.

TANEY'S DECISION WAS ALREADY SO DISCREDITED THAT NO ONE BROUGHT IT UP.

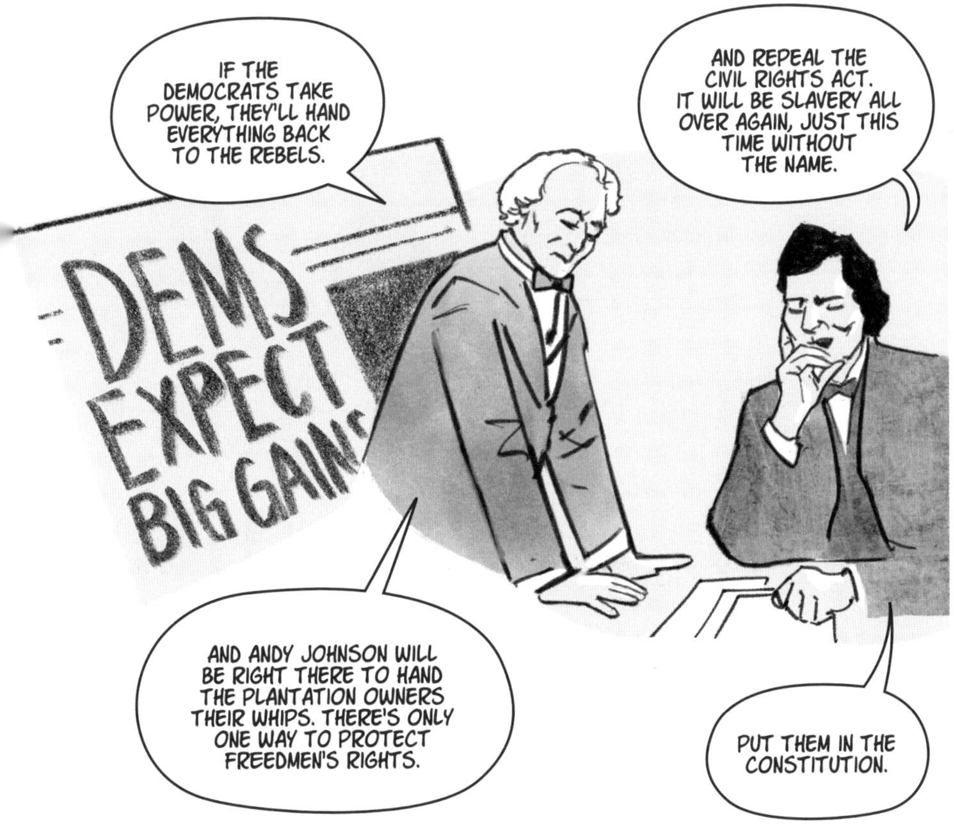
IF THE DEMOCRATS TAKE POWER, THEY'LL HAND EVERYTHING BACK TO THE REBELS.
AND REPEAL THE CIVIL RIGHTS ACT. IT WILL BE SLAVERY ALL OVER AGAIN, JUST THIS TIME WITHOUT THE NAME.
DEMS EXPECT BIG GAINS
AND ANDY JOHNSON WILL BE RIGHT THERE TO HAND THE PLANTATION OWNERS THEIR WHIPS. THERE'S ONLY ONE WAY TO PROTECT FREEDMEN'S RIGHTS.
PUT THEM IN THE CONSTITUTION.

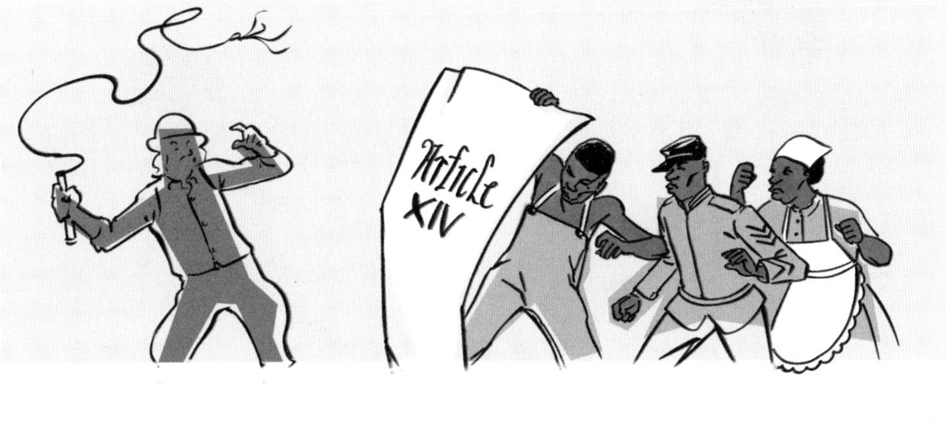
Article XIV

AND SO THE FOURTEENTH AMENDMENT WAS BORN. THE FIRST SECTION, WRITTEN BY JOHN BINGHAM OF OHIO, GUARANTEED THAT EVERY PERSON BORN IN THE UNITED STATES WOULD BE A UNITED STATES CITIZEN, NO MATTER WHAT THEIR COLOR OR THEIR RELIGION, WHETHER THEIR PARENTS WERE CITIZENS ON NOT. IT ALSO SAID THAT EVERY "PERSON," NOT JUST CITIZENS, WOULD BE GUARANTEED "DUE PROCESS OF LAW" AND "EQUAL PROTECTION OF THE LAWS."

THE FIRST SECTION OF THE FOURTEENTH AMENDMENT WOULD BECOME ONE OF THE MOST CONTROVERSIAL PASSAGES IN THE UNITED STATES CONSTITUTION AND SPAWN A SERIES OF HIGHLY CHARGED CASES UNIQUE IN AMERICAN HISTORY—EVERYTHING FROM VOTER REGISTRATION TO LIMITS ON WORKING HOURS TO ABORTION RIGHTS TO THE RIGHTS OF AN ACCUSED TO...

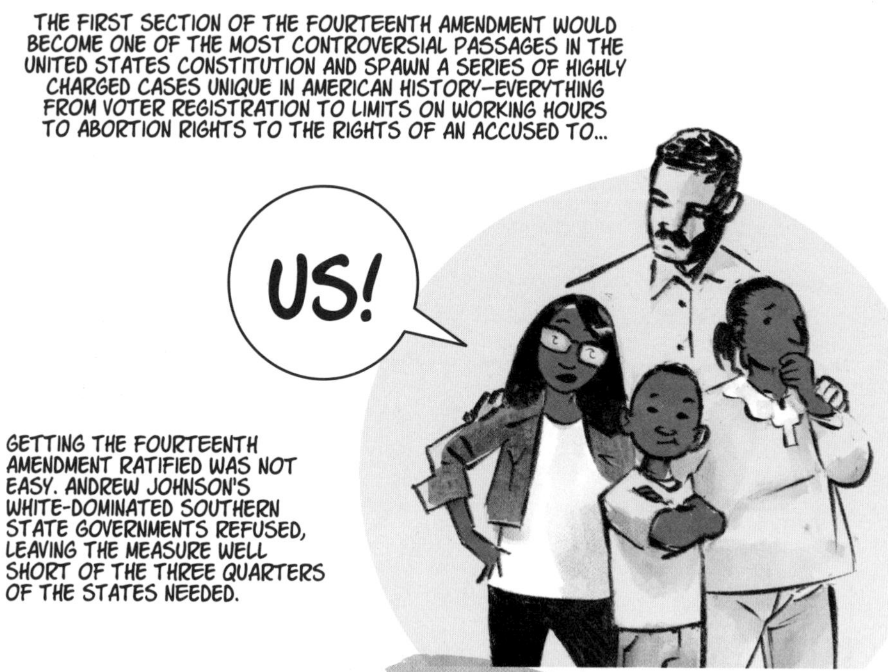
US!

GETTING THE FOURTEENTH AMENDMENT RATIFIED WAS NOT EASY. ANDREW JOHNSON'S WHITE-DOMINATED SOUTHERN STATE GOVERNMENTS REFUSED, LEAVING THE MEASURE WELL SHORT OF THE THREE QUARTERS OF THE STATES NEEDED.

WITH ONLY WHITE PEOPLE VOTING, THAT WAS NOT LIKELY TO CHANGE.

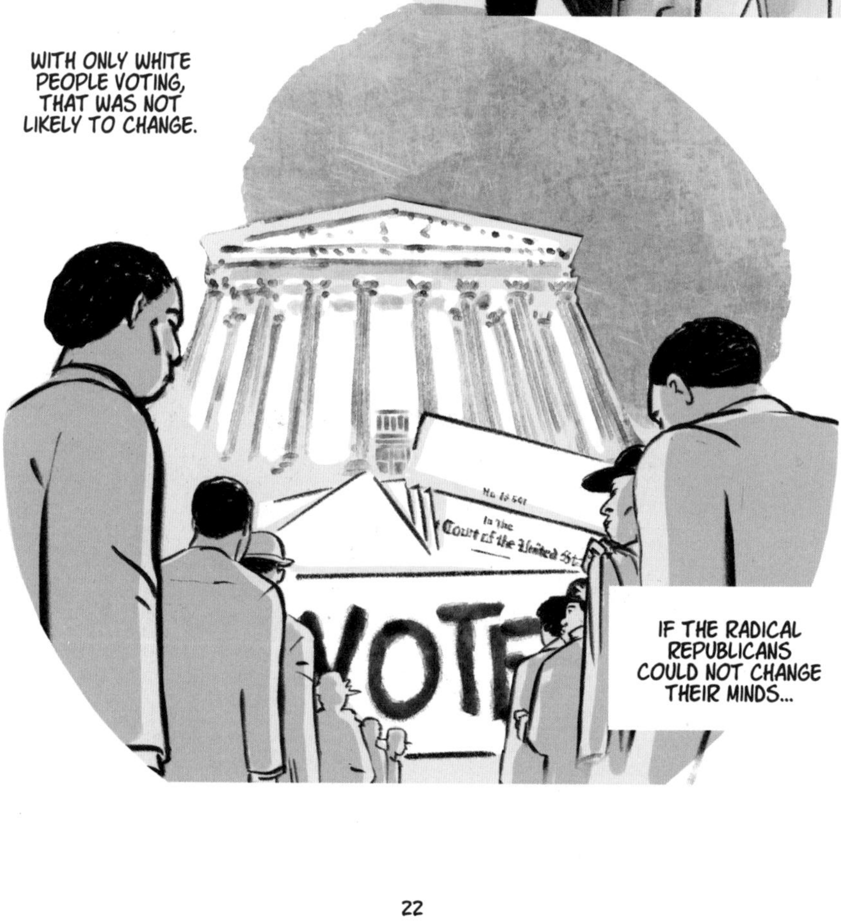
VOTE

IF THE RADICAL REPUBLICANS COULD NOT CHANGE THEIR MINDS...

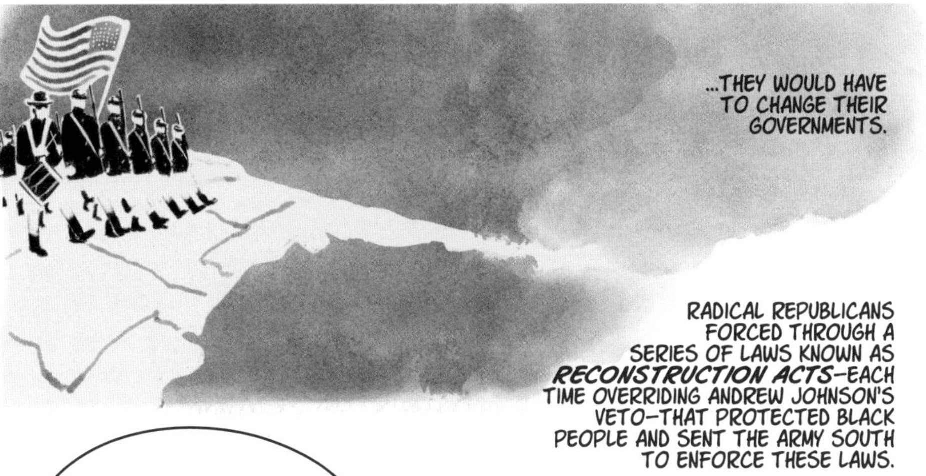
...THEY WOULD HAVE TO CHANGE THEIR GOVERNMENTS.
RADICAL REPUBLICANS FORCED THROUGH A SERIES OF LAWS KNOWN AS ***RECONSTRUCTION ACTS***—EACH TIME OVERRIDING ANDREW JOHNSON'S VETO—THAT PROTECTED BLACK PEOPLE AND SENT THE ARMY SOUTH TO ENFORCE THESE LAWS.

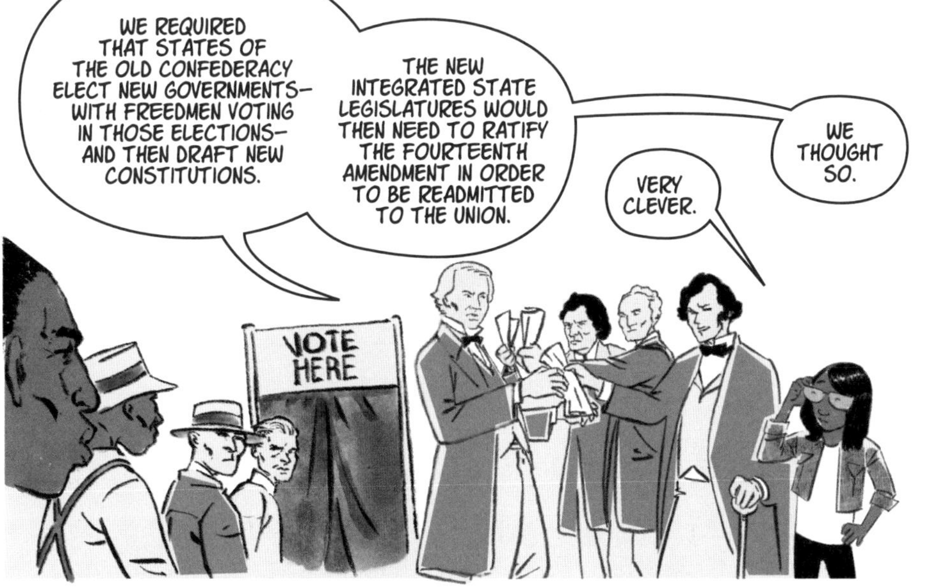
WE REQUIRED THAT STATES OF THE OLD CONFEDERACY ELECT NEW GOVERNMENTS—WITH FREEDMEN VOTING IN THOSE ELECTIONS—AND THEN DRAFT NEW CONSTITUTIONS.
THE NEW INTEGRATED STATE LEGISLATURES WOULD THEN NEED TO RATIFY THE FOURTEENTH AMENDMENT IN ORDER TO BE READMITTED TO THE UNION.
VERY CLEVER.
WE THOUGHT SO.
VOTE HERE

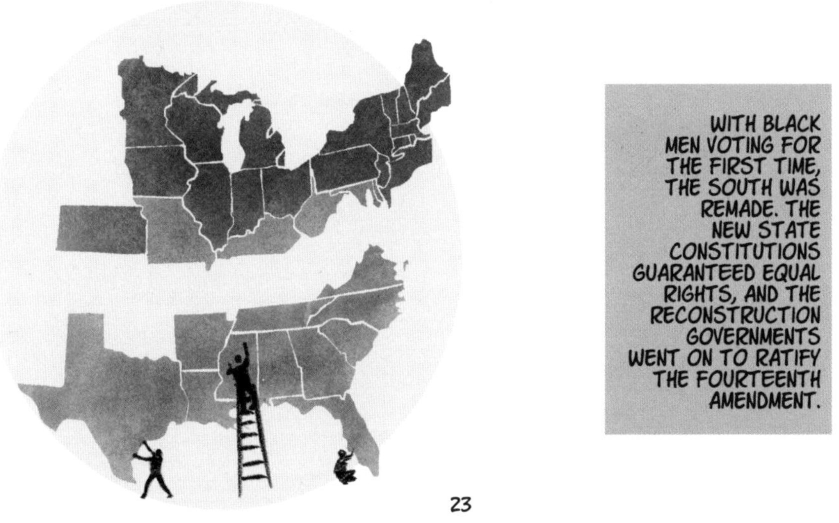
WITH BLACK MEN VOTING FOR THE FIRST TIME, THE SOUTH WAS REMADE. THE NEW STATE CONSTITUTIONS GUARANTEED EQUAL RIGHTS, AND THE RECONSTRUCTION GOVERNMENTS WENT ON TO RATIFY THE FOURTEENTH AMENDMENT.

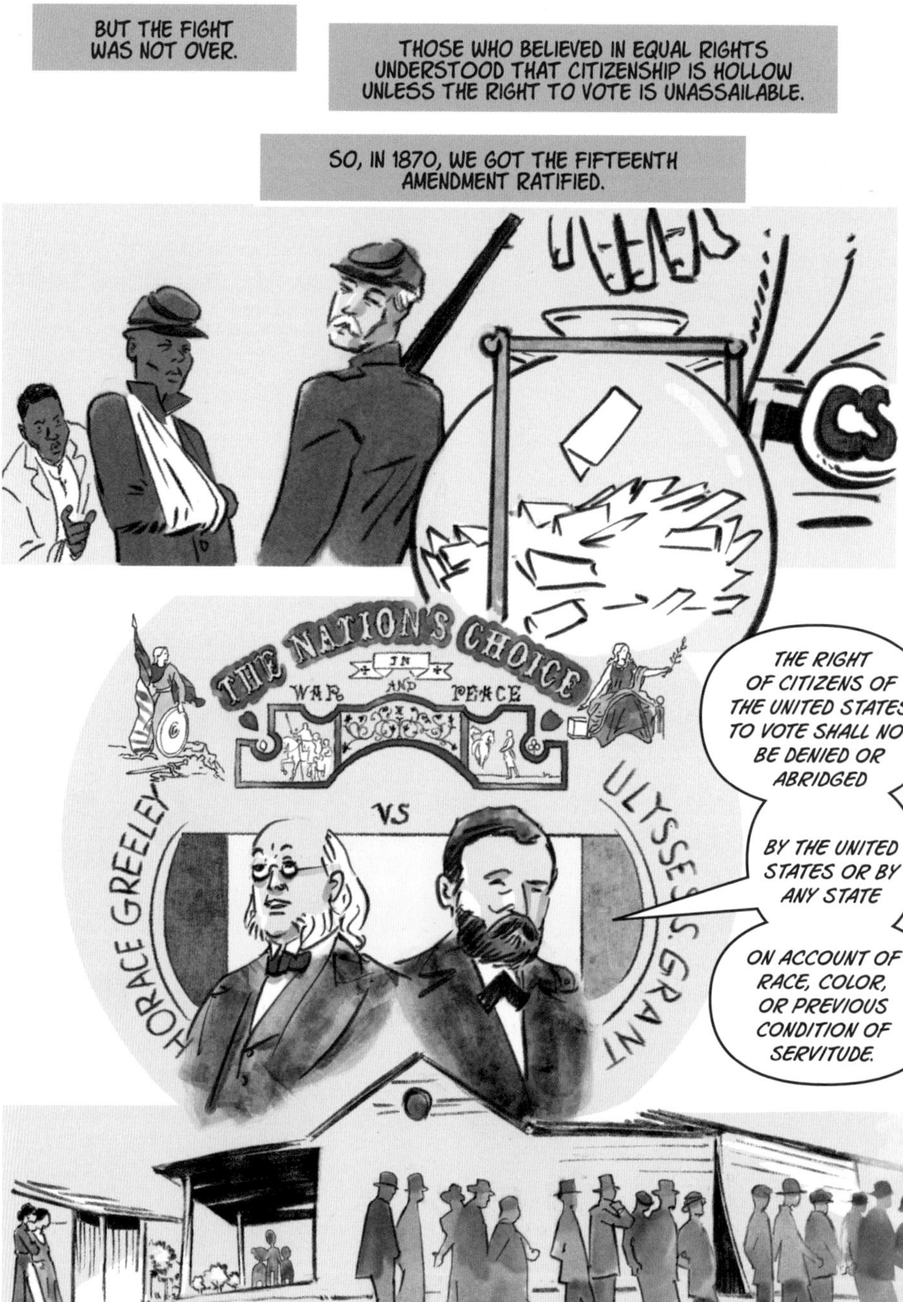
BUT THE FIGHT WAS NOT OVER.
THOSE WHO BELIEVED IN EQUAL RIGHTS UNDERSTOOD THAT CITIZENSHIP IS HOLLOW UNLESS THE RIGHT TO VOTE IS UNASSAILABLE.
SO, IN 1870, WE GOT THE FIFTEENTH AMENDMENT RATIFIED.
CS
THE NATION'S CHOICE
IN
WAR AND PEACE
HORACE GREELEY
VS
ULYSSES S. GRANT
THE RIGHT OF CITIZENS OF THE UNITED STATES TO VOTE SHALL NOT BE DENIED OR ABRIDGED
BY THE UNITED STATES OR BY ANY STATE
ON ACCOUNT OF RACE, COLOR, OR PREVIOUS CONDITION OF SERVITUDE.
ALMOST ONE-HALF MILLION BLACK MEN WOULD REGISTER TO VOTE. THEIR PARTICIPATION CHANGED THE FACE OF AMERICAN DEMOCRACY, PERHAPS MAKING THE GOVERNMENT FOR THE FIRST TIME THE VOICE OF THE (MALE) PEOPLE.

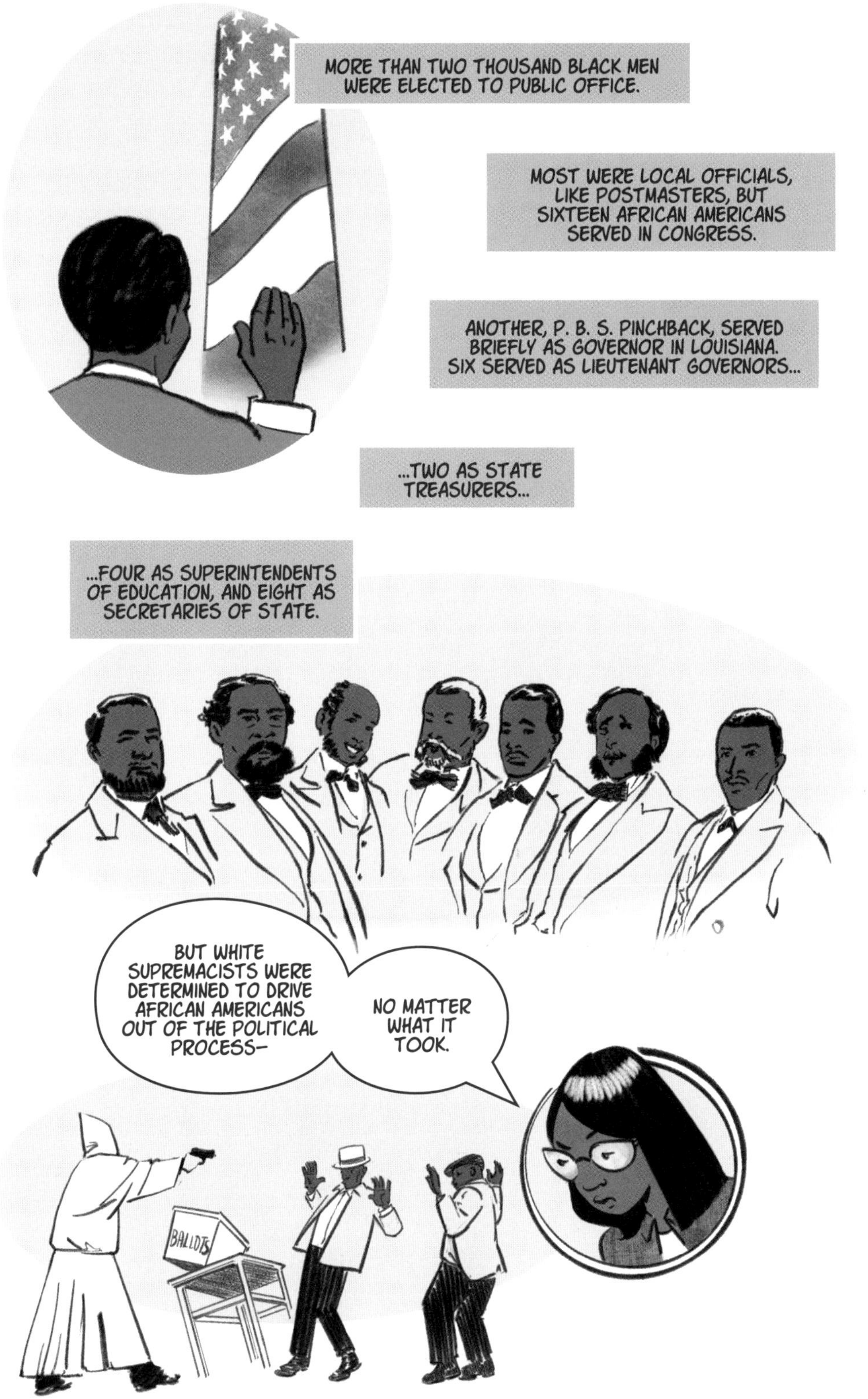
MORE THAN TWO THOUSAND BLACK MEN WERE ELECTED TO PUBLIC OFFICE.
MOST WERE LOCAL OFFICIALS, LIKE POSTMASTERS, BUT SIXTEEN AFRICAN AMERICANS SERVED IN CONGRESS.
ANOTHER, P. B. S. PINCHBACK, SERVED BRIEFLY AS GOVERNOR IN LOUISIANA. SIX SERVED AS LIEUTENANT GOVERNORS...
...TWO AS STATE TREASURERS...
...FOUR AS SUPERINTENDENTS OF EDUCATION, AND EIGHT AS SECRETARIES OF STATE.
BUT WHITE SUPREMACISTS WERE DETERMINED TO DRIVE AFRICAN AMERICANS OUT OF THE POLITICAL PROCESS–
NO MATTER WHAT IT TOOK.
BALLOTS

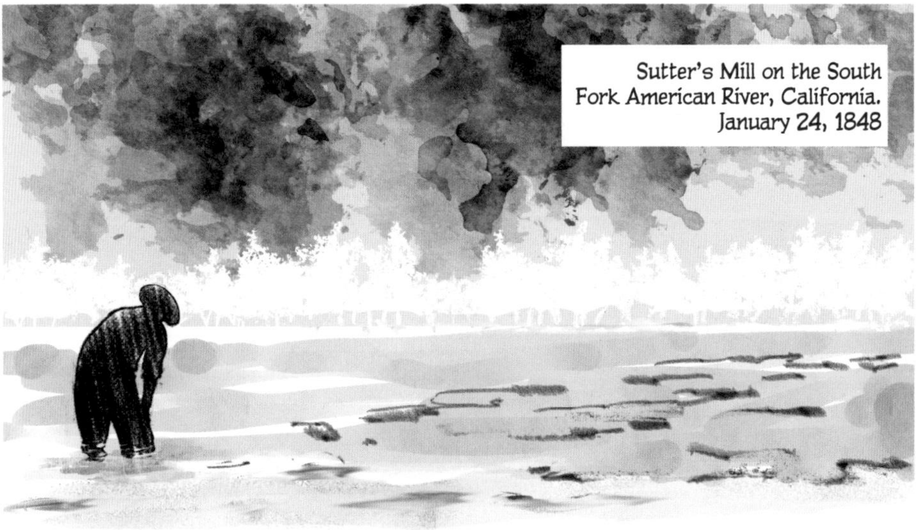
Sutter's Mill on the South Fork American River, California. January 24, 1848

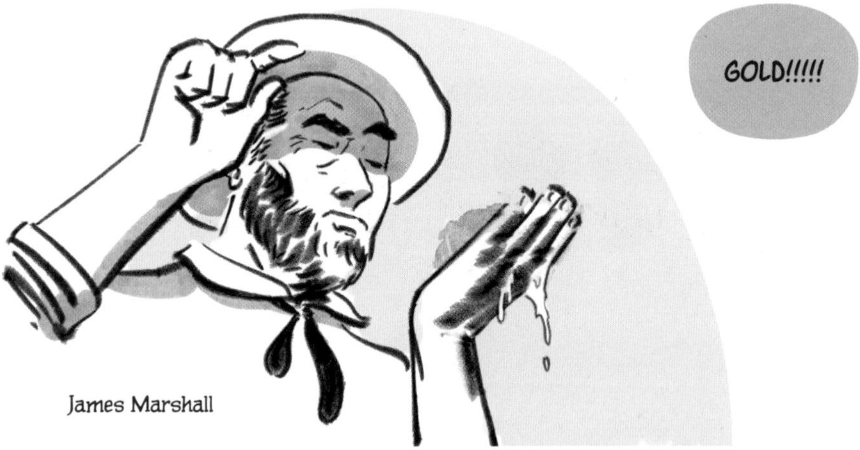
GOLD!!!!!
James Marshall

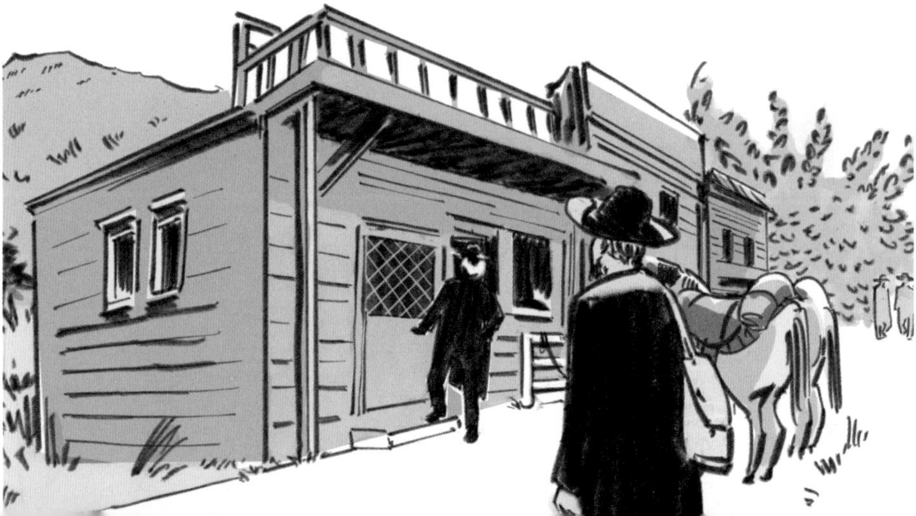

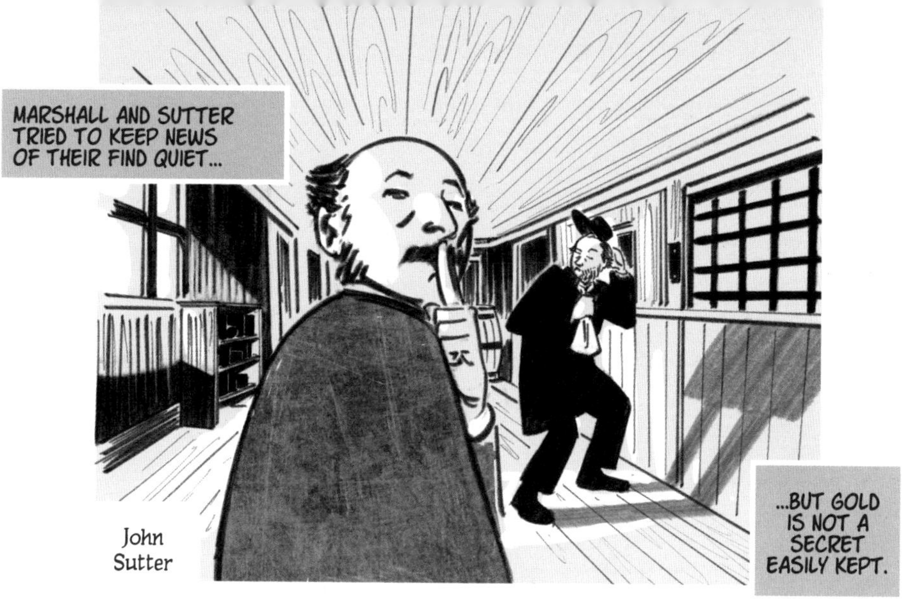
MARSHALL AND SUTTER TRIED TO KEEP NEWS OF THEIR FIND QUIET...
John Sutter
...BUT GOLD IS NOT A SECRET EASILY KEPT.

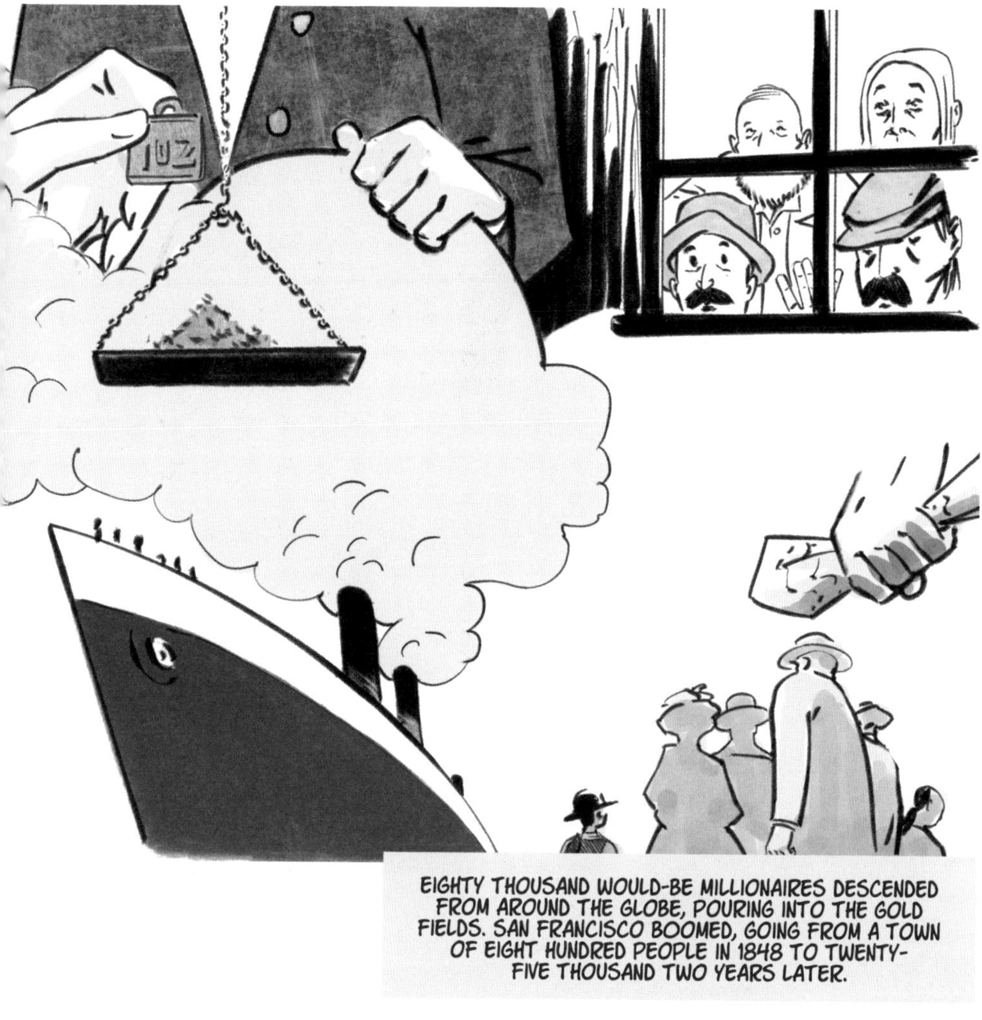
1OZ
EIGHTY THOUSAND WOULD-BE MILLIONAIRES DESCENDED FROM AROUND THE GLOBE, POURING INTO THE GOLD FIELDS. SAN FRANCISCO BOOMED, GOING FROM A TOWN OF EIGHT HUNDRED PEOPLE IN 1848 TO TWENTY-FIVE THOUSAND TWO YEARS LATER.

China

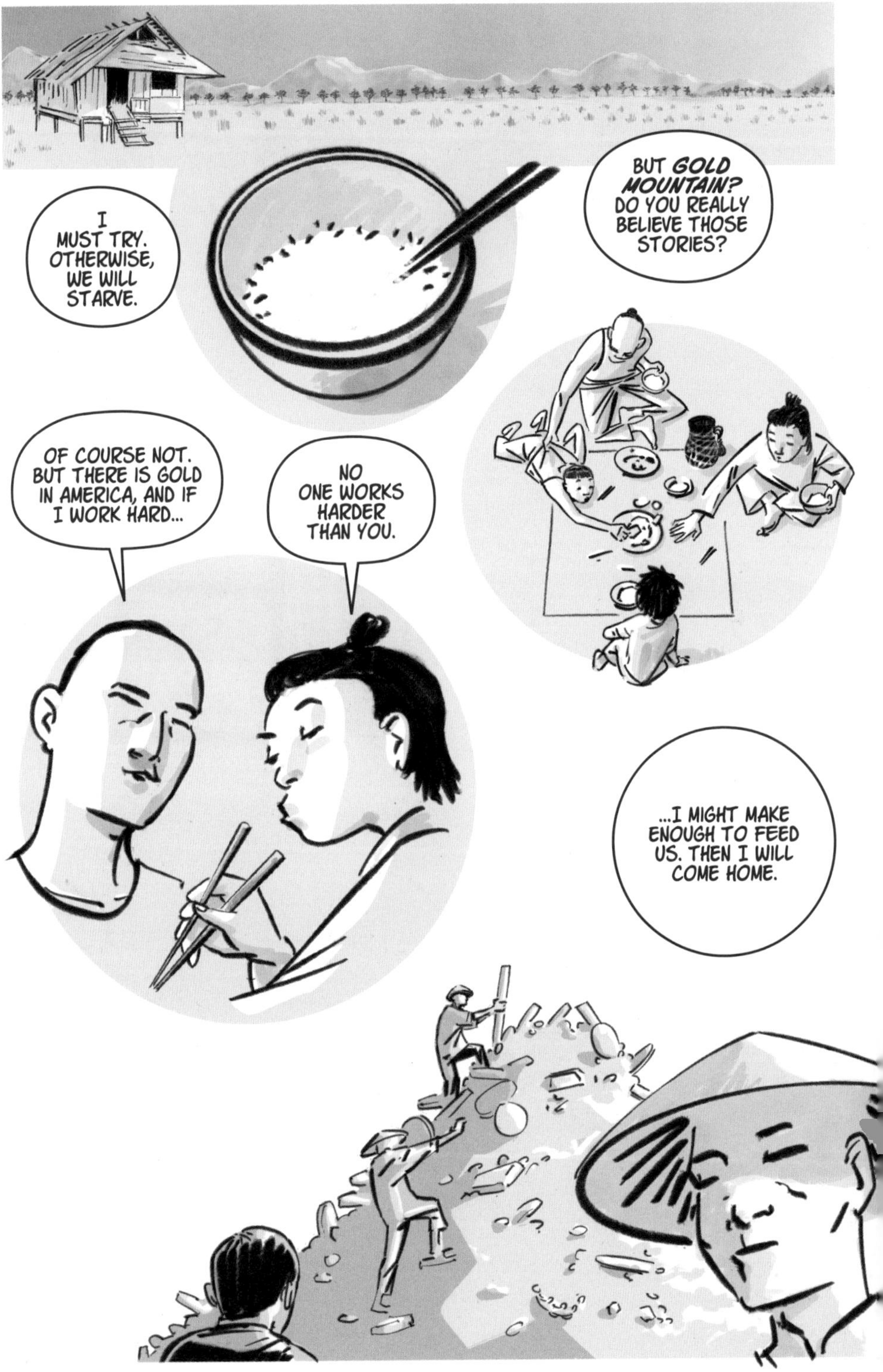

I MUST TRY. OTHERWISE, WE WILL STARVE.
BUT GOLD MOUNTAIN? DO YOU REALLY BELIEVE THOSE STORIES?
OF COURSE NOT. BUT THERE IS GOLD IN AMERICA, AND IF I WORK HARD...
NO ONE WORKS HARDER THAN YOU.
...I MIGHT MAKE ENOUGH TO FEED US. THEN I WILL COME HOME.

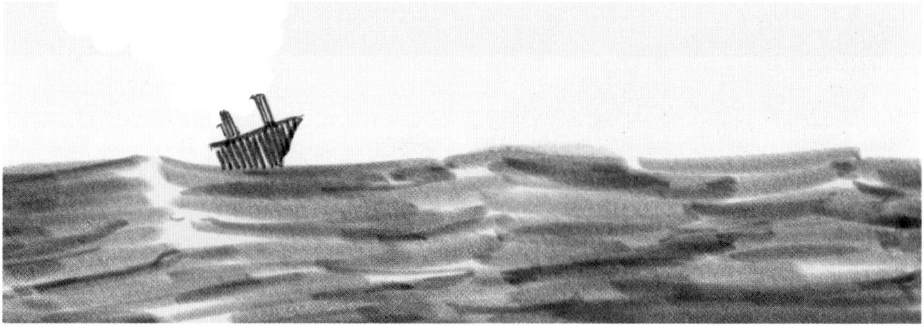

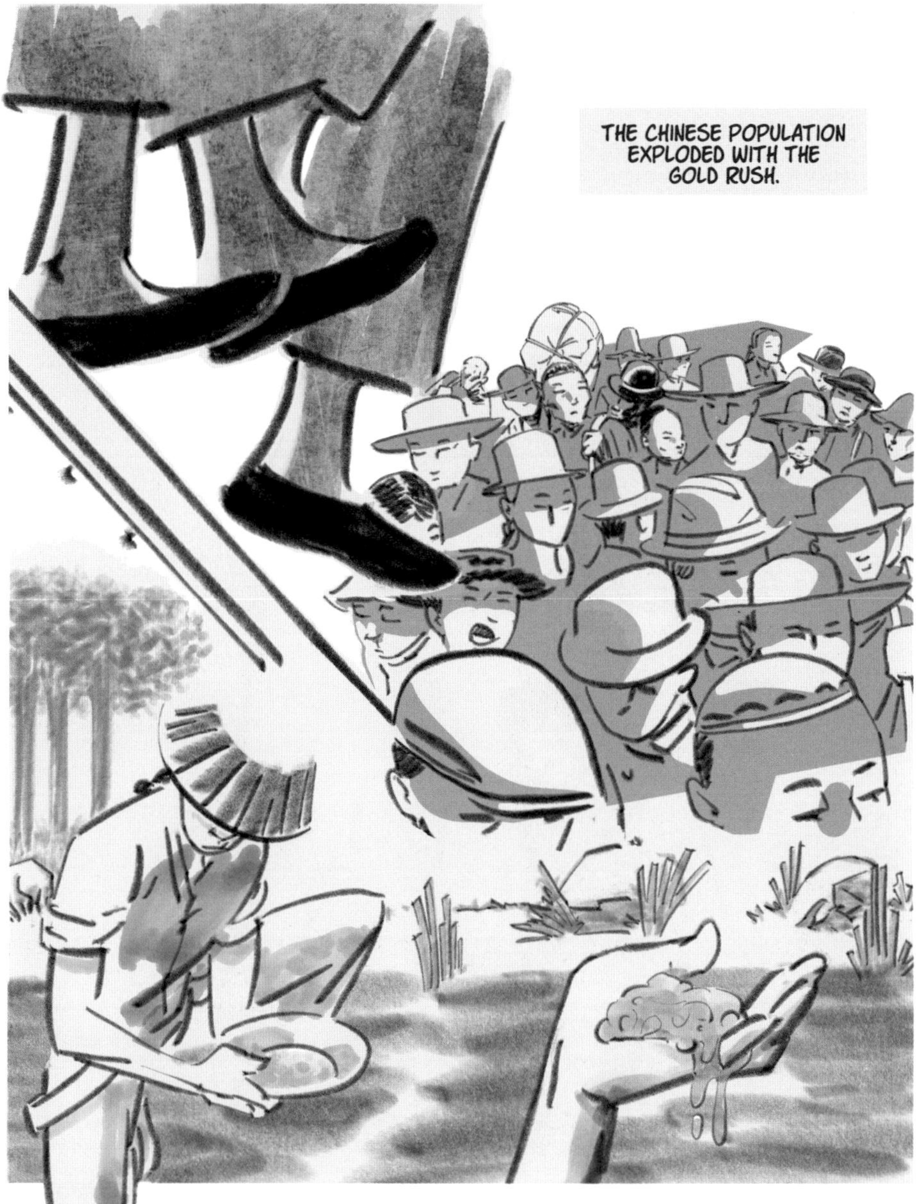
THE CHINESE POPULATION EXPLODED WITH THE GOLD RUSH.

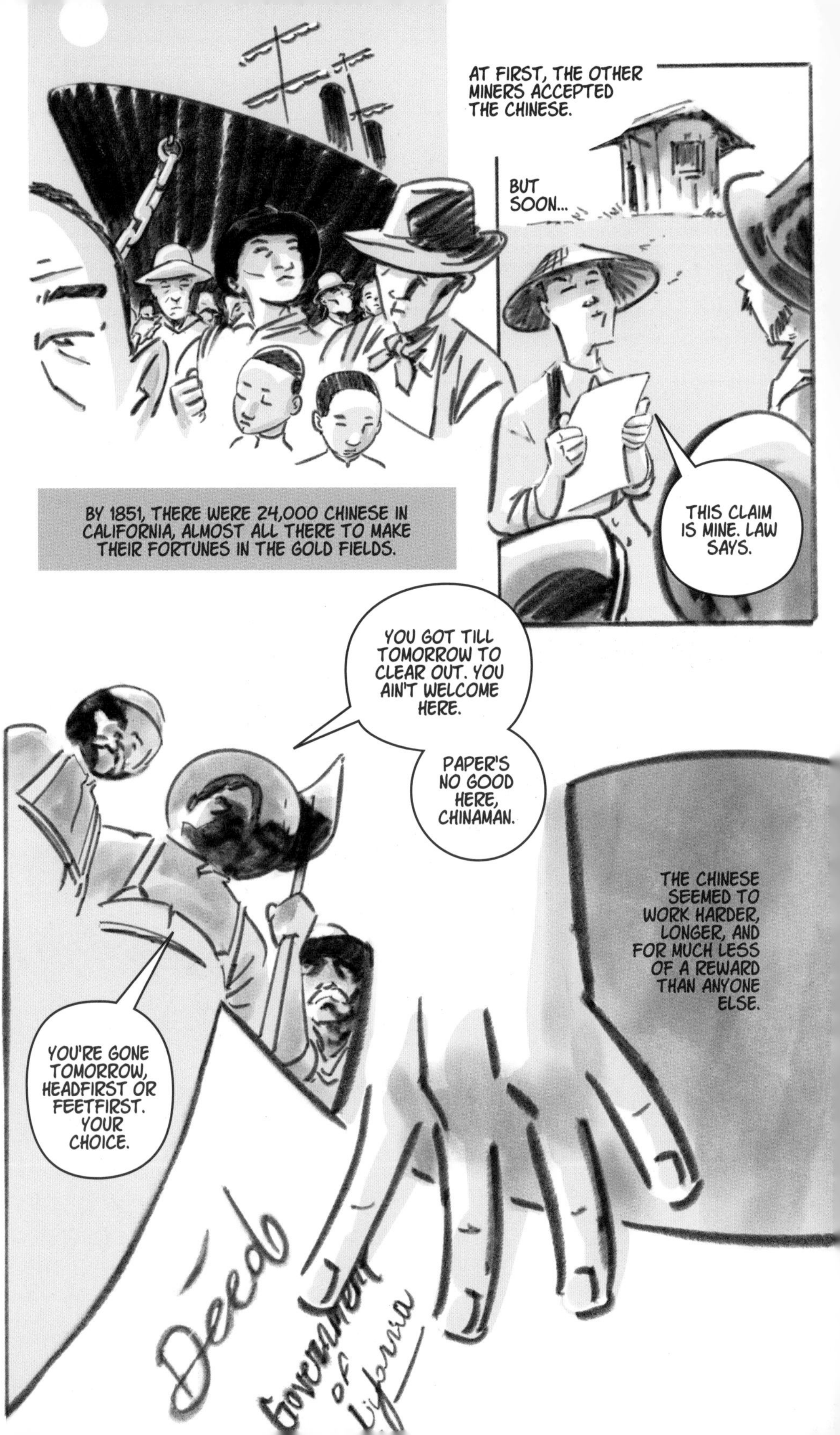
BY 1851, THERE WERE 24,000 CHINESE IN CALIFORNIA, ALMOST ALL THERE TO MAKE THEIR FORTUNES IN THE GOLD FIELDS.
AT FIRST, THE OTHER MINERS ACCEPTED THE CHINESE.
BUT SOON...
THIS CLAIM IS MINE. LAW SAYS.
YOU GOT TILL TOMORROW TO CLEAR OUT. YOU AIN'T WELCOME HERE.
PAPER'S NO GOOD HERE, CHINAMAN.
YOU'RE GONE TOMORROW, HEADFIRST OR FEETFIRST. YOUR CHOICE.
THE CHINESE SEEMED TO WORK HARDER, LONGER, AND FOR MUCH LESS OF A REWARD THAN ANYONE ELSE.
Deed
Government of

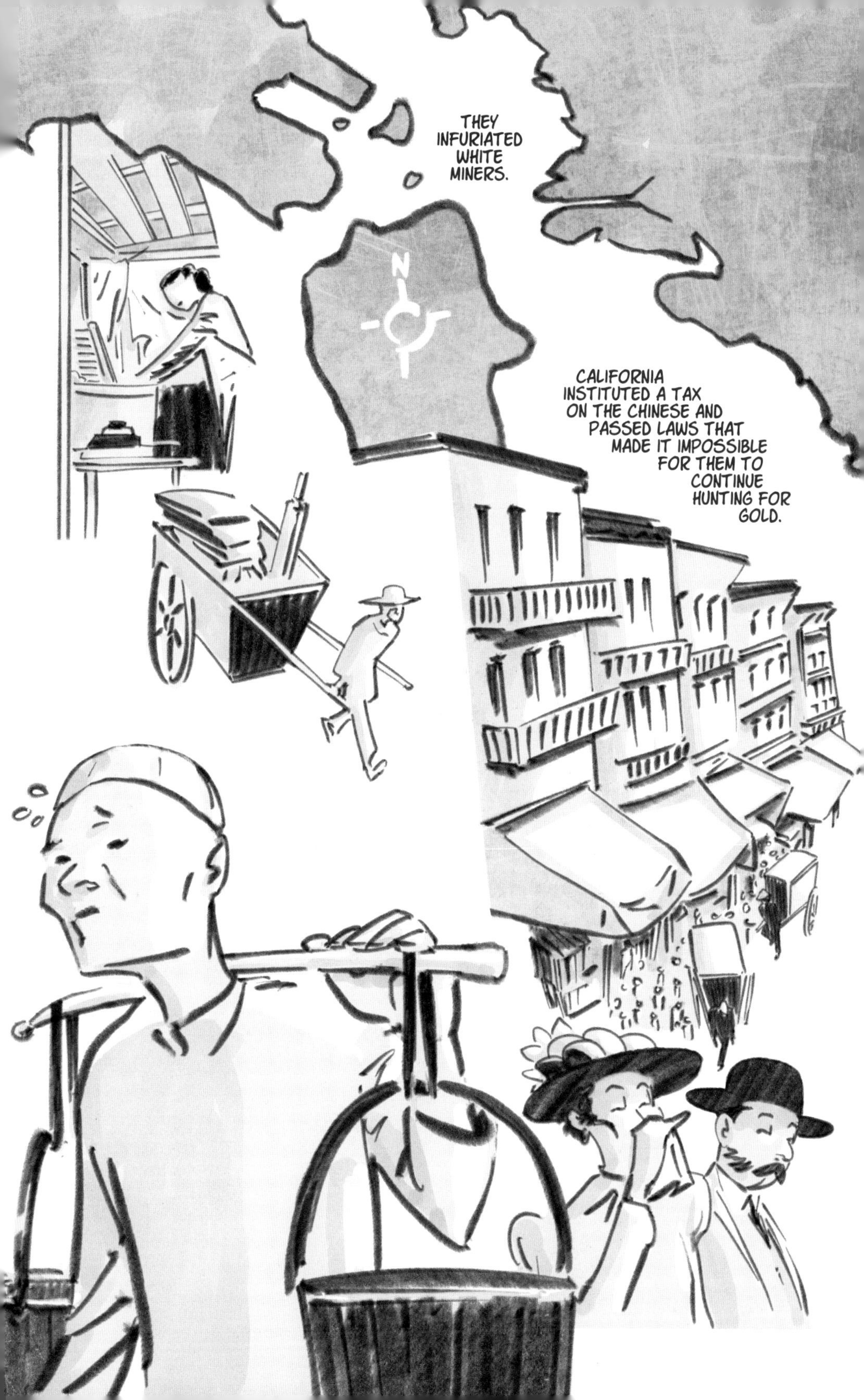
THEY INFURIATED WHITE MINERS.
CALIFORNIA INSTITUTED A TAX ON THE CHINESE AND PASSED LAWS THAT MADE IT IMPOSSIBLE FOR THEM TO CONTINUE HUNTING FOR GOLD.

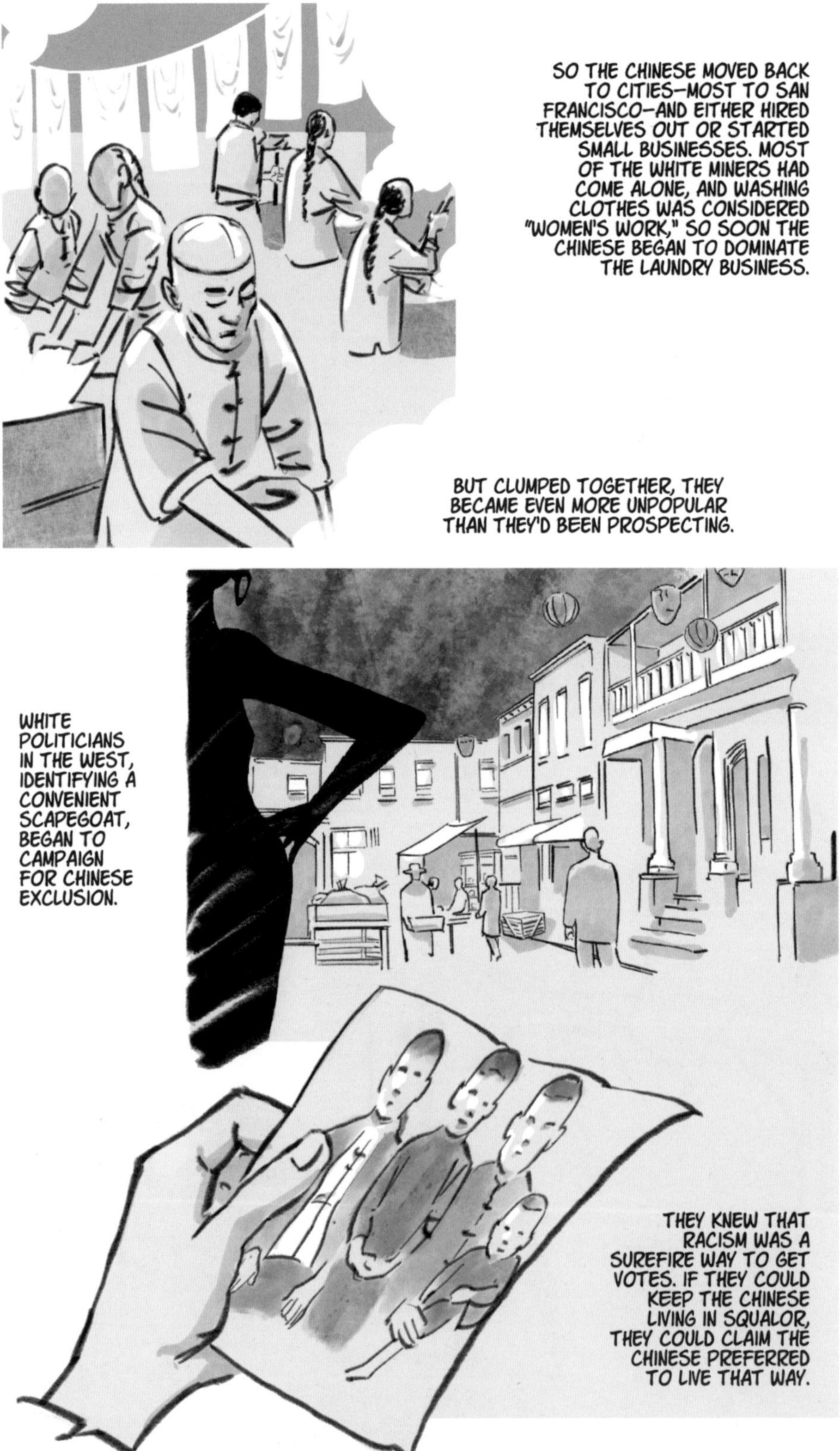
SO THE CHINESE MOVED BACK TO CITIES—MOST TO SAN FRANCISCO—AND EITHER HIRED THEMSELVES OUT OR STARTED SMALL BUSINESSES. MOST OF THE WHITE MINERS HAD COME ALONE, AND WASHING CLOTHES WAS CONSIDERED "WOMEN'S WORK," SO SOON THE CHINESE BEGAN TO DOMINATE THE LAUNDRY BUSINESS.
BUT CLUMPED TOGETHER, THEY BECAME EVEN MORE UNPOPULAR THAN THEY'D BEEN PROSPECTING.
WHITE POLITICIANS IN THE WEST, IDENTIFYING A CONVENIENT SCAPEGOAT, BEGAN TO CAMPAIGN FOR CHINESE EXCLUSION.
THEY KNEW THAT RACISM WAS A SUREFIRE WAY TO GET VOTES. IF THEY COULD KEEP THE CHINESE LIVING IN SQUALOR, THEY COULD CLAIM THE CHINESE PREFERRED TO LIVE THAT WAY.

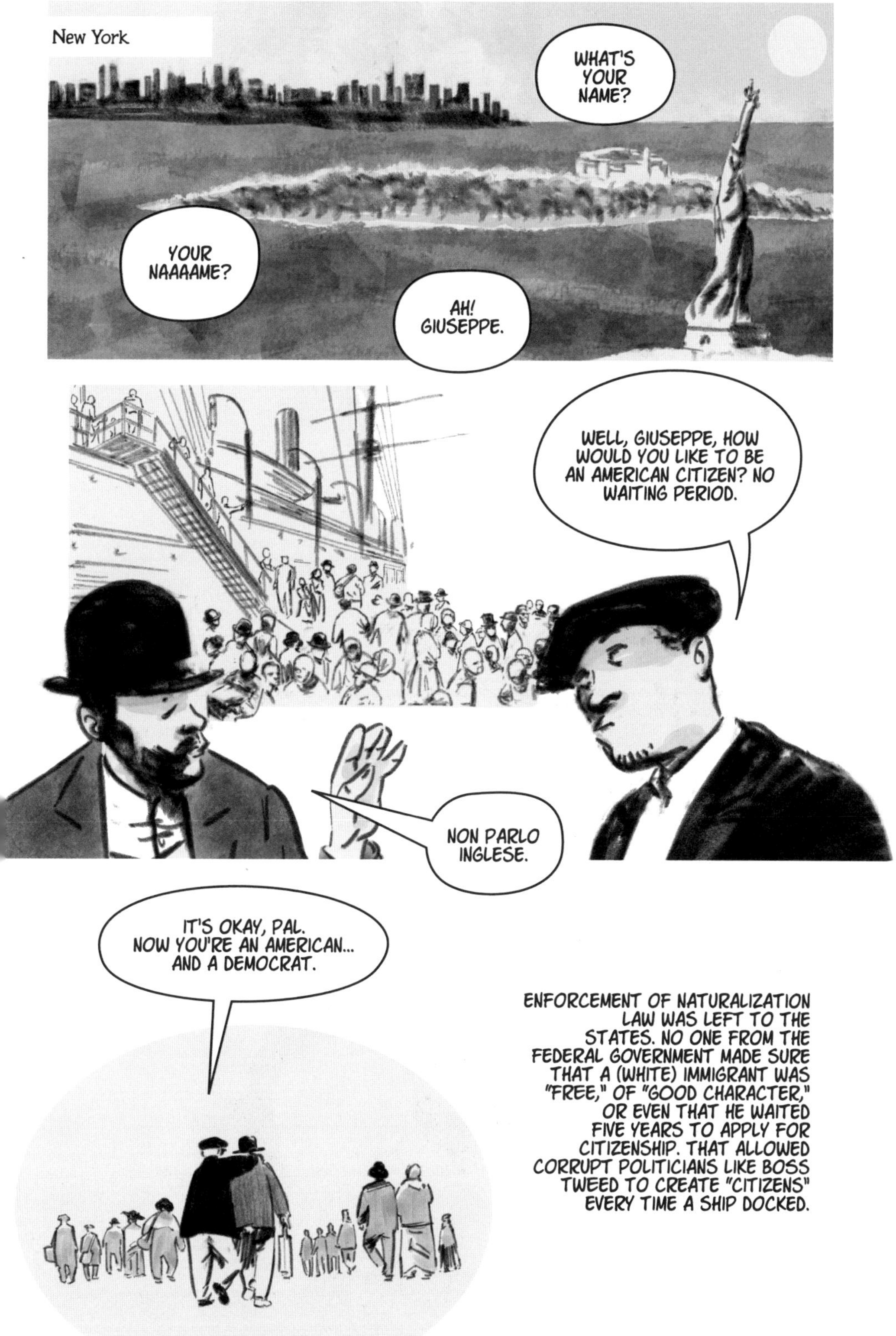
New York
WHAT'S YOUR NAME?
YOUR NAAAAME?
AH! GIUSEPPE.
WELL, GIUSEPPE, HOW WOULD YOU LIKE TO BE AN AMERICAN CITIZEN? NO WAITING PERIOD.
NON PARLO INGLESE.
IT'S OKAY, PAL. NOW YOU'RE AN AMERICAN... AND A DEMOCRAT.
ENFORCEMENT OF NATURALIZATION LAW WAS LEFT TO THE STATES. NO ONE FROM THE FEDERAL GOVERNMENT MADE SURE THAT A (WHITE) IMMIGRANT WAS "FREE," OF "GOOD CHARACTER," OR EVEN THAT HE WAITED FIVE YEARS TO APPLY FOR CITIZENSHIP. THAT ALLOWED CORRUPT POLITICIANS LIKE BOSS TWEED TO CREATE "CITIZENS" EVERY TIME A SHIP DOCKED.

FRAUD BECAME RAMPANT, ESPECIALLY IN NEW YORK, WHERE IMMIGRANTS USED FALSE NATURALIZATION PAPERS TO VOTE FOR DEMOCRATS AND KEEP THE TWEED RING IN POWER.

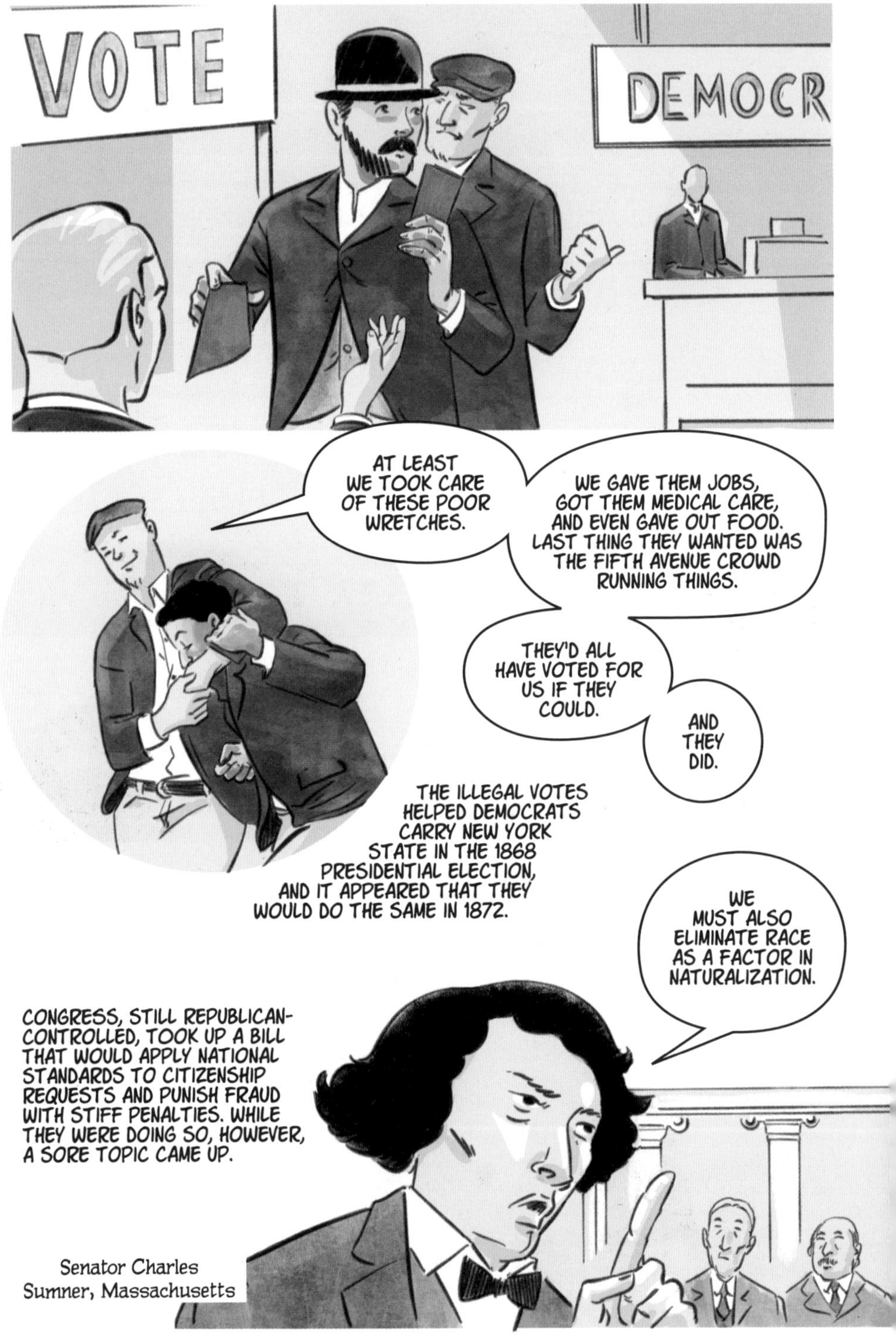
VOTE
DEMOCR
AT LEAST WE TOOK CARE OF THESE POOR WRETCHES.
WE GAVE THEM JOBS, GOT THEM MEDICAL CARE, AND EVEN GAVE OUT FOOD. LAST THING THEY WANTED WAS THE FIFTH AVENUE CROWD RUNNING THINGS.
THEY'D ALL HAVE VOTED FOR US IF THEY COULD.
AND THEY DID.
THE ILLEGAL VOTES HELPED DEMOCRATS CARRY NEW YORK STATE IN THE 1868 PRESIDENTIAL ELECTION, AND IT APPEARED THAT THEY WOULD DO THE SAME IN 1872.
WE MUST ALSO ELIMINATE RACE AS A FACTOR IN NATURALIZATION.
CONGRESS, STILL REPUBLICAN-CONTROLLED, TOOK UP A BILL THAT WOULD APPLY NATIONAL STANDARDS TO CITIZENSHIP REQUESTS AND PUNISH FRAUD WITH STIFF PENALTIES. WHILE THEY WERE DOING SO, HOWEVER, A SORE TOPIC CAME UP.
Senator Charles Sumner, Massachusetts

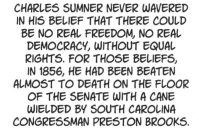

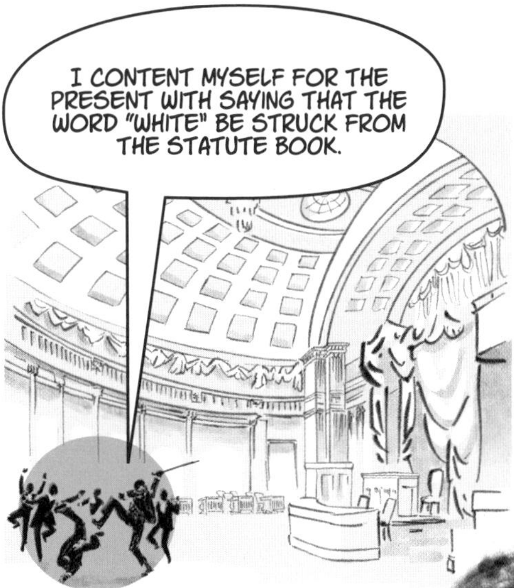
I CONTENT MYSELF FOR THE PRESENT WITH SAYING THAT THE WORD "WHITE" BE STRUCK FROM THE STATUTE BOOK.

CHARLES SUMNER NEVER WAVERED IN HIS BELIEF THAT THERE COULD BE NO REAL FREEDOM, NO REAL DEMOCRACY, WITHOUT EQUAL RIGHTS. FOR THOSE BELIEFS, IN 1856, HE HAD BEEN BEATEN ALMOST TO DEATH ON THE FLOOR OF THE SENATE WITH A CANE WIELDED BY SOUTH CAROLINA CONGRESSMAN PRESTON BROOKS.

NOW THE UNCONQUERABLE SUMNER WAS DETERMINED TO USE THE NEW BILL TO RIGHT AN OLD WRONG.

HE HAD SUPPORTERS.

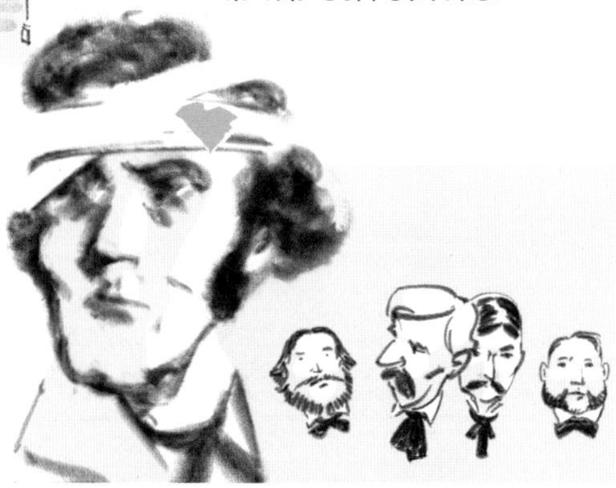

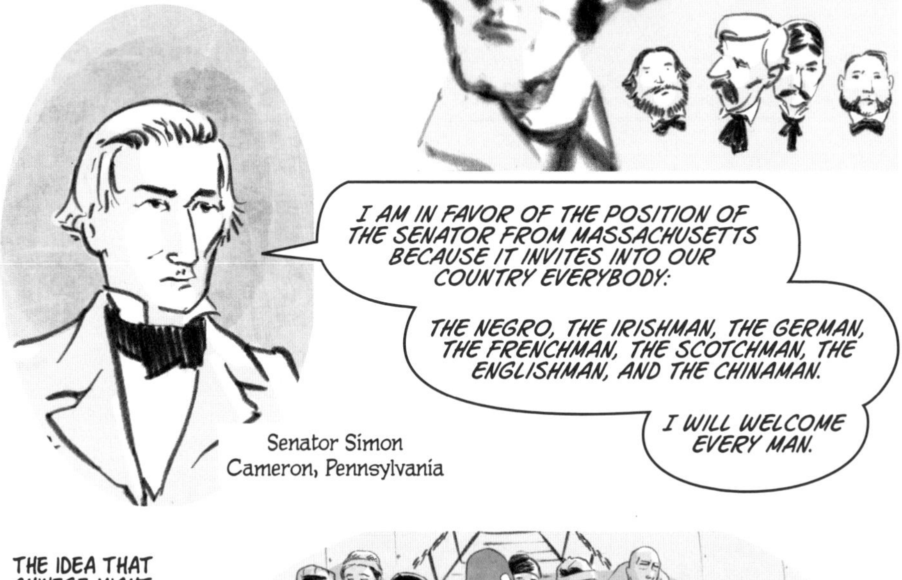
I AM IN FAVOR OF THE POSITION OF THE SENATOR FROM MASSACHUSETTS BECAUSE IT INVITES INTO OUR COUNTRY EVERYBODY:
THE NEGRO, THE IRISHMAN, THE GERMAN, THE FRENCHMAN, THE SCOTCHMAN, THE ENGLISHMAN, AND THE CHINAMAN.
I WILL WELCOME EVERY MAN.

Senator Simon Cameron, Pennsylvania

THE IDEA THAT CHINESE MIGHT BE FREE TO ENTER THE COUNTRY AND THEN BECOME CITIZENS INFURIATED WESTERNERS, WHO WERE TRYING TO GET RID OF THE CHINESE ALREADY THERE.

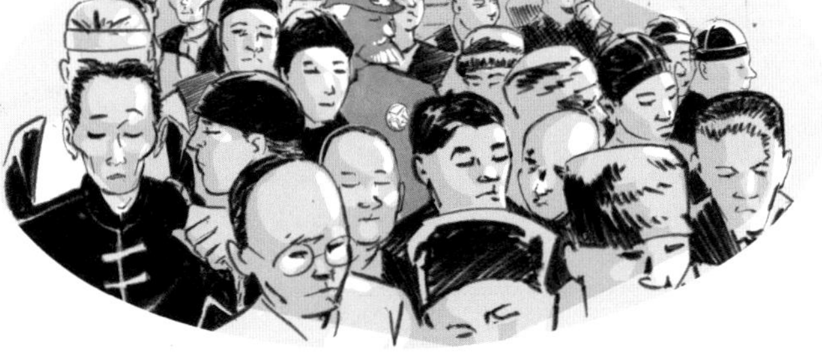

Representative James Johnson, California

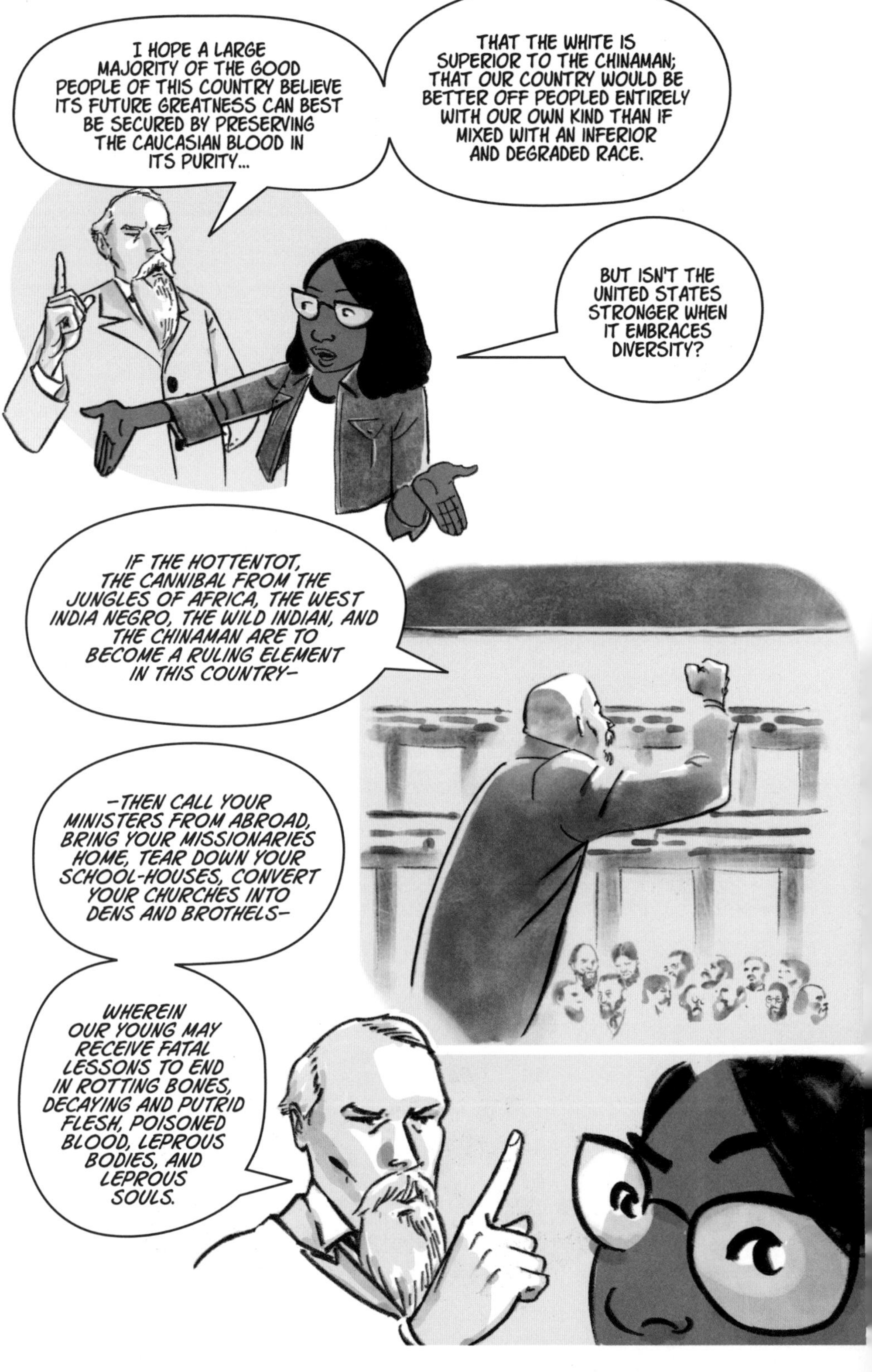
I HOPE A LARGE MAJORITY OF THE GOOD PEOPLE OF THIS COUNTRY BELIEVE ITS FUTURE GREATNESS CAN BEST BE SECURED BY PRESERVING THE CAUCASIAN BLOOD IN ITS PURITY...
THAT THE WHITE IS SUPERIOR TO THE CHINAMAN; THAT OUR COUNTRY WOULD BE BETTER OFF PEOPLED ENTIRELY WITH OUR OWN KIND THAN IF MIXED WITH AN INFERIOR AND DEGRADED RACE.
BUT ISN'T THE UNITED STATES STRONGER WHEN IT EMBRACES DIVERSITY?
IF THE HOTTENTOT, THE CANNIBAL FROM THE JUNGLES OF AFRICA, THE WEST INDIA NEGRO, THE WILD INDIAN, AND THE CHINAMAN ARE TO BECOME A RULING ELEMENT IN THIS COUNTRY–
–THEN CALL YOUR MINISTERS FROM ABROAD, BRING YOUR MISSIONARIES HOME, TEAR DOWN YOUR SCHOOL-HOUSES, CONVERT YOUR CHURCHES INTO DENS AND BROTHELS–
WHEREIN OUR YOUNG MAY RECEIVE FATAL LESSONS TO END IN ROTTING BONES, DECAYING AND PUTRID FLESH, POISONED BLOOD, LEPROUS BODIES, AND LEPROUS SOULS.

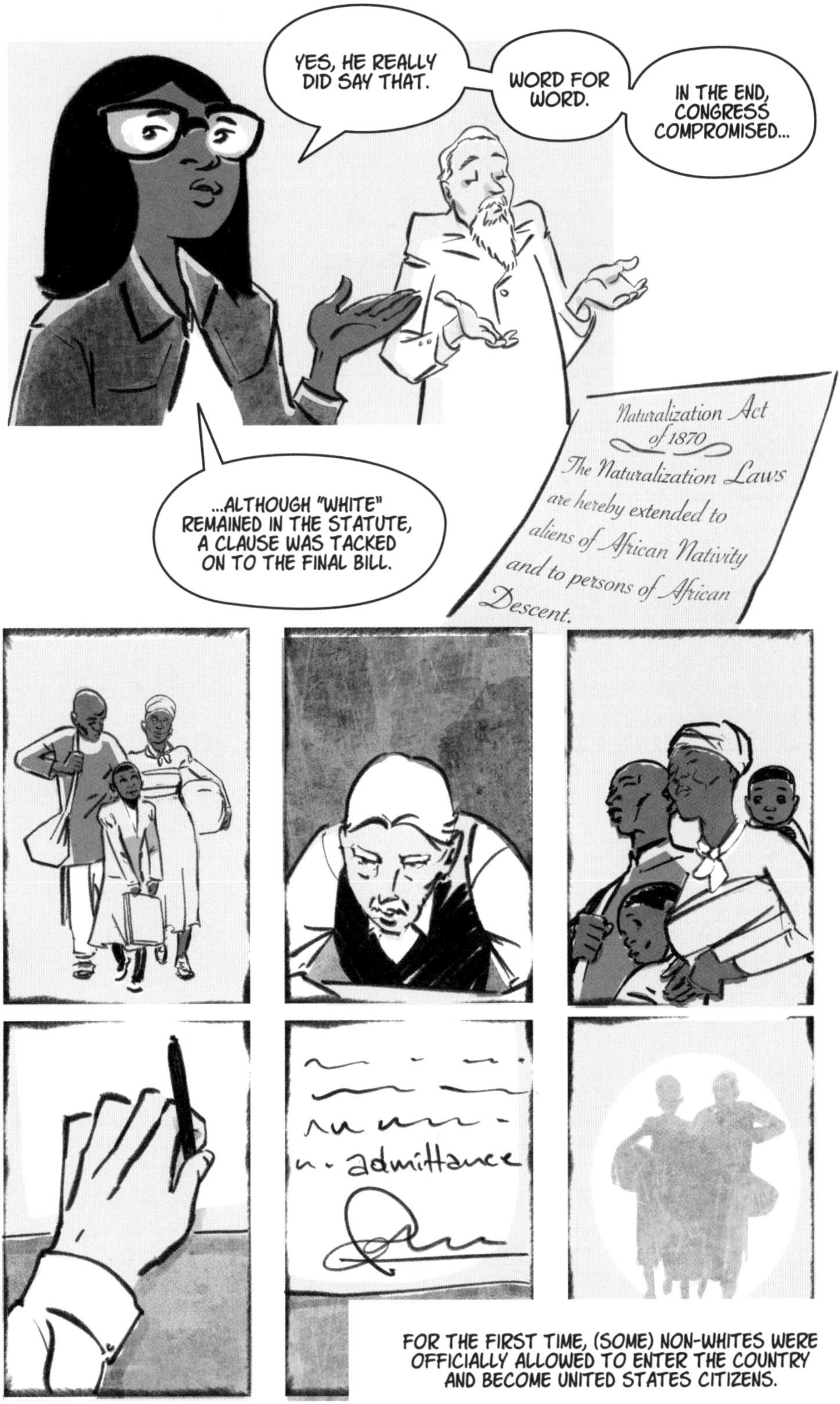
YES, HE REALLY DID SAY THAT.
WORD FOR WORD.
IN THE END, CONGRESS COMPROMISED...
...ALTHOUGH "WHITE" REMAINED IN THE STATUTE, A CLAUSE WAS TACKED ON TO THE FINAL BILL.
Naturalization Act of 1870
The Naturalization Laws are hereby extended to aliens of African Nativity and to persons of African Descent.
admittance
FOR THE FIRST TIME, (SOME) NON-WHITES WERE OFFICIALLY ALLOWED TO ENTER THE COUNTRY AND BECOME UNITED STATES CITIZENS.

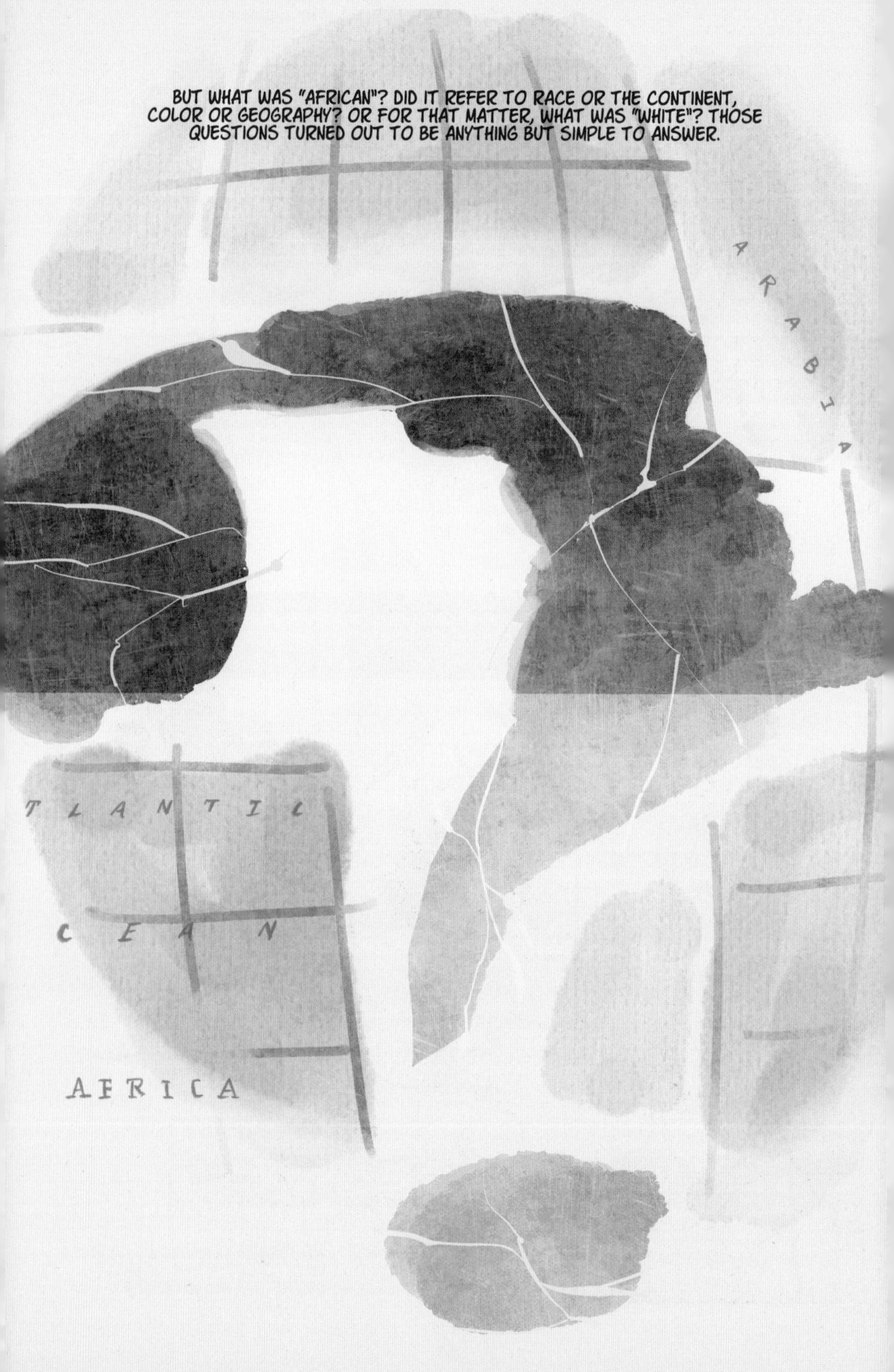
BUT WHAT WAS "AFRICAN"? DID IT REFER TO RACE OR THE CONTINENT, COLOR OR GEOGRAPHY? OR FOR THAT MATTER, WHAT WAS "WHITE"? THOSE QUESTIONS TURNED OUT TO BE ANYTHING BUT SIMPLE TO ANSWER.
ARABIA
TLANTIC
CEAN
AFRICA

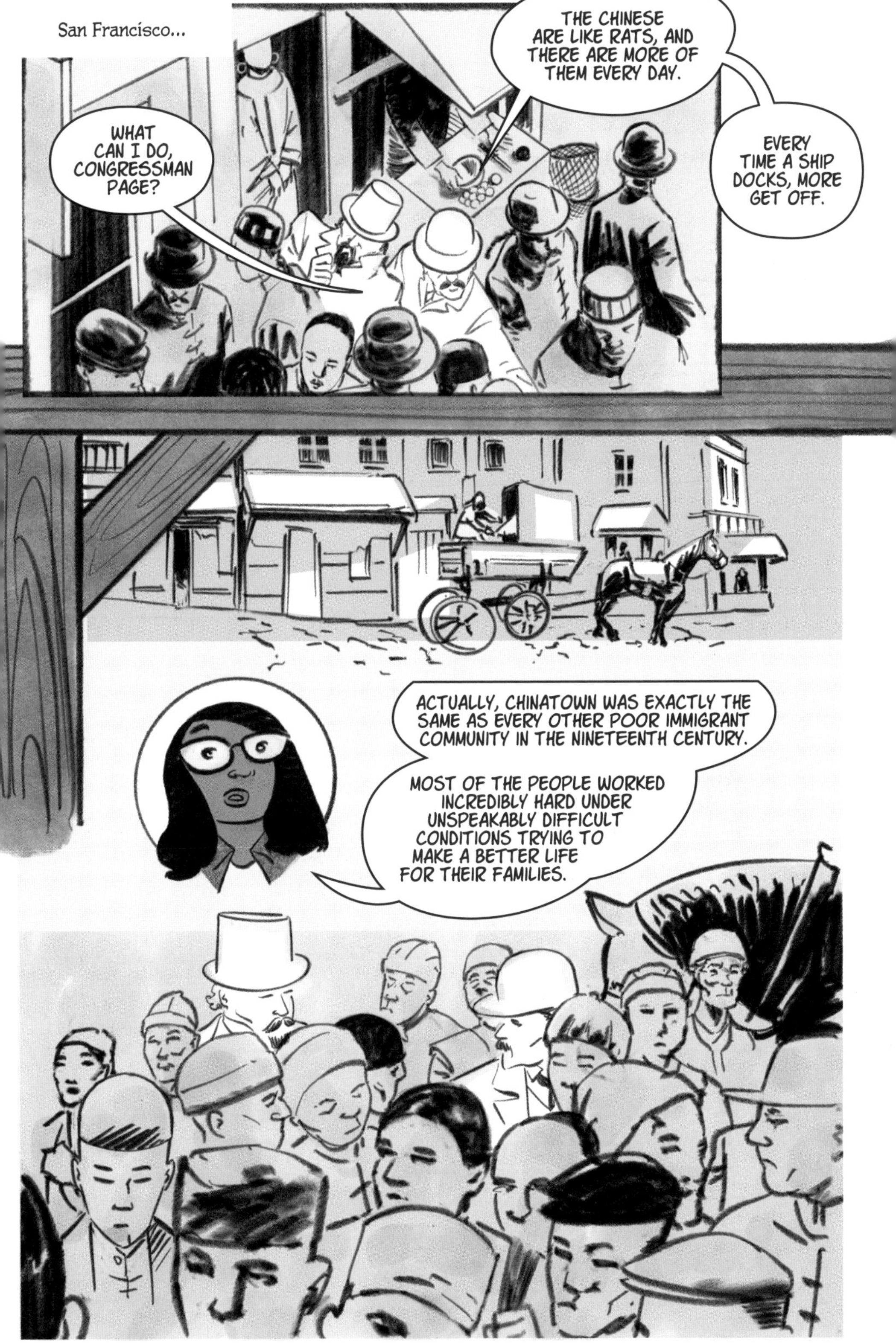
San Francisco...
WHAT CAN I DO, CONGRESSMAN PAGE?
THE CHINESE ARE LIKE RATS, AND THERE ARE MORE OF THEM EVERY DAY.
EVERY TIME A SHIP DOCKS, MORE GET OFF.
ACTUALLY, CHINATOWN WAS EXACTLY THE SAME AS EVERY OTHER POOR IMMIGRANT COMMUNITY IN THE NINETEENTH CENTURY.
MOST OF THE PEOPLE WORKED INCREDIBLY HARD UNDER UNSPEAKABLY DIFFICULT CONDITIONS TRYING TO MAKE A BETTER LIFE FOR THEIR FAMILIES.

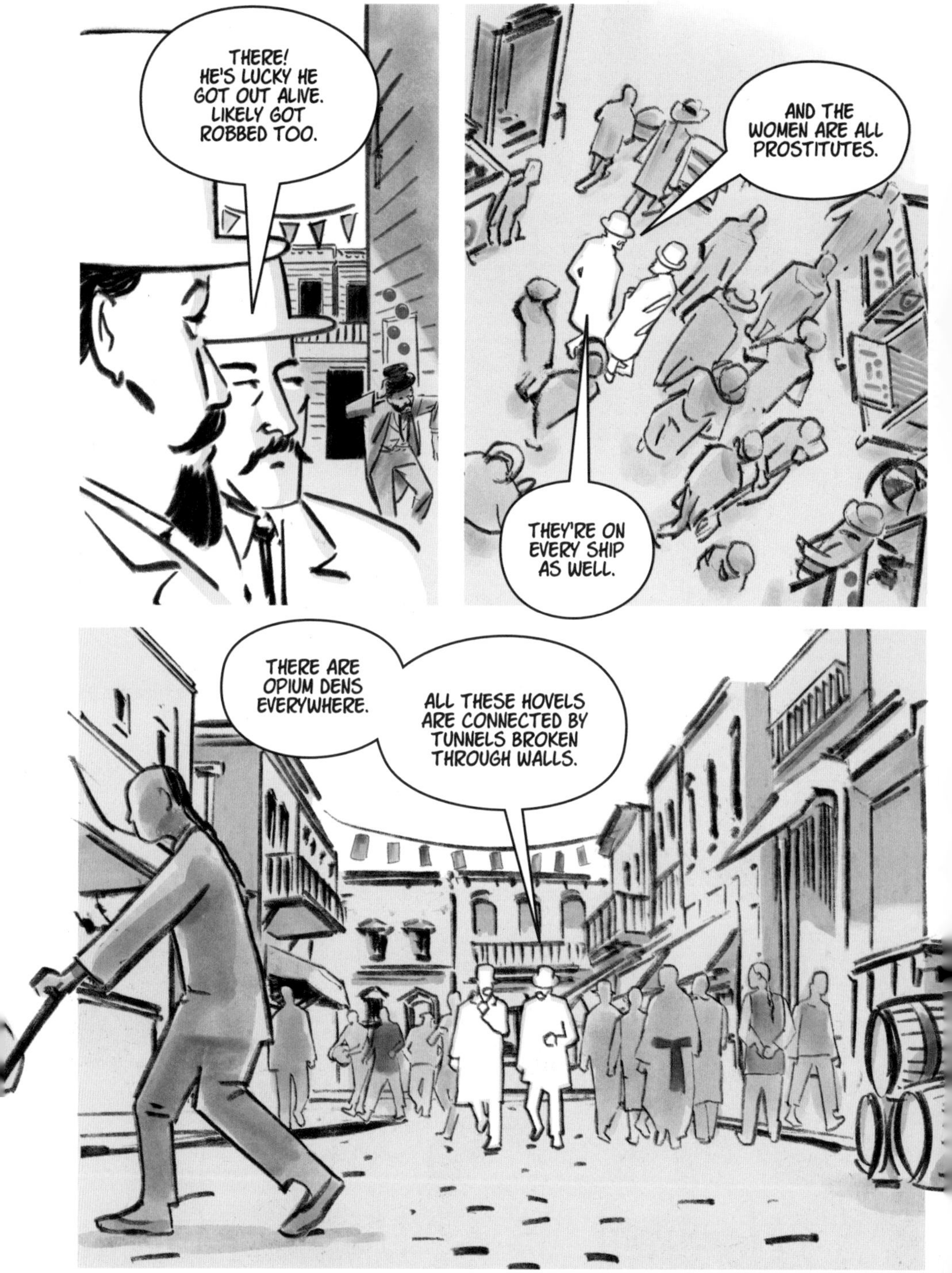
THERE! HE'S LUCKY HE GOT OUT ALIVE. LIKELY GOT ROBBED TOO.
AND THE WOMEN ARE ALL PROSTITUTES.
THEY'RE ON EVERY SHIP AS WELL.
THERE ARE OPIUM DENS EVERYWHERE.
ALL THESE HOVELS ARE CONNECTED BY TUNNELS BROKEN THROUGH WALLS.

AND, LIKE EVERY OTHER POOR IMMIGRANT COMMUNITY, CHINATOWN WAS ALSO CRIME-RIDDEN, ALTHOUGH THE RESIDENTS WERE THE VICTIMS FAR MORE OFTEN THAN VISITORS.

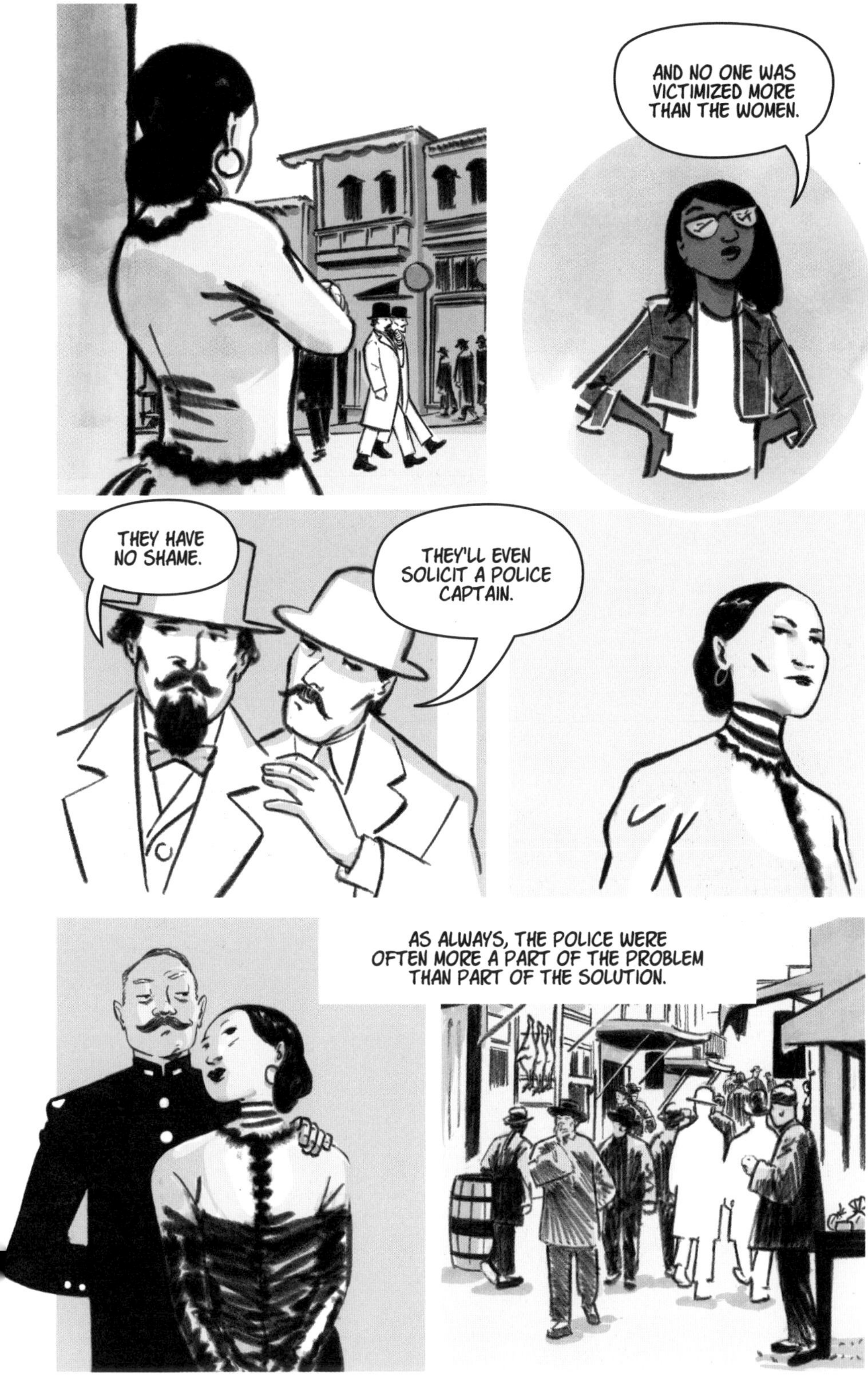
AND NO ONE WAS VICTIMIZED MORE THAN THE WOMEN.
THEY HAVE NO SHAME.
THEY'LL EVEN SOLICIT A POLICE CAPTAIN.
AS ALWAYS, THE POLICE WERE OFTEN MORE A PART OF THE PROBLEM THAN PART OF THE SOLUTION.

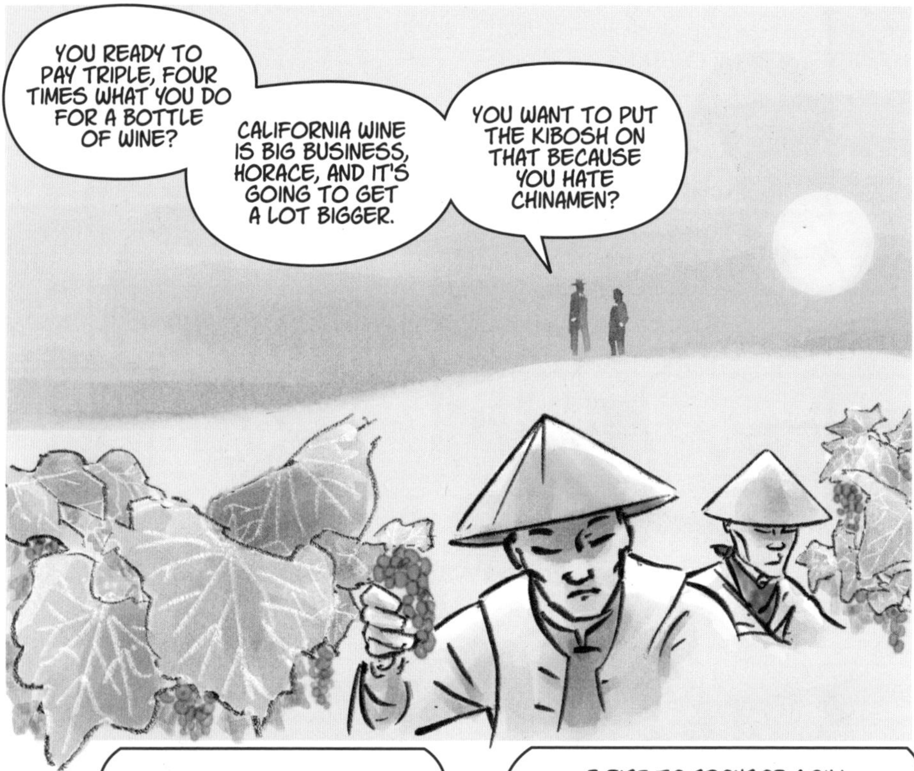
YOU READY TO PAY TRIPLE, FOUR TIMES WHAT YOU DO FOR A BOTTLE OF WINE?
CALIFORNIA WINE IS BIG BUSINESS, HORACE, AND IT'S GOING TO GET A LOT BIGGER.
YOU WANT TO PUT THE KIBOSH ON THAT BECAUSE YOU HATE CHINAMEN?

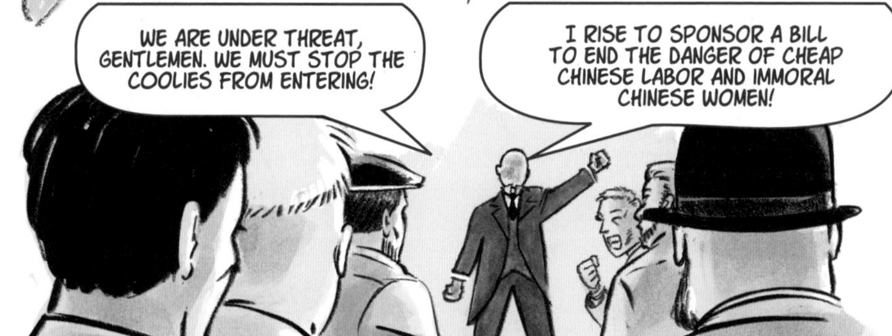
WE ARE UNDER THREAT, GENTLEMEN. WE MUST STOP THE COOLIES FROM ENTERING!
I RISE TO SPONSOR A BILL TO END THE DANGER OF CHEAP CHINESE LABOR AND IMMORAL CHINESE WOMEN!

THE BILL EASILY PASSED IN BOTH HOUSES OF CONGRESS AND WAS SIGNED INTO LAW BY PRESIDENT ULYSSES S. GRANT ON MARCH 3, 1875.

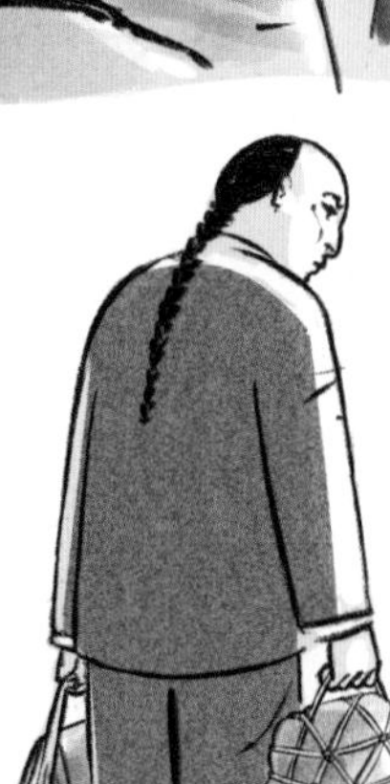

THE PAGE ACT BECAME THE FIRST LAW IN AMERICAN HISTORY THAT RESTRICTED THE ENTRY OF SPECIFIC "UNDESIRABLE" ELEMENTS.

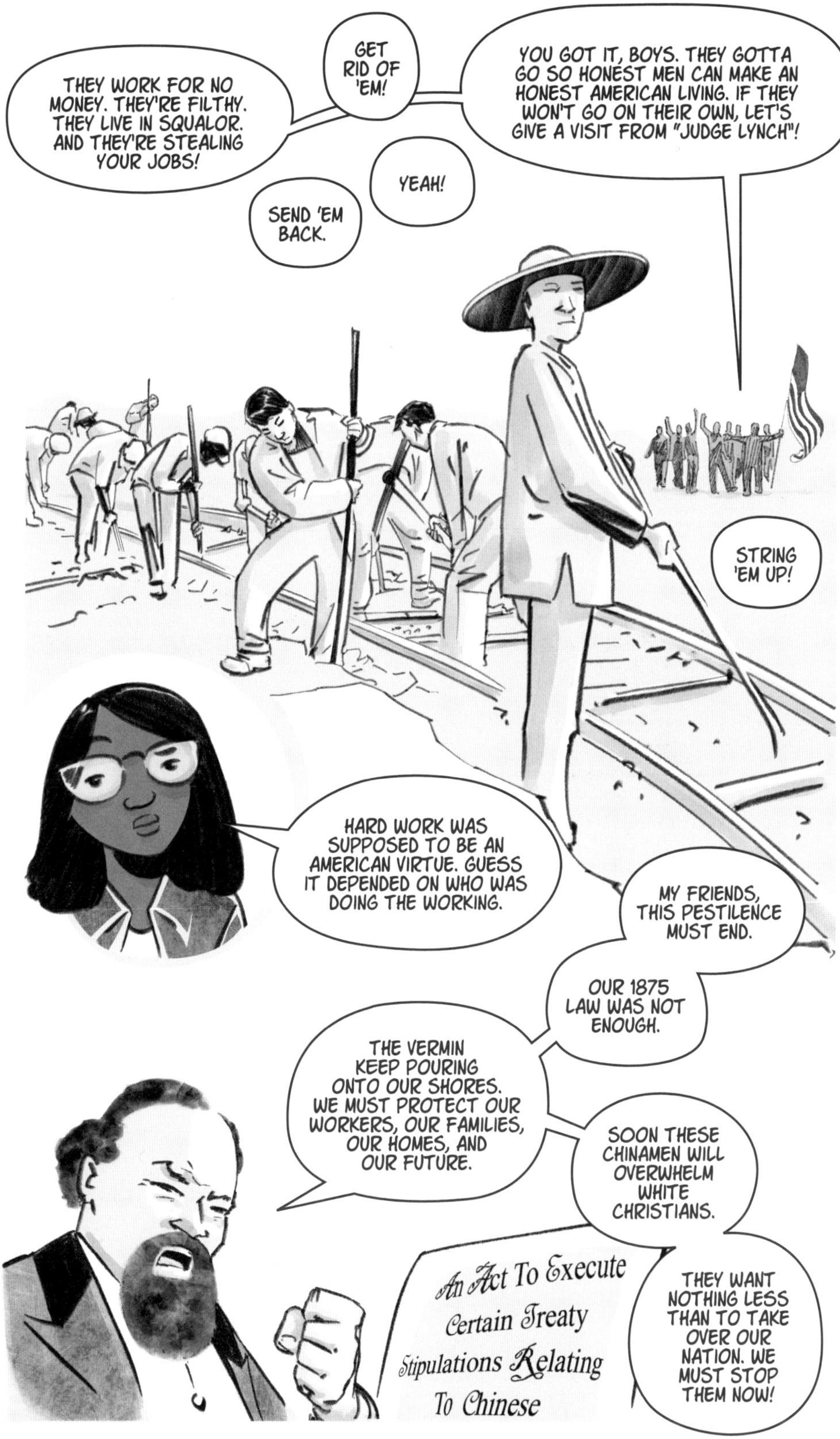
THEY WORK FOR NO MONEY. THEY'RE FILTHY. THEY LIVE IN SQUALOR. AND THEY'RE STEALING YOUR JOBS!
GET RID OF 'EM!
YOU GOT IT, BOYS. THEY GOTTA GO SO HONEST MEN CAN MAKE AN HONEST AMERICAN LIVING. IF THEY WON'T GO ON THEIR OWN, LET'S GIVE A VISIT FROM "JUDGE LYNCH"!
YEAH!
SEND 'EM BACK.
STRING 'EM UP!
HARD WORK WAS SUPPOSED TO BE AN AMERICAN VIRTUE. GUESS IT DEPENDED ON WHO WAS DOING THE WORKING.
MY FRIENDS, THIS PESTILENCE MUST END.
OUR 1875 LAW WAS NOT ENOUGH.
THE VERMIN KEEP POURING ONTO OUR SHORES. WE MUST PROTECT OUR WORKERS, OUR FAMILIES, OUR HOMES, AND OUR FUTURE.
SOON THESE CHINAMEN WILL OVERWHELM WHITE CHRISTIANS.
An Act To Execute Certain Treaty Stipulations Relating To Chinese
THEY WANT NOTHING LESS THAN TO TAKE OVER OUR NATION. WE MUST STOP THEM NOW!

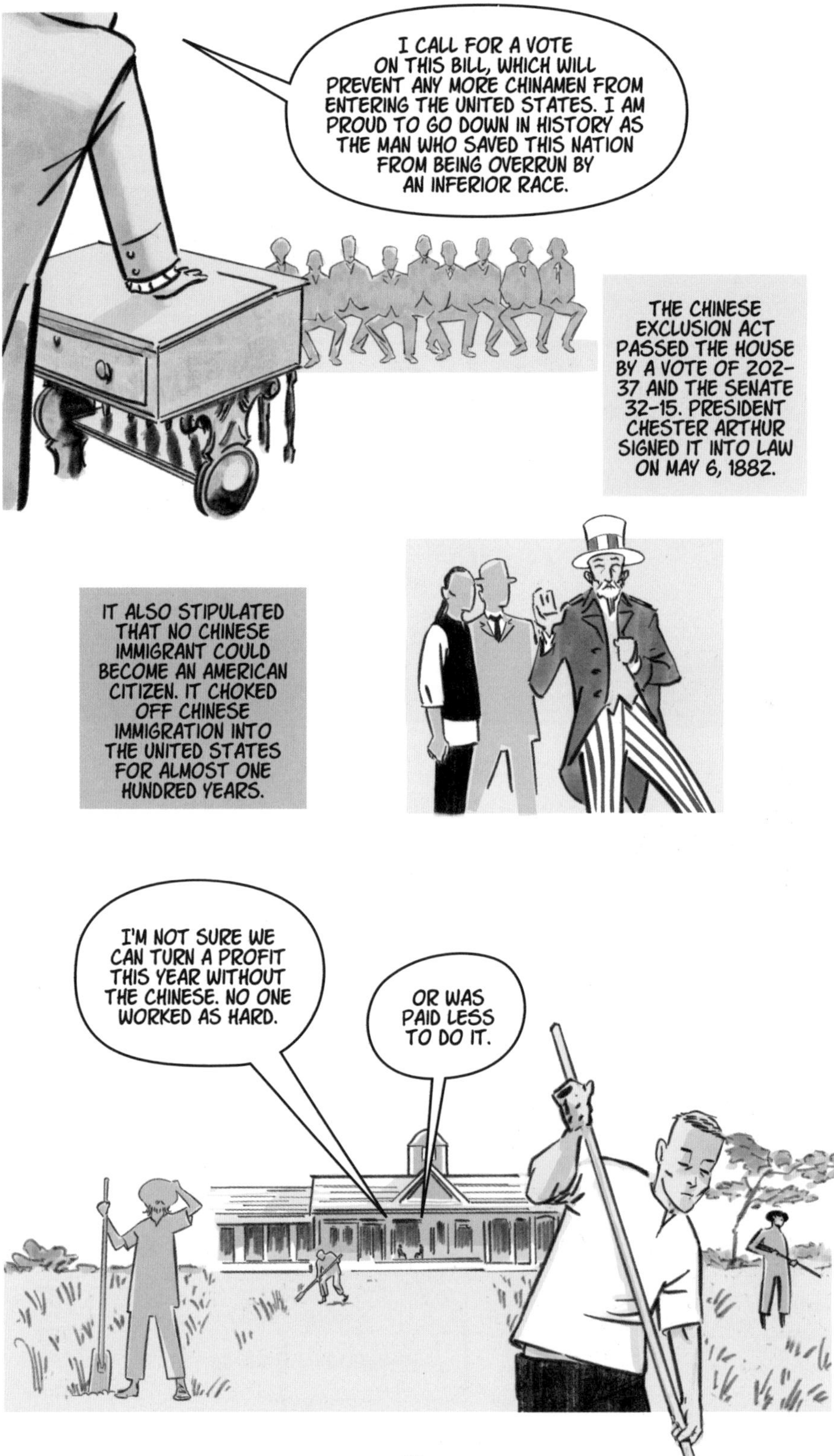
I CALL FOR A VOTE ON THIS BILL, WHICH WILL PREVENT ANY MORE CHINAMEN FROM ENTERING THE UNITED STATES. I AM PROUD TO GO DOWN IN HISTORY AS THE MAN WHO SAVED THIS NATION FROM BEING OVERRUN BY AN INFERIOR RACE.
THE CHINESE EXCLUSION ACT PASSED THE HOUSE BY A VOTE OF 202-37 AND THE SENATE 32-15. PRESIDENT CHESTER ARTHUR SIGNED IT INTO LAW ON MAY 6, 1882.
IT ALSO STIPULATED THAT NO CHINESE IMMIGRANT COULD BECOME AN AMERICAN CITIZEN. IT CHOKED OFF CHINESE IMMIGRATION INTO THE UNITED STATES FOR ALMOST ONE HUNDRED YEARS.
I'M NOT SURE WE CAN TURN A PROFIT THIS YEAR WITHOUT THE CHINESE. NO ONE WORKED AS HARD.
OR WAS PAID LESS TO DO IT.

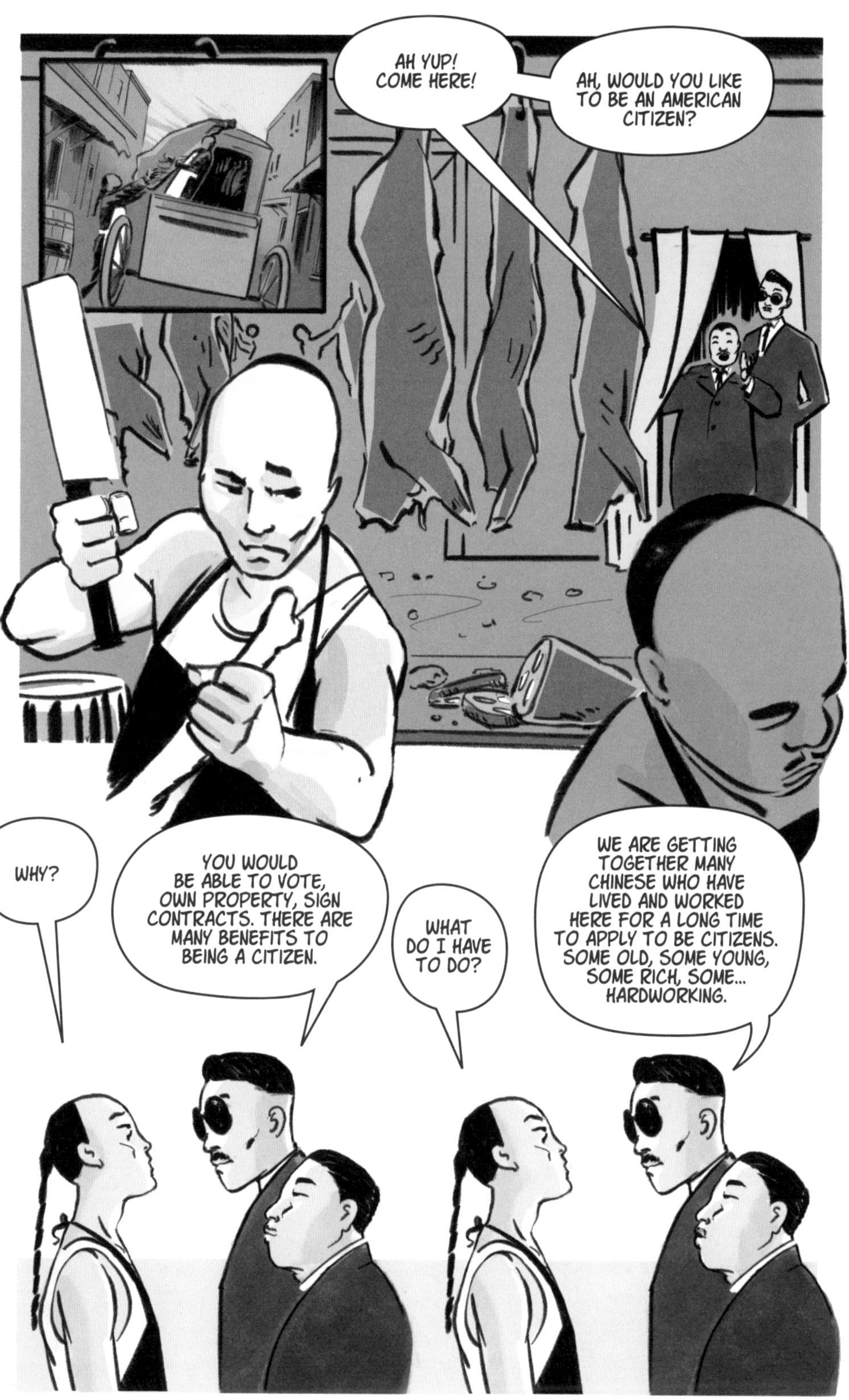
AH YUP! COME HERE!
AH, WOULD YOU LIKE TO BE AN AMERICAN CITIZEN?
WHY?
YOU WOULD BE ABLE TO VOTE, OWN PROPERTY, SIGN CONTRACTS. THERE ARE MANY BENEFITS TO BEING A CITIZEN.
WHAT DO I HAVE TO DO?
WE ARE GETTING TOGETHER MANY CHINESE WHO HAVE LIVED AND WORKED HERE FOR A LONG TIME TO APPLY TO BE CITIZENS. SOME OLD, SOME YOUNG, SOME RICH, SOME... HARDWORKING.

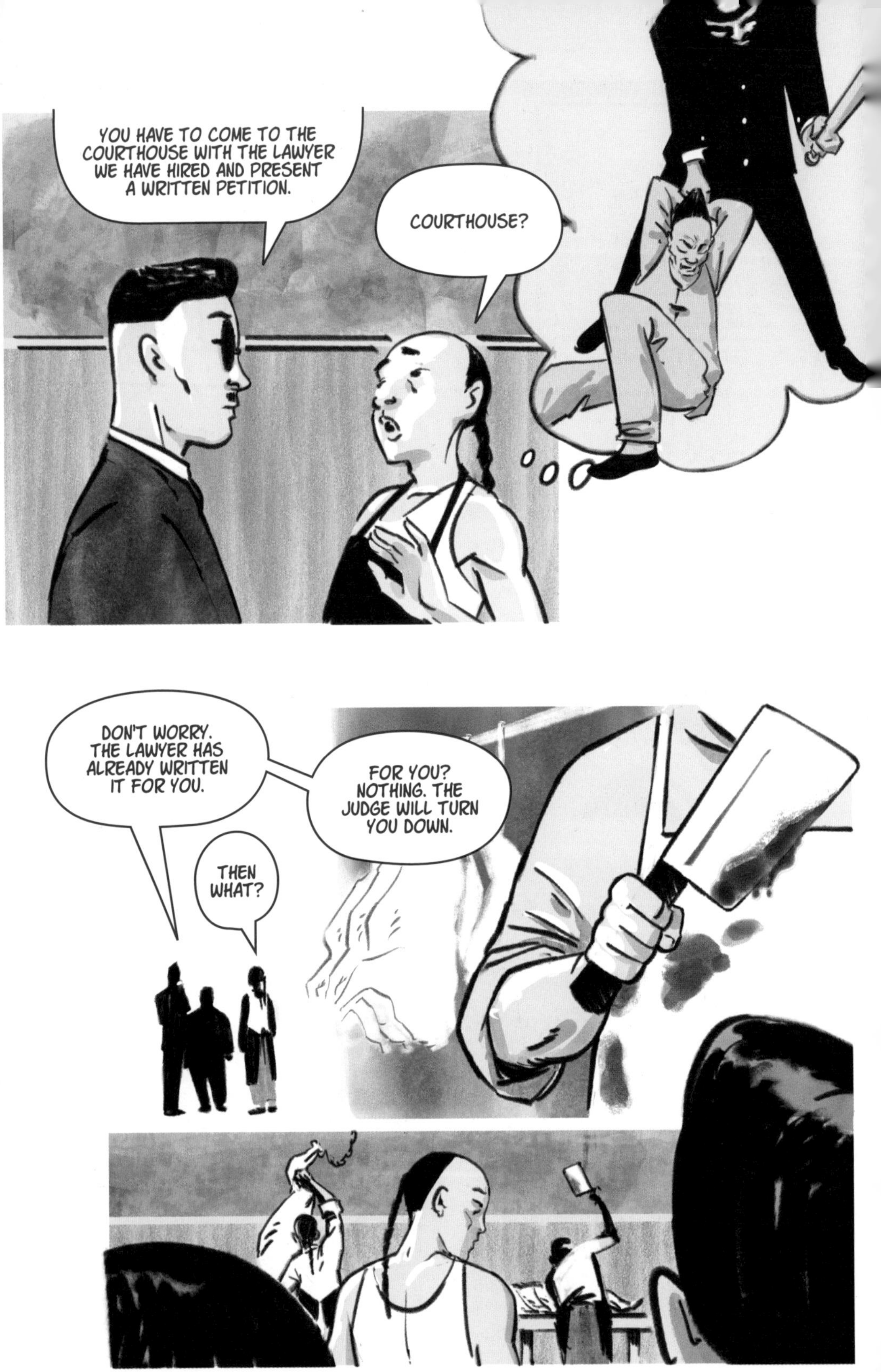
YOU HAVE TO COME TO THE COURTHOUSE WITH THE LAWYER WE HAVE HIRED AND PRESENT A WRITTEN PETITION.
COURTHOUSE?
DON'T WORRY. THE LAWYER HAS ALREADY WRITTEN IT FOR YOU.
THEN WHAT?
FOR YOU? NOTHING. THE JUDGE WILL TURN YOU DOWN.

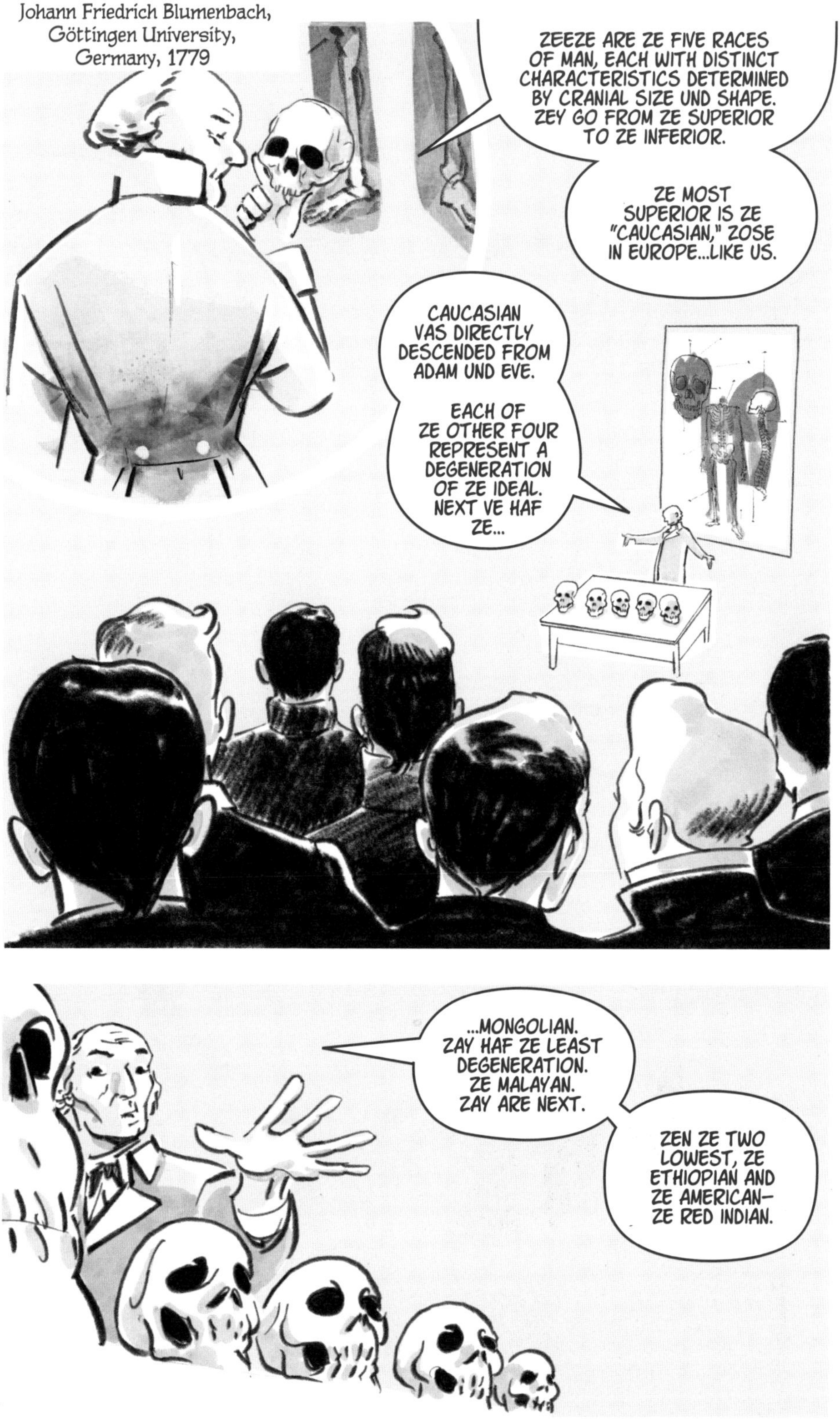
Johann Friedrich Blumenbach, Göttingen University, Germany, 1779
ZEEZE ARE ZE FIVE RACES OF MAN, EACH WITH DISTINCT CHARACTERISTICS DETERMINED BY CRANIAL SIZE UND SHAPE. ZEY GO FROM ZE SUPERIOR TO ZE INFERIOR.
ZE MOST SUPERIOR IS ZE "CAUCASIAN," ZOSE IN EUROPE...LIKE US.
CAUCASIAN VAS DIRECTLY DESCENDED FROM ADAM UND EVE.
EACH OF ZE OTHER FOUR REPRESENT A DEGENERATION OF ZE IDEAL. NEXT VE HAF ZE...
...MONGOLIAN. ZAY HAF ZE LEAST DEGENERATION. ZE MALAYAN. ZAY ARE NEXT.
ZEN ZE TWO LOWEST, ZE ETHIOPIAN AND ZE AMERICAN– ZE RED INDIAN.

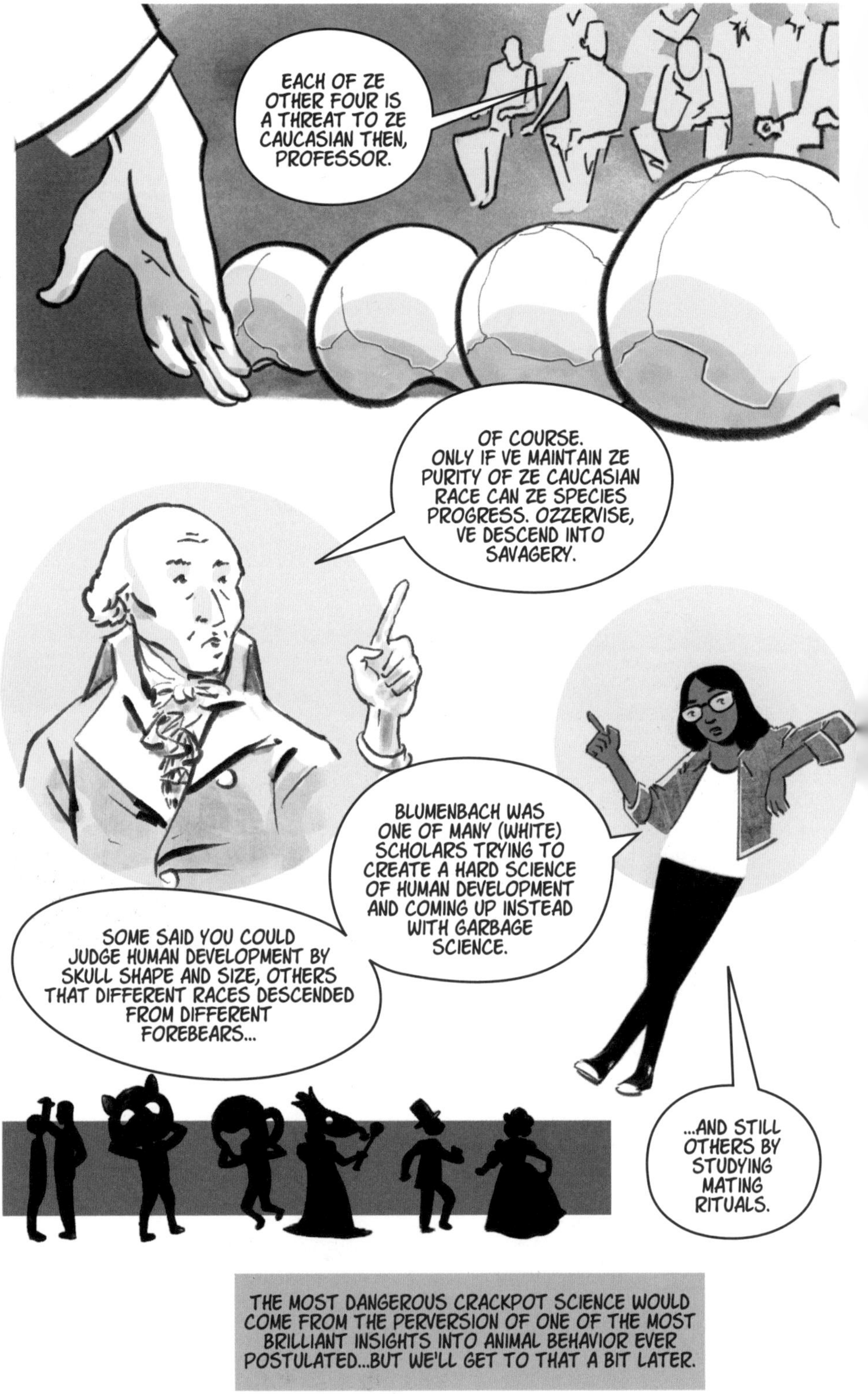
EACH OF ZE OTHER FOUR IS A THREAT TO ZE CAUCASIAN THEN, PROFESSOR.
OF COURSE. ONLY IF VE MAINTAIN ZE PURITY OF ZE CAUCASIAN RACE CAN ZE SPECIES PROGRESS. OZZERVISE, VE DESCEND INTO SAVAGERY.
BLUMENBACH WAS ONE OF MANY (WHITE) SCHOLARS TRYING TO CREATE A HARD SCIENCE OF HUMAN DEVELOPMENT AND COMING UP INSTEAD WITH GARBAGE SCIENCE.
SOME SAID YOU COULD JUDGE HUMAN DEVELOPMENT BY SKULL SHAPE AND SIZE, OTHERS THAT DIFFERENT RACES DESCENDED FROM DIFFERENT FOREBEARS...
...AND STILL OTHERS BY STUDYING MATING RITUALS.
THE MOST DANGEROUS CRACKPOT SCIENCE WOULD COME FROM THE PERVERSION OF ONE OF THE MOST BRILLIANT INSIGHTS INTO ANIMAL BEHAVIOR EVER POSTULATED...BUT WE'LL GET TO THAT A BIT LATER.

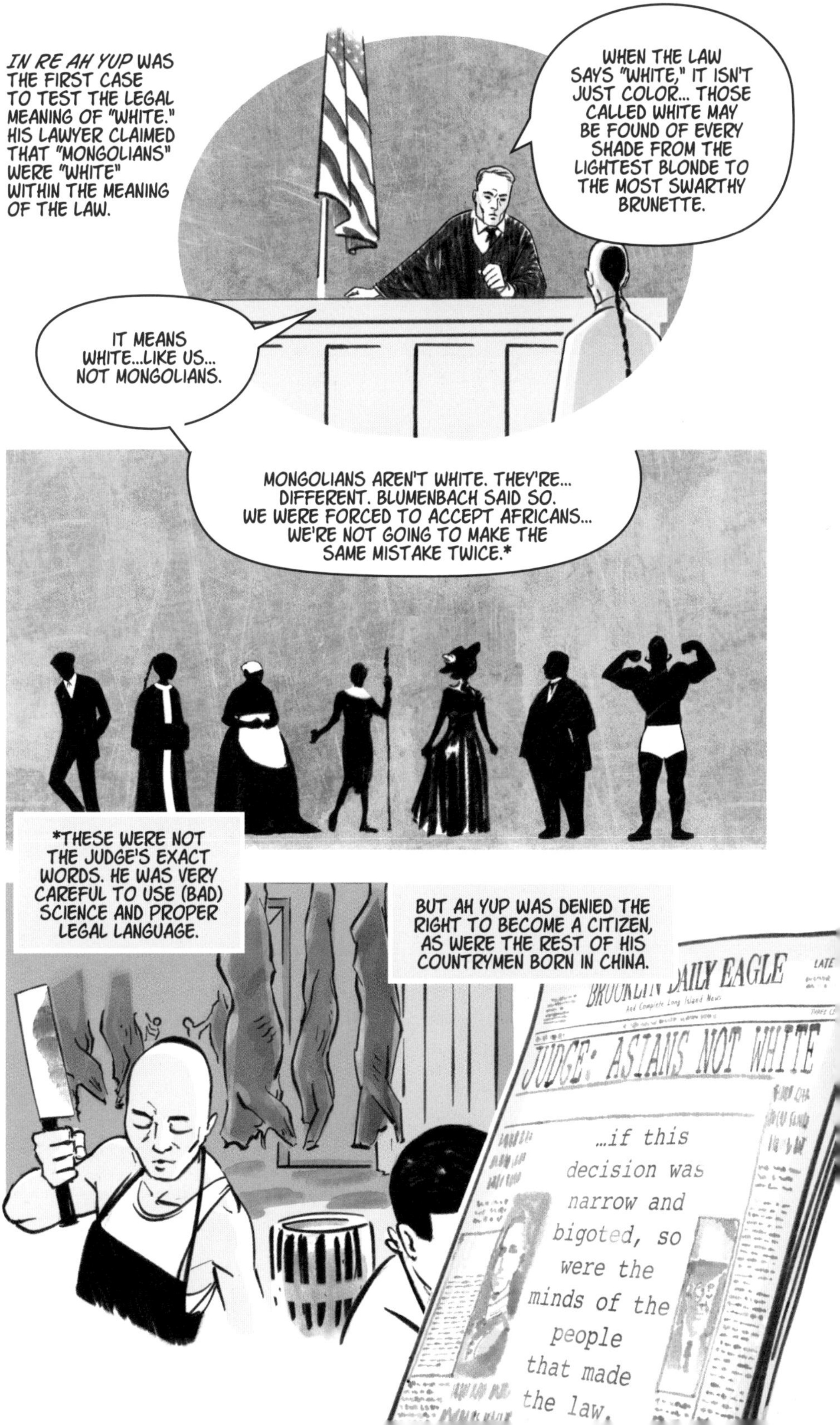

IN RE AH YUP WAS THE FIRST CASE TO TEST THE LEGAL MEANING OF "WHITE." HIS LAWYER CLAIMED THAT "MONGOLIANS" WERE "WHITE" WITHIN THE MEANING OF THE LAW.
WHEN THE LAW SAYS "WHITE," IT ISN'T JUST COLOR... THOSE CALLED WHITE MAY BE FOUND OF EVERY SHADE FROM THE LIGHTEST BLONDE TO THE MOST SWARTHY BRUNETTE.
IT MEANS WHITE...LIKE US... NOT MONGOLIANS.
MONGOLIANS AREN'T WHITE. THEY'RE... DIFFERENT. BLUMENBACH SAID SO. WE WERE FORCED TO ACCEPT AFRICANS... WE'RE NOT GOING TO MAKE THE SAME MISTAKE TWICE.*
*THESE WERE NOT THE JUDGE'S EXACT WORDS. HE WAS VERY CAREFUL TO USE (BAD) SCIENCE AND PROPER LEGAL LANGUAGE.
BUT AH YUP WAS DENIED THE RIGHT TO BECOME A CITIZEN, AS WERE THE REST OF HIS COUNTRYMEN BORN IN CHINA.
BROOKLYN DAILY EAGLE
And Complete Long Island News
JUDGE: ASIANS NOT WHITE
...if this decision was narrow and bigoted, so were the minds of the people that made the law.

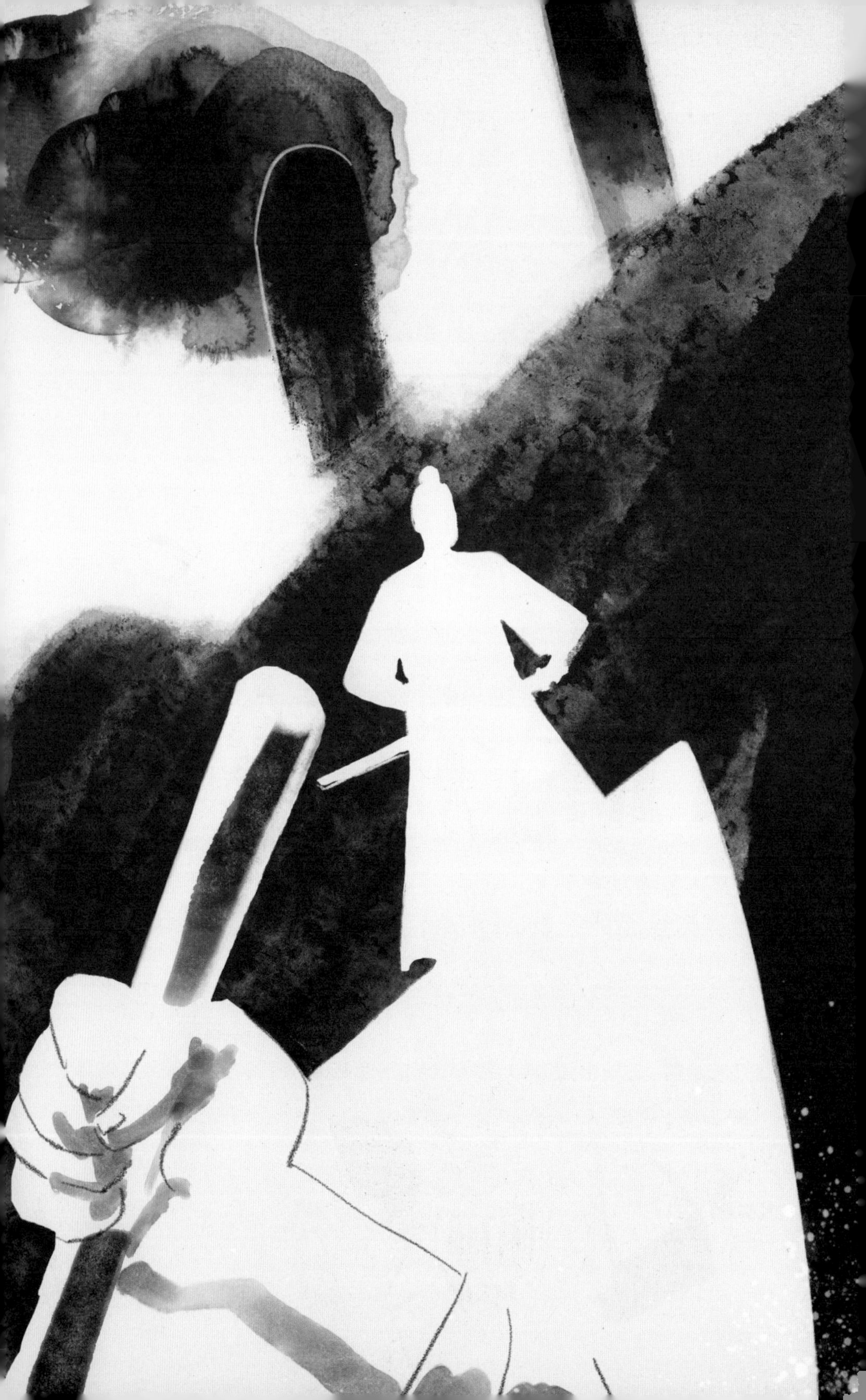

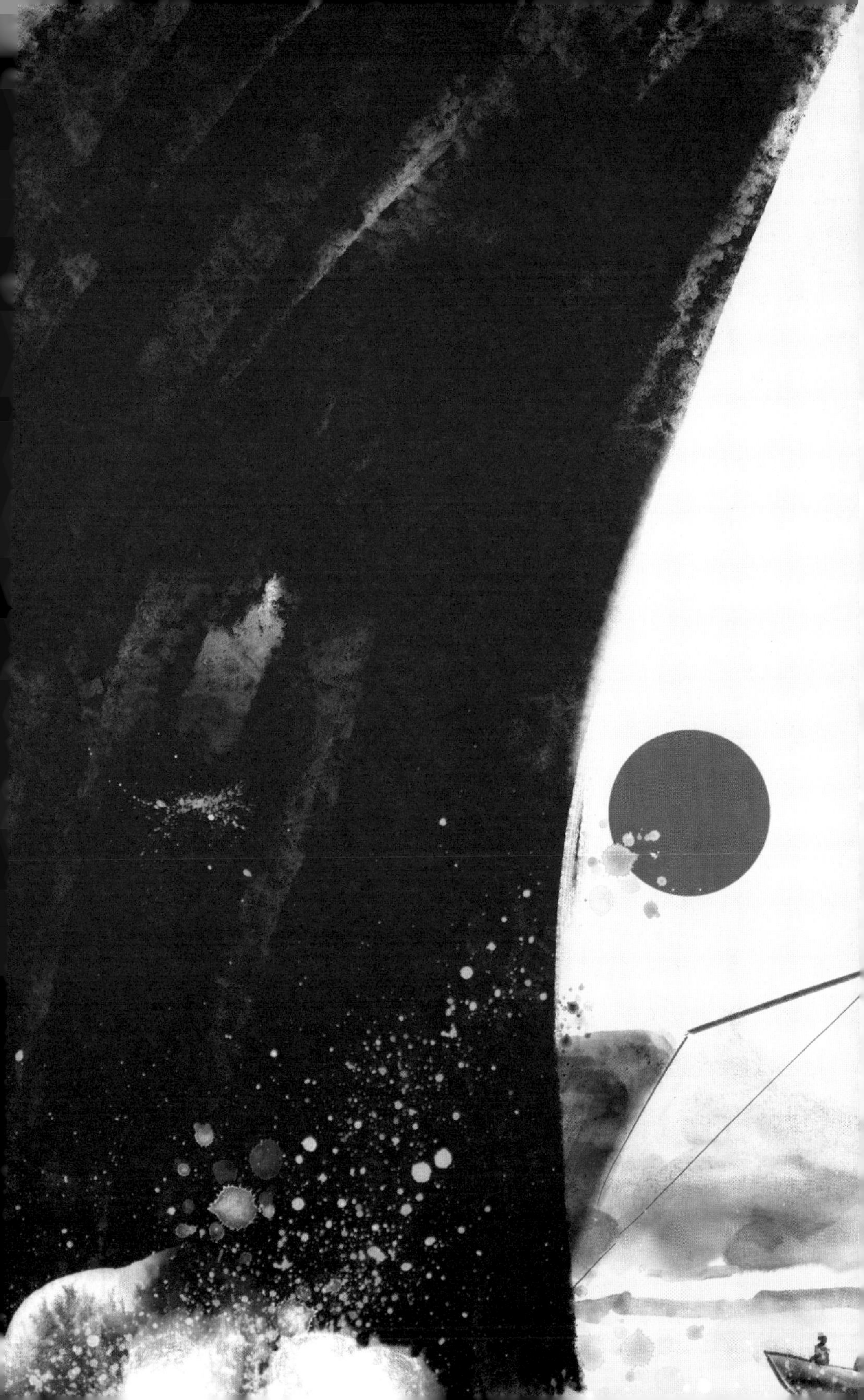

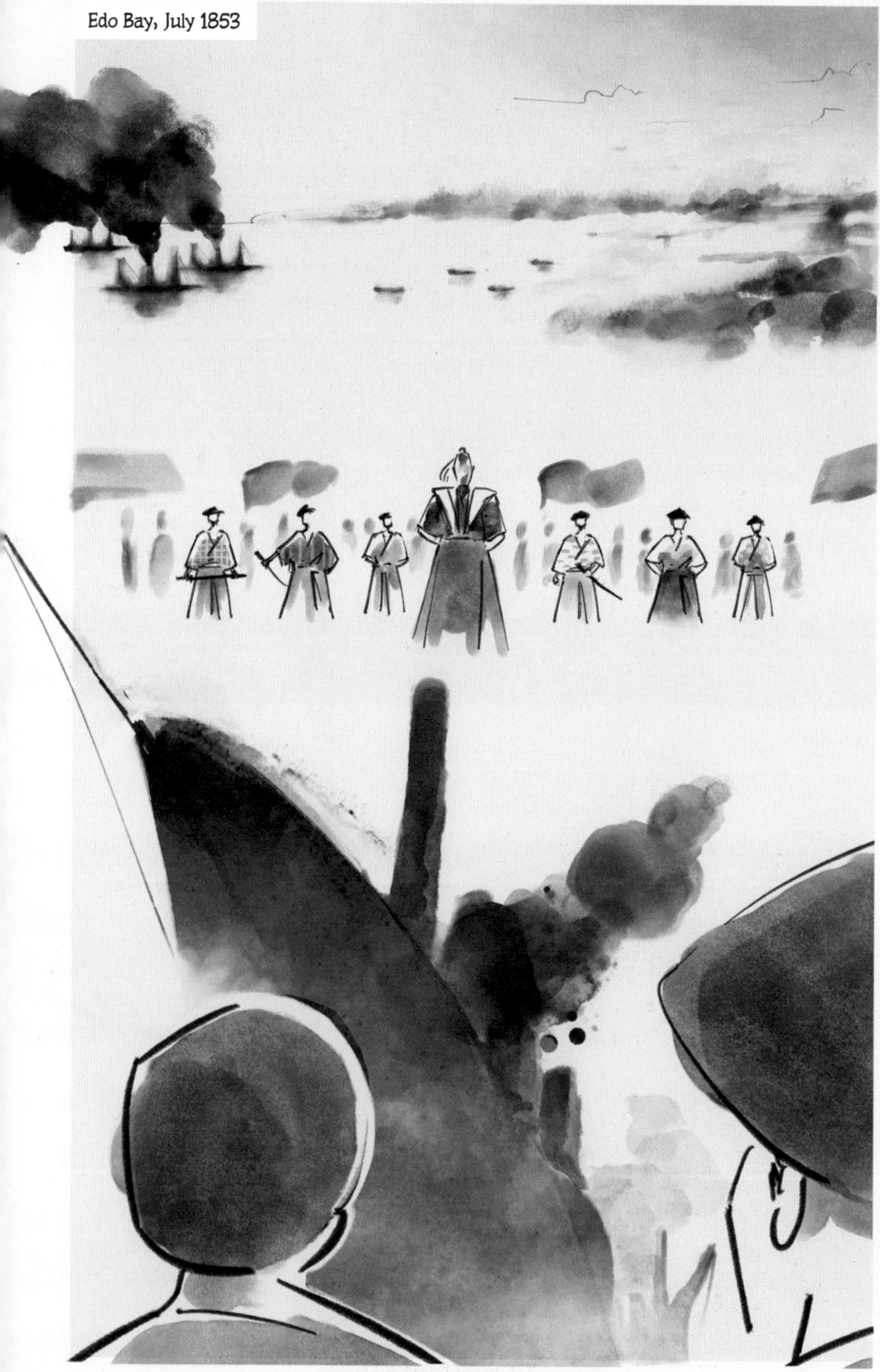
Edo Bay, July 1853

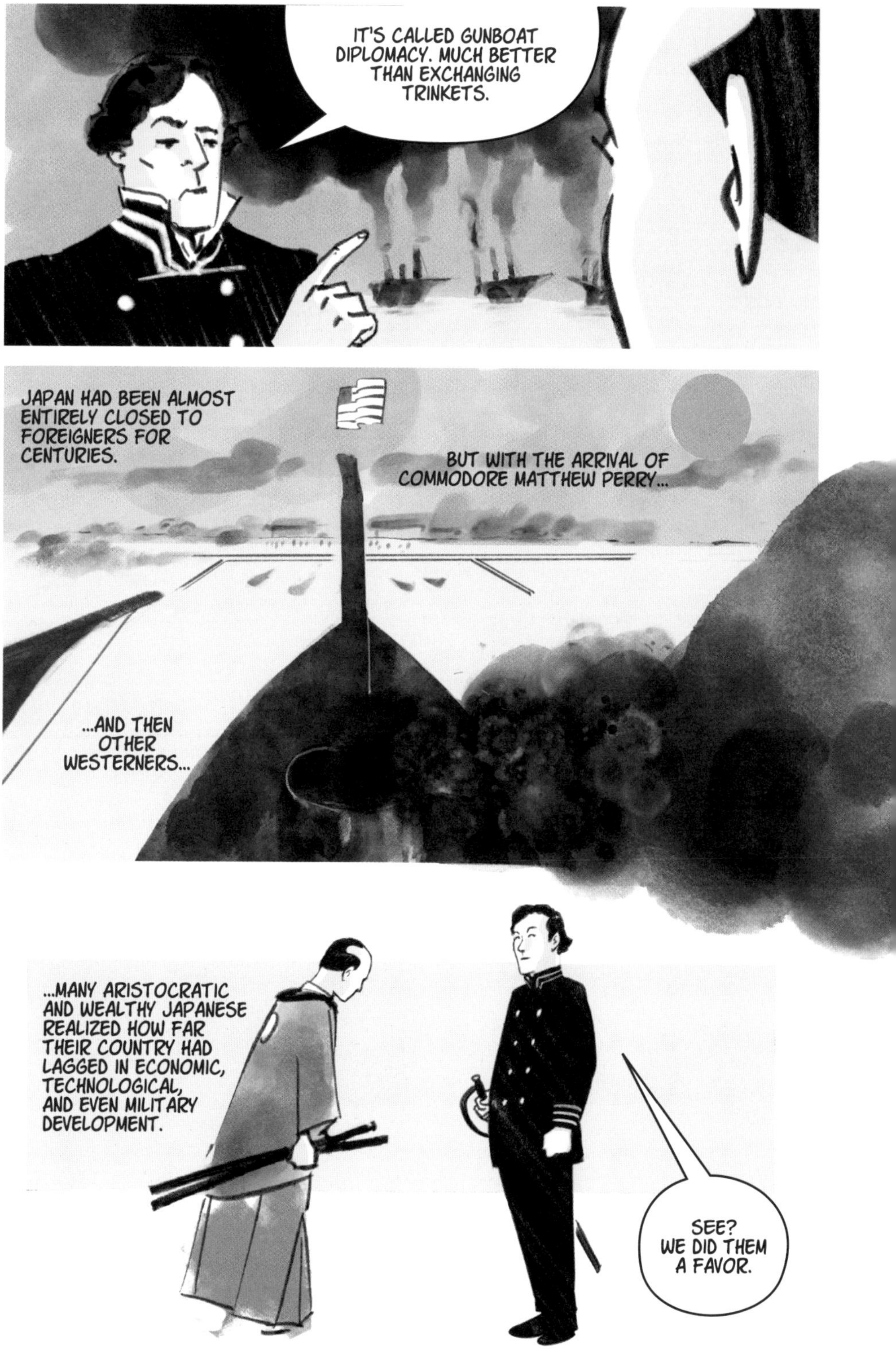
IT'S CALLED GUNBOAT DIPLOMACY. MUCH BETTER THAN EXCHANGING TRINKETS.
JAPAN HAD BEEN ALMOST ENTIRELY CLOSED TO FOREIGNERS FOR CENTURIES.
BUT WITH THE ARRIVAL OF COMMODORE MATTHEW PERRY...
...AND THEN OTHER WESTERNERS...
...MANY ARISTOCRATIC AND WEALTHY JAPANESE REALIZED HOW FAR THEIR COUNTRY HAD LAGGED IN ECONOMIC, TECHNOLOGICAL, AND EVEN MILITARY DEVELOPMENT.
SEE? WE DID THEM A FAVOR.

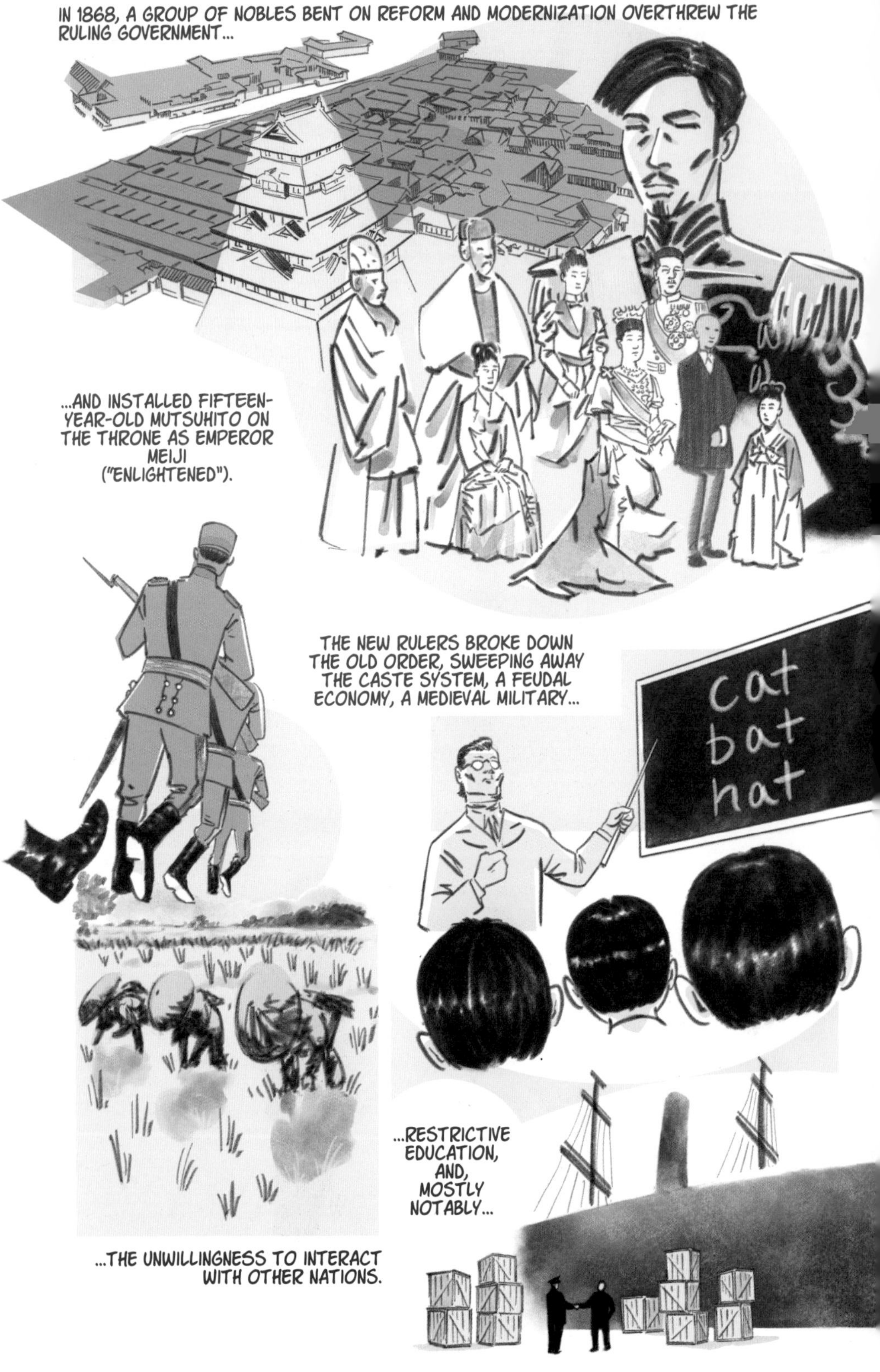
IN 1868, A GROUP OF NOBLES BENT ON REFORM AND MODERNIZATION OVERTHREW THE RULING GOVERNMENT...
...AND INSTALLED FIFTEEN-YEAR-OLD MUTSUHITO ON THE THRONE AS EMPEROR MEIJI ("ENLIGHTENED").
THE NEW RULERS BROKE DOWN THE OLD ORDER, SWEEPING AWAY THE CASTE SYSTEM, A FEUDAL ECONOMY, A MEDIEVAL MILITARY...
cat
bat
hat
...RESTRICTIVE EDUCATION, AND, MOSTLY NOTABLY...
...THE UNWILLINGNESS TO INTERACT WITH OTHER NATIONS.

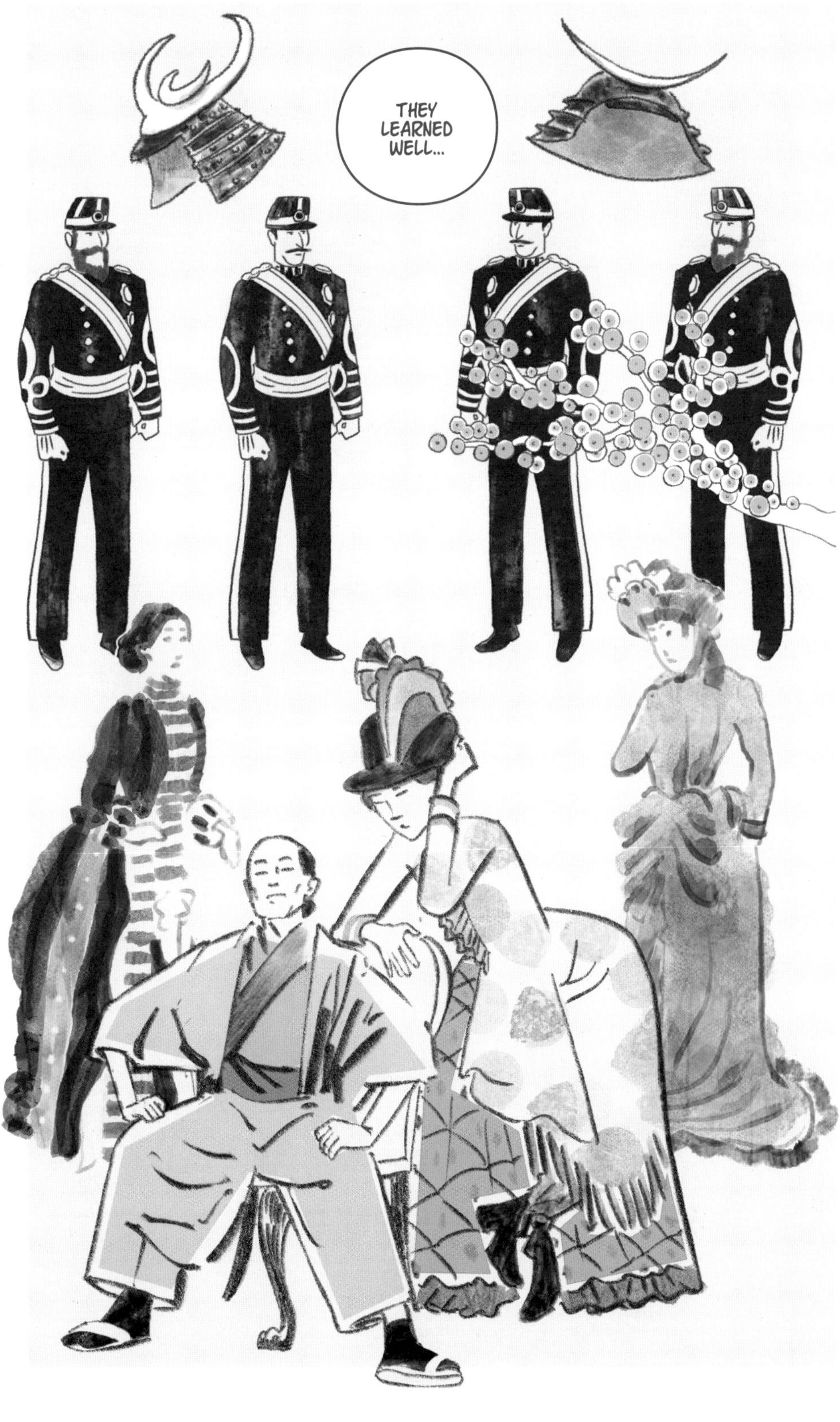
THEY LEARNED WELL...

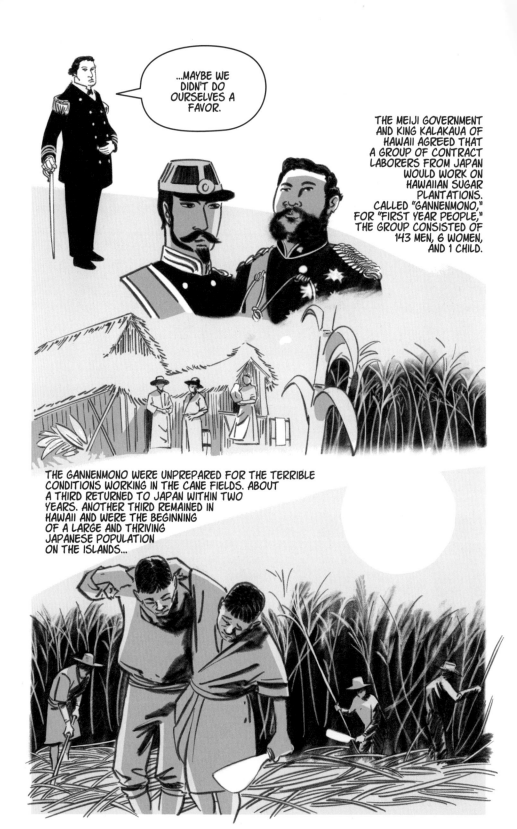

...MAYBE WE DIDN'T DO OURSELVES A FAVOR.

THE MEIJI GOVERNMENT AND KING KALAKAUA OF HAWAII AGREED THAT A GROUP OF CONTRACT LABORERS FROM JAPAN WOULD WORK ON HAWAIIAN SUGAR PLANTATIONS. CALLED "GANNENMONO," FOR "FIRST YEAR PEOPLE," THE GROUP CONSISTED OF 143 MEN, 6 WOMEN, AND 1 CHILD.

THE GANNENMONO WERE UNPREPARED FOR THE TERRIBLE CONDITIONS WORKING IN THE CANE FIELDS. ABOUT A THIRD RETURNED TO JAPAN WITHIN TWO YEARS. ANOTHER THIRD REMAINED IN HAWAII AND WERE THE BEGINNING OF A LARGE AND THRIVING JAPANESE POPULATION ON THE ISLANDS...

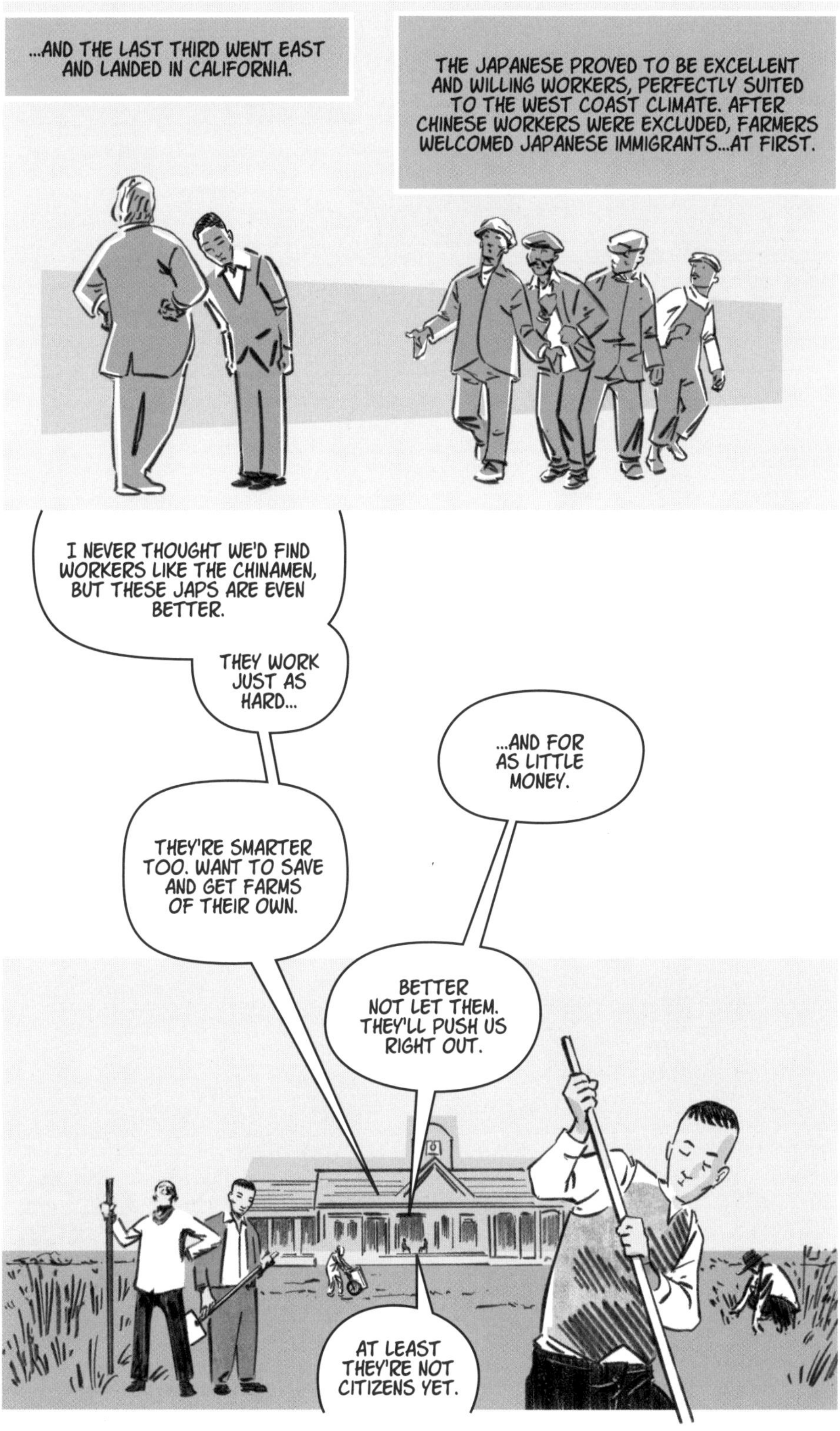
...AND THE LAST THIRD WENT EAST AND LANDED IN CALIFORNIA.
THE JAPANESE PROVED TO BE EXCELLENT AND WILLING WORKERS, PERFECTLY SUITED TO THE WEST COAST CLIMATE. AFTER CHINESE WORKERS WERE EXCLUDED, FARMERS WELCOMED JAPANESE IMMIGRANTS...AT FIRST.
I NEVER THOUGHT WE'D FIND WORKERS LIKE THE CHINAMEN, BUT THESE JAPS ARE EVEN BETTER.
THEY WORK JUST AS HARD...
...AND FOR AS LITTLE MONEY.
THEY'RE SMARTER TOO. WANT TO SAVE AND GET FARMS OF THEIR OWN.
BETTER NOT LET THEM. THEY'LL PUSH US RIGHT OUT.
AT LEAST THEY'RE NOT CITIZENS YET.

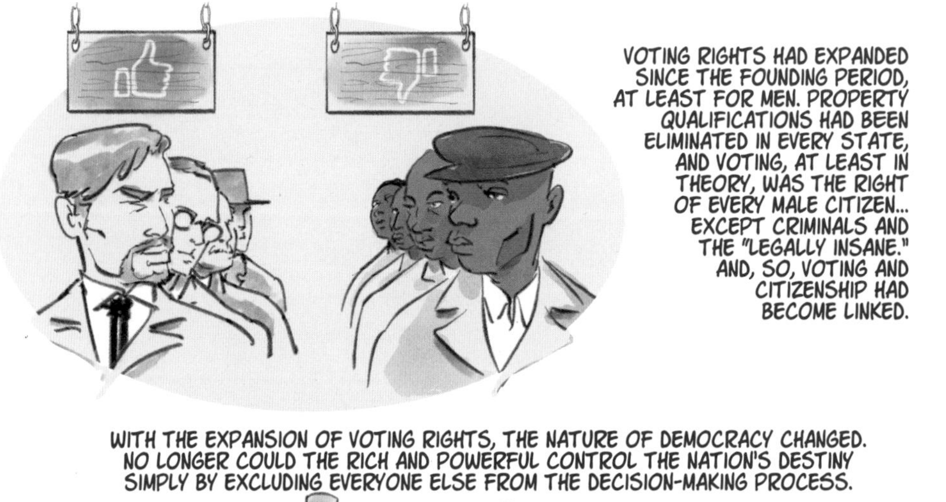

VOTING RIGHTS HAD EXPANDED SINCE THE FOUNDING PERIOD, AT LEAST FOR MEN. PROPERTY QUALIFICATIONS HAD BEEN ELIMINATED IN EVERY STATE, AND VOTING, AT LEAST IN THEORY, WAS THE RIGHT OF EVERY MALE CITIZEN... EXCEPT CRIMINALS AND THE "LEGALLY INSANE." AND, SO, VOTING AND CITIZENSHIP HAD BECOME LINKED.

WITH THE EXPANSION OF VOTING RIGHTS, THE NATURE OF DEMOCRACY CHANGED. NO LONGER COULD THE RICH AND POWERFUL CONTROL THE NATION'S DESTINY SIMPLY BY EXCLUDING EVERYONE ELSE FROM THE DECISION-MAKING PROCESS.

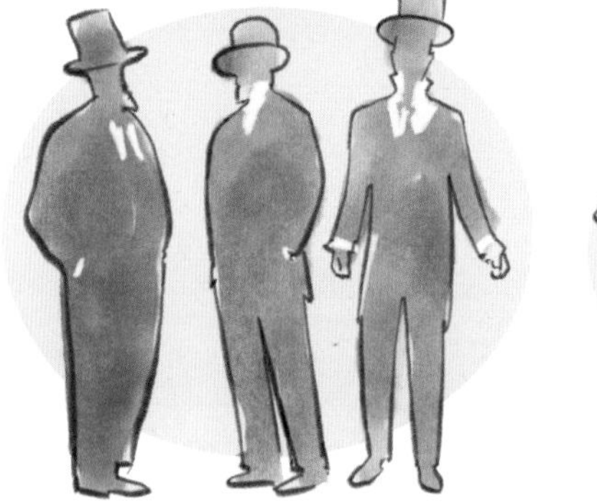

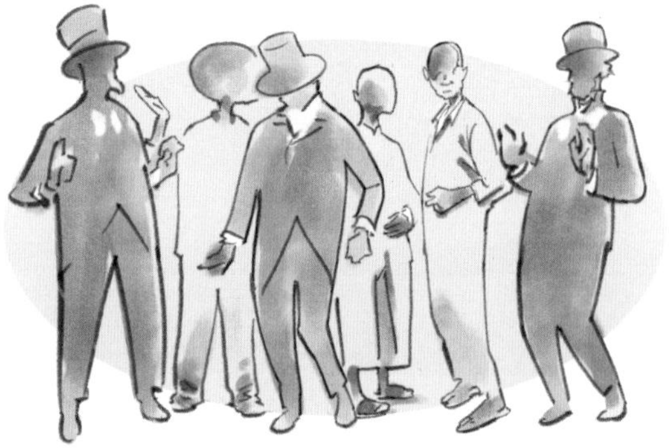

OF COURSE, THE RICH AND POWERFUL COULD STILL EXERT CONTROL, BUT THEY WERE OFTEN FORCED TO FIND WAYS TO APPEAL TO THE COMMON FOLK TO DO IT.

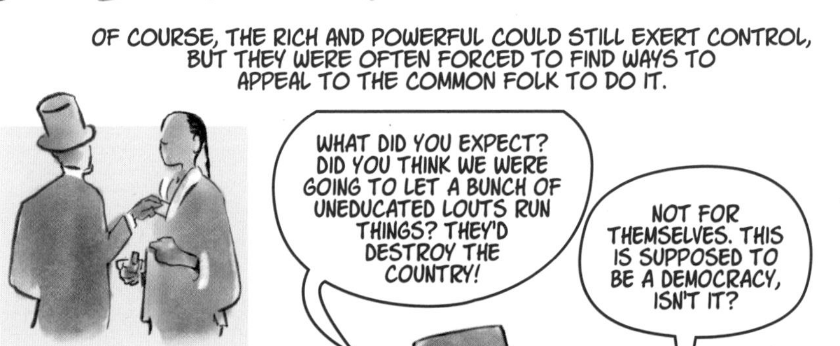

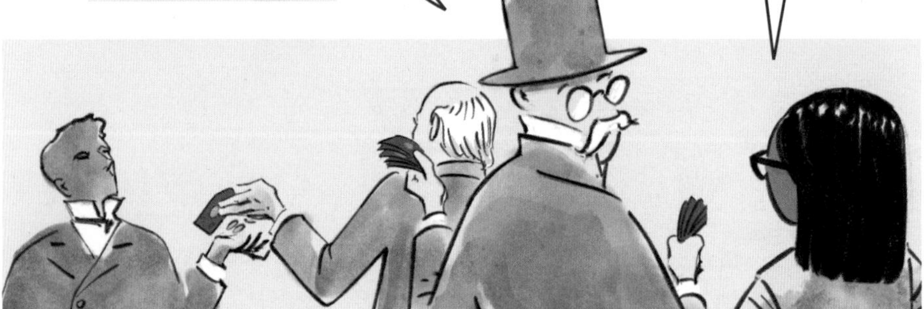
WHAT DID YOU EXPECT? DID YOU THINK WE WERE GOING TO LET A BUNCH OF UNEDUCATED LOUTS RUN THINGS? THEY'D DESTROY THE COUNTRY!
NOT FOR THEMSELVES. THIS IS SUPPOSED TO BE A DEMOCRACY, ISN'T IT?

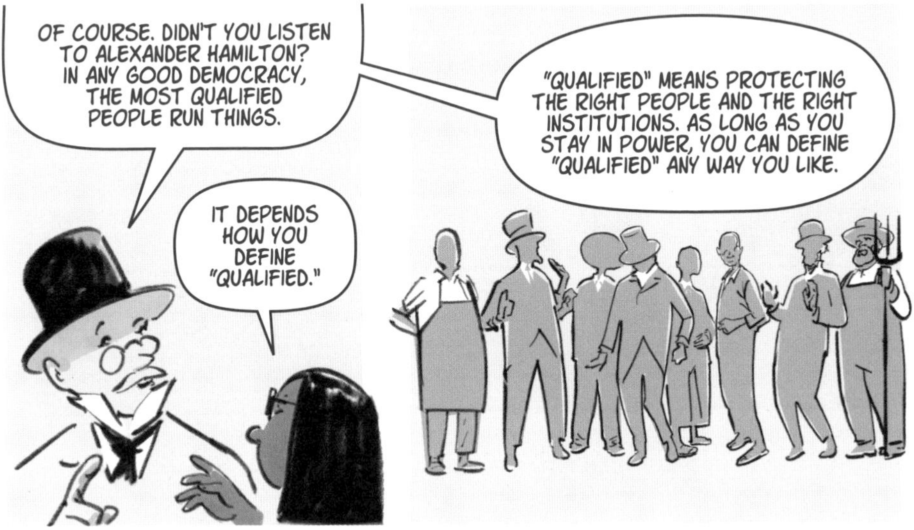
OF COURSE. DIDN'T YOU LISTEN TO ALEXANDER HAMILTON? IN ANY GOOD DEMOCRACY, THE MOST QUALIFIED PEOPLE RUN THINGS.
IT DEPENDS HOW YOU DEFINE "QUALIFIED."
"QUALIFIED" MEANS PROTECTING THE RIGHT PEOPLE AND THE RIGHT INSTITUTIONS. AS LONG AS YOU STAY IN POWER, YOU CAN DEFINE "QUALIFIED" ANY WAY YOU LIKE.

THERE WERE GROUPS, HOWEVER, THAT SAW THOSE INSTITUTIONS AS INHERENTLY UNFAIR. NEWLY ENFRANCHISED AFRICAN AMERICANS, POOR FARMERS, MOST OF THEM DEBTORS, AND WORKERS WHO WERE IN THE FOREFRONT OF THE UNION MOVEMENT WERE DETERMINED TO INCREASE THEIR OWN POWER AT THE EXPENSE OF THE TRADITIONAL ELITES.

THEY WOULD HAVE A MUCH BETTER CHANCE IF THEY WERE JOINED BY HORDES OF THOSE NEWLY ARRIVED, HOPING TO FULFILL THE AMERICAN DREAM.

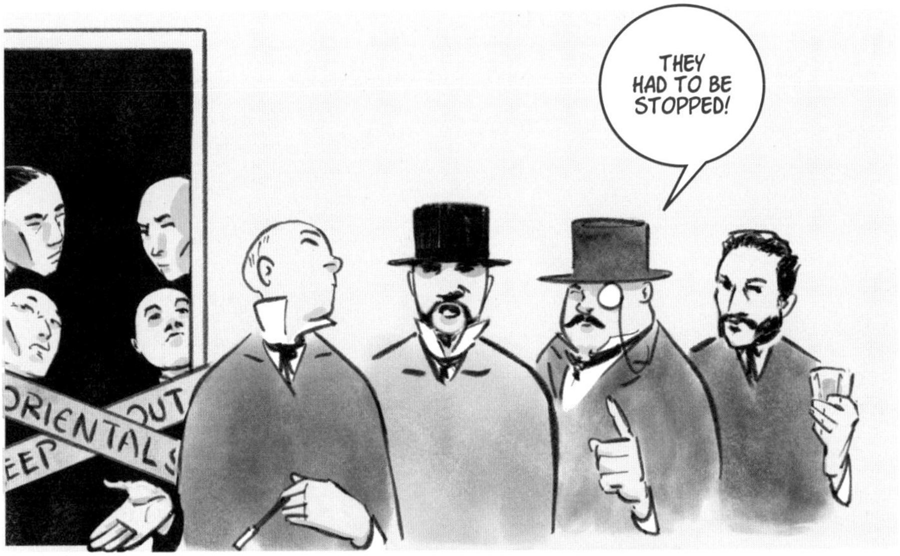
THEY HAD TO BE STOPPED!
ORIENTAL

MUCH OF THE EFFORT TO DENY VOTING RIGHTS WAS AIMED AT AFRICAN AMERICANS.

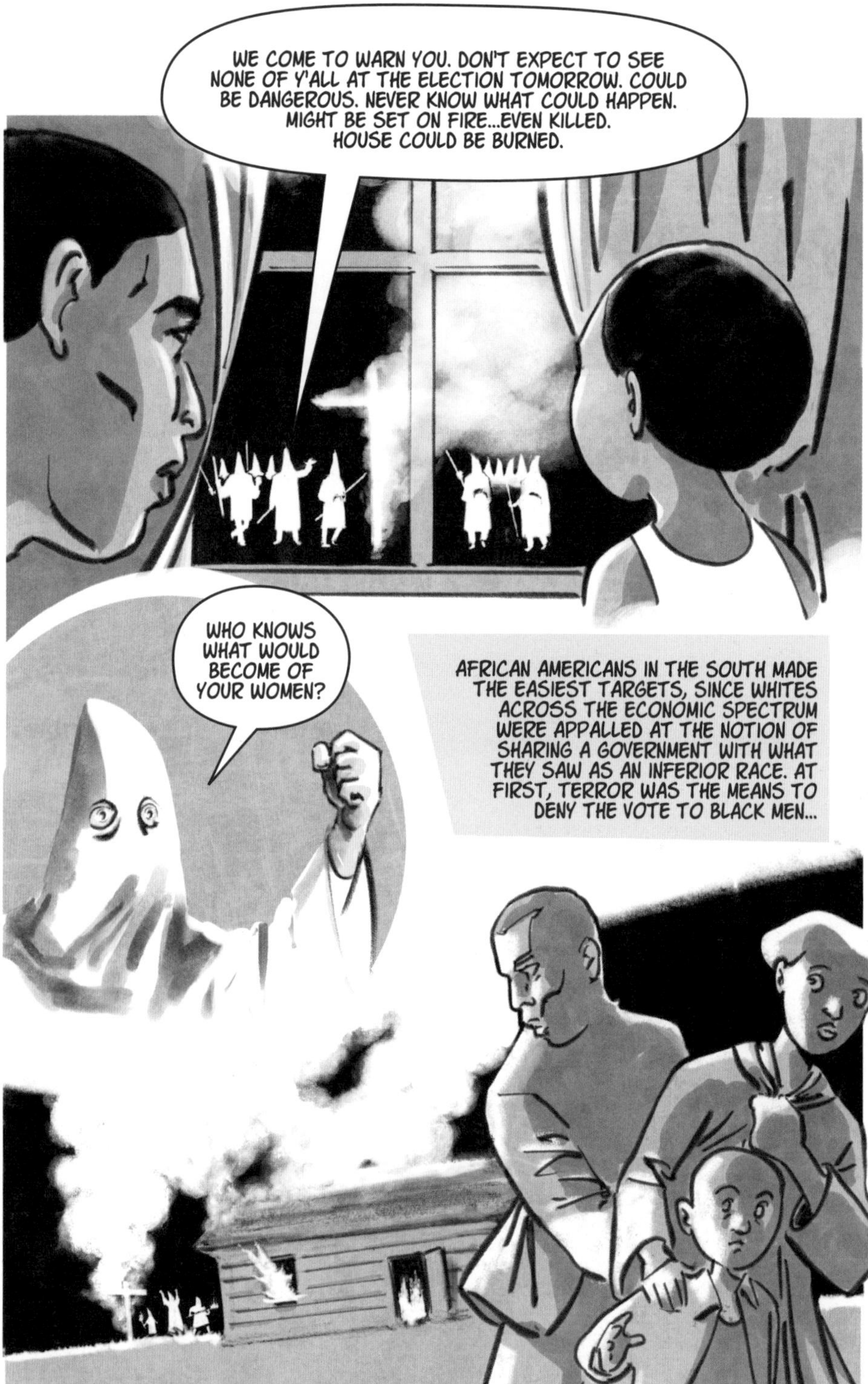
WE COME TO WARN YOU. DON'T EXPECT TO SEE NONE OF Y'ALL AT THE ELECTION TOMORROW. COULD BE DANGEROUS. NEVER KNOW WHAT COULD HAPPEN. MIGHT BE SET ON FIRE...EVEN KILLED. HOUSE COULD BE BURNED.
WHO KNOWS WHAT WOULD BECOME OF YOUR WOMEN?
AFRICAN AMERICANS IN THE SOUTH MADE THE EASIEST TARGETS, SINCE WHITES ACROSS THE ECONOMIC SPECTRUM WERE APPALLED AT THE NOTION OF SHARING A GOVERNMENT WITH WHAT THEY SAW AS AN INFERIOR RACE. AT FIRST, TERROR WAS THE MEANS TO DENY THE VOTE TO BLACK MEN...

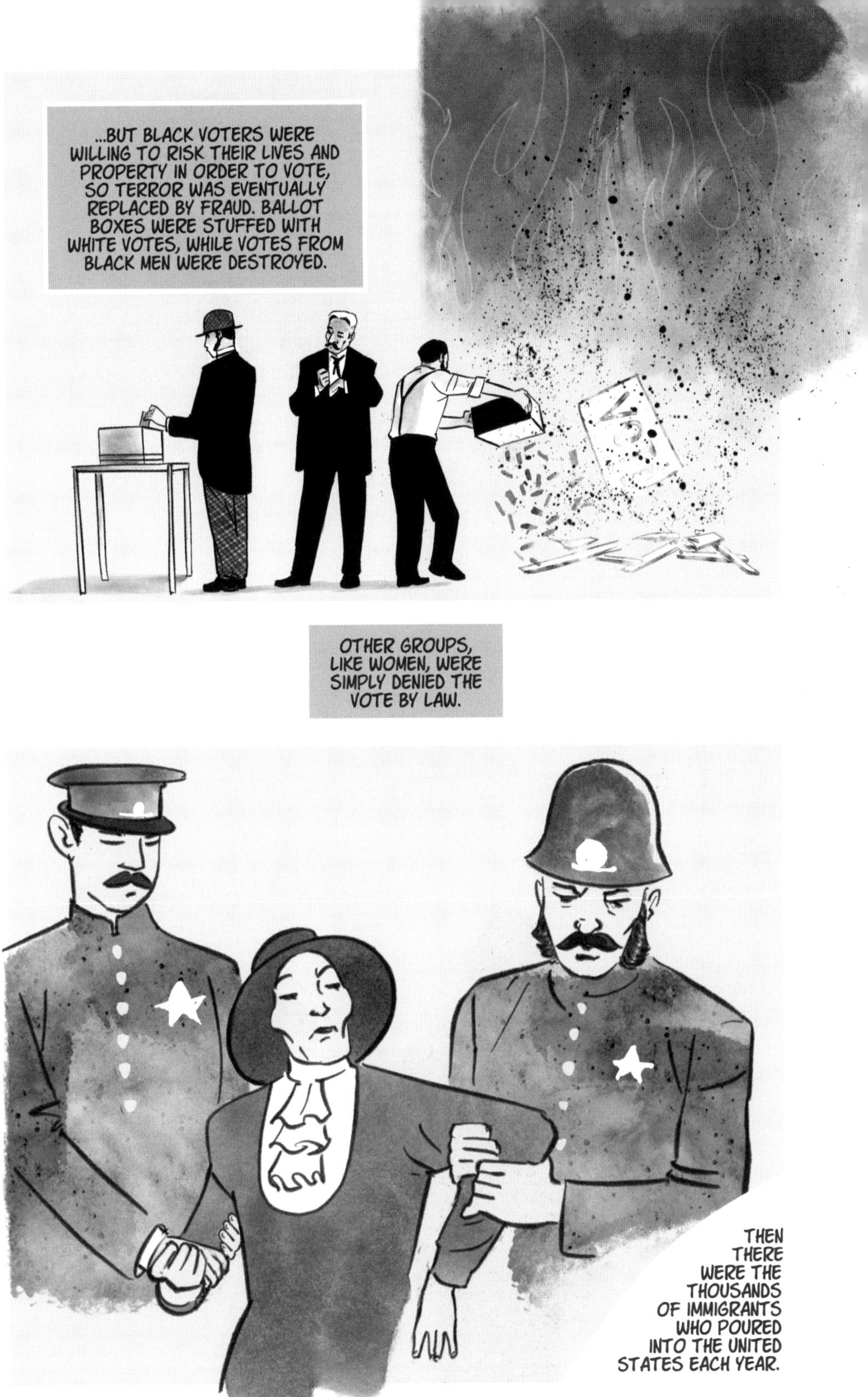
...BUT BLACK VOTERS WERE WILLING TO RISK THEIR LIVES AND PROPERTY IN ORDER TO VOTE, SO TERROR WAS EVENTUALLY REPLACED BY FRAUD. BALLOT BOXES WERE STUFFED WITH WHITE VOTES, WHILE VOTES FROM BLACK MEN WERE DESTROYED.
OTHER GROUPS, LIKE WOMEN, WERE SIMPLY DENIED THE VOTE BY LAW.
THEN THERE WERE THE THOUSANDS OF IMMIGRANTS WHO POURED INTO THE UNITED STATES EACH YEAR.

IMMIGRANTS FROM "DESIRABLE" PARTS OF THE WORLD, LIKE NORTHERN EUROPE, WERE CONSIDERED PEOPLE TO HELP MAINTAIN "THE AMERICAN WAY OF LIFE"...

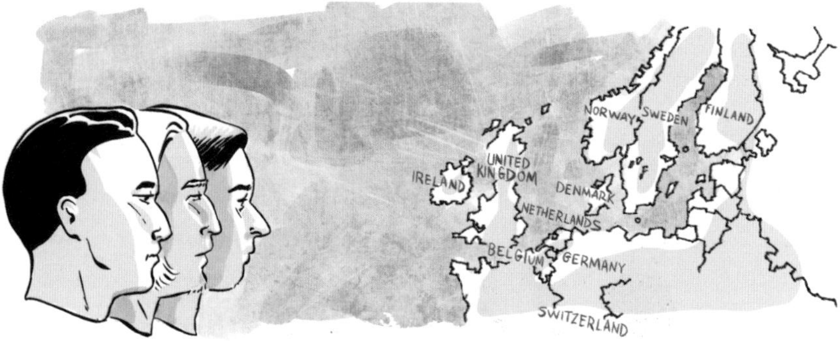
NORWAY
SWEDEN
FINLAND
UNITED KINGDOM
IRELAND
DENMARK
NETHERLANDS
BELGIUM
GERMANY
SWITZERLAND

IMMIGRANTS FROM "UNDESIRABLE" PARTS OF THE WORLD, LIKE ASIA OR SOUTHERN AND EASTERN EUROPE, WOULD DESTROY IT. EVEN IF THEY REMAINED NONCITIZEN LABORERS, LIKE THE CHINESE AND THE JAPANESE, THEY WOULD OVERRUN WHITE SOCIETY IF ALLOWED TO ENTER THE UNITED STATES IN SUFFICIENT NUMBERS.

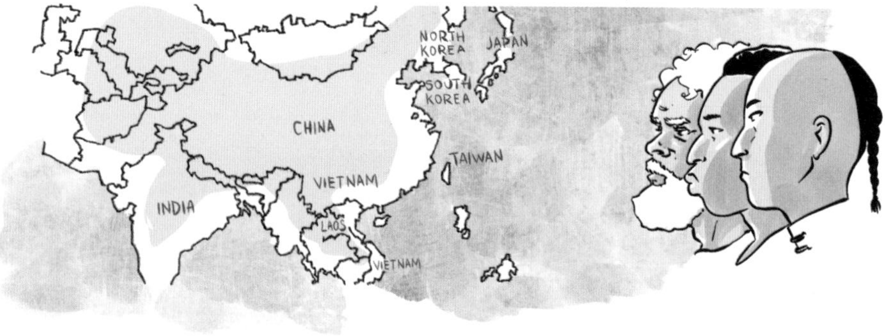
NORTH KOREA
JAPAN
SOUTH KOREA
CHINA
TAIWAN
VIETNAM
INDIA
LAOS
VIETNAM

SO IMMIGRATION BECAME AN ADDITIONAL LINK IN THE CITIZENSHIP-VOTING CHAIN.

SINCE THE WRONG KIND OF IMMIGRANT COULD BECOME THE WRONG KIND OF CITIZEN AND VOTE FOR THE WRONG KIND OF CANDIDATE, IT WAS BETTER TO KEEP THEM OUT TO START WITH.

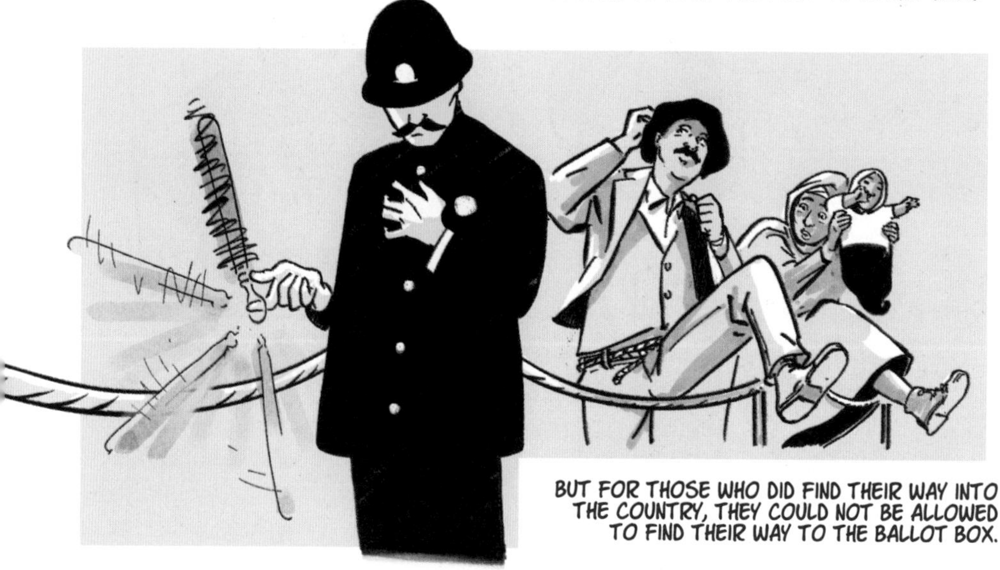

BUT FOR THOSE WHO DID FIND THEIR WAY INTO THE COUNTRY, THEY COULD NOT BE ALLOWED TO FIND THEIR WAY TO THE BALLOT BOX.

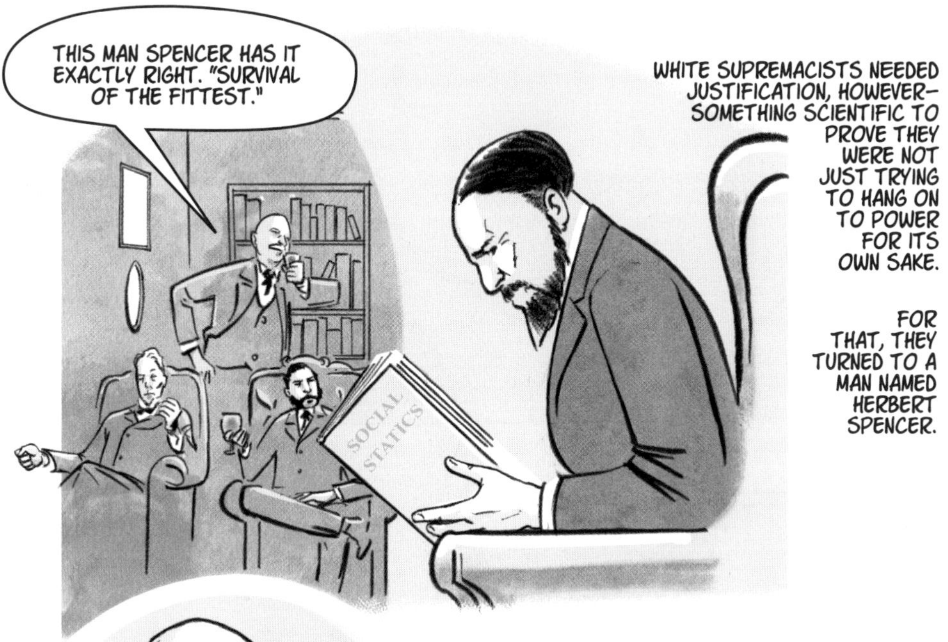
THIS MAN SPENCER HAS IT EXACTLY RIGHT. "SURVIVAL OF THE FITTEST."
WHITE SUPREMACISTS NEEDED JUSTIFICATION, HOWEVER– SOMETHING SCIENTIFIC TO PROVE THEY WERE NOT JUST TRYING TO HANG ON TO POWER FOR ITS OWN SAKE.
SOCIAL STATICS
FOR THAT, THEY TURNED TO A MAN NAMED HERBERT SPENCER.

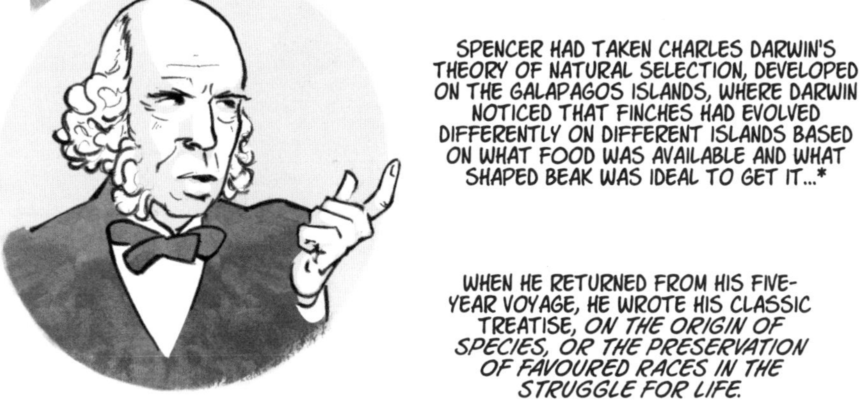
SPENCER HAD TAKEN CHARLES DARWIN'S THEORY OF NATURAL SELECTION, DEVELOPED ON THE GALAPAGOS ISLANDS, WHERE DARWIN NOTICED THAT FINCHES HAD EVOLVED DIFFERENTLY ON DIFFERENT ISLANDS BASED ON WHAT FOOD WAS AVAILABLE AND WHAT SHAPED BEAK WAS IDEAL TO GET IT...*
WHEN HE RETURNED FROM HIS FIVE-YEAR VOYAGE, HE WROTE HIS CLASSIC TREATISE, *ON THE ORIGIN OF SPECIES, OR THE PRESERVATION OF FAVOURED RACES IN THE STRUGGLE FOR LIFE.*

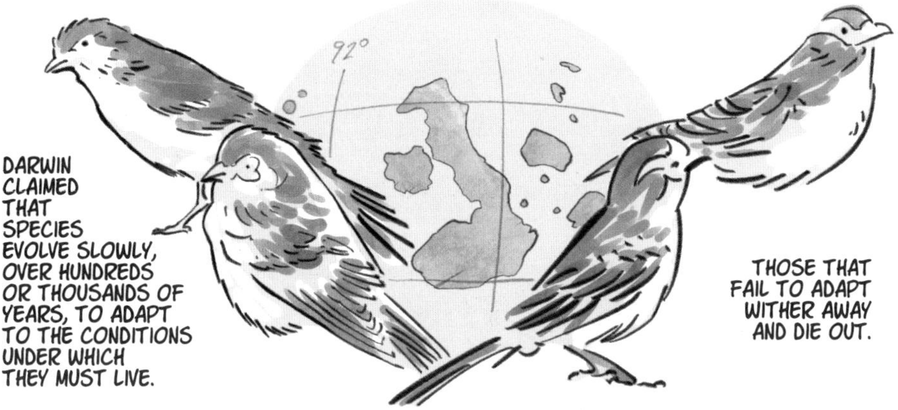
92°
DARWIN CLAIMED THAT SPECIES EVOLVE SLOWLY, OVER HUNDREDS OR THOUSANDS OF YEARS, TO ADAPT TO THE CONDITIONS UNDER WHICH THEY MUST LIVE.
THOSE THAT FAIL TO ADAPT WITHER AWAY AND DIE OUT.

*DARWIN WAS BORN ON FEBRUARY 12, 1809, THE SAME DAY AS ABRAHAM LINCOLN.

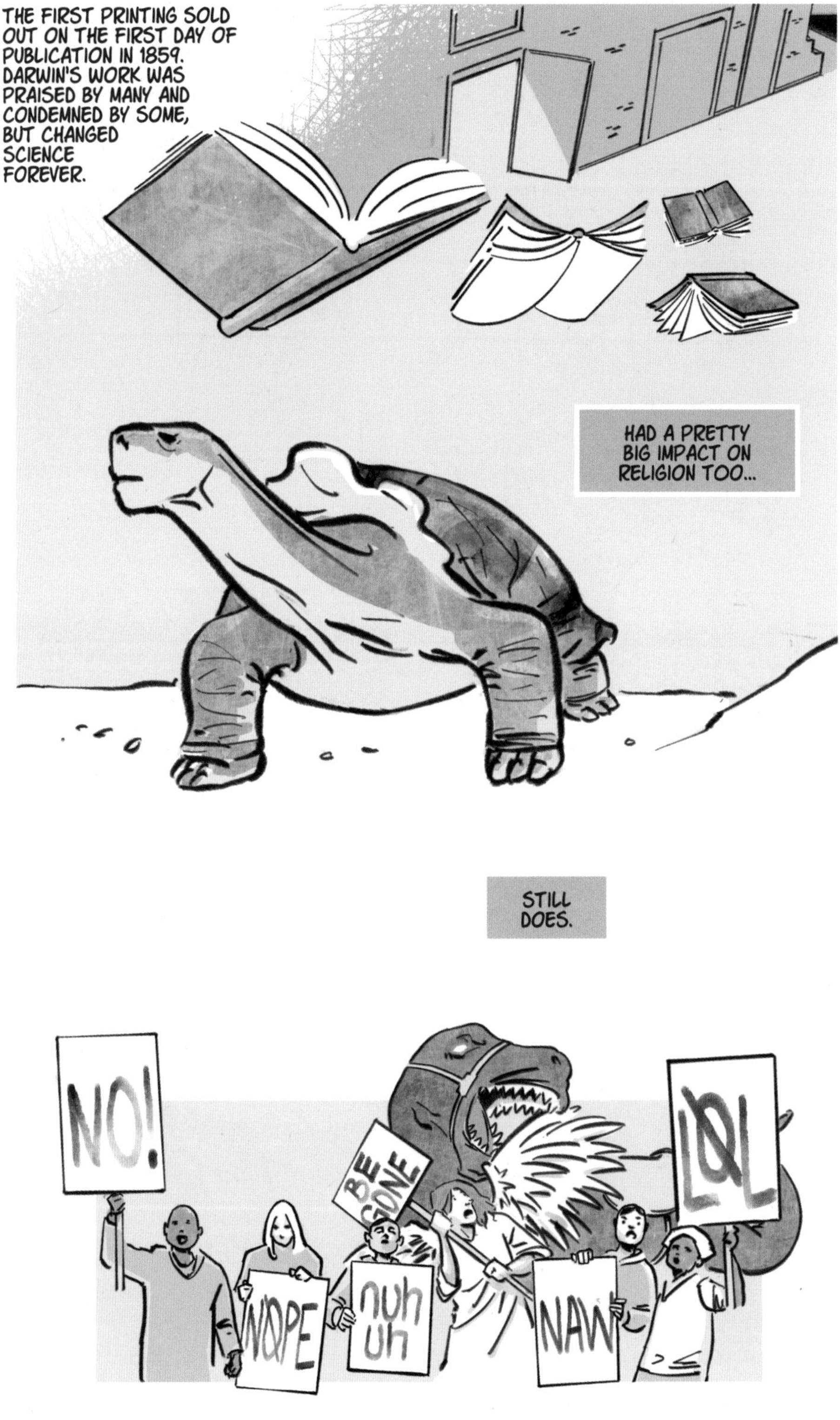
THE FIRST PRINTING SOLD OUT ON THE FIRST DAY OF PUBLICATION IN 1859. DARWIN'S WORK WAS PRAISED BY MANY AND CONDEMNED BY SOME, BUT CHANGED SCIENCE FOREVER.
HAD A PRETTY BIG IMPACT ON RELIGION TOO...
STILL DOES.
NO!
BE GONE
LOL
NOPE
nuh uh
NAW

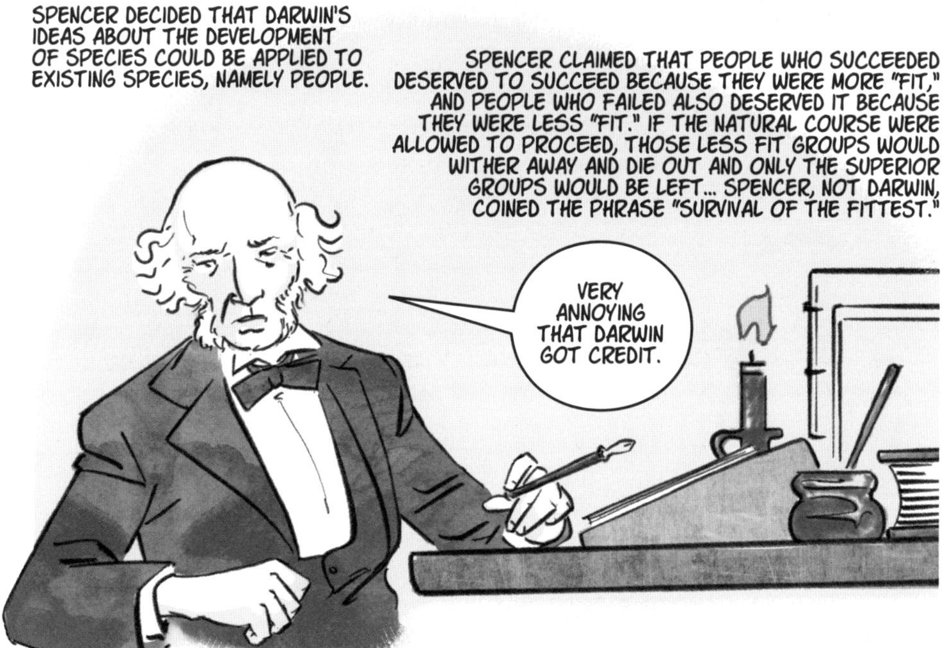
SPENCER DECIDED THAT DARWIN'S IDEAS ABOUT THE DEVELOPMENT OF SPECIES COULD BE APPLIED TO EXISTING SPECIES, NAMELY PEOPLE.
SPENCER CLAIMED THAT PEOPLE WHO SUCCEEDED DESERVED TO SUCCEED BECAUSE THEY WERE MORE "FIT," AND PEOPLE WHO FAILED ALSO DESERVED IT BECAUSE THEY WERE LESS "FIT." IF THE NATURAL COURSE WERE ALLOWED TO PROCEED, THOSE LESS FIT GROUPS WOULD WITHER AWAY AND DIE OUT AND ONLY THE SUPERIOR GROUPS WOULD BE LEFT... SPENCER, NOT DARWIN, COINED THE PHRASE "SURVIVAL OF THE FITTEST."
VERY ANNOYING THAT DARWIN GOT CREDIT.

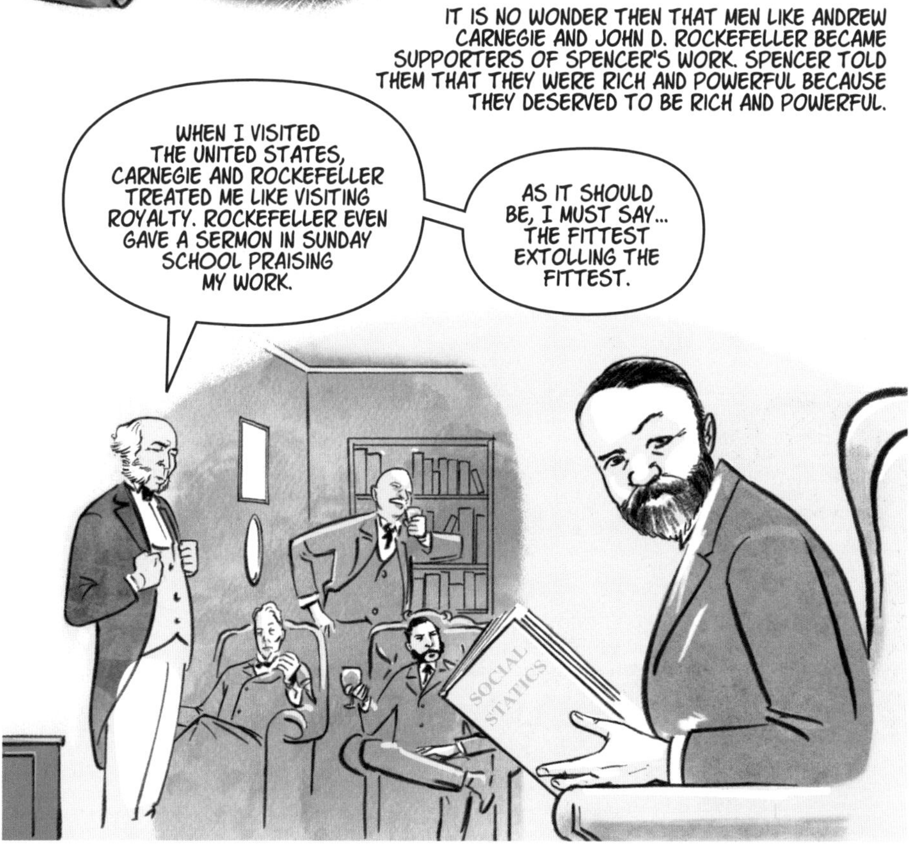
IT IS NO WONDER THEN THAT MEN LIKE ANDREW CARNEGIE AND JOHN D. ROCKEFELLER BECAME SUPPORTERS OF SPENCER'S WORK. SPENCER TOLD THEM THAT THEY WERE RICH AND POWERFUL BECAUSE THEY DESERVED TO BE RICH AND POWERFUL.
WHEN I VISITED THE UNITED STATES, CARNEGIE AND ROCKEFELLER TREATED ME LIKE VISITING ROYALTY. ROCKEFELLER EVEN GAVE A SERMON IN SUNDAY SCHOOL PRAISING MY WORK.
AS IT SHOULD BE, I MUST SAY... THE FITTEST EXTOLLING THE FITTEST.
SOCIAL STATICS

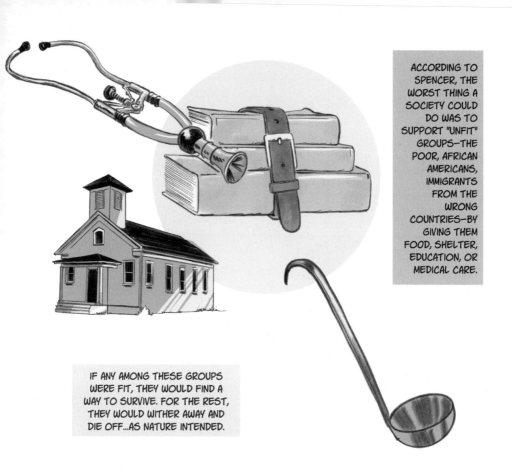

ACCORDING TO SPENCER, THE WORST THING A SOCIETY COULD DO WAS TO SUPPORT "UNFIT" GROUPS—THE POOR, AFRICAN AMERICANS, IMMIGRANTS FROM THE WRONG COUNTRIES—BY GIVING THEM FOOD, SHELTER, EDUCATION, OR MEDICAL CARE.

IF ANY AMONG THESE GROUPS WERE FIT, THEY WOULD FIND A WAY TO SURVIVE. FOR THE REST, THEY WOULD WITHER AWAY AND DIE OFF...AS NATURE INTENDED.

IF YOU HELPED THEM BREED AND PROLIFERATE, IT WOULD MEAN THE DESTRUCTION OF SOCIETY. THE UNFIT WOULD OVERWHELM THE EARTH...

VERY APPEALING THEORY TO SOME...

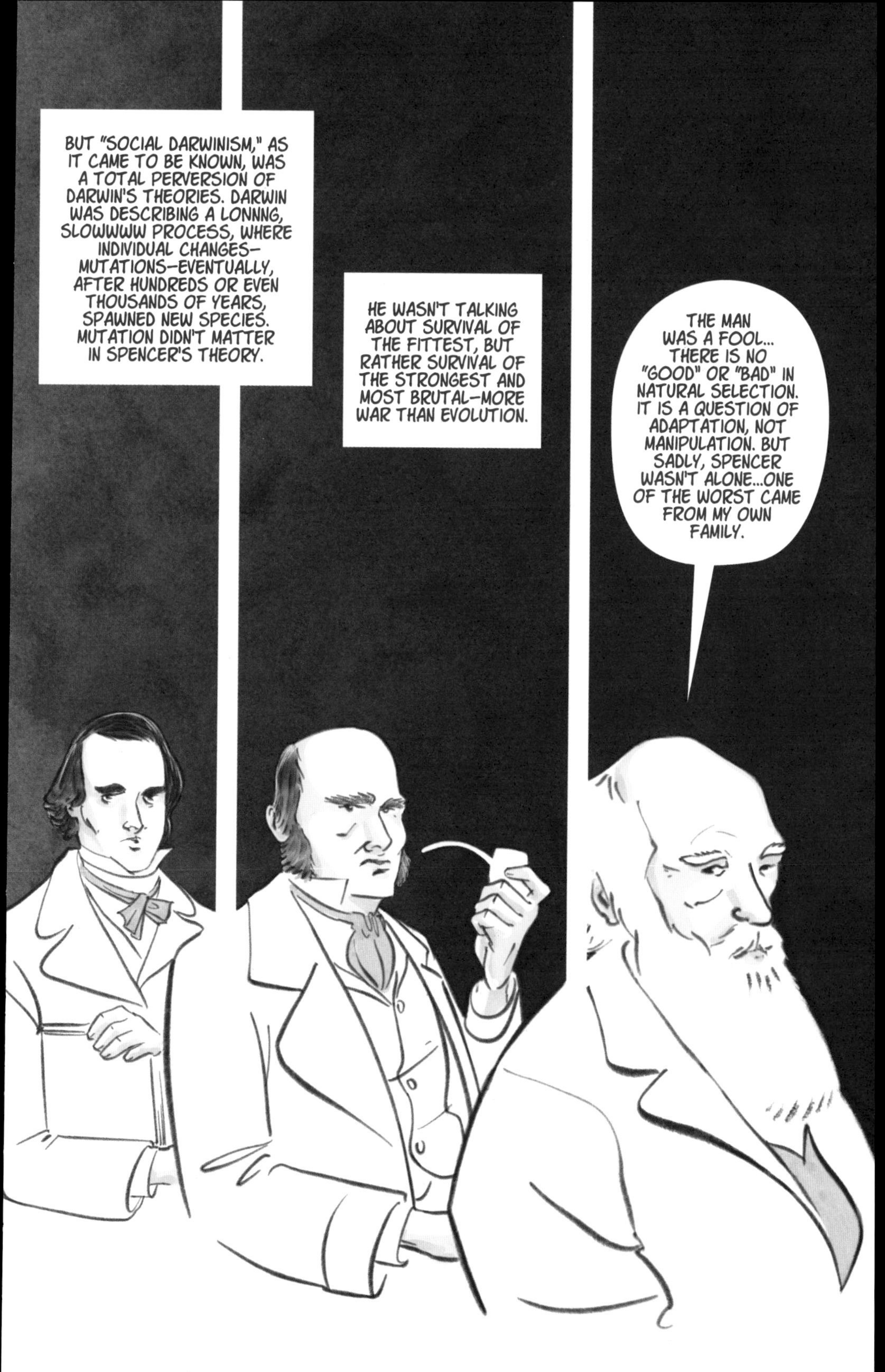
BUT "SOCIAL DARWINISM," AS IT CAME TO BE KNOWN, WAS A TOTAL PERVERSION OF DARWIN'S THEORIES. DARWIN WAS DESCRIBING A LONNNG, SLOWWWW PROCESS, WHERE INDIVIDUAL CHANGES—MUTATIONS—EVENTUALLY, AFTER HUNDREDS OR EVEN THOUSANDS OF YEARS, SPAWNED NEW SPECIES. MUTATION DIDN'T MATTER IN SPENCER'S THEORY.
HE WASN'T TALKING ABOUT SURVIVAL OF THE FITTEST, BUT RATHER SURVIVAL OF THE STRONGEST AND MOST BRUTAL—MORE WAR THAN EVOLUTION.
THE MAN WAS A FOOL... THERE IS NO "GOOD" OR "BAD" IN NATURAL SELECTION. IT IS A QUESTION OF ADAPTATION, NOT MANIPULATION. BUT SADLY, SPENCER WASN'T ALONE...ONE OF THE WORST CAME FROM MY OWN FAMILY.

ANOTHER PLACE RICH AND POWERFUL AMERICANS LOOKED TO JUSTIFY KEEPING THE NATION "PURE"...MEANING "WHITE"...WAS THE EUGENICS MOVEMENT, WHICH SAID THE HUMAN RACE WOULD BE IMPROVED BY SELECTIVE BREEDING AND HARMED IF THE INFERIOR WERE ALLOWED TO BREED WITH THE SUPERIOR.

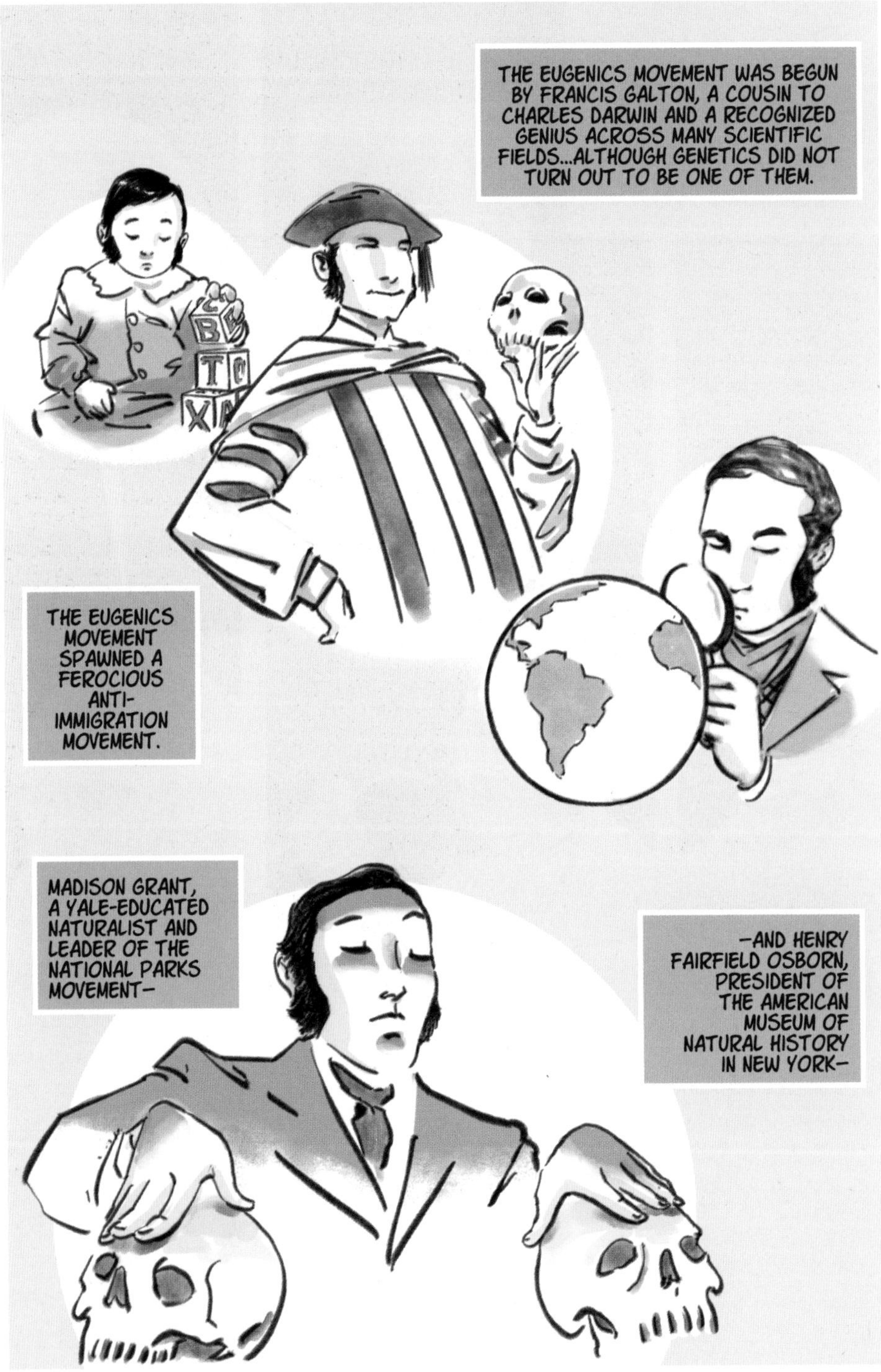
THE EUGENICS MOVEMENT WAS BEGUN BY FRANCIS GALTON, A COUSIN TO CHARLES DARWIN AND A RECOGNIZED GENIUS ACROSS MANY SCIENTIFIC FIELDS...ALTHOUGH GENETICS DID NOT TURN OUT TO BE ONE OF THEM.
THE EUGENICS MOVEMENT SPAWNED A FEROCIOUS ANTI-IMMIGRATION MOVEMENT.
MADISON GRANT, A YALE-EDUCATED NATURALIST AND LEADER OF THE NATIONAL PARKS MOVEMENT–
–AND HENRY FAIRFIELD OSBORN, PRESIDENT OF THE AMERICAN MUSEUM OF NATURAL HISTORY IN NEW YORK–

–PUSHED TO DENY ENTRY TO "INFERIOR RACES" TO PREVENT THE NATION FROM DESCENDING INTO "A RACIAL ABYSS."

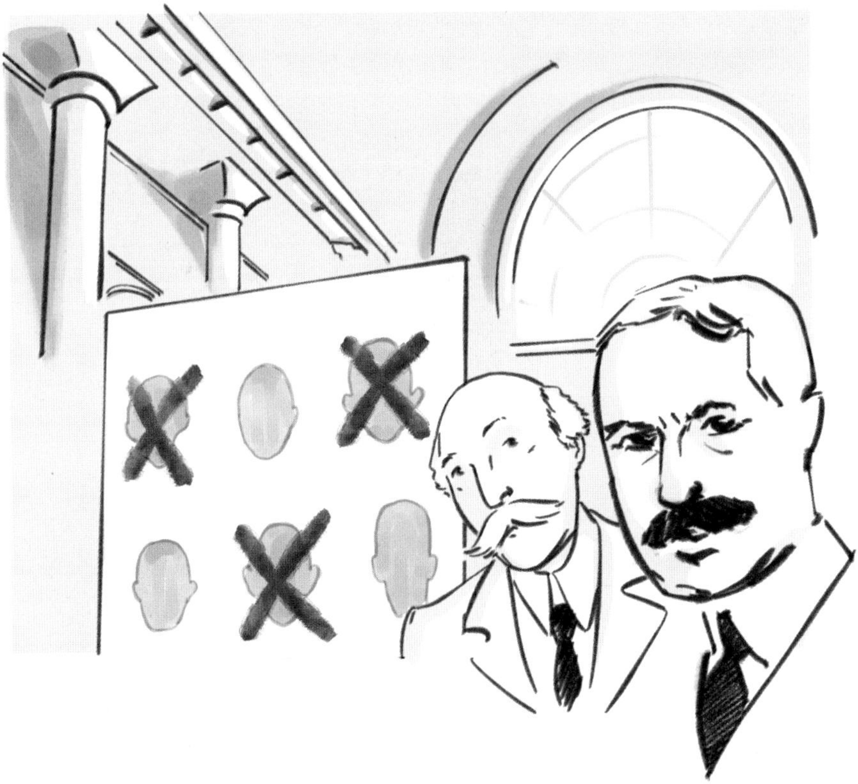

GRANT'S BOOK WOULD BECOME POPULAR ON BOTH SIDES OF THE ATLANTIC.

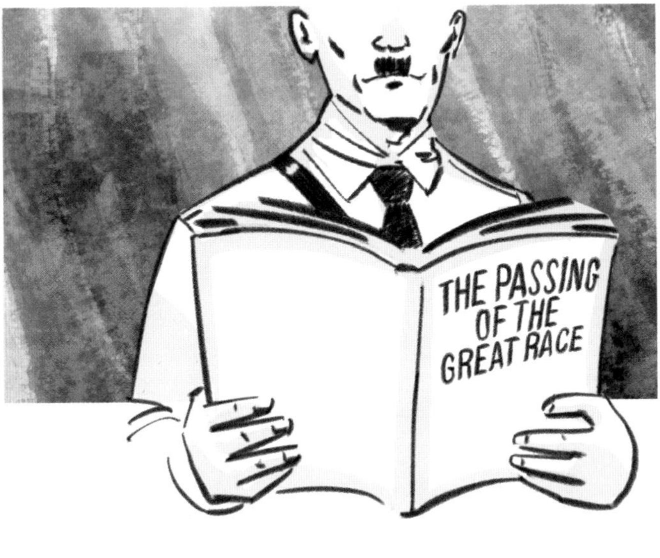
THE PASSING OF THE GREAT RACE

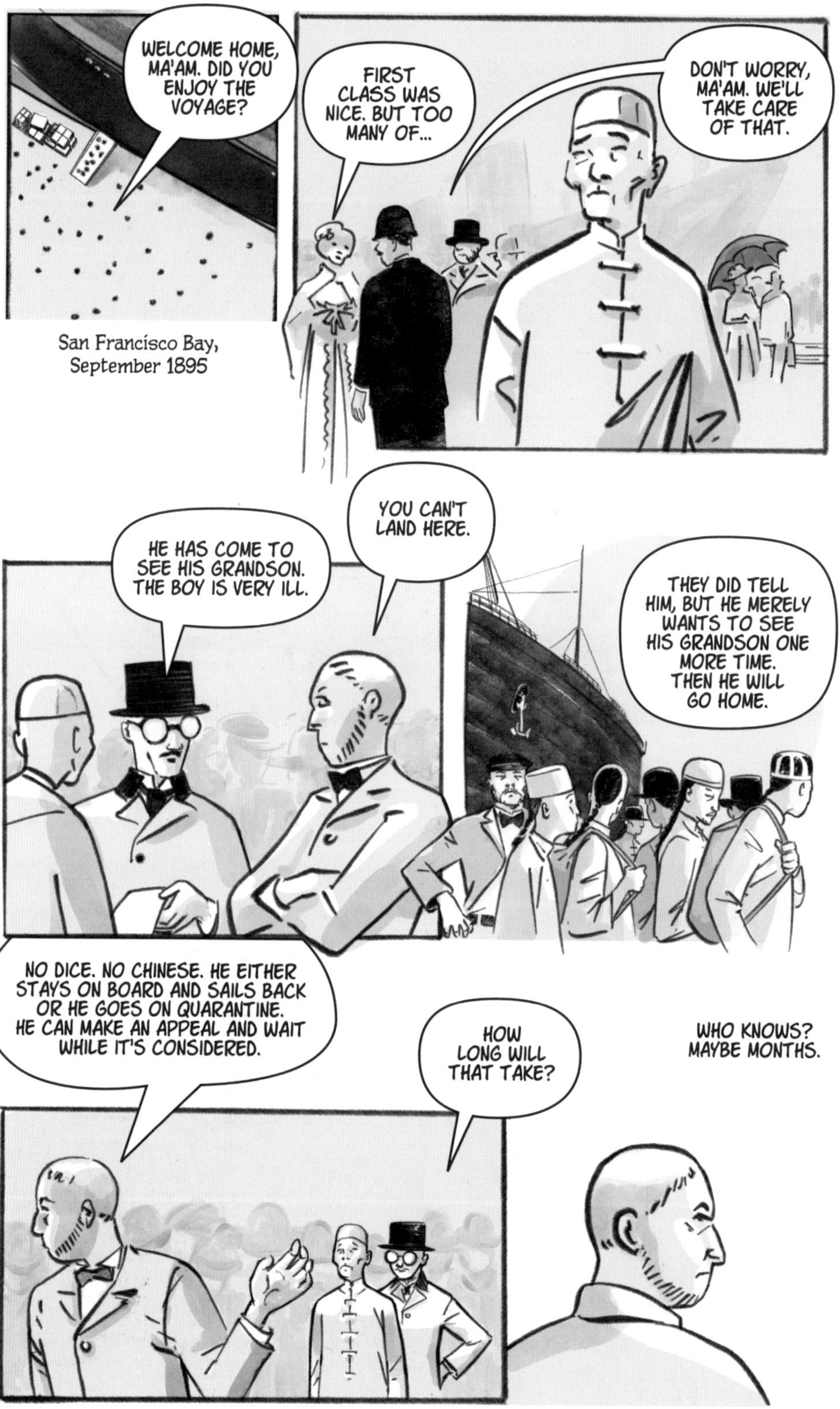
WELCOME HOME, MA'AM. DID YOU ENJOY THE VOYAGE?
San Francisco Bay, September 1895
FIRST CLASS WAS NICE. BUT TOO MANY OF...
DON'T WORRY, MA'AM. WE'LL TAKE CARE OF THAT.
HE HAS COME TO SEE HIS GRANDSON. THE BOY IS VERY ILL.
YOU CAN'T LAND HERE.
THEY DID TELL HIM, BUT HE MERELY WANTS TO SEE HIS GRANDSON ONE MORE TIME. THEN HE WILL GO HOME.
NO DICE. NO CHINESE. HE EITHER STAYS ON BOARD AND SAILS BACK OR HE GOES ON QUARANTINE. HE CAN MAKE AN APPEAL AND WAIT WHILE IT'S CONSIDERED.
HOW LONG WILL THAT TAKE?
WHO KNOWS? MAYBE MONTHS.

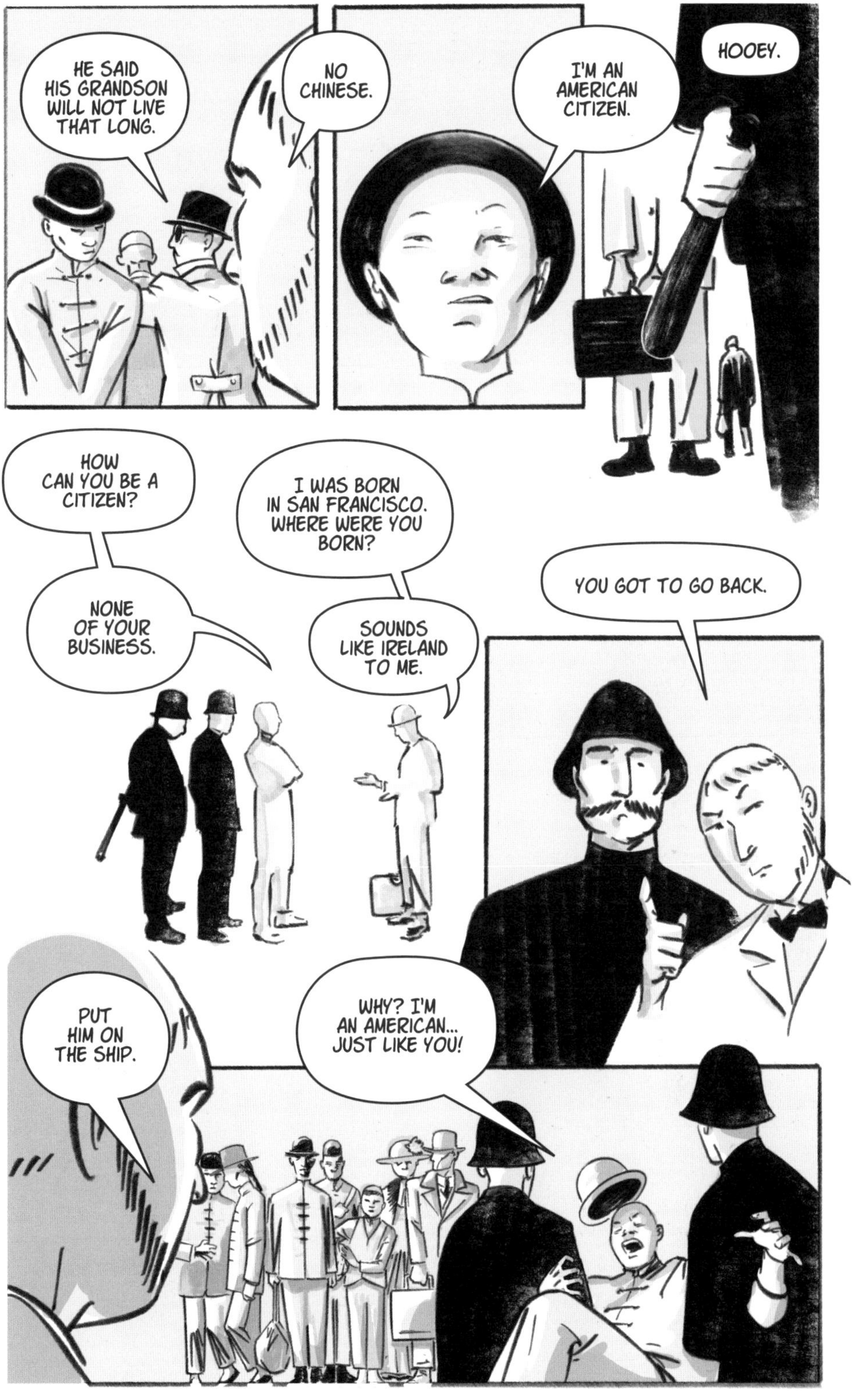
HE SAID HIS GRANDSON WILL NOT LIVE THAT LONG.
NO CHINESE.
I'M AN AMERICAN CITIZEN.
HOOEY.
HOW CAN YOU BE A CITIZEN?
NONE OF YOUR BUSINESS.
I WAS BORN IN SAN FRANCISCO. WHERE WERE YOU BORN?
SOUNDS LIKE IRELAND TO ME.
YOU GOT TO GO BACK.
PUT HIM ON THE SHIP.
WHY? I'M AN AMERICAN... JUST LIKE YOU!

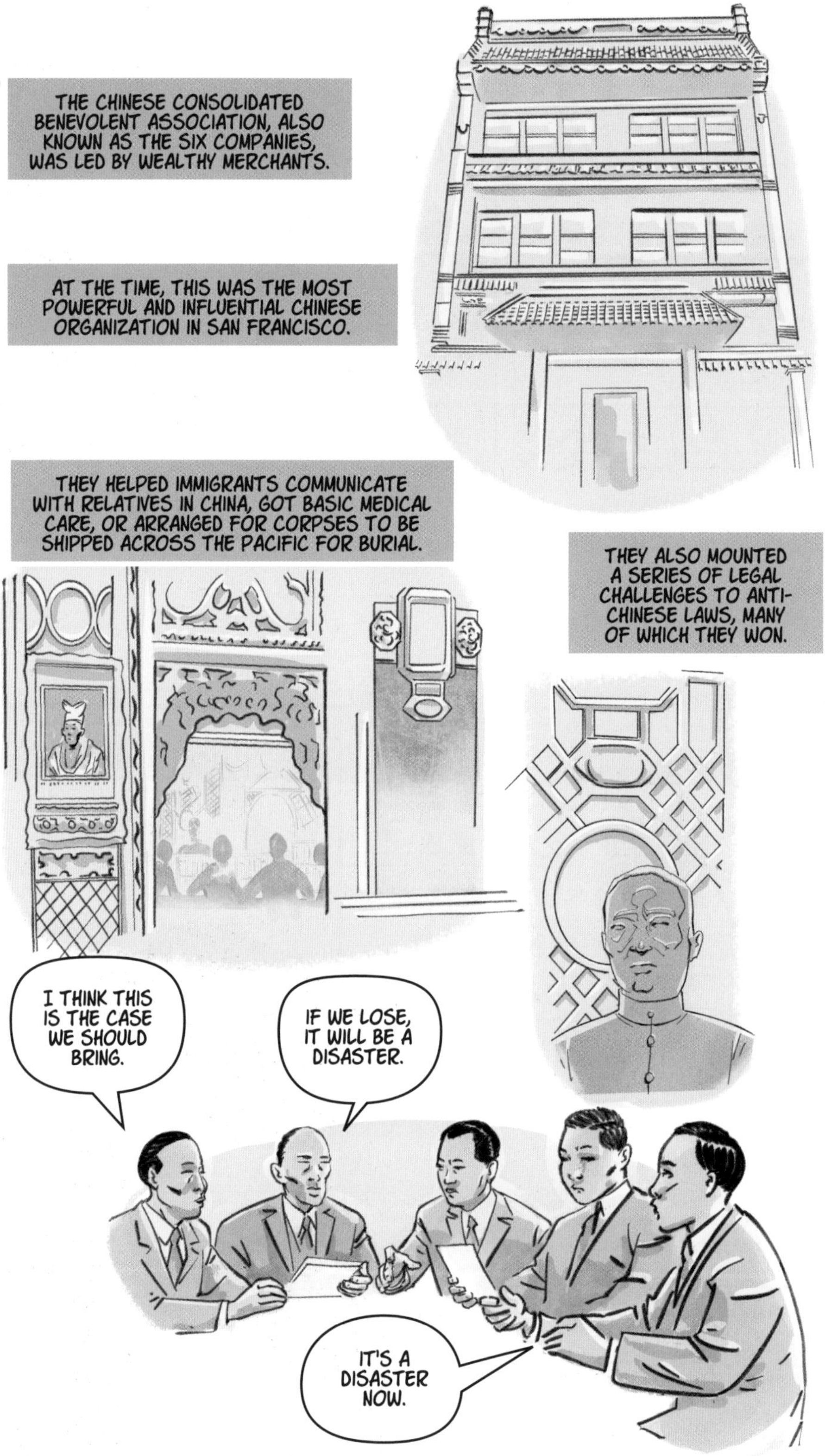
THE CHINESE CONSOLIDATED BENEVOLENT ASSOCIATION, ALSO KNOWN AS THE SIX COMPANIES, WAS LED BY WEALTHY MERCHANTS.
AT THE TIME, THIS WAS THE MOST POWERFUL AND INFLUENTIAL CHINESE ORGANIZATION IN SAN FRANCISCO.
THEY HELPED IMMIGRANTS COMMUNICATE WITH RELATIVES IN CHINA, GOT BASIC MEDICAL CARE, OR ARRANGED FOR CORPSES TO BE SHIPPED ACROSS THE PACIFIC FOR BURIAL.
THEY ALSO MOUNTED A SERIES OF LEGAL CHALLENGES TO ANTI-CHINESE LAWS, MANY OF WHICH THEY WON.
I THINK THIS IS THE CASE WE SHOULD BRING.
IF WE LOSE, IT WILL BE A DISASTER.
IT'S A DISASTER NOW.

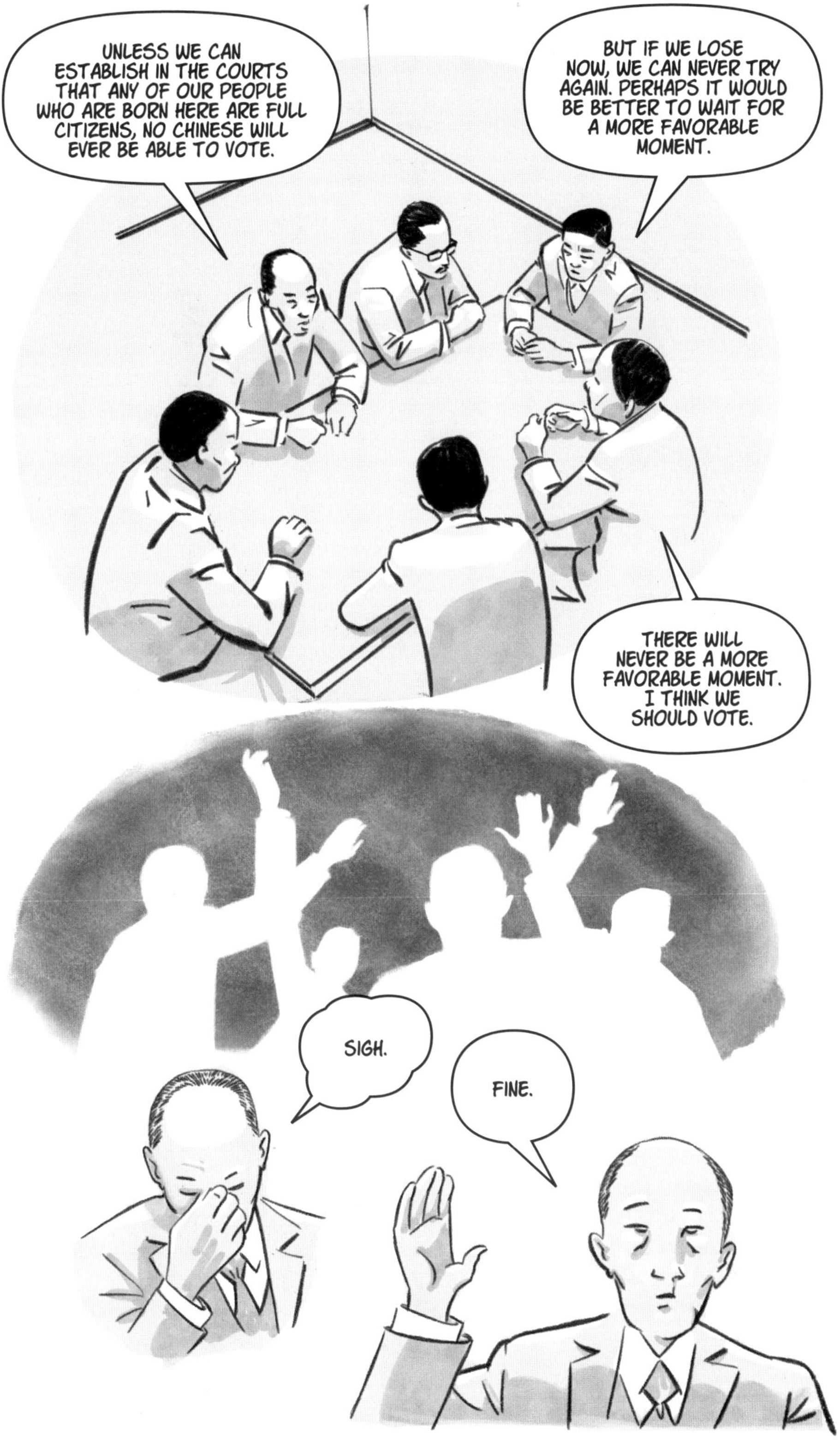
UNLESS WE CAN ESTABLISH IN THE COURTS THAT ANY OF OUR PEOPLE WHO ARE BORN HERE ARE FULL CITIZENS, NO CHINESE WILL EVER BE ABLE TO VOTE.
BUT IF WE LOSE NOW, WE CAN NEVER TRY AGAIN. PERHAPS IT WOULD BE BETTER TO WAIT FOR A MORE FAVORABLE MOMENT.
THERE WILL NEVER BE A MORE FAVORABLE MOMENT. I THINK WE SHOULD VOTE.
SIGH.
FINE.

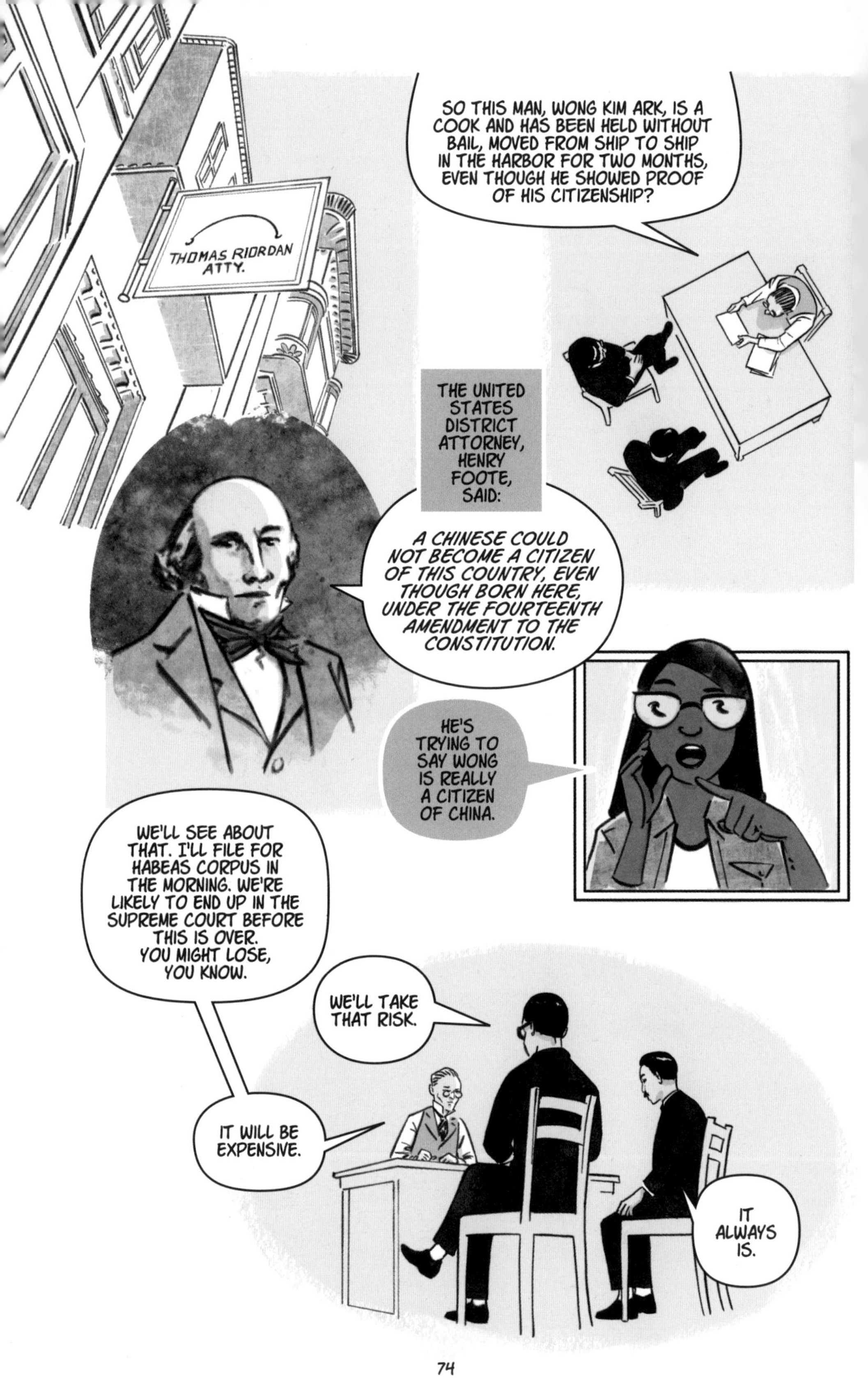

THOMAS RIORDAN ATTY.
SO THIS MAN, WONG KIM ARK, IS A COOK AND HAS BEEN HELD WITHOUT BAIL, MOVED FROM SHIP TO SHIP IN THE HARBOR FOR TWO MONTHS, EVEN THOUGH HE SHOWED PROOF OF HIS CITIZENSHIP?
THE UNITED STATES DISTRICT ATTORNEY, HENRY FOOTE, SAID:
A CHINESE COULD NOT BECOME A CITIZEN OF THIS COUNTRY, EVEN THOUGH BORN HERE, UNDER THE FOURTEENTH AMENDMENT TO THE CONSTITUTION.
HE'S TRYING TO SAY WONG IS REALLY A CITIZEN OF CHINA.
WE'LL SEE ABOUT THAT. I'LL FILE FOR HABEAS CORPUS IN THE MORNING. WE'RE LIKELY TO END UP IN THE SUPREME COURT BEFORE THIS IS OVER. YOU MIGHT LOSE, YOU KNOW.
WE'LL TAKE THAT RISK.
IT WILL BE EXPENSIVE.
IT ALWAYS IS.

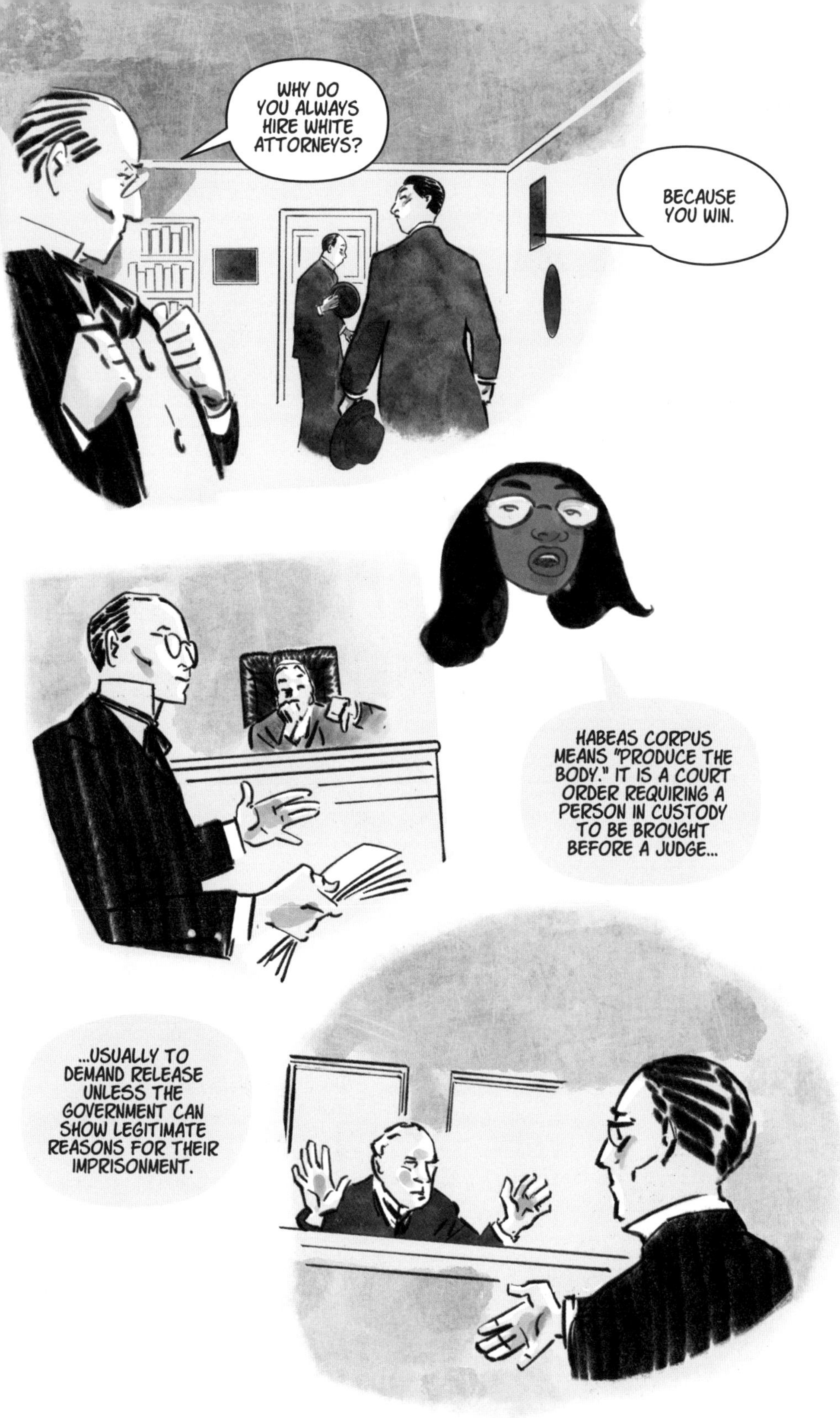
WHY DO YOU ALWAYS HIRE WHITE ATTORNEYS?
BECAUSE YOU WIN.
HABEAS CORPUS MEANS "PRODUCE THE BODY." IT IS A COURT ORDER REQUIRING A PERSON IN CUSTODY TO BE BROUGHT BEFORE A JUDGE...
...USUALLY TO DEMAND RELEASE UNLESS THE GOVERNMENT CAN SHOW LEGITIMATE REASONS FOR THEIR IMPRISONMENT.

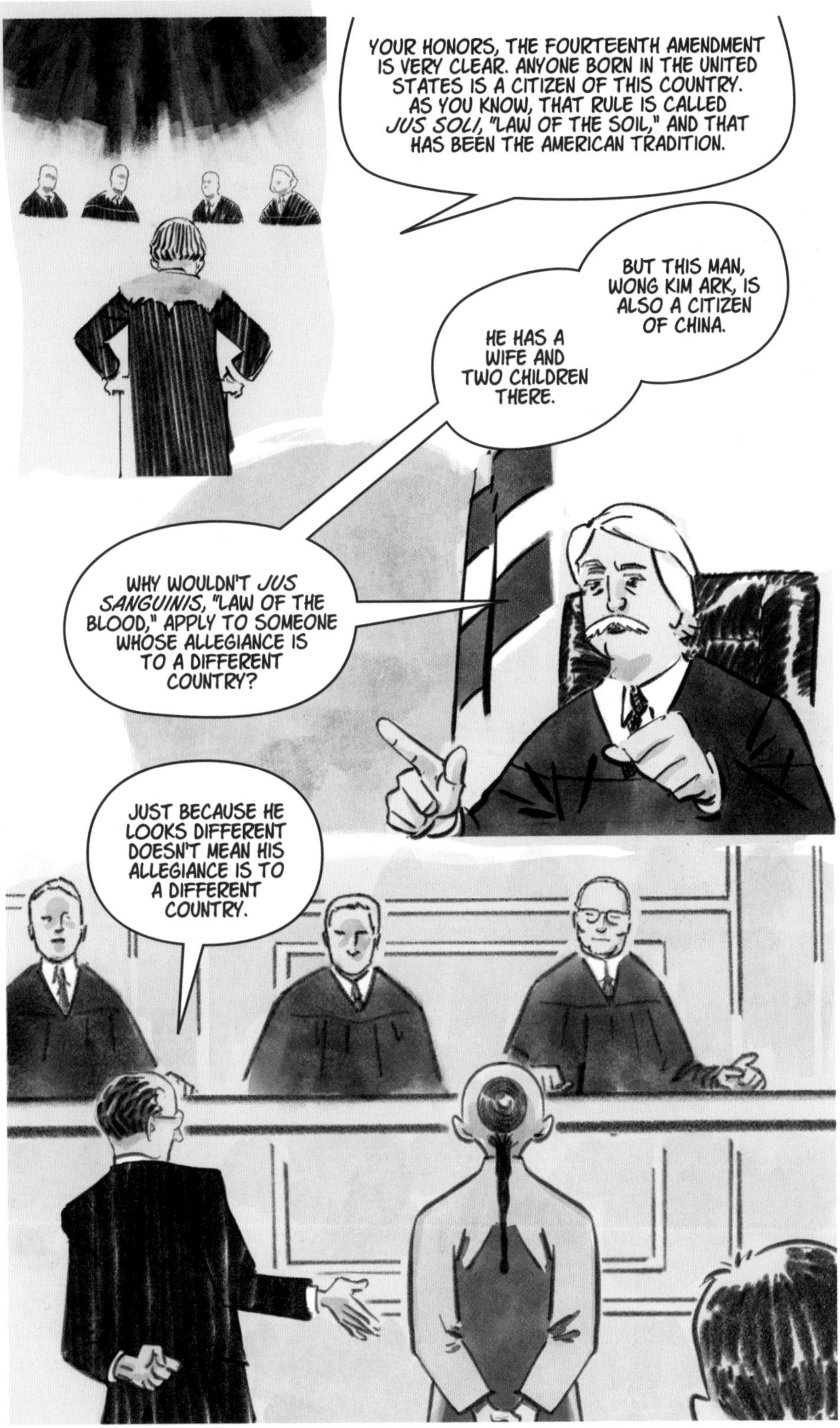
YOUR HONORS, THE FOURTEENTH AMENDMENT IS VERY CLEAR. ANYONE BORN IN THE UNITED STATES IS A CITIZEN OF THIS COUNTRY. AS YOU KNOW, THAT RULE IS CALLED *JUS SOLI*, "LAW OF THE SOIL," AND THAT HAS BEEN THE AMERICAN TRADITION.
BUT THIS MAN, WONG KIM ARK, IS ALSO A CITIZEN OF CHINA.
HE HAS A WIFE AND TWO CHILDREN THERE.
WHY WOULDN'T *JUS SANGUINIS*, "LAW OF THE BLOOD," APPLY TO SOMEONE WHOSE ALLEGIANCE IS TO A DIFFERENT COUNTRY?
JUST BECAUSE HE LOOKS DIFFERENT DOESN'T MEAN HIS ALLEGIANCE IS TO A DIFFERENT COUNTRY.

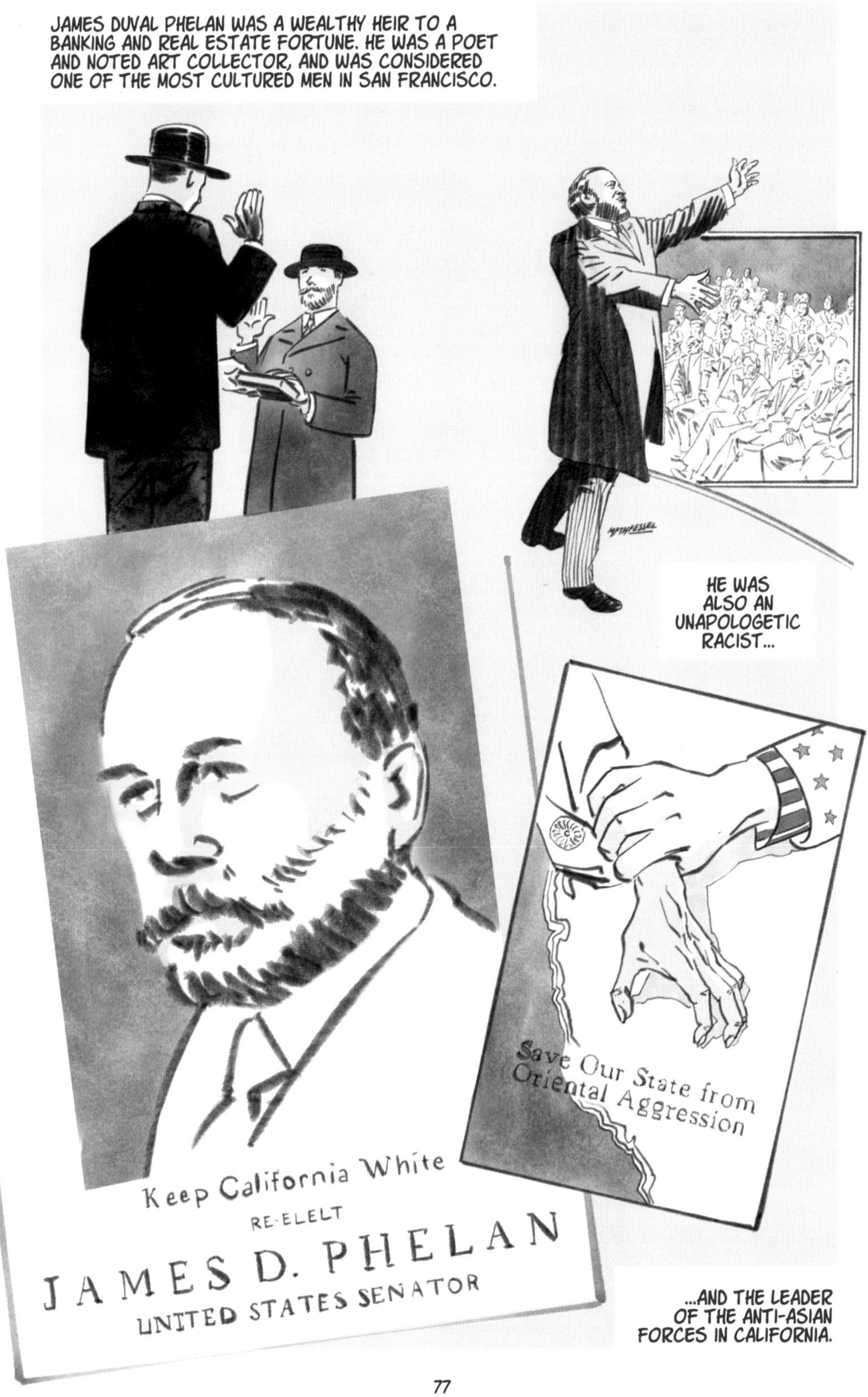
JAMES DUVAL PHELAN WAS A WEALTHY HEIR TO A BANKING AND REAL ESTATE FORTUNE. HE WAS A POET AND NOTED ART COLLECTOR, AND WAS CONSIDERED ONE OF THE MOST CULTURED MEN IN SAN FRANCISCO.
HE WAS ALSO AN UNAPOLOGETIC RACIST...
Keep California White
RE-ELELT
JAMES D. PHELAN
UNITED STATES SENATOR
Save Our State from Oriental Aggression
...AND THE LEADER OF THE ANTI-ASIAN FORCES IN CALIFORNIA.

HE WAS ELECTED MAYOR IN 1896 TO STAMP OUT GRAFT AND CORRUPTION BUT SOON REALIZED THAT THE BEST WAY TO APPEAL TO WHITE VOTERS WAS BY ATTACKING ASIAN IMMIGRANTS. HE WOULD LATER RUN FOR NATIONAL OFFICE WITH THE SLOGAN "KEEP CALIFORNIA WHITE."

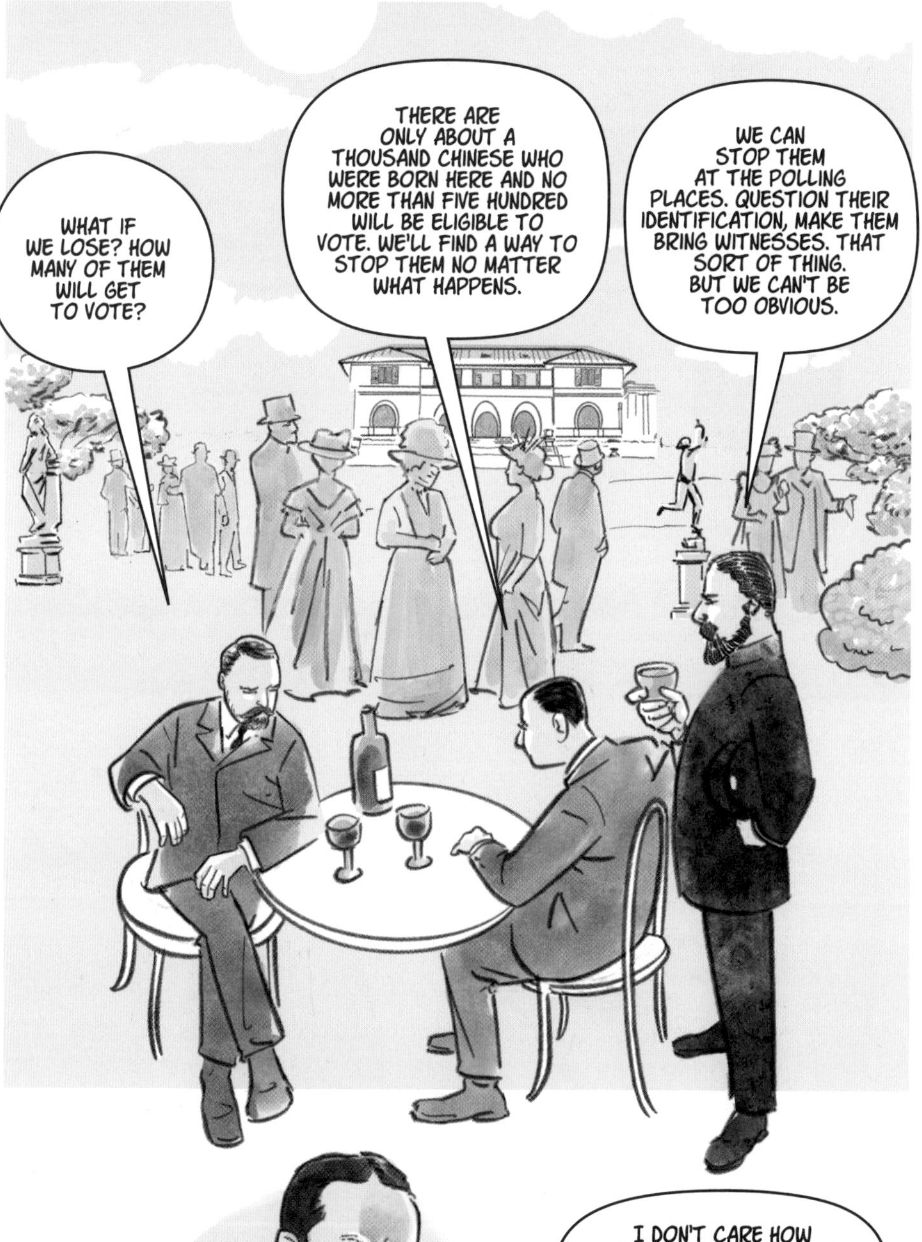

WHAT IF WE LOSE? HOW MANY OF THEM WILL GET TO VOTE?
THERE ARE ONLY ABOUT A THOUSAND CHINESE WHO WERE BORN HERE AND NO MORE THAN FIVE HUNDRED WILL BE ELIGIBLE TO VOTE. WE'LL FIND A WAY TO STOP THEM NO MATTER WHAT HAPPENS.
WE CAN STOP THEM AT THE POLLING PLACES. QUESTION THEIR IDENTIFICATION, MAKE THEM BRING WITNESSES. THAT SORT OF THING. BUT WE CAN'T BE TOO OBVIOUS.

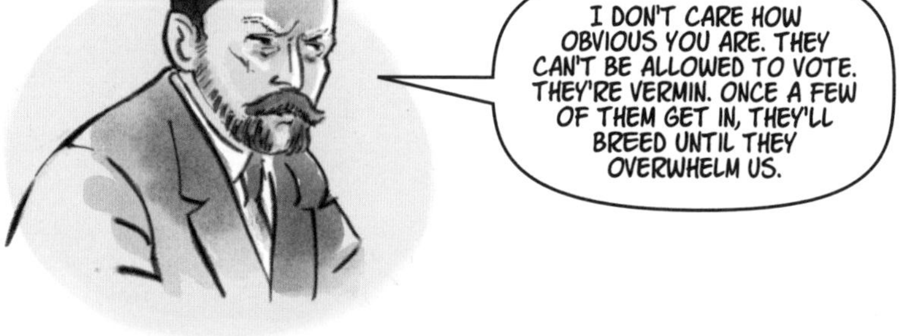

I DON'T CARE HOW OBVIOUS YOU ARE. THEY CAN'T BE ALLOWED TO VOTE. THEY'RE VERMIN. ONCE A FEW OF THEM GET IN, THEY'LL BREED UNTIL THEY OVERWHELM US.

IN THE CASE OF *UNITED STATES V. WONG KIM ARK,* WE FIND THE RESPONDENT, HAVING BEEN BORN IN THE UNITED STATES, IS, UNDER THE FOURTEENTH AMENDMENT, A CITIZEN...

TO HOLD THAT THE FOURTEENTH AMENDMENT OF THE CONSTITUTION EXCLUDES FROM CITIZENSHIP THE CHILDREN BORN IN THE UNITED STATES OF CITIZENS OR SUBJECTS OF OTHER COUNTRIES—

—WOULD BE TO DENY CITIZENSHIP TO THOUSANDS OF PERSONS OF ENGLISH, SCOTCH, IRISH, GERMAN, OR OTHER EUROPEAN PARENTAGE WHO HAVE ALWAYS BEEN CONSIDERED AND TREATED AS CITIZENS OF THE UNITED STATES.

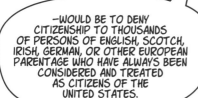

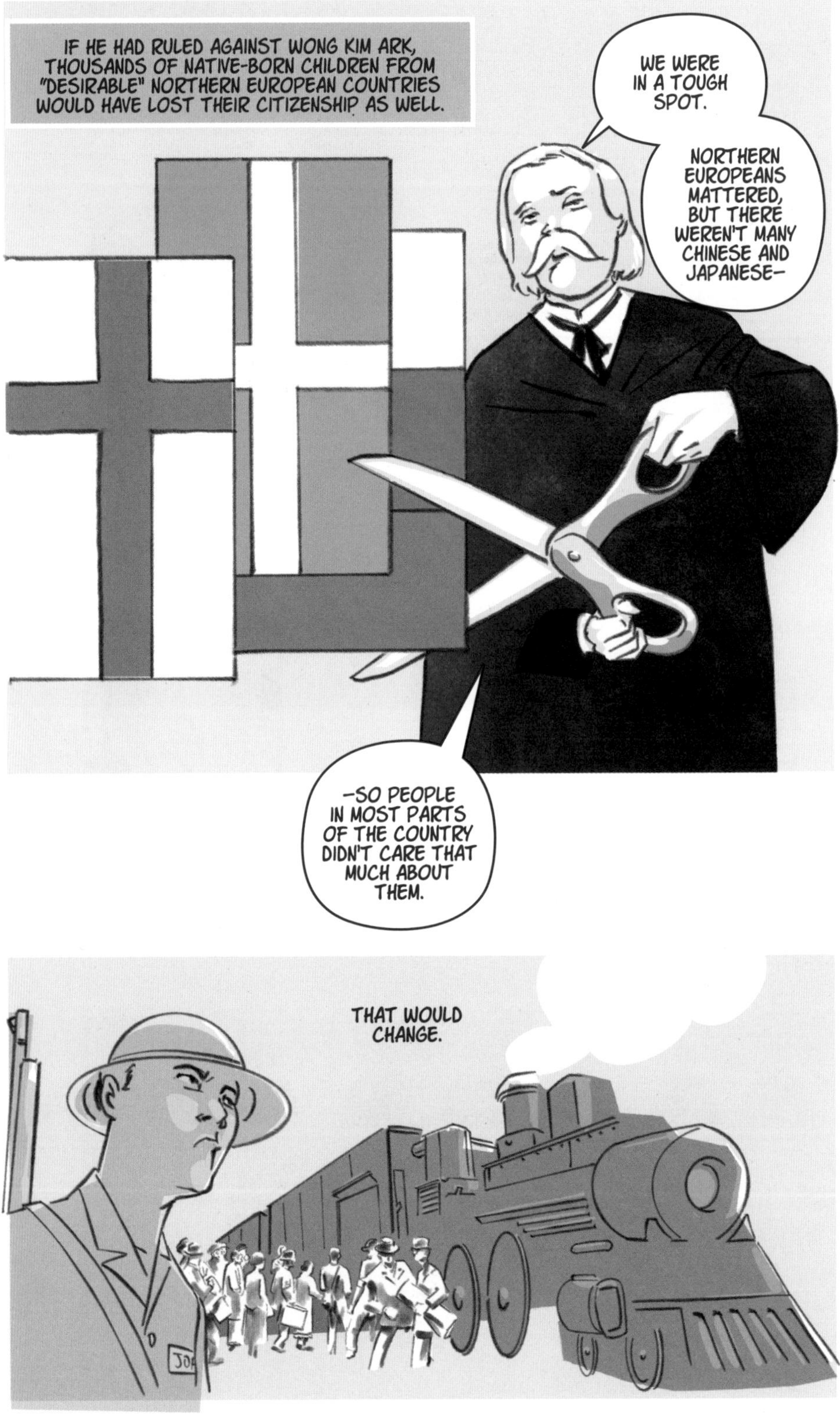
IF HE HAD RULED AGAINST WONG KIM ARK, THOUSANDS OF NATIVE-BORN CHILDREN FROM "DESIRABLE" NORTHERN EUROPEAN COUNTRIES WOULD HAVE LOST THEIR CITIZENSHIP AS WELL.
WE WERE IN A TOUGH SPOT.
NORTHERN EUROPEANS MATTERED, BUT THERE WEREN'T MANY CHINESE AND JAPANESE–
–SO PEOPLE IN MOST PARTS OF THE COUNTRY DIDN'T CARE THAT MUCH ABOUT THEM.
THAT WOULD CHANGE.

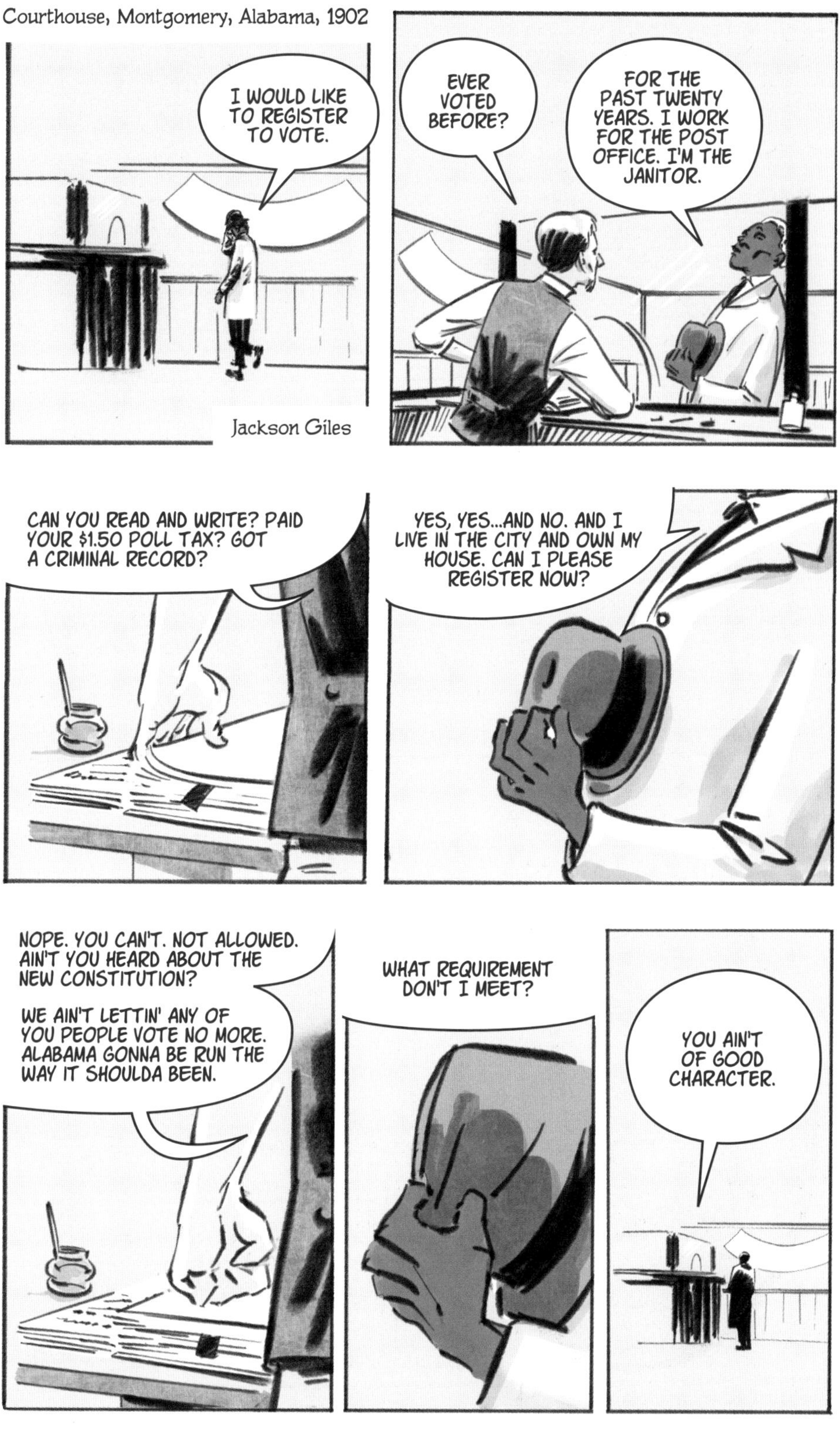
Courthouse, Montgomery, Alabama, 1902
I WOULD LIKE TO REGISTER TO VOTE.
Jackson Giles
EVER VOTED BEFORE?
FOR THE PAST TWENTY YEARS. I WORK FOR THE POST OFFICE. I'M THE JANITOR.
CAN YOU READ AND WRITE? PAID YOUR $1.50 POLL TAX? GOT A CRIMINAL RECORD?
YES, YES...AND NO. AND I LIVE IN THE CITY AND OWN MY HOUSE. CAN I PLEASE REGISTER NOW?
NOPE. YOU CAN'T. NOT ALLOWED. AIN'T YOU HEARD ABOUT THE NEW CONSTITUTION?
WE AIN'T LETTIN' ANY OF YOU PEOPLE VOTE NO MORE. ALABAMA GONNA BE RUN THE WAY IT SHOULDA BEEN.
WHAT REQUIREMENT DON'T I MEET?
YOU AIN'T OF GOOD CHARACTER.

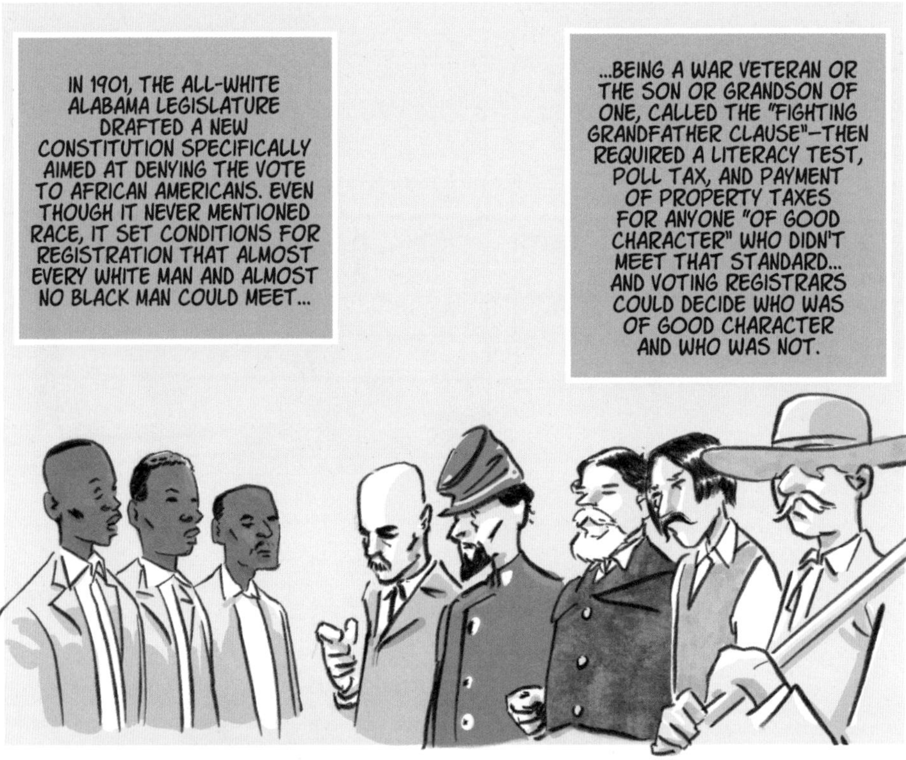
IN 1901, THE ALL-WHITE ALABAMA LEGISLATURE DRAFTED A NEW CONSTITUTION SPECIFICALLY AIMED AT DENYING THE VOTE TO AFRICAN AMERICANS. EVEN THOUGH IT NEVER MENTIONED RACE, IT SET CONDITIONS FOR REGISTRATION THAT ALMOST EVERY WHITE MAN AND ALMOST NO BLACK MAN COULD MEET...
...BEING A WAR VETERAN OR THE SON OR GRANDSON OF ONE, CALLED THE "FIGHTING GRANDFATHER CLAUSE"—THEN REQUIRED A LITERACY TEST, POLL TAX, AND PAYMENT OF PROPERTY TAXES FOR ANYONE "OF GOOD CHARACTER" WHO DIDN'T MEET THAT STANDARD... AND VOTING REGISTRARS COULD DECIDE WHO WAS OF GOOD CHARACTER AND WHO WAS NOT.

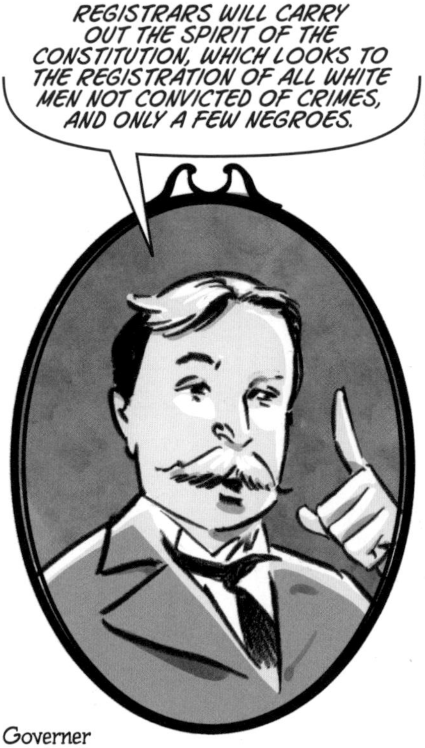
REGISTRARS WILL CARRY OUT THE SPIRIT OF THE CONSTITUTION, WHICH LOOKS TO THE REGISTRATION OF ALL WHITE MEN NOT CONVICTED OF CRIMES, AND ONLY A FEW NEGROES.

Governer
William Dorsey Jelks, Alabama

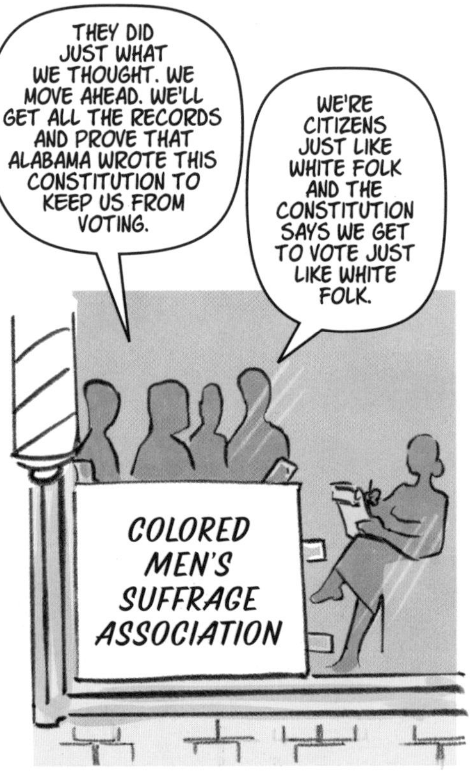
THEY DID JUST WHAT WE THOUGHT. WE MOVE AHEAD. WE'LL GET ALL THE RECORDS AND PROVE THAT ALABAMA WROTE THIS CONSTITUTION TO KEEP US FROM VOTING.
WE'RE CITIZENS JUST LIKE WHITE FOLK AND THE CONSTITUTION SAYS WE GET TO VOTE JUST LIKE WHITE FOLK.
COLORED MEN'S SUFFRAGE ASSOCIATION

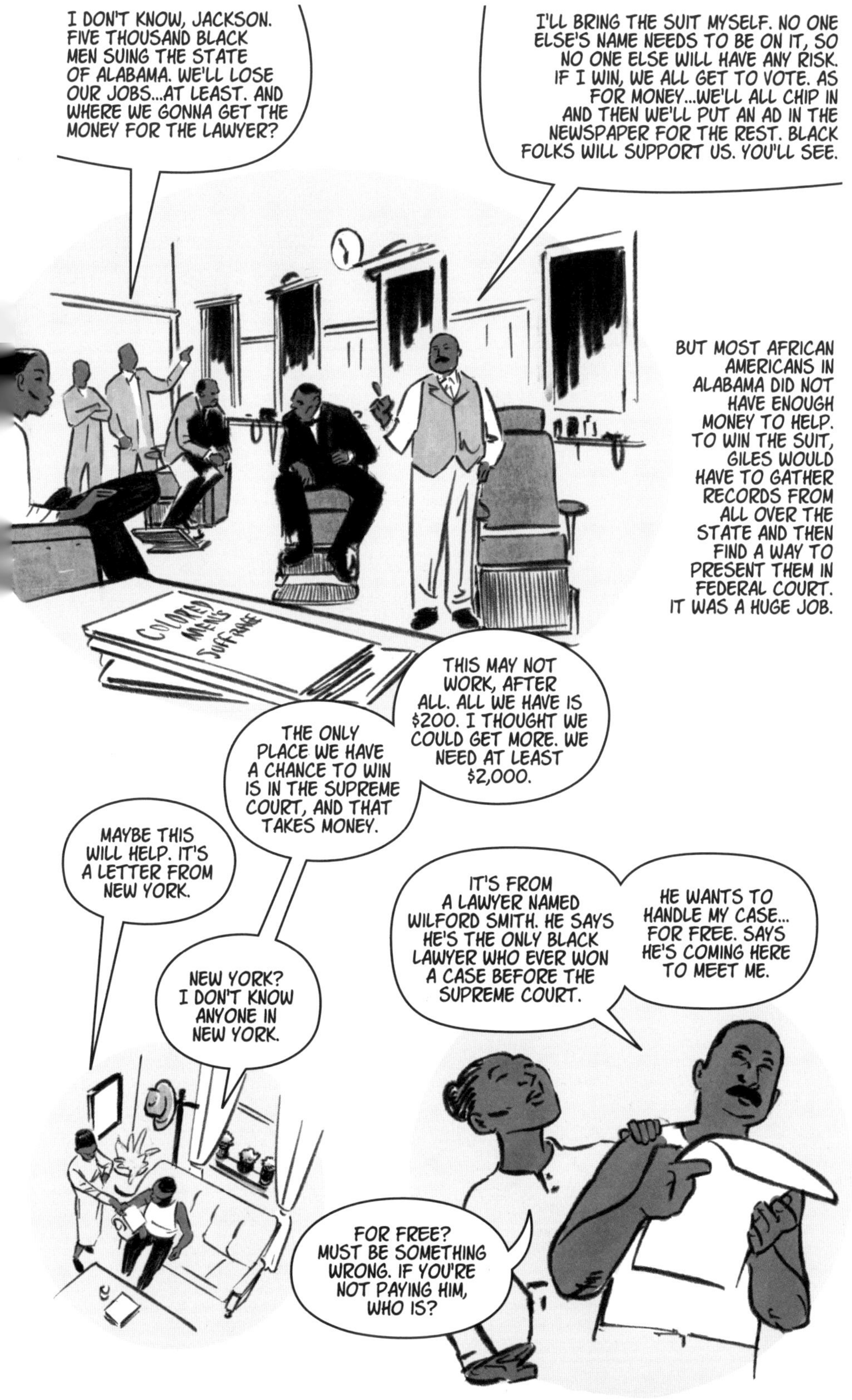
I DON'T KNOW, JACKSON. FIVE THOUSAND BLACK MEN SUING THE STATE OF ALABAMA. WE'LL LOSE OUR JOBS...AT LEAST. AND WHERE WE GONNA GET THE MONEY FOR THE LAWYER?
I'LL BRING THE SUIT MYSELF. NO ONE ELSE'S NAME NEEDS TO BE ON IT, SO NO ONE ELSE WILL HAVE ANY RISK. IF I WIN, WE ALL GET TO VOTE. AS FOR MONEY...WE'LL ALL CHIP IN AND THEN WE'LL PUT AN AD IN THE NEWSPAPER FOR THE REST. BLACK FOLKS WILL SUPPORT US. YOU'LL SEE.
COLORED MEN'S SUFFRAGE
BUT MOST AFRICAN AMERICANS IN ALABAMA DID NOT HAVE ENOUGH MONEY TO HELP. TO WIN THE SUIT, GILES WOULD HAVE TO GATHER RECORDS FROM ALL OVER THE STATE AND THEN FIND A WAY TO PRESENT THEM IN FEDERAL COURT. IT WAS A HUGE JOB.
THIS MAY NOT WORK, AFTER ALL. ALL WE HAVE IS $200. I THOUGHT WE COULD GET MORE. WE NEED AT LEAST $2,000.
THE ONLY PLACE WE HAVE A CHANCE TO WIN IS IN THE SUPREME COURT, AND THAT TAKES MONEY.
MAYBE THIS WILL HELP. IT'S A LETTER FROM NEW YORK.
NEW YORK? I DON'T KNOW ANYONE IN NEW YORK.
IT'S FROM A LAWYER NAMED WILFORD SMITH. HE SAYS HE'S THE ONLY BLACK LAWYER WHO EVER WON A CASE BEFORE THE SUPREME COURT.
HE WANTS TO HANDLE MY CASE... FOR FREE. SAYS HE'S COMING HERE TO MEET ME.
FOR FREE? MUST BE SOMETHING WRONG. IF YOU'RE NOT PAYING HIM, WHO IS?

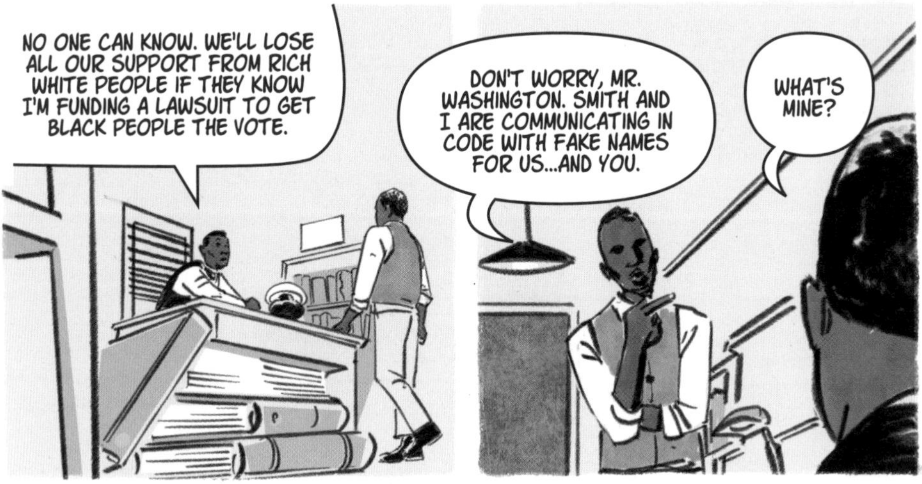
NO ONE CAN KNOW. WE'LL LOSE ALL OUR SUPPORT FROM RICH WHITE PEOPLE IF THEY KNOW I'M FUNDING A LAWSUIT TO GET BLACK PEOPLE THE VOTE.
DON'T WORRY, MR. WASHINGTON. SMITH AND I ARE COMMUNICATING IN CODE WITH FAKE NAMES FOR US...AND YOU.
WHAT'S MINE?

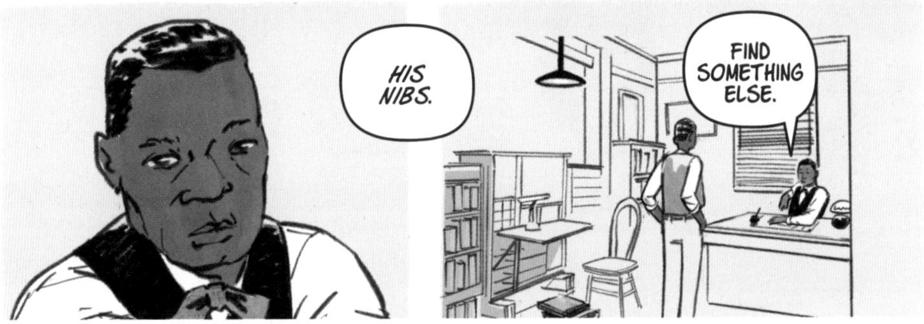
HIS NIBS.
FIND SOMETHING ELSE.

BOOKER T. WASHINGTON WAS BOTH FAMOUS AND NOTORIOUS AS AN "ACCOMMODATIONIST" WILLING TO ACCEPT SEGREGATION AND ENCOURAGE BLACK PEOPLE TO LEARN SIMPLE TASKS AND BUILD THEMSELVES UP SLOWLY. HE WAS EVEN WILLING FOR POOR, ILLITERATE BLACK MEN NOT TO HAVE THE VOTE—AS LONG AS POOR, ILLITERATE WHITE MEN DIDN'T HAVE IT EITHER.

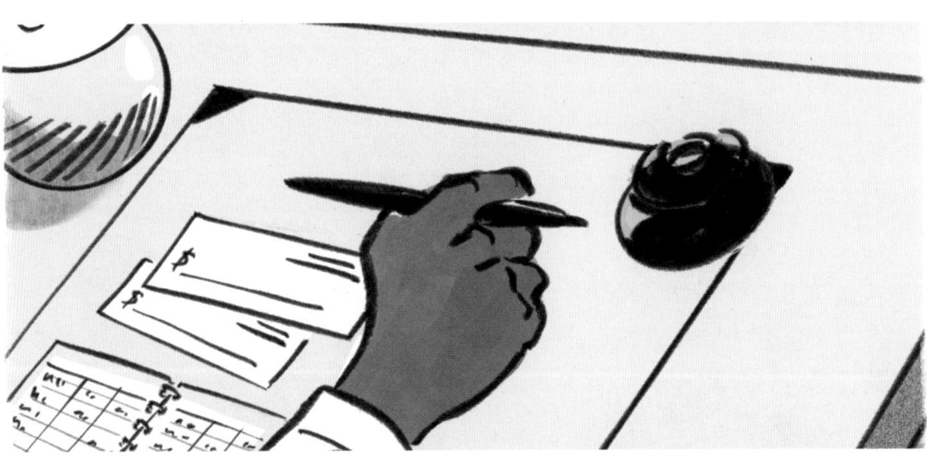

ALTHOUGH HIS PHILOSOPHY OF SLOW, STEADY GROWTH WAS EVENTUALLY DISCREDITED AND SUPPLANTED BY THE MORE ACTIVIST METHODS ADVOCATED BY PEOPLE SUCH AS W. E. B. DU BOIS, WASHINGTON PROVIDED A CADRE OF EDUCATED MEN AND WOMEN TO HELP MOVE THE EARLY CIVIL RIGHTS MOVEMENT FORWARD.

ON FEBRUARY 24, 1903, *GILES V. HARRIS* REACHED THE SUPREME COURT. WILFORD SMITH PRESENTED OVERWHELMING EVIDENCE THAT DISCRIMINATION AGAINST HIS CLIENT SPRUNG DIRECTLY FROM THE 1901 ALABAMA CONSTITUTION.

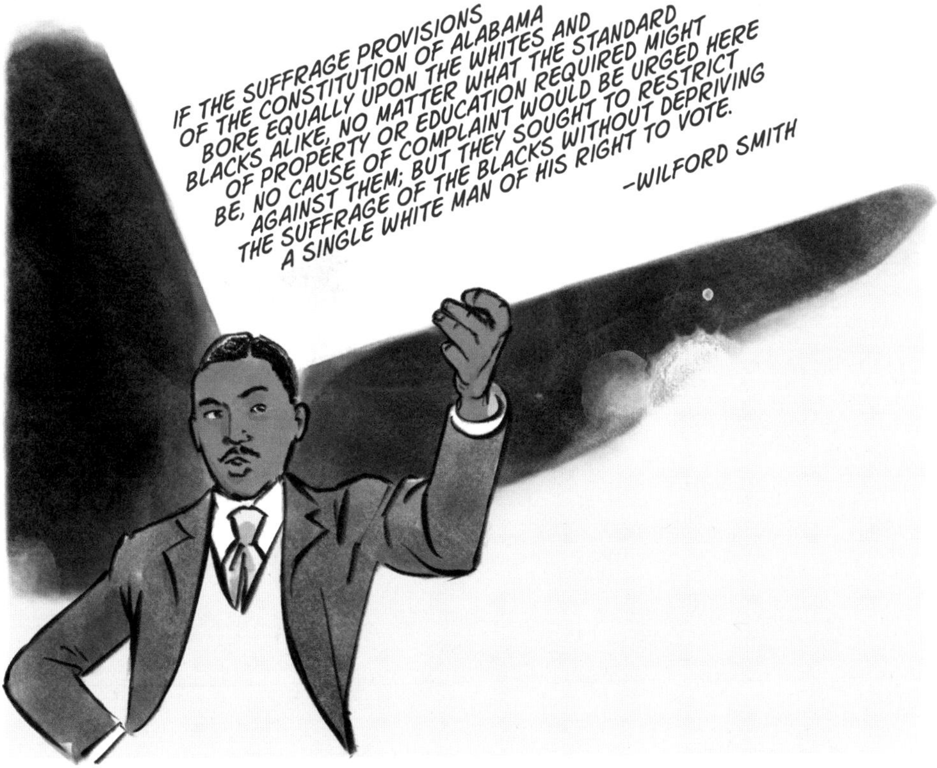
IF THE SUFFRAGE PROVISIONS
OF THE CONSTITUTION OF ALABAMA
BORE EQUALLY UPON THE WHITES AND
BLACKS ALIKE, NO MATTER WHAT THE STANDARD
OF PROPERTY OR EDUCATION REQUIRED MIGHT
BE, NO CAUSE OF COMPLAINT WOULD BE URGED HERE
AGAINST THEM; BUT THEY SOUGHT TO RESTRICT
THE SUFFRAGE OF THE BLACKS WITHOUT DEPRIVING
A SINGLE WHITE MAN OF HIS RIGHT TO VOTE.
-WILFORD SMITH

AMONG THE NINE JUSTICES SMITH WOULD NEED TO PERSUADE WAS A NEW APPOINTEE, ONE OF THE MOST HIGHLY PRAISED MEN EVER TO SIT ON THE SUPREME COURT. OLIVER WENDELL HOLMES JR., A CELEBRATED LEGAL PHILOSOPHER AND FORMER WAR HERO, HAD ARRIVED ON THE COURT JUST TWO MONTHS BEFORE.

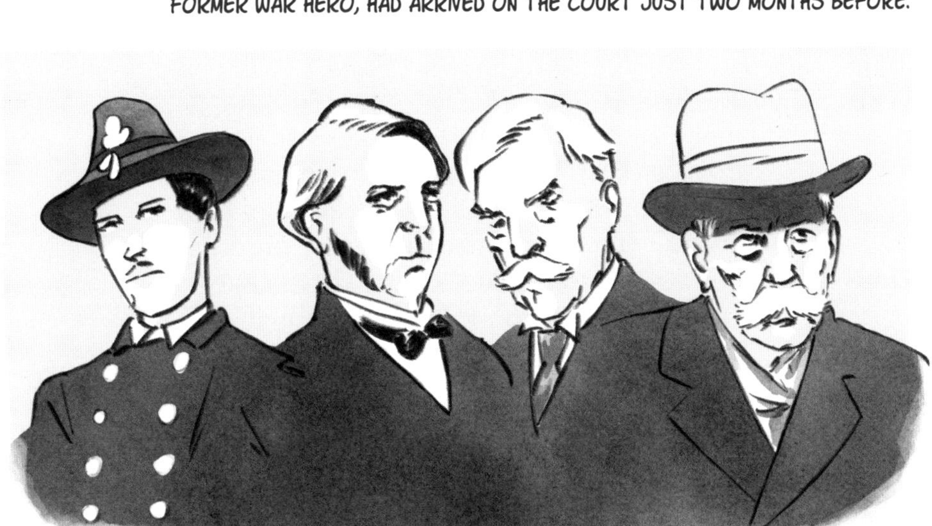

NAMED FOR HIS PHYSICIAN, PHILOSOPHER, AND WRITER FATHER—WHOSE NAME WAS BORROWED BY ARTHUR CONAN DOYLE FOR A FICTIONAL DETECTIVE—HOLMES JR. WAS WOUNDED THREE TIMES FIGHTING FOR THE UNION DURING THE CIVIL WAR. HE BECAME A DISTINGUISHED LAWYER AND JUDGE AND WAS EVENTUALLY NOMINATED BY THEODORE ROOSEVELT TO THE SUPREME COURT. HOLMES IS OFTEN CALLED ONE OF THE GREATEST LEGAL MINDS IN AMERICAN HISTORY.

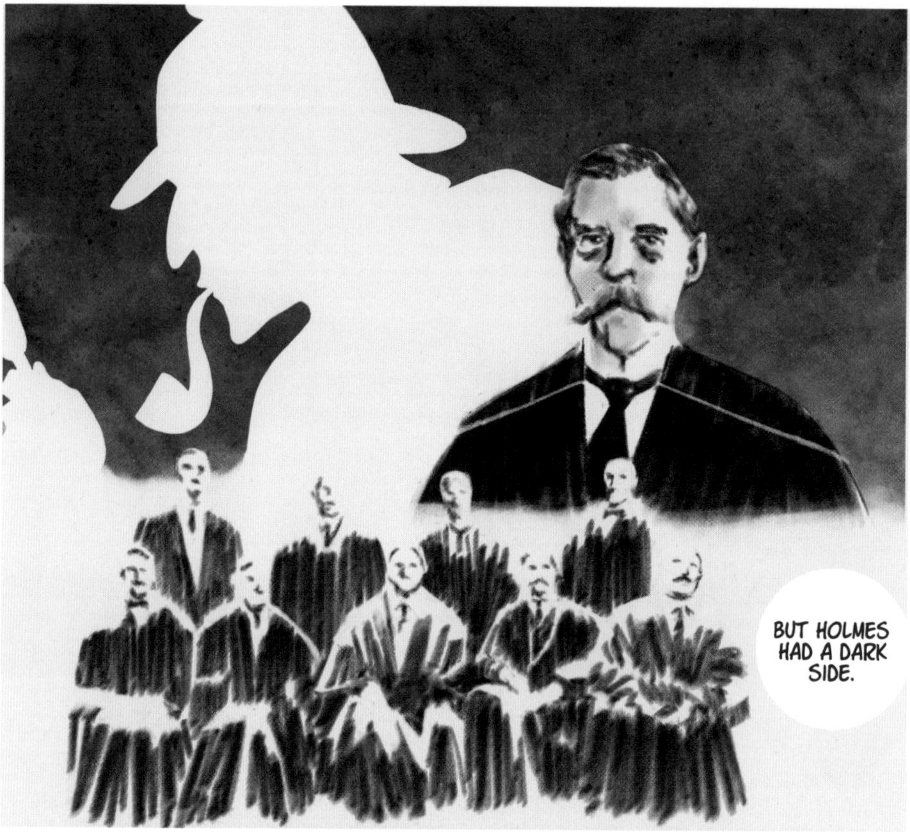
BUT HOLMES HAD A DARK SIDE.

IN 1927, HOLMES WROTE A DECISION UPHOLDING THE FORCED STERILIZATION OF CARRIE BUCK, A NINETEEN-YEAR-OLD WOMAN IN VIRGINIA WHO WAS, WRONGLY AS IT TURNED OUT, THOUGHT TO HAVE AN INTELLECTUAL DISABILITY. HE WROTE...

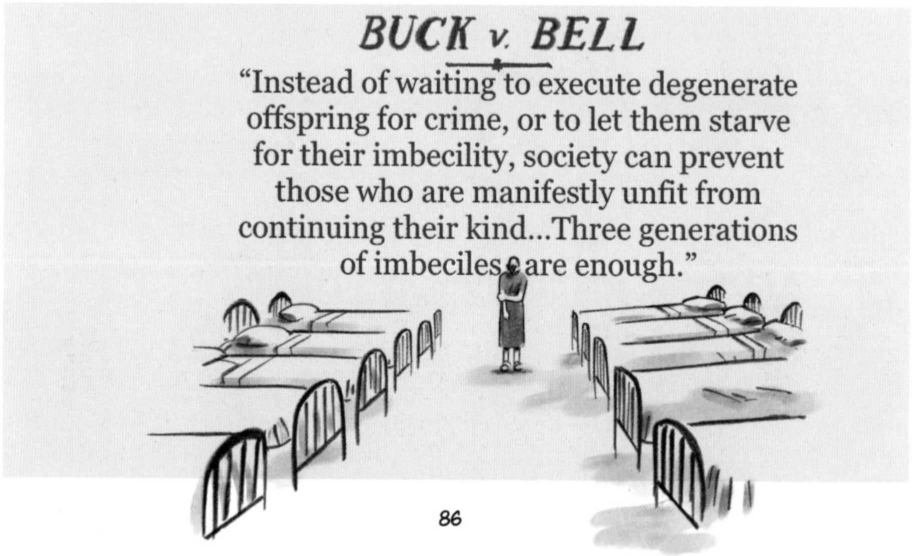
BUCK v. BELL
"Instead of waiting to execute degenerate offspring for crime, or to let them starve for their imbecility, society can prevent those who are manifestly unfit from continuing their kind...Three generations of imbeciles are enough."

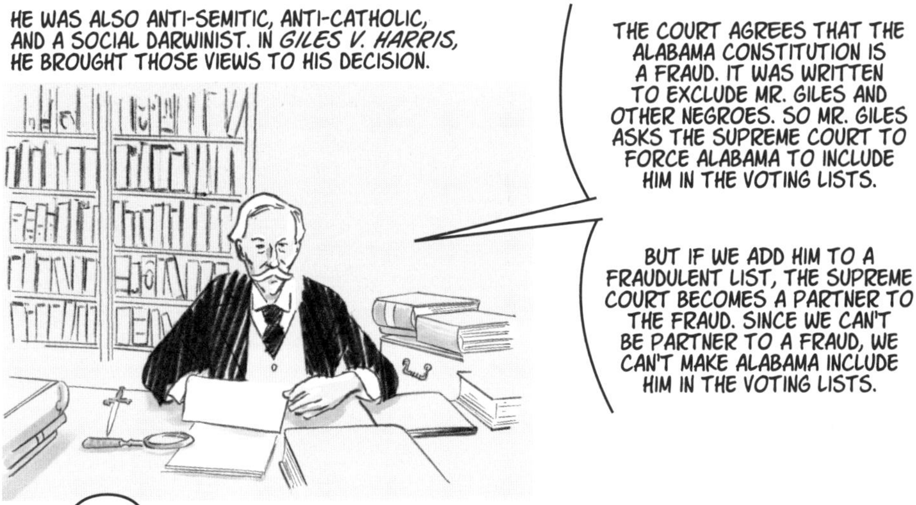
HE WAS ALSO ANTI-SEMITIC, ANTI-CATHOLIC, AND A SOCIAL DARWINIST. IN *GILES V. HARRIS,* HE BROUGHT THOSE VIEWS TO HIS DECISION.
THE COURT AGREES THAT THE ALABAMA CONSTITUTION IS A FRAUD. IT WAS WRITTEN TO EXCLUDE MR. GILES AND OTHER NEGROES. SO MR. GILES ASKS THE SUPREME COURT TO FORCE ALABAMA TO INCLUDE HIM IN THE VOTING LISTS.
BUT IF WE ADD HIM TO A FRAUDULENT LIST, THE SUPREME COURT BECOMES A PARTNER TO THE FRAUD. SINCE WE CAN'T BE PARTNER TO A FRAUD, WE CAN'T MAKE ALABAMA INCLUDE HIM IN THE VOTING LISTS.

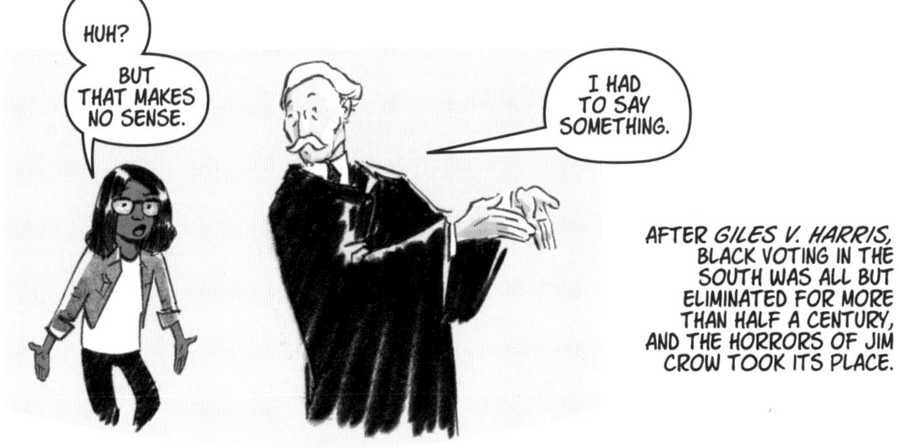
HUH?
BUT THAT MAKES NO SENSE.
I HAD TO SAY SOMETHING.
AFTER *GILES V. HARRIS,* BLACK VOTING IN THE SOUTH WAS ALL BUT ELIMINATED FOR MORE THAN HALF A CENTURY, AND THE HORRORS OF JIM CROW TOOK ITS PLACE.

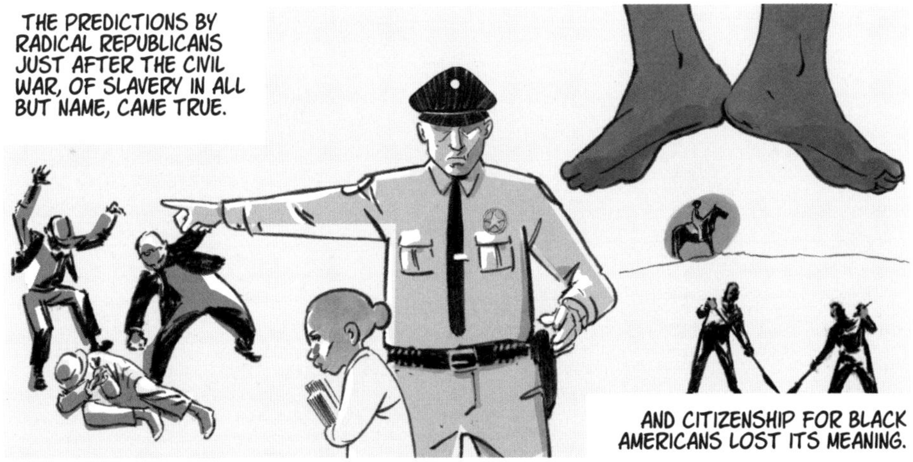
THE PREDICTIONS BY RADICAL REPUBLICANS JUST AFTER THE CIVIL WAR, OF SLAVERY IN ALL BUT NAME, CAME TRUE.
AND CITIZENSHIP FOR BLACK AMERICANS LOST ITS MEANING.

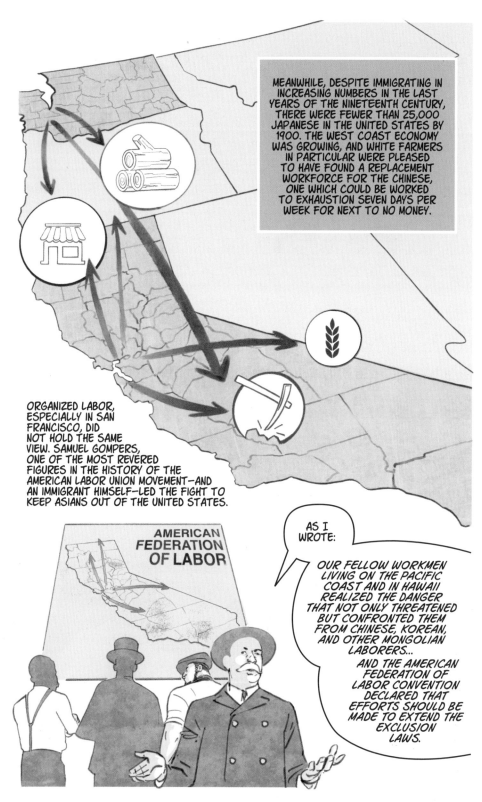

MEANWHILE, DESPITE IMMIGRATING IN INCREASING NUMBERS IN THE LAST YEARS OF THE NINETEENTH CENTURY, THERE WERE FEWER THAN 25,000 JAPANESE IN THE UNITED STATES BY 1900. THE WEST COAST ECONOMY WAS GROWING, AND WHITE FARMERS IN PARTICULAR WERE PLEASED TO HAVE FOUND A REPLACEMENT WORKFORCE FOR THE CHINESE, ONE WHICH COULD BE WORKED TO EXHAUSTION SEVEN DAYS PER WEEK FOR NEXT TO NO MONEY.

ORGANIZED LABOR, ESPECIALLY IN SAN FRANCISCO, DID NOT HOLD THE SAME VIEW. SAMUEL GOMPERS, ONE OF THE MOST REVERED FIGURES IN THE HISTORY OF THE AMERICAN LABOR UNION MOVEMENT—AND AN IMMIGRANT HIMSELF—LED THE FIGHT TO KEEP ASIANS OUT OF THE UNITED STATES.

AMERICAN FEDERATION OF LABOR

AS I WROTE:

OUR FELLOW WORKMEN LIVING ON THE PACIFIC COAST AND IN HAWAII REALIZED THE DANGER THAT NOT ONLY THREATENED BUT CONFRONTED THEM FROM CHINESE, KOREAN, AND OTHER MONGOLIAN LABORERS...

AND THE AMERICAN FEDERATION OF LABOR CONVENTION DECLARED THAT EFFORTS SHOULD BE MADE TO EXTEND THE EXCLUSION LAWS.

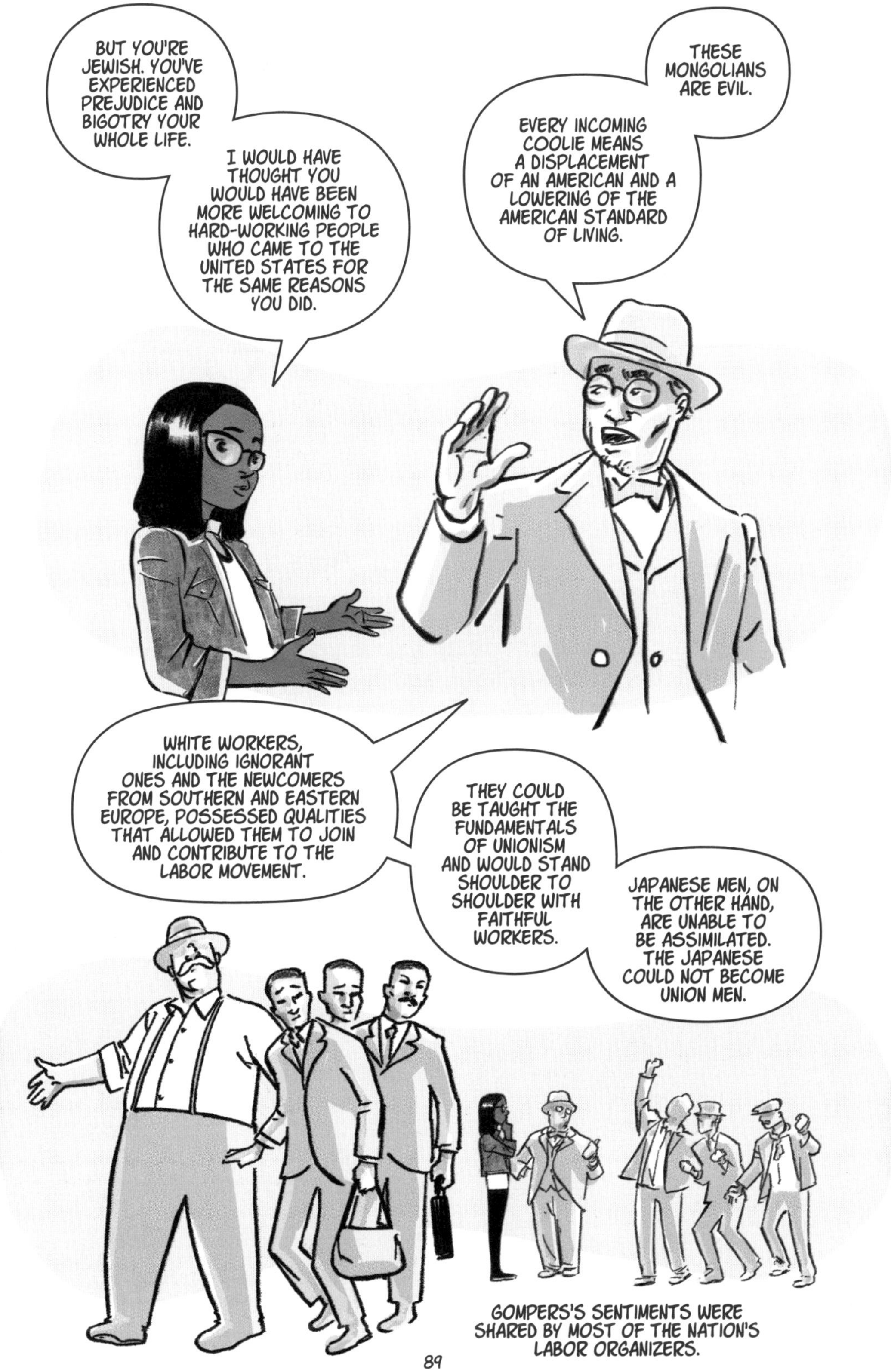
BUT YOU'RE JEWISH. YOU'VE EXPERIENCED PREJUDICE AND BIGOTRY YOUR WHOLE LIFE.
I WOULD HAVE THOUGHT YOU WOULD HAVE BEEN MORE WELCOMING TO HARD-WORKING PEOPLE WHO CAME TO THE UNITED STATES FOR THE SAME REASONS YOU DID.
THESE MONGOLIANS ARE EVIL.
EVERY INCOMING COOLIE MEANS A DISPLACEMENT OF AN AMERICAN AND A LOWERING OF THE AMERICAN STANDARD OF LIVING.
WHITE WORKERS, INCLUDING IGNORANT ONES AND THE NEWCOMERS FROM SOUTHERN AND EASTERN EUROPE, POSSESSED QUALITIES THAT ALLOWED THEM TO JOIN AND CONTRIBUTE TO THE LABOR MOVEMENT.
THEY COULD BE TAUGHT THE FUNDAMENTALS OF UNIONISM AND WOULD STAND SHOULDER TO SHOULDER WITH FAITHFUL WORKERS.
JAPANESE MEN, ON THE OTHER HAND, ARE UNABLE TO BE ASSIMILATED. THE JAPANESE COULD NOT BECOME UNION MEN.
GOMPERS'S SENTIMENTS WERE SHARED BY MOST OF THE NATION'S LABOR ORGANIZERS.

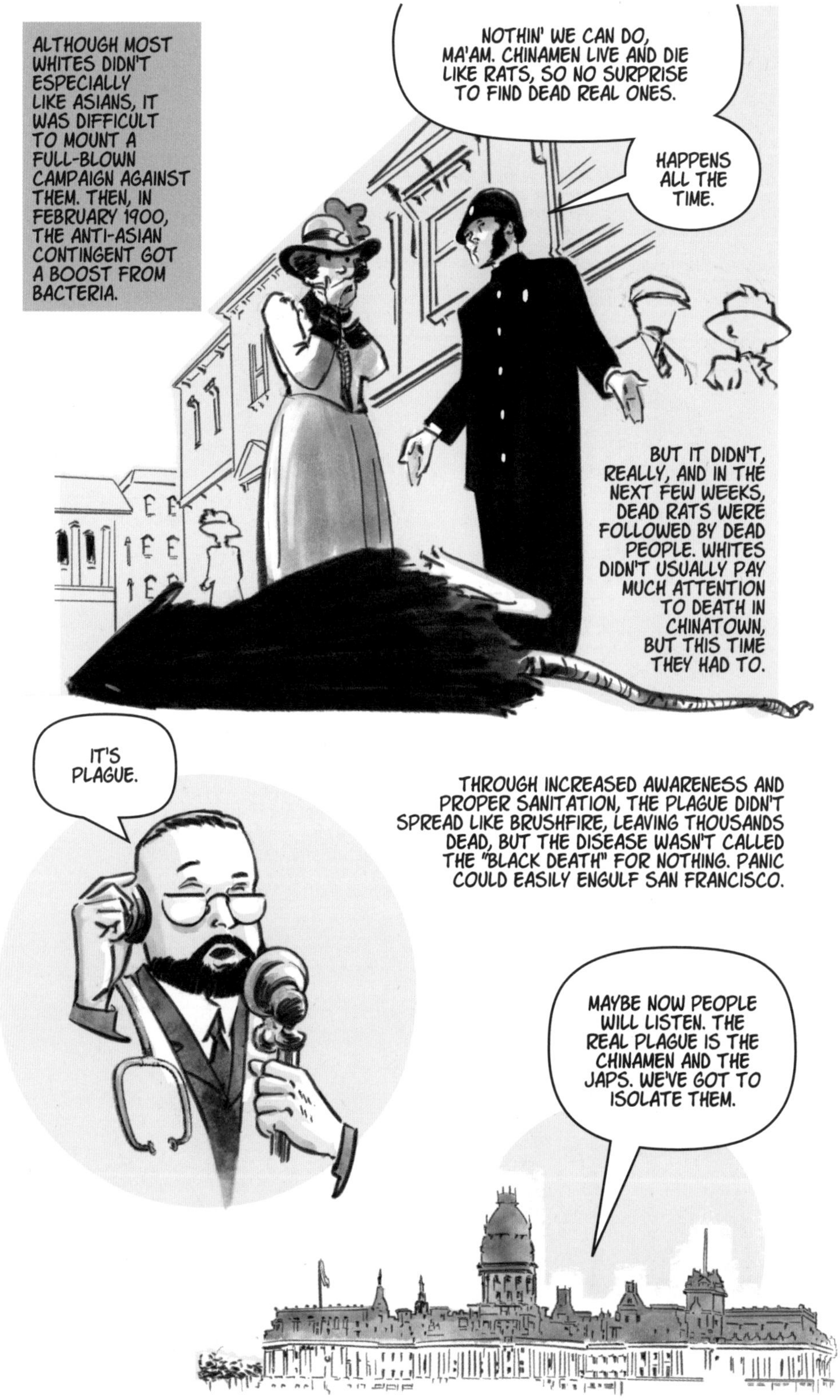

ALTHOUGH MOST WHITES DIDN'T ESPECIALLY LIKE ASIANS, IT WAS DIFFICULT TO MOUNT A FULL-BLOWN CAMPAIGN AGAINST THEM. THEN, IN FEBRUARY 1900, THE ANTI-ASIAN CONTINGENT GOT A BOOST FROM BACTERIA.
NOTHIN' WE CAN DO, MA'AM. CHINAMEN LIVE AND DIE LIKE RATS, SO NO SURPRISE TO FIND DEAD REAL ONES.
HAPPENS ALL THE TIME.
BUT IT DIDN'T, REALLY, AND IN THE NEXT FEW WEEKS, DEAD RATS WERE FOLLOWED BY DEAD PEOPLE. WHITES DIDN'T USUALLY PAY MUCH ATTENTION TO DEATH IN CHINATOWN, BUT THIS TIME THEY HAD TO.
IT'S PLAGUE.
THROUGH INCREASED AWARENESS AND PROPER SANITATION, THE PLAGUE DIDN'T SPREAD LIKE BRUSHFIRE, LEAVING THOUSANDS DEAD, BUT THE DISEASE WASN'T CALLED THE "BLACK DEATH" FOR NOTHING. PANIC COULD EASILY ENGULF SAN FRANCISCO.
MAYBE NOW PEOPLE WILL LISTEN. THE REAL PLAGUE IS THE CHINAMEN AND THE JAPS. WE'VE GOT TO ISOLATE THEM.

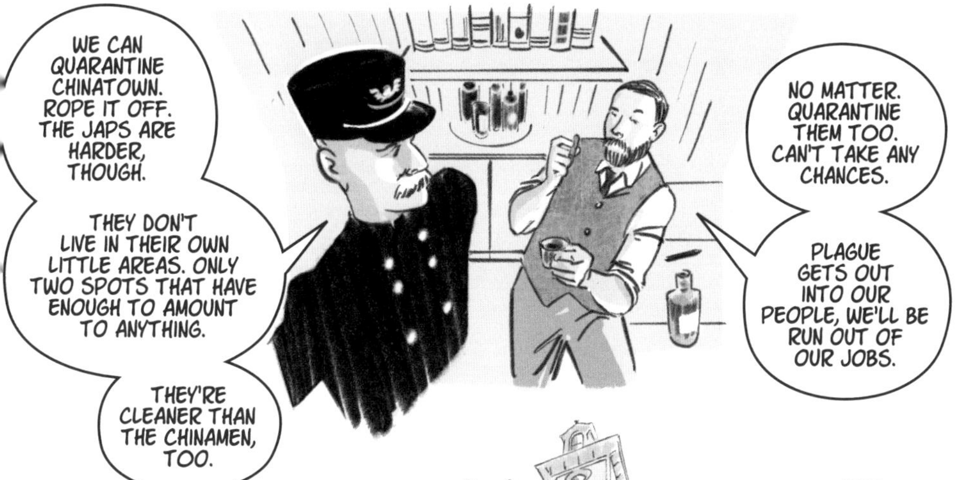
WE CAN QUARANTINE CHINATOWN. ROPE IT OFF. THE JAPS ARE HARDER, THOUGH.
THEY DON'T LIVE IN THEIR OWN LITTLE AREAS. ONLY TWO SPOTS THAT HAVE ENOUGH TO AMOUNT TO ANYTHING.
THEY'RE CLEANER THAN THE CHINAMEN, TOO.
NO MATTER. QUARANTINE THEM TOO. CAN'T TAKE ANY CHANCES.
PLAGUE GETS OUT INTO OUR PEOPLE, WE'LL BE RUN OUT OF OUR JOBS.

BUT THE MAYOR'S ORDER CAUSED PROBLEMS AND FROM AN UNEXPECTED SOURCE.

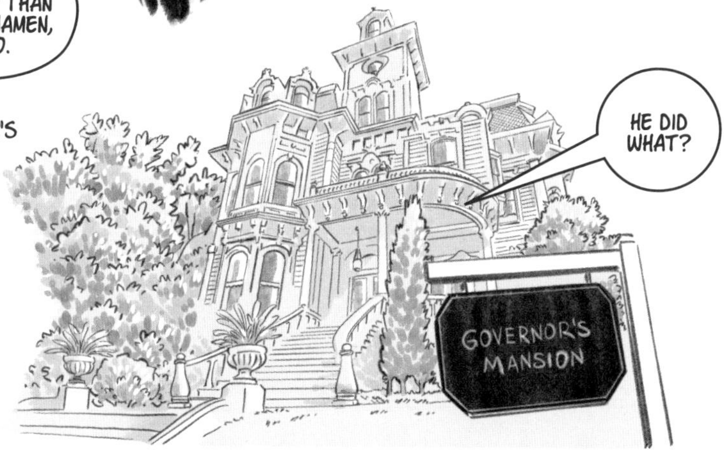
HE DID WHAT?
GOVERNOR'S MANSION

PLAGUE IS NOT GOOD FOR THE ECONOMY. SAN FRANCISCO WAS THE MOST IMPORTANT CITY ON THE WEST COAST, AND GOVERNOR HENRY GAGE FURIOUSLY DENIED THAT PLAGUE HAD INVADED THE CITY. HE USED THE TIME-HONORED EXCUSE THAT THE REPORTS WERE POLITICALLY MOTIVATED.

SAN FRANCISCO NEWSPAPERS BACKED UP THE GOVERNOR AND ATTACKED THE MAYOR. *THE SAN FRANCISCO CALL*, USUALLY A PHELAN CHEERLEADER, RAN AN ARTICLE THE DAY AFTER THE QUARANTINE.

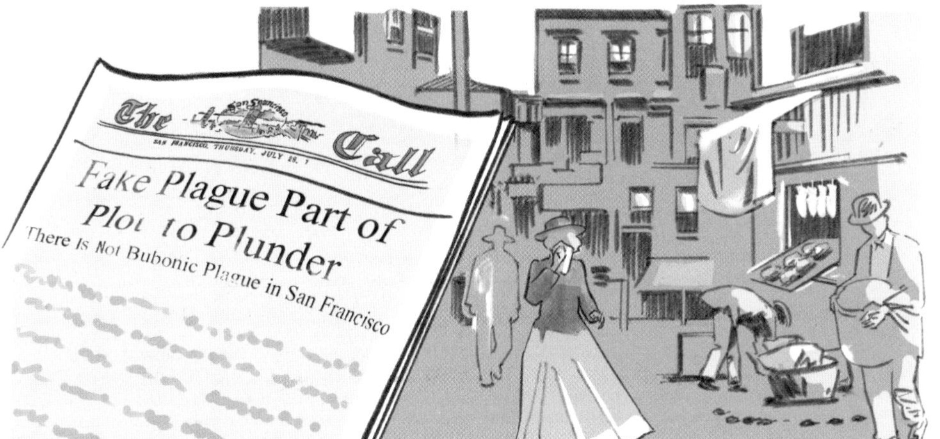
The Call
Fake Plague Part of Plot to Plunder
There Is Not Bubonic Plague in San Francisco

IT WENT ON TO ACCUSE THOSE WHO PUT FORTH SUCH A RIDICULOUS NOTION OF MAKING "A BOLD ATTEMPT TO BLACKMAIL THE CITY OUT OF FUNDS TO FEED A HORDE OF HUNGRY OFFICE-SEEKERS WHO COMPOSE MAYOR PHELAN'S ONLY FOLLOWING."

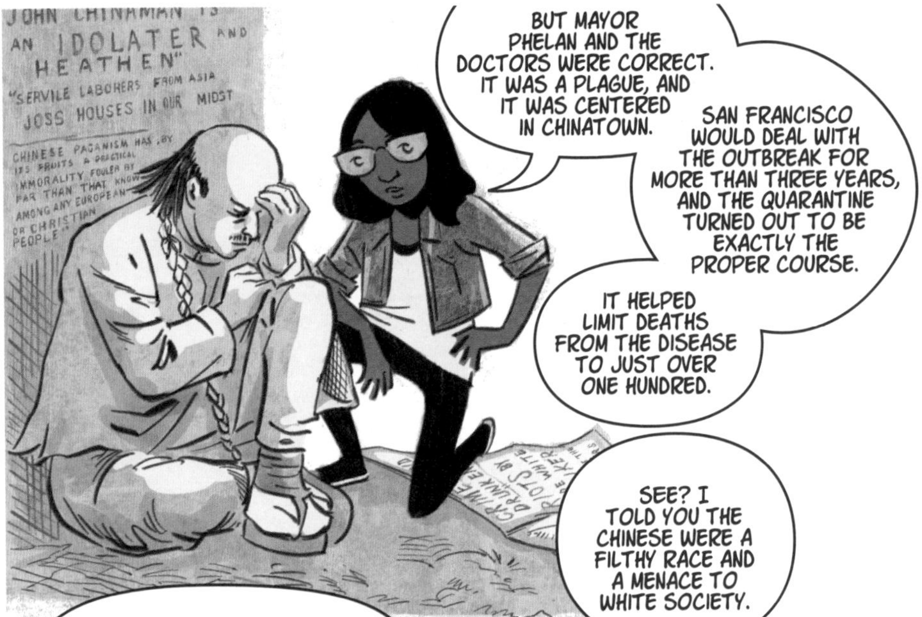
BUT MAYOR PHELAN AND THE DOCTORS WERE CORRECT. IT WAS A PLAGUE, AND IT WAS CENTERED IN CHINATOWN.
SAN FRANCISCO WOULD DEAL WITH THE OUTBREAK FOR MORE THAN THREE YEARS, AND THE QUARANTINE TURNED OUT TO BE EXACTLY THE PROPER COURSE.
IT HELPED LIMIT DEATHS FROM THE DISEASE TO JUST OVER ONE HUNDRED.
SEE? I TOLD YOU THE CHINESE WERE A FILTHY RACE AND A MENACE TO WHITE SOCIETY.

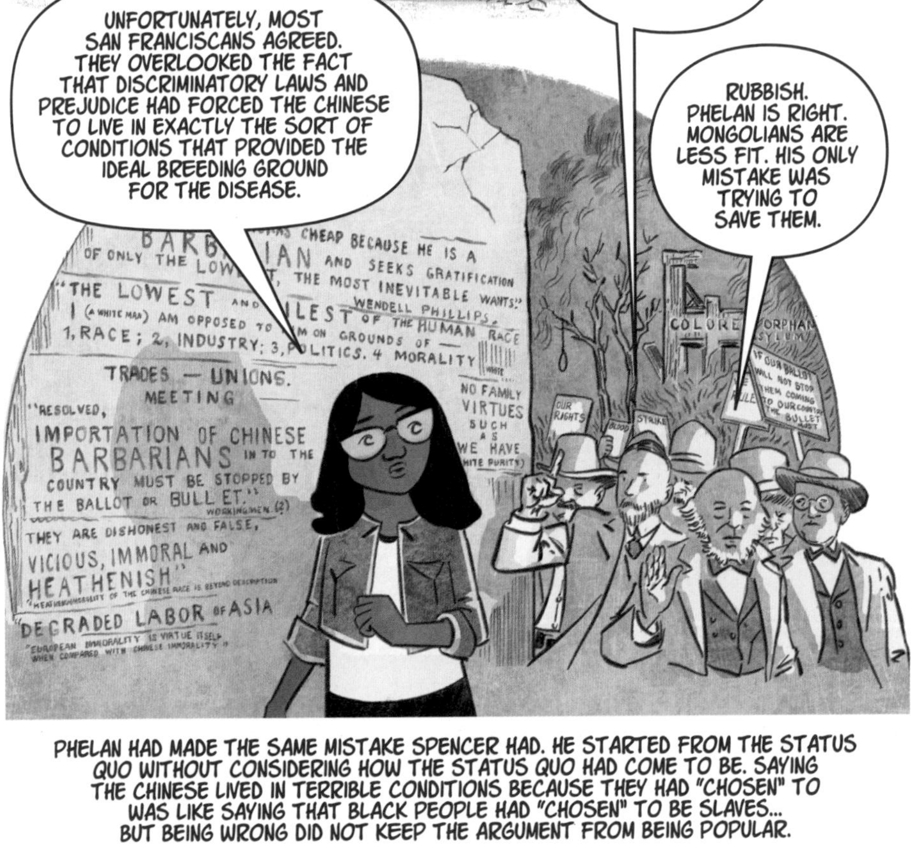
UNFORTUNATELY, MOST SAN FRANCISCANS AGREED. THEY OVERLOOKED THE FACT THAT DISCRIMINATORY LAWS AND PREJUDICE HAD FORCED THE CHINESE TO LIVE IN EXACTLY THE SORT OF CONDITIONS THAT PROVIDED THE IDEAL BREEDING GROUND FOR THE DISEASE.
RUBBISH. PHELAN IS RIGHT. MONGOLIANS ARE LESS FIT. HIS ONLY MISTAKE WAS TRYING TO SAVE THEM.
TRADES — UNIONS. MEETING
"RESOLVED, IMPORTATION OF CHINESE BARBARIANS IN TO THE COUNTRY MUST BE STOPPED BY THE BALLOT OR BULLET."
THEY ARE DISHONEST AND FALSE, VICIOUS, IMMORAL AND HEATHENISH"
DEGRADED LABOR OF ASIA

PHELAN HAD MADE THE SAME MISTAKE SPENCER HAD. HE STARTED FROM THE STATUS QUO WITHOUT CONSIDERING HOW THE STATUS QUO HAD COME TO BE. SAYING THE CHINESE LIVED IN TERRIBLE CONDITIONS BECAUSE THEY HAD "CHOSEN" TO WAS LIKE SAYING THAT BLACK PEOPLE HAD "CHOSEN" TO BE SLAVES... BUT BEING WRONG DID NOT KEEP THE ARGUMENT FROM BEING POPULAR.

UNION LEADERS COMPLAINED THAT BIRTHRIGHT CHINESE, SUCH AS WONG KIM ARK, WERE STEALING THE VOTE. THEY DEMANDED EXPULSION, IGNORING THE INCONVENIENCE OF THEM BEING UNITED STATES CITIZENS. THEY GOT SUPPORT FROM A PREDICTABLE ALLY.

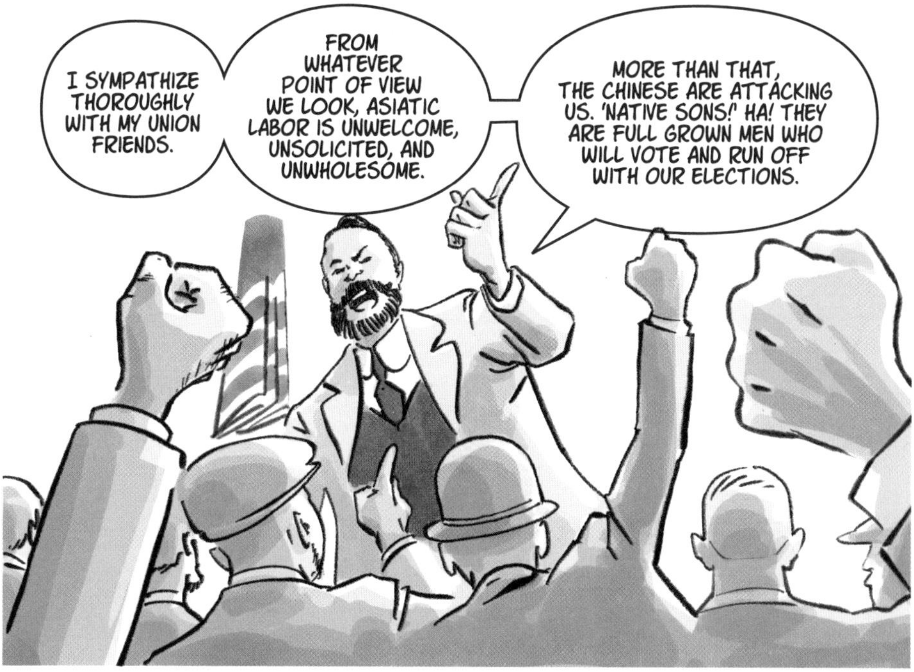
I SYMPATHIZE THOROUGHLY WITH MY UNION FRIENDS.
FROM WHATEVER POINT OF VIEW WE LOOK, ASIATIC LABOR IS UNWELCOME, UNSOLICITED, AND UNWHOLESOME.
MORE THAN THAT, THE CHINESE ARE ATTACKING US. 'NATIVE SONS!' HA! THEY ARE FULL GROWN MEN WHO WILL VOTE AND RUN OFF WITH OUR ELECTIONS.

BUT EVEN MORE IMPORTANT THAN PHELAN'S SUPPORT WAS THAT OF STANFORD SOCIOLOGY PROFESSOR, EDWARD A. ROSS, A NOTED PROGRESSIVE.

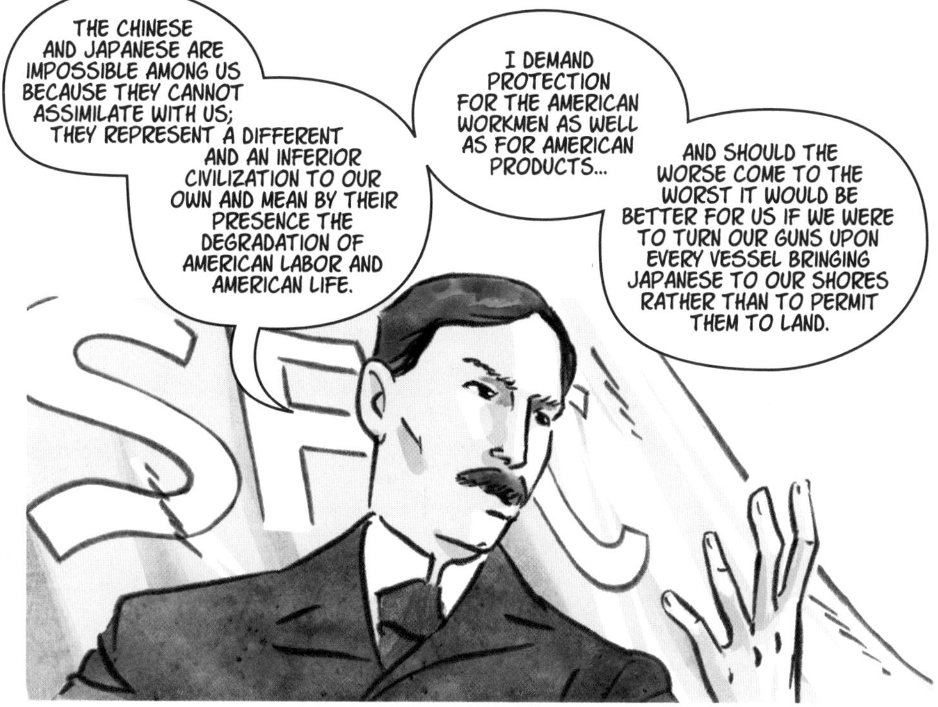
THE CHINESE AND JAPANESE ARE IMPOSSIBLE AMONG US BECAUSE THEY CANNOT ASSIMILATE WITH US; THEY REPRESENT A DIFFERENT AND AN INFERIOR CIVILIZATION TO OUR OWN AND MEAN BY THEIR PRESENCE THE DEGRADATION OF AMERICAN LABOR AND AMERICAN LIFE.
I DEMAND PROTECTION FOR THE AMERICAN WORKMEN AS WELL AS FOR AMERICAN PRODUCTS...
AND SHOULD THE WORSE COME TO THE WORST IT WOULD BE BETTER FOR US IF WE WERE TO TURN OUR GUNS UPON EVERY VESSEL BRINGING JAPANESE TO OUR SHORES RATHER THAN TO PERMIT THEM TO LAND.

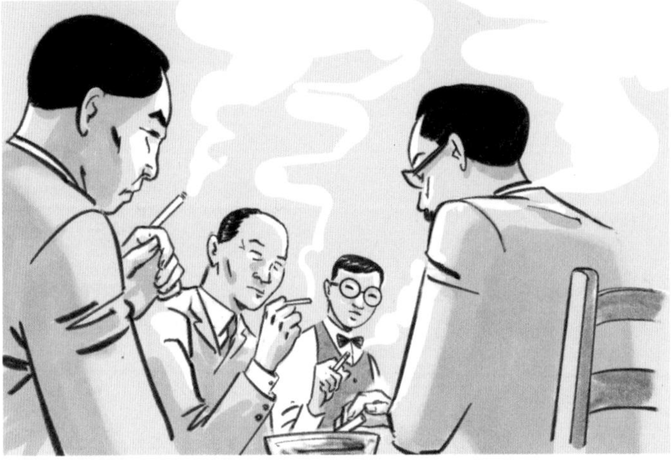

HAVING A STANFORD PROFESSOR ON THEIR SIDE WAS JUST WHAT THE UNIONS NEEDED. THEY DRAFTED A SERIES OF RESOLUTIONS THAT INCLUDED, FOR THE FIRST TIME, JAPANESE AS WELL AS CHINESE.

THE LABOR COUNCIL DEMANDED THAT CONGRESS UPDATE THE CHINESE EXCLUSION ACT "TO MAKE IT FULLY EFFECTIVE FOR THE PROTECTION OF AMERICAN LABOR," AND THAT TOTAL EXCLUSION BE APPLIED ALSO TO THE JAPANESE. THE JAPANESE WERE PARTICULARLY DANGEROUS BECAUSE:

THEIR PARTIAL ADOPTION OF AMERICAN CUSTOMS MAKE THEM THE MORE DANGEROUS AS COMPETITORS.

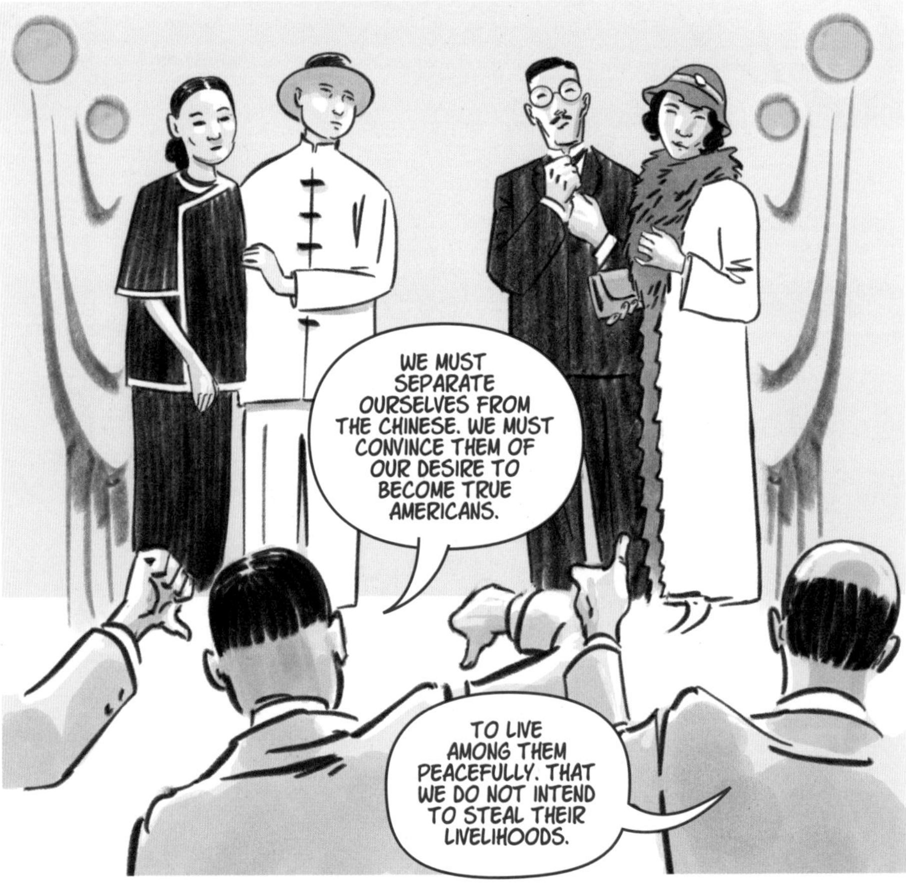
WE MUST SEPARATE OURSELVES FROM THE CHINESE. WE MUST CONVINCE THEM OF OUR DESIRE TO BECOME TRUE AMERICANS.
TO LIVE AMONG THEM PEACEFULLY. THAT WE DO NOT INTEND TO STEAL THEIR LIVELIHOODS.

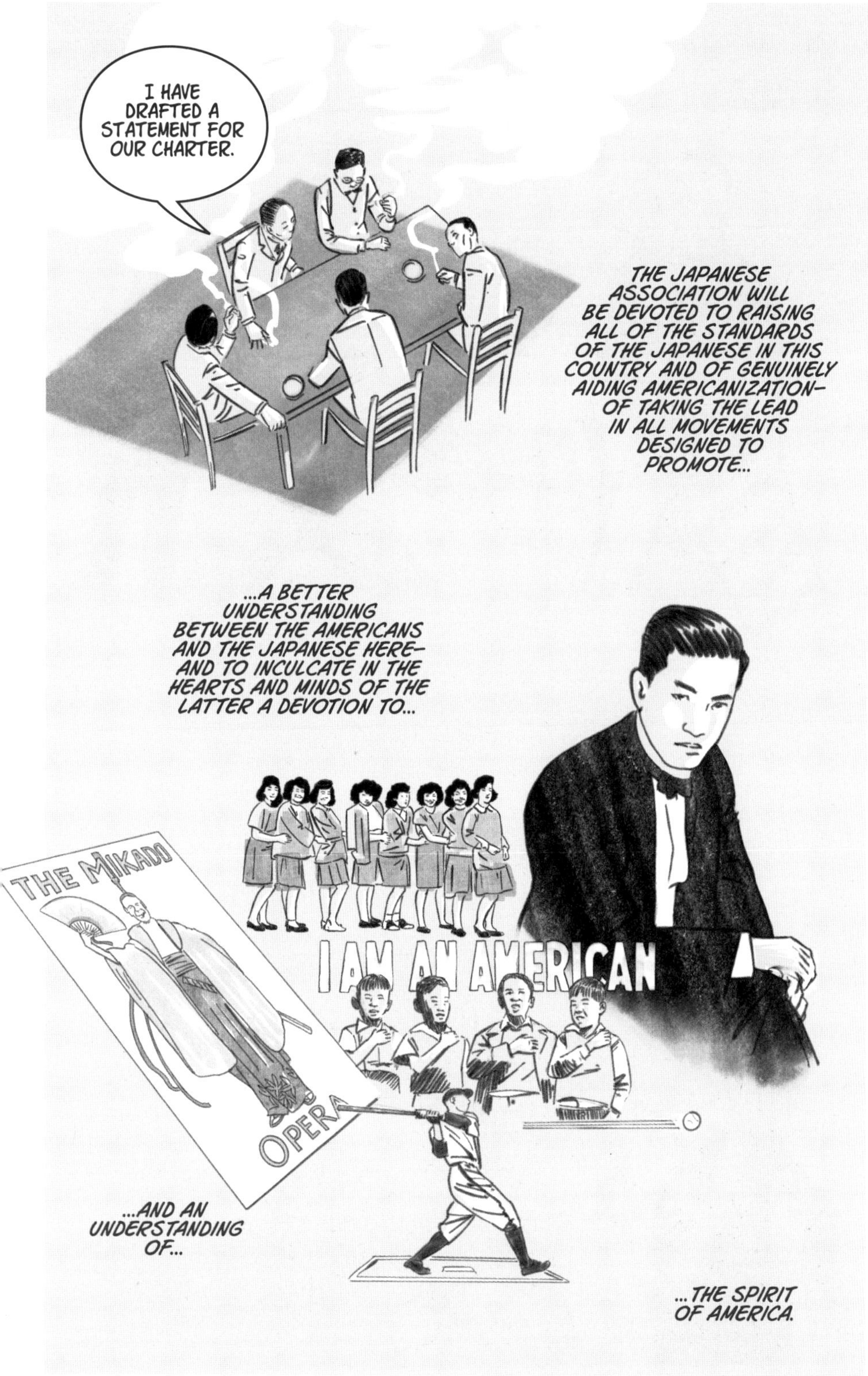
I HAVE DRAFTED A STATEMENT FOR OUR CHARTER.
THE JAPANESE ASSOCIATION WILL BE DEVOTED TO RAISING ALL OF THE STANDARDS OF THE JAPANESE IN THIS COUNTRY AND OF GENUINELY AIDING AMERICANIZATION– OF TAKING THE LEAD IN ALL MOVEMENTS DESIGNED TO PROMOTE...
...A BETTER UNDERSTANDING BETWEEN THE AMERICANS AND THE JAPANESE HERE– AND TO INCULCATE IN THE HEARTS AND MINDS OF THE LATTER A DEVOTION TO...
THE MIKADO
OPERA
I AM AN AMERICAN
...AND AN UNDERSTANDING OF...
...THE SPIRIT OF AMERICA.

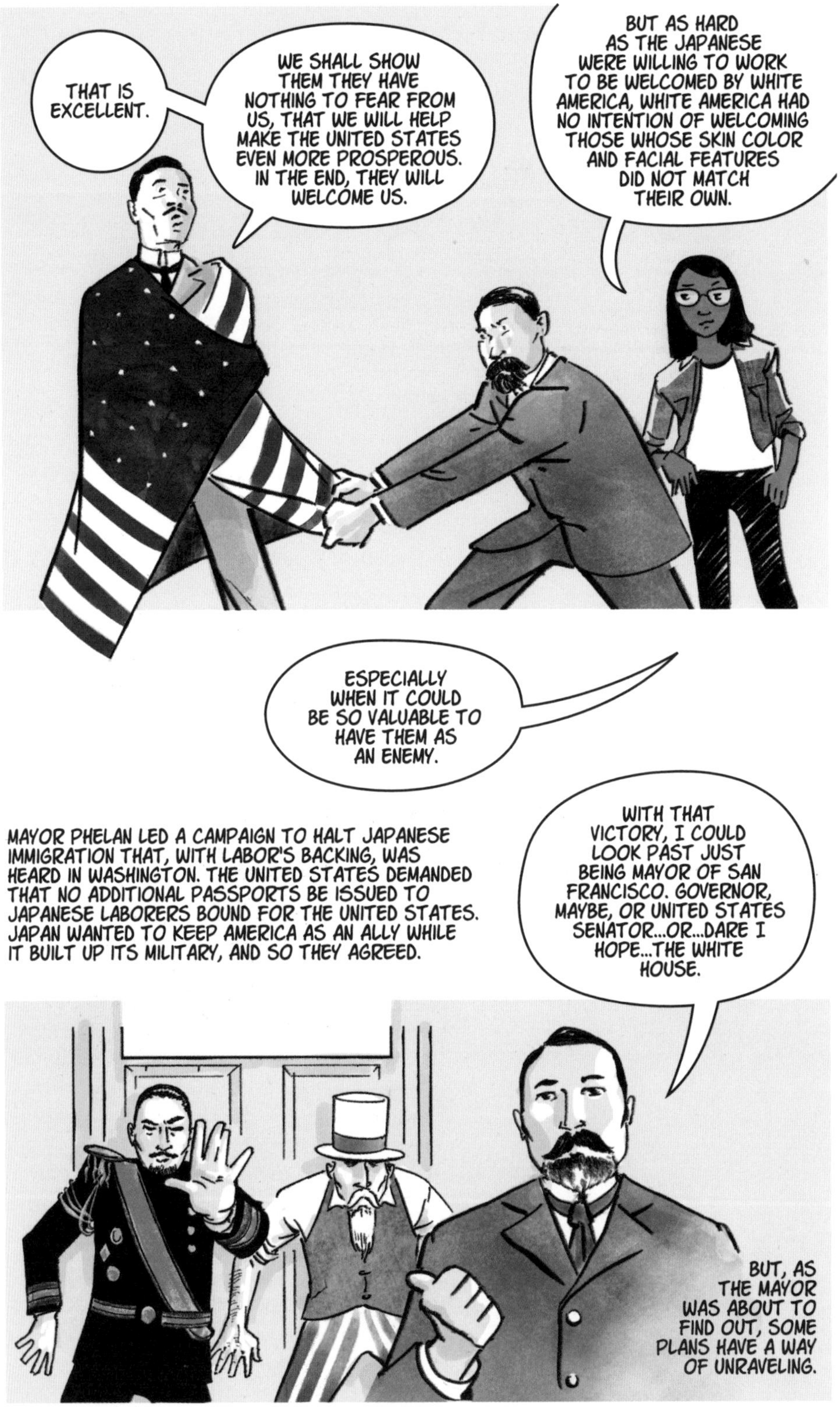
THAT IS EXCELLENT.
WE SHALL SHOW THEM THEY HAVE NOTHING TO FEAR FROM US, THAT WE WILL HELP MAKE THE UNITED STATES EVEN MORE PROSPEROUS. IN THE END, THEY WILL WELCOME US.
BUT AS HARD AS THE JAPANESE WERE WILLING TO WORK TO BE WELCOMED BY WHITE AMERICA, WHITE AMERICA HAD NO INTENTION OF WELCOMING THOSE WHOSE SKIN COLOR AND FACIAL FEATURES DID NOT MATCH THEIR OWN.
ESPECIALLY WHEN IT COULD BE SO VALUABLE TO HAVE THEM AS AN ENEMY.
MAYOR PHELAN LED A CAMPAIGN TO HALT JAPANESE IMMIGRATION THAT, WITH LABOR'S BACKING, WAS HEARD IN WASHINGTON. THE UNITED STATES DEMANDED THAT NO ADDITIONAL PASSPORTS BE ISSUED TO JAPANESE LABORERS BOUND FOR THE UNITED STATES. JAPAN WANTED TO KEEP AMERICA AS AN ALLY WHILE IT BUILT UP ITS MILITARY, AND SO THEY AGREED.
WITH THAT VICTORY, I COULD LOOK PAST JUST BEING MAYOR OF SAN FRANCISCO. GOVERNOR, MAYBE, OR UNITED STATES SENATOR...OR...DARE I HOPE...THE WHITE HOUSE.
BUT, AS THE MAYOR WAS ABOUT TO FIND OUT, SOME PLANS HAVE A WAY OF UNRAVELING.

September 1900, freight yard of McNab & Smith, one of San Francisco's biggest hauling firms.

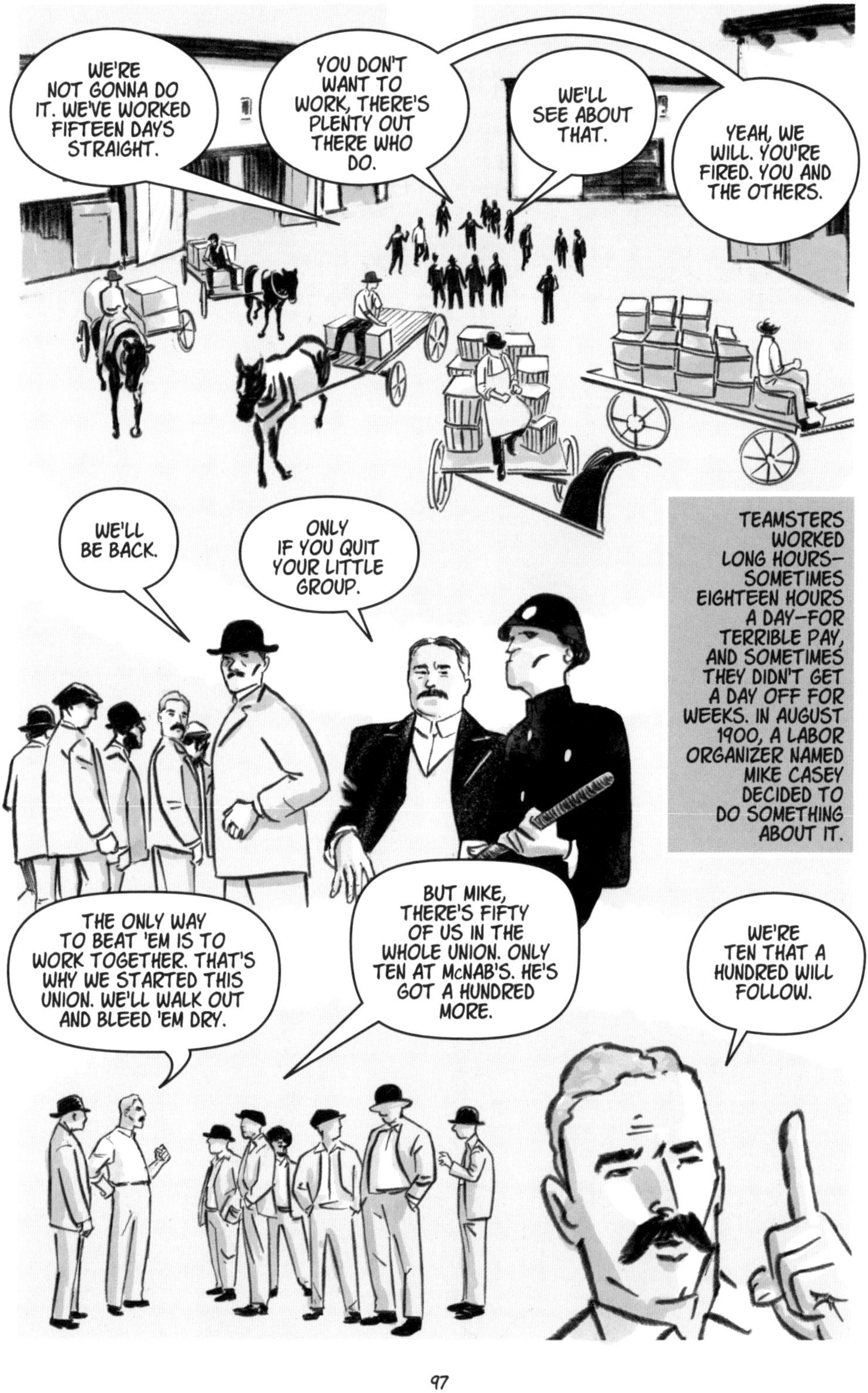
WE'RE NOT GONNA DO IT. WE'VE WORKED FIFTEEN DAYS STRAIGHT.
YOU DON'T WANT TO WORK, THERE'S PLENTY OUT THERE WHO DO.
WE'LL SEE ABOUT THAT.
YEAH, WE WILL. YOU'RE FIRED. YOU AND THE OTHERS.
WE'LL BE BACK.
ONLY IF YOU QUIT YOUR LITTLE GROUP.
TEAMSTERS WORKED LONG HOURS—SOMETIMES EIGHTEEN HOURS A DAY—FOR TERRIBLE PAY, AND SOMETIMES THEY DIDN'T GET A DAY OFF FOR WEEKS. IN AUGUST 1900, A LABOR ORGANIZER NAMED MIKE CASEY DECIDED TO DO SOMETHING ABOUT IT.
THE ONLY WAY TO BEAT 'EM IS TO WORK TOGETHER. THAT'S WHY WE STARTED THIS UNION. WE'LL WALK OUT AND BLEED 'EM DRY.
BUT MIKE, THERE'S FIFTY OF US IN THE WHOLE UNION. ONLY TEN AT McNAB'S. HE'S GOT A HUNDRED MORE.
WE'RE TEN THAT A HUNDRED WILL FOLLOW.

AND THE HUNDRED DID. THE NEXT DAY, EVERY DRIVER AT McNAB & SMITH'S JOINED THE STRIKE.

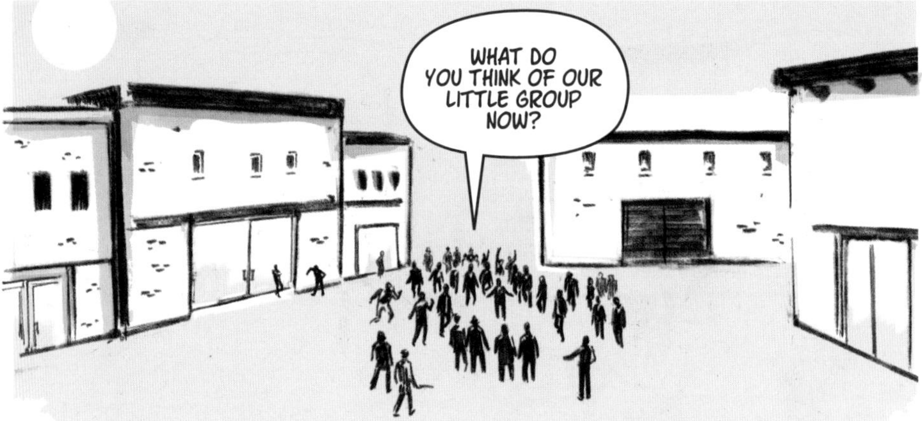
WHAT DO YOU THINK OF OUR LITTLE GROUP NOW?

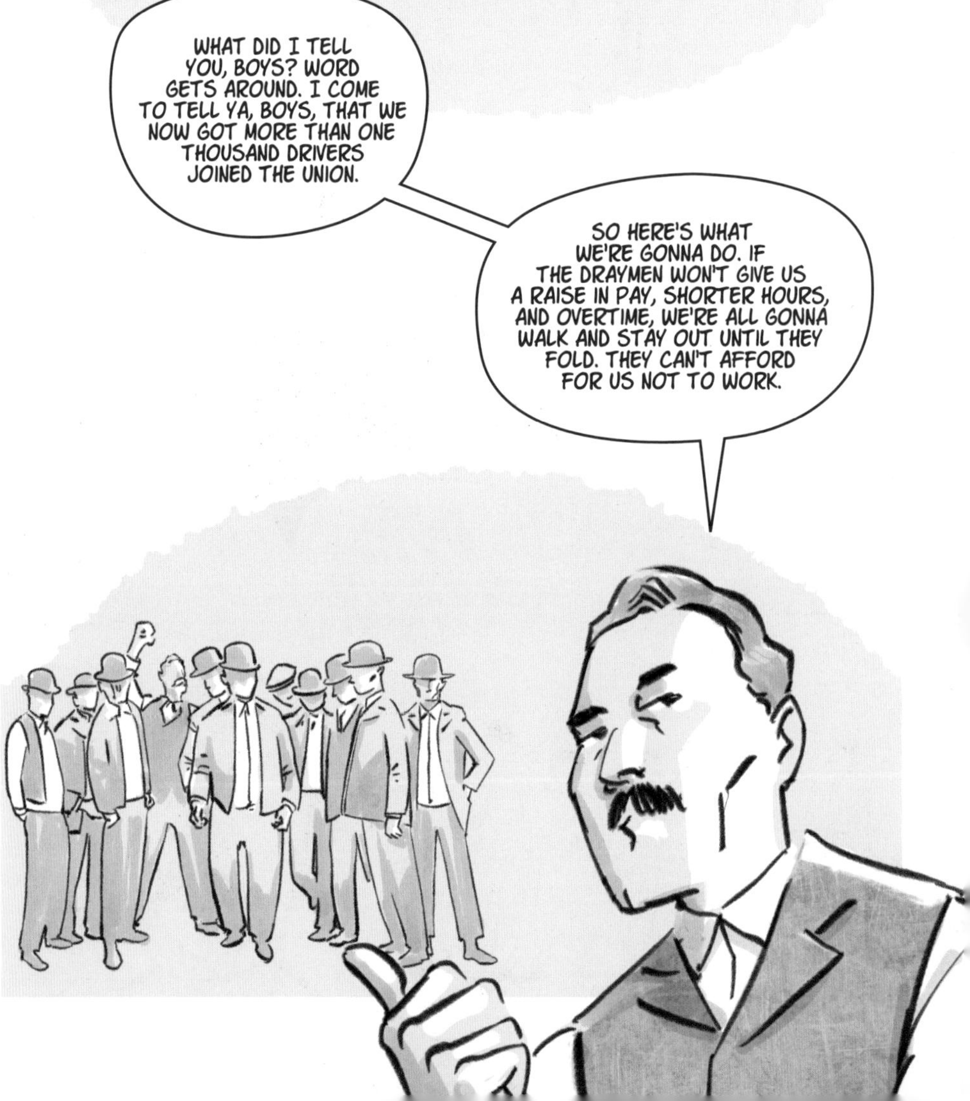
WHAT DID I TELL YOU, BOYS? WORD GETS AROUND. I COME TO TELL YA, BOYS, THAT WE NOW GOT MORE THAN ONE THOUSAND DRIVERS JOINED THE UNION.
SO HERE'S WHAT WE'RE GONNA DO. IF THE DRAYMEN WON'T GIVE US A RAISE IN PAY, SHORTER HOURS, AND OVERTIME, WE'RE ALL GONNA WALK AND STAY OUT UNTIL THEY FOLD. THEY CAN'T AFFORD FOR US NOT TO WORK.

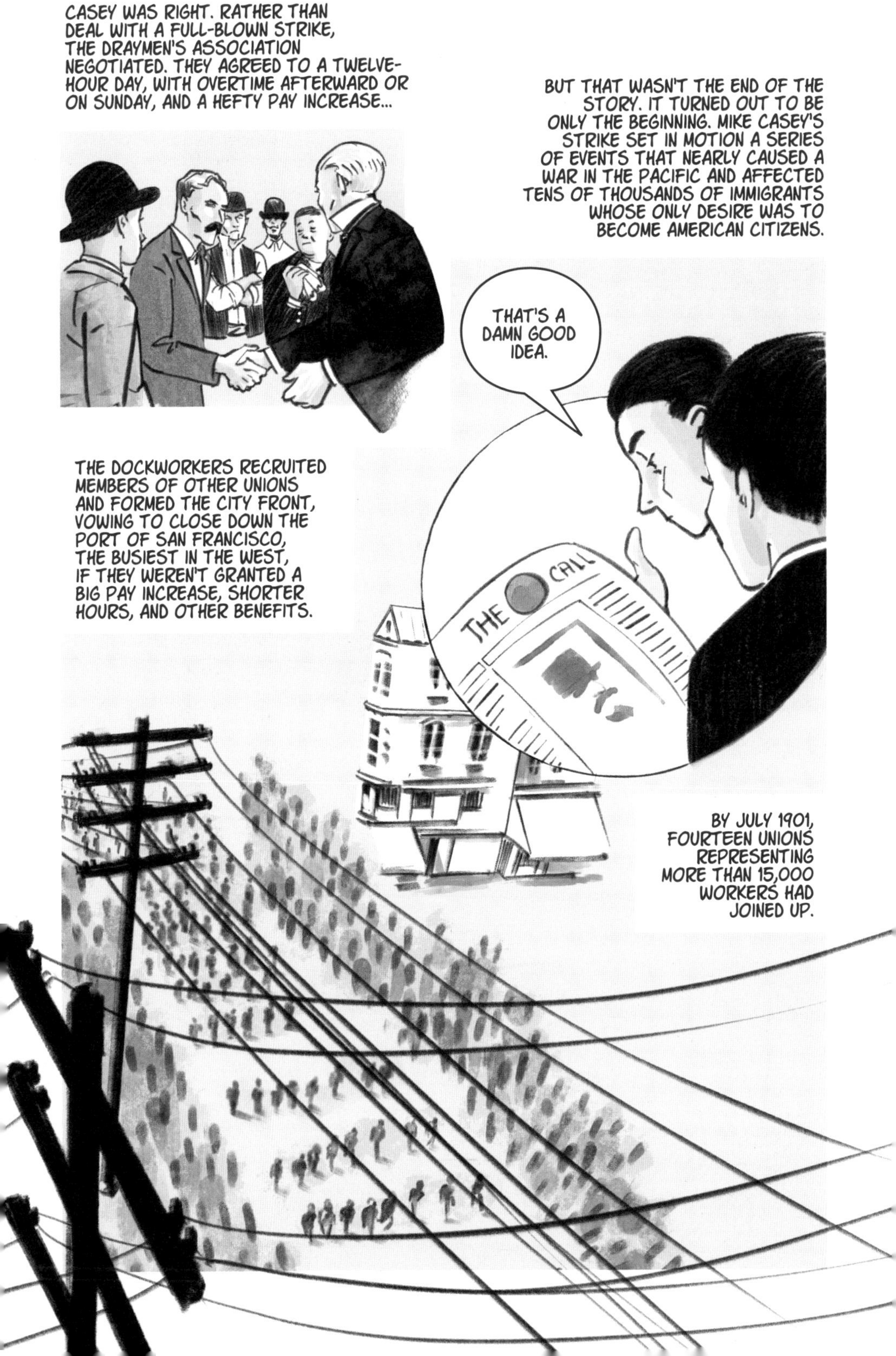
CASEY WAS RIGHT. RATHER THAN DEAL WITH A FULL-BLOWN STRIKE, THE DRAYMEN'S ASSOCIATION NEGOTIATED. THEY AGREED TO A TWELVE-HOUR DAY, WITH OVERTIME AFTERWARD OR ON SUNDAY, AND A HEFTY PAY INCREASE...
BUT THAT WASN'T THE END OF THE STORY. IT TURNED OUT TO BE ONLY THE BEGINNING. MIKE CASEY'S STRIKE SET IN MOTION A SERIES OF EVENTS THAT NEARLY CAUSED A WAR IN THE PACIFIC AND AFFECTED TENS OF THOUSANDS OF IMMIGRANTS WHOSE ONLY DESIRE WAS TO BECOME AMERICAN CITIZENS.
THAT'S A DAMN GOOD IDEA.
THE DOCKWORKERS RECRUITED MEMBERS OF OTHER UNIONS AND FORMED THE CITY FRONT, VOWING TO CLOSE DOWN THE PORT OF SAN FRANCISCO, THE BUSIEST IN THE WEST, IF THEY WEREN'T GRANTED A BIG PAY INCREASE, SHORTER HOURS, AND OTHER BENEFITS.
THE CALL
BY JULY 1901, FOURTEEN UNIONS REPRESENTING MORE THAN 15,000 WORKERS HAD JOINED UP.

AT THE SAME TIME, IN SECRET, BUSINESS OWNERS FORMED THE EMPLOYERS ASSOCIATION TO "CHECK THE GROWING EVILS...OF STRIKES AND BOYCOTTS." BY JULY 1901, HUNDREDS HAD JOINED UP, EACH KICKING IN $1,000, PREPARED TO USE ANY MEANS NECESSARY TO CRUSH THE UNIONS.

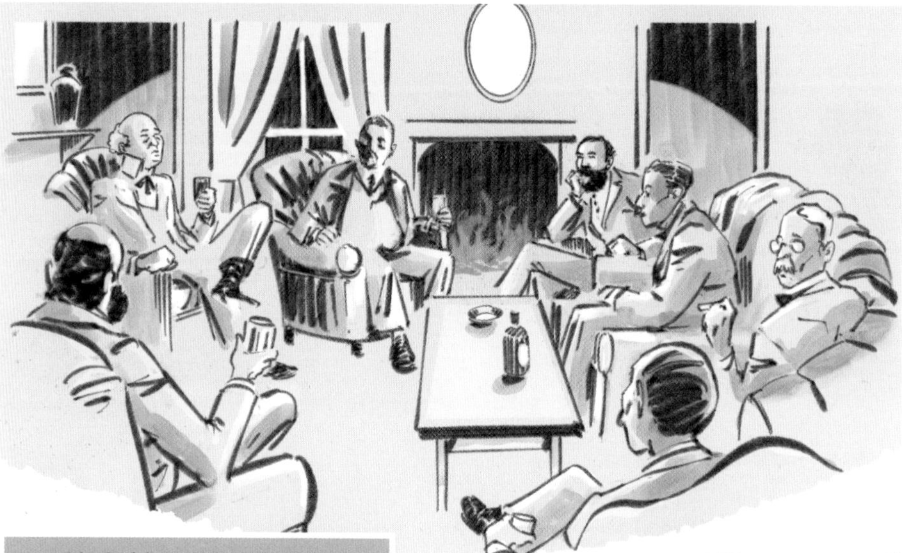

THE RESULT WAS INEVITABLE, AND IT WAS AGAIN MIKE CASEY'S UNION THAT LIT THE FUSE.

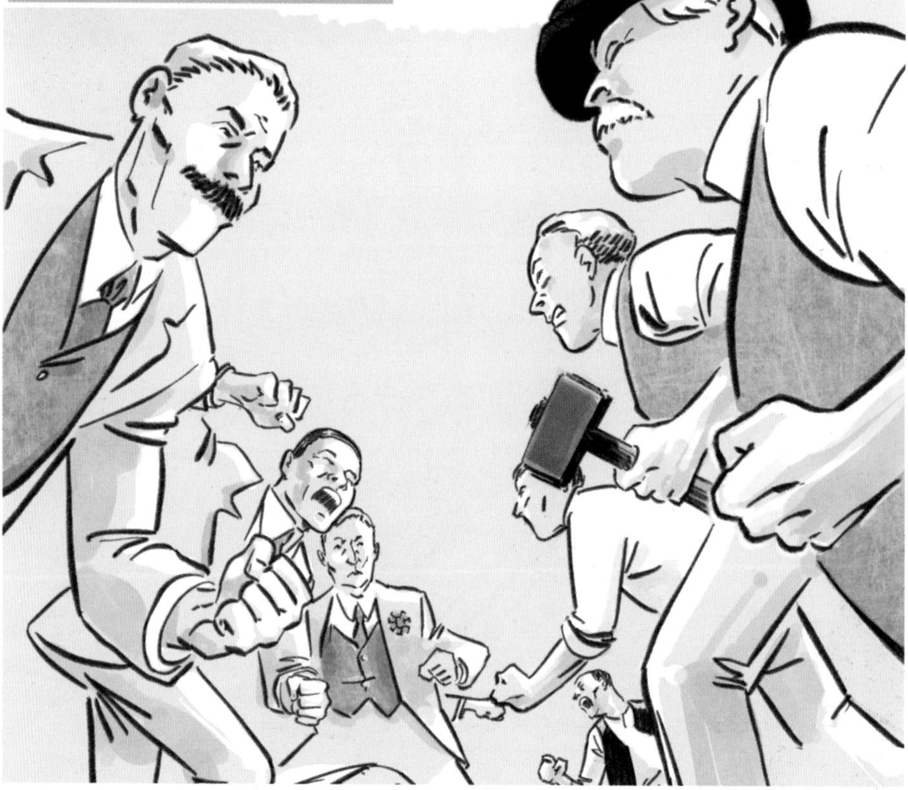

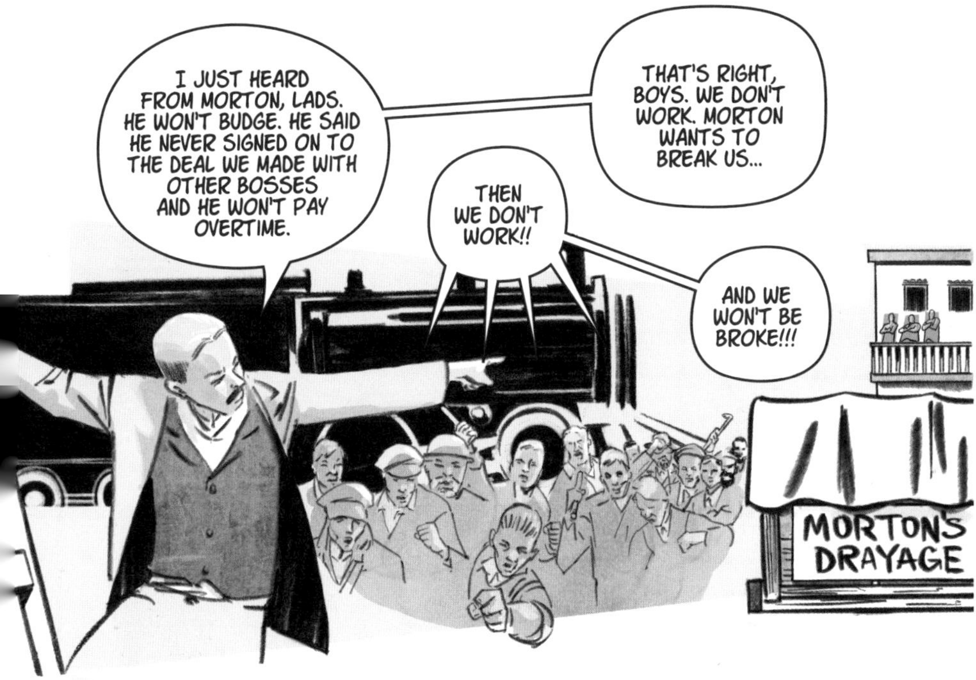
I JUST HEARD FROM MORTON, LADS. HE WON'T BUDGE. HE SAID HE NEVER SIGNED ON TO THE DEAL WE MADE WITH OTHER BOSSES AND HE WON'T PAY OVERTIME.
THAT'S RIGHT, BOYS. WE DON'T WORK. MORTON WANTS TO BREAK US...
THEN WE DON'T WORK!!
AND WE WON'T BE BROKE!!!
MORTON'S DRAYAGE

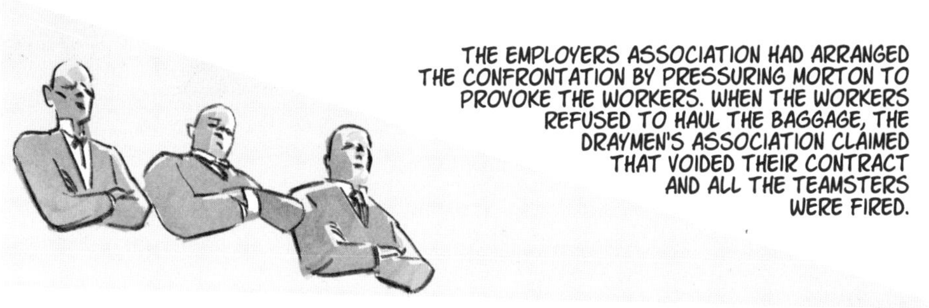
THE EMPLOYERS ASSOCIATION HAD ARRANGED THE CONFRONTATION BY PRESSURING MORTON TO PROVOKE THE WORKERS. WHEN THE WORKERS REFUSED TO HAUL THE BAGGAGE, THE DRAYMEN'S ASSOCIATION CLAIMED THAT VOIDED THEIR CONTRACT AND ALL THE TEAMSTERS WERE FIRED.

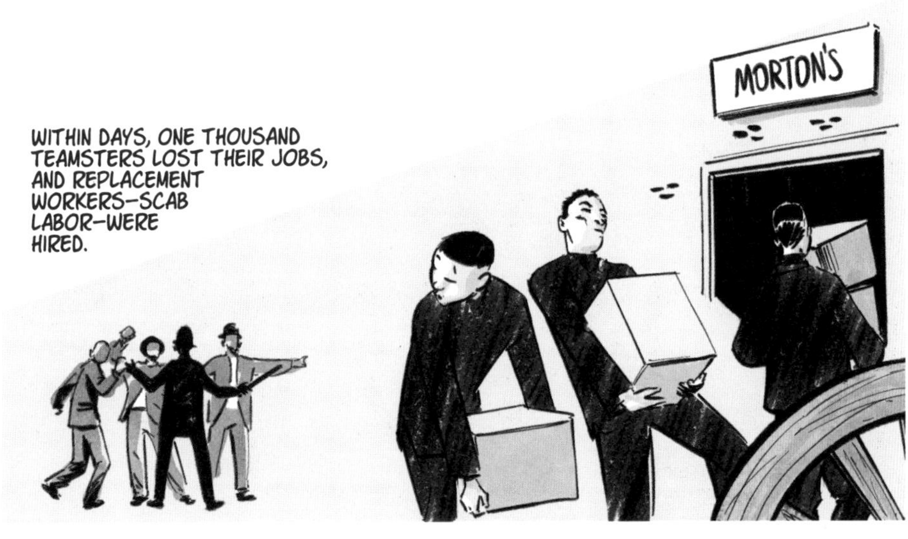
MORTON'S
WITHIN DAYS, ONE THOUSAND TEAMSTERS LOST THEIR JOBS, AND REPLACEMENT WORKERS—SCAB LABOR—WERE HIRED.

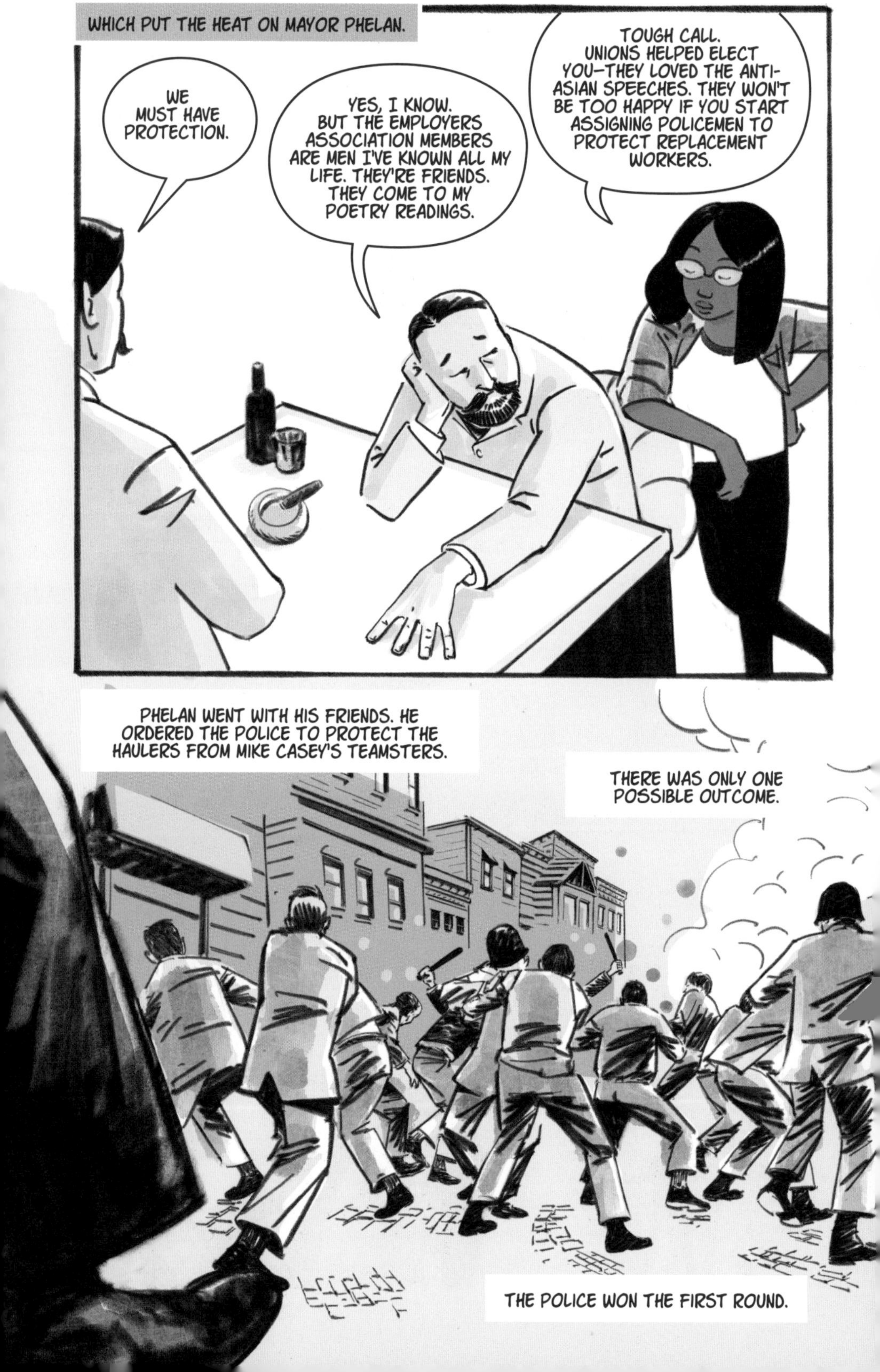
WHICH PUT THE HEAT ON MAYOR PHELAN.
WE MUST HAVE PROTECTION.
YES, I KNOW. BUT THE EMPLOYERS ASSOCIATION MEMBERS ARE MEN I'VE KNOWN ALL MY LIFE. THEY'RE FRIENDS. THEY COME TO MY POETRY READINGS.
TOUGH CALL. UNIONS HELPED ELECT YOU—THEY LOVED THE ANTI-ASIAN SPEECHES. THEY WON'T BE TOO HAPPY IF YOU START ASSIGNING POLICEMEN TO PROTECT REPLACEMENT WORKERS.
PHELAN WENT WITH HIS FRIENDS. HE ORDERED THE POLICE TO PROTECT THE HAULERS FROM MIKE CASEY'S TEAMSTERS.
THERE WAS ONLY ONE POSSIBLE OUTCOME.
THE POLICE WON THE FIRST ROUND.

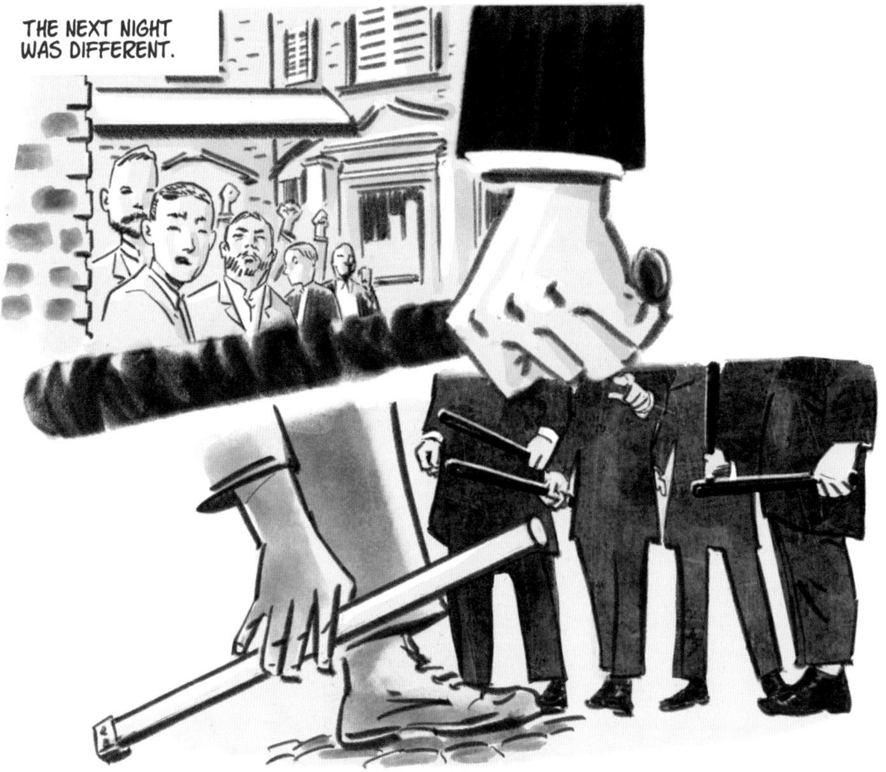
THE NEXT NIGHT WAS DIFFERENT.

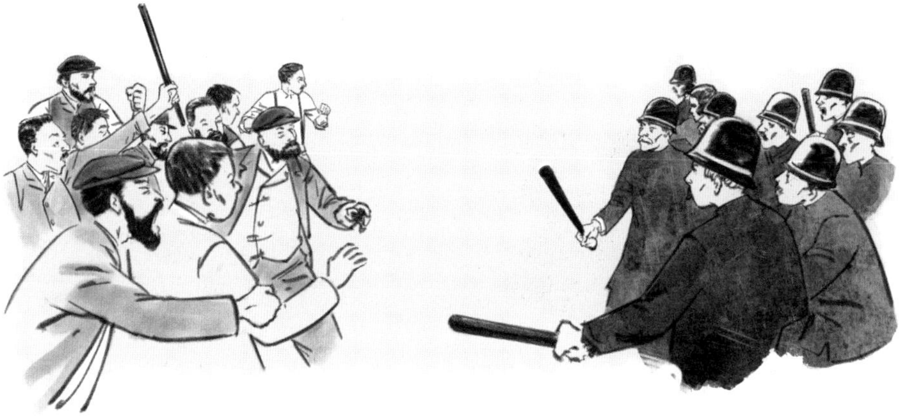

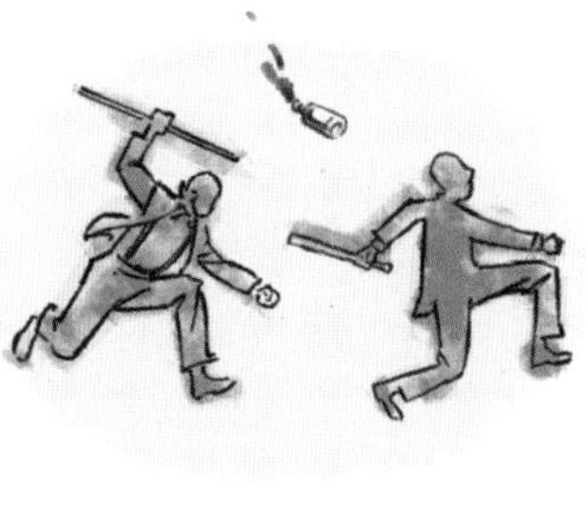

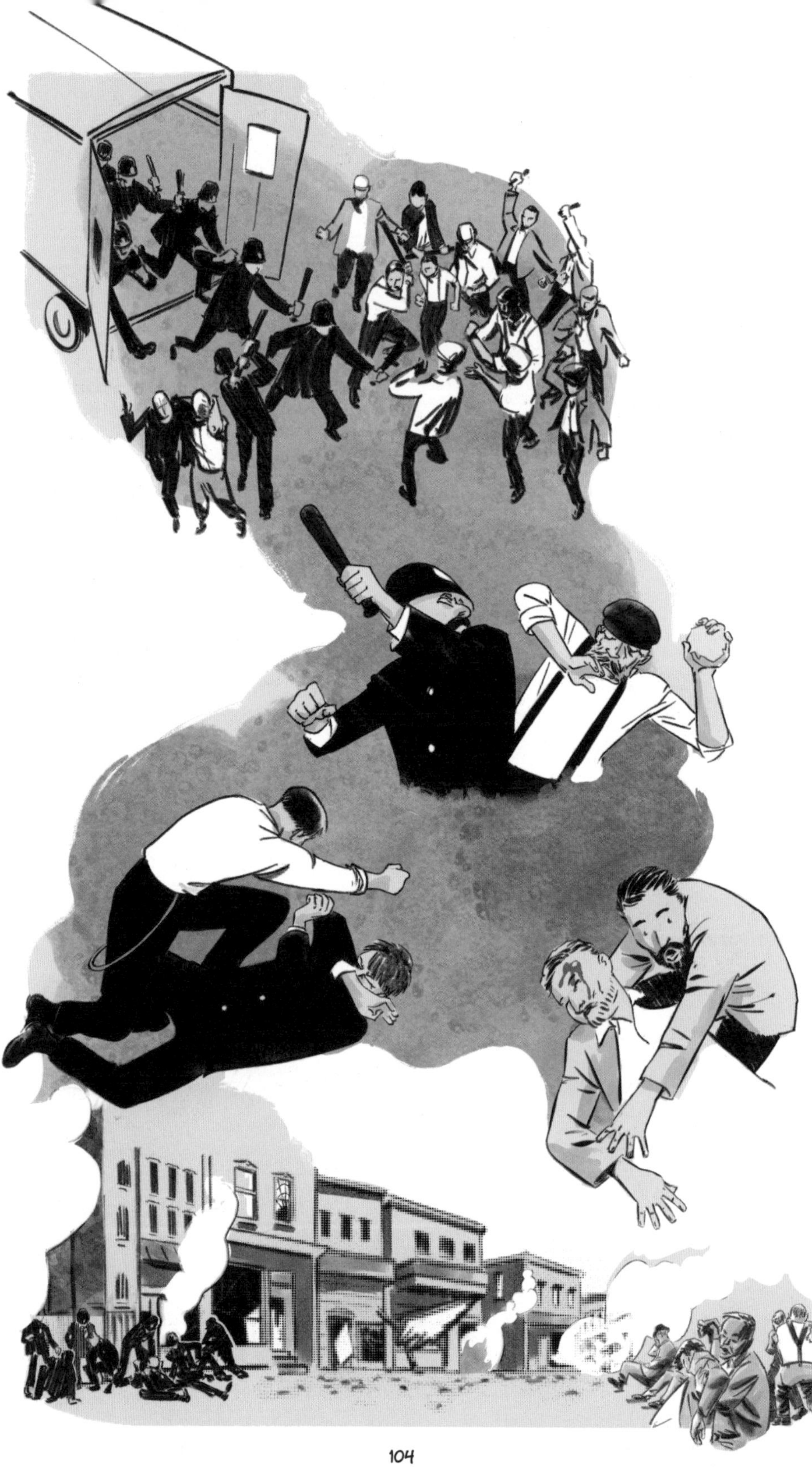

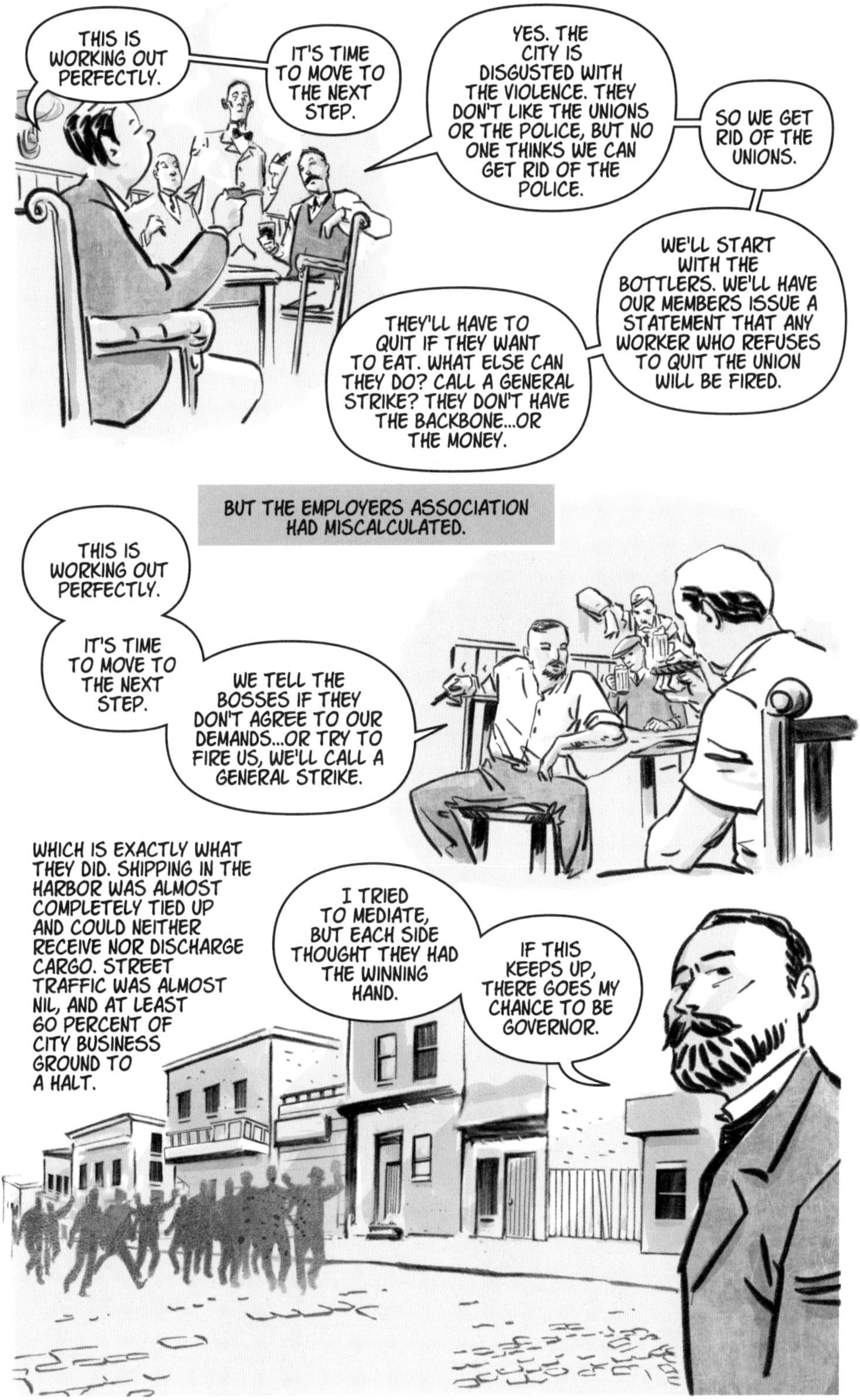
THIS IS WORKING OUT PERFECTLY.
IT'S TIME TO MOVE TO THE NEXT STEP.
YES. THE CITY IS DISGUSTED WITH THE VIOLENCE. THEY DON'T LIKE THE UNIONS OR THE POLICE, BUT NO ONE THINKS WE CAN GET RID OF THE POLICE.
SO WE GET RID OF THE UNIONS.
WE'LL START WITH THE BOTTLERS. WE'LL HAVE OUR MEMBERS ISSUE A STATEMENT THAT ANY WORKER WHO REFUSES TO QUIT THE UNION WILL BE FIRED.
THEY'LL HAVE TO QUIT IF THEY WANT TO EAT. WHAT ELSE CAN THEY DO? CALL A GENERAL STRIKE? THEY DON'T HAVE THE BACKBONE...OR THE MONEY.
BUT THE EMPLOYERS ASSOCIATION HAD MISCALCULATED.
THIS IS WORKING OUT PERFECTLY.
IT'S TIME TO MOVE TO THE NEXT STEP.
WE TELL THE BOSSES IF THEY DON'T AGREE TO OUR DEMANDS...OR TRY TO FIRE US, WE'LL CALL A GENERAL STRIKE.
WHICH IS EXACTLY WHAT THEY DID. SHIPPING IN THE HARBOR WAS ALMOST COMPLETELY TIED UP AND COULD NEITHER RECEIVE NOR DISCHARGE CARGO. STREET TRAFFIC WAS ALMOST NIL, AND AT LEAST 60 PERCENT OF CITY BUSINESS GROUND TO A HALT.
I TRIED TO MEDIATE, BUT EACH SIDE THOUGHT THEY HAD THE WINNING HAND.
IF THIS KEEPS UP, THERE GOES MY CHANCE TO BE GOVERNOR.

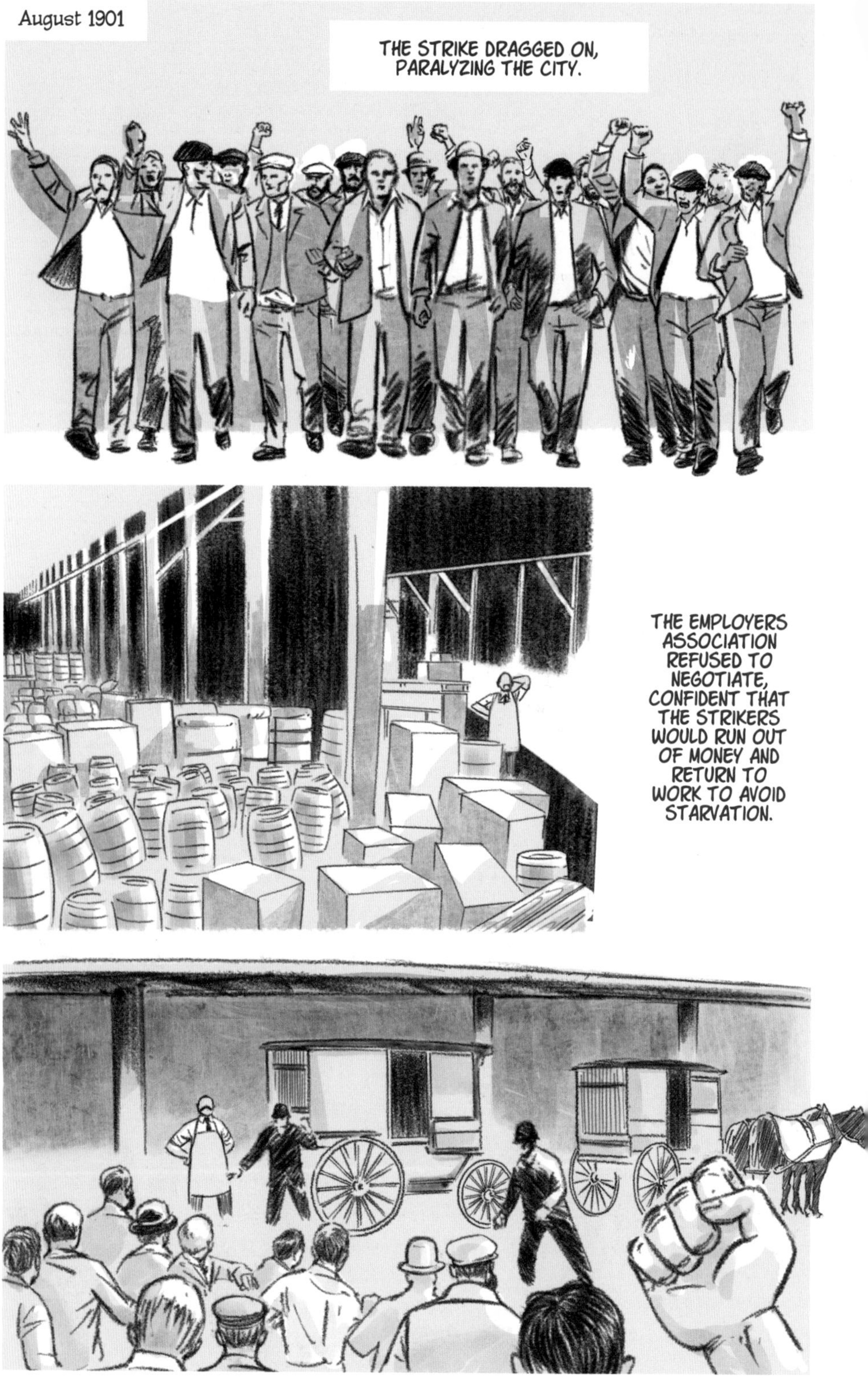
August 1901
THE STRIKE DRAGGED ON, PARALYZING THE CITY.
THE EMPLOYERS ASSOCIATION REFUSED TO NEGOTIATE, CONFIDENT THAT THE STRIKERS WOULD RUN OUT OF MONEY AND RETURN TO WORK TO AVOID STARVATION.

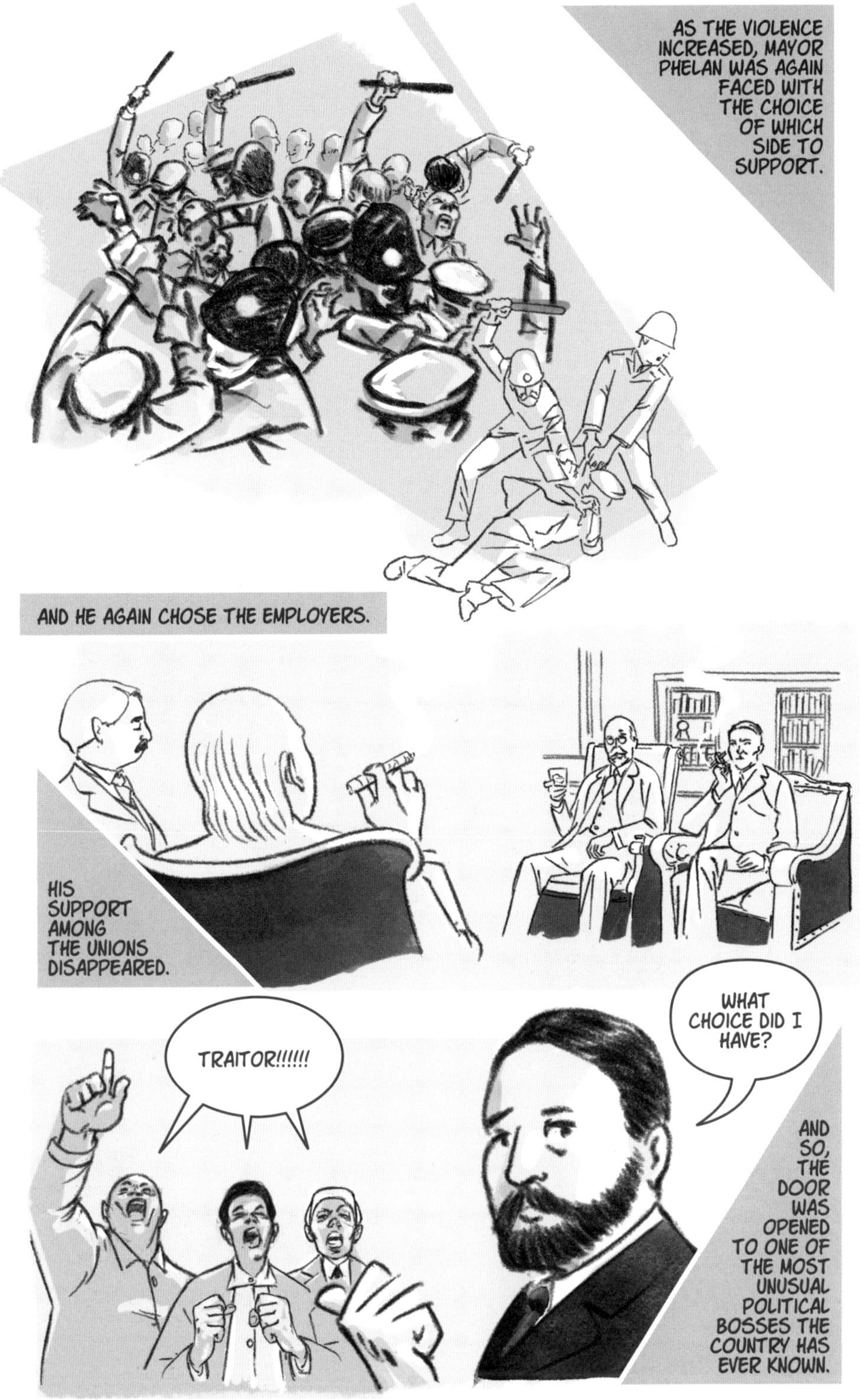

AS THE VIOLENCE INCREASED, MAYOR PHELAN WAS AGAIN FACED WITH THE CHOICE OF WHICH SIDE TO SUPPORT.
AND HE AGAIN CHOSE THE EMPLOYERS.
HIS SUPPORT AMONG THE UNIONS DISAPPEARED.
TRAITOR!!!!!!
WHAT CHOICE DID I HAVE?
AND SO, THE DOOR WAS OPENED TO ONE OF THE MOST UNUSUAL POLITICAL BOSSES THE COUNTRY HAS EVER KNOWN.

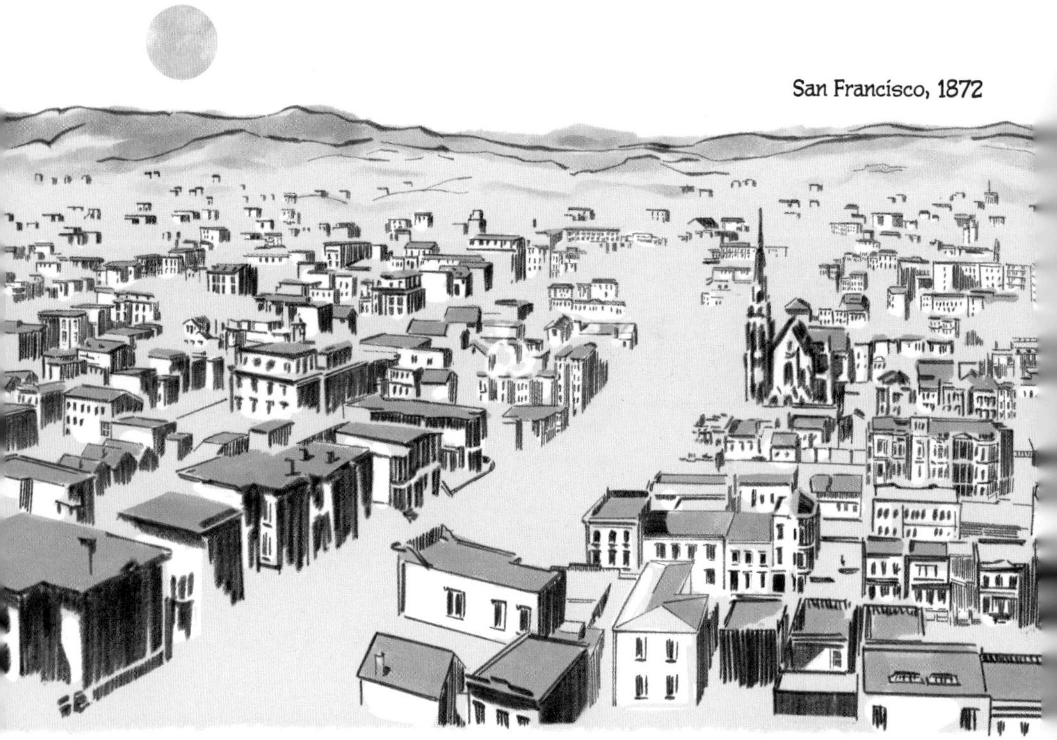
San Francisco, 1872

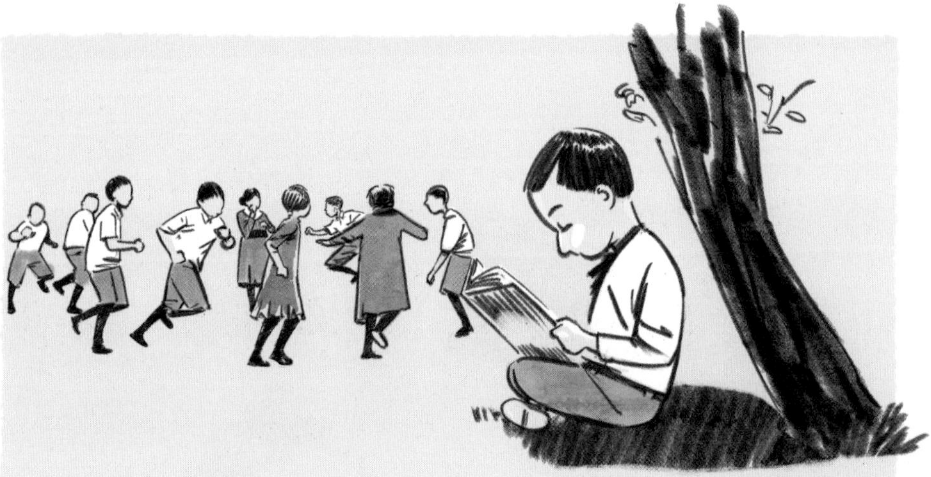

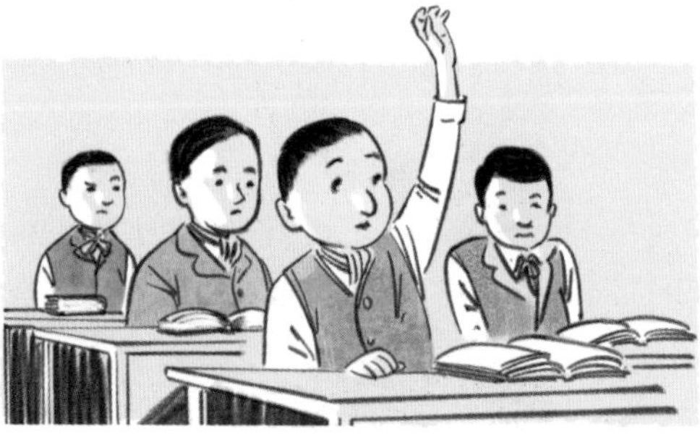

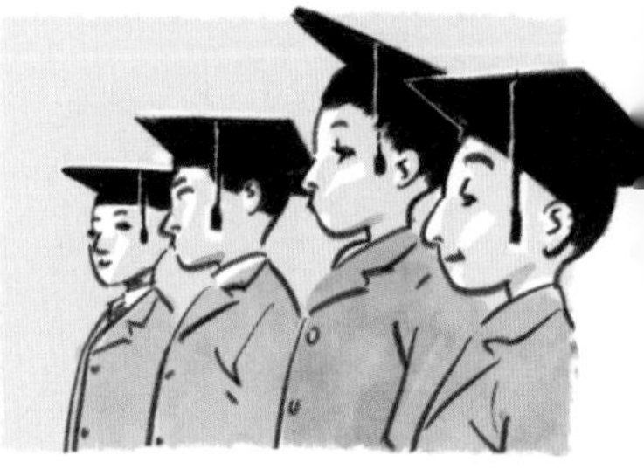

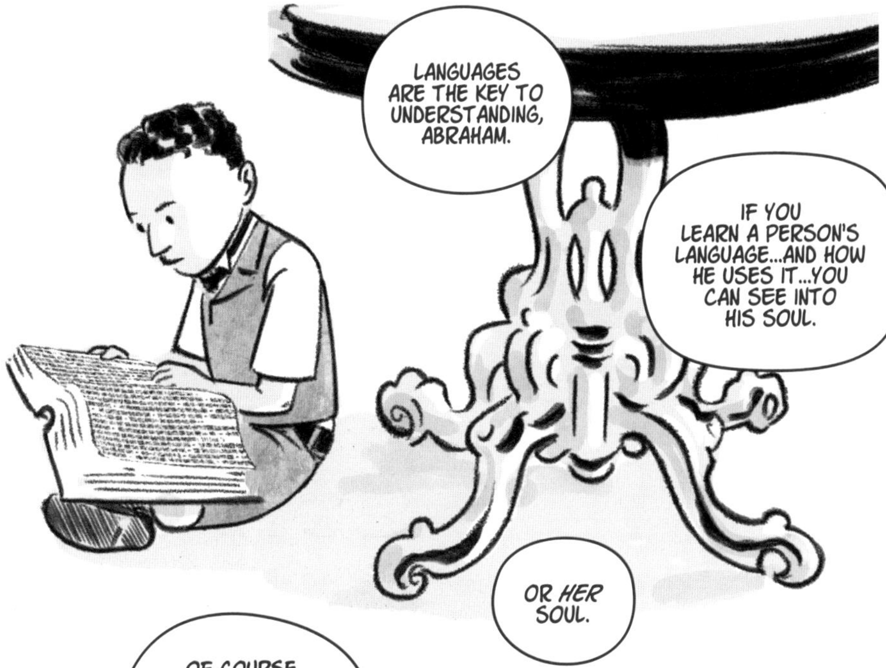
LANGUAGES ARE THE KEY TO UNDERSTANDING, ABRAHAM.
IF YOU LEARN A PERSON'S LANGUAGE...AND HOW HE USES IT...YOU CAN SEE INTO HIS SOUL.
OR *HER* SOUL.

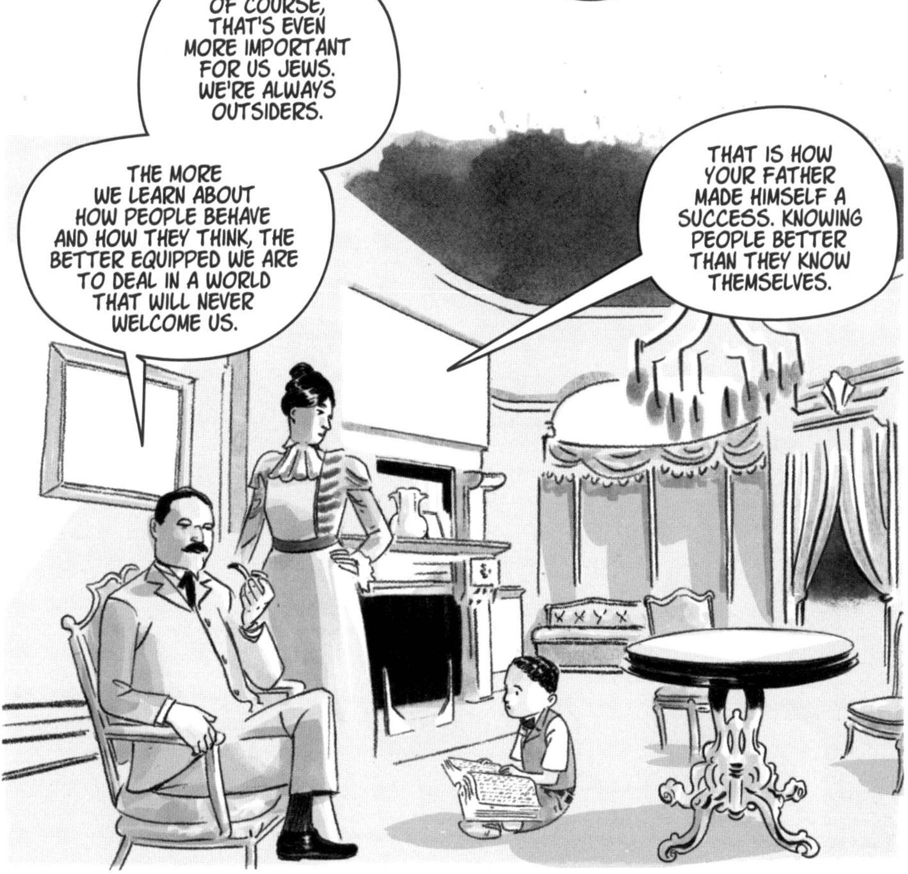
OF COURSE, THAT'S EVEN MORE IMPORTANT FOR US JEWS. WE'RE ALWAYS OUTSIDERS.
THE MORE WE LEARN ABOUT HOW PEOPLE BEHAVE AND HOW THEY THINK, THE BETTER EQUIPPED WE ARE TO DEAL IN A WORLD THAT WILL NEVER WELCOME US.
THAT IS HOW YOUR FATHER MADE HIMSELF A SUCCESS. KNOWING PEOPLE BETTER THAN THEY KNOW THEMSELVES.

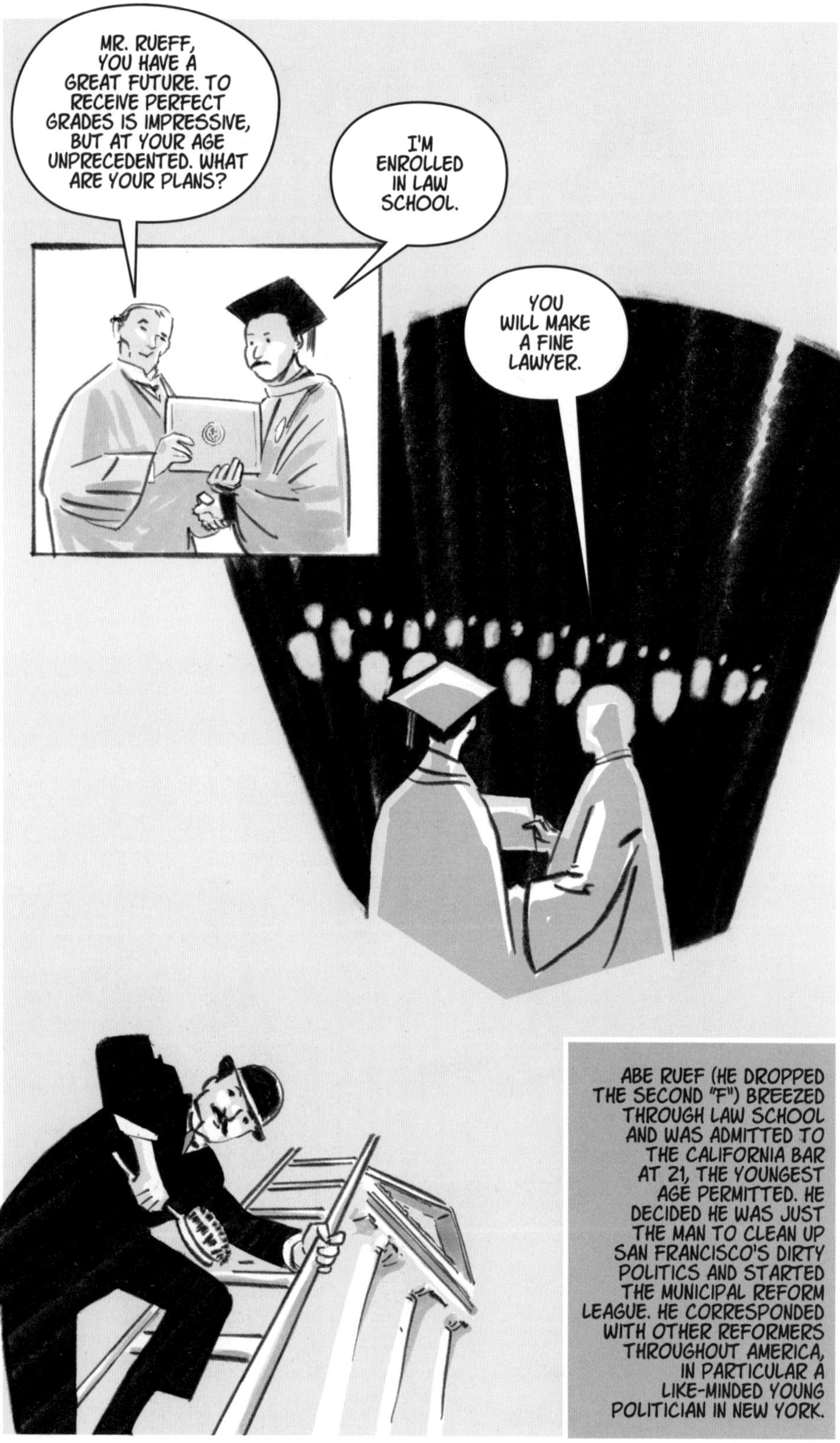
MR. RUEFF, YOU HAVE A GREAT FUTURE. TO RECEIVE PERFECT GRADES IS IMPRESSIVE, BUT AT YOUR AGE UNPRECEDENTED. WHAT ARE YOUR PLANS?
I'M ENROLLED IN LAW SCHOOL.
YOU WILL MAKE A FINE LAWYER.
ABE RUEF (HE DROPPED THE SECOND "F") BREEZED THROUGH LAW SCHOOL AND WAS ADMITTED TO THE CALIFORNIA BAR AT 21, THE YOUNGEST AGE PERMITTED. HE DECIDED HE WAS JUST THE MAN TO CLEAN UP SAN FRANCISCO'S DIRTY POLITICS AND STARTED THE MUNICIPAL REFORM LEAGUE. HE CORRESPONDED WITH OTHER REFORMERS THROUGHOUT AMERICA, IN PARTICULAR A LIKE-MINDED YOUNG POLITICIAN IN NEW YORK.

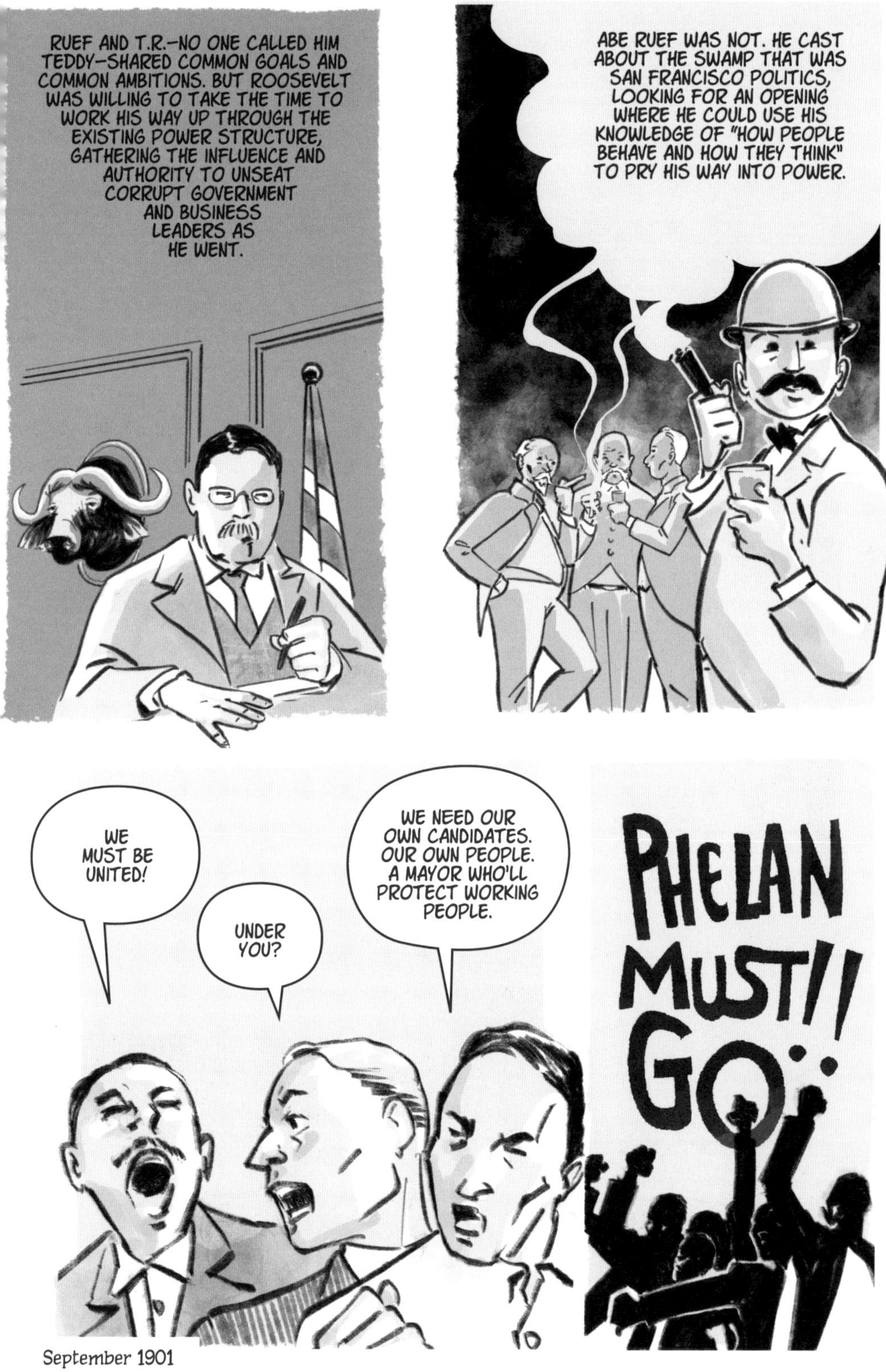
RUEF AND T.R.—NO ONE CALLED HIM TEDDY—SHARED COMMON GOALS AND COMMON AMBITIONS. BUT ROOSEVELT WAS WILLING TO TAKE THE TIME TO WORK HIS WAY UP THROUGH THE EXISTING POWER STRUCTURE, GATHERING THE INFLUENCE AND AUTHORITY TO UNSEAT CORRUPT GOVERNMENT AND BUSINESS LEADERS AS HE WENT.
ABE RUEF WAS NOT. HE CAST ABOUT THE SWAMP THAT WAS SAN FRANCISCO POLITICS, LOOKING FOR AN OPENING WHERE HE COULD USE HIS KNOWLEDGE OF "HOW PEOPLE BEHAVE AND HOW THEY THINK" TO PRY HIS WAY INTO POWER.
WE MUST BE UNITED!
UNDER YOU?
WE NEED OUR OWN CANDIDATES. OUR OWN PEOPLE. A MAYOR WHO'LL PROTECT WORKING PEOPLE.
PHELAN MUST GO!!!
September 1901

WHEN RUEF HEARD OF THE NEW UNION LABOR PARTY, HE KNEW HE HAD FOUND HIS OPPORTUNITY.

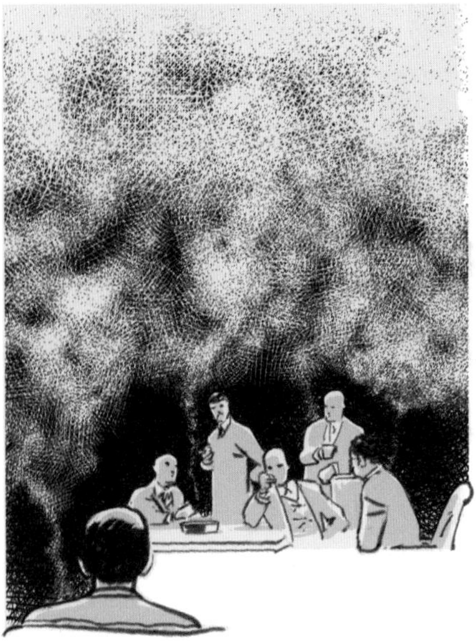

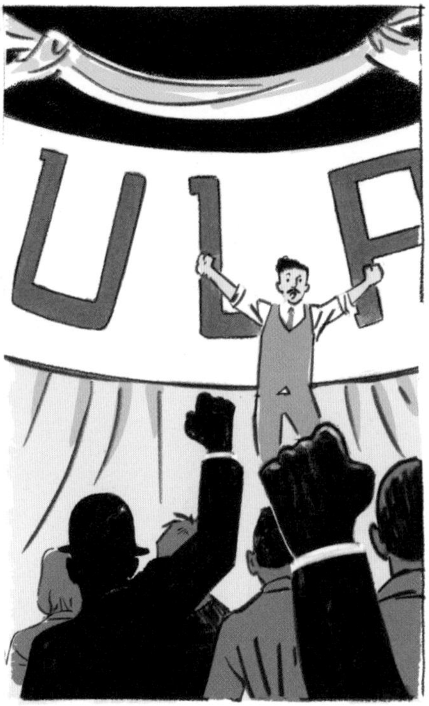

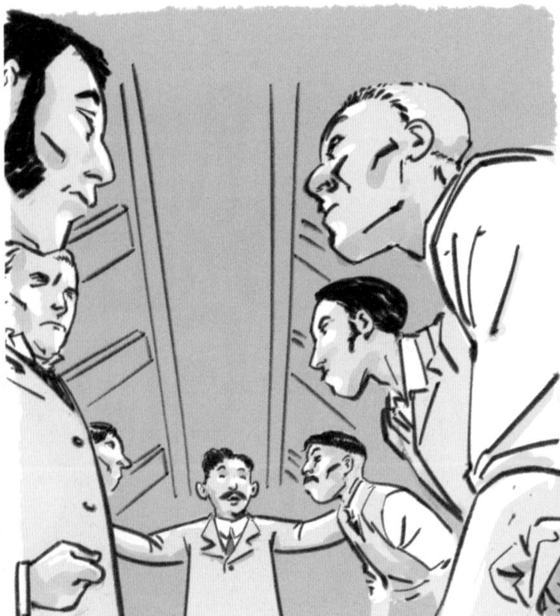

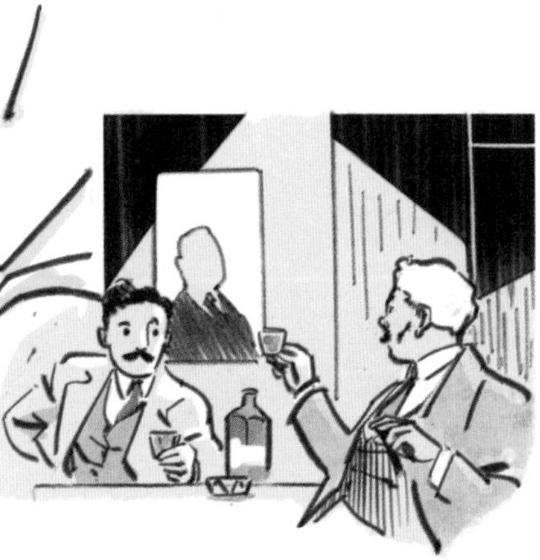

THE PARTY CALLED FOR A CONVENTION IN SEPTEMBER TO DRAW UP A SLATE OF CANDIDATES TO RUN FOR CITY OFFICE. THE EMPLOYERS ASSOCIATION THOUGHT THE UNION LABOR PARTY WAS A JOKE, A BUNCH OF AMATEURS WHO WOULD BE EASY TO BRUSH ASIDE ON ELECTION DAY. NO ONE IN SAN FRANCISCO GAVE THIS GROUP OF HARD-DRINKING, TWO-FISTED WORKING MEN ANY CHANCE AT ALL OF DEFEATING EITHER OF THE TWO MAJOR PARTIES.

THEY WERE WRONG.

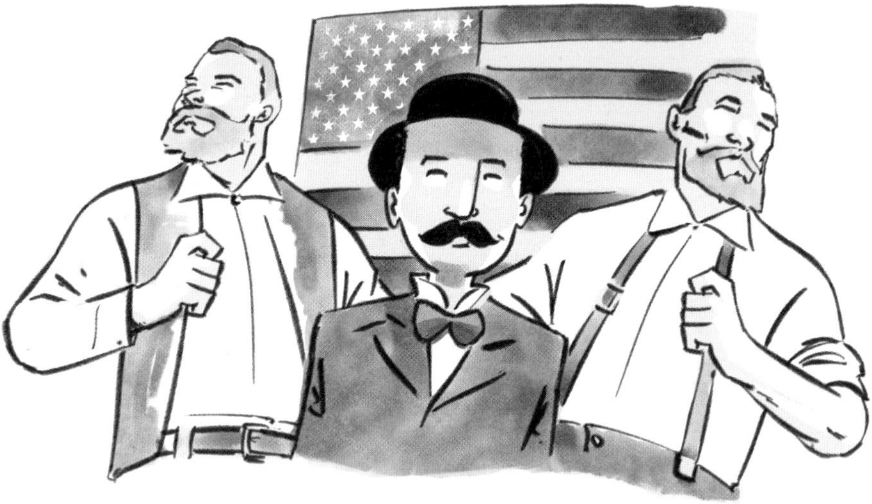

USING BRAINS, POLITICAL SAVVY, AND CHARM, RUEF TOOK OVER.

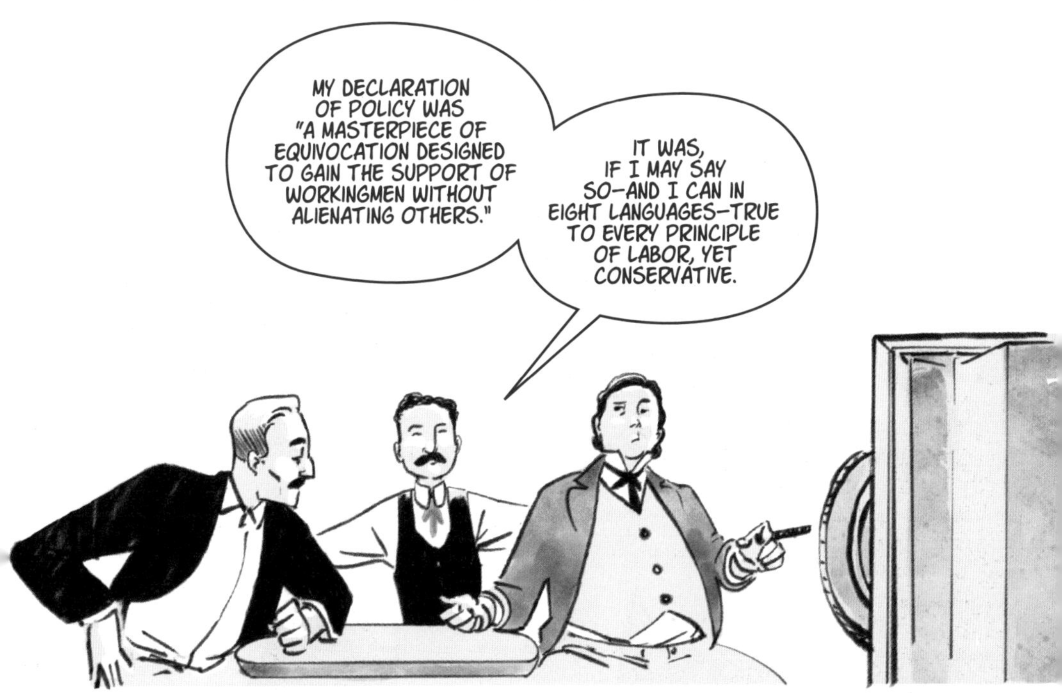
MY DECLARATION OF POLICY WAS "A MASTERPIECE OF EQUIVOCATION DESIGNED TO GAIN THE SUPPORT OF WORKINGMEN WITHOUT ALIENATING OTHERS."
IT WAS, IF I MAY SAY SO—AND I CAN IN EIGHT LANGUAGES—TRUE TO EVERY PRINCIPLE OF LABOR, YET CONSERVATIVE.

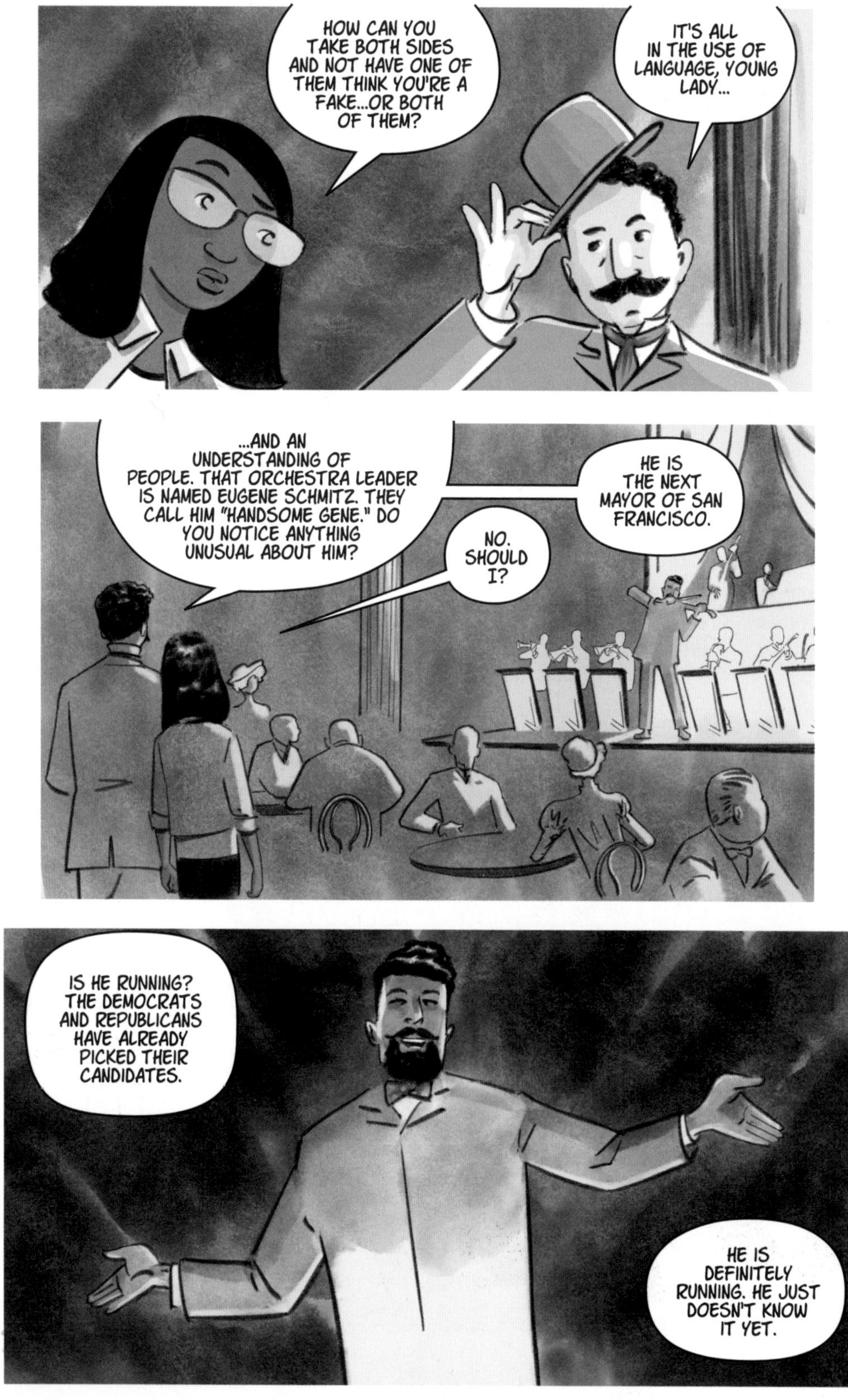
HOW CAN YOU TAKE BOTH SIDES AND NOT HAVE ONE OF THEM THINK YOU'RE A FAKE...OR BOTH OF THEM?
IT'S ALL IN THE USE OF LANGUAGE, YOUNG LADY...
...AND AN UNDERSTANDING OF PEOPLE. THAT ORCHESTRA LEADER IS NAMED EUGENE SCHMITZ. THEY CALL HIM "HANDSOME GENE." DO YOU NOTICE ANYTHING UNUSUAL ABOUT HIM?
NO. SHOULD I?
HE IS THE NEXT MAYOR OF SAN FRANCISCO.
IS HE RUNNING? THE DEMOCRATS AND REPUBLICANS HAVE ALREADY PICKED THEIR CANDIDATES.
HE IS DEFINITELY RUNNING. HE JUST DOESN'T KNOW IT YET.

BUT ABE RUEF KNEW IT. SCHMITZ WAS A VIOLINIST AND HEAD OF THE MUSICIANS' UNION. HE HAD NOT A TRACE OF POLITICAL EXPERIENCE AND NO INTENTION OF ACQUIRING ANY. THAT MADE HIM THE PERFECT BLANK SLATE FOR RUEF TO FILL IN.

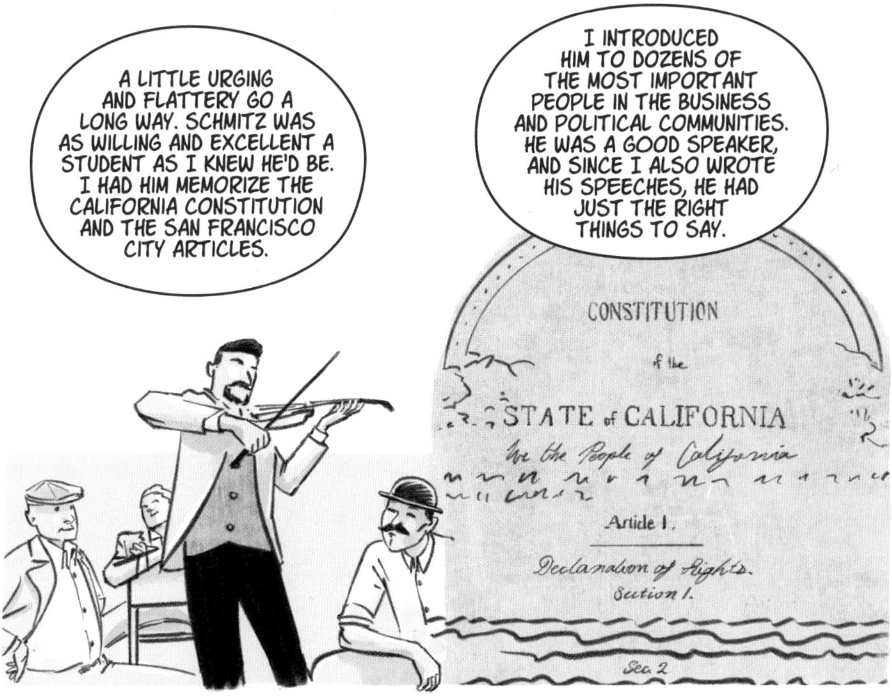

A LITTLE URGING AND FLATTERY GO A LONG WAY. SCHMITZ WAS AS WILLING AND EXCELLENT A STUDENT AS I KNEW HE'D BE. I HAD HIM MEMORIZE THE CALIFORNIA CONSTITUTION AND THE SAN FRANCISCO CITY ARTICLES.
I INTRODUCED HIM TO DOZENS OF THE MOST IMPORTANT PEOPLE IN THE BUSINESS AND POLITICAL COMMUNITIES. HE WAS A GOOD SPEAKER, AND SINCE I ALSO WROTE HIS SPEECHES, HE HAD JUST THE RIGHT THINGS TO SAY.
CONSTITUTION
of the
STATE of CALIFORNIA
We the People of California
Article I.
Declaration of Rights.
Section 1.
Sec. 2

BUT THE STRIKES HAD NOT ENDED. ON THE STREETS, THE WORKERS WERE GROWING DESPERATE. AS THE EMPLOYERS ASSOCIATION HAD PREDICTED, AS THEIR MONEY RAN OUT AND THEY NEEDED TO PAY FOR FOOD AND OTHER NECESSITIES, MANY OF THE STRIKERS BEGAN TO TALK OF SETTLEMENT. SOME BEGAN DRIFTING BACK TO WORK.

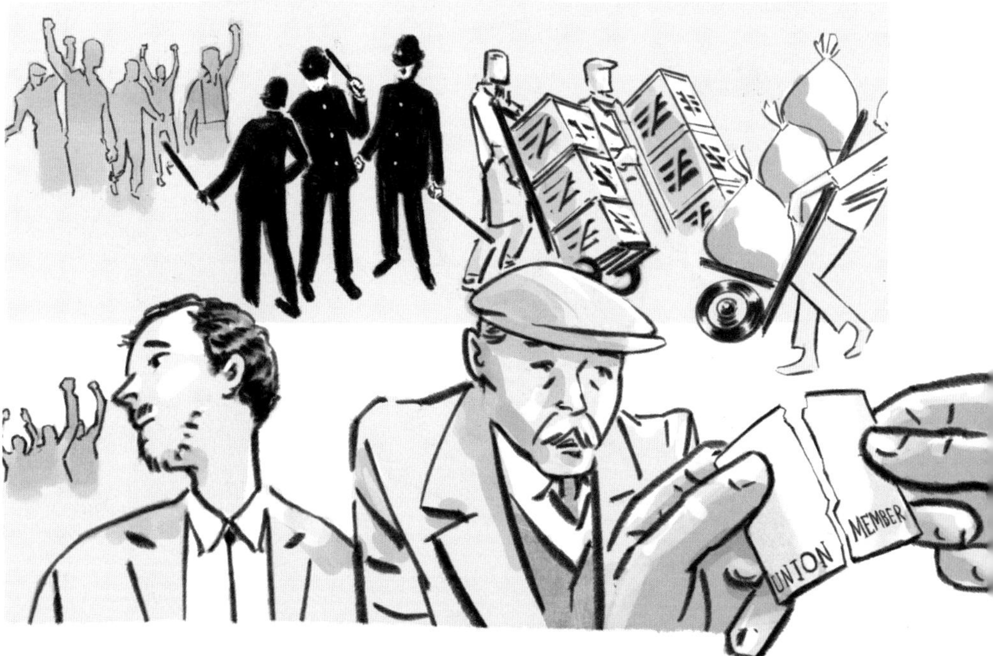

UNION
MEMBER

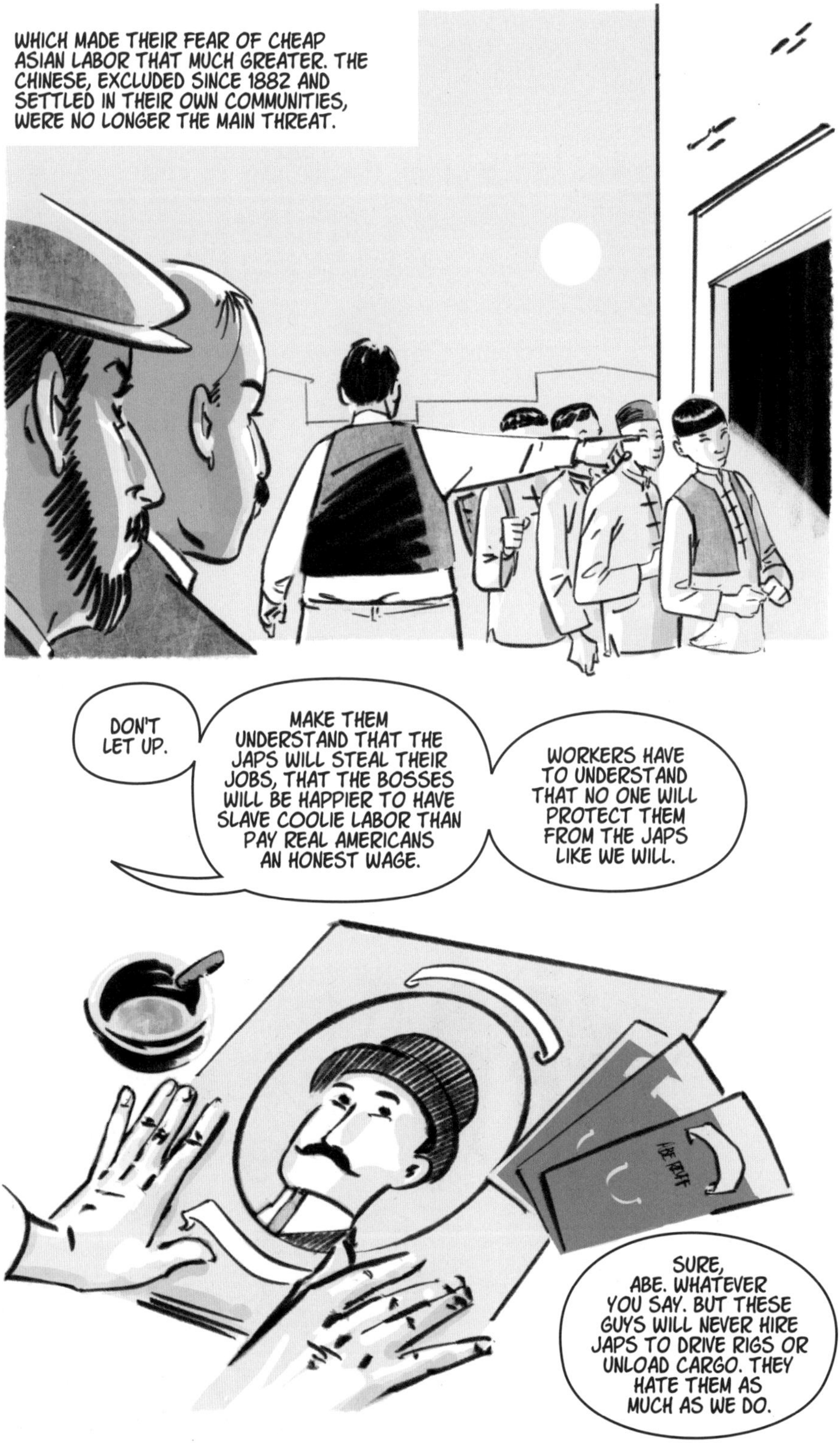
WHICH MADE THEIR FEAR OF CHEAP ASIAN LABOR THAT MUCH GREATER. THE CHINESE, EXCLUDED SINCE 1882 AND SETTLED IN THEIR OWN COMMUNITIES, WERE NO LONGER THE MAIN THREAT.
DON'T LET UP.
MAKE THEM UNDERSTAND THAT THE JAPS WILL STEAL THEIR JOBS, THAT THE BOSSES WILL BE HAPPIER TO HAVE SLAVE COOLIE LABOR THAN PAY REAL AMERICANS AN HONEST WAGE.
WORKERS HAVE TO UNDERSTAND THAT NO ONE WILL PROTECT THEM FROM THE JAPS LIKE WE WILL.
SURE, ABE. WHATEVER YOU SAY. BUT THESE GUYS WILL NEVER HIRE JAPS TO DRIVE RIGS OR UNLOAD CARGO. THEY HATE THEM AS MUCH AS WE DO.

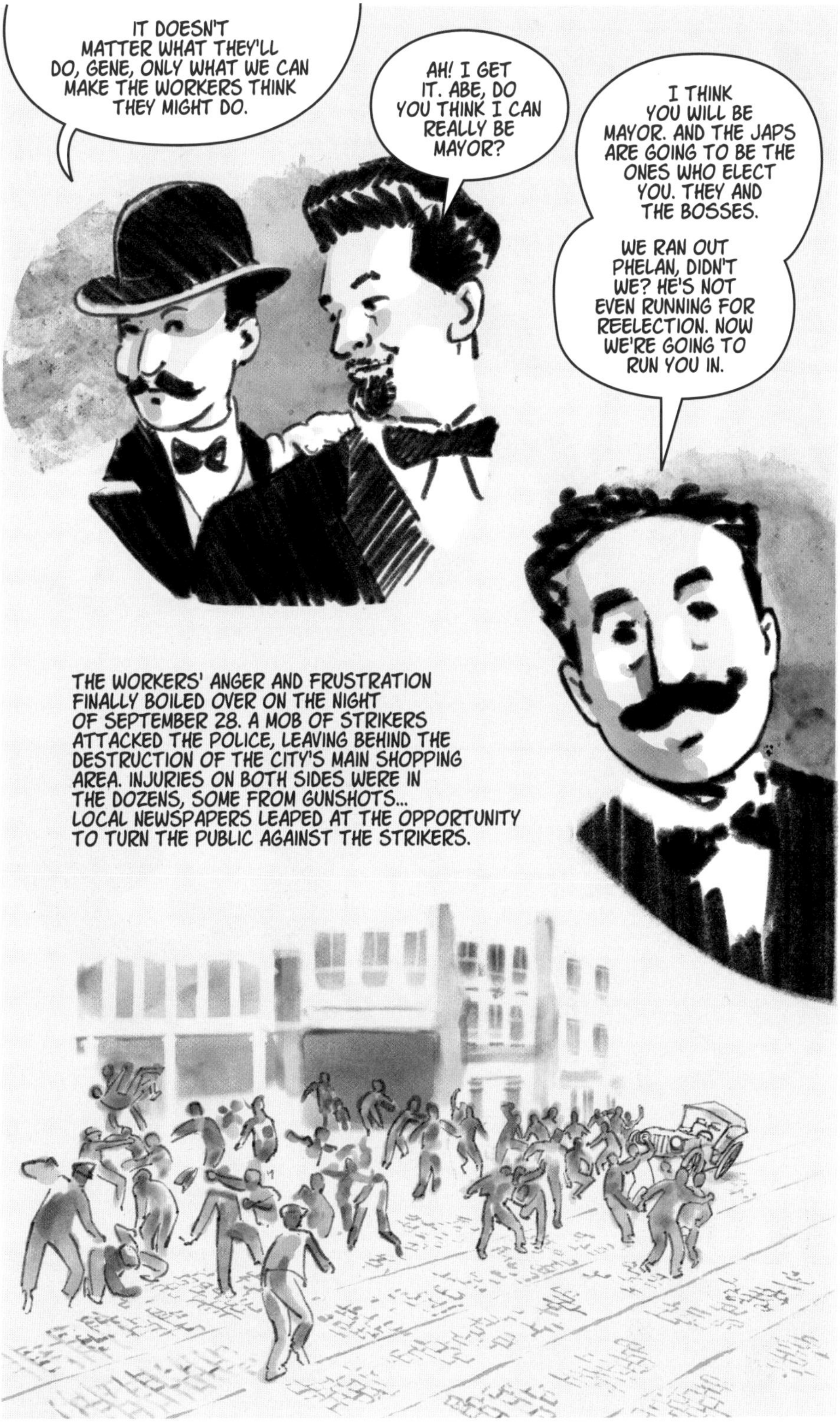
IT DOESN'T MATTER WHAT THEY'LL DO, GENE, ONLY WHAT WE CAN MAKE THE WORKERS THINK THEY MIGHT DO.
AH! I GET IT. ABE, DO YOU THINK I CAN REALLY BE MAYOR?
I THINK YOU WILL BE MAYOR. AND THE JAPS ARE GOING TO BE THE ONES WHO ELECT YOU. THEY AND THE BOSSES.
WE RAN OUT PHELAN, DIDN'T WE? HE'S NOT EVEN RUNNING FOR REELECTION. NOW WE'RE GOING TO RUN YOU IN.
THE WORKERS' ANGER AND FRUSTRATION FINALLY BOILED OVER ON THE NIGHT OF SEPTEMBER 28. A MOB OF STRIKERS ATTACKED THE POLICE, LEAVING BEHIND THE DESTRUCTION OF THE CITY'S MAIN SHOPPING AREA. INJURIES ON BOTH SIDES WERE IN THE DOZENS, SOME FROM GUNSHOTS... LOCAL NEWSPAPERS LEAPED AT THE OPPORTUNITY TO TURN THE PUBLIC AGAINST THE STRIKERS.

Reported in *The San Francisco Call:*

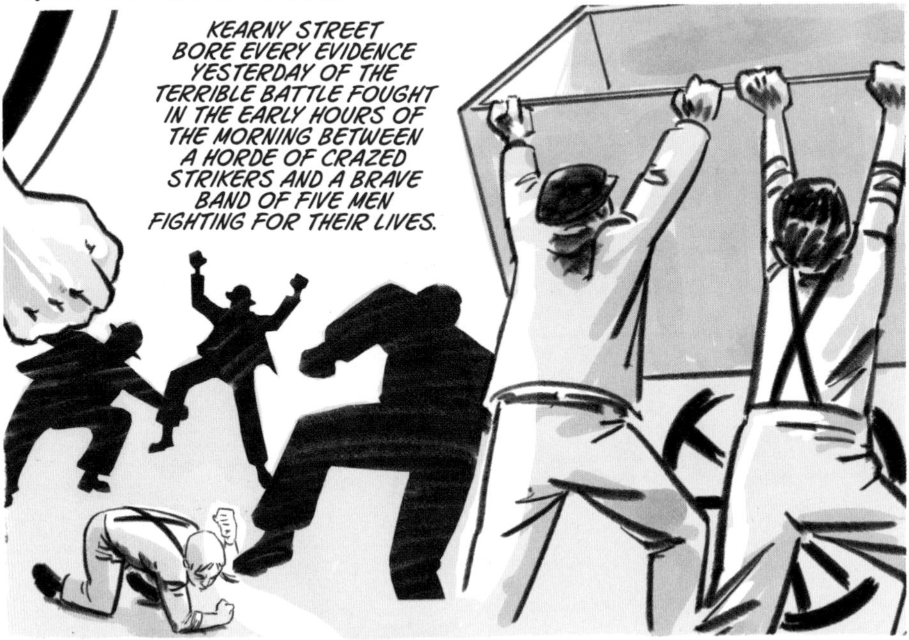
KEARNY STREET BORE EVERY EVIDENCE YESTERDAY OF THE TERRIBLE BATTLE FOUGHT IN THE EARLY HOURS OF THE MORNING BETWEEN A HORDE OF CRAZED STRIKERS AND A BRAVE BAND OF FIVE MEN FIGHTING FOR THEIR LIVES.

WINDOWS SHATTERED, SIGNS INDENTED, AWNINGS RIPPED...AND BUILDINGS FURROWED WITH BULLETS WERE THE MUTE EVIDENCES OF THE LATEST RIOT THAT DARKENS THE PAGES OF THE HISTORY OF SAN FRANCISCO.

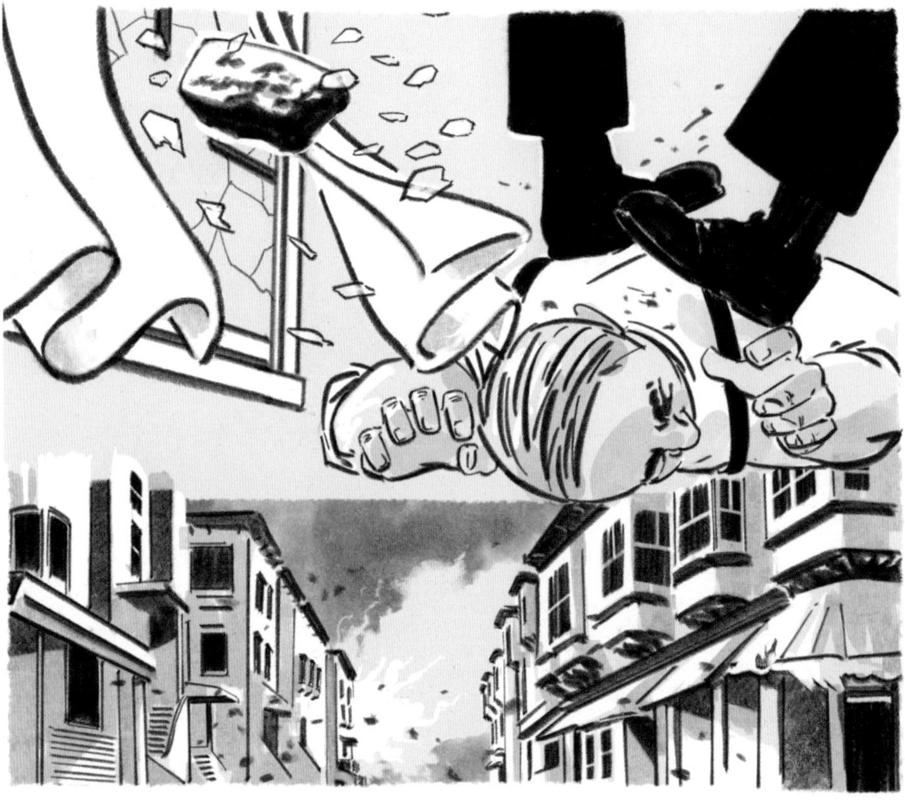

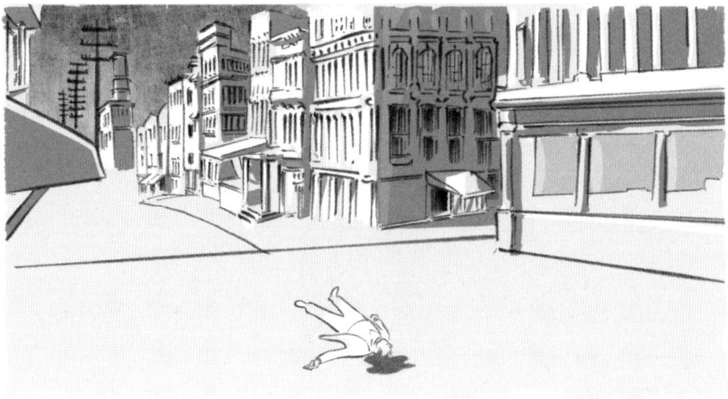

THE KEARNY STREET BATTLE WAS A PUBLIC RELATIONS DISASTER FOR THE UNIONS. THE EMPLOYERS ASSOCIATION DONATED $200,000 TO THE POLICE TO INCREASE MANPOWER. THE CITY FRONT SWORE THE STRIKE WOULD NEVER BE BROKEN. THE CITY BRACED FOR WAR.

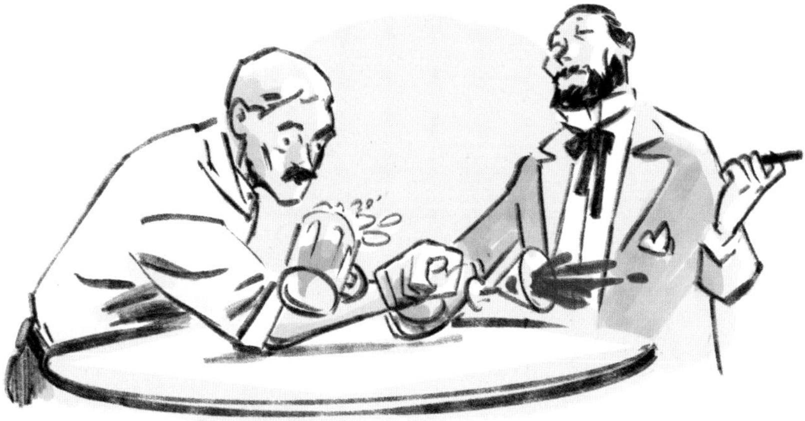

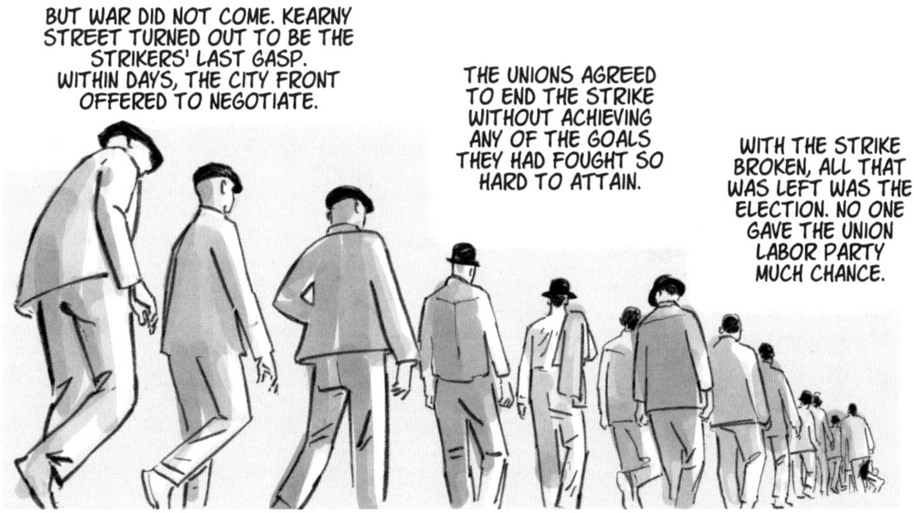
BUT WAR DID NOT COME. KEARNY STREET TURNED OUT TO BE THE STRIKERS' LAST GASP. WITHIN DAYS, THE CITY FRONT OFFERED TO NEGOTIATE.
THE UNIONS AGREED TO END THE STRIKE WITHOUT ACHIEVING ANY OF THE GOALS THEY HAD FOUGHT SO HARD TO ATTAIN.
WITH THE STRIKE BROKEN, ALL THAT WAS LEFT WAS THE ELECTION. NO ONE GAVE THE UNION LABOR PARTY MUCH CHANCE.

BUT ONCE AGAIN, THE ESTABLISHED POWERS IN THE CITY HAD GROSSLY UNDERESTIMATED ABE RUEF.

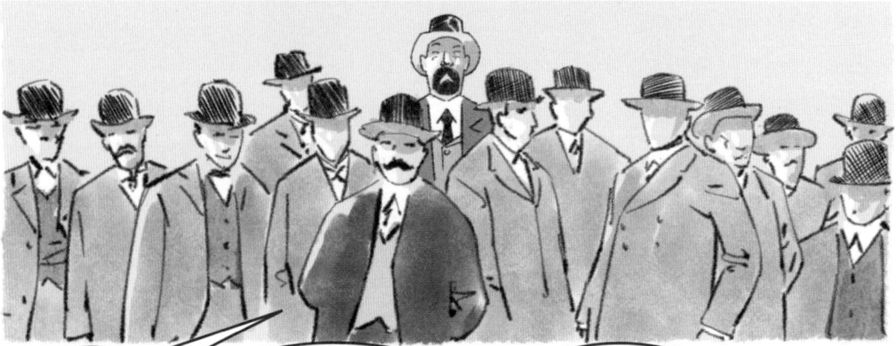
IT IS MUCH EASIER TO WIN WHEN NO ONE IS PAYING ATTENTION TO WHAT YOU ARE DOING TO TRY TO WIN.
WE WERE ABLE TO ORGANIZE, TO GET WORKERS TO VOTE, BECAUSE BOTH THE DEMOCRATS AND REPUBLICANS ASSUMED, HAVING JUST SURRENDERED TO THE BOSSES, THAT THE WORKERS WOULD SIMPLY GIVE UP AND STAY HOME.
BUT I KNEW THEY WOULD BE MOTIVATED TO VOTE SPECIFICALLY BECAUSE THEY HAD JUST SURRENDERED TO THE BOSSES.
I TOLD THEM THIS WAS THE WAY THEY COULD TURN A DEFEAT INTO A VICTORY... AND THEY DID.

IN THE END, IT WASN'T CLOSE. SCHMITZ WON EASILY.

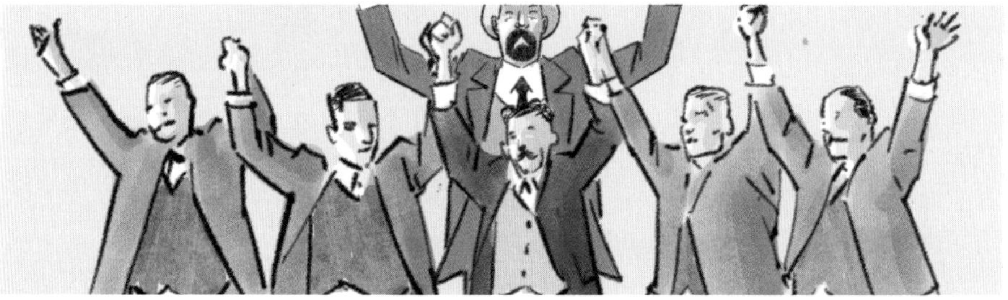

IN HIS VICTORY SPEECH, HE CLAIMED HE WOULD BE A REFORMER.

WORDS WRITTEN FOR HIM BY THE CITY'S NEXT AND PERHAPS MOST PREDATORY POLITICAL BOSS.

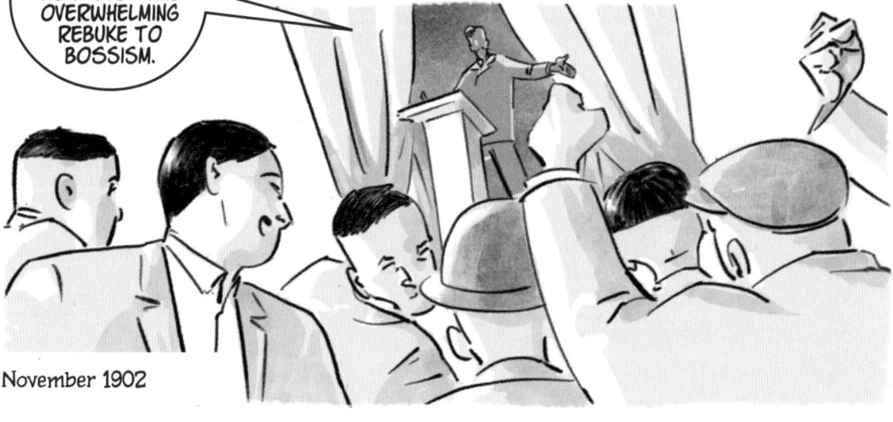
I REGARD MY ELECTION AS A JUST AND OVERWHELMING REBUKE TO BOSSISM.

November 1902

FOR THE NEXT FIVE YEARS, RUEF AND HIS CRONIES, INCLUDING THE ONCE-HONEST SCHMITZ, WOULD LOOT THE CITY ON AN UNPRECEDENTED SCALE.

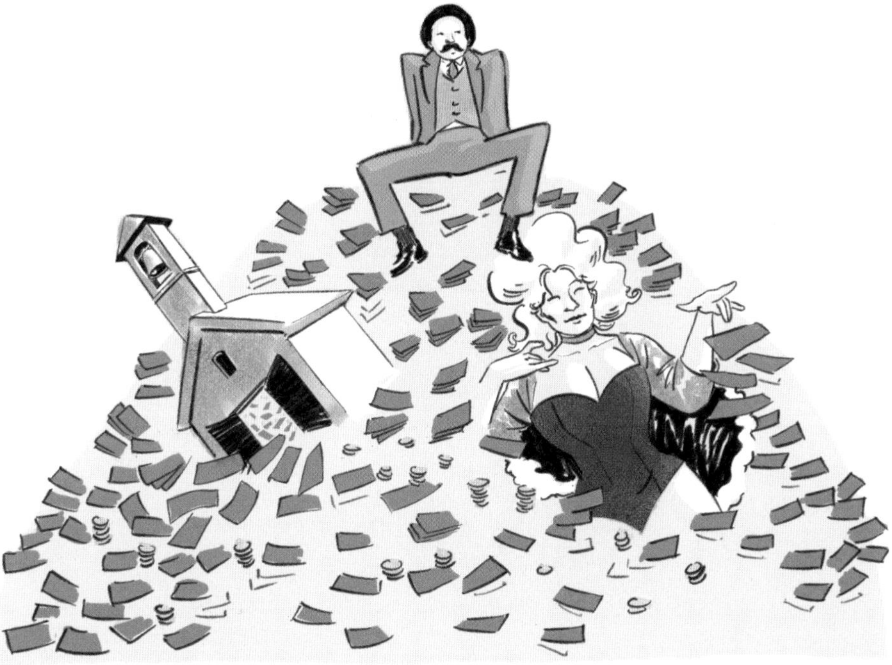

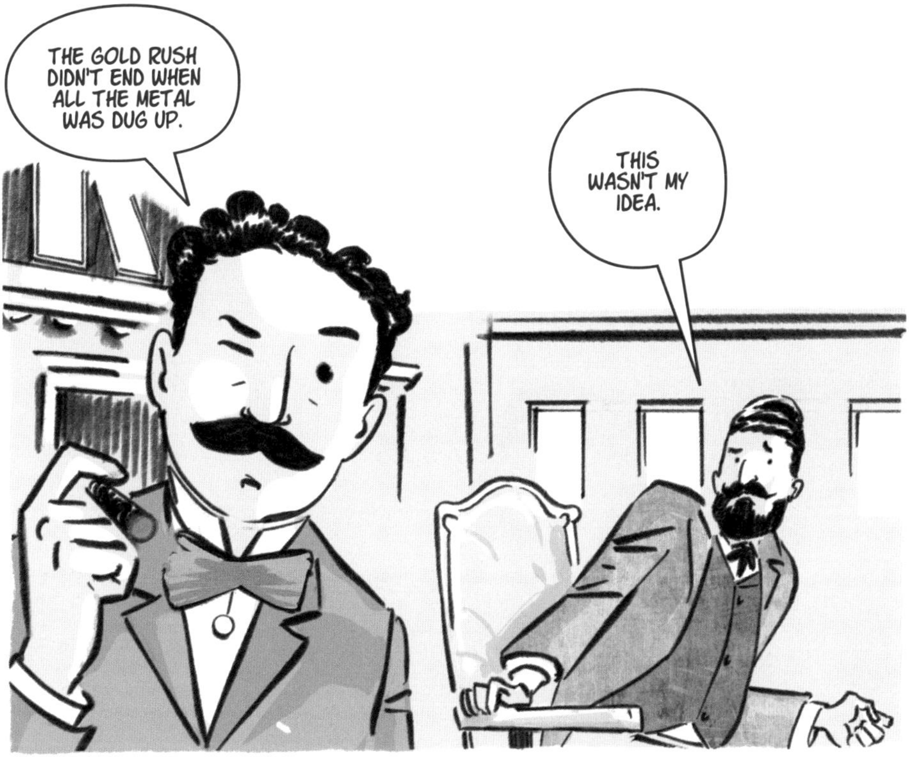
THE GOLD RUSH DIDN'T END WHEN ALL THE METAL WAS DUG UP.
THIS WASN'T MY IDEA.

HERE IS HOW A LOCAL WRITER DESCRIBED THE SITUATION:

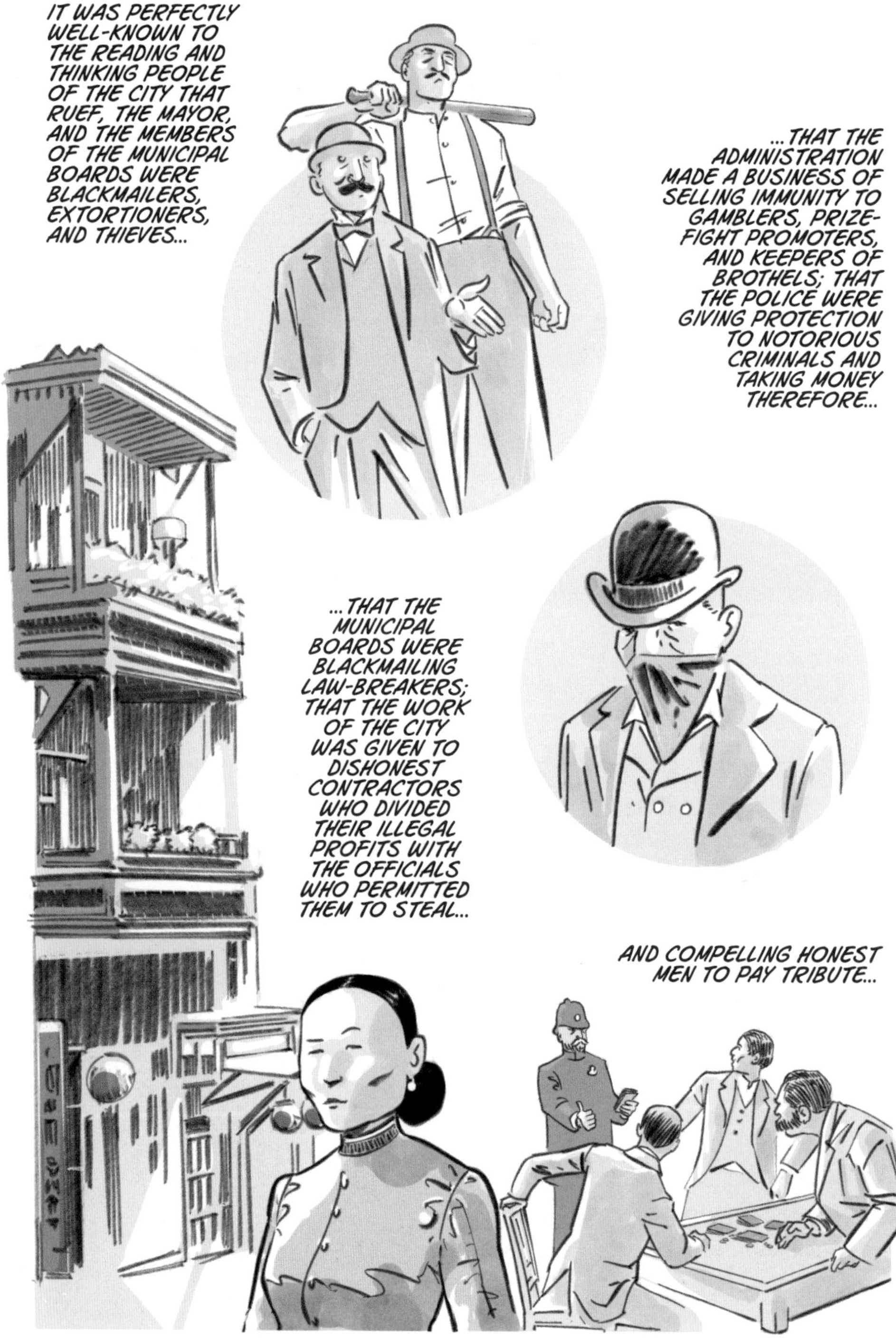
IT WAS PERFECTLY WELL-KNOWN TO THE READING AND THINKING PEOPLE OF THE CITY THAT RUEF, THE MAYOR, AND THE MEMBERS OF THE MUNICIPAL BOARDS WERE BLACKMAILERS, EXTORTIONERS, AND THIEVES...
...THAT THE ADMINISTRATION MADE A BUSINESS OF SELLING IMMUNITY TO GAMBLERS, PRIZE-FIGHT PROMOTERS, AND KEEPERS OF BROTHELS; THAT THE POLICE WERE GIVING PROTECTION TO NOTORIOUS CRIMINALS AND TAKING MONEY THEREFORE...
...THAT THE MUNICIPAL BOARDS WERE BLACKMAILING LAW-BREAKERS; THAT THE WORK OF THE CITY WAS GIVEN TO DISHONEST CONTRACTORS WHO DIVIDED THEIR ILLEGAL PROFITS WITH THE OFFICIALS WHO PERMITTED THEM TO STEAL...
AND COMPELLING HONEST MEN TO PAY TRIBUTE...

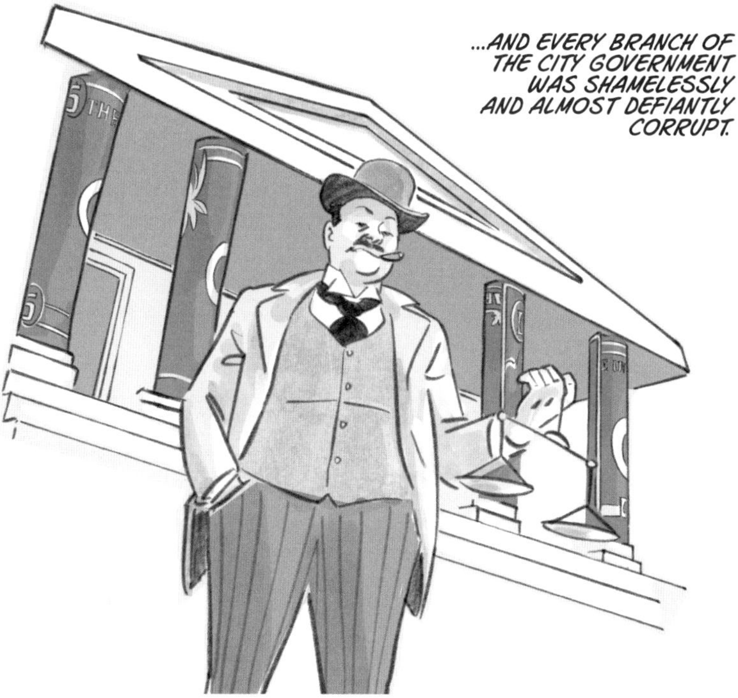
...AND EVERY BRANCH OF THE CITY GOVERNMENT WAS SHAMELESSLY AND ALMOST DEFIANTLY CORRUPT.

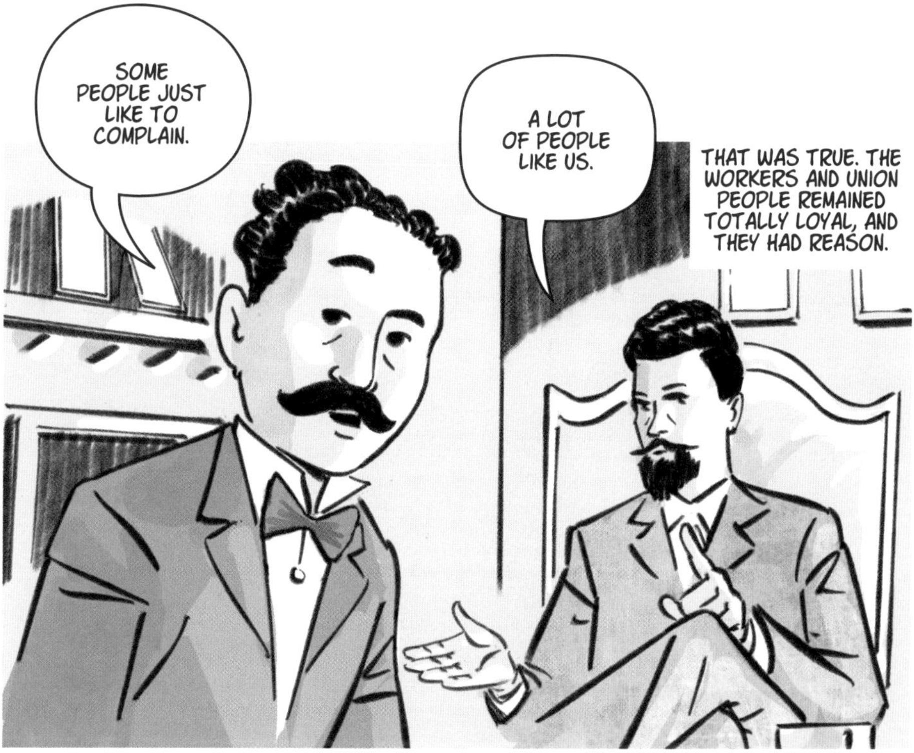
SOME PEOPLE JUST LIKE TO COMPLAIN.
A LOT OF PEOPLE LIKE US.
THAT WAS TRUE. THE WORKERS AND UNION PEOPLE REMAINED TOTALLY LOYAL, AND THEY HAD REASON.

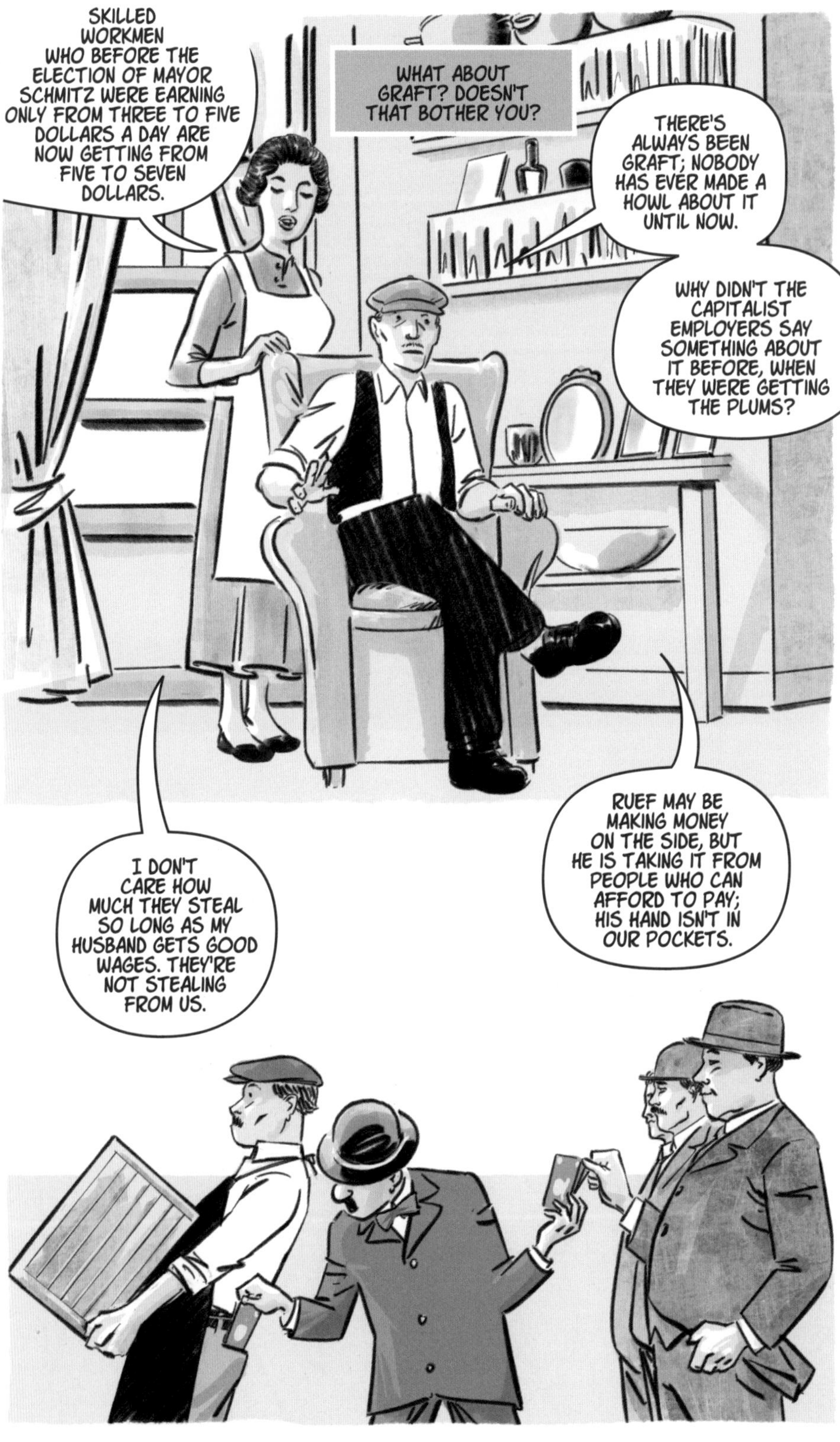
SKILLED WORKMEN WHO BEFORE THE ELECTION OF MAYOR SCHMITZ WERE EARNING ONLY FROM THREE TO FIVE DOLLARS A DAY ARE NOW GETTING FROM FIVE TO SEVEN DOLLARS.
WHAT ABOUT GRAFT? DOESN'T THAT BOTHER YOU?
THERE'S ALWAYS BEEN GRAFT; NOBODY HAS EVER MADE A HOWL ABOUT IT UNTIL NOW.
WHY DIDN'T THE CAPITALIST EMPLOYERS SAY SOMETHING ABOUT IT BEFORE, WHEN THEY WERE GETTING THE PLUMS?
I DON'T CARE HOW MUCH THEY STEAL SO LONG AS MY HUSBAND GETS GOOD WAGES. THEY'RE NOT STEALING FROM US.
RUEF MAY BE MAKING MONEY ON THE SIDE, BUT HE IS TAKING IT FROM PEOPLE WHO CAN AFFORD TO PAY; HIS HAND ISN'T IN OUR POCKETS.

A COUPLE OF YEARS LATER, ON THE OTHER SIDE OF THE PACIFIC OCEAN, JAPAN AND RUSSIA FOUGHT IT OUT FOR EIGHTEEN MONTHS BETWEEN 1904 AND 1905. RUSSIA WANTED PORT ARTHUR AS A WARM WEATHER PORT. THE JAPANESE HAD BECOME FULLY MODERNIZED SINCE EMPEROR MEIJI HAD SENT JAPAN ON ITS WESTERNIZED COURSE, AND THE JAPANESE WERE READY TO SHOW THE WORLD HOW POWERFUL THEY HAD BECOME.

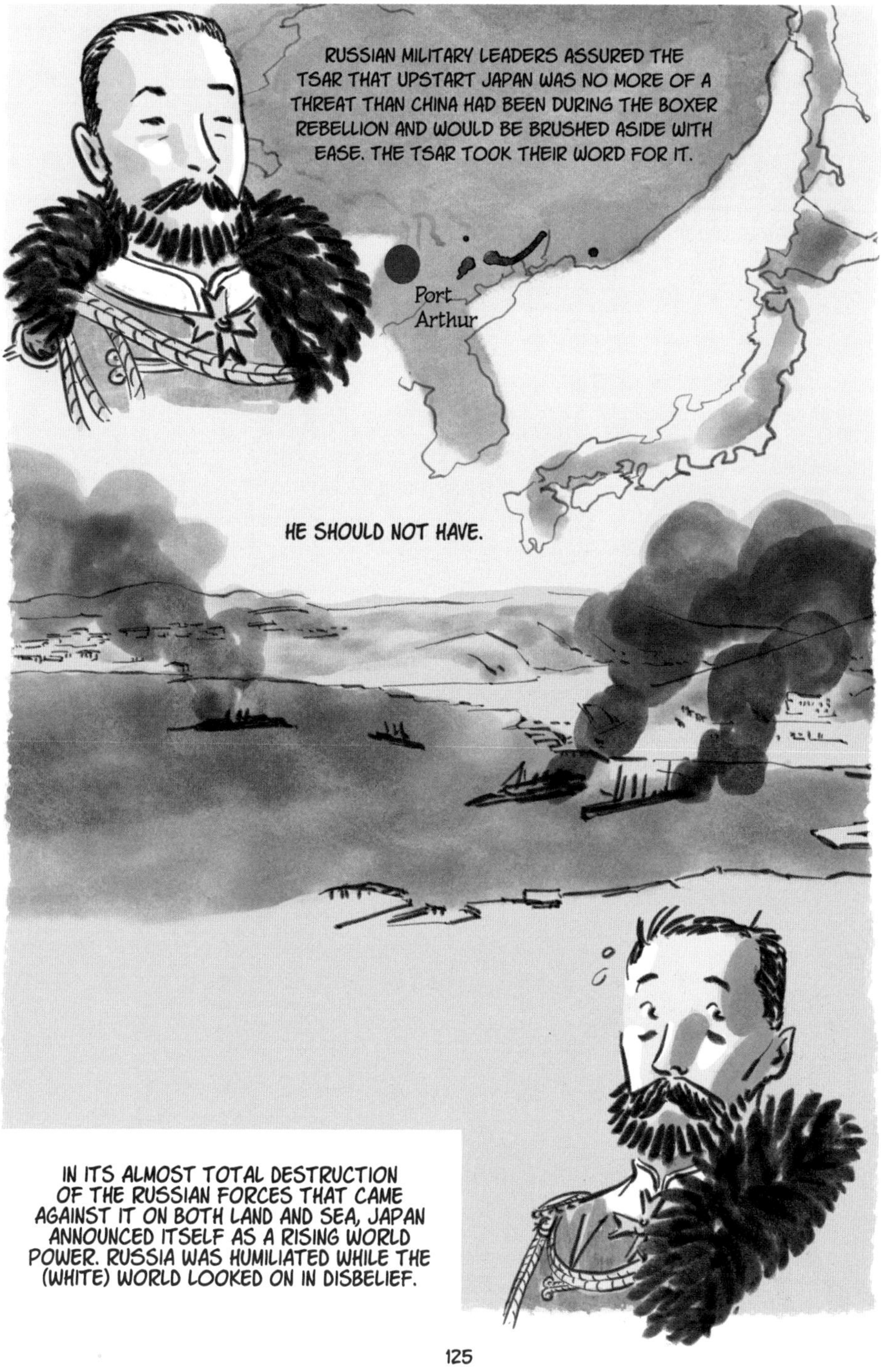
RUSSIAN MILITARY LEADERS ASSURED THE TSAR THAT UPSTART JAPAN WAS NO MORE OF A THREAT THAN CHINA HAD BEEN DURING THE BOXER REBELLION AND WOULD BE BRUSHED ASIDE WITH EASE. THE TSAR TOOK THEIR WORD FOR IT.
Port Arthur
HE SHOULD NOT HAVE.
IN ITS ALMOST TOTAL DESTRUCTION OF THE RUSSIAN FORCES THAT CAME AGAINST IT ON BOTH LAND AND SEA, JAPAN ANNOUNCED ITSELF AS A RISING WORLD POWER. RUSSIA WAS HUMILIATED WHILE THE (WHITE) WORLD LOOKED ON IN DISBELIEF.

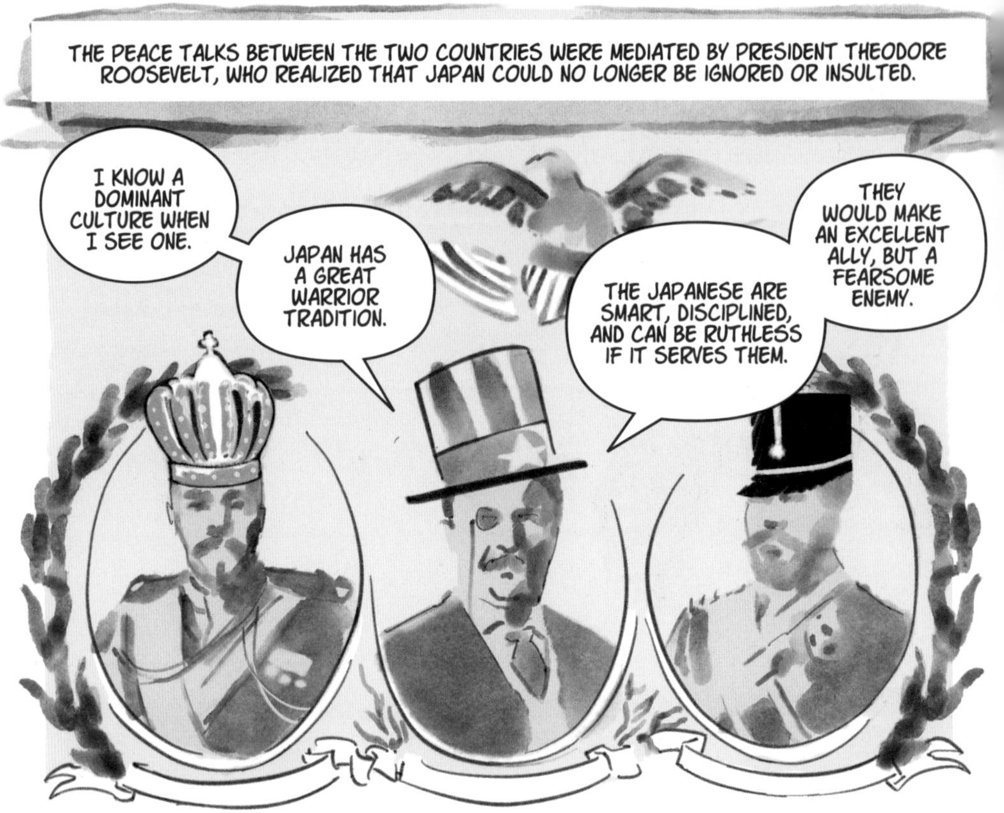
THE PEACE TALKS BETWEEN THE TWO COUNTRIES WERE MEDIATED BY PRESIDENT THEODORE ROOSEVELT, WHO REALIZED THAT JAPAN COULD NO LONGER BE IGNORED OR INSULTED.
I KNOW A DOMINANT CULTURE WHEN I SEE ONE.
JAPAN HAS A GREAT WARRIOR TRADITION.
THE JAPANESE ARE SMART, DISCIPLINED, AND CAN BE RUTHLESS IF IT SERVES THEM.
THEY WOULD MAKE AN EXCELLENT ALLY, BUT A FEARSOME ENEMY.

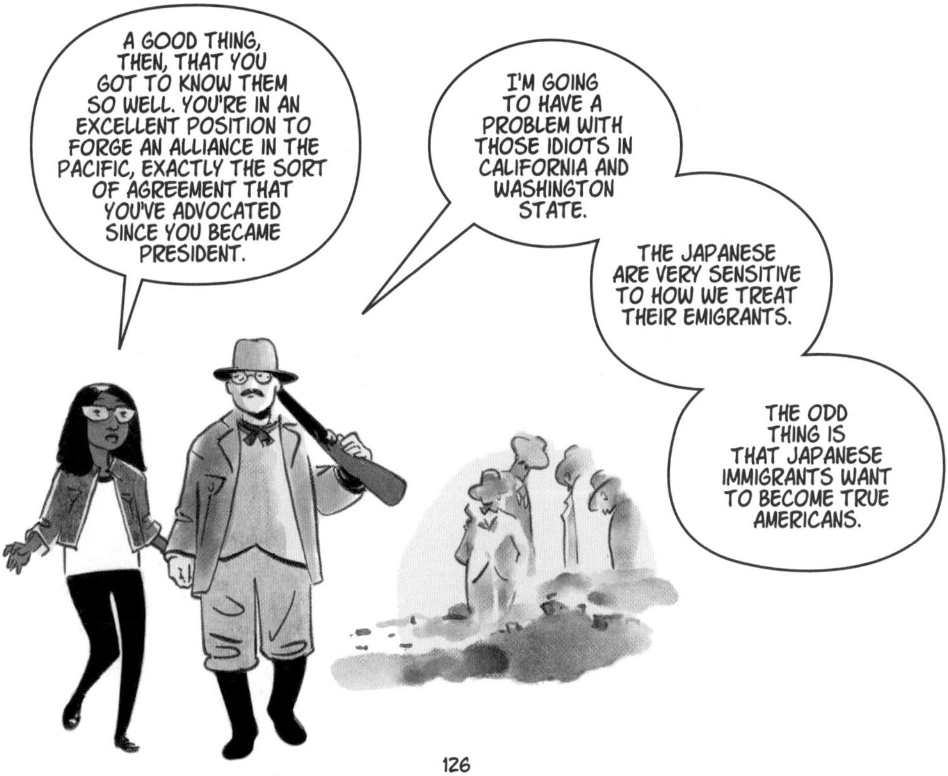
A GOOD THING, THEN, THAT YOU GOT TO KNOW THEM SO WELL. YOU'RE IN AN EXCELLENT POSITION TO FORGE AN ALLIANCE IN THE PACIFIC, EXACTLY THE SORT OF AGREEMENT THAT YOU'VE ADVOCATED SINCE YOU BECAME PRESIDENT.
I'M GOING TO HAVE A PROBLEM WITH THOSE IDIOTS IN CALIFORNIA AND WASHINGTON STATE.
THE JAPANESE ARE VERY SENSITIVE TO HOW WE TREAT THEIR EMIGRANTS.
THE ODD THING IS THAT JAPANESE IMMIGRANTS WANT TO BECOME TRUE AMERICANS.

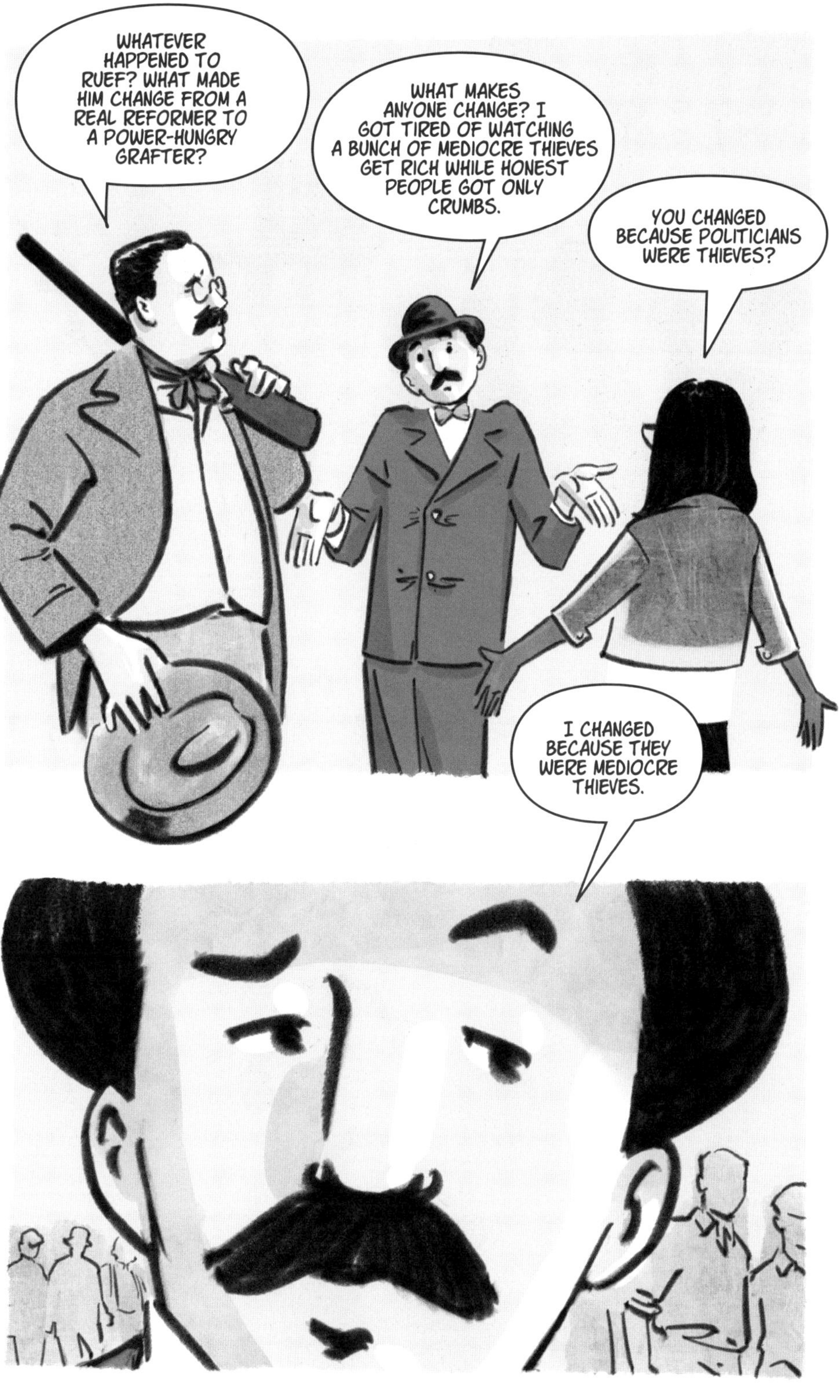
WHATEVER HAPPENED TO RUEF? WHAT MADE HIM CHANGE FROM A REAL REFORMER TO A POWER-HUNGRY GRAFTER?
WHAT MAKES ANYONE CHANGE? I GOT TIRED OF WATCHING A BUNCH OF MEDIOCRE THIEVES GET RICH WHILE HONEST PEOPLE GOT ONLY CRUMBS.
YOU CHANGED BECAUSE POLITICIANS WERE THIEVES?
I CHANGED BECAUSE THEY WERE MEDIOCRE THIEVES.

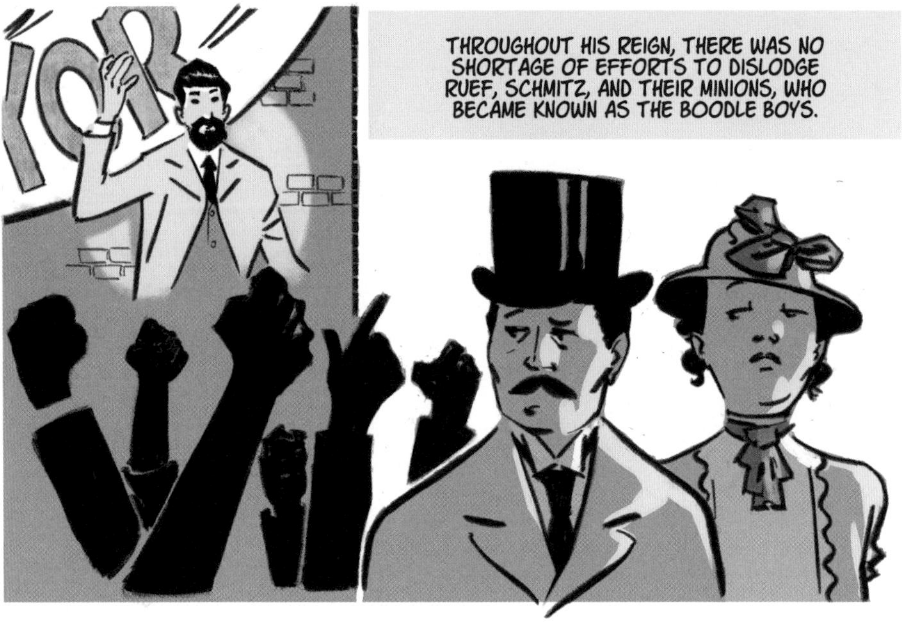
THROUGHOUT HIS REIGN, THERE WAS NO SHORTAGE OF EFFORTS TO DISLODGE RUEF, SCHMITZ, AND THEIR MINIONS, WHO BECAME KNOWN AS THE BOODLE BOYS.

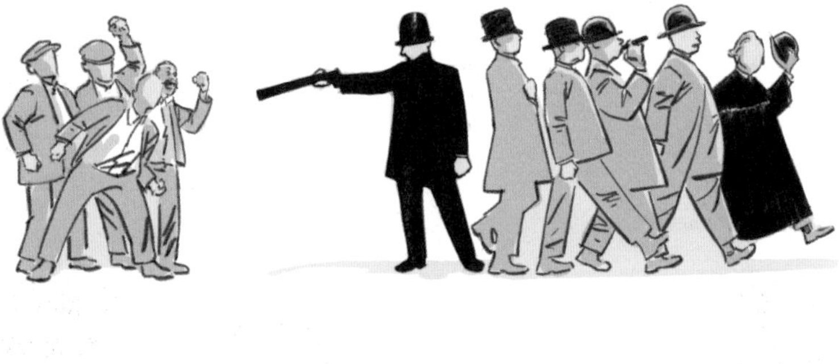

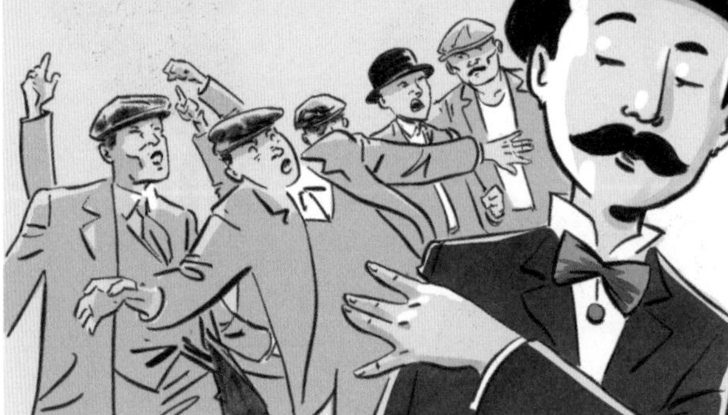

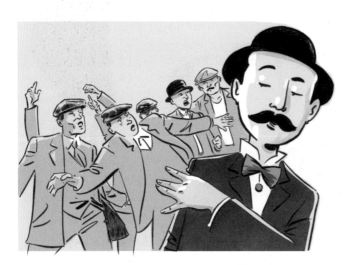

NONE WERE SUCCESSFUL. WHAT MADE RUEF DIFFERENT FROM SO MANY OTHER BIG-CITY POLITICAL BOSSES WAS THAT HE ALMOST NEVER RESORTED TO VIOLENCE. HE PREFERRED USING STRATEGY AND GUILE, AND HE WAS A MASTER AT IT.

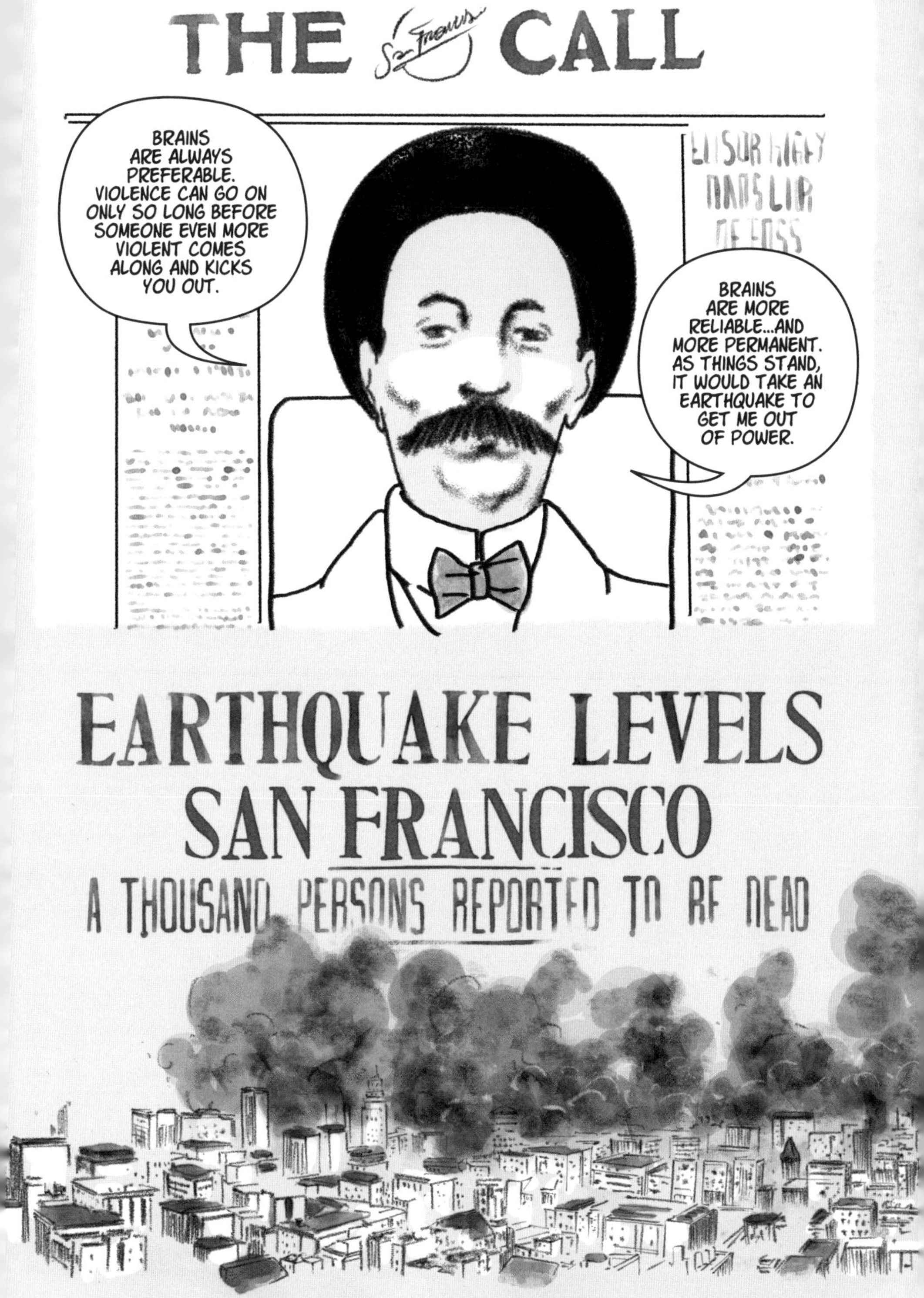
THE San Francisco CALL
BRAINS ARE ALWAYS PREFERABLE. VIOLENCE CAN GO ON ONLY SO LONG BEFORE SOMEONE EVEN MORE VIOLENT COMES ALONG AND KICKS YOU OUT.
BRAINS ARE MORE RELIABLE...AND MORE PERMANENT. AS THINGS STAND, IT WOULD TAKE AN EARTHQUAKE TO GET ME OUT OF POWER.
EARTHQUAKE LEVELS SAN FRANCISCO
A THOUSAND PERSONS REPORTED TO BE DEAD

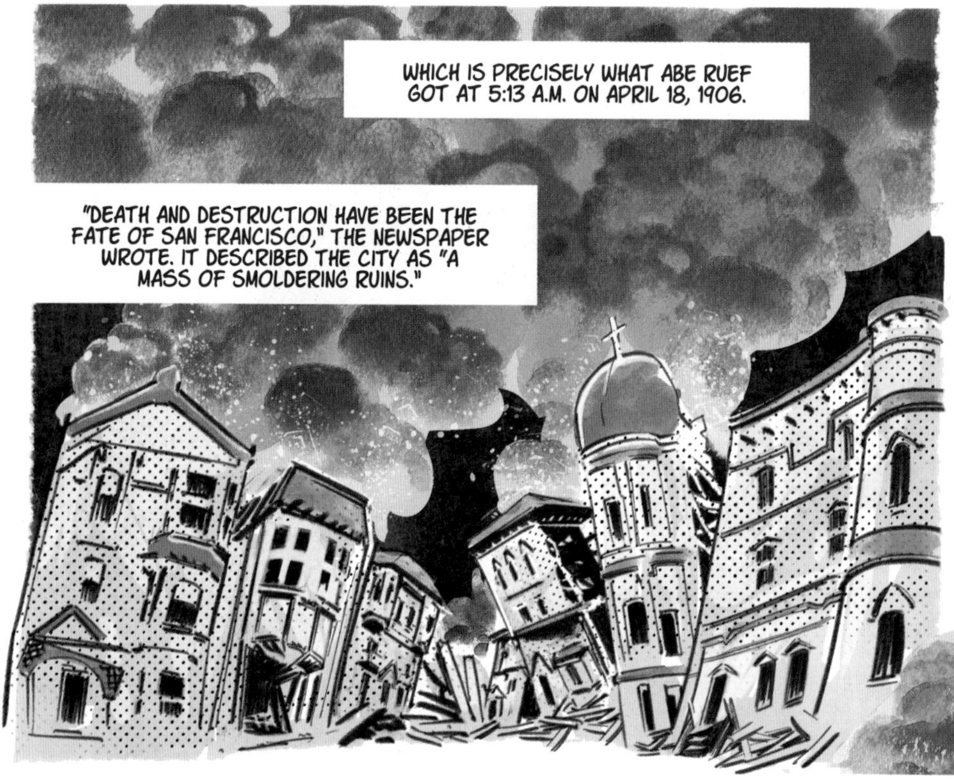
WHICH IS PRECISELY WHAT ABE RUEF GOT AT 5:13 A.M. ON APRIL 18, 1906.
"DEATH AND DESTRUCTION HAVE BEEN THE FATE OF SAN FRANCISCO," THE NEWSPAPER WROTE. IT DESCRIBED THE CITY AS "A MASS OF SMOLDERING RUINS."

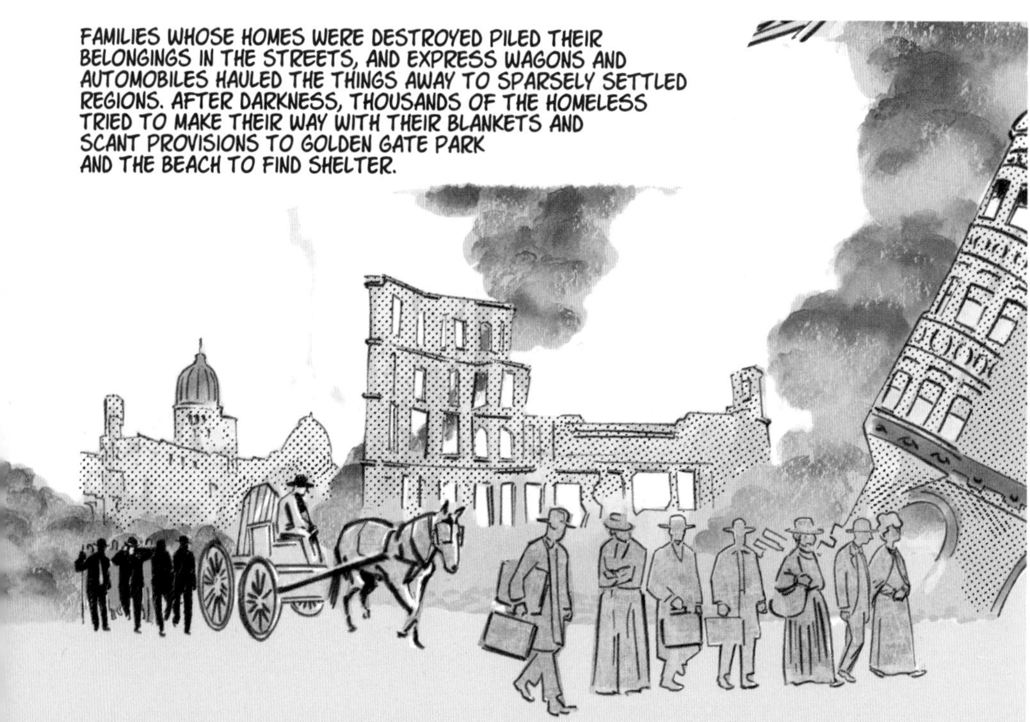
FAMILIES WHOSE HOMES WERE DESTROYED PILED THEIR BELONGINGS IN THE STREETS, AND EXPRESS WAGONS AND AUTOMOBILES HAULED THE THINGS AWAY TO SPARSELY SETTLED REGIONS. AFTER DARKNESS, THOUSANDS OF THE HOMELESS TRIED TO MAKE THEIR WAY WITH THEIR BLANKETS AND SCANT PROVISIONS TO GOLDEN GATE PARK AND THE BEACH TO FIND SHELTER.

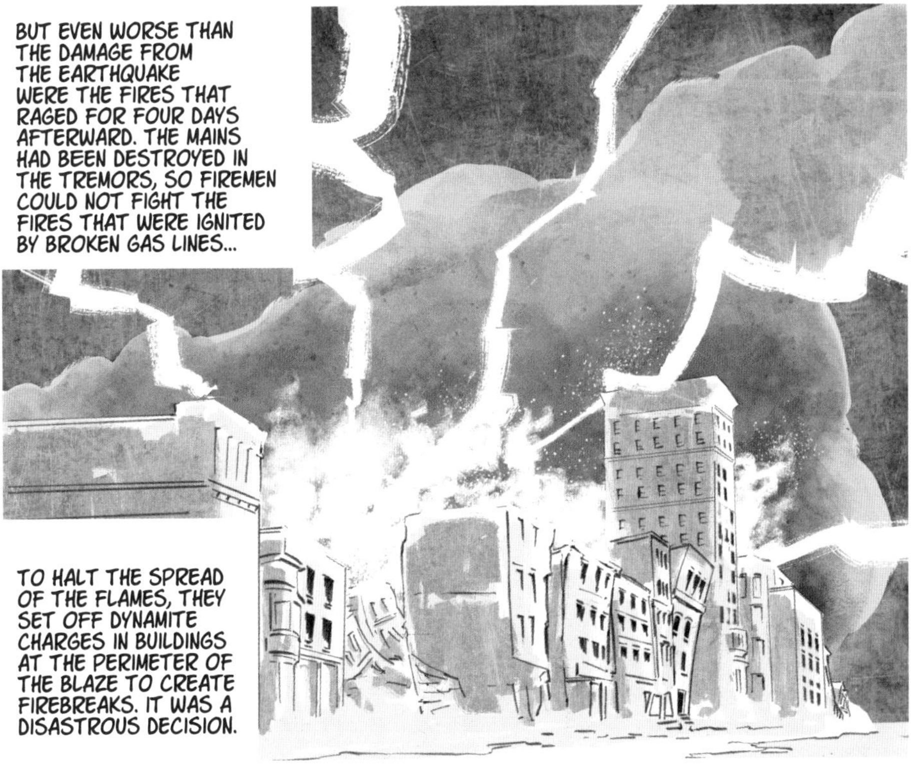
BUT EVEN WORSE THAN THE DAMAGE FROM THE EARTHQUAKE WERE THE FIRES THAT RAGED FOR FOUR DAYS AFTERWARD. THE MAINS HAD BEEN DESTROYED IN THE TREMORS, SO FIREMEN COULD NOT FIGHT THE FIRES THAT WERE IGNITED BY BROKEN GAS LINES...
TO HALT THE SPREAD OF THE FLAMES, THEY SET OFF DYNAMITE CHARGES IN BUILDINGS AT THE PERIMETER OF THE BLAZE TO CREATE FIREBREAKS. IT WAS A DISASTROUS DECISION.

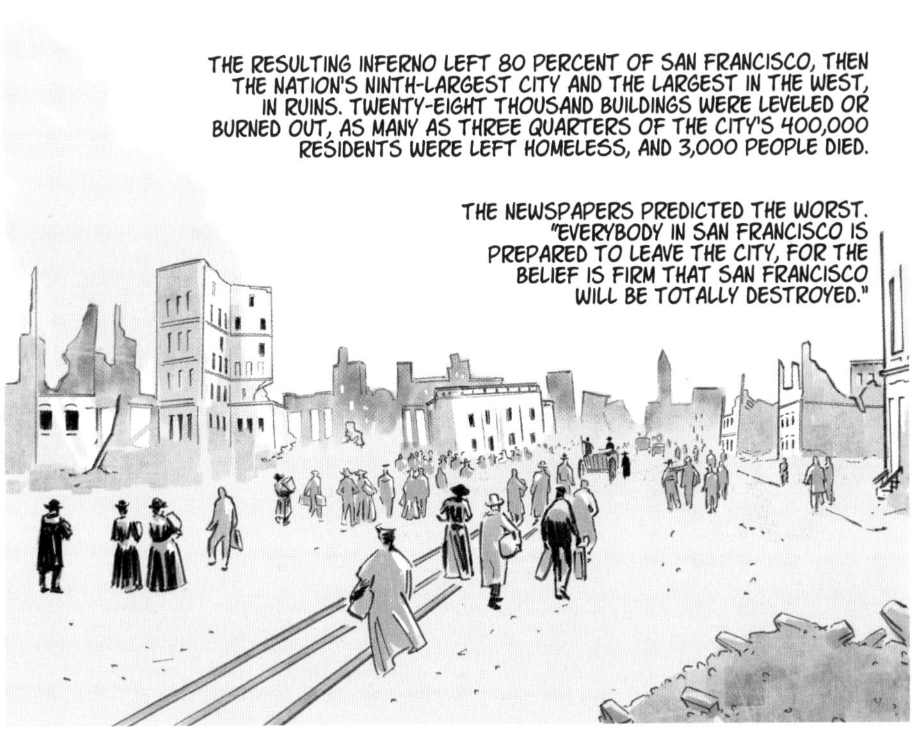
THE RESULTING INFERNO LEFT 80 PERCENT OF SAN FRANCISCO, THEN THE NATION'S NINTH-LARGEST CITY AND THE LARGEST IN THE WEST, IN RUINS. TWENTY-EIGHT THOUSAND BUILDINGS WERE LEVELED OR BURNED OUT, AS MANY AS THREE QUARTERS OF THE CITY'S 400,000 RESIDENTS WERE LEFT HOMELESS, AND 3,000 PEOPLE DIED.
THE NEWSPAPERS PREDICTED THE WORST. "EVERYBODY IN SAN FRANCISCO IS PREPARED TO LEAVE THE CITY, FOR THE BELIEF IS FIRM THAT SAN FRANCISCO WILL BE TOTALLY DESTROYED."

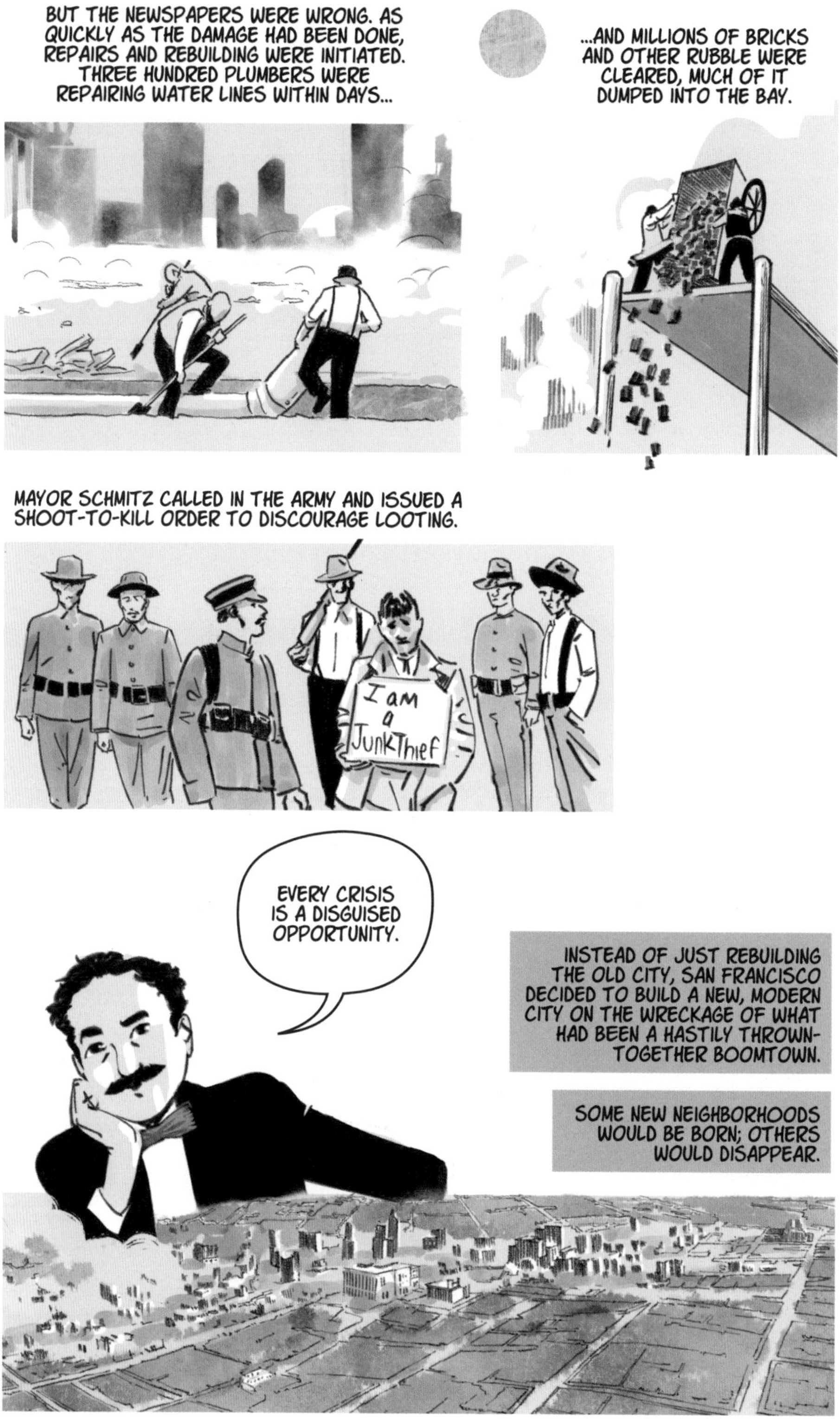

BUT THE NEWSPAPERS WERE WRONG. AS QUICKLY AS THE DAMAGE HAD BEEN DONE, REPAIRS AND REBUILDING WERE INITIATED. THREE HUNDRED PLUMBERS WERE REPAIRING WATER LINES WITHIN DAYS...
...AND MILLIONS OF BRICKS AND OTHER RUBBLE WERE CLEARED, MUCH OF IT DUMPED INTO THE BAY.
MAYOR SCHMITZ CALLED IN THE ARMY AND ISSUED A SHOOT-TO-KILL ORDER TO DISCOURAGE LOOTING.
I am a JunkThief
EVERY CRISIS IS A DISGUISED OPPORTUNITY.
INSTEAD OF JUST REBUILDING THE OLD CITY, SAN FRANCISCO DECIDED TO BUILD A NEW, MODERN CITY ON THE WRECKAGE OF WHAT HAD BEEN A HASTILY THROWN-TOGETHER BOOMTOWN.
SOME NEW NEIGHBORHOODS WOULD BE BORN; OTHERS WOULD DISAPPEAR.

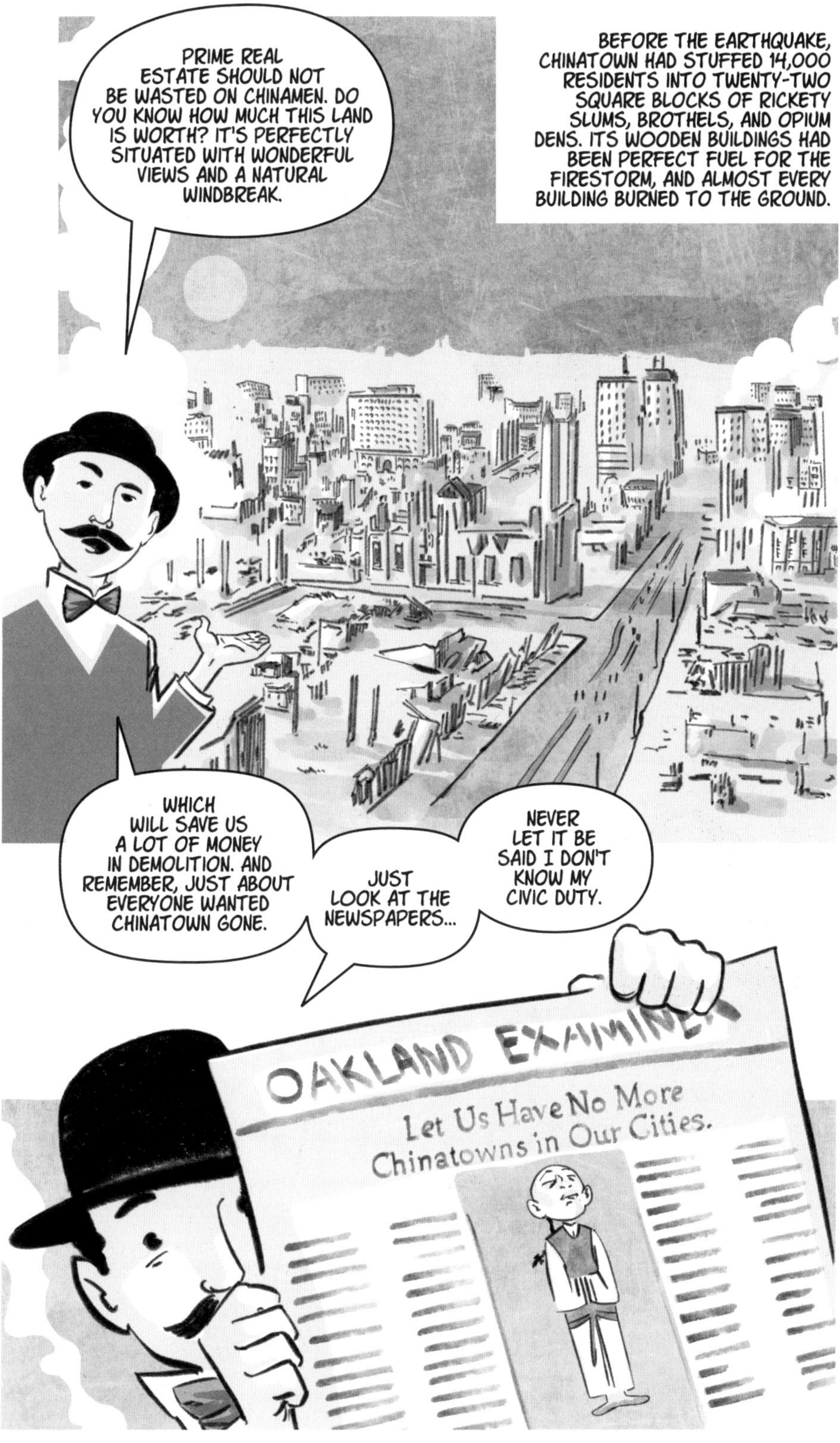
PRIME REAL ESTATE SHOULD NOT BE WASTED ON CHINAMEN. DO YOU KNOW HOW MUCH THIS LAND IS WORTH? IT'S PERFECTLY SITUATED WITH WONDERFUL VIEWS AND A NATURAL WINDBREAK.
BEFORE THE EARTHQUAKE, CHINATOWN HAD STUFFED 14,000 RESIDENTS INTO TWENTY-TWO SQUARE BLOCKS OF RICKETY SLUMS, BROTHELS, AND OPIUM DENS. ITS WOODEN BUILDINGS HAD BEEN PERFECT FUEL FOR THE FIRESTORM, AND ALMOST EVERY BUILDING BURNED TO THE GROUND.
WHICH WILL SAVE US A LOT OF MONEY IN DEMOLITION. AND REMEMBER, JUST ABOUT EVERYONE WANTED CHINATOWN GONE.
NEVER LET IT BE SAID I DON'T KNOW MY CIVIC DUTY.
JUST LOOK AT THE NEWSPAPERS...
OAKLAND EXAMINER
Let Us Have No More Chinatowns in Our Cities.

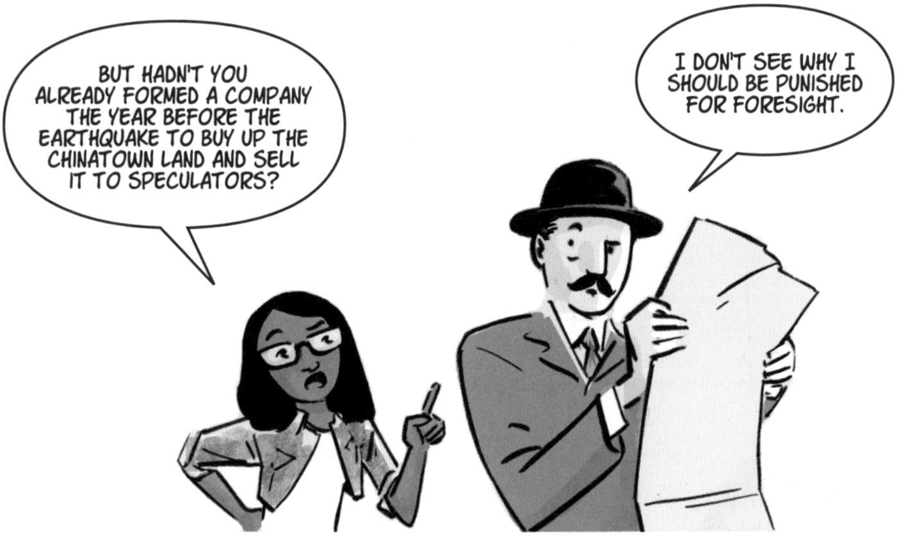
BUT HADN'T YOU ALREADY FORMED A COMPANY THE YEAR BEFORE THE EARTHQUAKE TO BUY UP THE CHINATOWN LAND AND SELL IT TO SPECULATORS?
I DON'T SEE WHY I SHOULD BE PUNISHED FOR FORESIGHT.

BUT EVEN ABE RUEF WAS AWARE THAT THE CHINESE HAD TO LIVE SOMEWHERE.

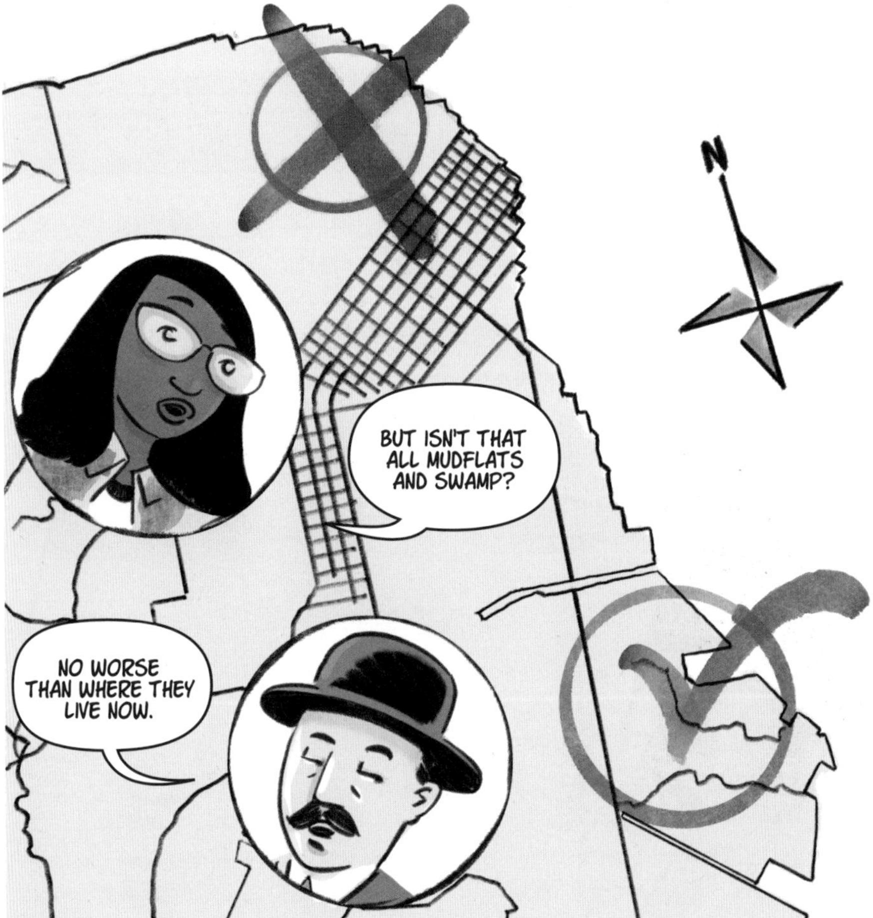
N
BUT ISN'T THAT ALL MUDFLATS AND SWAMP?
NO WORSE THAN WHERE THEY LIVE NOW.

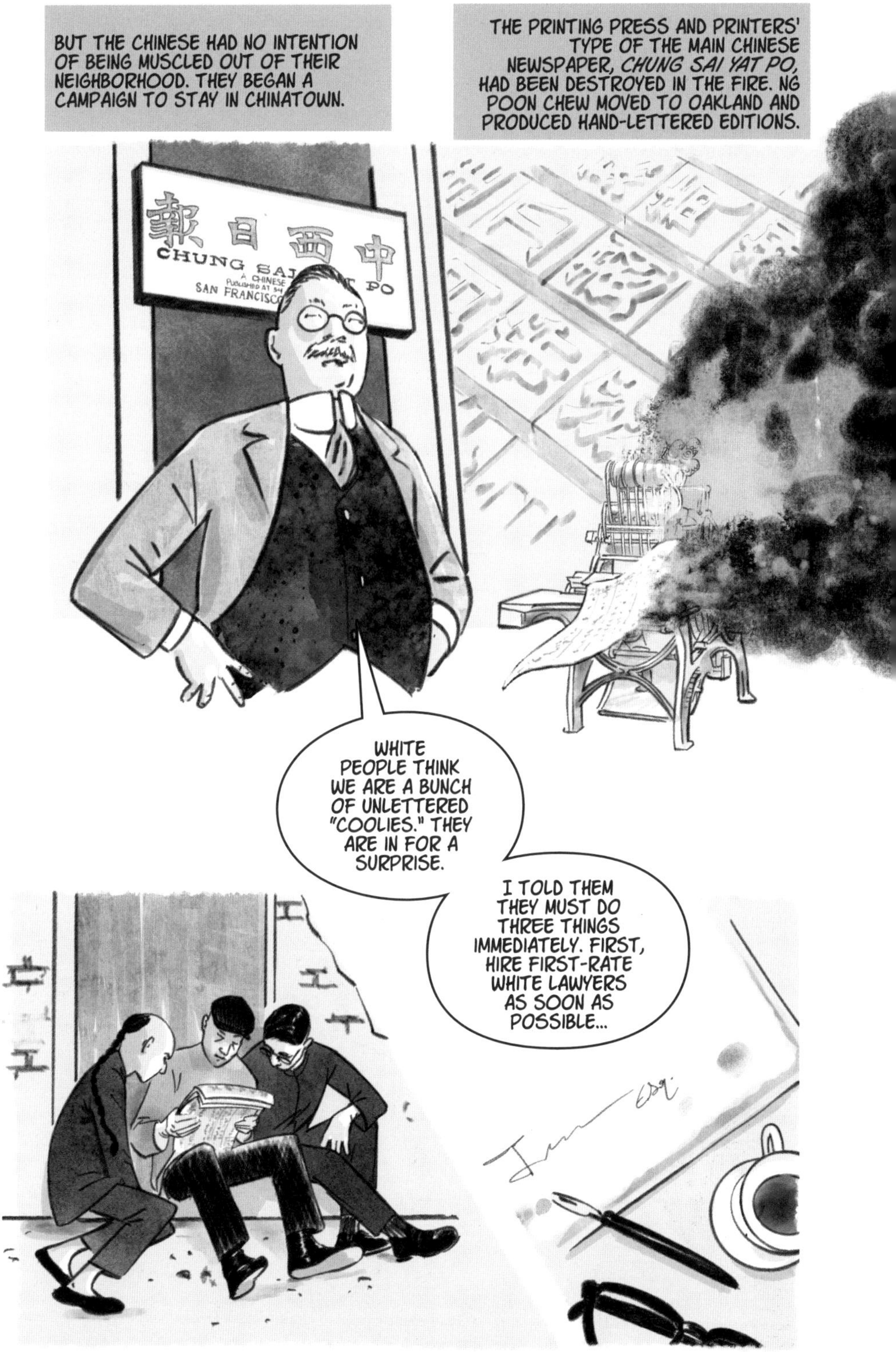

BUT THE CHINESE HAD NO INTENTION OF BEING MUSCLED OUT OF THEIR NEIGHBORHOOD. THEY BEGAN A CAMPAIGN TO STAY IN CHINATOWN.
THE PRINTING PRESS AND PRINTERS' TYPE OF THE MAIN CHINESE NEWSPAPER, *CHUNG SAI YAT PO,* HAD BEEN DESTROYED IN THE FIRE. NG POON CHEW MOVED TO OAKLAND AND PRODUCED HAND-LETTERED EDITIONS.
WHITE PEOPLE THINK WE ARE A BUNCH OF UNLETTERED "COOLIES." THEY ARE IN FOR A SURPRISE.
I TOLD THEM THEY MUST DO THREE THINGS IMMEDIATELY. FIRST, HIRE FIRST-RATE WHITE LAWYERS AS SOON AS POSSIBLE...

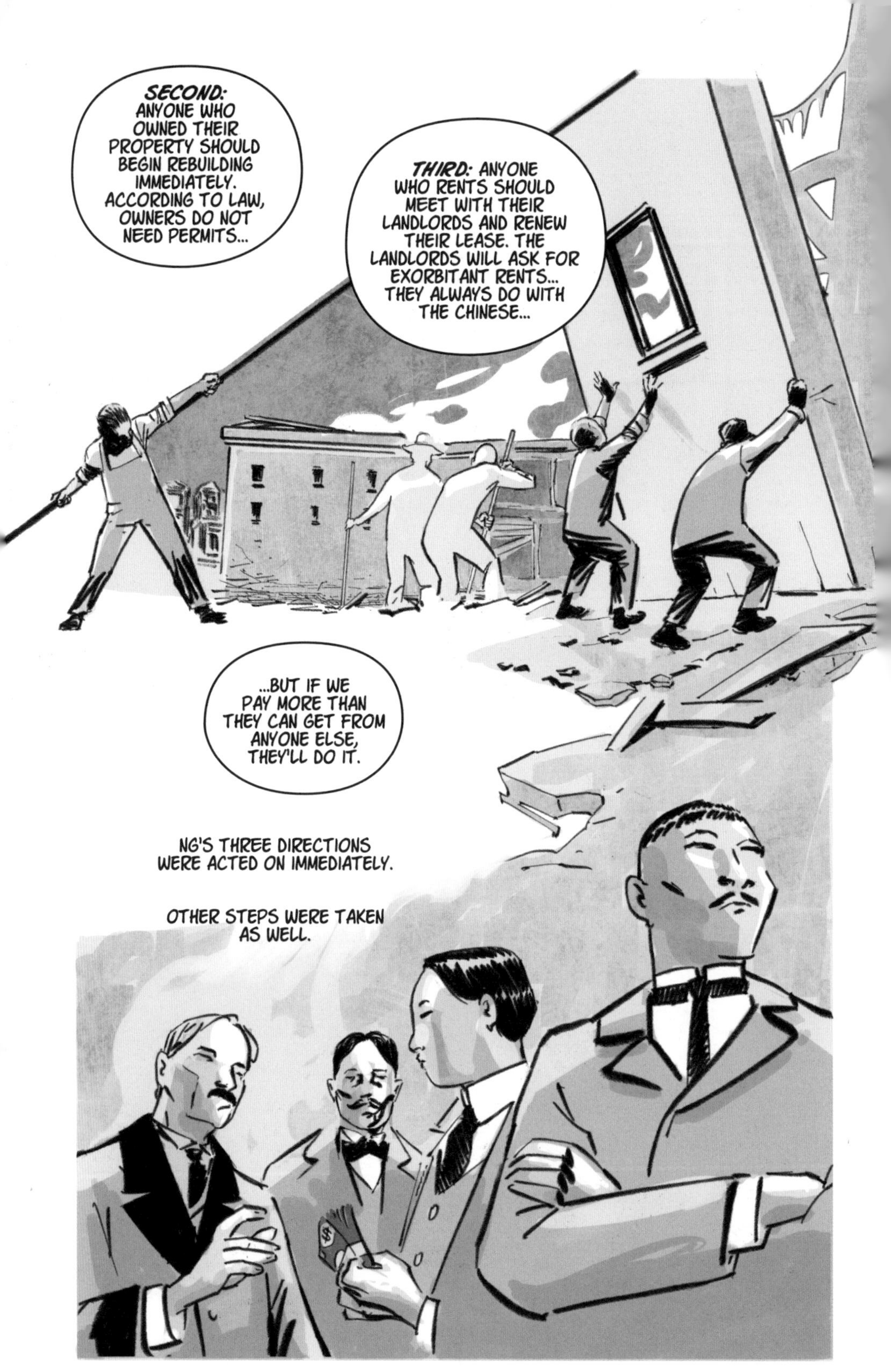
SECOND: ANYONE WHO OWNED THEIR PROPERTY SHOULD BEGIN REBUILDING IMMEDIATELY. ACCORDING TO LAW, OWNERS DO NOT NEED PERMITS...
THIRD: ANYONE WHO RENTS SHOULD MEET WITH THEIR LANDLORDS AND RENEW THEIR LEASE. THE LANDLORDS WILL ASK FOR EXORBITANT RENTS... THEY ALWAYS DO WITH THE CHINESE...
...BUT IF WE PAY MORE THAN THEY CAN GET FROM ANYONE ELSE, THEY'LL DO IT.
NG'S THREE DIRECTIONS WERE ACTED ON IMMEDIATELY.
OTHER STEPS WERE TAKEN AS WELL.

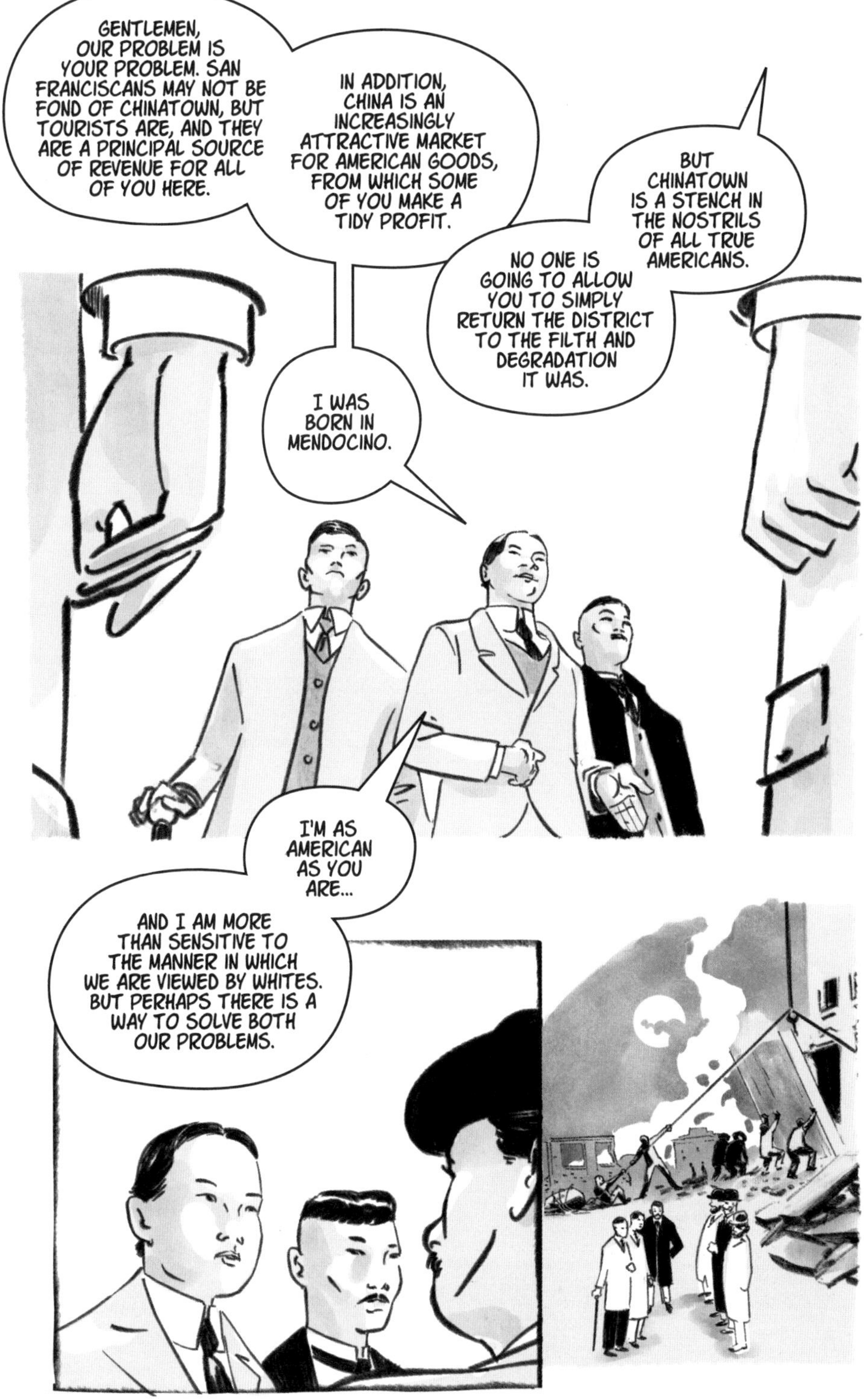
GENTLEMEN, OUR PROBLEM IS YOUR PROBLEM. SAN FRANCISCANS MAY NOT BE FOND OF CHINATOWN, BUT TOURISTS ARE, AND THEY ARE A PRINCIPAL SOURCE OF REVENUE FOR ALL OF YOU HERE.
IN ADDITION, CHINA IS AN INCREASINGLY ATTRACTIVE MARKET FOR AMERICAN GOODS, FROM WHICH SOME OF YOU MAKE A TIDY PROFIT.
BUT CHINATOWN IS A STENCH IN THE NOSTRILS OF ALL TRUE AMERICANS.
NO ONE IS GOING TO ALLOW YOU TO SIMPLY RETURN THE DISTRICT TO THE FILTH AND DEGRADATION IT WAS.
I WAS BORN IN MENDOCINO.
I'M AS AMERICAN AS YOU ARE...
AND I AM MORE THAN SENSITIVE TO THE MANNER IN WHICH WE ARE VIEWED BY WHITES. BUT PERHAPS THERE IS A WAY TO SOLVE BOTH OUR PROBLEMS.

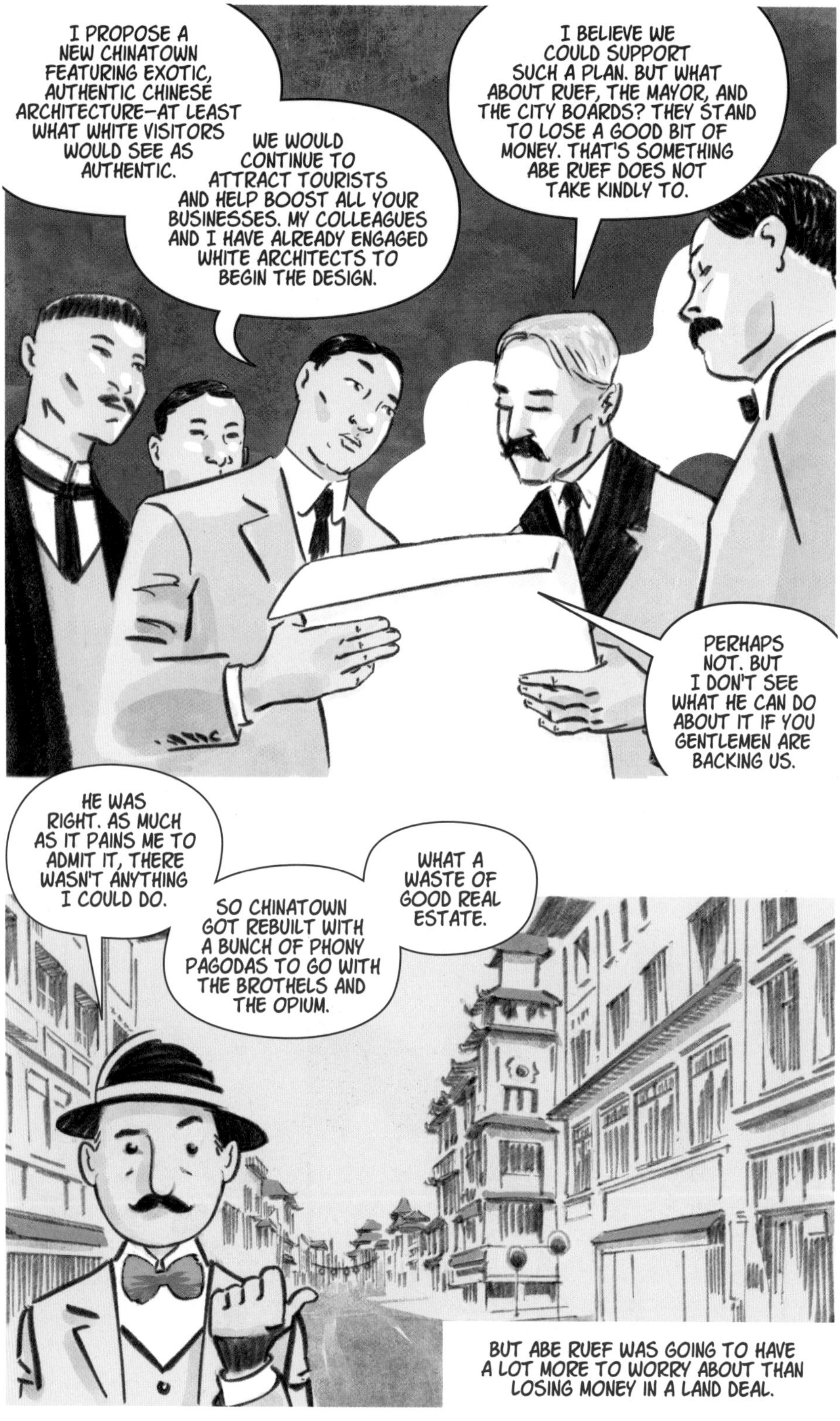
I PROPOSE A NEW CHINATOWN FEATURING EXOTIC, AUTHENTIC CHINESE ARCHITECTURE—AT LEAST WHAT WHITE VISITORS WOULD SEE AS AUTHENTIC.
WE WOULD CONTINUE TO ATTRACT TOURISTS AND HELP BOOST ALL YOUR BUSINESSES. MY COLLEAGUES AND I HAVE ALREADY ENGAGED WHITE ARCHITECTS TO BEGIN THE DESIGN.
I BELIEVE WE COULD SUPPORT SUCH A PLAN. BUT WHAT ABOUT RUEF, THE MAYOR, AND THE CITY BOARDS? THEY STAND TO LOSE A GOOD BIT OF MONEY. THAT'S SOMETHING ABE RUEF DOES NOT TAKE KINDLY TO.
PERHAPS NOT. BUT I DON'T SEE WHAT HE CAN DO ABOUT IT IF YOU GENTLEMEN ARE BACKING US.
HE WAS RIGHT. AS MUCH AS IT PAINS ME TO ADMIT IT, THERE WASN'T ANYTHING I COULD DO.
SO CHINATOWN GOT REBUILT WITH A BUNCH OF PHONY PAGODAS TO GO WITH THE BROTHELS AND THE OPIUM.
WHAT A WASTE OF GOOD REAL ESTATE.
BUT ABE RUEF WAS GOING TO HAVE A LOT MORE TO WORRY ABOUT THAN LOSING MONEY IN A LAND DEAL.

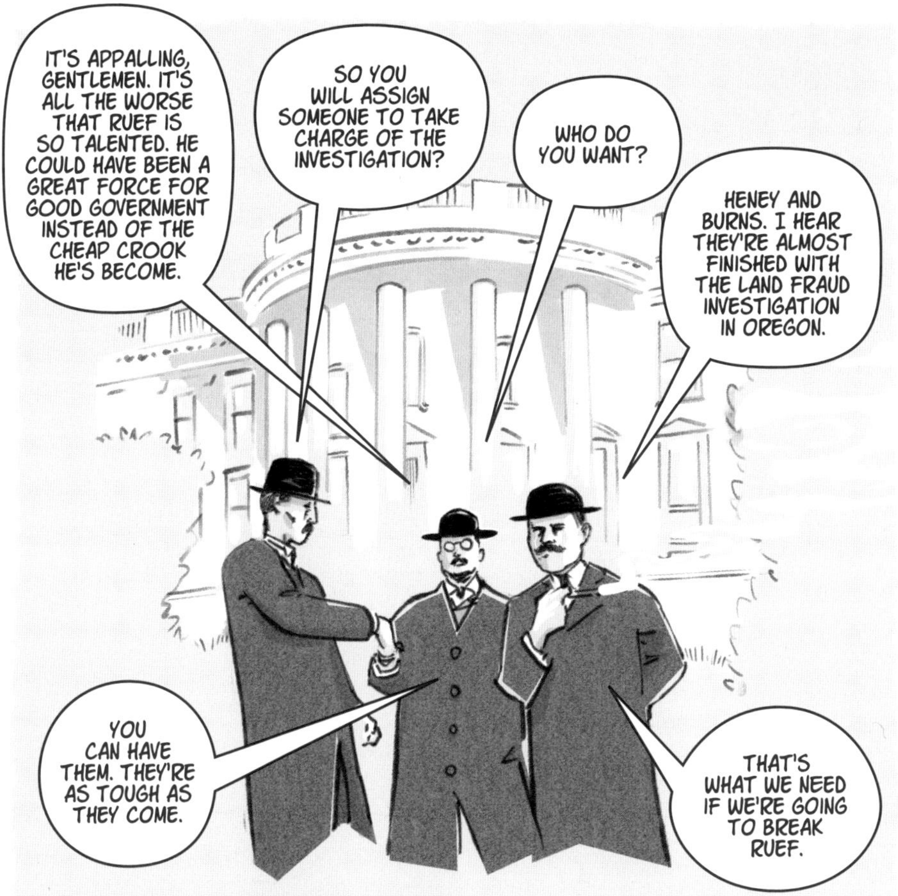
IT'S APPALLING, GENTLEMEN. IT'S ALL THE WORSE THAT RUEF IS SO TALENTED. HE COULD HAVE BEEN A GREAT FORCE FOR GOOD GOVERNMENT INSTEAD OF THE CHEAP CROOK HE'S BECOME.
SO YOU WILL ASSIGN SOMEONE TO TAKE CHARGE OF THE INVESTIGATION?
WHO DO YOU WANT?
HENEY AND BURNS. I HEAR THEY'RE ALMOST FINISHED WITH THE LAND FRAUD INVESTIGATION IN OREGON.
YOU CAN HAVE THEM. THEY'RE AS TOUGH AS THEY COME.
THAT'S WHAT WE NEED IF WE'RE GOING TO BREAK RUEF.

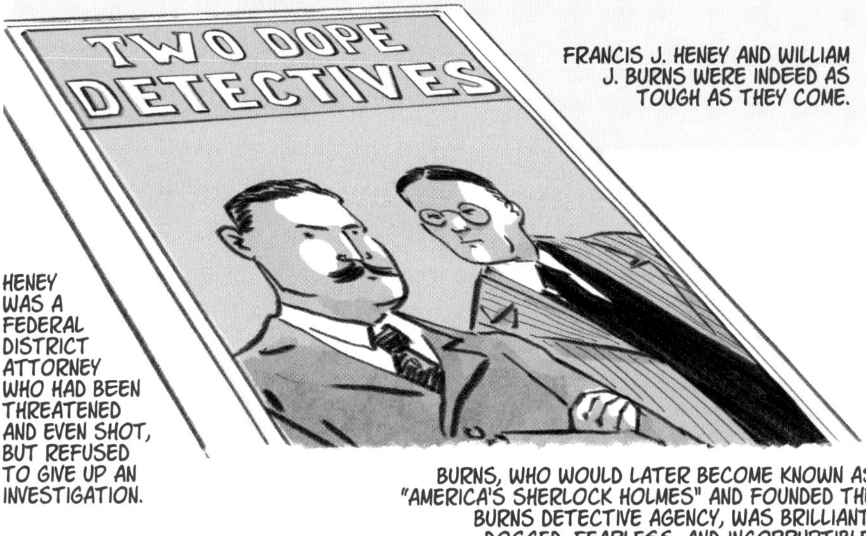
TWO DOPE DETECTIVES

FRANCIS J. HENEY AND WILLIAM J. BURNS WERE INDEED AS TOUGH AS THEY COME.

HENEY WAS A FEDERAL DISTRICT ATTORNEY WHO HAD BEEN THREATENED AND EVEN SHOT, BUT REFUSED TO GIVE UP AN INVESTIGATION.

BURNS, WHO WOULD LATER BECOME KNOWN AS "AMERICA'S SHERLOCK HOLMES" AND FOUNDED THE BURNS DETECTIVE AGENCY, WAS BRILLIANT, DOGGED, FEARLESS, AND INCORRUPTIBLE.

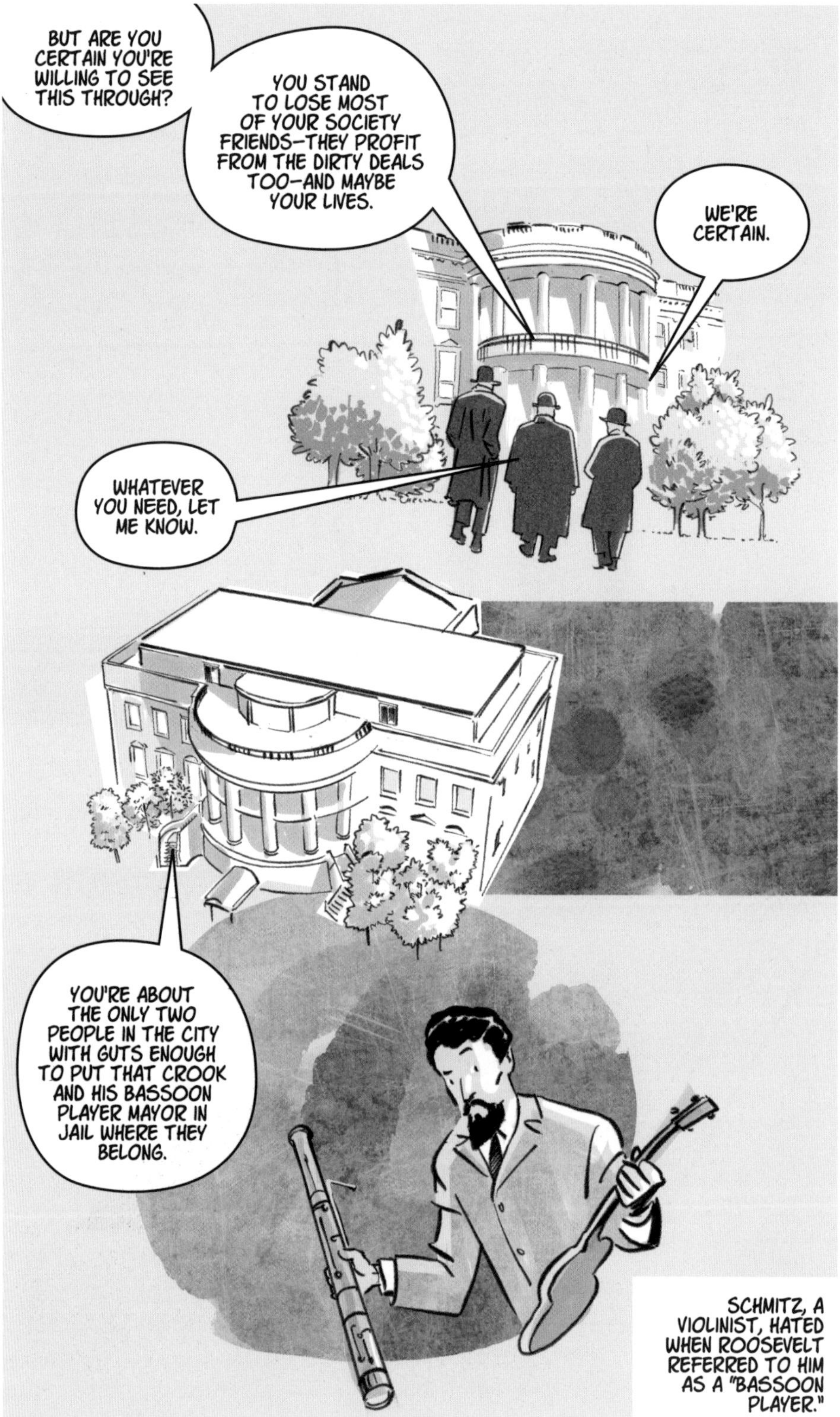
BUT ARE YOU CERTAIN YOU'RE WILLING TO SEE THIS THROUGH?
YOU STAND TO LOSE MOST OF YOUR SOCIETY FRIENDS—THEY PROFIT FROM THE DIRTY DEALS TOO—AND MAYBE YOUR LIVES.
WE'RE CERTAIN.
WHATEVER YOU NEED, LET ME KNOW.
YOU'RE ABOUT THE ONLY TWO PEOPLE IN THE CITY WITH GUTS ENOUGH TO PUT THAT CROOK AND HIS BASSOON PLAYER MAYOR IN JAIL WHERE THEY BELONG.
SCHMITZ, A VIOLINIST, HATED WHEN ROOSEVELT REFERRED TO HIM AS A "BASSOON PLAYER."

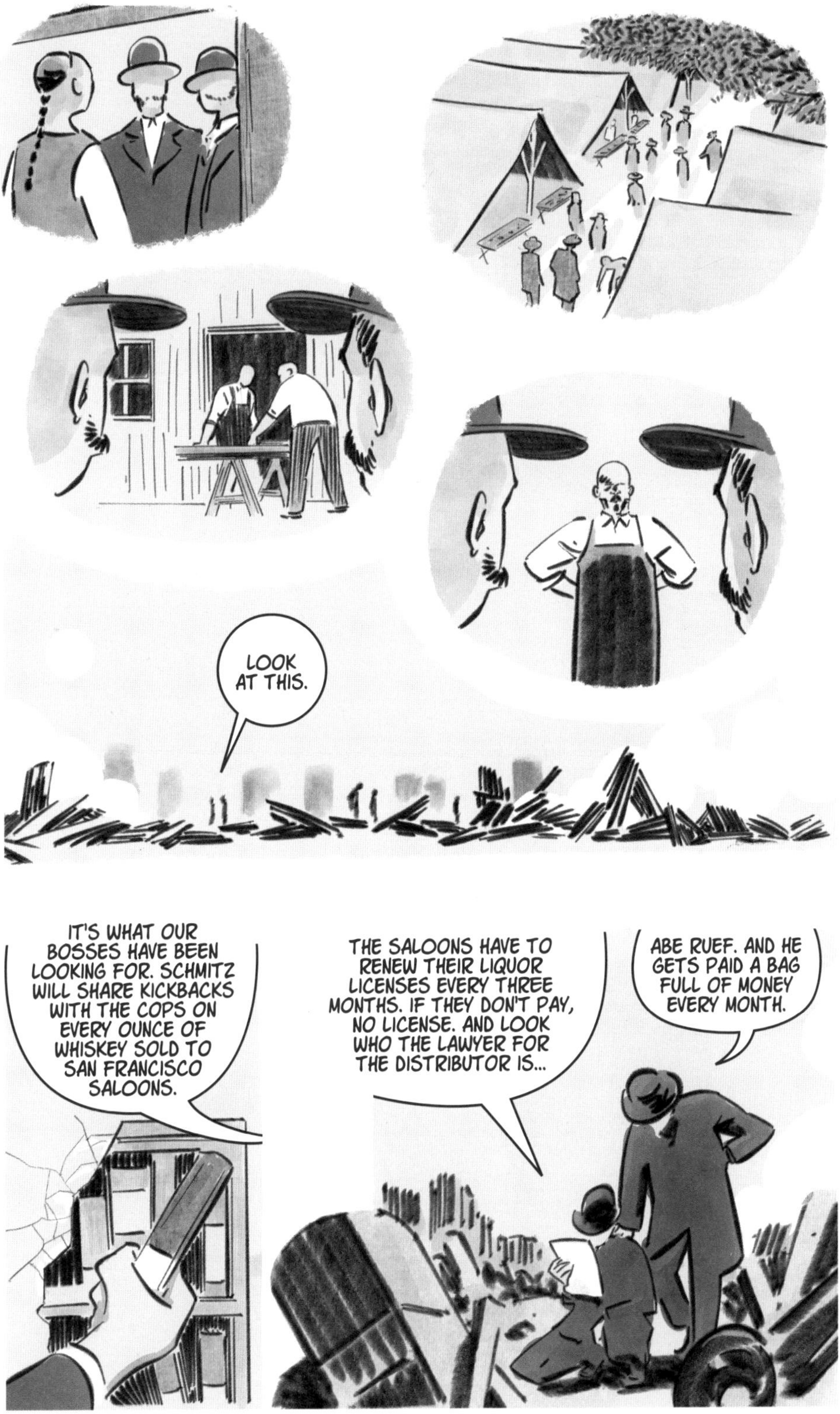
LOOK AT THIS.
IT'S WHAT OUR BOSSES HAVE BEEN LOOKING FOR. SCHMITZ WILL SHARE KICKBACKS WITH THE COPS ON EVERY OUNCE OF WHISKEY SOLD TO SAN FRANCISCO SALOONS.
THE SALOONS HAVE TO RENEW THEIR LIQUOR LICENSES EVERY THREE MONTHS. IF THEY DON'T PAY, NO LICENSE. AND LOOK WHO THE LAWYER FOR THE DISTRIBUTOR IS...
ABE RUEF. AND HE GETS PAID A BAG FULL OF MONEY EVERY MONTH.

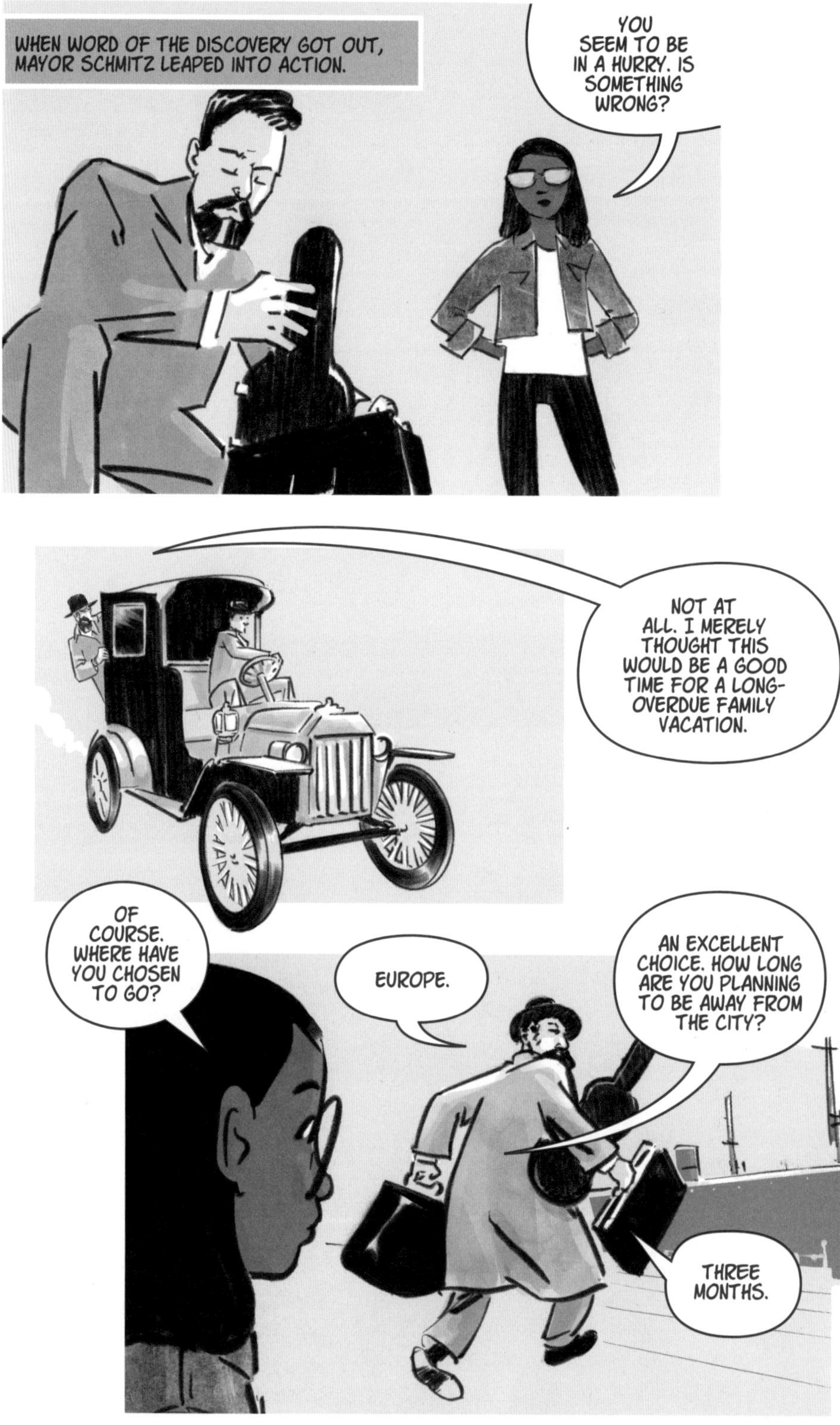
WHEN WORD OF THE DISCOVERY GOT OUT, MAYOR SCHMITZ LEAPED INTO ACTION.
YOU SEEM TO BE IN A HURRY. IS SOMETHING WRONG?
NOT AT ALL. I MERELY THOUGHT THIS WOULD BE A GOOD TIME FOR A LONG-OVERDUE FAMILY VACATION.
OF COURSE. WHERE HAVE YOU CHOSEN TO GO?
EUROPE.
AN EXCELLENT CHOICE. HOW LONG ARE YOU PLANNING TO BE AWAY FROM THE CITY?
THREE MONTHS.

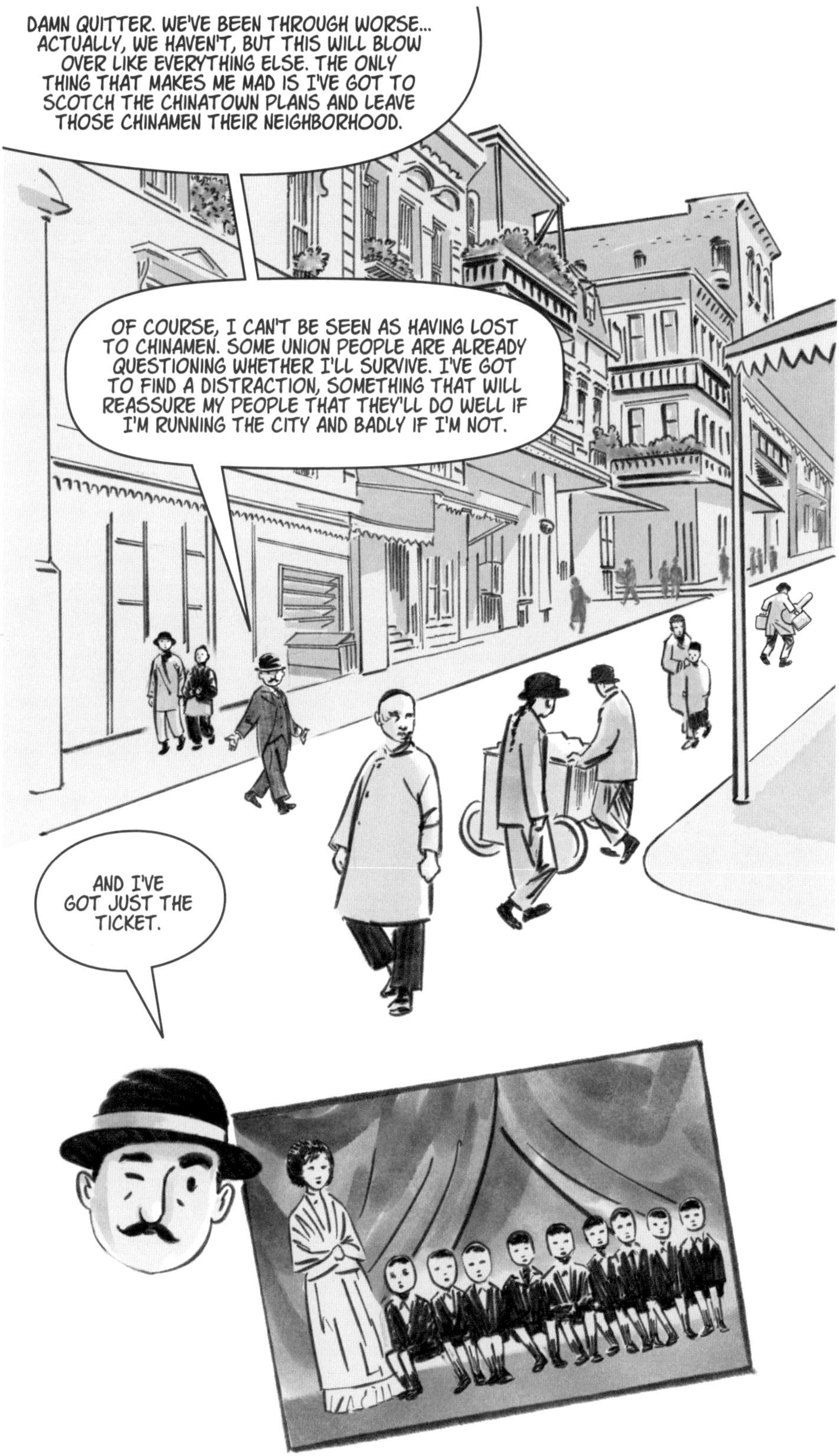
DAMN QUITTER. WE'VE BEEN THROUGH WORSE... ACTUALLY, WE HAVEN'T, BUT THIS WILL BLOW OVER LIKE EVERYTHING ELSE. THE ONLY THING THAT MAKES ME MAD IS I'VE GOT TO SCOTCH THE CHINATOWN PLANS AND LEAVE THOSE CHINAMEN THEIR NEIGHBORHOOD.
OF COURSE, I CAN'T BE SEEN AS HAVING LOST TO CHINAMEN. SOME UNION PEOPLE ARE ALREADY QUESTIONING WHETHER I'LL SURVIVE. I'VE GOT TO FIND A DISTRACTION, SOMETHING THAT WILL REASSURE MY PEOPLE THAT THEY'LL DO WELL IF I'M RUNNING THE CITY AND BADLY IF I'M NOT.
AND I'VE GOT JUST THE TICKET.

Offices of the San Francisco School Board, October 11, 1906

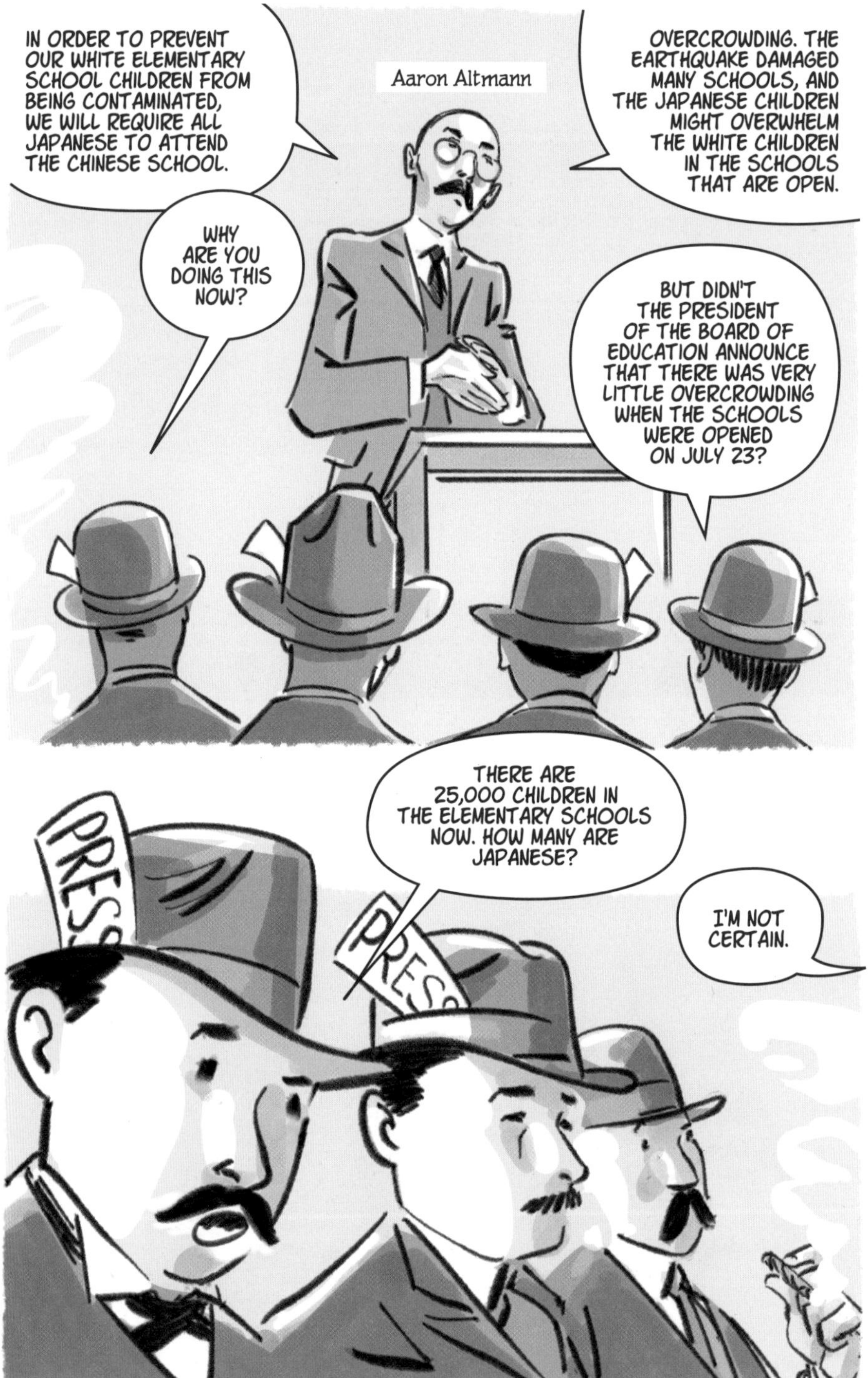
IN ORDER TO PREVENT OUR WHITE ELEMENTARY SCHOOL CHILDREN FROM BEING CONTAMINATED, WE WILL REQUIRE ALL JAPANESE TO ATTEND THE CHINESE SCHOOL.
Aaron Altmann
WHY ARE YOU DOING THIS NOW?
OVERCROWDING. THE EARTHQUAKE DAMAGED MANY SCHOOLS, AND THE JAPANESE CHILDREN MIGHT OVERWHELM THE WHITE CHILDREN IN THE SCHOOLS THAT ARE OPEN.
BUT DIDN'T THE PRESIDENT OF THE BOARD OF EDUCATION ANNOUNCE THAT THERE WAS VERY LITTLE OVERCROWDING WHEN THE SCHOOLS WERE OPENED ON JULY 23?
THERE ARE 25,000 CHILDREN IN THE ELEMENTARY SCHOOLS NOW. HOW MANY ARE JAPANESE?
I'M NOT CERTAIN.

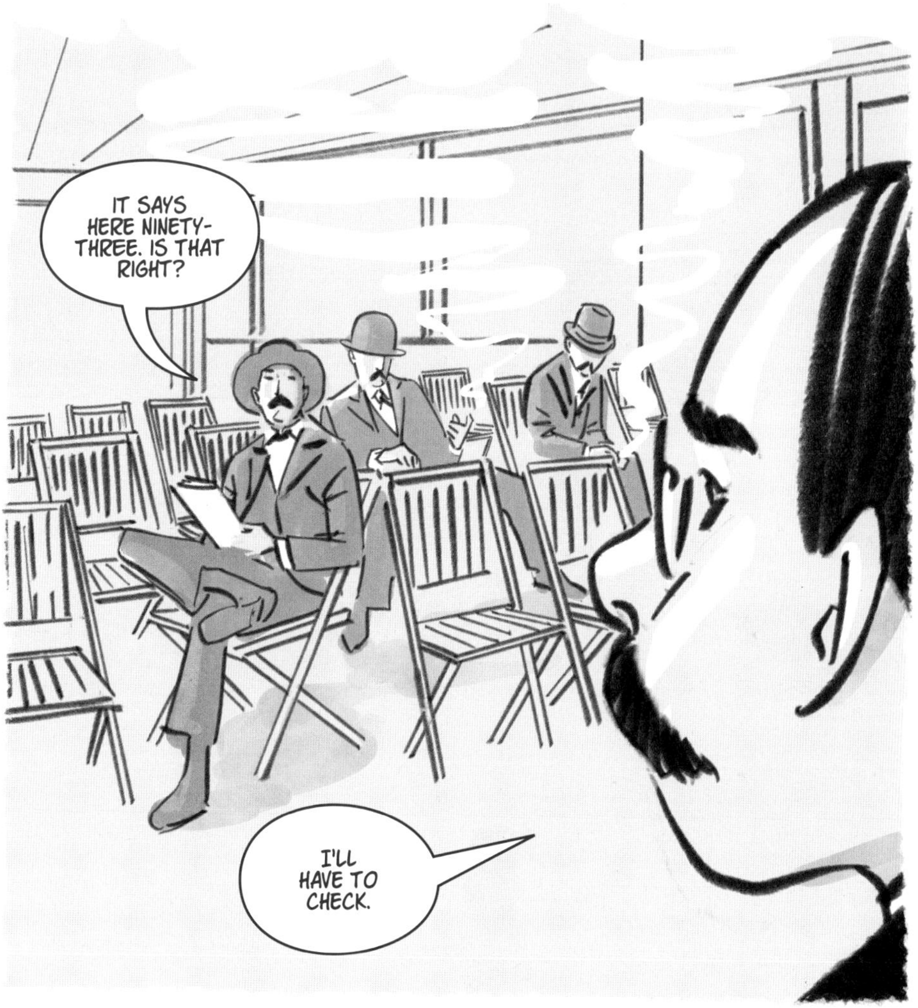
IT SAYS HERE NINETY-THREE. IS THAT RIGHT?
I'LL HAVE TO CHECK.

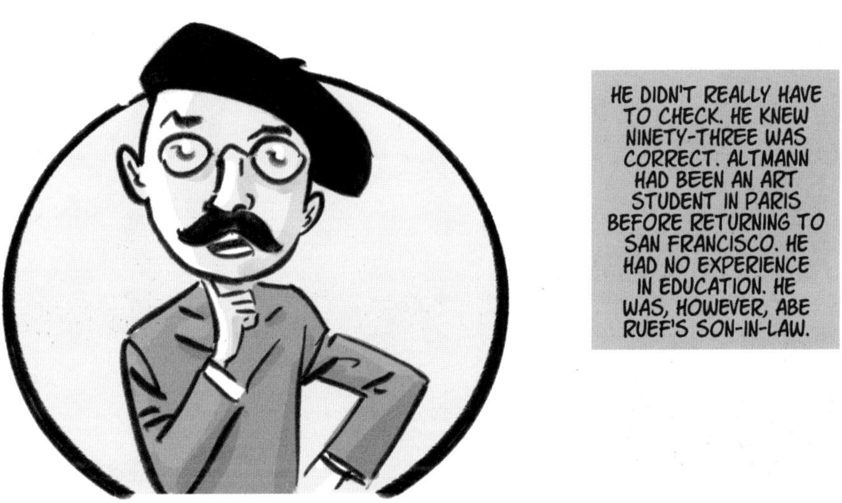
HE DIDN'T REALLY HAVE TO CHECK. HE KNEW NINETY-THREE WAS CORRECT. ALTMANN HAD BEEN AN ART STUDENT IN PARIS BEFORE RETURNING TO SAN FRANCISCO. HE HAD NO EXPERIENCE IN EDUCATION. HE WAS, HOWEVER, ABE RUEF'S SON-IN-LAW.

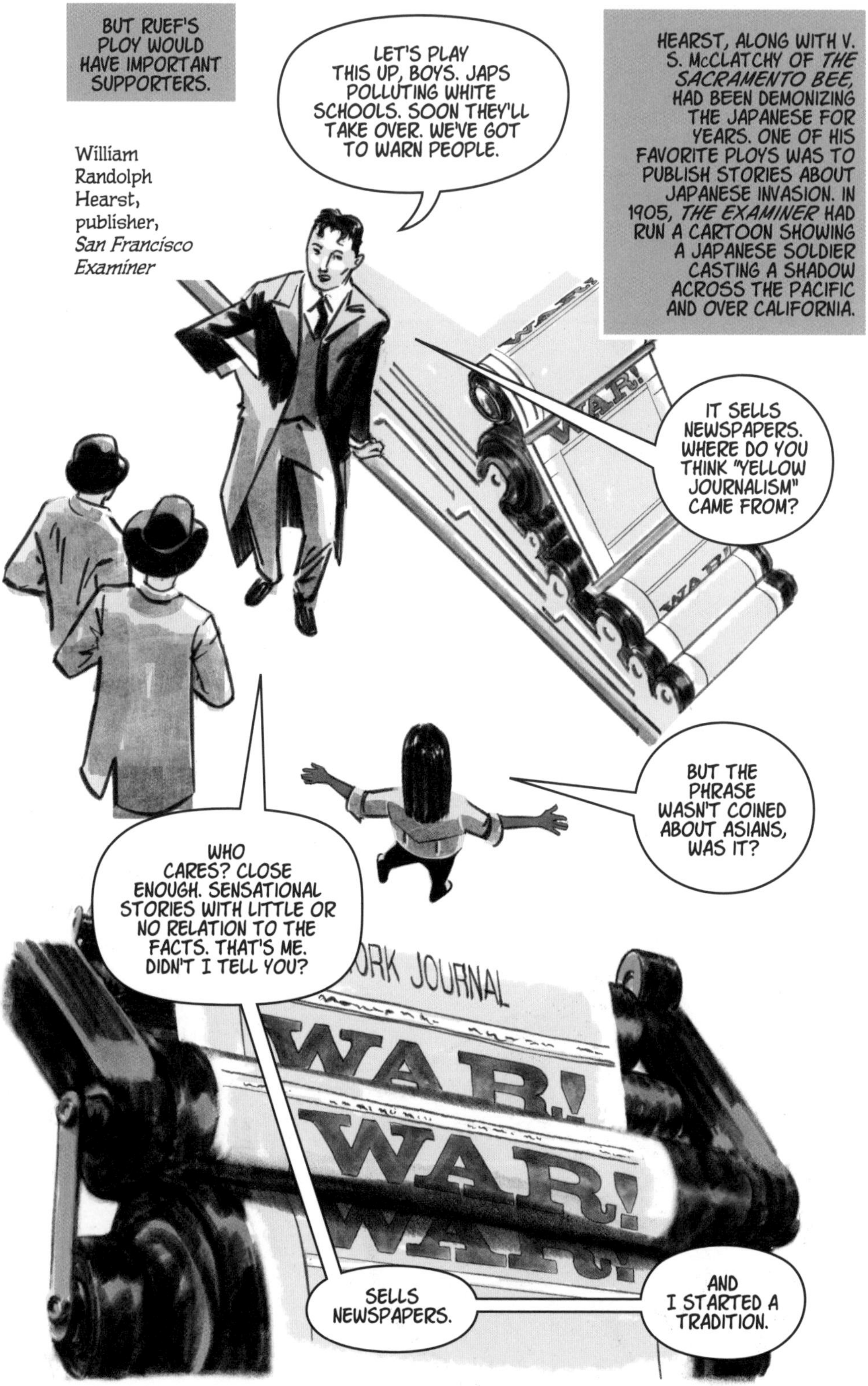
BUT RUEF'S PLOY WOULD HAVE IMPORTANT SUPPORTERS.
LET'S PLAY THIS UP, BOYS. JAPS POLLUTING WHITE SCHOOLS. SOON THEY'LL TAKE OVER. WE'VE GOT TO WARN PEOPLE.
HEARST, ALONG WITH V. S. McCLATCHY OF *THE SACRAMENTO BEE,* HAD BEEN DEMONIZING THE JAPANESE FOR YEARS. ONE OF HIS FAVORITE PLOYS WAS TO PUBLISH STORIES ABOUT JAPANESE INVASION. IN 1905, *THE EXAMINER* HAD RUN A CARTOON SHOWING A JAPANESE SOLDIER CASTING A SHADOW ACROSS THE PACIFIC AND OVER CALIFORNIA.
William Randolph Hearst, publisher, *San Francisco Examiner*
IT SELLS NEWSPAPERS. WHERE DO YOU THINK "YELLOW JOURNALISM" CAME FROM?
BUT THE PHRASE WASN'T COINED ABOUT ASIANS, WAS IT?
WHO CARES? CLOSE ENOUGH. SENSATIONAL STORIES WITH LITTLE OR NO RELATION TO THE FACTS. THAT'S ME. DIDN'T I TELL YOU?
ORK JOURNAL
WAR!
WAR!
SELLS NEWSPAPERS.
AND I STARTED A TRADITION.

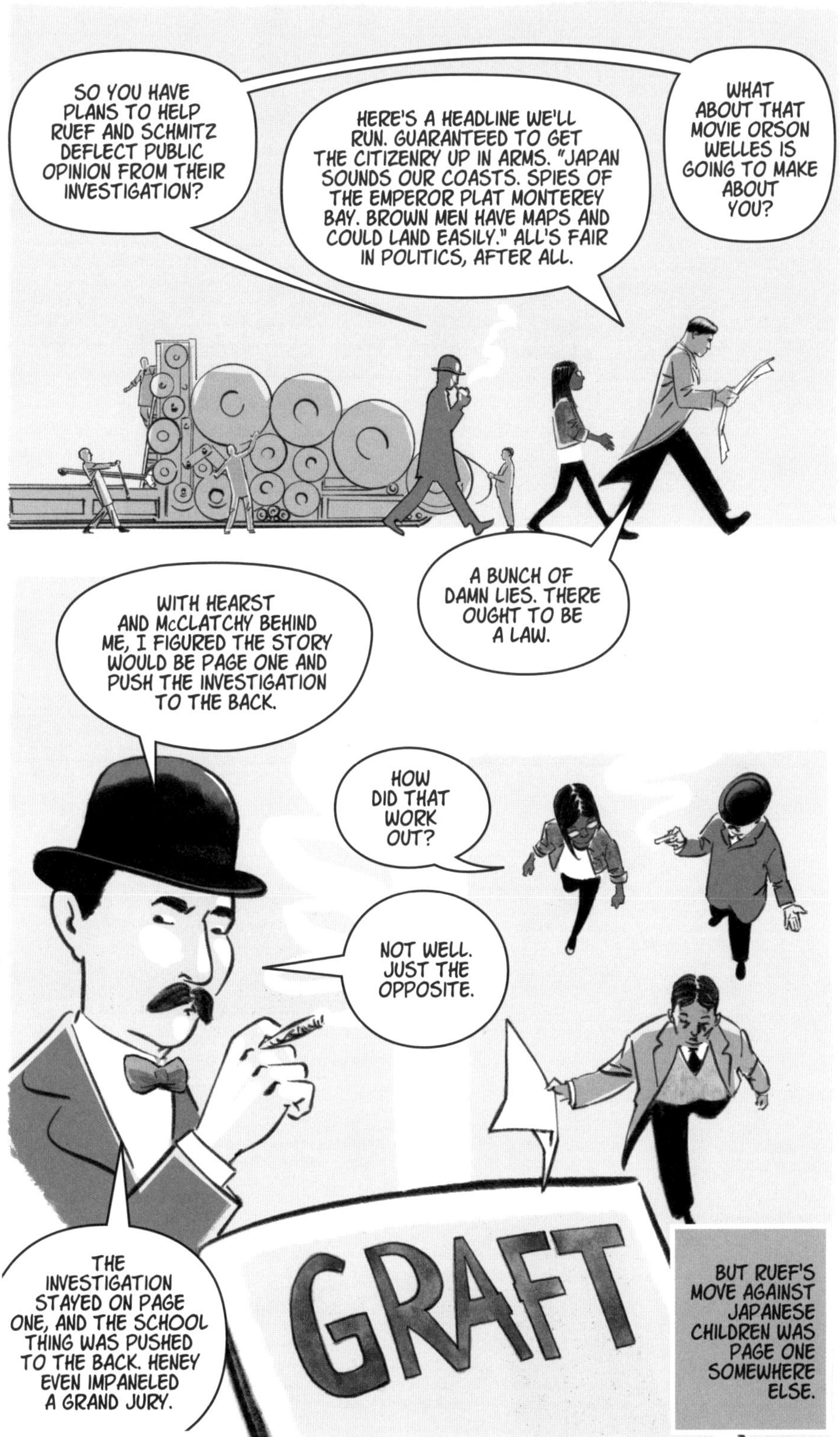
SO YOU HAVE PLANS TO HELP RUEF AND SCHMITZ DEFLECT PUBLIC OPINION FROM THEIR INVESTIGATION?
HERE'S A HEADLINE WE'LL RUN. GUARANTEED TO GET THE CITIZENRY UP IN ARMS. "JAPAN SOUNDS OUR COASTS. SPIES OF THE EMPEROR PLAT MONTEREY BAY. BROWN MEN HAVE MAPS AND COULD LAND EASILY." ALL'S FAIR IN POLITICS, AFTER ALL.
WHAT ABOUT THAT MOVIE ORSON WELLES IS GOING TO MAKE ABOUT YOU?
A BUNCH OF DAMN LIES. THERE OUGHT TO BE A LAW.
WITH HEARST AND McCLATCHY BEHIND ME, I FIGURED THE STORY WOULD BE PAGE ONE AND PUSH THE INVESTIGATION TO THE BACK.
HOW DID THAT WORK OUT?
NOT WELL. JUST THE OPPOSITE.
THE INVESTIGATION STAYED ON PAGE ONE, AND THE SCHOOL THING WAS PUSHED TO THE BACK. HENEY EVEN IMPANELED A GRAND JURY.
GRAFT
BUT RUEF'S MOVE AGAINST JAPANESE CHILDREN WAS PAGE ONE SOMEWHERE ELSE.

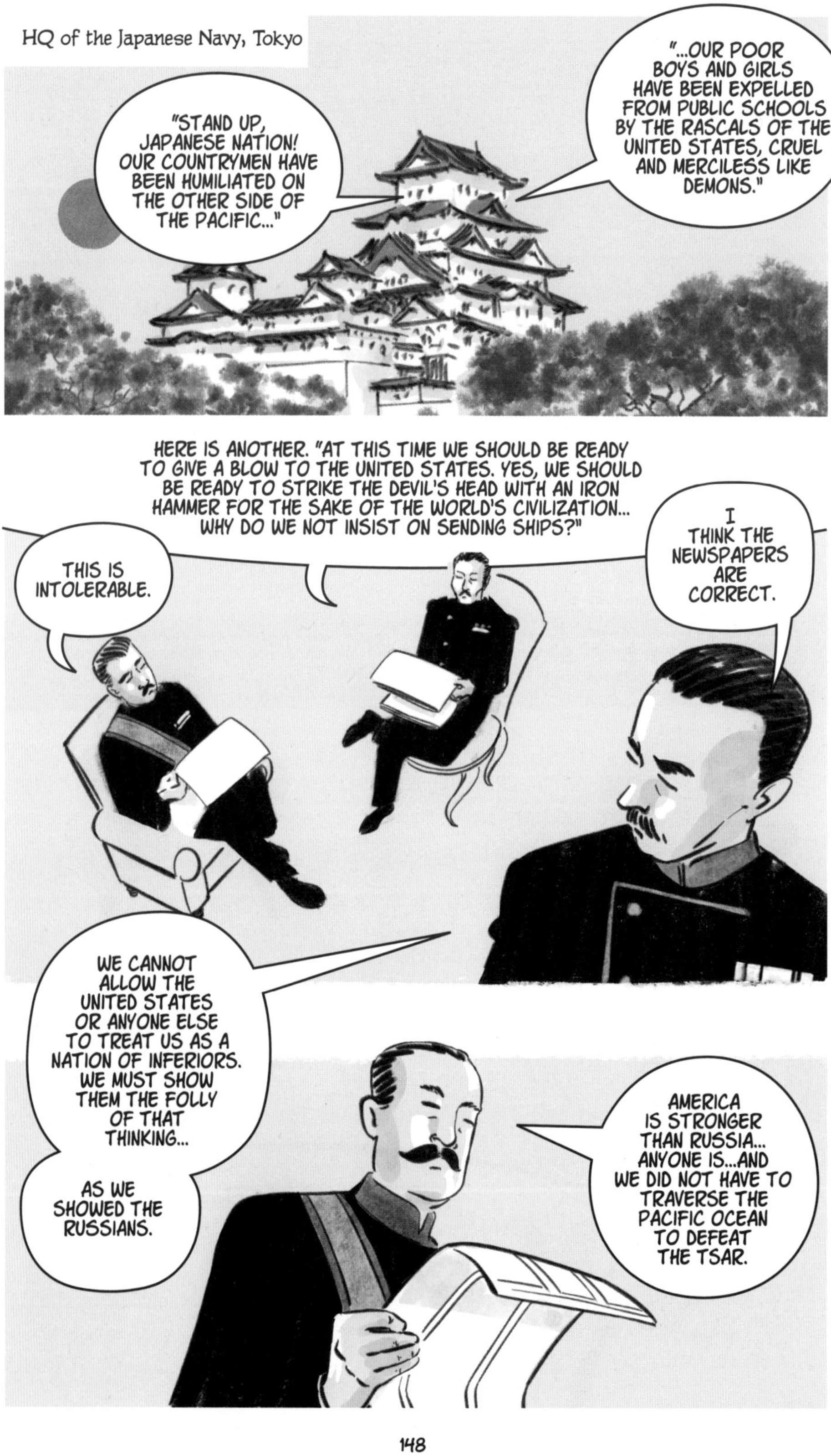
HQ of the Japanese Navy, Tokyo
"STAND UP, JAPANESE NATION! OUR COUNTRYMEN HAVE BEEN HUMILIATED ON THE OTHER SIDE OF THE PACIFIC..."
"...OUR POOR BOYS AND GIRLS HAVE BEEN EXPELLED FROM PUBLIC SCHOOLS BY THE RASCALS OF THE UNITED STATES, CRUEL AND MERCILESS LIKE DEMONS."
HERE IS ANOTHER. "AT THIS TIME WE SHOULD BE READY TO GIVE A BLOW TO THE UNITED STATES. YES, WE SHOULD BE READY TO STRIKE THE DEVIL'S HEAD WITH AN IRON HAMMER FOR THE SAKE OF THE WORLD'S CIVILIZATION... WHY DO WE NOT INSIST ON SENDING SHIPS?"
THIS IS INTOLERABLE.
I THINK THE NEWSPAPERS ARE CORRECT.
WE CANNOT ALLOW THE UNITED STATES OR ANYONE ELSE TO TREAT US AS A NATION OF INFERIORS. WE MUST SHOW THEM THE FOLLY OF THAT THINKING...
AS WE SHOWED THE RUSSIANS.
AMERICA IS STRONGER THAN RUSSIA... ANYONE IS...AND WE DID NOT HAVE TO TRAVERSE THE PACIFIC OCEAN TO DEFEAT THE TSAR.

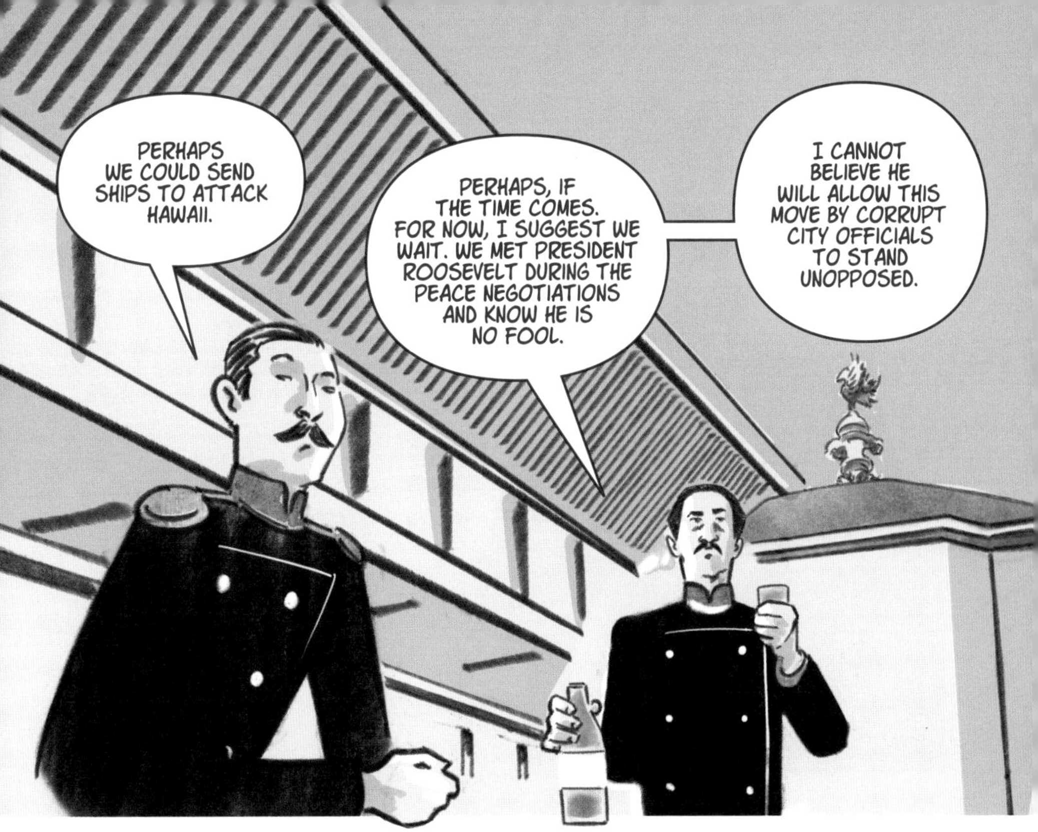
PERHAPS WE COULD SEND SHIPS TO ATTACK HAWAII.
PERHAPS, IF THE TIME COMES. FOR NOW, I SUGGEST WE WAIT. WE MET PRESIDENT ROOSEVELT DURING THE PEACE NEGOTIATIONS AND KNOW HE IS NO FOOL.
I CANNOT BELIEVE HE WILL ALLOW THIS MOVE BY CORRUPT CITY OFFICIALS TO STAND UNOPPOSED.

THE ADMIRAL WAS CORRECT.

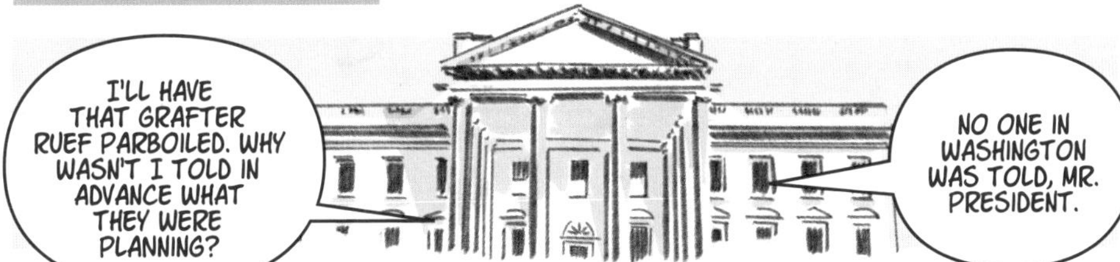
I'LL HAVE THAT GRAFTER RUEF PARBOILED. WHY WASN'T I TOLD IN ADVANCE WHAT THEY WERE PLANNING?
NO ONE IN WASHINGTON WAS TOLD, MR. PRESIDENT.

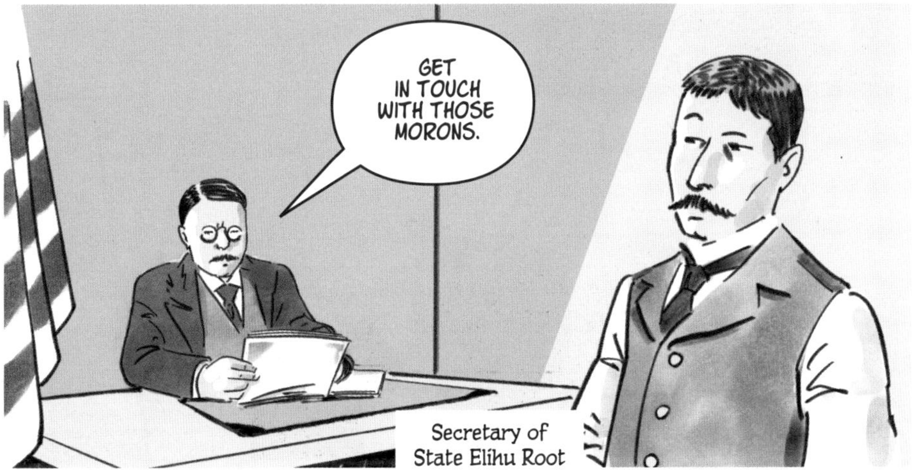
GET IN TOUCH WITH THOSE MORONS.
Secretary of State Elihu Root

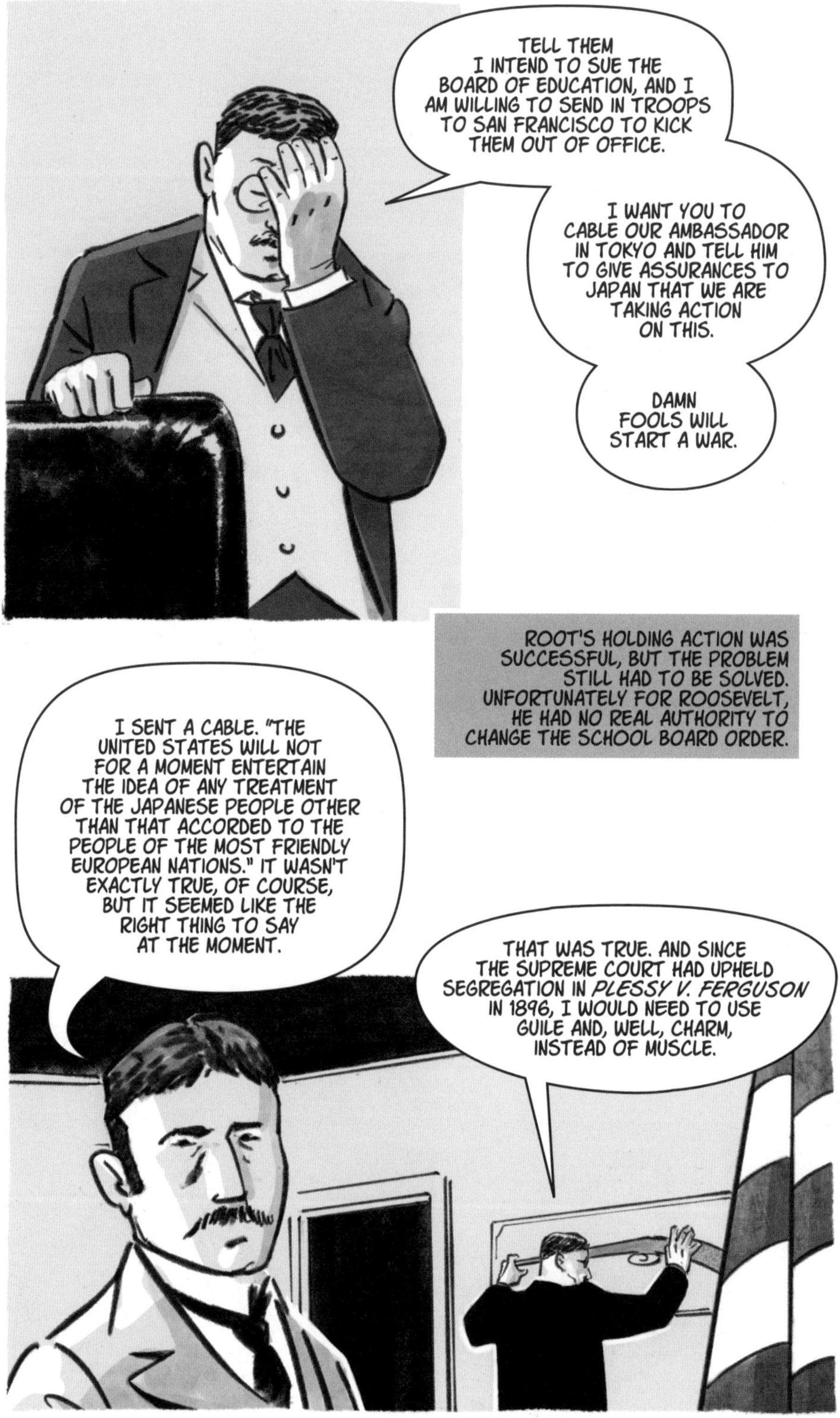
TELL THEM I INTEND TO SUE THE BOARD OF EDUCATION, AND I AM WILLING TO SEND IN TROOPS TO SAN FRANCISCO TO KICK THEM OUT OF OFFICE.
I WANT YOU TO CABLE OUR AMBASSADOR IN TOKYO AND TELL HIM TO GIVE ASSURANCES TO JAPAN THAT WE ARE TAKING ACTION ON THIS.
DAMN FOOLS WILL START A WAR.
ROOT'S HOLDING ACTION WAS SUCCESSFUL, BUT THE PROBLEM STILL HAD TO BE SOLVED. UNFORTUNATELY FOR ROOSEVELT, HE HAD NO REAL AUTHORITY TO CHANGE THE SCHOOL BOARD ORDER.
I SENT A CABLE. "THE UNITED STATES WILL NOT FOR A MOMENT ENTERTAIN THE IDEA OF ANY TREATMENT OF THE JAPANESE PEOPLE OTHER THAN THAT ACCORDED TO THE PEOPLE OF THE MOST FRIENDLY EUROPEAN NATIONS." IT WASN'T EXACTLY TRUE, OF COURSE, BUT IT SEEMED LIKE THE RIGHT THING TO SAY AT THE MOMENT.
THAT WAS TRUE. AND SINCE THE SUPREME COURT HAD UPHELD SEGREGATION IN *PLESSY V. FERGUSON* IN 1896, I WOULD NEED TO USE GUILE AND, WELL, CHARM, INSTEAD OF MUSCLE.

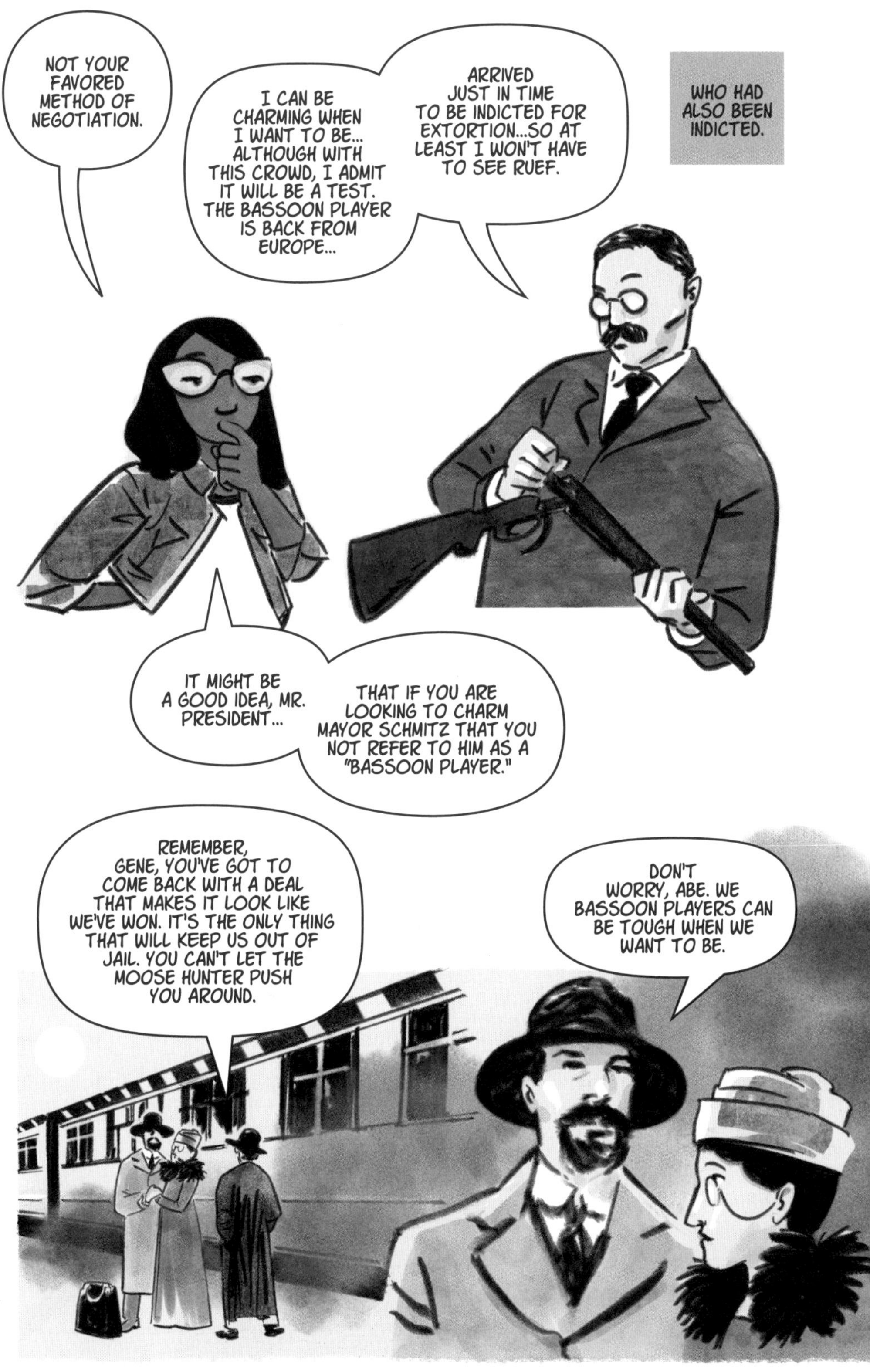
NOT YOUR FAVORED METHOD OF NEGOTIATION.
I CAN BE CHARMING WHEN I WANT TO BE... ALTHOUGH WITH THIS CROWD, I ADMIT IT WILL BE A TEST. THE BASSOON PLAYER IS BACK FROM EUROPE...
ARRIVED JUST IN TIME TO BE INDICTED FOR EXTORTION...SO AT LEAST I WON'T HAVE TO SEE RUEF.
WHO HAD ALSO BEEN INDICTED.
IT MIGHT BE A GOOD IDEA, MR. PRESIDENT...
THAT IF YOU ARE LOOKING TO CHARM MAYOR SCHMITZ THAT YOU NOT REFER TO HIM AS A "BASSOON PLAYER."
REMEMBER, GENE, YOU'VE GOT TO COME BACK WITH A DEAL THAT MAKES IT LOOK LIKE WE'VE WON. IT'S THE ONLY THING THAT WILL KEEP US OUT OF JAIL. YOU CAN'T LET THE MOOSE HUNTER PUSH YOU AROUND.
DON'T WORRY, ABE. WE BASSOON PLAYERS CAN BE TOUGH WHEN WE WANT TO BE.

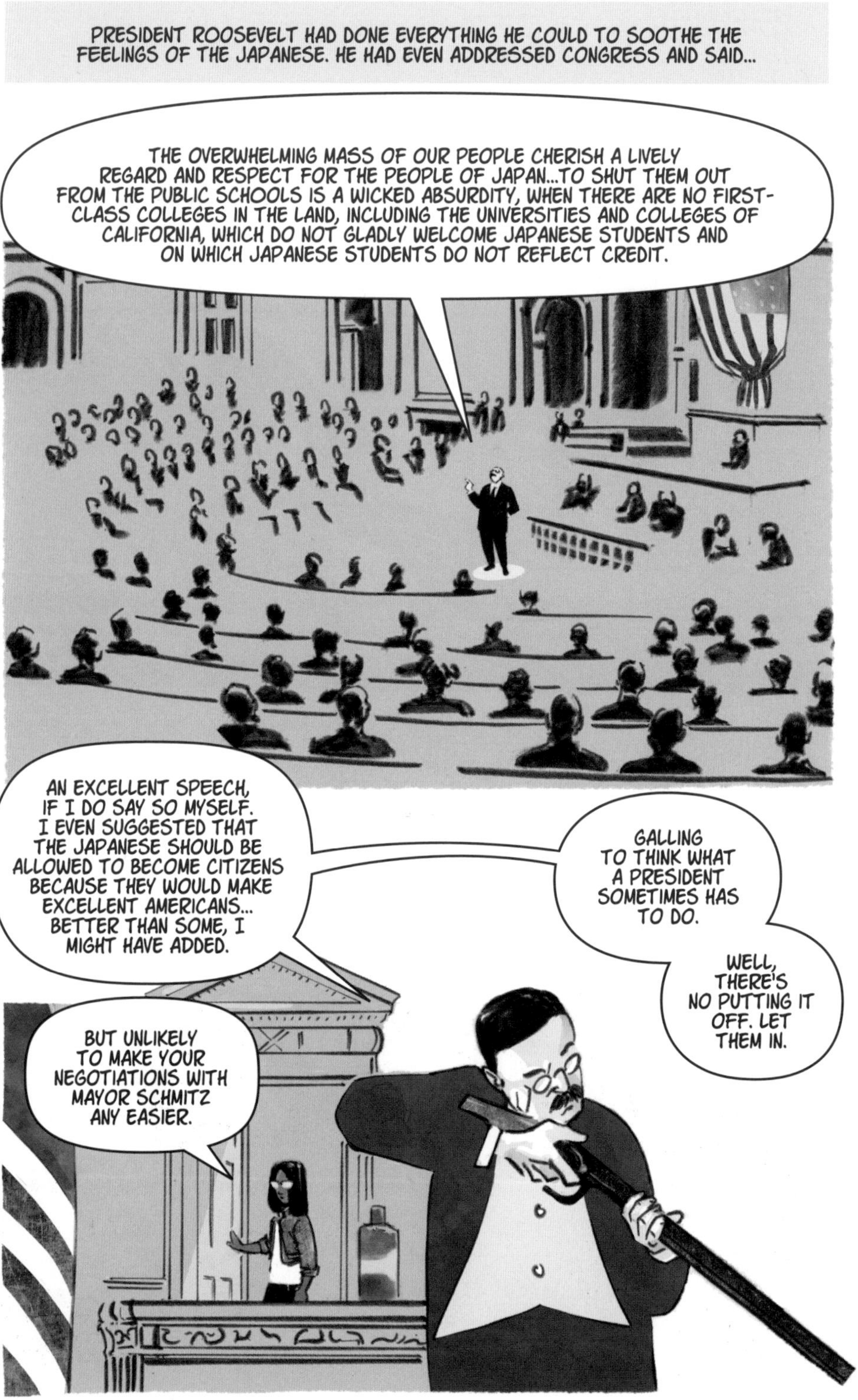
PRESIDENT ROOSEVELT HAD DONE EVERYTHING HE COULD TO SOOTHE THE FEELINGS OF THE JAPANESE. HE HAD EVEN ADDRESSED CONGRESS AND SAID...
THE OVERWHELMING MASS OF OUR PEOPLE CHERISH A LIVELY REGARD AND RESPECT FOR THE PEOPLE OF JAPAN...TO SHUT THEM OUT FROM THE PUBLIC SCHOOLS IS A WICKED ABSURDITY, WHEN THERE ARE NO FIRST-CLASS COLLEGES IN THE LAND, INCLUDING THE UNIVERSITIES AND COLLEGES OF CALIFORNIA, WHICH DO NOT GLADLY WELCOME JAPANESE STUDENTS AND ON WHICH JAPANESE STUDENTS DO NOT REFLECT CREDIT.
AN EXCELLENT SPEECH, IF I DO SAY SO MYSELF. I EVEN SUGGESTED THAT THE JAPANESE SHOULD BE ALLOWED TO BECOME CITIZENS BECAUSE THEY WOULD MAKE EXCELLENT AMERICANS... BETTER THAN SOME, I MIGHT HAVE ADDED.
GALLING TO THINK WHAT A PRESIDENT SOMETIMES HAS TO DO.
BUT UNLIKELY TO MAKE YOUR NEGOTIATIONS WITH MAYOR SCHMITZ ANY EASIER.
WELL, THERE'S NO PUTTING IT OFF. LET THEM IN.

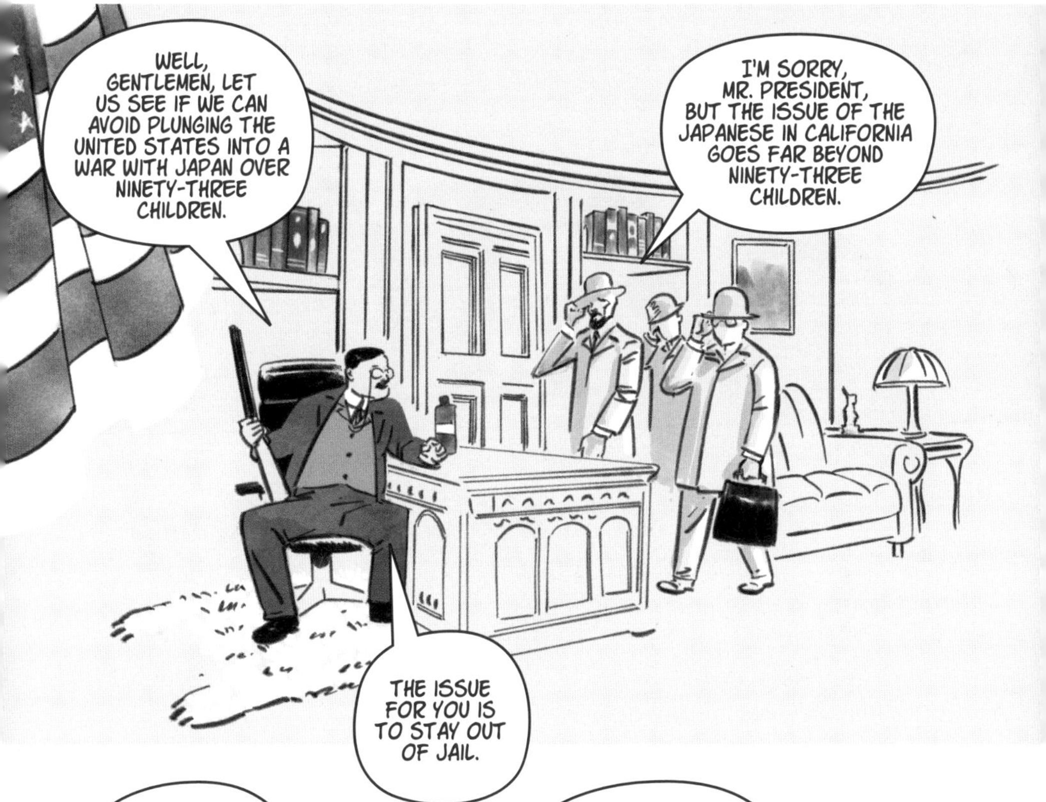
WELL, GENTLEMEN, LET US SEE IF WE CAN AVOID PLUNGING THE UNITED STATES INTO A WAR WITH JAPAN OVER NINETY-THREE CHILDREN.
I'M SORRY, MR. PRESIDENT, BUT THE ISSUE OF THE JAPANESE IN CALIFORNIA GOES FAR BEYOND NINETY-THREE CHILDREN.
THE ISSUE FOR YOU IS TO STAY OUT OF JAIL.

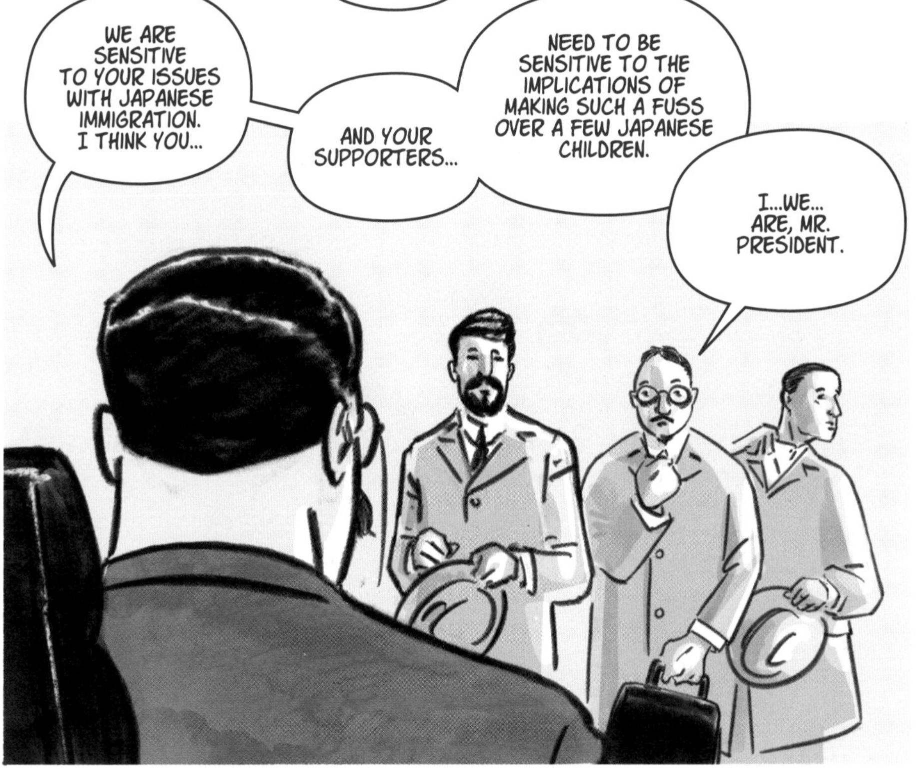
WE ARE SENSITIVE TO YOUR ISSUES WITH JAPANESE IMMIGRATION. I THINK YOU...
AND YOUR SUPPORTERS...
NEED TO BE SENSITIVE TO THE IMPLICATIONS OF MAKING SUCH A FUSS OVER A FEW JAPANESE CHILDREN.
I...WE... ARE, MR. PRESIDENT.

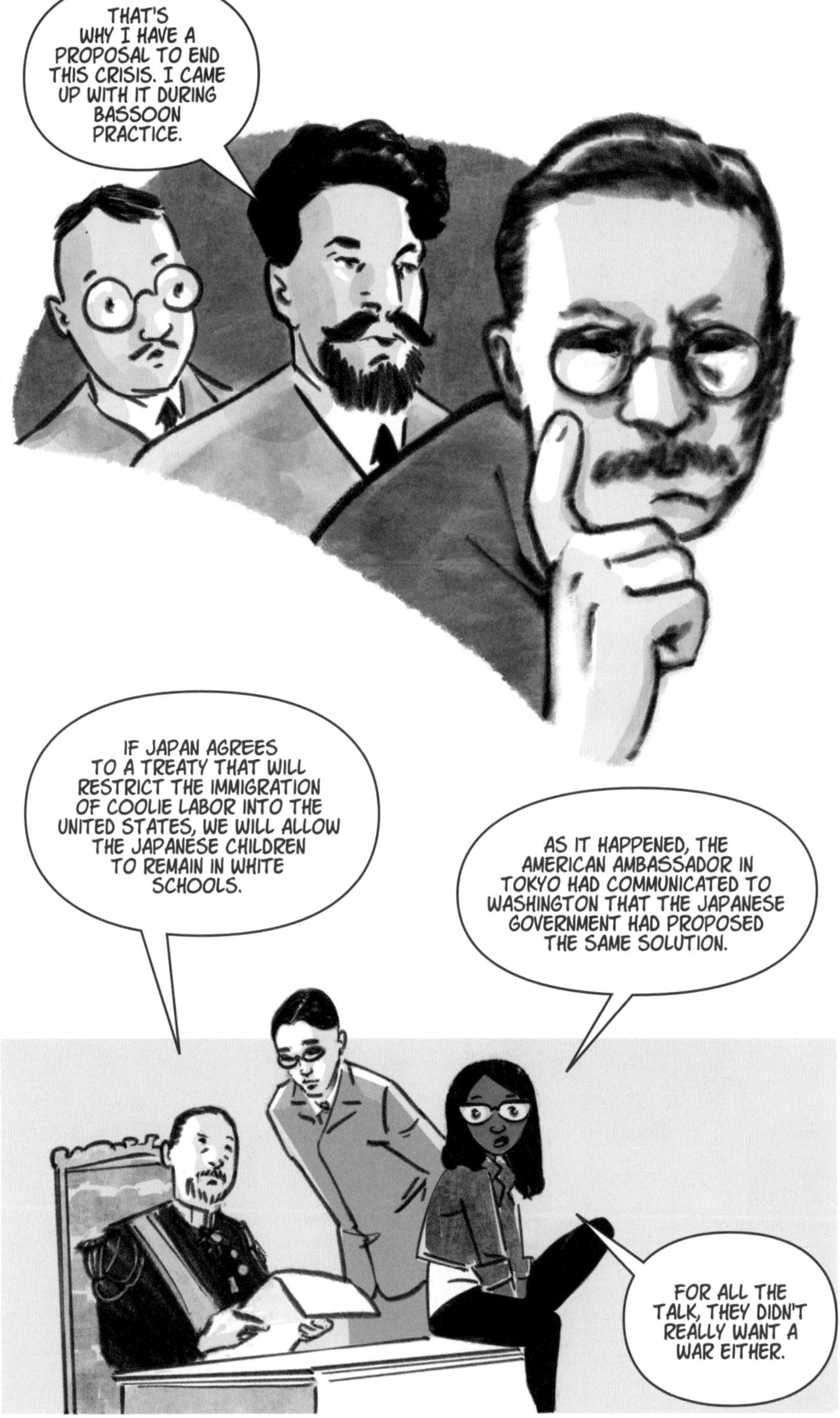
THAT'S WHY I HAVE A PROPOSAL TO END THIS CRISIS. I CAME UP WITH IT DURING BASSOON PRACTICE.
IF JAPAN AGREES TO A TREATY THAT WILL RESTRICT THE IMMIGRATION OF COOLIE LABOR INTO THE UNITED STATES, WE WILL ALLOW THE JAPANESE CHILDREN TO REMAIN IN WHITE SCHOOLS.
AS IT HAPPENED, THE AMERICAN AMBASSADOR IN TOKYO HAD COMMUNICATED TO WASHINGTON THAT THE JAPANESE GOVERNMENT HAD PROPOSED THE SAME SOLUTION.
FOR ALL THE TALK, THEY DIDN'T REALLY WANT A WAR EITHER.

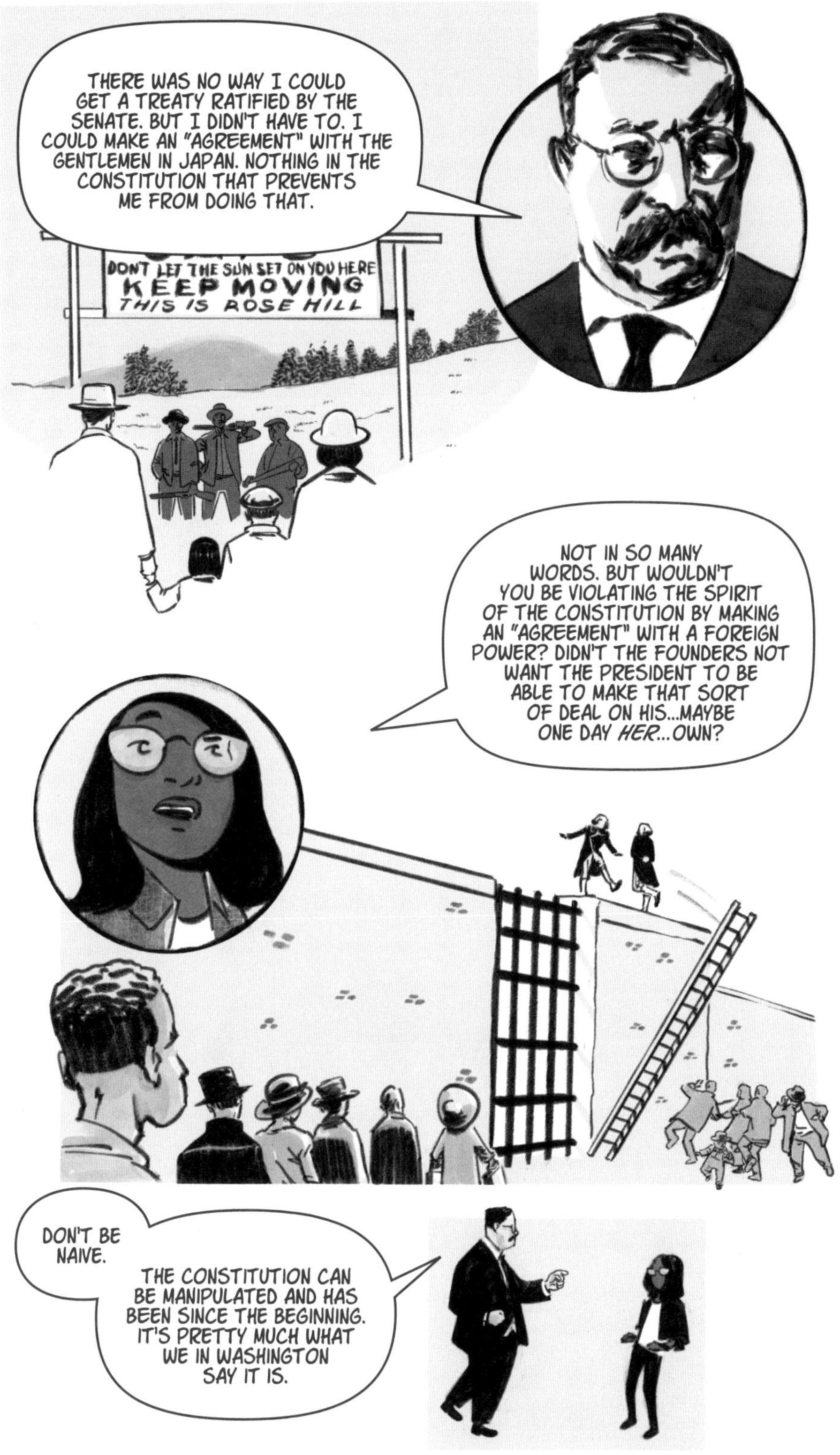
THERE WAS NO WAY I COULD GET A TREATY RATIFIED BY THE SENATE. BUT I DIDN'T HAVE TO. I COULD MAKE AN "AGREEMENT" WITH THE GENTLEMEN IN JAPAN. NOTHING IN THE CONSTITUTION THAT PREVENTS ME FROM DOING THAT.
DON'T LET THE SUN SET ON YOU HERE
KEEP MOVING
THIS IS ROSE HILL
NOT IN SO MANY WORDS. BUT WOULDN'T YOU BE VIOLATING THE SPIRIT OF THE CONSTITUTION BY MAKING AN "AGREEMENT" WITH A FOREIGN POWER? DIDN'T THE FOUNDERS NOT WANT THE PRESIDENT TO BE ABLE TO MAKE THAT SORT OF DEAL ON HIS...MAYBE ONE DAY *HER*...OWN?
DON'T BE NAIVE.
THE CONSTITUTION CAN BE MANIPULATED AND HAS BEEN SINCE THE BEGINNING. IT'S PRETTY MUCH WHAT WE IN WASHINGTON SAY IT IS.

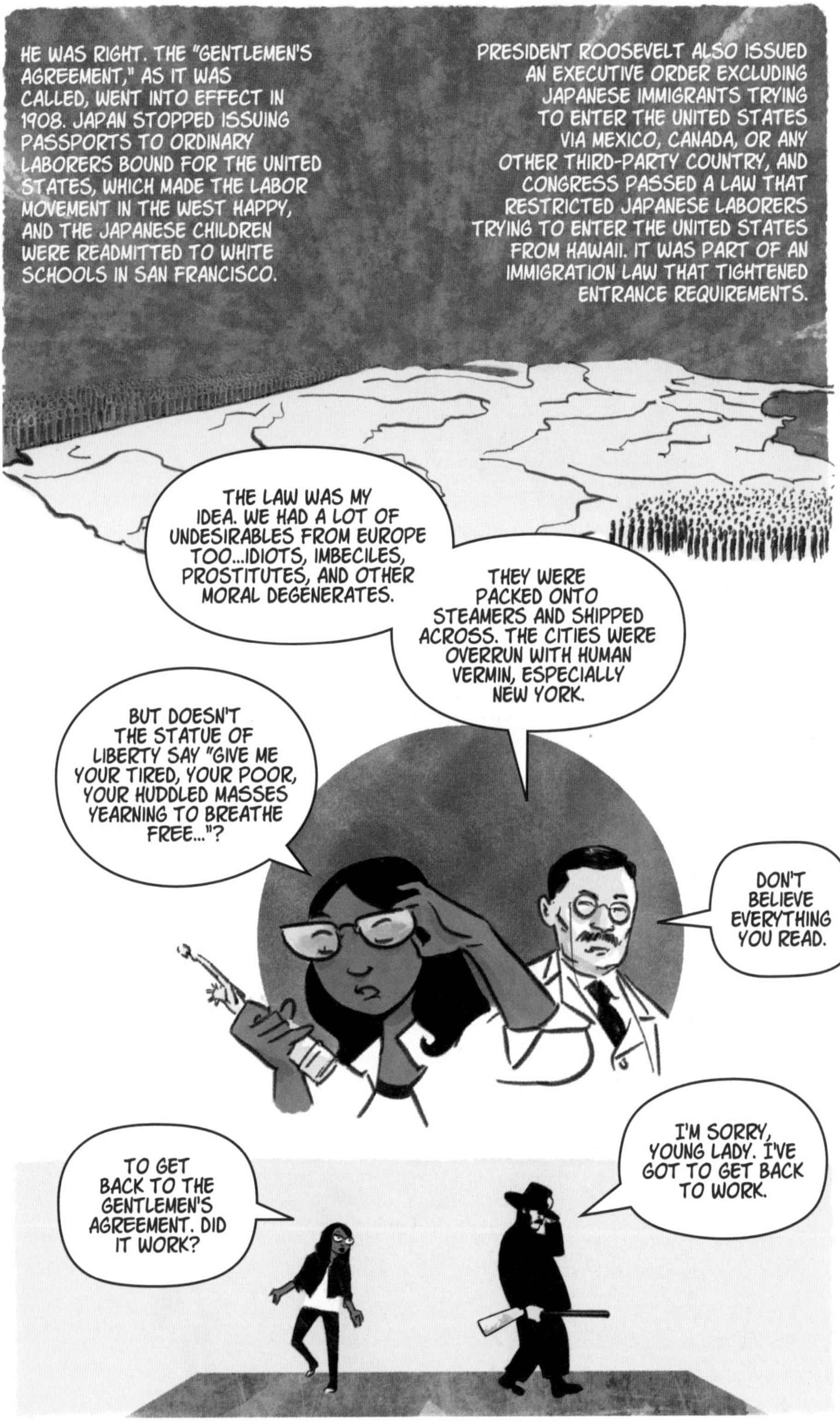
HE WAS RIGHT. THE "GENTLEMEN'S AGREEMENT," AS IT WAS CALLED, WENT INTO EFFECT IN 1908. JAPAN STOPPED ISSUING PASSPORTS TO ORDINARY LABORERS BOUND FOR THE UNITED STATES, WHICH MADE THE LABOR MOVEMENT IN THE WEST HAPPY, AND THE JAPANESE CHILDREN WERE READMITTED TO WHITE SCHOOLS IN SAN FRANCISCO.
PRESIDENT ROOSEVELT ALSO ISSUED AN EXECUTIVE ORDER EXCLUDING JAPANESE IMMIGRANTS TRYING TO ENTER THE UNITED STATES VIA MEXICO, CANADA, OR ANY OTHER THIRD-PARTY COUNTRY, AND CONGRESS PASSED A LAW THAT RESTRICTED JAPANESE LABORERS TRYING TO ENTER THE UNITED STATES FROM HAWAII. IT WAS PART OF AN IMMIGRATION LAW THAT TIGHTENED ENTRANCE REQUIREMENTS.
THE LAW WAS MY IDEA. WE HAD A LOT OF UNDESIRABLES FROM EUROPE TOO...IDIOTS, IMBECILES, PROSTITUTES, AND OTHER MORAL DEGENERATES.
THEY WERE PACKED ONTO STEAMERS AND SHIPPED ACROSS. THE CITIES WERE OVERRUN WITH HUMAN VERMIN, ESPECIALLY NEW YORK.
BUT DOESN'T THE STATUE OF LIBERTY SAY "GIVE ME YOUR TIRED, YOUR POOR, YOUR HUDDLED MASSES YEARNING TO BREATHE FREE..."?
DON'T BELIEVE EVERYTHING YOU READ.
TO GET BACK TO THE GENTLEMEN'S AGREEMENT. DID IT WORK?
I'M SORRY, YOUNG LADY. I'VE GOT TO GET BACK TO WORK.

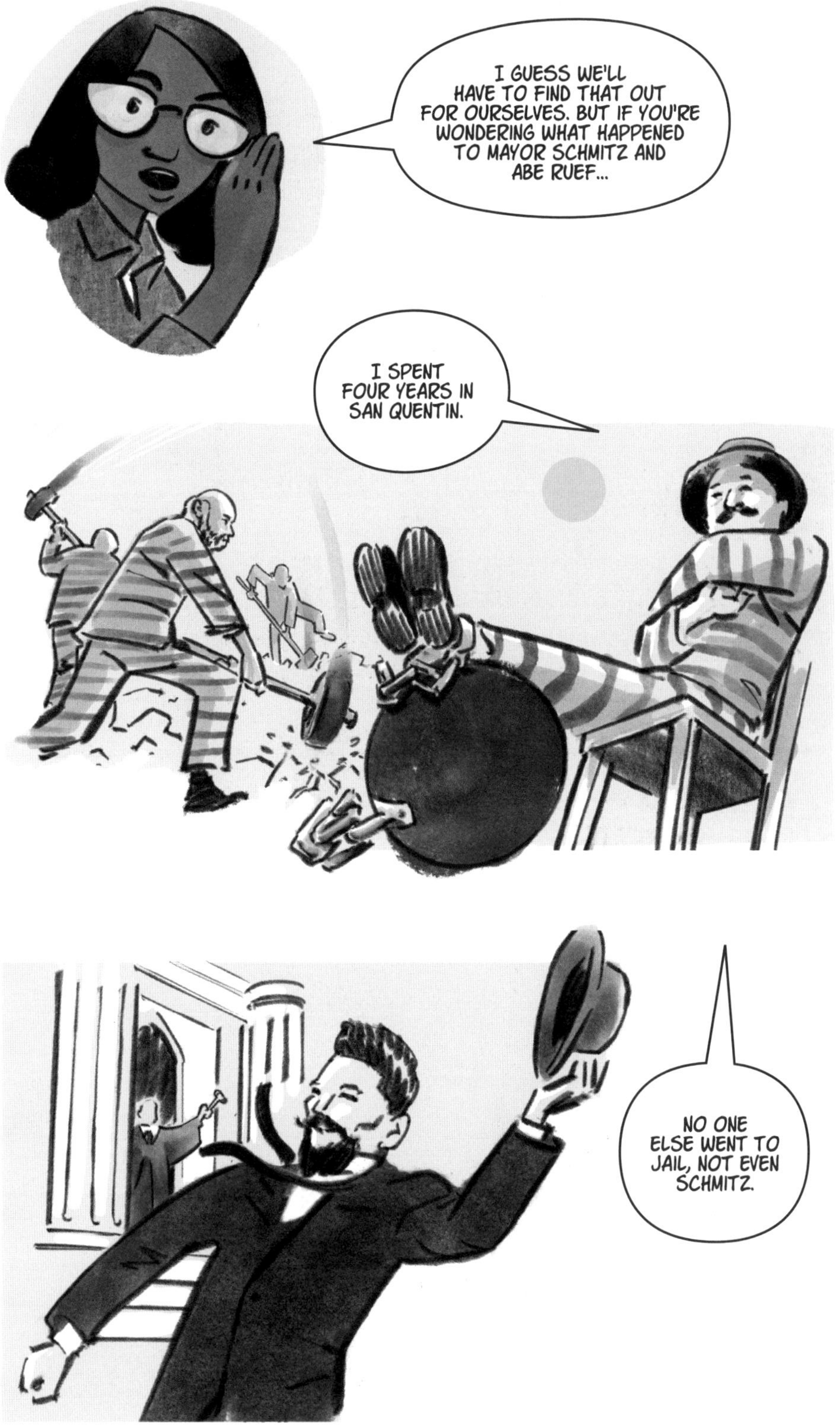
I GUESS WE'LL HAVE TO FIND THAT OUT FOR OURSELVES. BUT IF YOU'RE WONDERING WHAT HAPPENED TO MAYOR SCHMITZ AND ABE RUEF...
I SPENT FOUR YEARS IN SAN QUENTIN.
NO ONE ELSE WENT TO JAIL, NOT EVEN SCHMITZ.

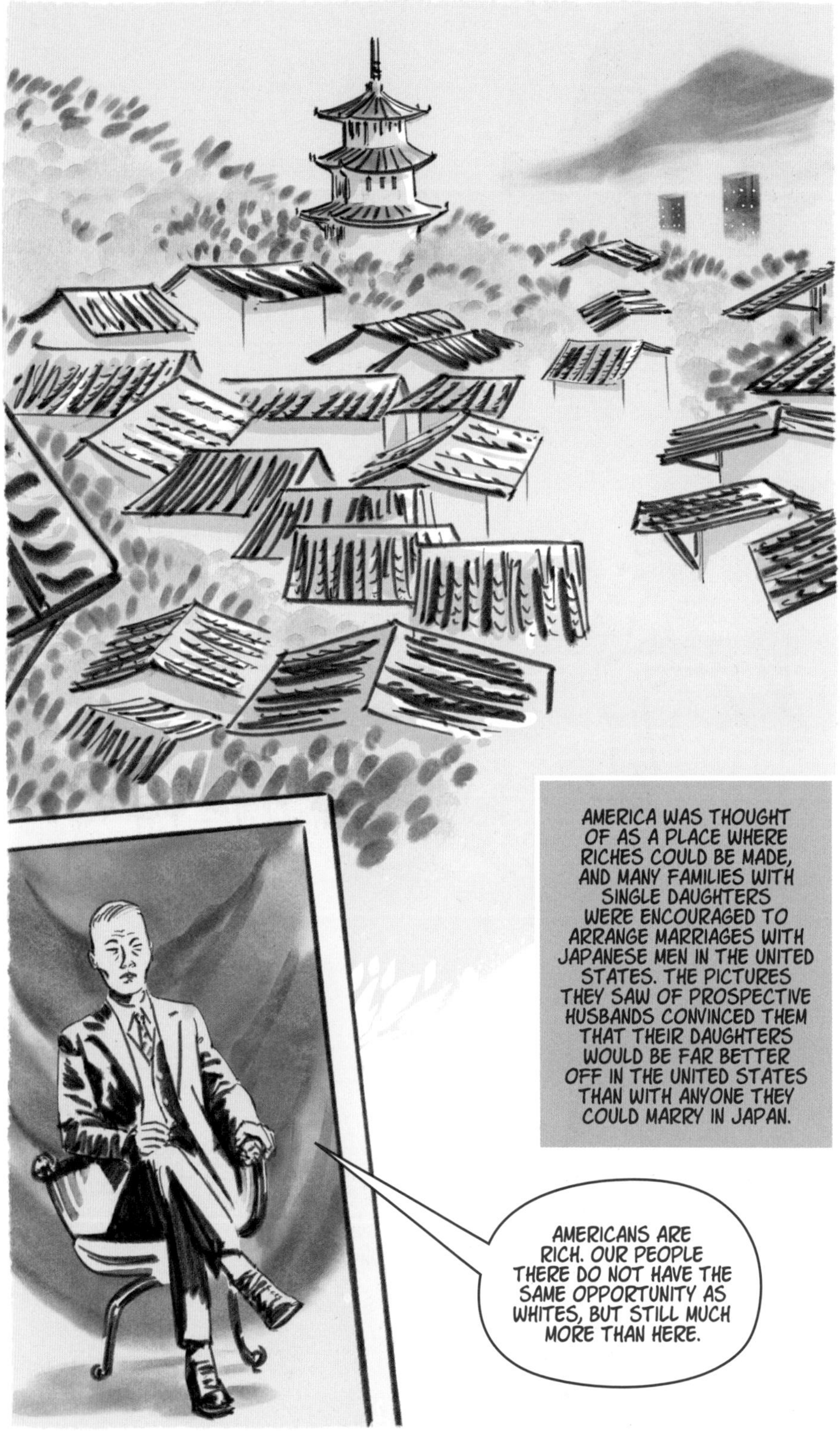
AMERICA WAS THOUGHT OF AS A PLACE WHERE RICHES COULD BE MADE, AND MANY FAMILIES WITH SINGLE DAUGHTERS WERE ENCOURAGED TO ARRANGE MARRIAGES WITH JAPANESE MEN IN THE UNITED STATES. THE PICTURES THEY SAW OF PROSPECTIVE HUSBANDS CONVINCED THEM THAT THEIR DAUGHTERS WOULD BE FAR BETTER OFF IN THE UNITED STATES THAN WITH ANYONE THEY COULD MARRY IN JAPAN.
AMERICANS ARE RICH. OUR PEOPLE THERE DO NOT HAVE THE SAME OPPORTUNITY AS WHITES, BUT STILL MUCH MORE THAN HERE.

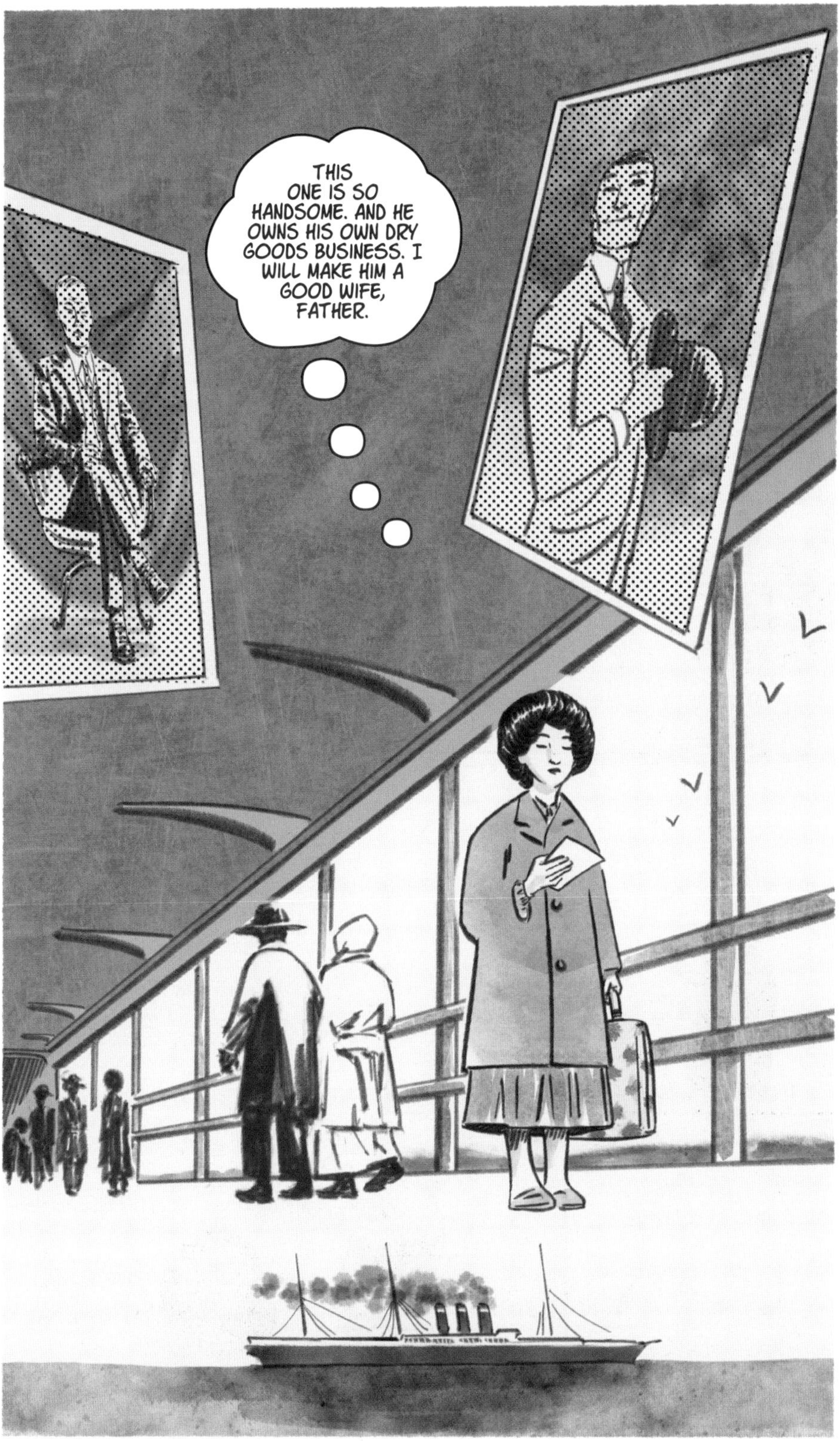
THIS ONE IS SO HANDSOME. AND HE OWNS HIS OWN DRY GOODS BUSINESS. I WILL MAKE HIM A GOOD WIFE, FATHER.

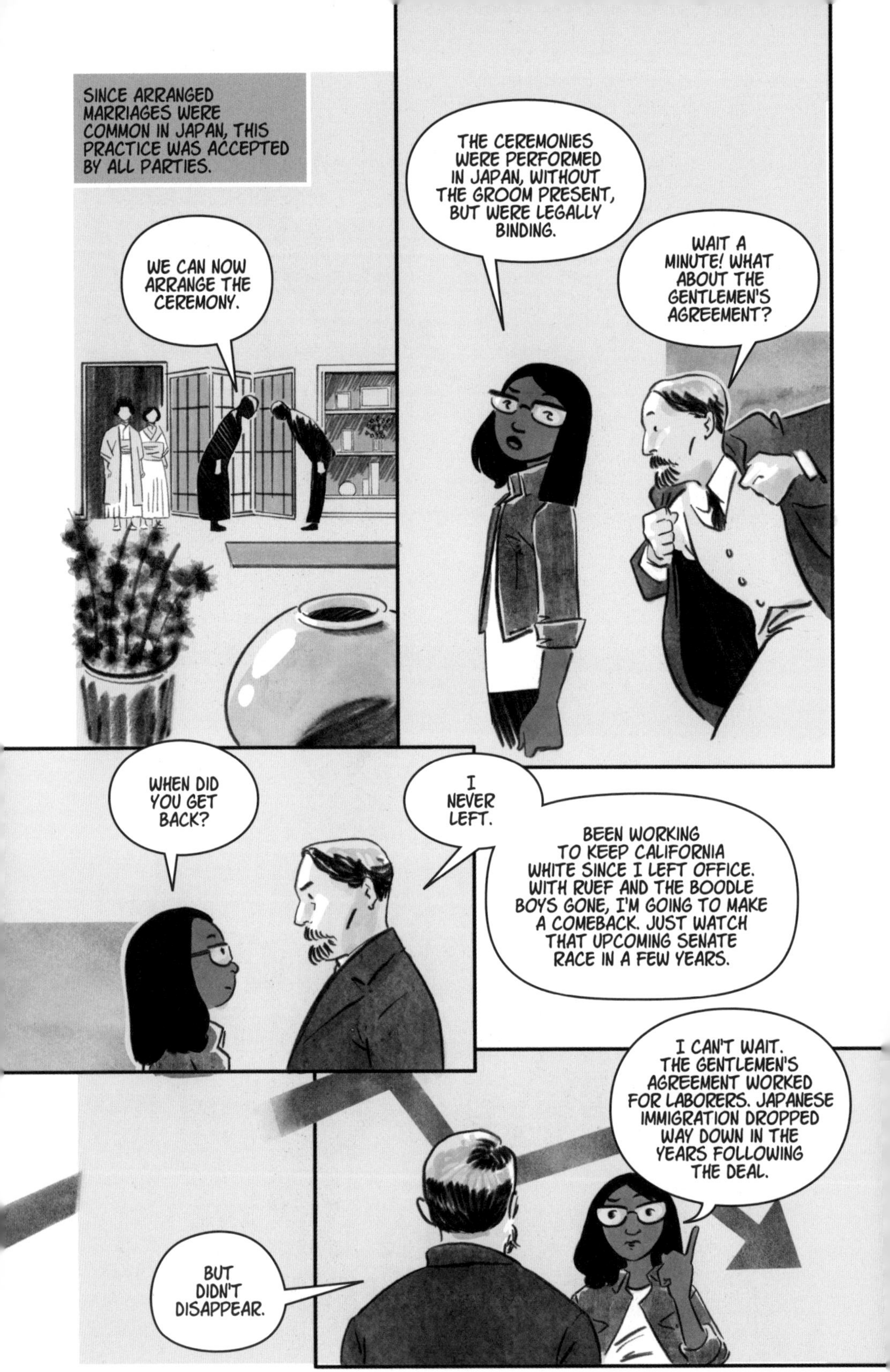
SINCE ARRANGED MARRIAGES WERE COMMON IN JAPAN, THIS PRACTICE WAS ACCEPTED BY ALL PARTIES.
WE CAN NOW ARRANGE THE CEREMONY.
THE CEREMONIES WERE PERFORMED IN JAPAN, WITHOUT THE GROOM PRESENT, BUT WERE LEGALLY BINDING.
WAIT A MINUTE! WHAT ABOUT THE GENTLEMEN'S AGREEMENT?
WHEN DID YOU GET BACK?
I NEVER LEFT.
BEEN WORKING TO KEEP CALIFORNIA WHITE SINCE I LEFT OFFICE. WITH RUEF AND THE BOODLE BOYS GONE, I'M GOING TO MAKE A COMEBACK. JUST WATCH THAT UPCOMING SENATE RACE IN A FEW YEARS.
I CAN'T WAIT. THE GENTLEMEN'S AGREEMENT WORKED FOR LABORERS. JAPANESE IMMIGRATION DROPPED WAY DOWN IN THE YEARS FOLLOWING THE DEAL.
BUT DIDN'T DISAPPEAR.

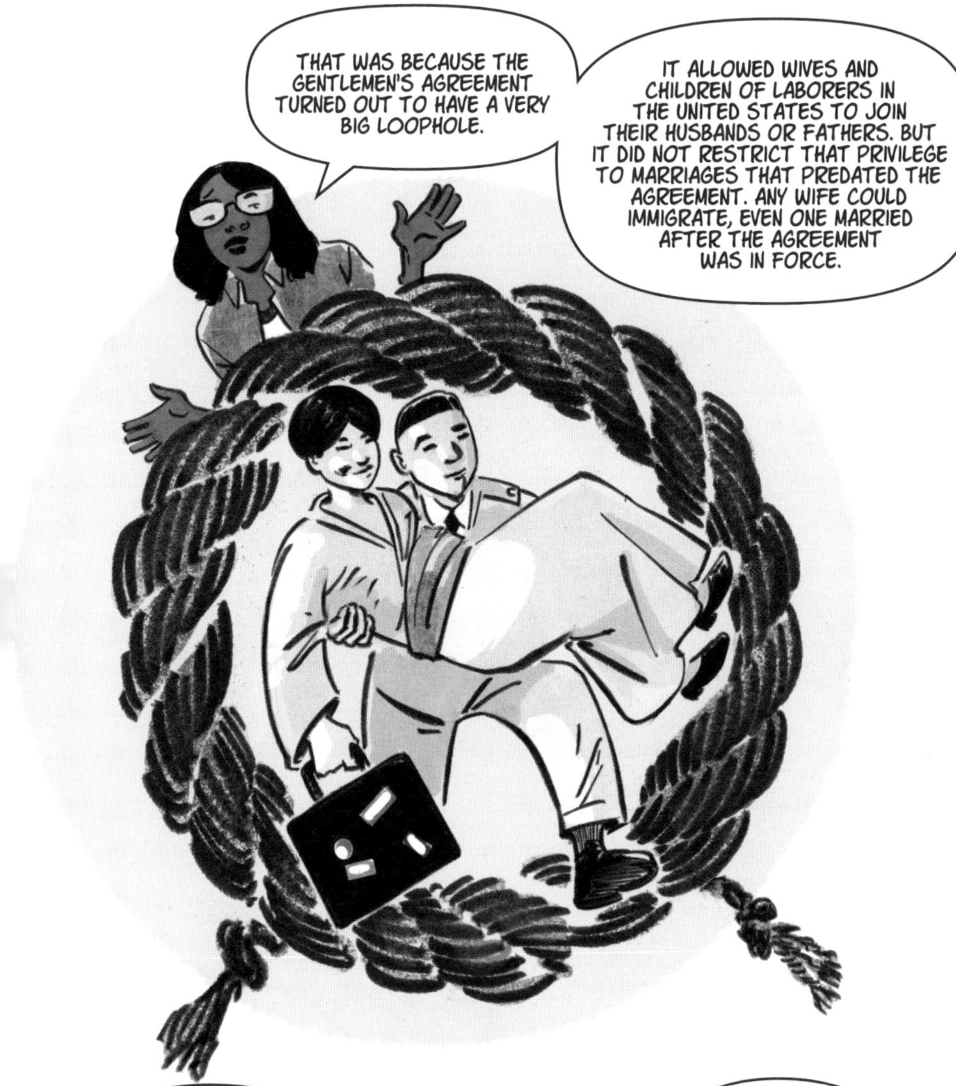
THAT WAS BECAUSE THE GENTLEMEN'S AGREEMENT TURNED OUT TO HAVE A VERY BIG LOOPHOLE.
IT ALLOWED WIVES AND CHILDREN OF LABORERS IN THE UNITED STATES TO JOIN THEIR HUSBANDS OR FATHERS. BUT IT DID NOT RESTRICT THAT PRIVILEGE TO MARRIAGES THAT PREDATED THE AGREEMENT. ANY WIFE COULD IMMIGRATE, EVEN ONE MARRIED AFTER THE AGREEMENT WAS IN FORCE.

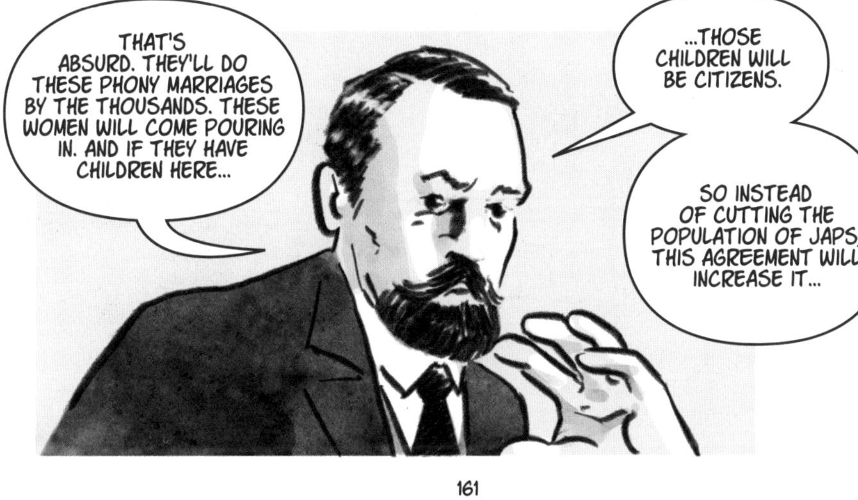
THAT'S ABSURD. THEY'LL DO THESE PHONY MARRIAGES BY THE THOUSANDS. THESE WOMEN WILL COME POURING IN. AND IF THEY HAVE CHILDREN HERE...
...THOSE CHILDREN WILL BE CITIZENS.
SO INSTEAD OF CUTTING THE POPULATION OF JAPS, THIS AGREEMENT WILL INCREASE IT...

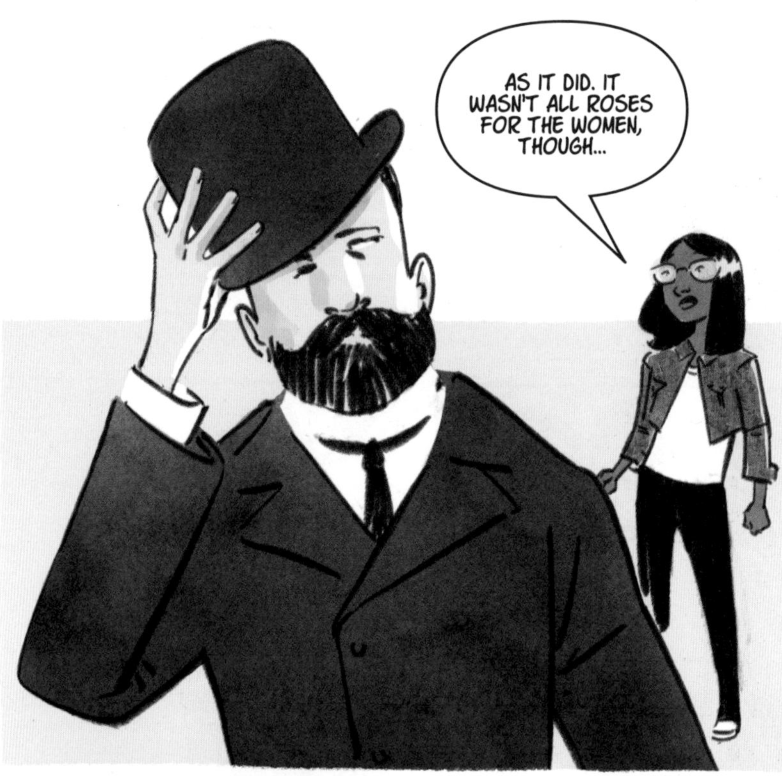
AS IT DID. IT WASN'T ALL ROSES FOR THE WOMEN, THOUGH...

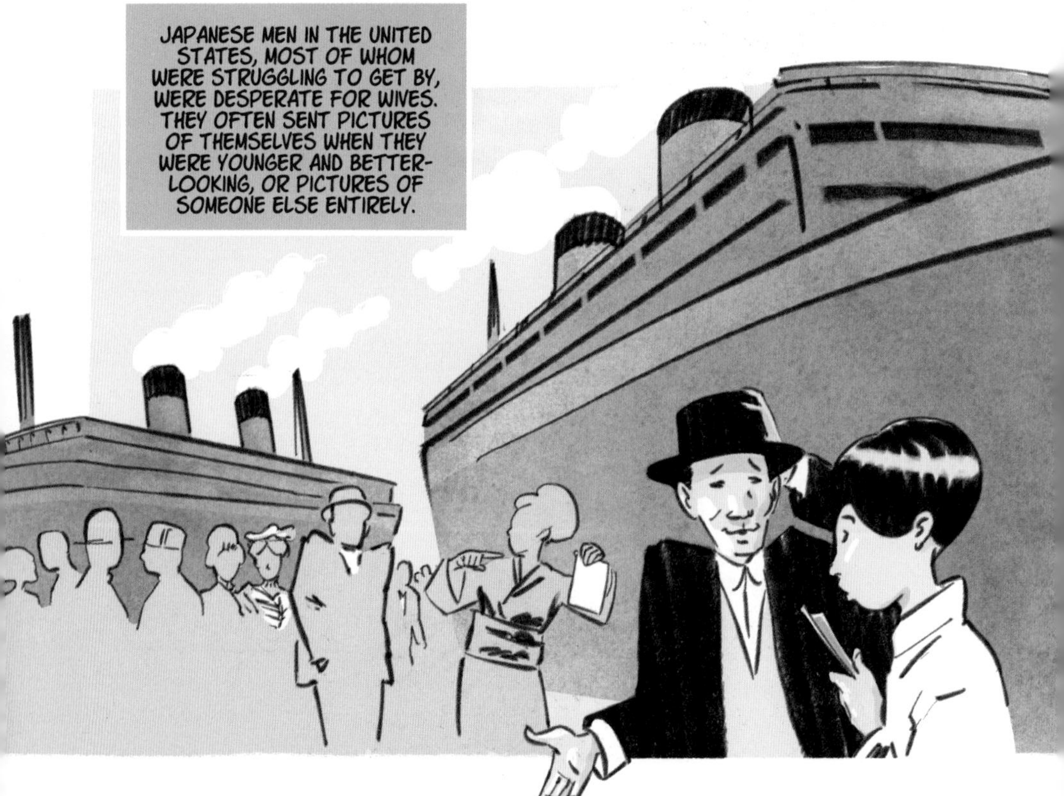
JAPANESE MEN IN THE UNITED STATES, MOST OF WHOM WERE STRUGGLING TO GET BY, WERE DESPERATE FOR WIVES. THEY OFTEN SENT PICTURES OF THEMSELVES WHEN THEY WERE YOUNGER AND BETTER-LOOKING, OR PICTURES OF SOMEONE ELSE ENTIRELY.

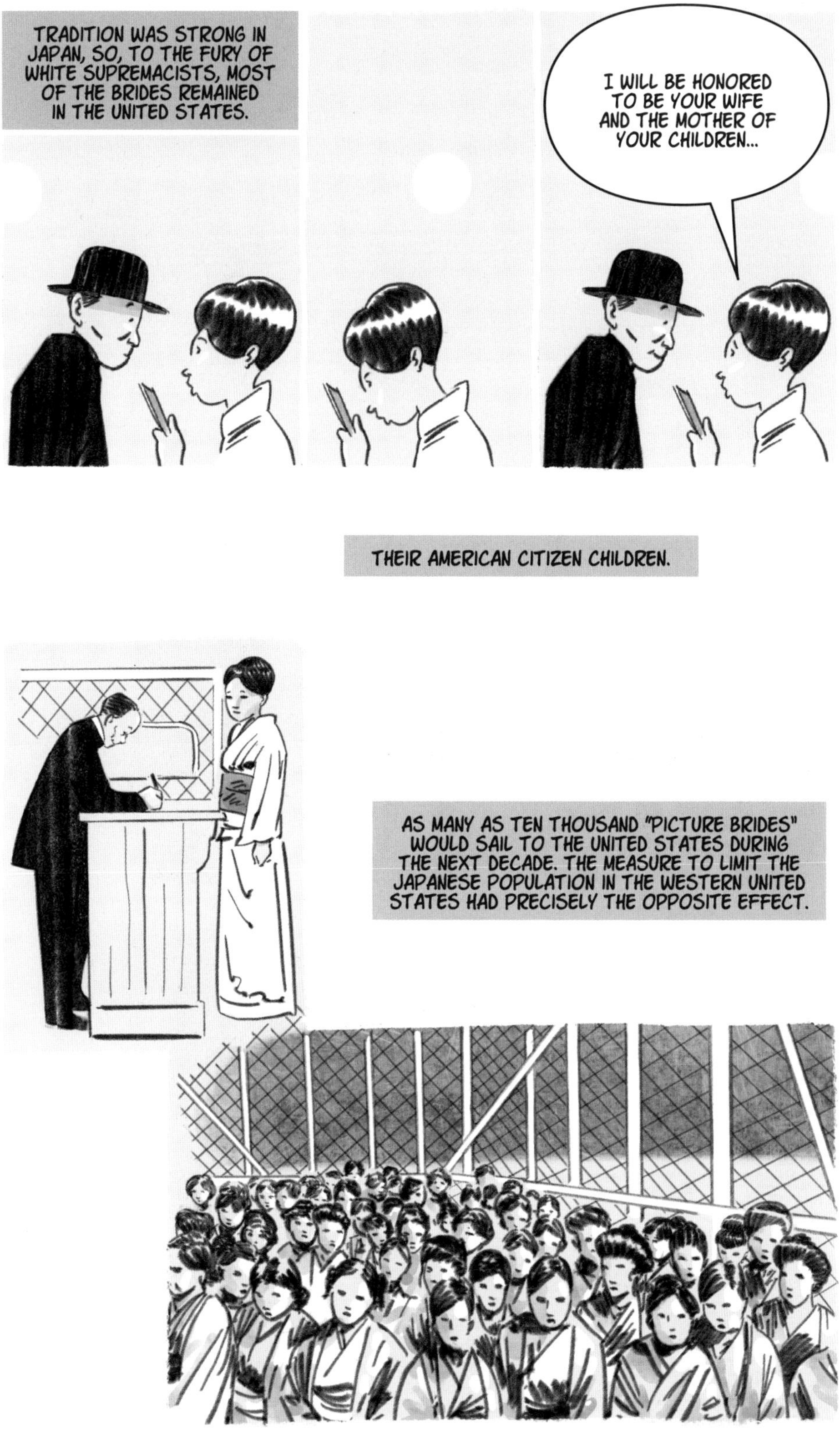
TRADITION WAS STRONG IN JAPAN, SO, TO THE FURY OF WHITE SUPREMACISTS, MOST OF THE BRIDES REMAINED IN THE UNITED STATES.
I WILL BE HONORED TO BE YOUR WIFE AND THE MOTHER OF YOUR CHILDREN...
THEIR AMERICAN CITIZEN CHILDREN.
AS MANY AS TEN THOUSAND "PICTURE BRIDES" WOULD SAIL TO THE UNITED STATES DURING THE NEXT DECADE. THE MEASURE TO LIMIT THE JAPANESE POPULATION IN THE WESTERN UNITED STATES HAD PRECISELY THE OPPOSITE EFFECT.

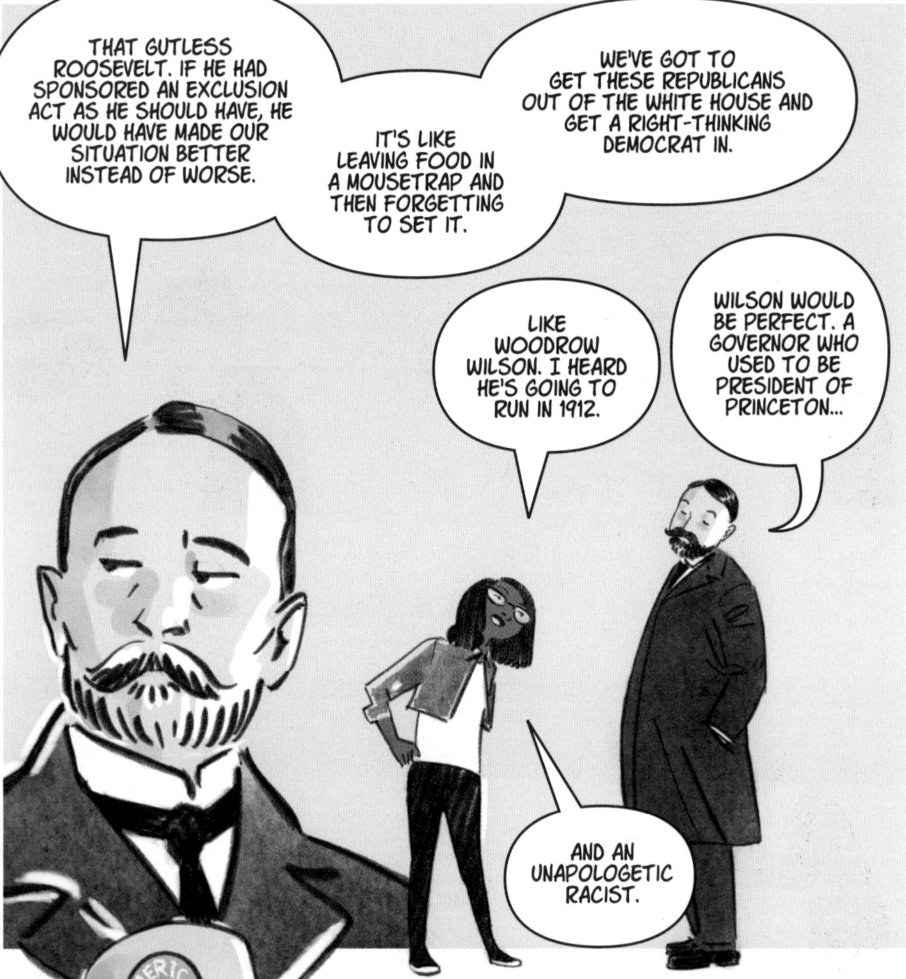
THAT GUTLESS ROOSEVELT. IF HE HAD SPONSORED AN EXCLUSION ACT AS HE SHOULD HAVE, HE WOULD HAVE MADE OUR SITUATION BETTER INSTEAD OF WORSE.
IT'S LIKE LEAVING FOOD IN A MOUSETRAP AND THEN FORGETTING TO SET IT.
WE'VE GOT TO GET THESE REPUBLICANS OUT OF THE WHITE HOUSE AND GET A RIGHT-THINKING DEMOCRAT IN.
LIKE WOODROW WILSON. I HEARD HE'S GOING TO RUN IN 1912.
WILSON WOULD BE PERFECT. A GOVERNOR WHO USED TO BE PRESIDENT OF PRINCETON...
AND AN UNAPOLOGETIC RACIST.

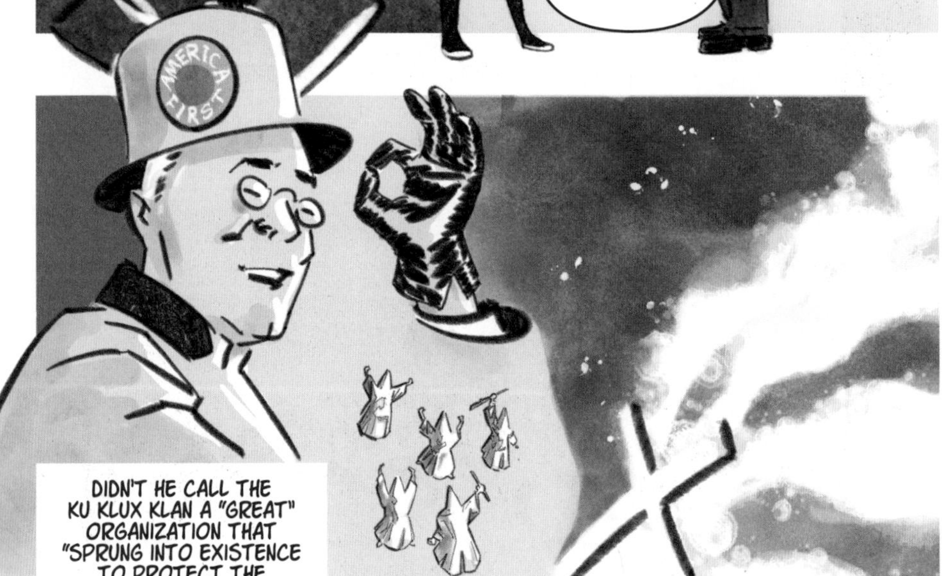
AMERICA FIRST
DIDN'T HE CALL THE KU KLUX KLAN A "GREAT" ORGANIZATION THAT "SPRUNG INTO EXISTENCE TO PROTECT THE SOUTHERN COUNTRY"?

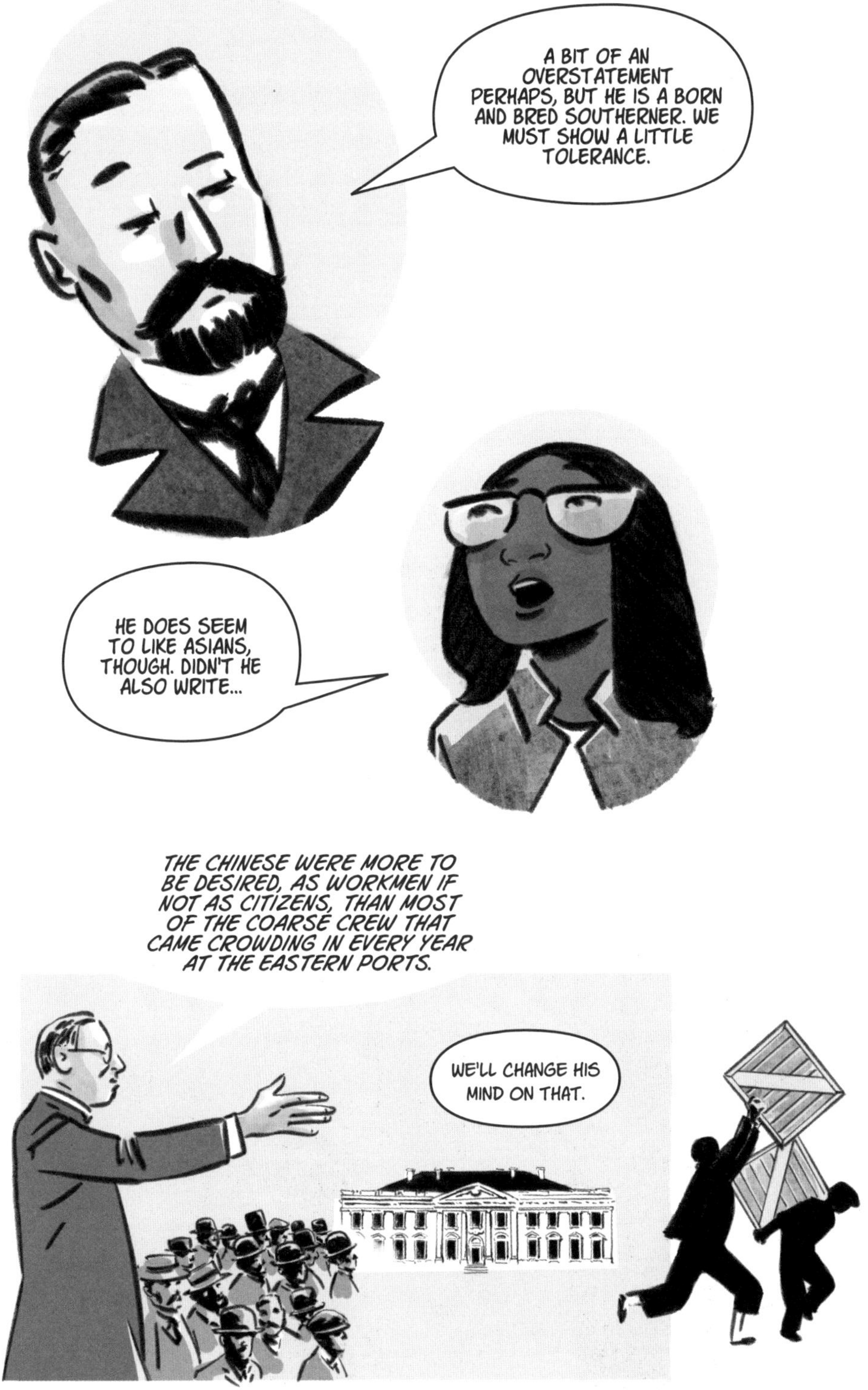
A BIT OF AN OVERSTATEMENT PERHAPS, BUT HE IS A BORN AND BRED SOUTHERNER. WE MUST SHOW A LITTLE TOLERANCE.
HE DOES SEEM TO LIKE ASIANS, THOUGH. DIDN'T HE ALSO WRITE...
THE CHINESE WERE MORE TO BE DESIRED, AS WORKMEN IF NOT AS CITIZENS, THAN MOST OF THE COARSE CREW THAT CAME CROWDING IN EVERY YEAR AT THE EASTERN PORTS.
WE'LL CHANGE HIS MIND ON THAT.

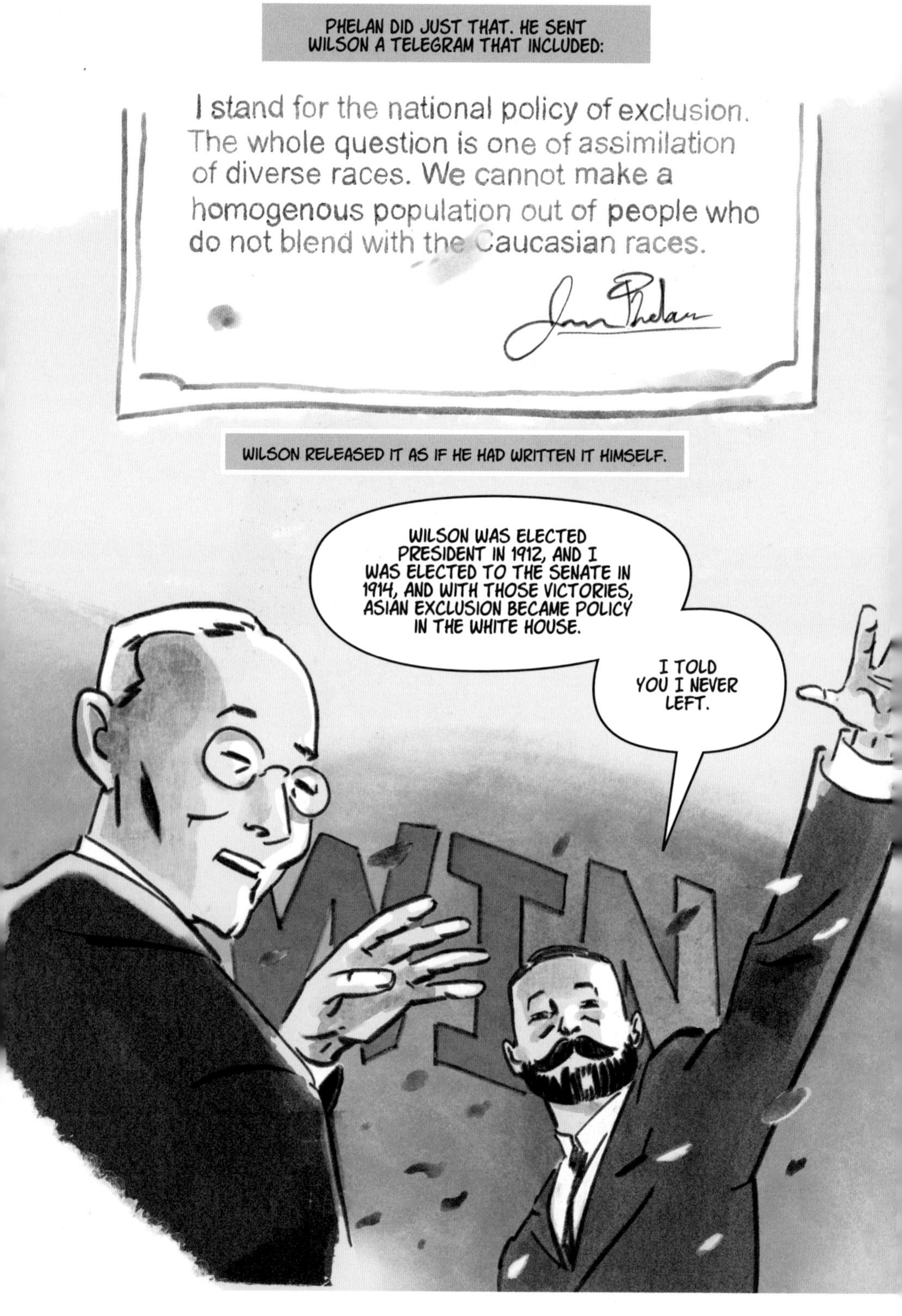
PHELAN DID JUST THAT. HE SENT WILSON A TELEGRAM THAT INCLUDED:
I stand for the national policy of exclusion. The whole question is one of assimilation of diverse races. We cannot make a homogenous population out of people who do not blend with the Caucasian races.
WILSON RELEASED IT AS IF HE HAD WRITTEN IT HIMSELF.
WILSON WAS ELECTED PRESIDENT IN 1912, AND I WAS ELECTED TO THE SENATE IN 1914, AND WITH THOSE VICTORIES, ASIAN EXCLUSION BECAME POLICY IN THE WHITE HOUSE.
I TOLD YOU I NEVER LEFT.

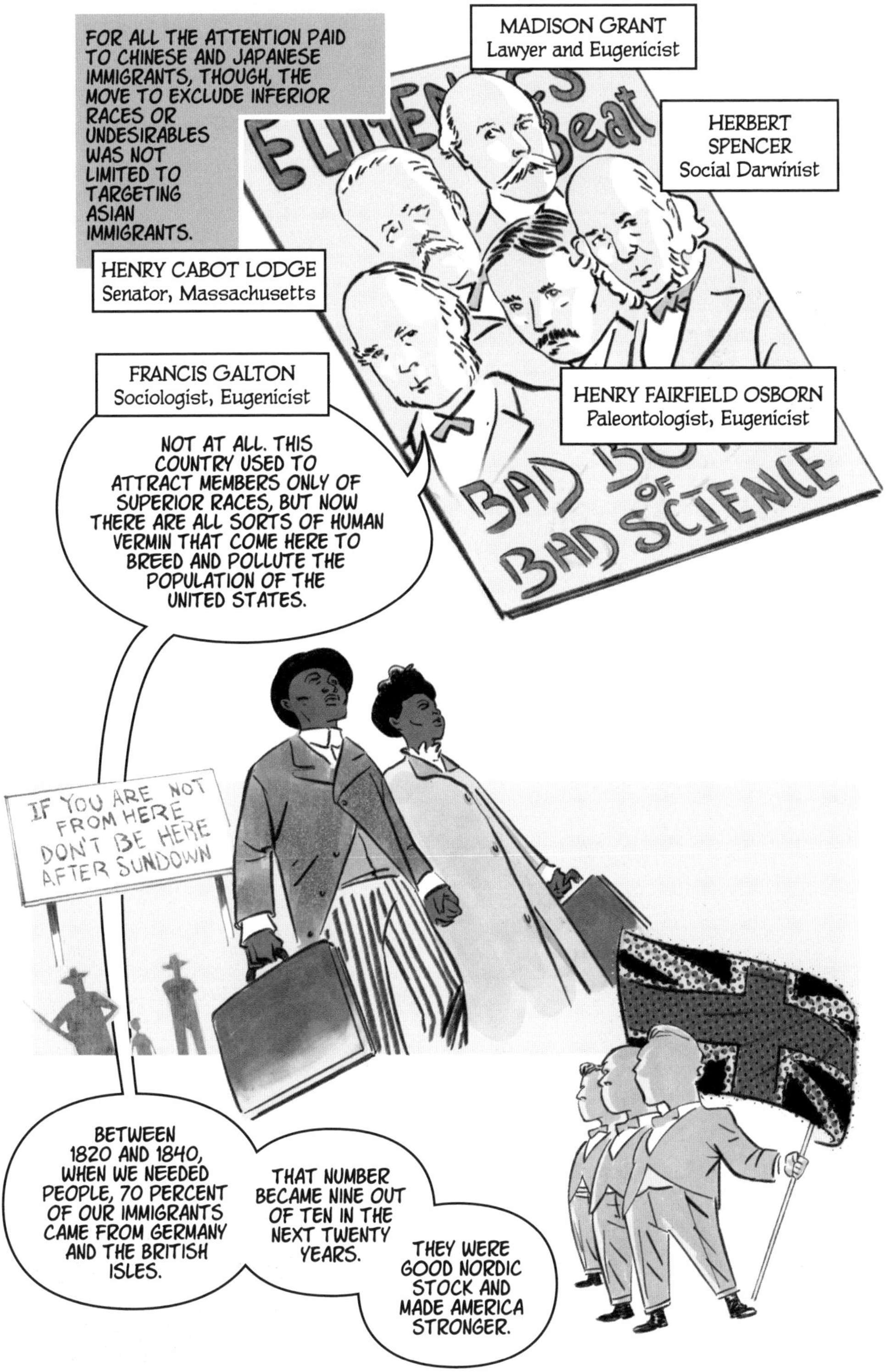
FOR ALL THE ATTENTION PAID TO CHINESE AND JAPANESE IMMIGRANTS, THOUGH, THE MOVE TO EXCLUDE INFERIOR RACES OR UNDESIRABLES WAS NOT LIMITED TO TARGETING ASIAN IMMIGRANTS.
MADISON GRANT Lawyer and Eugenicist
HERBERT SPENCER Social Darwinist
HENRY CABOT LODGE Senator, Massachusetts
FRANCIS GALTON Sociologist, Eugenicist
HENRY FAIRFIELD OSBORN Paleontologist, Eugenicist
NOT AT ALL. THIS COUNTRY USED TO ATTRACT MEMBERS ONLY OF SUPERIOR RACES, BUT NOW THERE ARE ALL SORTS OF HUMAN VERMIN THAT COME HERE TO BREED AND POLLUTE THE POPULATION OF THE UNITED STATES.
BAD SCIENCE
IF YOU ARE NOT FROM HERE DON'T BE HERE AFTER SUNDOWN
BETWEEN 1820 AND 1840, WHEN WE NEEDED PEOPLE, 70 PERCENT OF OUR IMMIGRANTS CAME FROM GERMANY AND THE BRITISH ISLES.
THAT NUMBER BECAME NINE OUT OF TEN IN THE NEXT TWENTY YEARS.
THEY WERE GOOD NORDIC STOCK AND MADE AMERICA STRONGER.

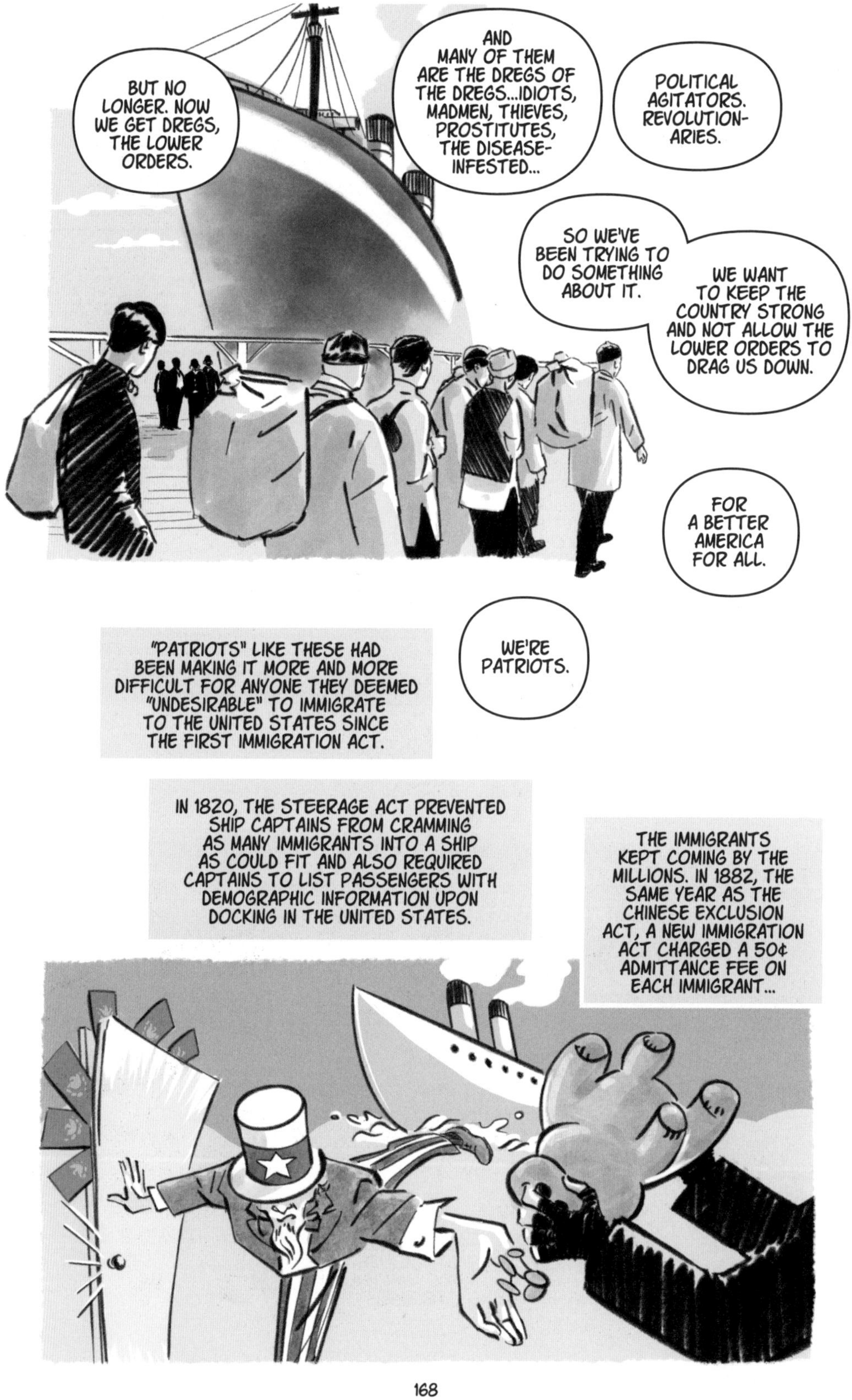
BUT NO LONGER. NOW WE GET DREGS, THE LOWER ORDERS.
AND MANY OF THEM ARE THE DREGS OF THE DREGS...IDIOTS, MADMEN, THIEVES, PROSTITUTES, THE DISEASE-INFESTED...
POLITICAL AGITATORS. REVOLUTION-ARIES.
SO WE'VE BEEN TRYING TO DO SOMETHING ABOUT IT.
WE WANT TO KEEP THE COUNTRY STRONG AND NOT ALLOW THE LOWER ORDERS TO DRAG US DOWN.
FOR A BETTER AMERICA FOR ALL.
WE'RE PATRIOTS.
"PATRIOTS" LIKE THESE HAD BEEN MAKING IT MORE AND MORE DIFFICULT FOR ANYONE THEY DEEMED "UNDESIRABLE" TO IMMIGRATE TO THE UNITED STATES SINCE THE FIRST IMMIGRATION ACT.
IN 1820, THE STEERAGE ACT PREVENTED SHIP CAPTAINS FROM CRAMMING AS MANY IMMIGRANTS INTO A SHIP AS COULD FIT AND ALSO REQUIRED CAPTAINS TO LIST PASSENGERS WITH DEMOGRAPHIC INFORMATION UPON DOCKING IN THE UNITED STATES.
THE IMMIGRANTS KEPT COMING BY THE MILLIONS. IN 1882, THE SAME YEAR AS THE CHINESE EXCLUSION ACT, A NEW IMMIGRATION ACT CHARGED A 50¢ ADMITTANCE FEE ON EACH IMMIGRANT...

...AND ALSO FORBADE THE ENTRY OF "ANY CONVICT, LUNATIC, IDIOT, OR ANY PERSON UNABLE TO TAKE CARE OF HIM OR HERSELF WITHOUT BECOMING A PUBLIC CHARGE."

IN 1885, ENTRY WAS DENIED TO CONTRACT LABORERS, MENIAL WORKERS OFTEN IMPORTED BY THE HUNDREDS, WHO HAD SIGNED CONTRACTS IN THEIR HOME COUNTRY TO WORK FOR VERY LOW WAGES. THE LAW WAS TOUGHENED IN 1887, AND A DEPORTATION CLAUSE WAS ADDED IN 1888. IN 1891, POLYGAMISTS WERE FORBIDDEN, AS WELL AS THOSE "SUFFERING FROM A LOATHSOME OR A DANGEROUS CONTAGIOUS DISEASE, OR WHO HAVE BEEN CONVICTED OF A MISDEMEANOR INVOLVING MORAL TURPITUDE."

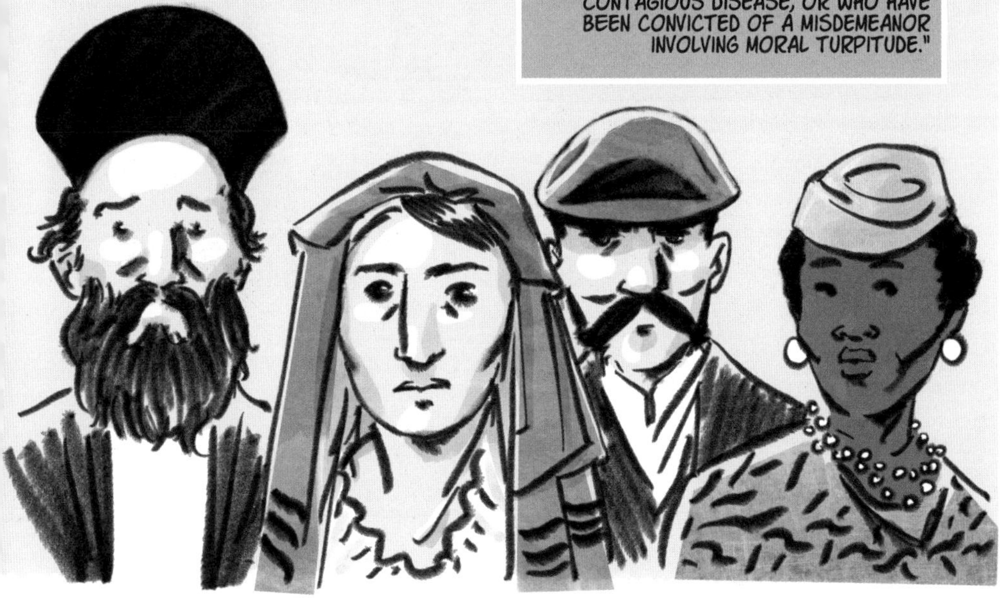

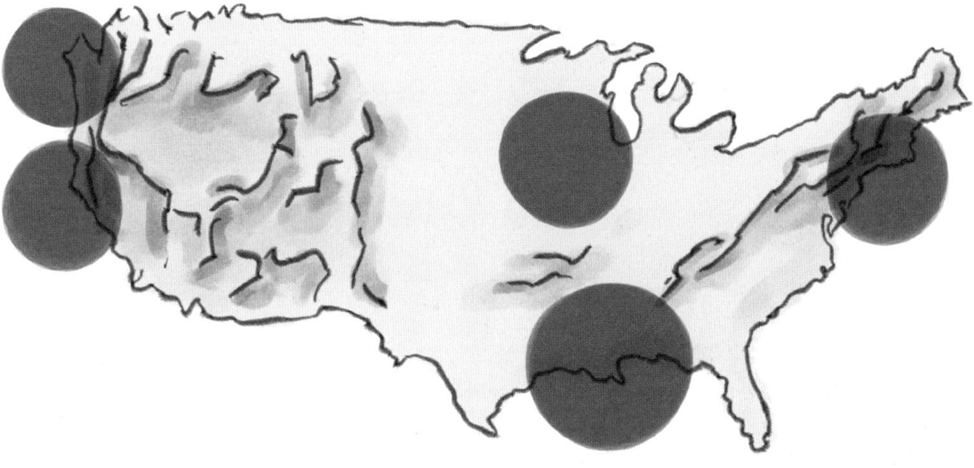

BUT STILL THEY KEPT COMING, MORE AND MORE FROM SOUTHERN AND EASTERN EUROPE.

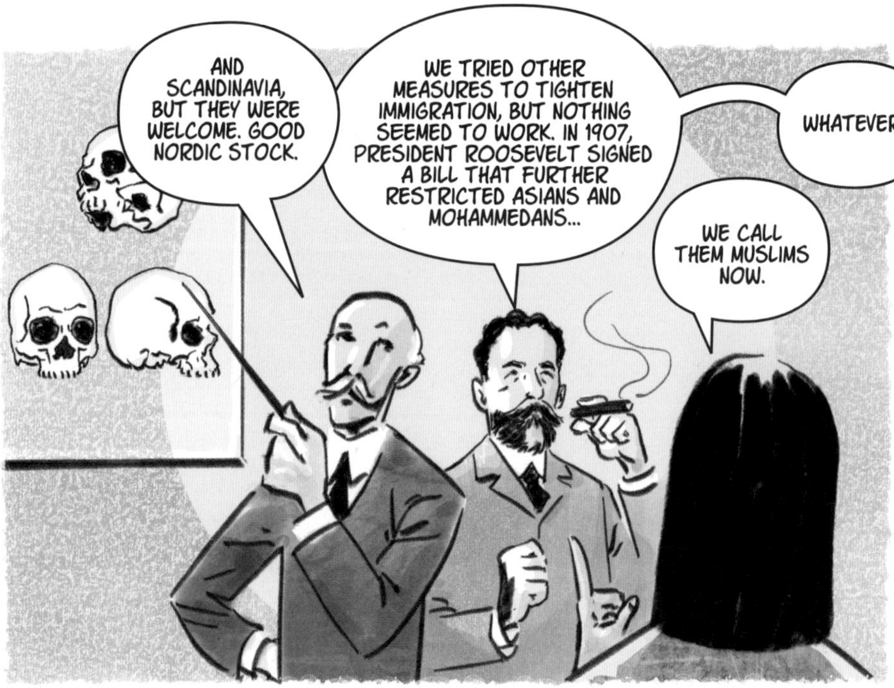
AND SCANDINAVIA, BUT THEY WERE WELCOME. GOOD NORDIC STOCK.
WE TRIED OTHER MEASURES TO TIGHTEN IMMIGRATION, BUT NOTHING SEEMED TO WORK. IN 1907, PRESIDENT ROOSEVELT SIGNED A BILL THAT FURTHER RESTRICTED ASIANS AND MOHAMMEDANS...
WHATEVER.
WE CALL THEM MUSLIMS NOW.

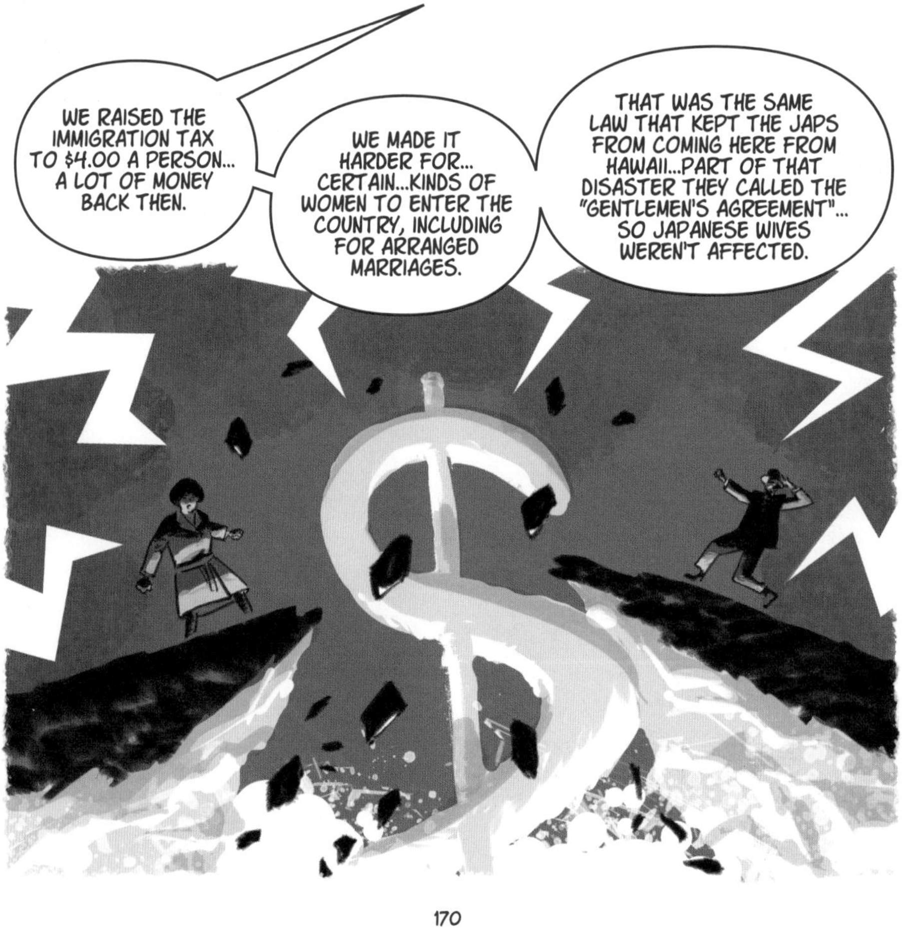
WE RAISED THE IMMIGRATION TAX TO $4.00 A PERSON... A LOT OF MONEY BACK THEN.
WE MADE IT HARDER FOR... CERTAIN...KINDS OF WOMEN TO ENTER THE COUNTRY, INCLUDING FOR ARRANGED MARRIAGES.
THAT WAS THE SAME LAW THAT KEPT THE JAPS FROM COMING HERE FROM HAWAII...PART OF THAT DISASTER THEY CALLED THE "GENTLEMEN'S AGREEMENT"... SO JAPANESE WIVES WEREN'T AFFECTED.

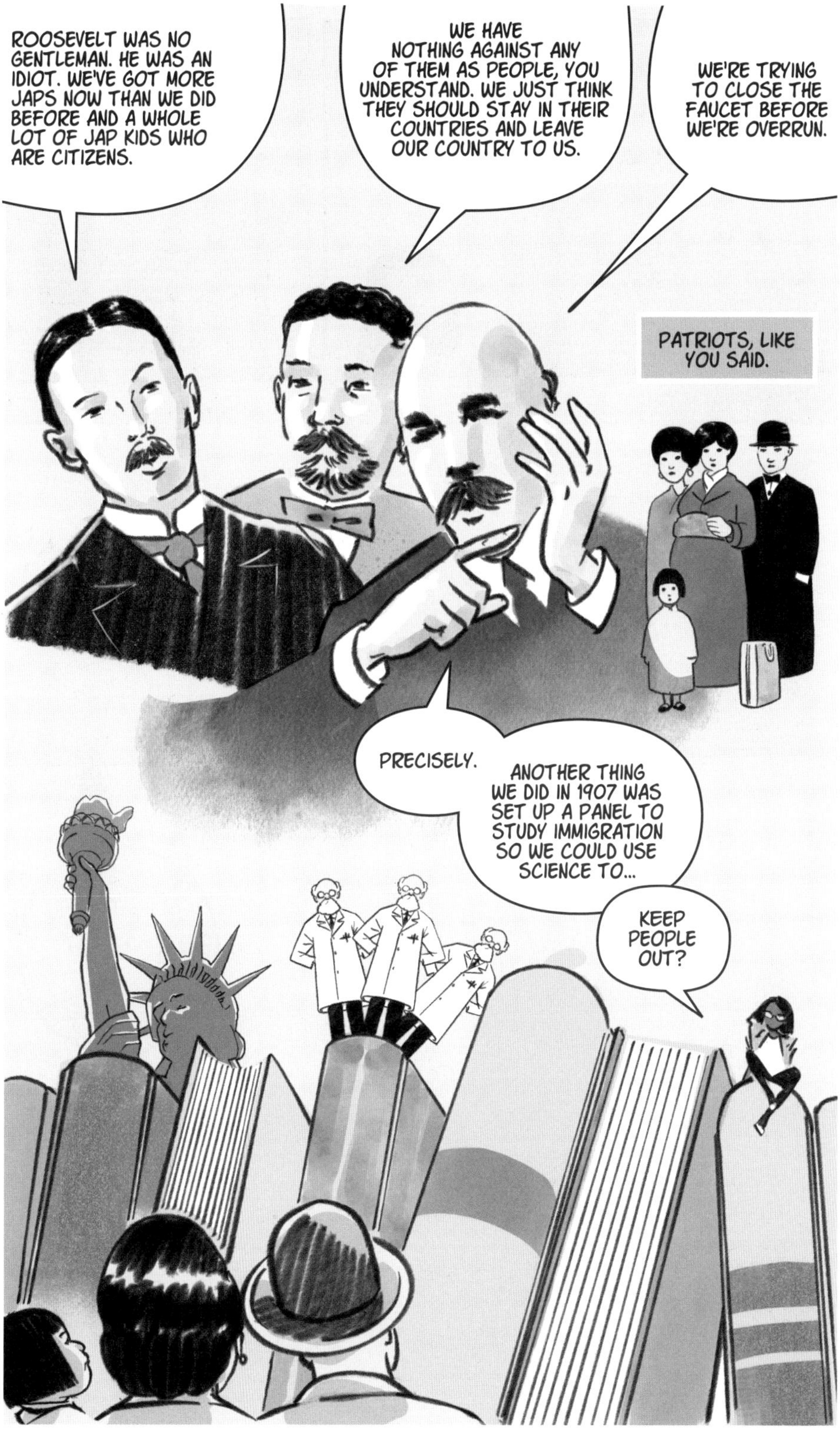
ROOSEVELT WAS NO GENTLEMAN. HE WAS AN IDIOT. WE'VE GOT MORE JAPS NOW THAN WE DID BEFORE AND A WHOLE LOT OF JAP KIDS WHO ARE CITIZENS.
WE HAVE NOTHING AGAINST ANY OF THEM AS PEOPLE, YOU UNDERSTAND. WE JUST THINK THEY SHOULD STAY IN THEIR COUNTRIES AND LEAVE OUR COUNTRY TO US.
WE'RE TRYING TO CLOSE THE FAUCET BEFORE WE'RE OVERRUN.
PATRIOTS, LIKE YOU SAID.
PRECISELY.
ANOTHER THING WE DID IN 1907 WAS SET UP A PANEL TO STUDY IMMIGRATION SO WE COULD USE SCIENCE TO...
KEEP PEOPLE OUT?

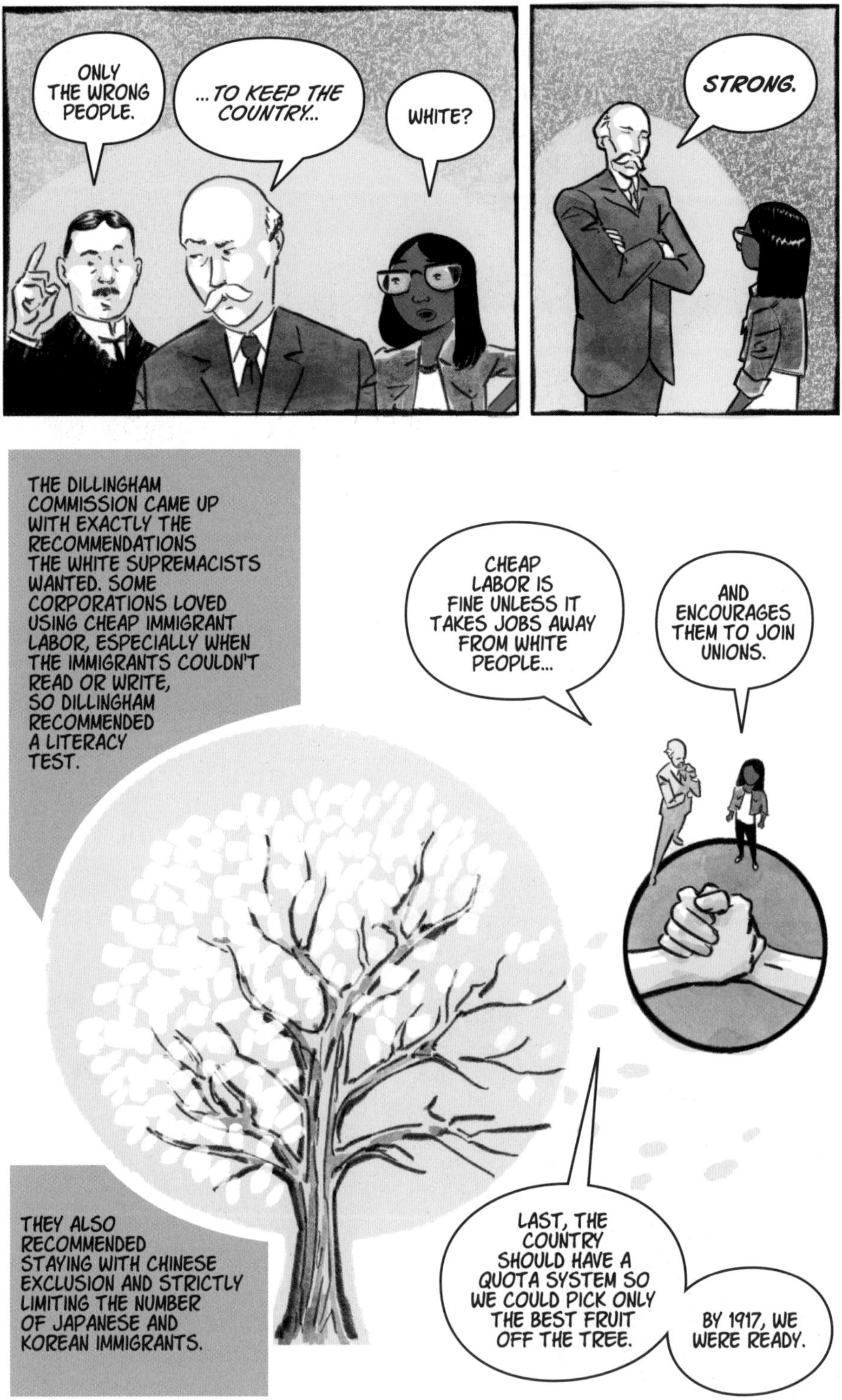
ONLY THE WRONG PEOPLE.
...TO KEEP THE COUNTRY...
WHITE?
STRONG.
THE DILLINGHAM COMMISSION CAME UP WITH EXACTLY THE RECOMMENDATIONS THE WHITE SUPREMACISTS WANTED. SOME CORPORATIONS LOVED USING CHEAP IMMIGRANT LABOR, ESPECIALLY WHEN THE IMMIGRANTS COULDN'T READ OR WRITE, SO DILLINGHAM RECOMMENDED A LITERACY TEST.
CHEAP LABOR IS FINE UNLESS IT TAKES JOBS AWAY FROM WHITE PEOPLE...
AND ENCOURAGES THEM TO JOIN UNIONS.
THEY ALSO RECOMMENDED STAYING WITH CHINESE EXCLUSION AND STRICTLY LIMITING THE NUMBER OF JAPANESE AND KOREAN IMMIGRANTS.
LAST, THE COUNTRY SHOULD HAVE A QUOTA SYSTEM SO WE COULD PICK ONLY THE BEST FRUIT OFF THE TREE.
BY 1917, WE WERE READY.

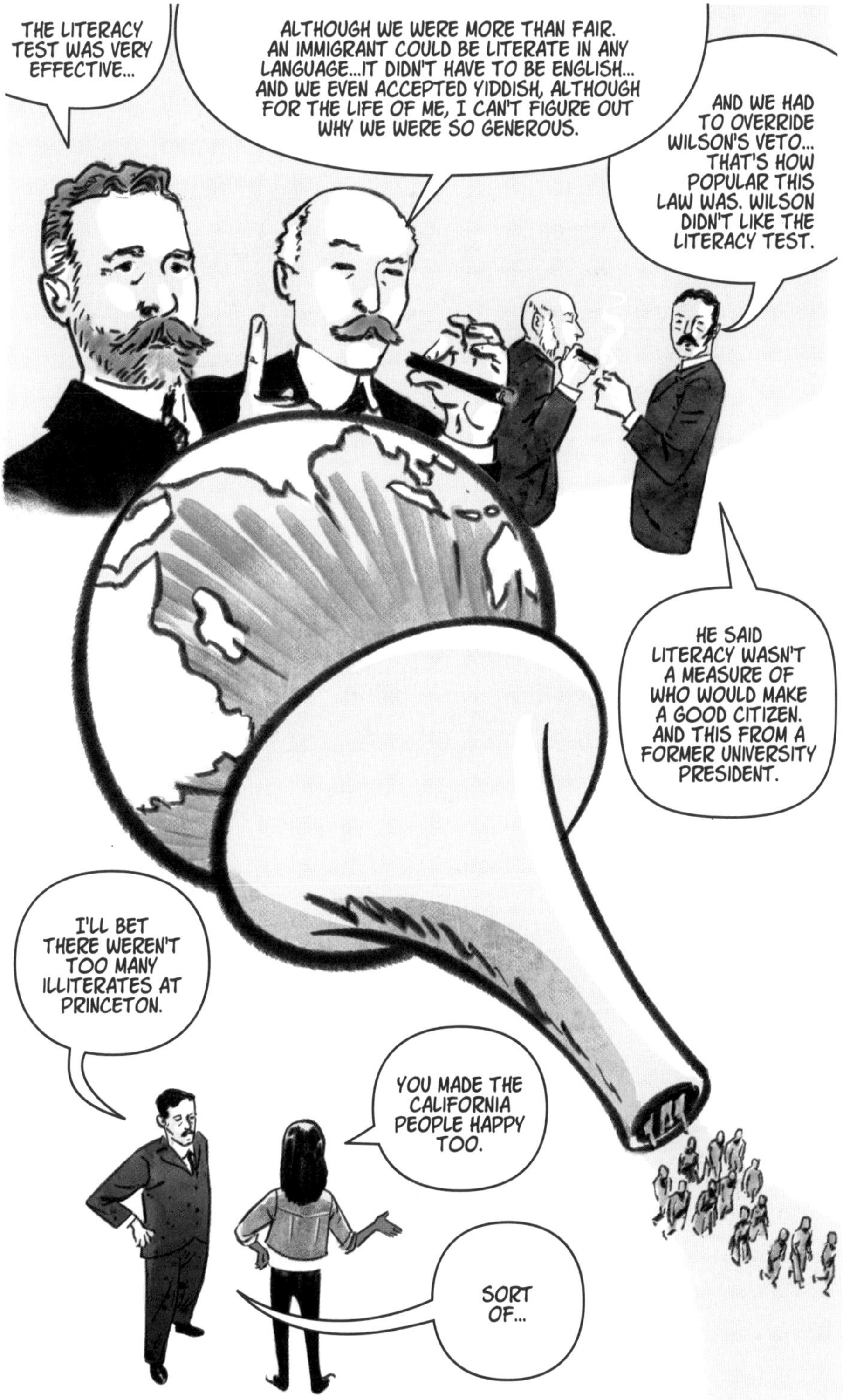
THE LITERACY TEST WAS VERY EFFECTIVE...
ALTHOUGH WE WERE MORE THAN FAIR. AN IMMIGRANT COULD BE LITERATE IN ANY LANGUAGE...IT DIDN'T HAVE TO BE ENGLISH... AND WE EVEN ACCEPTED YIDDISH, ALTHOUGH FOR THE LIFE OF ME, I CAN'T FIGURE OUT WHY WE WERE SO GENEROUS.
AND WE HAD TO OVERRIDE WILSON'S VETO... THAT'S HOW POPULAR THIS LAW WAS. WILSON DIDN'T LIKE THE LITERACY TEST.
HE SAID LITERACY WASN'T A MEASURE OF WHO WOULD MAKE A GOOD CITIZEN. AND THIS FROM A FORMER UNIVERSITY PRESIDENT.
I'LL BET THERE WEREN'T TOO MANY ILLITERATES AT PRINCETON.
YOU MADE THE CALIFORNIA PEOPLE HAPPY TOO.
SORT OF...

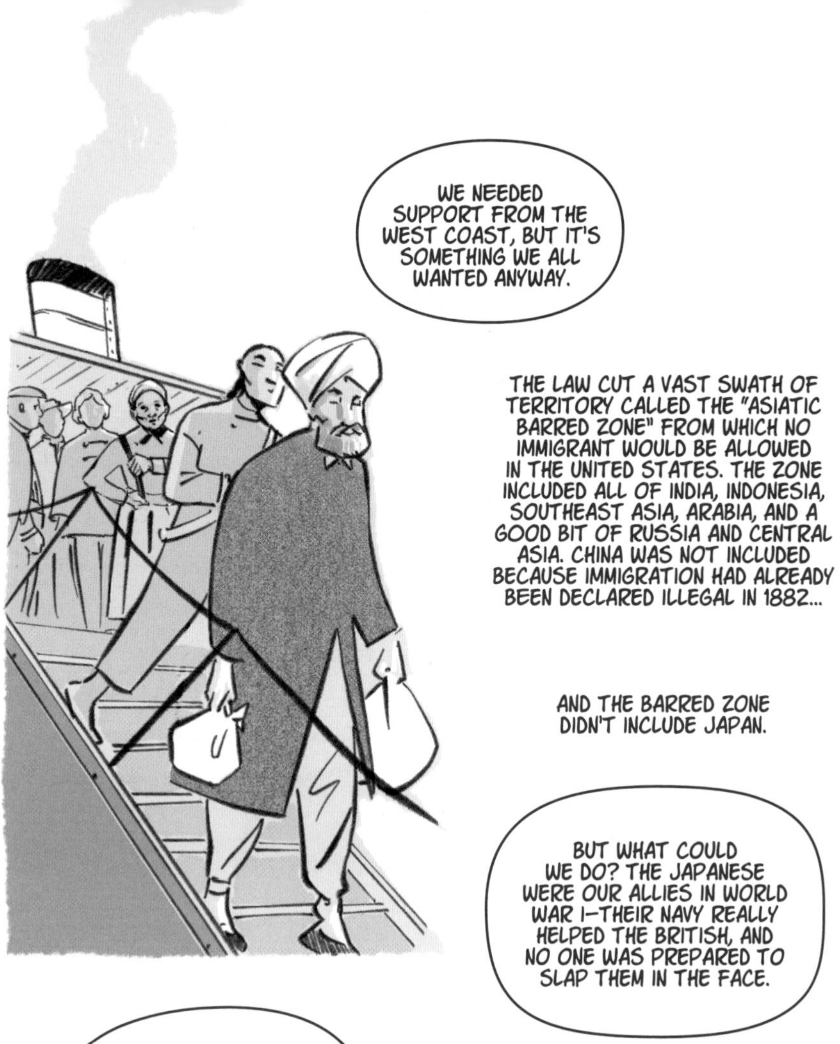
WE NEEDED SUPPORT FROM THE WEST COAST, BUT IT'S SOMETHING WE ALL WANTED ANYWAY.
THE LAW CUT A VAST SWATH OF TERRITORY CALLED THE "ASIATIC BARRED ZONE" FROM WHICH NO IMMIGRANT WOULD BE ALLOWED IN THE UNITED STATES. THE ZONE INCLUDED ALL OF INDIA, INDONESIA, SOUTHEAST ASIA, ARABIA, AND A GOOD BIT OF RUSSIA AND CENTRAL ASIA. CHINA WAS NOT INCLUDED BECAUSE IMMIGRATION HAD ALREADY BEEN DECLARED ILLEGAL IN 1882...
AND THE BARRED ZONE DIDN'T INCLUDE JAPAN.
BUT WHAT COULD WE DO? THE JAPANESE WERE OUR ALLIES IN WORLD WAR I—THEIR NAVY REALLY HELPED THE BRITISH, AND NO ONE WAS PREPARED TO SLAP THEM IN THE FACE.

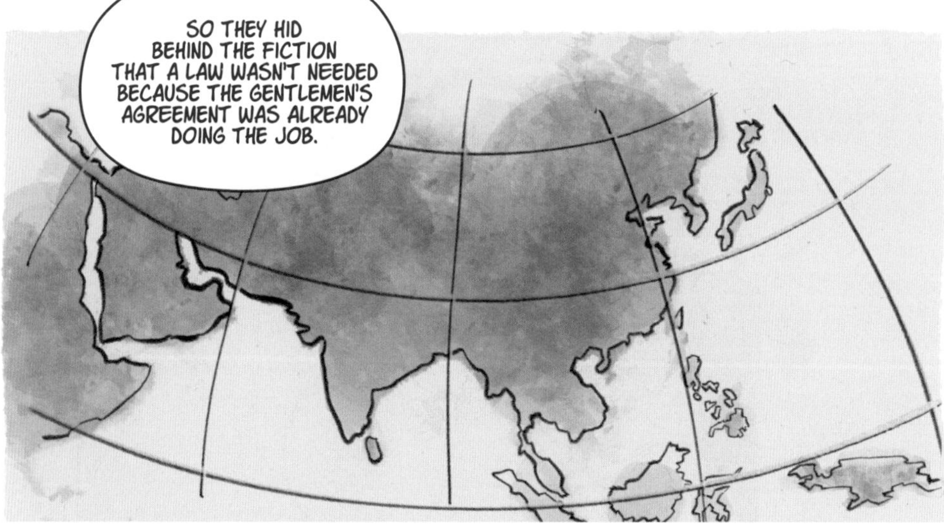
SO THEY HID BEHIND THE FICTION THAT A LAW WASN'T NEEDED BECAUSE THE GENTLEMEN'S AGREEMENT WAS ALREADY DOING THE JOB.

WHEN THE WAR ENDED, HOWEVER, THE WHITE SUPREMACISTS GOT BACK TO WORK.

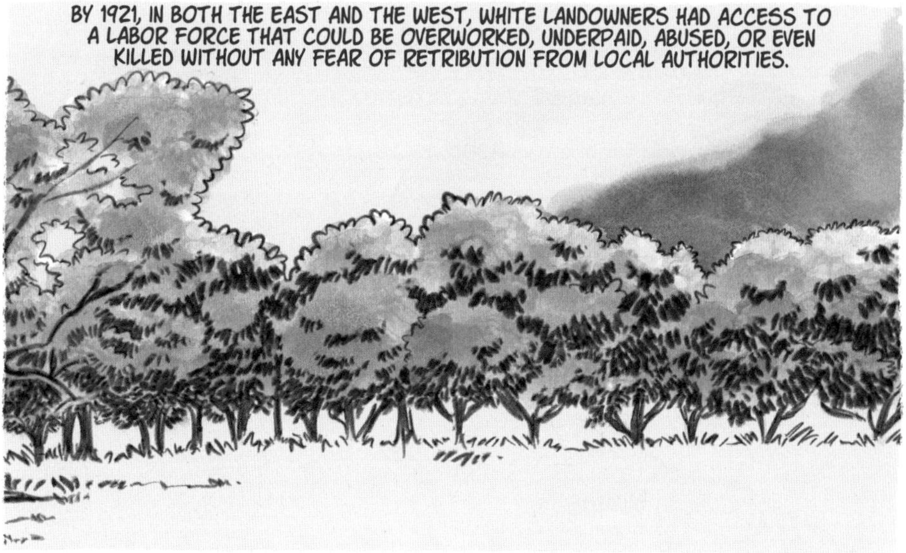
BY 1921, IN BOTH THE EAST AND THE WEST, WHITE LANDOWNERS HAD ACCESS TO A LABOR FORCE THAT COULD BE OVERWORKED, UNDERPAID, ABUSED, OR EVEN KILLED WITHOUT ANY FEAR OF RETRIBUTION FROM LOCAL AUTHORITIES.

THERE WERE DIFFERENCES, HOWEVER. AFRICAN AMERICANS IN THE SOUTH WERE AMERICAN CITIZENS, BUT PREVENTED THROUGH TERROR AND LEGAL TRICKERY FROM EXERCISING EVEN THE MOST BASIC RIGHTS OF CITIZENSHIP. MOST WERE DOOMED TO WORK THE LAND FOR WHITE MASTERS WITH LITTLE DIFFERENCE FROM WHEN THEY WERE SLAVES.

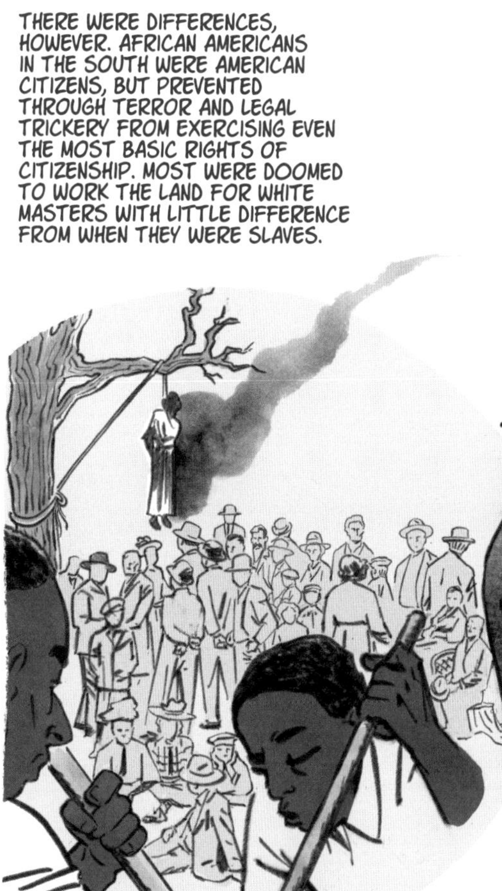

THE JAPANESE IN THE WEST WERE NOT CITIZENS, BUT A FEW MANAGED TO EXPLOIT LOOPHOLES IN THE LAW TO EITHER BUY LAND THEMSELVES OR DO SO THROUGH CONTRIVANCES, SUCH AS LEASES OR DUMMY CORPORATIONS.

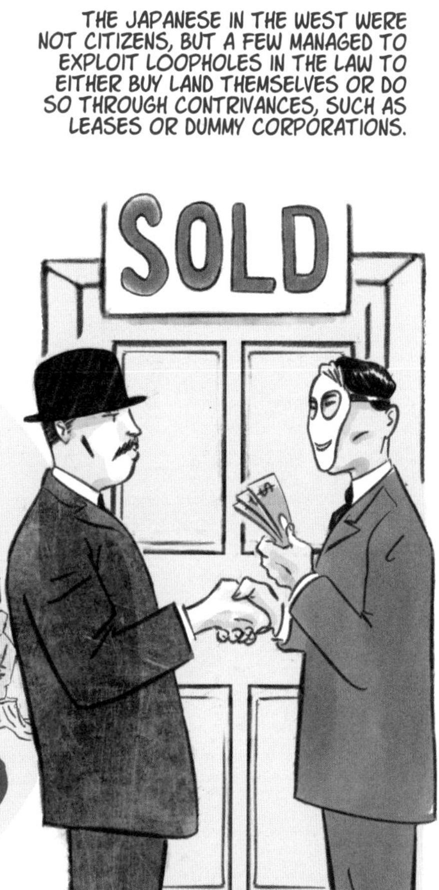
SOLD

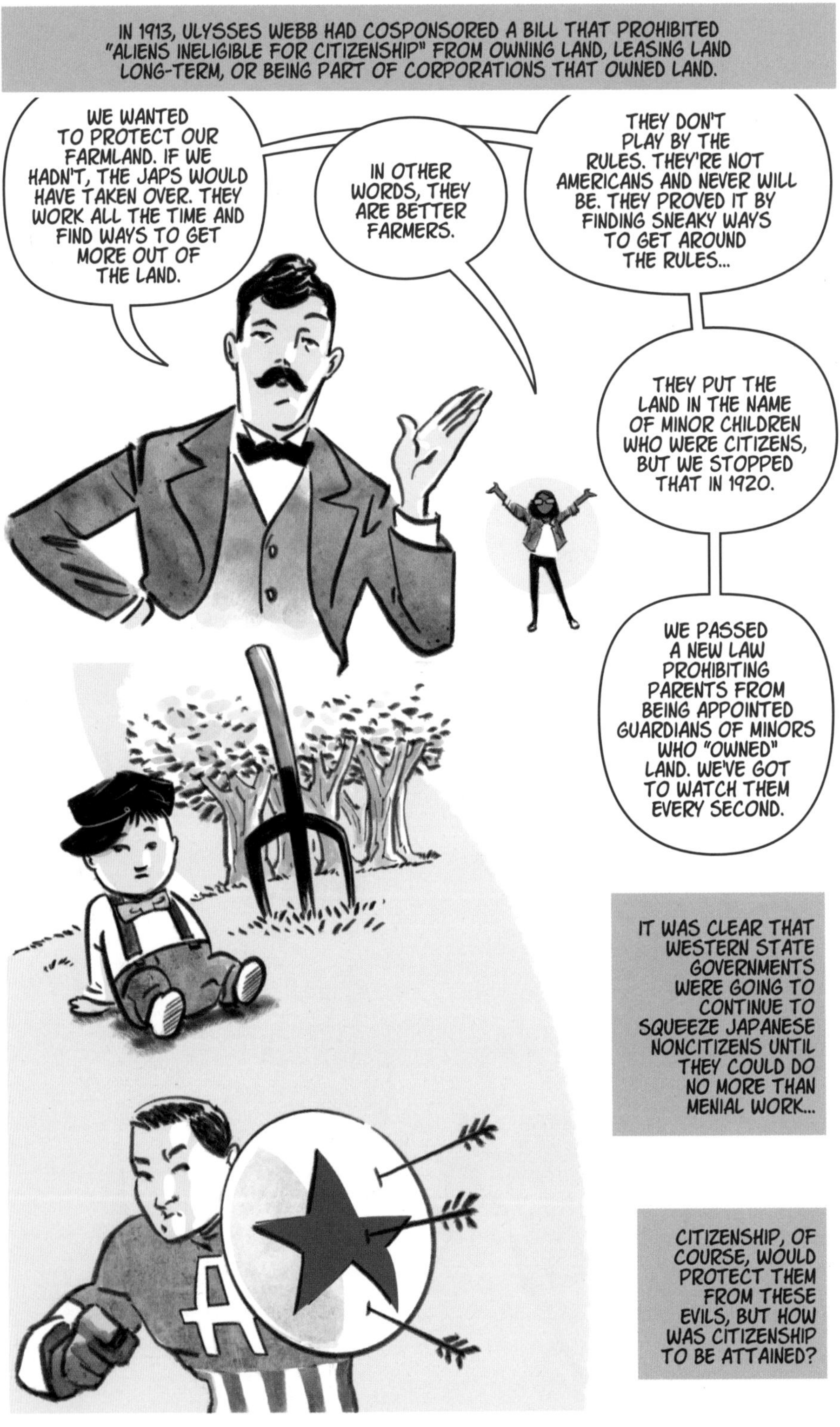
IN 1913, ULYSSES WEBB HAD COSPONSORED A BILL THAT PROHIBITED "ALIENS INELIGIBLE FOR CITIZENSHIP" FROM OWNING LAND, LEASING LAND LONG-TERM, OR BEING PART OF CORPORATIONS THAT OWNED LAND.
WE WANTED TO PROTECT OUR FARMLAND. IF WE HADN'T, THE JAPS WOULD HAVE TAKEN OVER. THEY WORK ALL THE TIME AND FIND WAYS TO GET MORE OUT OF THE LAND.
IN OTHER WORDS, THEY ARE BETTER FARMERS.
THEY DON'T PLAY BY THE RULES. THEY'RE NOT AMERICANS AND NEVER WILL BE. THEY PROVED IT BY FINDING SNEAKY WAYS TO GET AROUND THE RULES...
THEY PUT THE LAND IN THE NAME OF MINOR CHILDREN WHO WERE CITIZENS, BUT WE STOPPED THAT IN 1920.
WE PASSED A NEW LAW PROHIBITING PARENTS FROM BEING APPOINTED GUARDIANS OF MINORS WHO "OWNED" LAND. WE'VE GOT TO WATCH THEM EVERY SECOND.
IT WAS CLEAR THAT WESTERN STATE GOVERNMENTS WERE GOING TO CONTINUE TO SQUEEZE JAPANESE NONCITIZENS UNTIL THEY COULD DO NO MORE THAN MENIAL WORK...
CITIZENSHIP, OF COURSE, WOULD PROTECT THEM FROM THESE EVILS, BUT HOW WAS CITIZENSHIP TO BE ATTAINED?
A

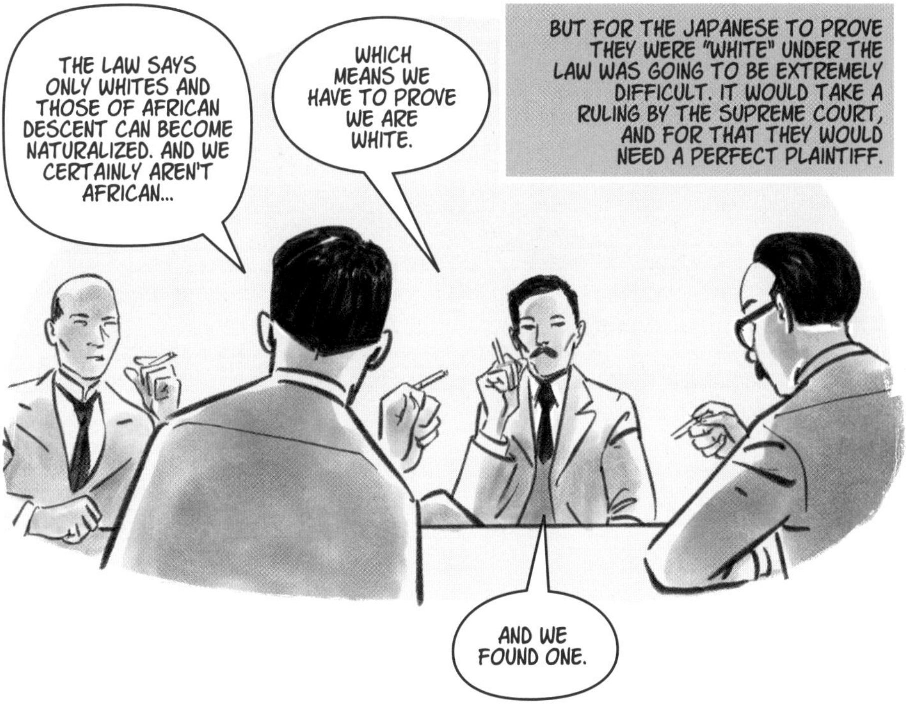
THE LAW SAYS ONLY WHITES AND THOSE OF AFRICAN DESCENT CAN BECOME NATURALIZED. AND WE CERTAINLY AREN'T AFRICAN...
WHICH MEANS WE HAVE TO PROVE WE ARE WHITE.
BUT FOR THE JAPANESE TO PROVE THEY WERE "WHITE" UNDER THE LAW WAS GOING TO BE EXTREMELY DIFFICULT. IT WOULD TAKE A RULING BY THE SUPREME COURT, AND FOR THAT THEY WOULD NEED A PERFECT PLAINTIFF.
AND WE FOUND ONE.

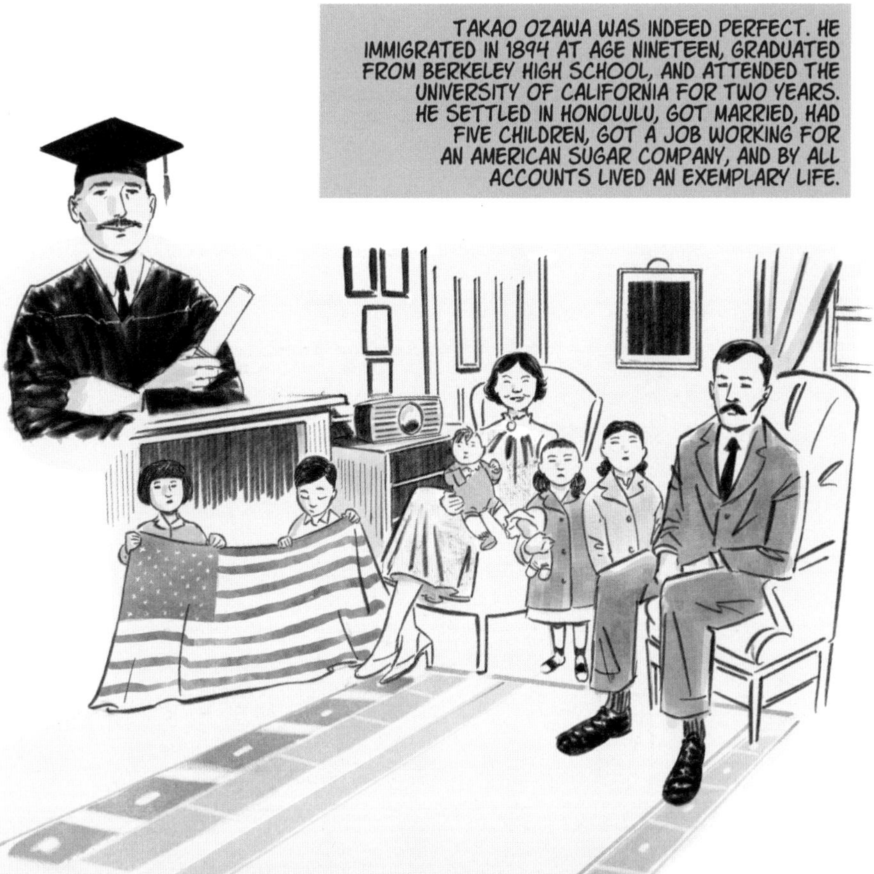
TAKAO OZAWA WAS INDEED PERFECT. HE IMMIGRATED IN 1894 AT AGE NINETEEN, GRADUATED FROM BERKELEY HIGH SCHOOL, AND ATTENDED THE UNIVERSITY OF CALIFORNIA FOR TWO YEARS. HE SETTLED IN HONOLULU, GOT MARRIED, HAD FIVE CHILDREN, GOT A JOB WORKING FOR AN AMERICAN SUGAR COMPANY, AND BY ALL ACCOUNTS LIVED AN EXEMPLARY LIFE.

HIS FAMILY WAS CHRISTIAN, ONLY ENGLISH WAS SPOKEN IN THEIR HOME, HE LIVED IN A MOSTLY WHITE NEIGHBORHOOD, AND HE WAS WELL-LIKED BY HIS MANY FRIENDS OF BOTH RACES.

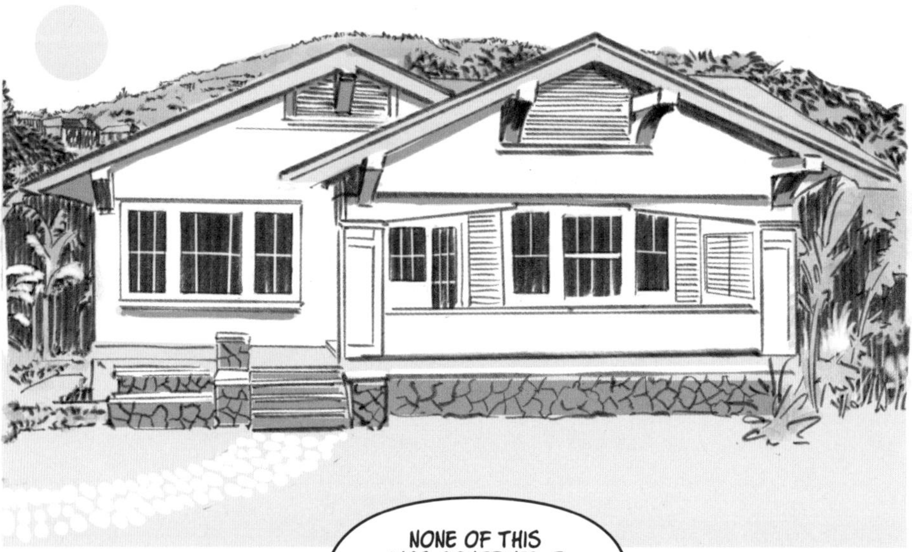

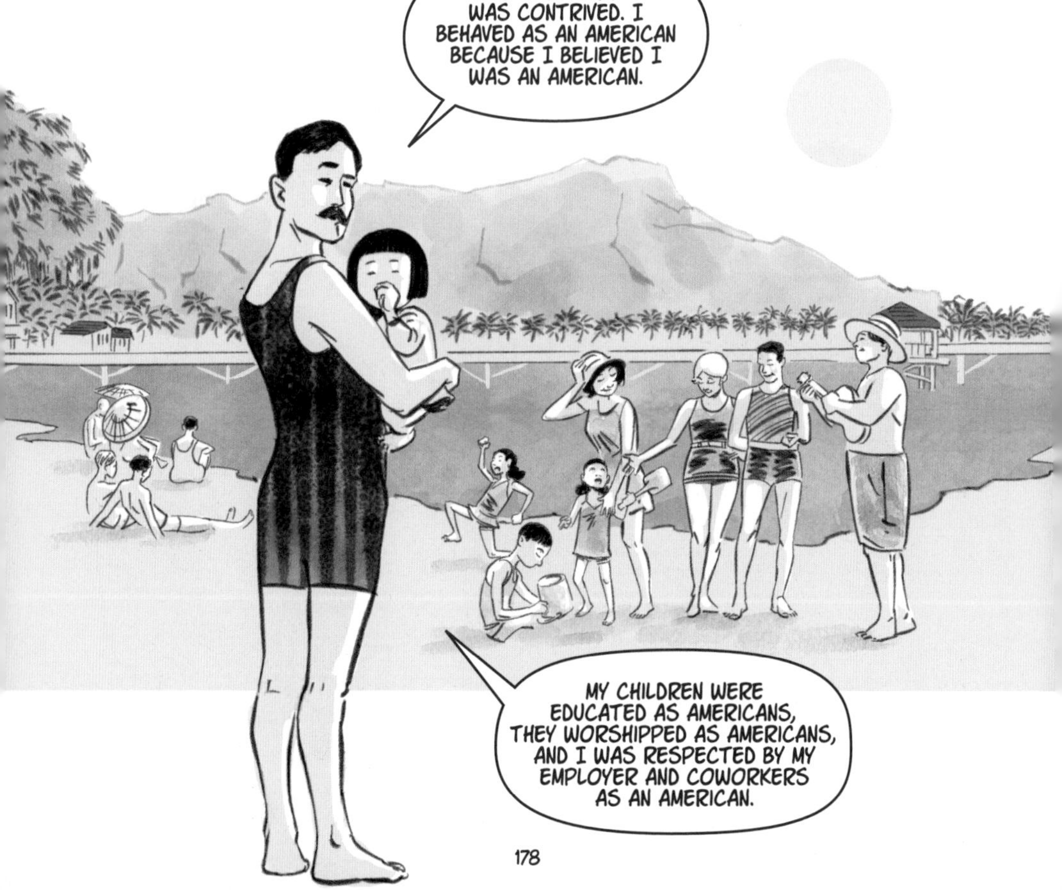
NONE OF THIS WAS CONTRIVED. I BEHAVED AS AN AMERICAN BECAUSE I BELIEVED I WAS AN AMERICAN.
MY CHILDREN WERE EDUCATED AS AMERICANS, THEY WORSHIPPED AS AMERICANS, AND I WAS RESPECTED BY MY EMPLOYER AND COWORKERS AS AN AMERICAN.

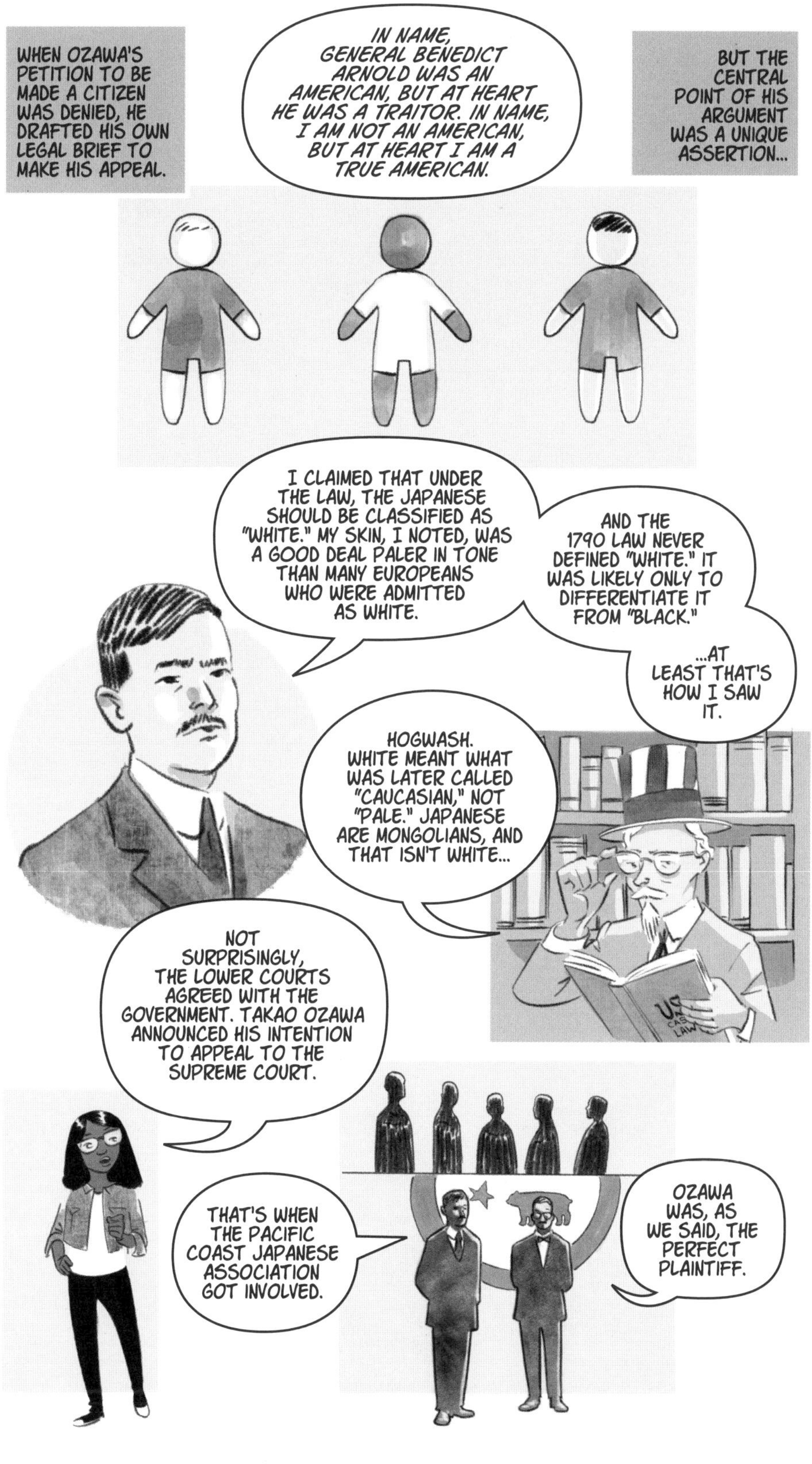
WHEN OZAWA'S PETITION TO BE MADE A CITIZEN WAS DENIED, HE DRAFTED HIS OWN LEGAL BRIEF TO MAKE HIS APPEAL.
IN NAME, GENERAL BENEDICT ARNOLD WAS AN AMERICAN, BUT AT HEART HE WAS A TRAITOR. IN NAME, I AM NOT AN AMERICAN, BUT AT HEART I AM A TRUE AMERICAN.
BUT THE CENTRAL POINT OF HIS ARGUMENT WAS A UNIQUE ASSERTION...
I CLAIMED THAT UNDER THE LAW, THE JAPANESE SHOULD BE CLASSIFIED AS "WHITE." MY SKIN, I NOTED, WAS A GOOD DEAL PALER IN TONE THAN MANY EUROPEANS WHO WERE ADMITTED AS WHITE.
AND THE 1790 LAW NEVER DEFINED "WHITE." IT WAS LIKELY ONLY TO DIFFERENTIATE IT FROM "BLACK."
...AT LEAST THAT'S HOW I SAW IT.
HOGWASH. WHITE MEANT WHAT WAS LATER CALLED "CAUCASIAN," NOT "PALE." JAPANESE ARE MONGOLIANS, AND THAT ISN'T WHITE...
NOT SURPRISINGLY, THE LOWER COURTS AGREED WITH THE GOVERNMENT. TAKAO OZAWA ANNOUNCED HIS INTENTION TO APPEAL TO THE SUPREME COURT.
THAT'S WHEN THE PACIFIC COAST JAPANESE ASSOCIATION GOT INVOLVED.
OZAWA WAS, AS WE SAID, THE PERFECT PLAINTIFF.

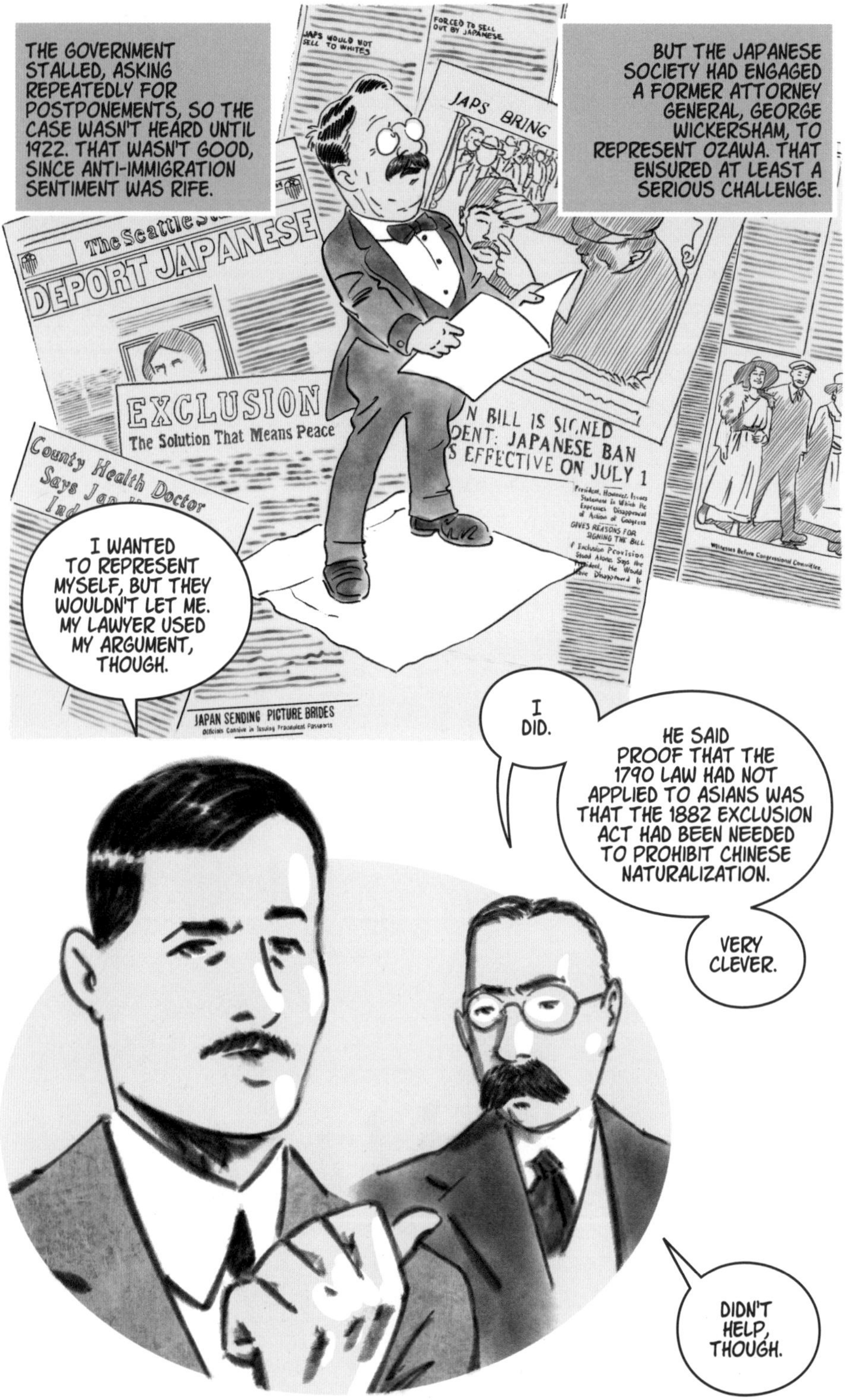
THE GOVERNMENT STALLED, ASKING REPEATEDLY FOR POSTPONEMENTS, SO THE CASE WASN'T HEARD UNTIL 1922. THAT WASN'T GOOD, SINCE ANTI-IMMIGRATION SENTIMENT WAS RIFE.
JAPS WOULD NOT SELL TO WHITES
FORCED TO SELL OUT BY JAPANESE
JAPS BRING
BUT THE JAPANESE SOCIETY HAD ENGAGED A FORMER ATTORNEY GENERAL, GEORGE WICKERSHAM, TO REPRESENT OZAWA. THAT ENSURED AT LEAST A SERIOUS CHALLENGE.
DEPORT JAPANESE
EXCLUSION
The Solution That Means Peace
County Health Doctor Says
JAPANESE BAN
EFFECTIVE ON JULY 1
I WANTED TO REPRESENT MYSELF, BUT THEY WOULDN'T LET ME. MY LAWYER USED MY ARGUMENT, THOUGH.
JAPAN SENDING PICTURE BRIDES
I DID.
HE SAID PROOF THAT THE 1790 LAW HAD NOT APPLIED TO ASIANS WAS THAT THE 1882 EXCLUSION ACT HAD BEEN NEEDED TO PROHIBIT CHINESE NATURALIZATION.
VERY CLEVER.
DIDN'T HELP, THOUGH.

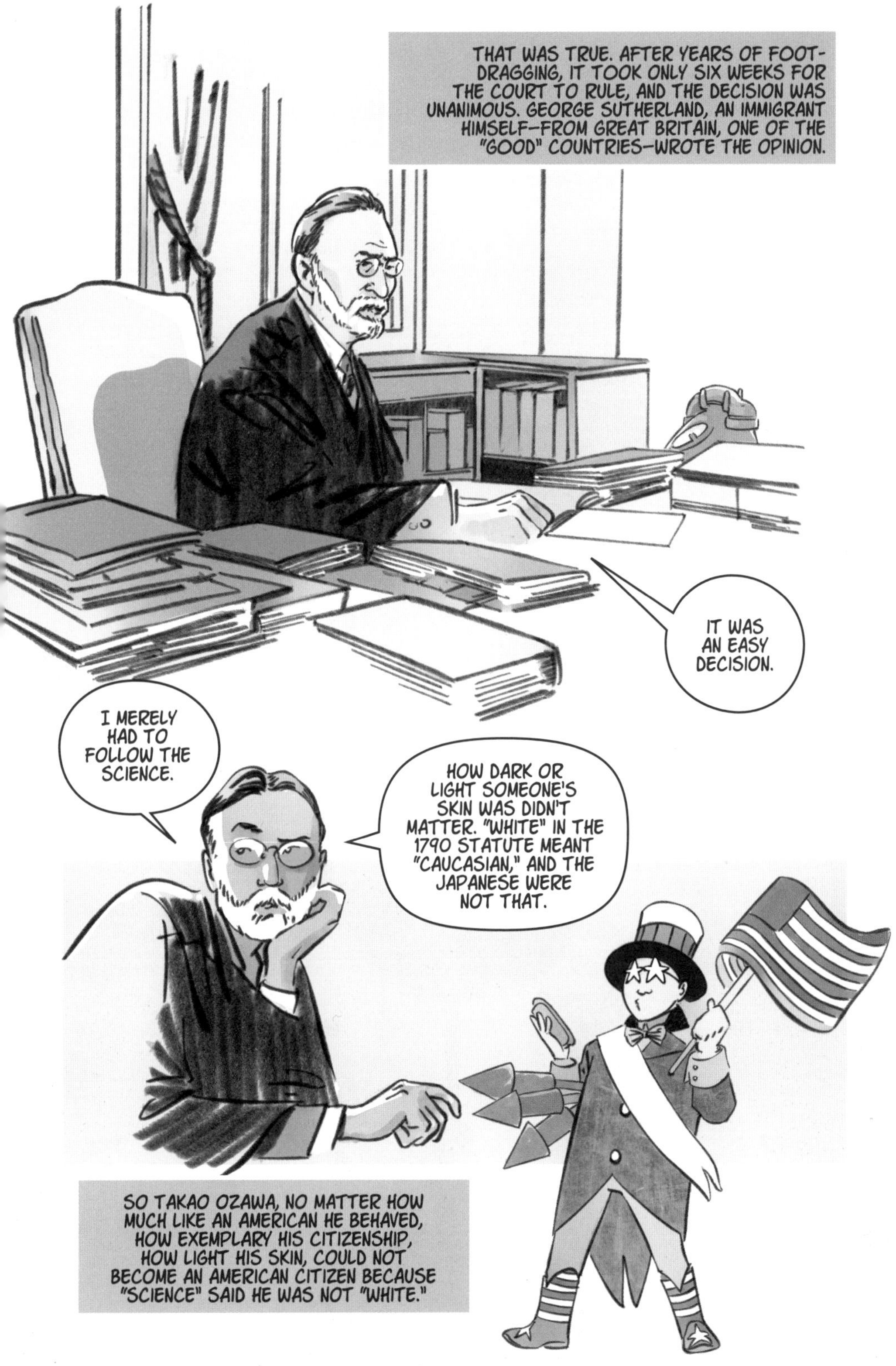
THAT WAS TRUE. AFTER YEARS OF FOOT-DRAGGING, IT TOOK ONLY SIX WEEKS FOR THE COURT TO RULE, AND THE DECISION WAS UNANIMOUS. GEORGE SUTHERLAND, AN IMMIGRANT HIMSELF—FROM GREAT BRITAIN, ONE OF THE "GOOD" COUNTRIES—WROTE THE OPINION.
IT WAS AN EASY DECISION.
I MERELY HAD TO FOLLOW THE SCIENCE.
HOW DARK OR LIGHT SOMEONE'S SKIN WAS DIDN'T MATTER. "WHITE" IN THE 1790 STATUTE MEANT "CAUCASIAN," AND THE JAPANESE WERE NOT THAT.
SO TAKAO OZAWA, NO MATTER HOW MUCH LIKE AN AMERICAN HE BEHAVED, HOW EXEMPLARY HIS CITIZENSHIP, HOW LIGHT HIS SKIN, COULD NOT BECOME AN AMERICAN CITIZEN BECAUSE "SCIENCE" SAID HE WAS NOT "WHITE."

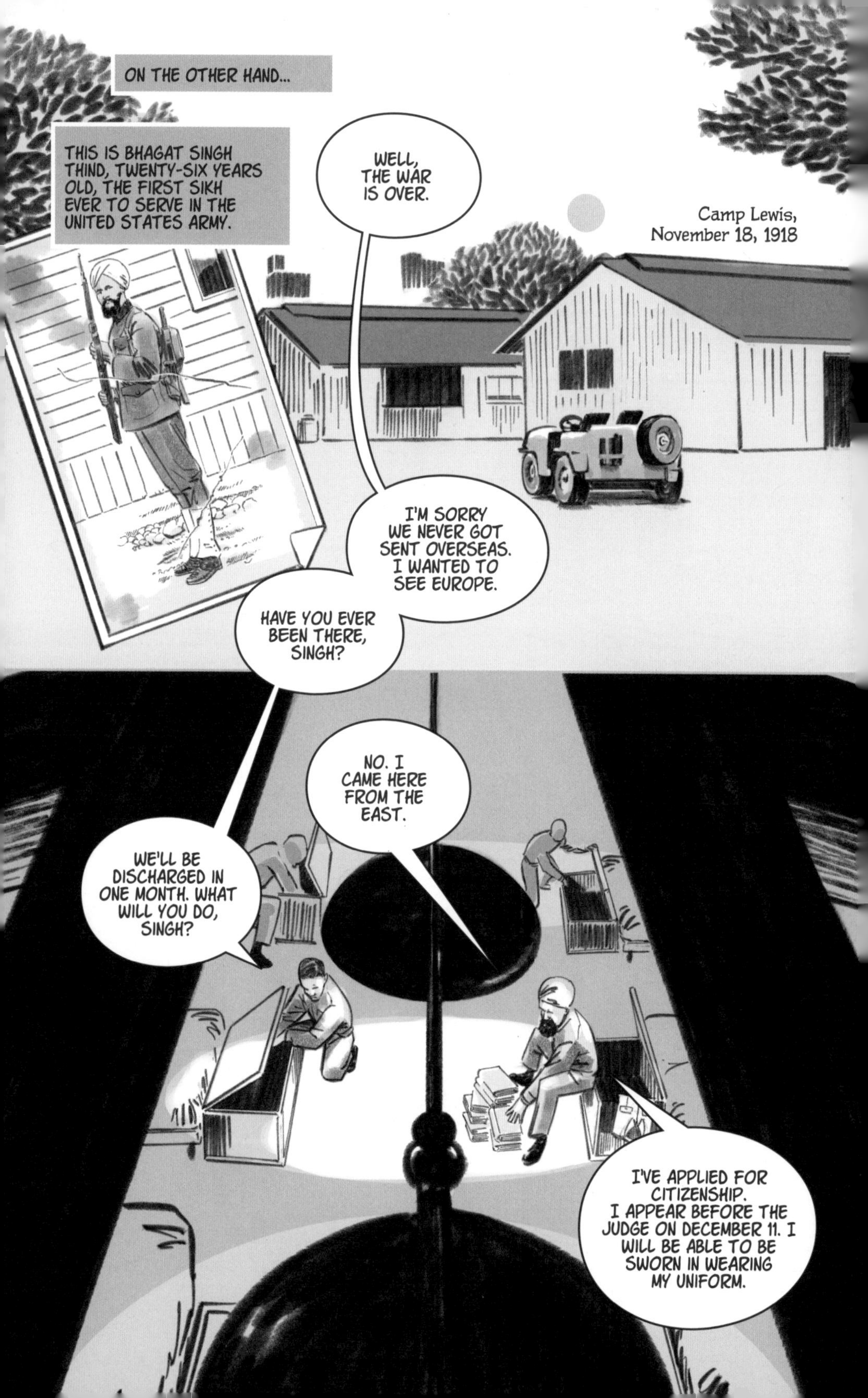
ON THE OTHER HAND...
THIS IS BHAGAT SINGH THIND, TWENTY-SIX YEARS OLD, THE FIRST SIKH EVER TO SERVE IN THE UNITED STATES ARMY.
WELL, THE WAR IS OVER.
Camp Lewis, November 18, 1918
I'M SORRY WE NEVER GOT SENT OVERSEAS. I WANTED TO SEE EUROPE.
HAVE YOU EVER BEEN THERE, SINGH?
NO. I CAME HERE FROM THE EAST.
WE'LL BE DISCHARGED IN ONE MONTH. WHAT WILL YOU DO, SINGH?
I'VE APPLIED FOR CITIZENSHIP. I APPEAR BEFORE THE JUDGE ON DECEMBER 11. I WILL BE ABLE TO BE SWORN IN WEARING MY UNIFORM.

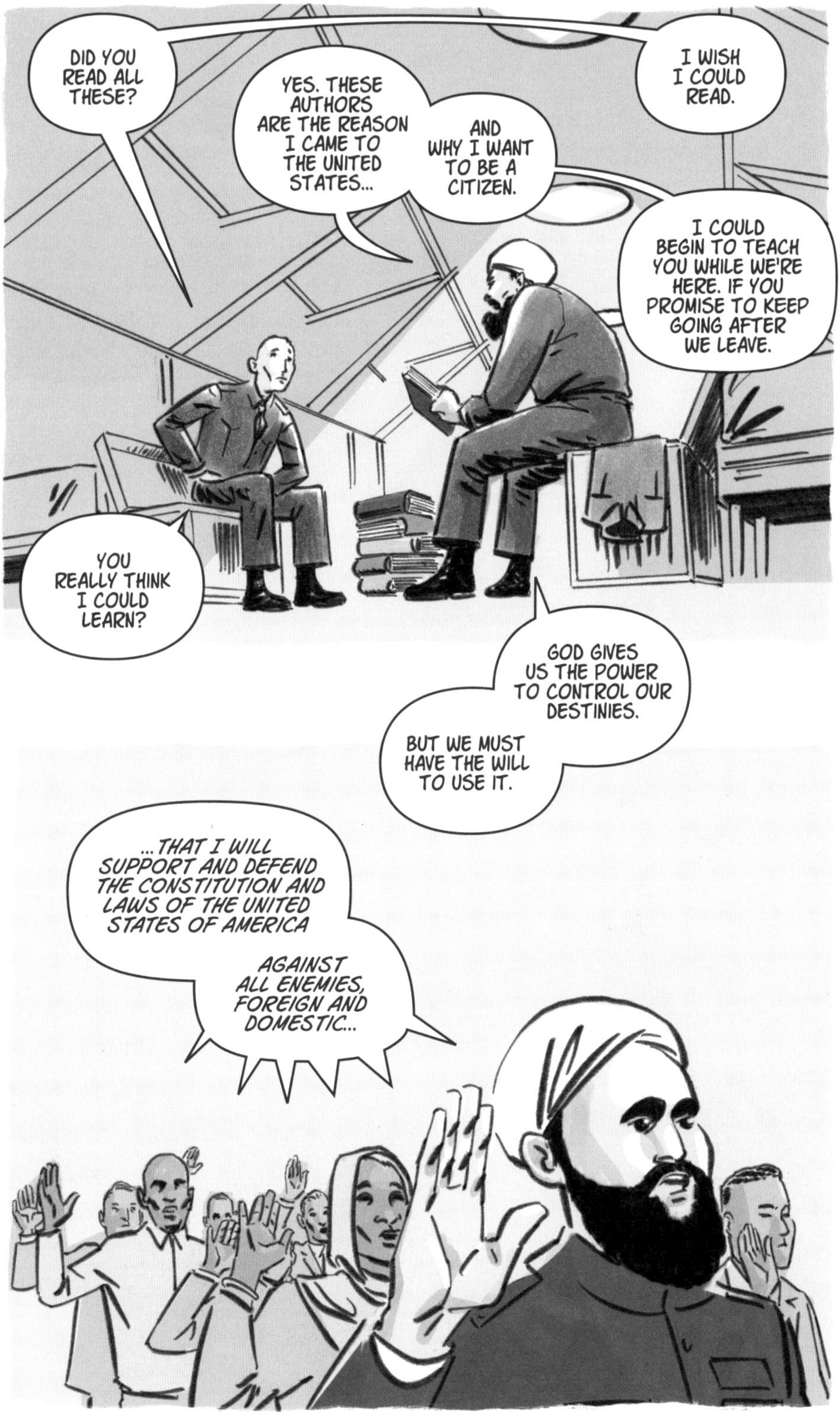
DID YOU READ ALL THESE?
YES. THESE AUTHORS ARE THE REASON I CAME TO THE UNITED STATES...
AND WHY I WANT TO BE A CITIZEN.
I WISH I COULD READ.
I COULD BEGIN TO TEACH YOU WHILE WE'RE HERE. IF YOU PROMISE TO KEEP GOING AFTER WE LEAVE.
YOU REALLY THINK I COULD LEARN?
GOD GIVES US THE POWER TO CONTROL OUR DESTINIES.
BUT WE MUST HAVE THE WILL TO USE IT.
...THAT I WILL SUPPORT AND DEFEND THE CONSTITUTION AND LAWS OF THE UNITED STATES OF AMERICA
AGAINST ALL ENEMIES, FOREIGN AND DOMESTIC...

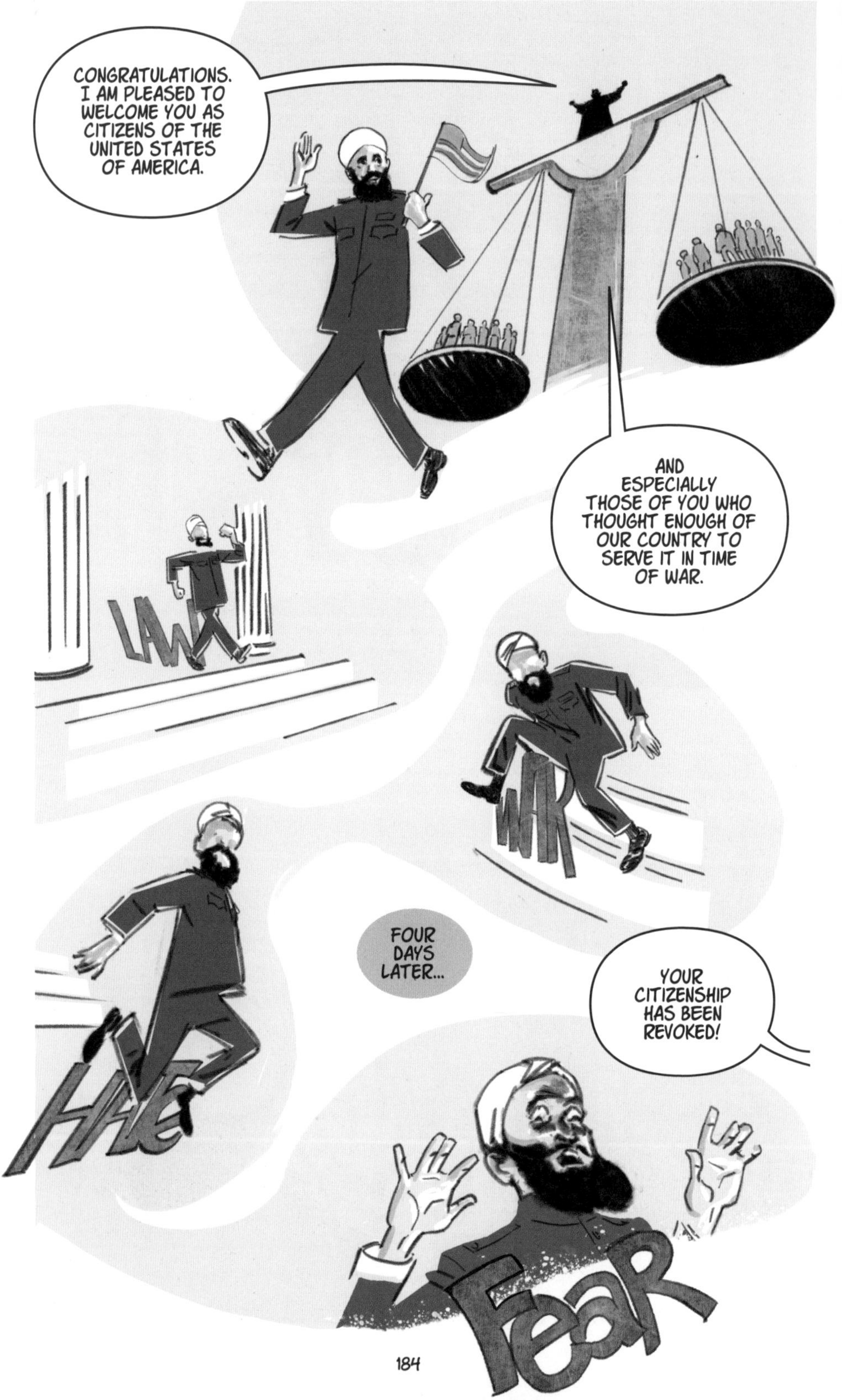
CONGRATULATIONS. I AM PLEASED TO WELCOME YOU AS CITIZENS OF THE UNITED STATES OF AMERICA.
AND ESPECIALLY THOSE OF YOU WHO THOUGHT ENOUGH OF OUR COUNTRY TO SERVE IT IN TIME OF WAR.
LAW
WAR
HATE
FOUR DAYS LATER...
YOUR CITIZENSHIP HAS BEEN REVOKED!
FEAR

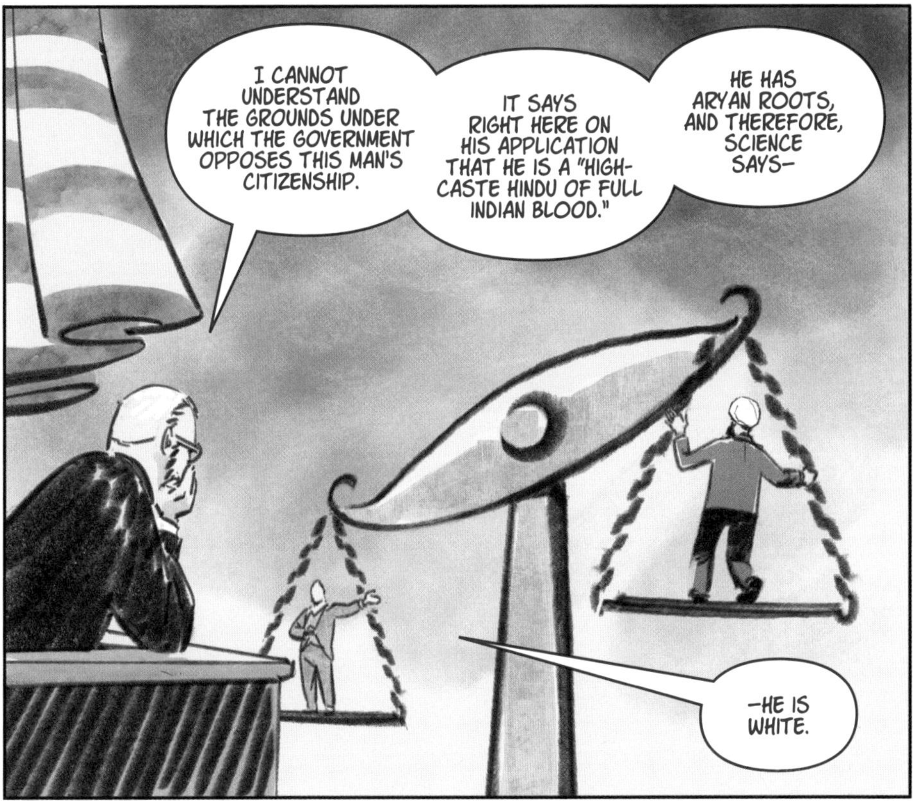
I CANNOT UNDERSTAND THE GROUNDS UNDER WHICH THE GOVERNMENT OPPOSES THIS MAN'S CITIZENSHIP.
IT SAYS RIGHT HERE ON HIS APPLICATION THAT HE IS A "HIGH-CASTE HINDU OF FULL INDIAN BLOOD."
HE HAS ARYAN ROOTS, AND THEREFORE, SCIENCE SAYS–
–HE IS WHITE.

ALTHOUGH THIND WAS A SIKH, ALL EAST ASIANS WERE CALLED "HINDUS" IN 1919. ACCORDING TO THE ETHNOLOGY OF THE PERIOD, "HIGH-CASTE HINDUS" WERE CONSIDERED CAUCASIAN, AND OTHERS HAD BECOME NATURALIZED CITIZENS.

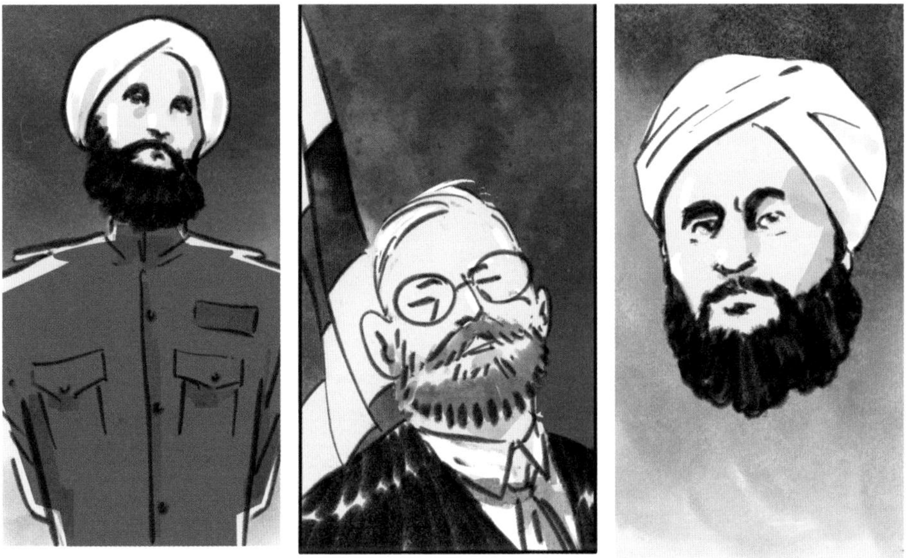

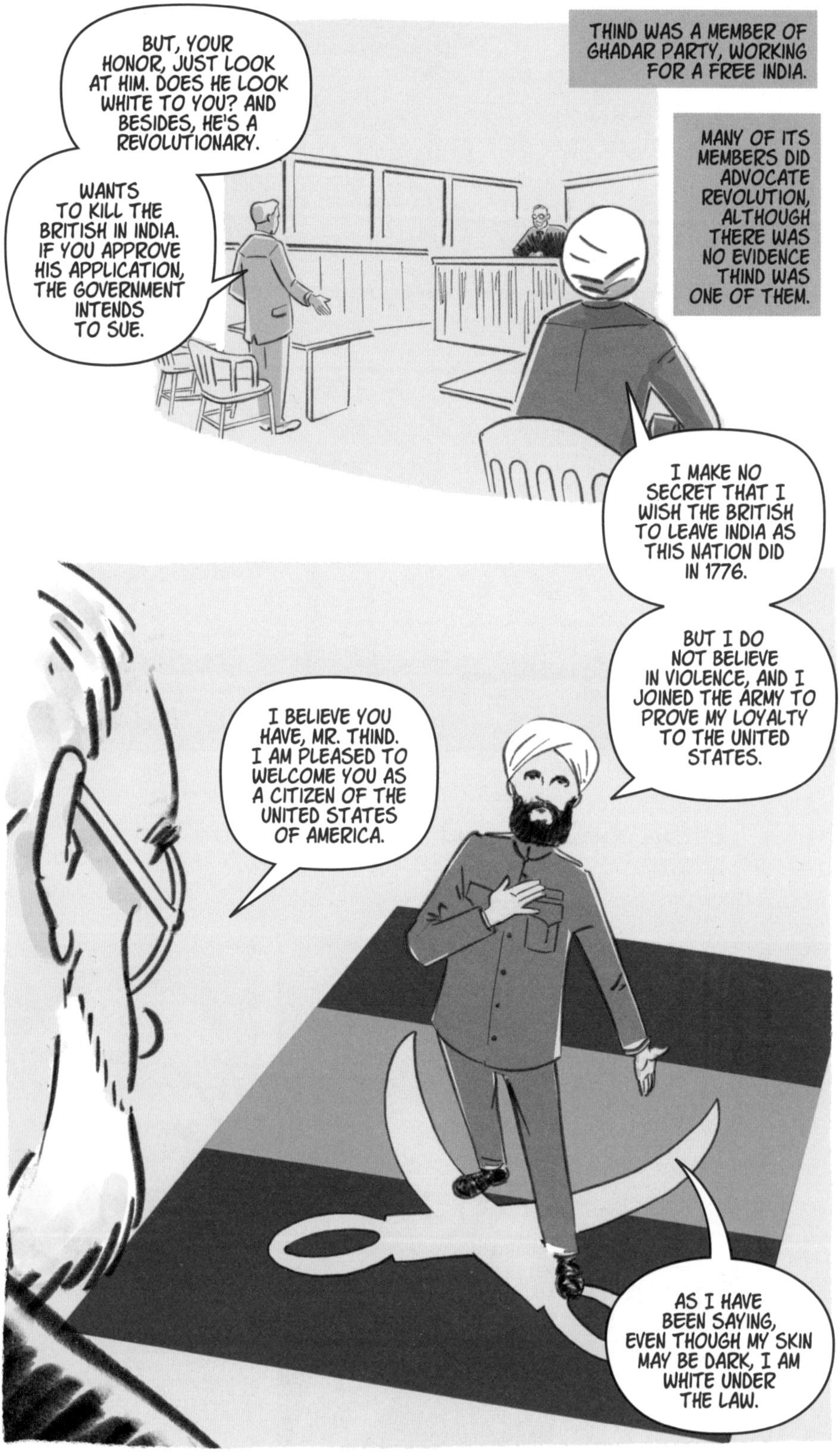
BUT, YOUR HONOR, JUST LOOK AT HIM. DOES HE LOOK WHITE TO YOU? AND BESIDES, HE'S A REVOLUTIONARY.
WANTS TO KILL THE BRITISH IN INDIA. IF YOU APPROVE HIS APPLICATION, THE GOVERNMENT INTENDS TO SUE.
THIND WAS A MEMBER OF GHADAR PARTY, WORKING FOR A FREE INDIA.
MANY OF ITS MEMBERS DID ADVOCATE REVOLUTION, ALTHOUGH THERE WAS NO EVIDENCE THIND WAS ONE OF THEM.
I MAKE NO SECRET THAT I WISH THE BRITISH TO LEAVE INDIA AS THIS NATION DID IN 1776.
BUT I DO NOT BELIEVE IN VIOLENCE, AND I JOINED THE ARMY TO PROVE MY LOYALTY TO THE UNITED STATES.
I BELIEVE YOU HAVE, MR. THIND. I AM PLEASED TO WELCOME YOU AS A CITIZEN OF THE UNITED STATES OF AMERICA.
AS I HAVE BEEN SAYING, EVEN THOUGH MY SKIN MAY BE DARK, I AM WHITE UNDER THE LAW.

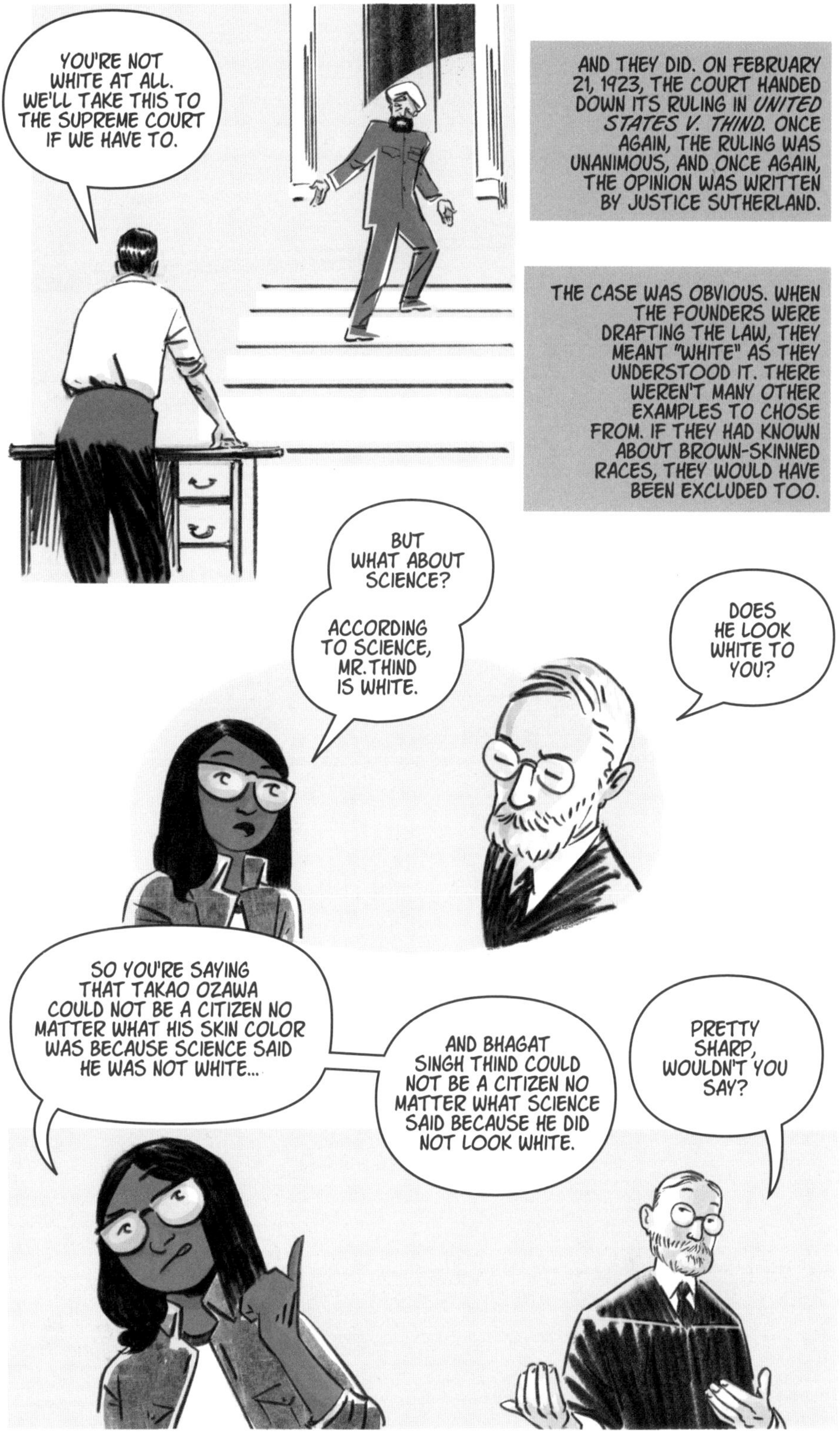

YOU'RE NOT WHITE AT ALL. WE'LL TAKE THIS TO THE SUPREME COURT IF WE HAVE TO.
AND THEY DID. ON FEBRUARY 21, 1923, THE COURT HANDED DOWN ITS RULING IN *UNITED STATES V. THIND*. ONCE AGAIN, THE RULING WAS UNANIMOUS, AND ONCE AGAIN, THE OPINION WAS WRITTEN BY JUSTICE SUTHERLAND.
THE CASE WAS OBVIOUS. WHEN THE FOUNDERS WERE DRAFTING THE LAW, THEY MEANT "WHITE" AS THEY UNDERSTOOD IT. THERE WEREN'T MANY OTHER EXAMPLES TO CHOSE FROM. IF THEY HAD KNOWN ABOUT BROWN-SKINNED RACES, THEY WOULD HAVE BEEN EXCLUDED TOO.
BUT WHAT ABOUT SCIENCE?
ACCORDING TO SCIENCE, MR.THIND IS WHITE.
DOES HE LOOK WHITE TO YOU?
SO YOU'RE SAYING THAT TAKAO OZAWA COULD NOT BE A CITIZEN NO MATTER WHAT HIS SKIN COLOR WAS BECAUSE SCIENCE SAID HE WAS NOT WHITE...
AND BHAGAT SINGH THIND COULD NOT BE A CITIZEN NO MATTER WHAT SCIENCE SAID BECAUSE HE DID NOT LOOK WHITE.
PRETTY SHARP, WOULDN'T YOU SAY?

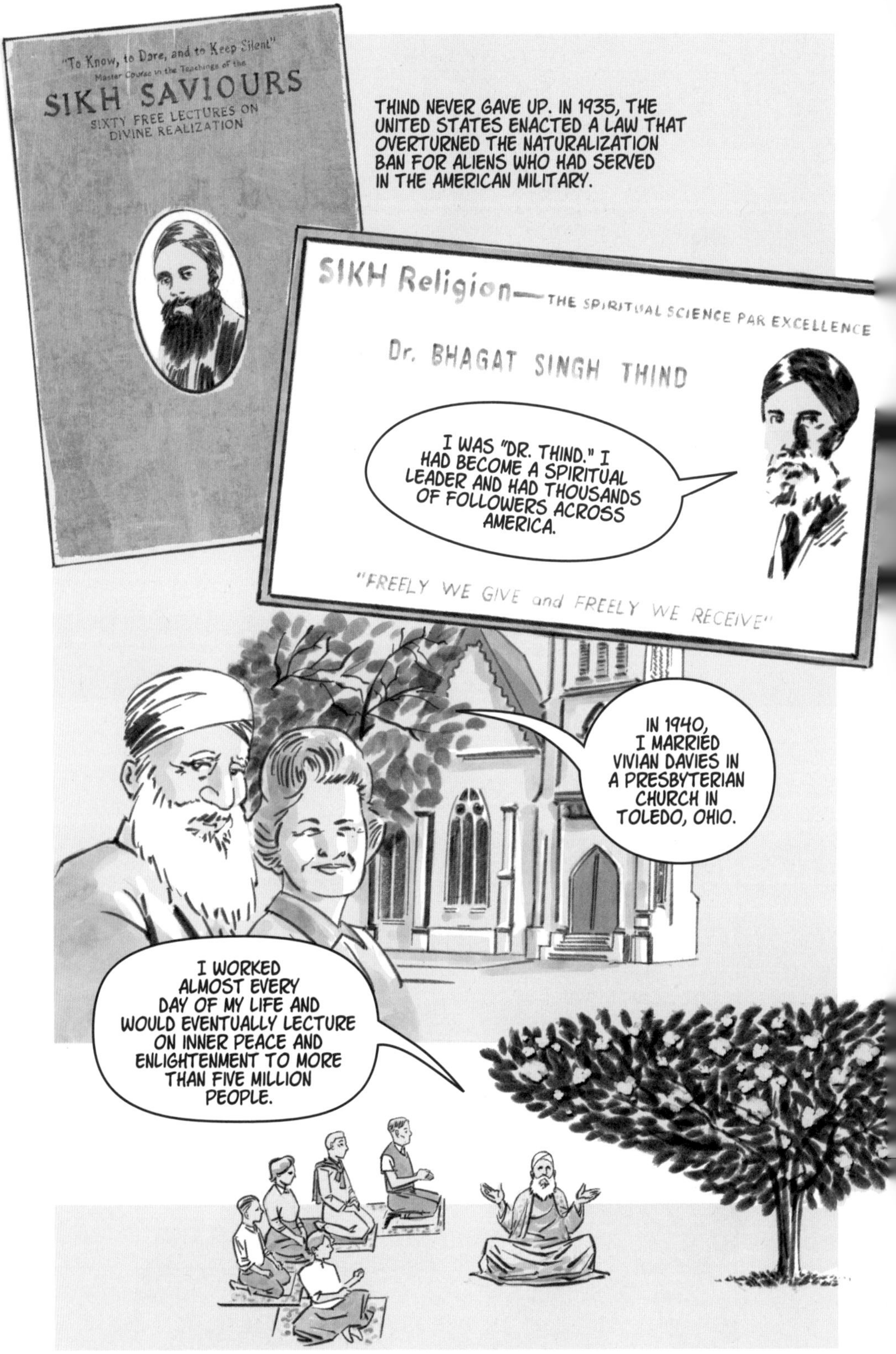
"To Know, to Dare, and to Keep Silent"
Master Course in the Teachings of the
SIKH SAVIOURS
SIXTY FREE LECTURES ON
DIVINE REALIZATION
THIND NEVER GAVE UP. IN 1935, THE UNITED STATES ENACTED A LAW THAT OVERTURNED THE NATURALIZATION BAN FOR ALIENS WHO HAD SERVED IN THE AMERICAN MILITARY.
SIKH Religion— THE SPIRITUAL SCIENCE PAR EXCELLENCE
Dr. BHAGAT SINGH THIND
I WAS "DR. THIND." I HAD BECOME A SPIRITUAL LEADER AND HAD THOUSANDS OF FOLLOWERS ACROSS AMERICA.
"FREELY WE GIVE and FREELY WE RECEIVE"
IN 1940, I MARRIED VIVIAN DAVIES IN A PRESBYTERIAN CHURCH IN TOLEDO, OHIO.
I WORKED ALMOST EVERY DAY OF MY LIFE AND WOULD EVENTUALLY LECTURE ON INNER PEACE AND ENLIGHTENMENT TO MORE THAN FIVE MILLION PEOPLE.

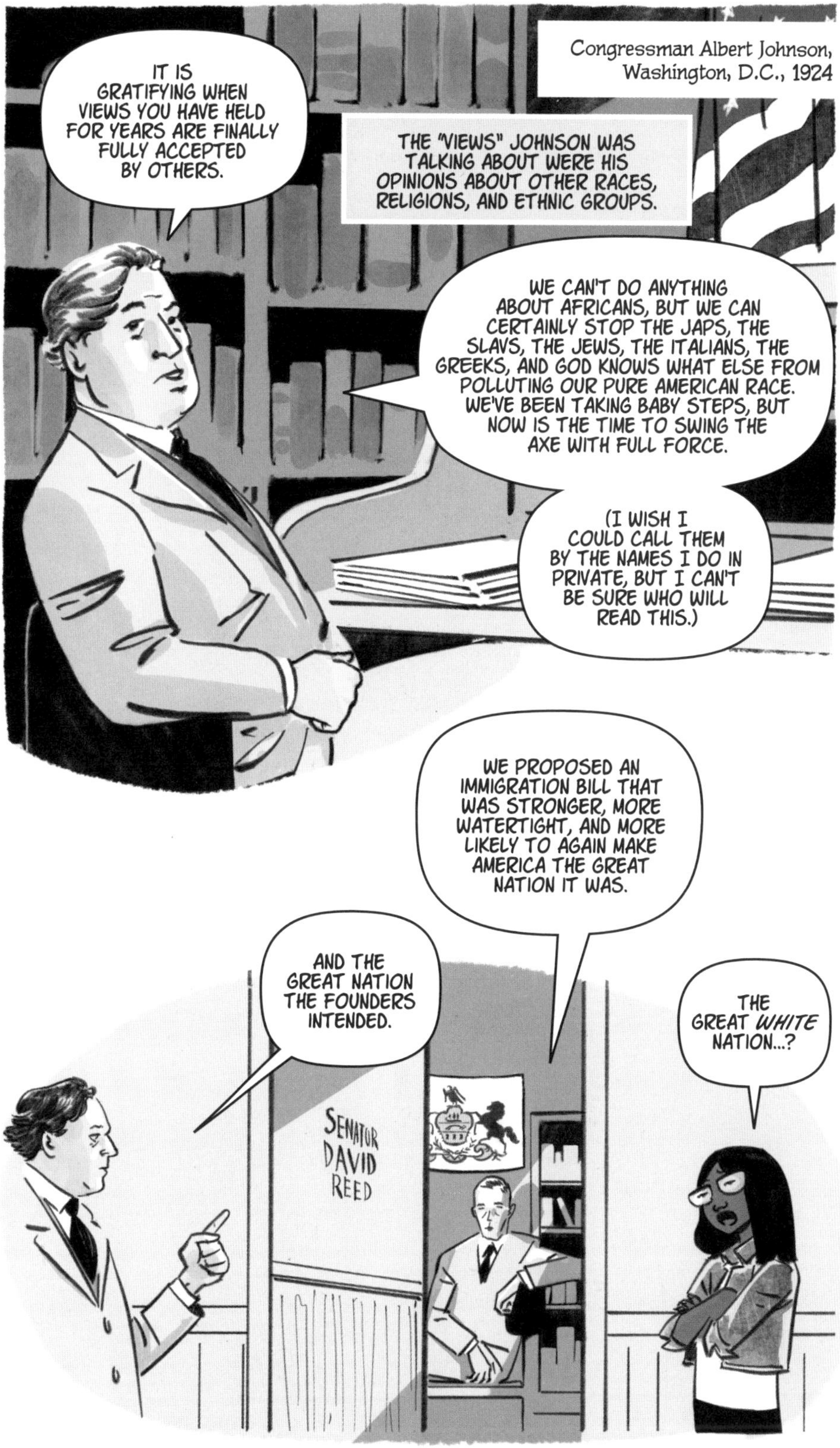
Congressman Albert Johnson, Washington, D.C., 1924
IT IS GRATIFYING WHEN VIEWS YOU HAVE HELD FOR YEARS ARE FINALLY FULLY ACCEPTED BY OTHERS.
THE "VIEWS" JOHNSON WAS TALKING ABOUT WERE HIS OPINIONS ABOUT OTHER RACES, RELIGIONS, AND ETHNIC GROUPS.
WE CAN'T DO ANYTHING ABOUT AFRICANS, BUT WE CAN CERTAINLY STOP THE JAPS, THE SLAVS, THE JEWS, THE ITALIANS, THE GREEKS, AND GOD KNOWS WHAT ELSE FROM POLLUTING OUR PURE AMERICAN RACE. WE'VE BEEN TAKING BABY STEPS, BUT NOW IS THE TIME TO SWING THE AXE WITH FULL FORCE.
(I WISH I COULD CALL THEM BY THE NAMES I DO IN PRIVATE, BUT I CAN'T BE SURE WHO WILL READ THIS.)
WE PROPOSED AN IMMIGRATION BILL THAT WAS STRONGER, MORE WATERTIGHT, AND MORE LIKELY TO AGAIN MAKE AMERICA THE GREAT NATION IT WAS.
AND THE GREAT NATION THE FOUNDERS INTENDED.
SENATOR DAVID REED
THE GREAT *WHITE* NATION...?

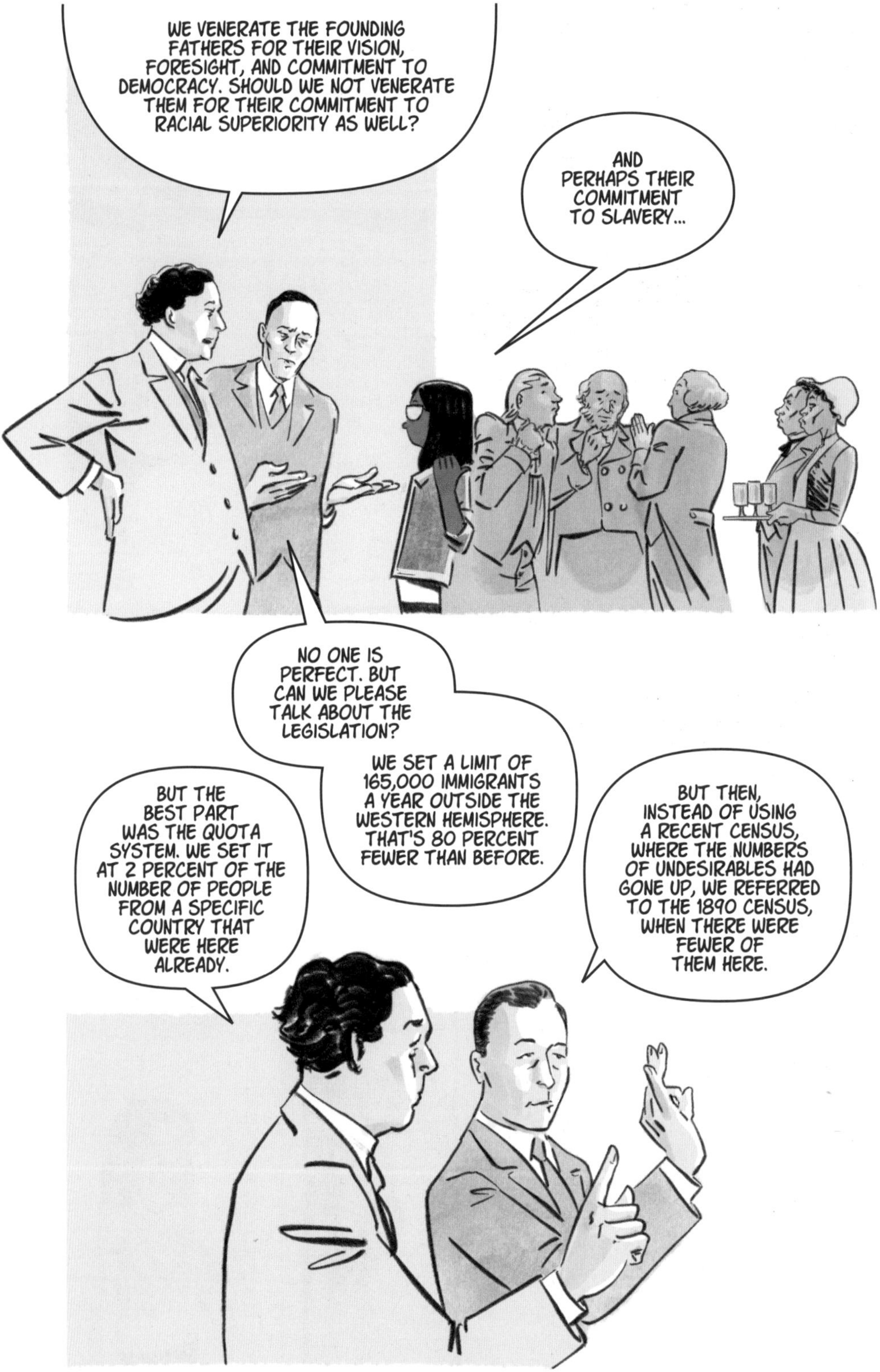
WE VENERATE THE FOUNDING FATHERS FOR THEIR VISION, FORESIGHT, AND COMMITMENT TO DEMOCRACY. SHOULD WE NOT VENERATE THEM FOR THEIR COMMITMENT TO RACIAL SUPERIORITY AS WELL?
AND PERHAPS THEIR COMMITMENT TO SLAVERY...
NO ONE IS PERFECT. BUT CAN WE PLEASE TALK ABOUT THE LEGISLATION?
WE SET A LIMIT OF 165,000 IMMIGRANTS A YEAR OUTSIDE THE WESTERN HEMISPHERE. THAT'S 80 PERCENT FEWER THAN BEFORE.
BUT THE BEST PART WAS THE QUOTA SYSTEM. WE SET IT AT 2 PERCENT OF THE NUMBER OF PEOPLE FROM A SPECIFIC COUNTRY THAT WERE HERE ALREADY.
BUT THEN, INSTEAD OF USING A RECENT CENSUS, WHERE THE NUMBERS OF UNDESIRABLES HAD GONE UP, WE REFERRED TO THE 1890 CENSUS, WHEN THERE WERE FEWER OF THEM HERE.

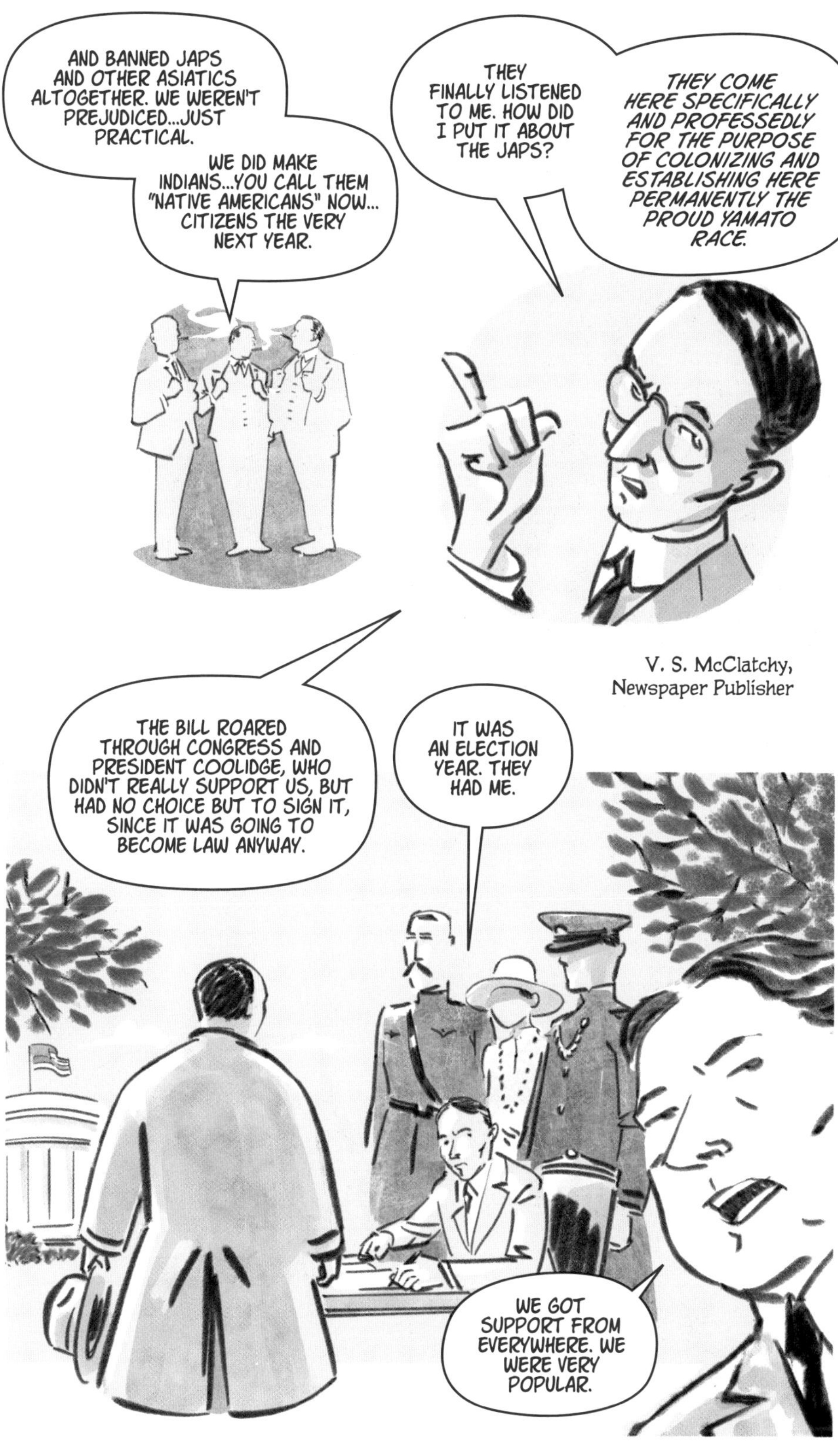
AND BANNED JAPS AND OTHER ASIATICS ALTOGETHER. WE WEREN'T PREJUDICED...JUST PRACTICAL.
WE DID MAKE INDIANS...YOU CALL THEM "NATIVE AMERICANS" NOW... CITIZENS THE VERY NEXT YEAR.
THEY FINALLY LISTENED TO ME. HOW DID I PUT IT ABOUT THE JAPS?
THEY COME HERE SPECIFICALLY AND PROFESSEDLY FOR THE PURPOSE OF COLONIZING AND ESTABLISHING HERE PERMANENTLY THE PROUD YAMATO RACE.
V. S. McClatchy, Newspaper Publisher
THE BILL ROARED THROUGH CONGRESS AND PRESIDENT COOLIDGE, WHO DIDN'T REALLY SUPPORT US, BUT HAD NO CHOICE BUT TO SIGN IT, SINCE IT WAS GOING TO BECOME LAW ANYWAY.
IT WAS AN ELECTION YEAR. THEY HAD ME.
WE GOT SUPPORT FROM EVERYWHERE. WE WERE VERY POPULAR.

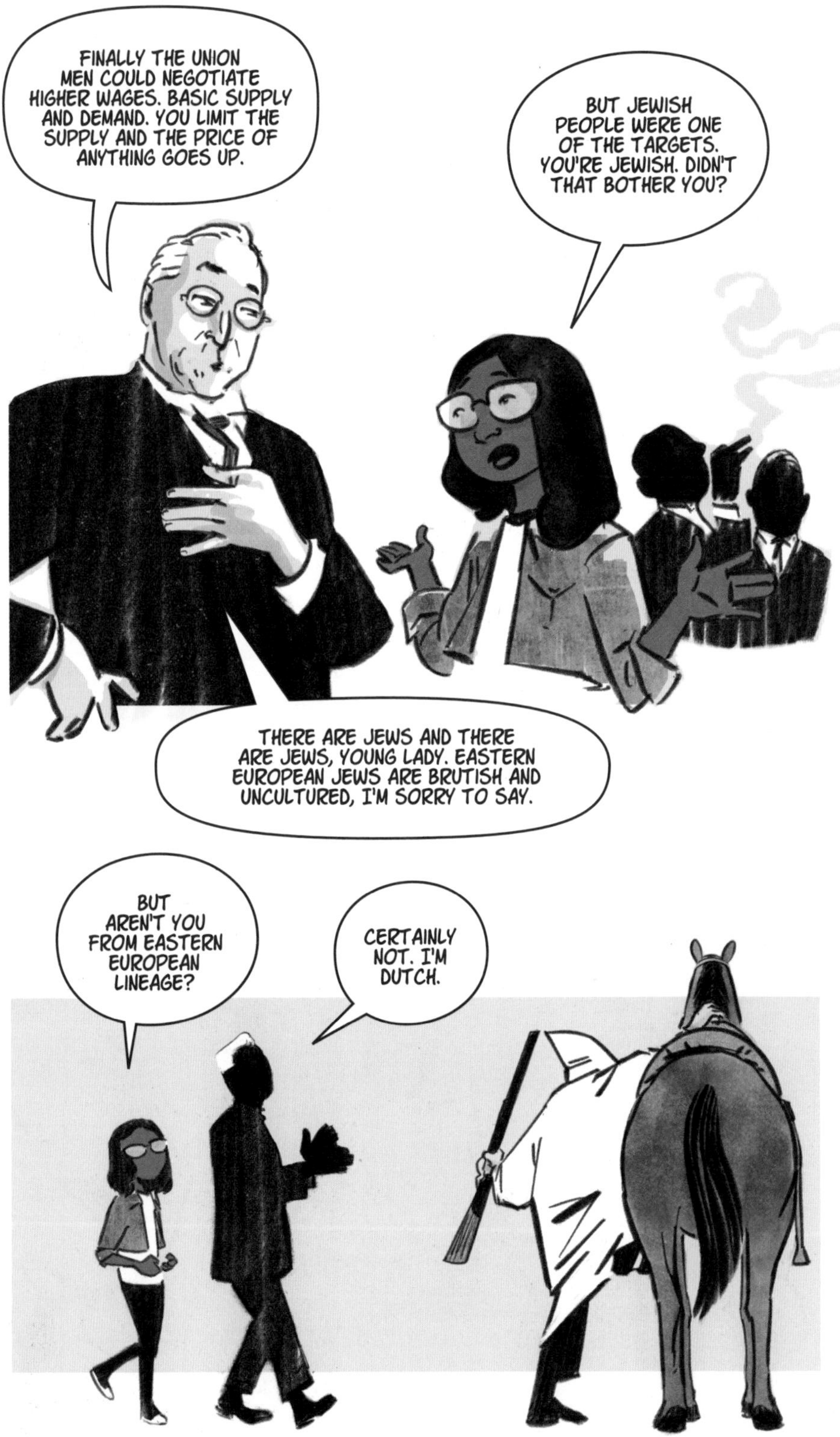
FINALLY THE UNION MEN COULD NEGOTIATE HIGHER WAGES. BASIC SUPPLY AND DEMAND. YOU LIMIT THE SUPPLY AND THE PRICE OF ANYTHING GOES UP.
BUT JEWISH PEOPLE WERE ONE OF THE TARGETS. YOU'RE JEWISH. DIDN'T THAT BOTHER YOU?
THERE ARE JEWS AND THERE ARE JEWS, YOUNG LADY. EASTERN EUROPEAN JEWS ARE BRUTISH AND UNCULTURED, I'M SORRY TO SAY.
BUT AREN'T YOU FROM EASTERN EUROPEAN LINEAGE?
CERTAINLY NOT. I'M DUTCH.

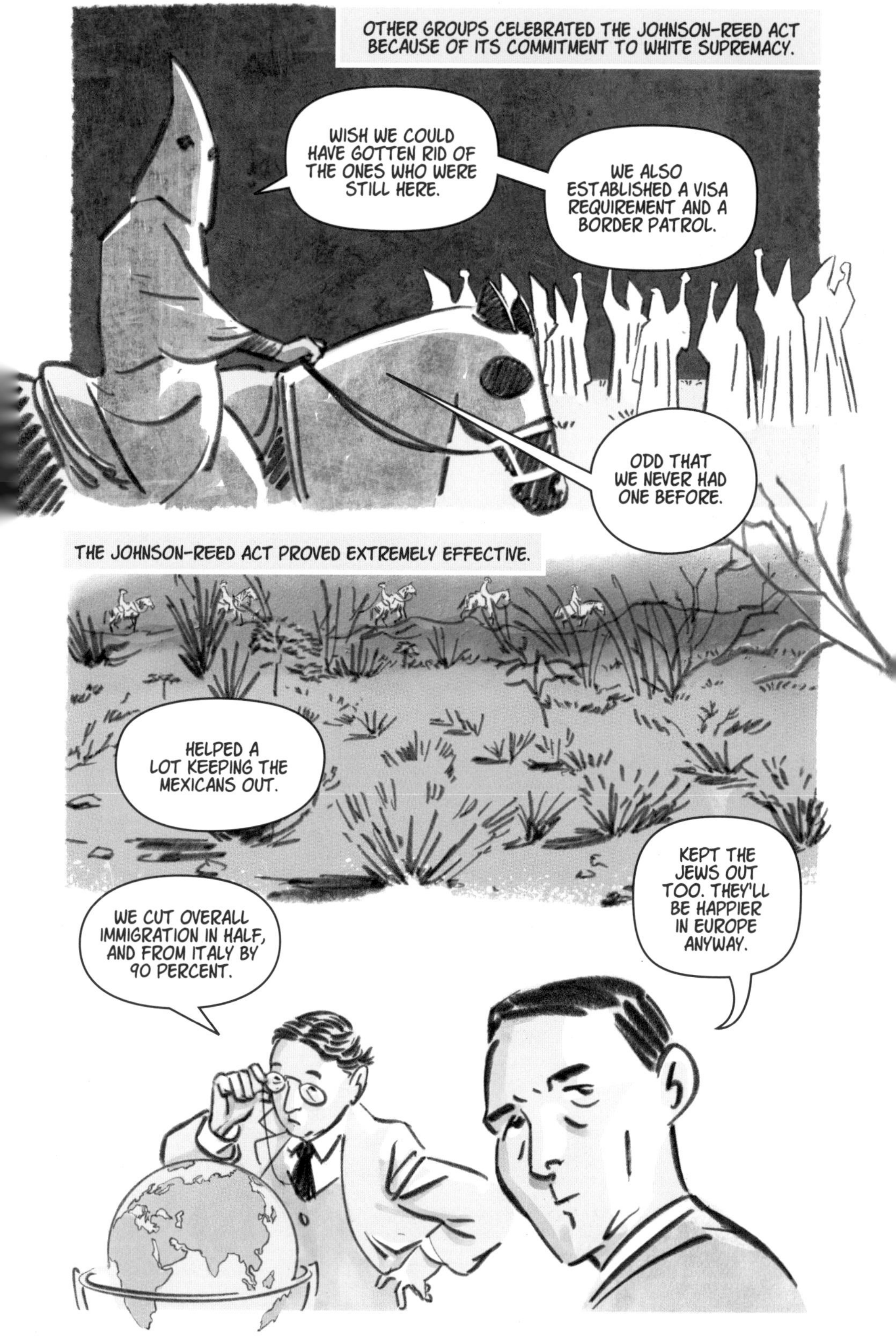

OTHER GROUPS CELEBRATED THE JOHNSON-REED ACT BECAUSE OF ITS COMMITMENT TO WHITE SUPREMACY.
WISH WE COULD HAVE GOTTEN RID OF THE ONES WHO WERE STILL HERE.
WE ALSO ESTABLISHED A VISA REQUIREMENT AND A BORDER PATROL.
ODD THAT WE NEVER HAD ONE BEFORE.
THE JOHNSON-REED ACT PROVED EXTREMELY EFFECTIVE.
HELPED A LOT KEEPING THE MEXICANS OUT.
WE CUT OVERALL IMMIGRATION IN HALF, AND FROM ITALY BY 90 PERCENT.
KEPT THE JEWS OUT TOO. THEY'LL BE HAPPIER IN EUROPE ANYWAY.

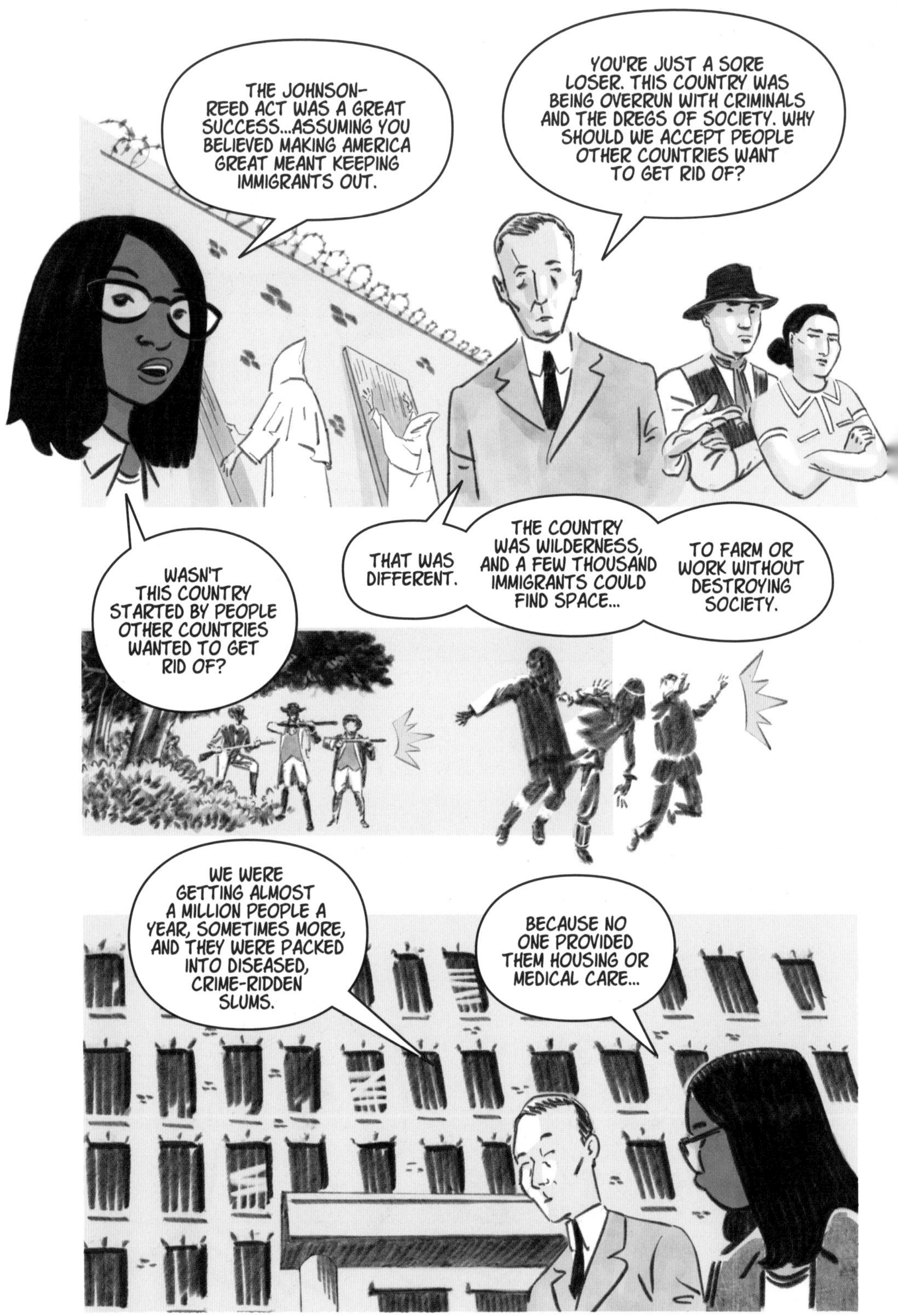
THE JOHNSON-REED ACT WAS A GREAT SUCCESS...ASSUMING YOU BELIEVED MAKING AMERICA GREAT MEANT KEEPING IMMIGRANTS OUT.
YOU'RE JUST A SORE LOSER. THIS COUNTRY WAS BEING OVERRUN WITH CRIMINALS AND THE DREGS OF SOCIETY. WHY SHOULD WE ACCEPT PEOPLE OTHER COUNTRIES WANT TO GET RID OF?
WASN'T THIS COUNTRY STARTED BY PEOPLE OTHER COUNTRIES WANTED TO GET RID OF?
THAT WAS DIFFERENT.
THE COUNTRY WAS WILDERNESS, AND A FEW THOUSAND IMMIGRANTS COULD FIND SPACE...
TO FARM OR WORK WITHOUT DESTROYING SOCIETY.
WE WERE GETTING ALMOST A MILLION PEOPLE A YEAR, SOMETIMES MORE, AND THEY WERE PACKED INTO DISEASED, CRIME-RIDDEN SLUMS.
BECAUSE NO ONE PROVIDED THEM HOUSING OR MEDICAL CARE...

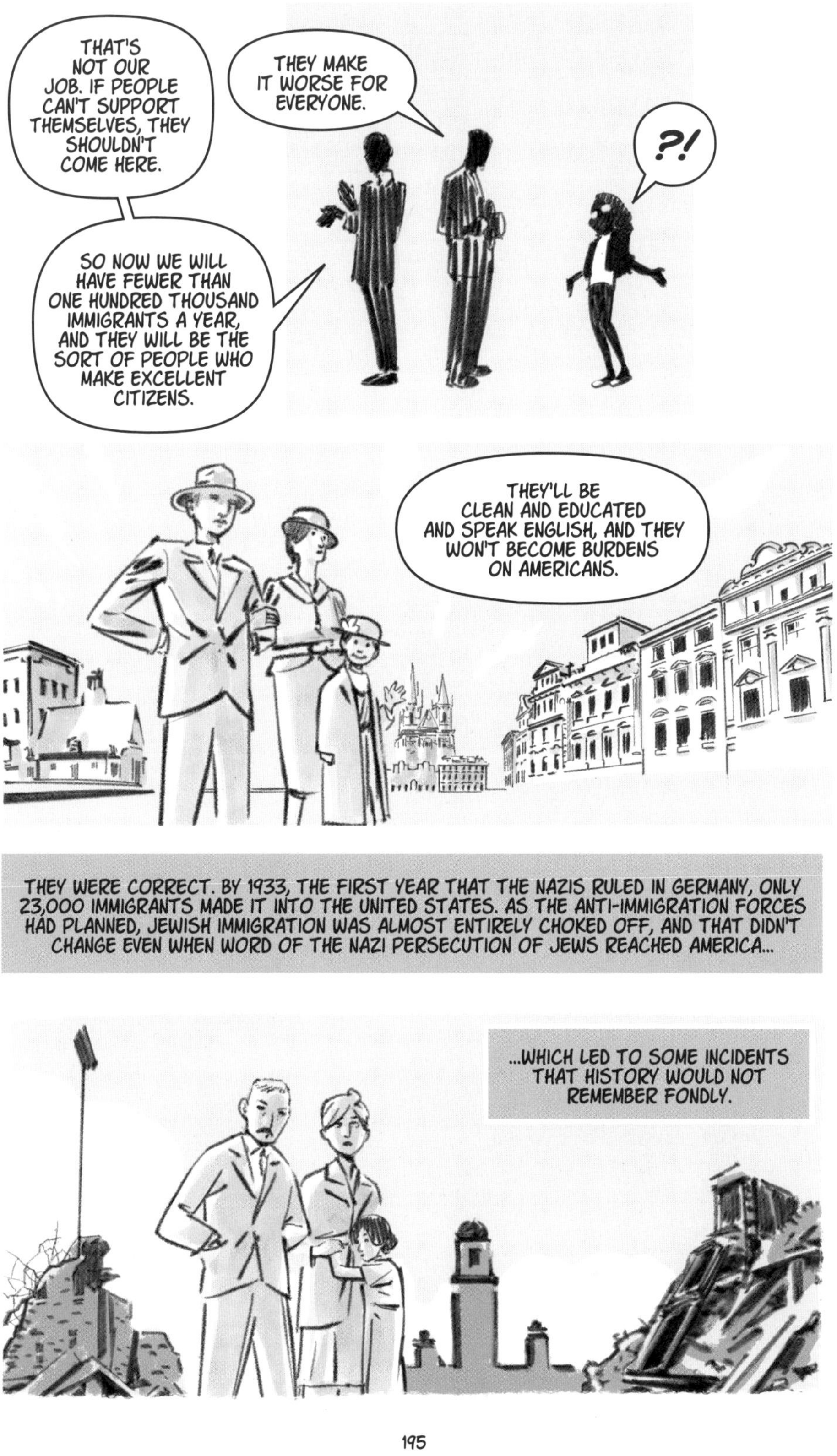
THAT'S NOT OUR JOB. IF PEOPLE CAN'T SUPPORT THEMSELVES, THEY SHOULDN'T COME HERE.
THEY MAKE IT WORSE FOR EVERYONE.
?!
SO NOW WE WILL HAVE FEWER THAN ONE HUNDRED THOUSAND IMMIGRANTS A YEAR, AND THEY WILL BE THE SORT OF PEOPLE WHO MAKE EXCELLENT CITIZENS.
THEY'LL BE CLEAN AND EDUCATED AND SPEAK ENGLISH, AND THEY WON'T BECOME BURDENS ON AMERICANS.
THEY WERE CORRECT. BY 1933, THE FIRST YEAR THAT THE NAZIS RULED IN GERMANY, ONLY 23,000 IMMIGRANTS MADE IT INTO THE UNITED STATES. AS THE ANTI-IMMIGRATION FORCES HAD PLANNED, JEWISH IMMIGRATION WAS ALMOST ENTIRELY CHOKED OFF, AND THAT DIDN'T CHANGE EVEN WHEN WORD OF THE NAZI PERSECUTION OF JEWS REACHED AMERICA...
...WHICH LED TO SOME INCIDENTS THAT HISTORY WOULD NOT REMEMBER FONDLY.

Havana, Cuba, 1939, on the ocean liner *St. Louis*.

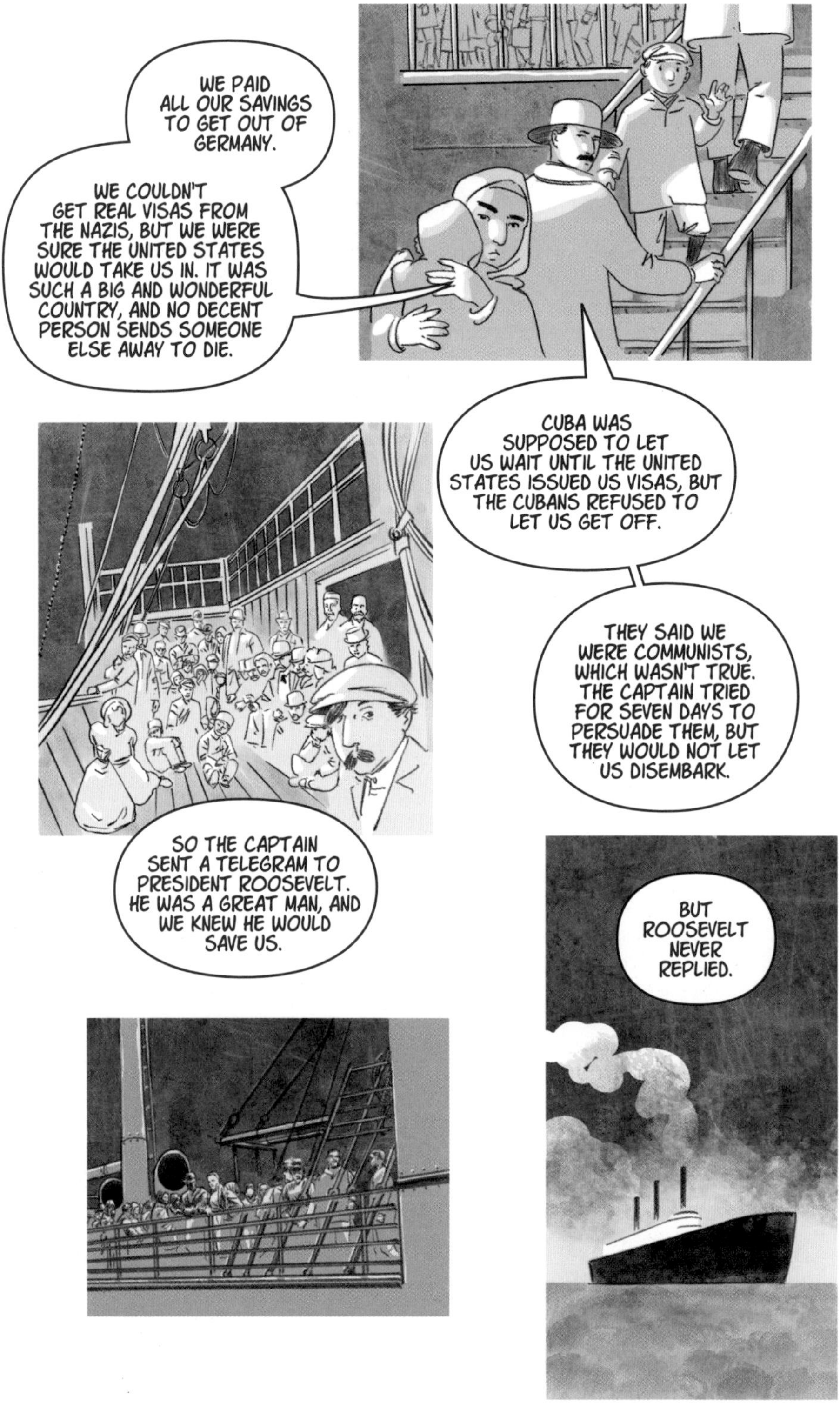
WE PAID ALL OUR SAVINGS TO GET OUT OF GERMANY.
WE COULDN'T GET REAL VISAS FROM THE NAZIS, BUT WE WERE SURE THE UNITED STATES WOULD TAKE US IN. IT WAS SUCH A BIG AND WONDERFUL COUNTRY, AND NO DECENT PERSON SENDS SOMEONE ELSE AWAY TO DIE.
CUBA WAS SUPPOSED TO LET US WAIT UNTIL THE UNITED STATES ISSUED US VISAS, BUT THE CUBANS REFUSED TO LET US GET OFF.
THEY SAID WE WERE COMMUNISTS, WHICH WASN'T TRUE. THE CAPTAIN TRIED FOR SEVEN DAYS TO PERSUADE THEM, BUT THEY WOULD NOT LET US DISEMBARK.
SO THE CAPTAIN SENT A TELEGRAM TO PRESIDENT ROOSEVELT. HE WAS A GREAT MAN, AND WE KNEW HE WOULD SAVE US.
BUT ROOSEVELT NEVER REPLIED.

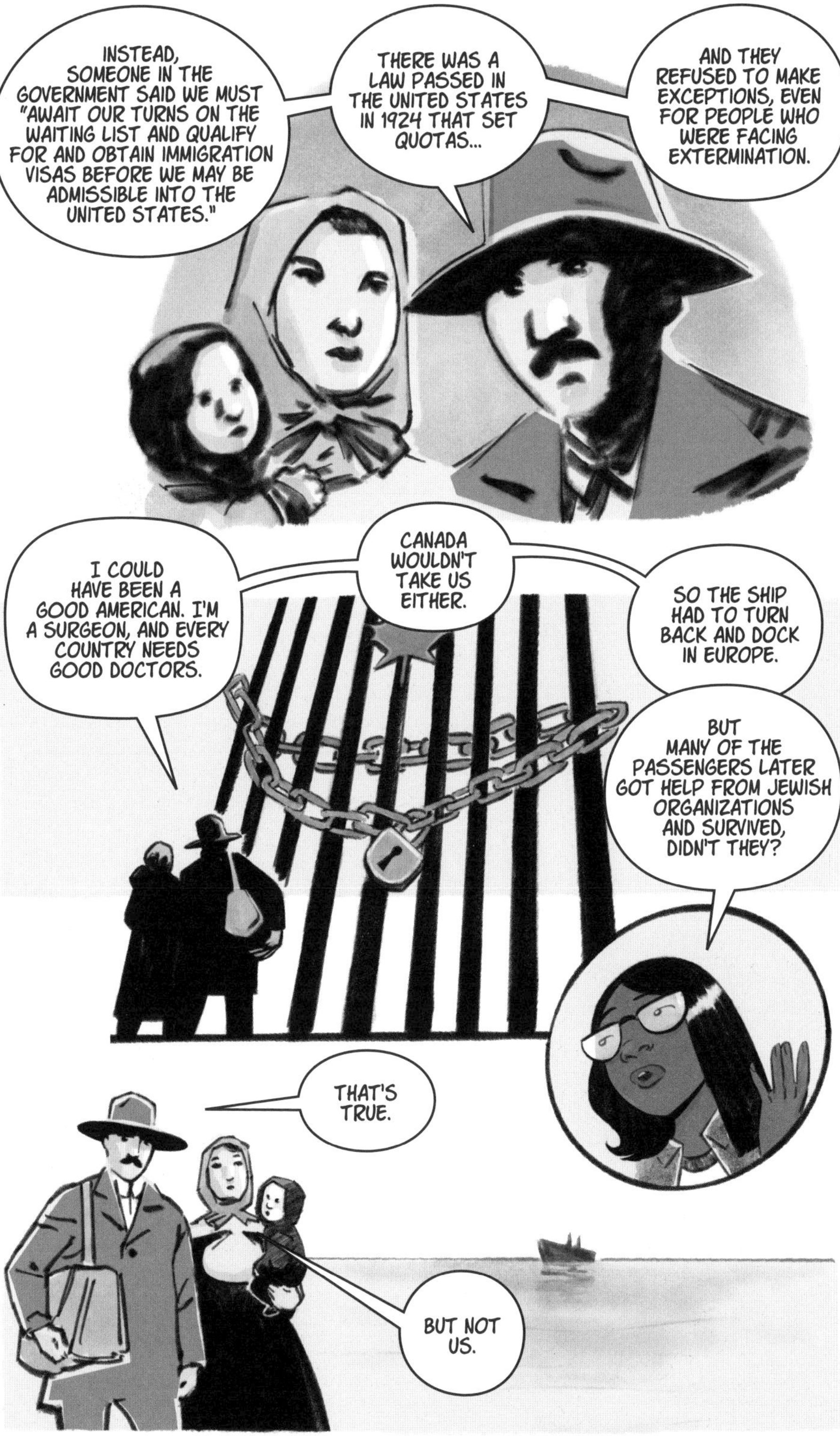
INSTEAD, SOMEONE IN THE GOVERNMENT SAID WE MUST "AWAIT OUR TURNS ON THE WAITING LIST AND QUALIFY FOR AND OBTAIN IMMIGRATION VISAS BEFORE WE MAY BE ADMISSIBLE INTO THE UNITED STATES."
THERE WAS A LAW PASSED IN THE UNITED STATES IN 1924 THAT SET QUOTAS...
AND THEY REFUSED TO MAKE EXCEPTIONS, EVEN FOR PEOPLE WHO WERE FACING EXTERMINATION.
I COULD HAVE BEEN A GOOD AMERICAN. I'M A SURGEON, AND EVERY COUNTRY NEEDS GOOD DOCTORS.
CANADA WOULDN'T TAKE US EITHER.
SO THE SHIP HAD TO TURN BACK AND DOCK IN EUROPE.
BUT MANY OF THE PASSENGERS LATER GOT HELP FROM JEWISH ORGANIZATIONS AND SURVIVED, DIDN'T THEY?
THAT'S TRUE.
BUT NOT US.

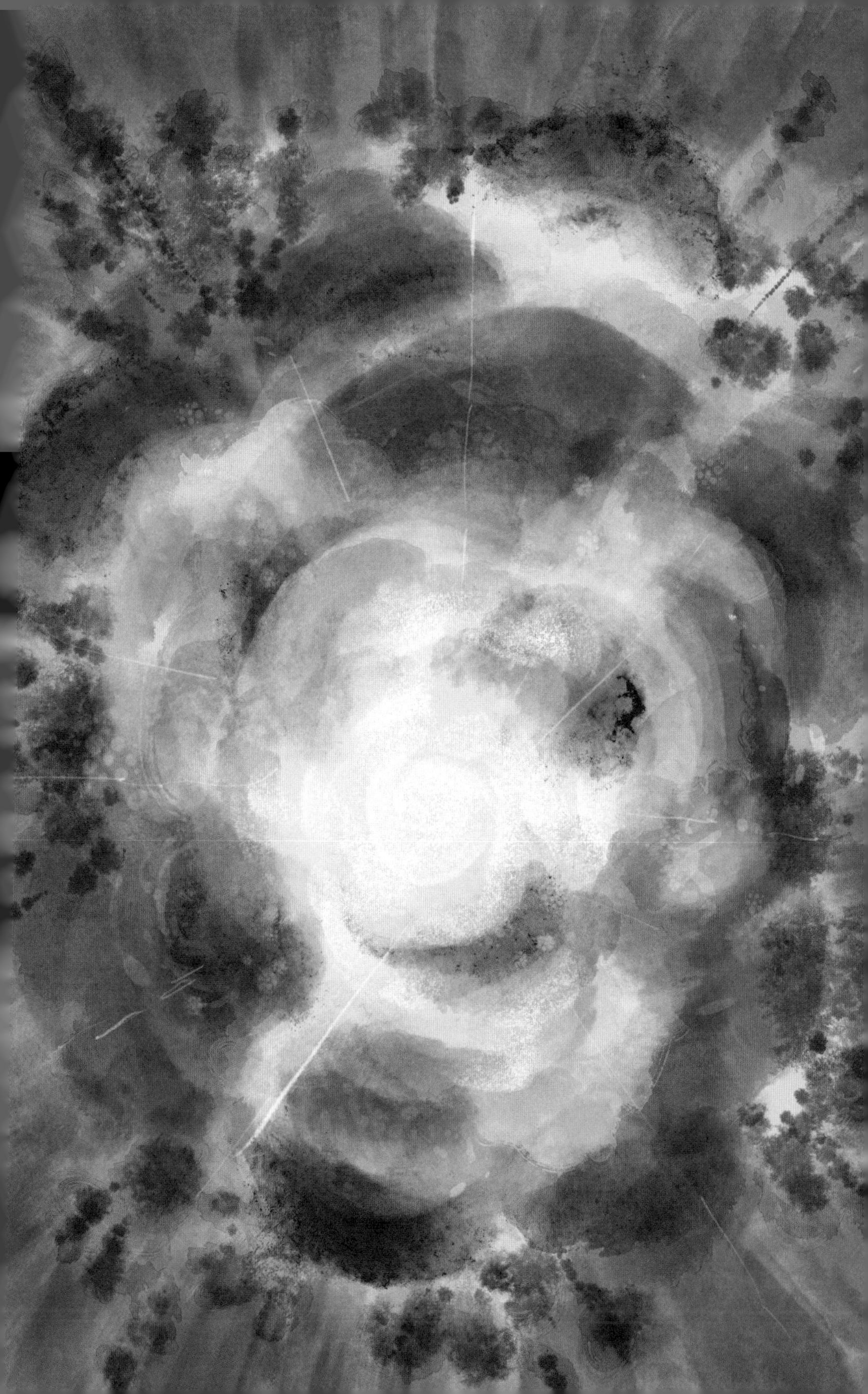

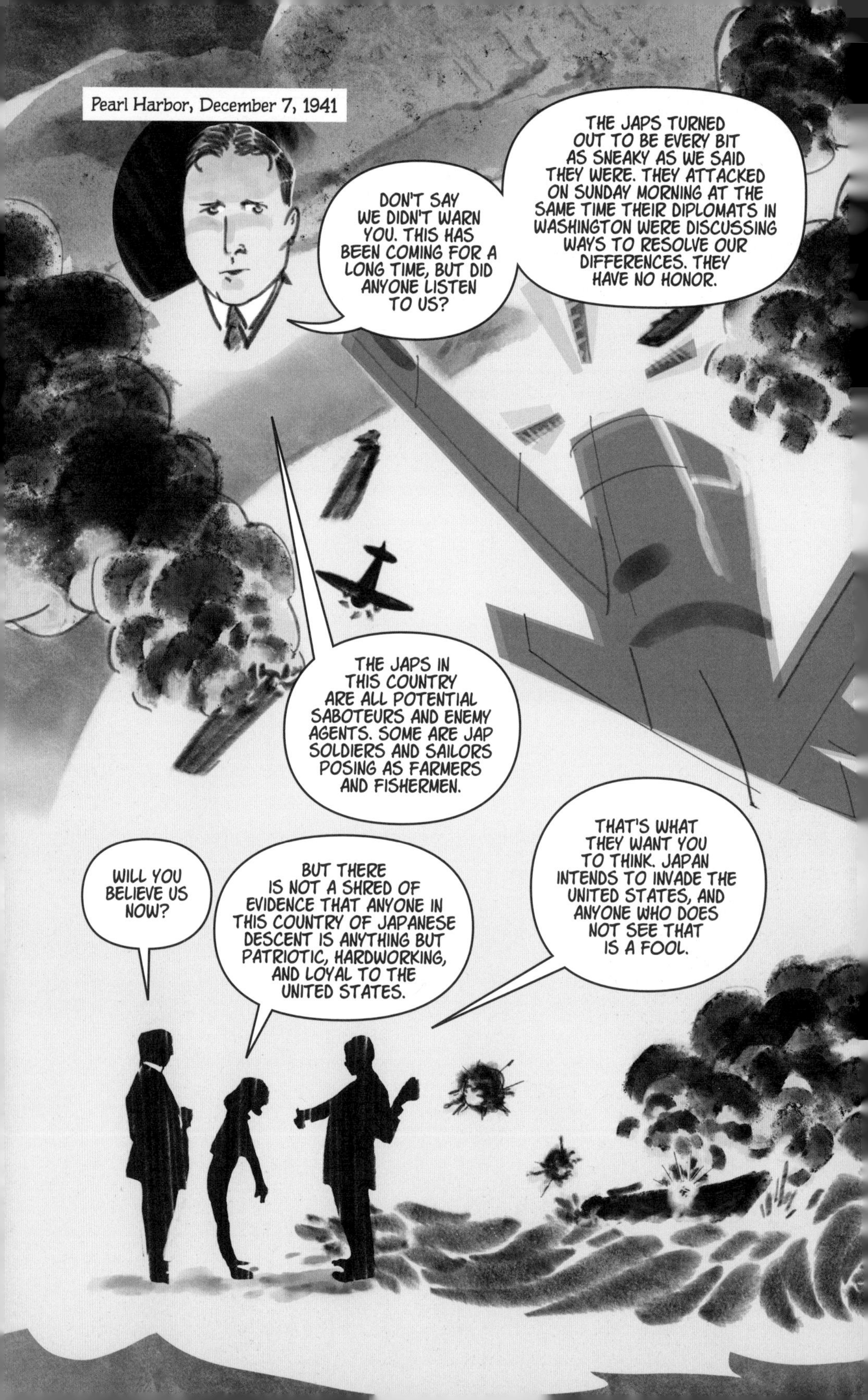
Pearl Harbor, December 7, 1941
DON'T SAY WE DIDN'T WARN YOU. THIS HAS BEEN COMING FOR A LONG TIME, BUT DID ANYONE LISTEN TO US?
THE JAPS TURNED OUT TO BE EVERY BIT AS SNEAKY AS WE SAID THEY WERE. THEY ATTACKED ON SUNDAY MORNING AT THE SAME TIME THEIR DIPLOMATS IN WASHINGTON WERE DISCUSSING WAYS TO RESOLVE OUR DIFFERENCES. THEY HAVE NO HONOR.
THE JAPS IN THIS COUNTRY ARE ALL POTENTIAL SABOTEURS AND ENEMY AGENTS. SOME ARE JAP SOLDIERS AND SAILORS POSING AS FARMERS AND FISHERMEN.
WILL YOU BELIEVE US NOW?
BUT THERE IS NOT A SHRED OF EVIDENCE THAT ANYONE IN THIS COUNTRY OF JAPANESE DESCENT IS ANYTHING BUT PATRIOTIC, HARDWORKING, AND LOYAL TO THE UNITED STATES.
THAT'S WHAT THEY WANT YOU TO THINK. JAPAN INTENDS TO INVADE THE UNITED STATES, AND ANYONE WHO DOES NOT SEE THAT IS A FOOL.

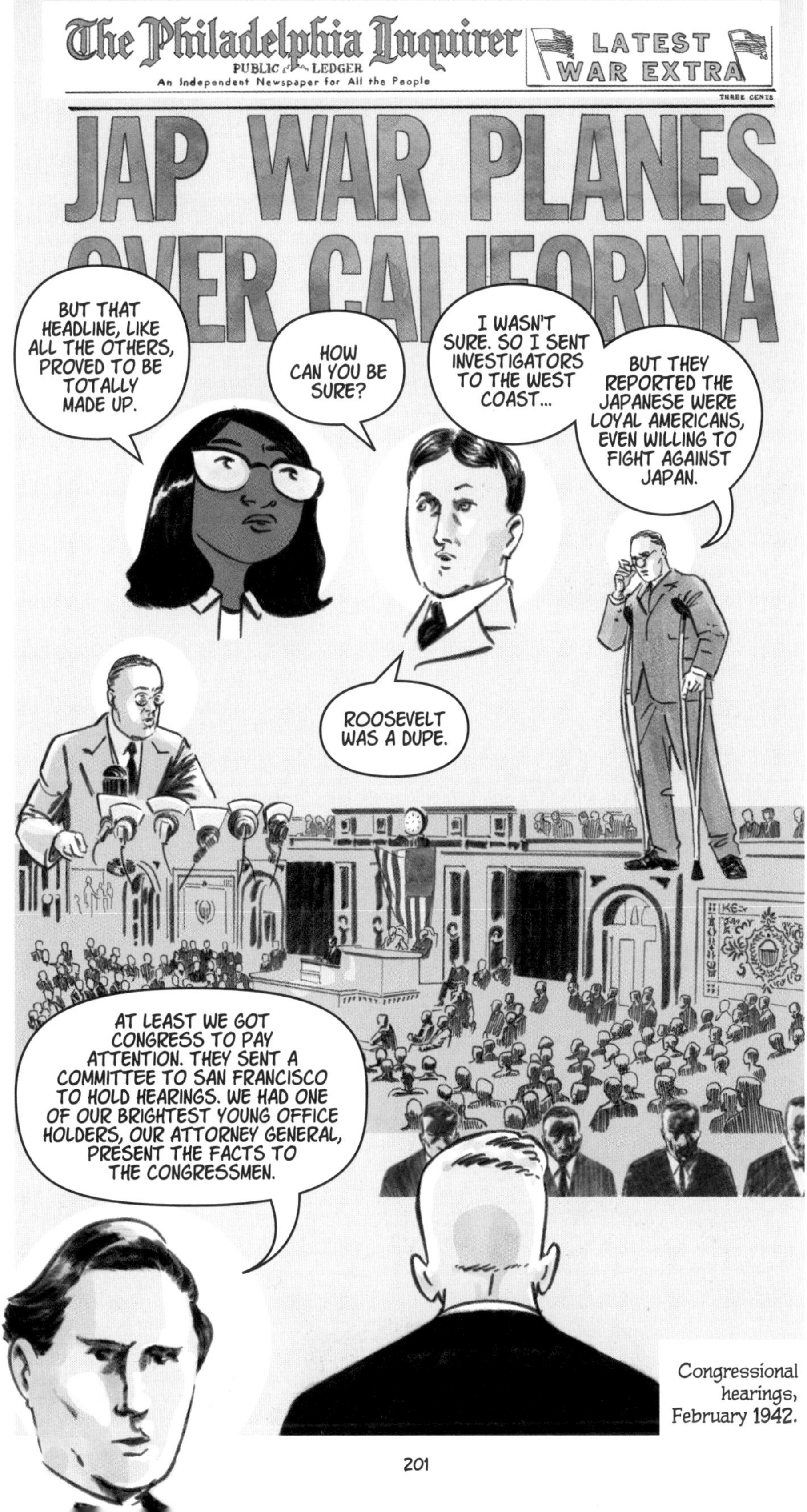
The Philadelphia Inquirer
PUBLIC LEDGER
An Independent Newspaper for All the People
LATEST WAR EXTRA
THREE CENTS
JAP WAR PLANES OVER CALIFORNIA
BUT THAT HEADLINE, LIKE ALL THE OTHERS, PROVED TO BE TOTALLY MADE UP.
HOW CAN YOU BE SURE?
I WASN'T SURE. SO I SENT INVESTIGATORS TO THE WEST COAST...
BUT THEY REPORTED THE JAPANESE WERE LOYAL AMERICANS, EVEN WILLING TO FIGHT AGAINST JAPAN.
ROOSEVELT WAS A DUPE.
AT LEAST WE GOT CONGRESS TO PAY ATTENTION. THEY SENT A COMMITTEE TO SAN FRANCISCO TO HOLD HEARINGS. WE HAD ONE OF OUR BRIGHTEST YOUNG OFFICE HOLDERS, OUR ATTORNEY GENERAL, PRESENT THE FACTS TO THE CONGRESSMEN.
Congressional hearings, February 1942.

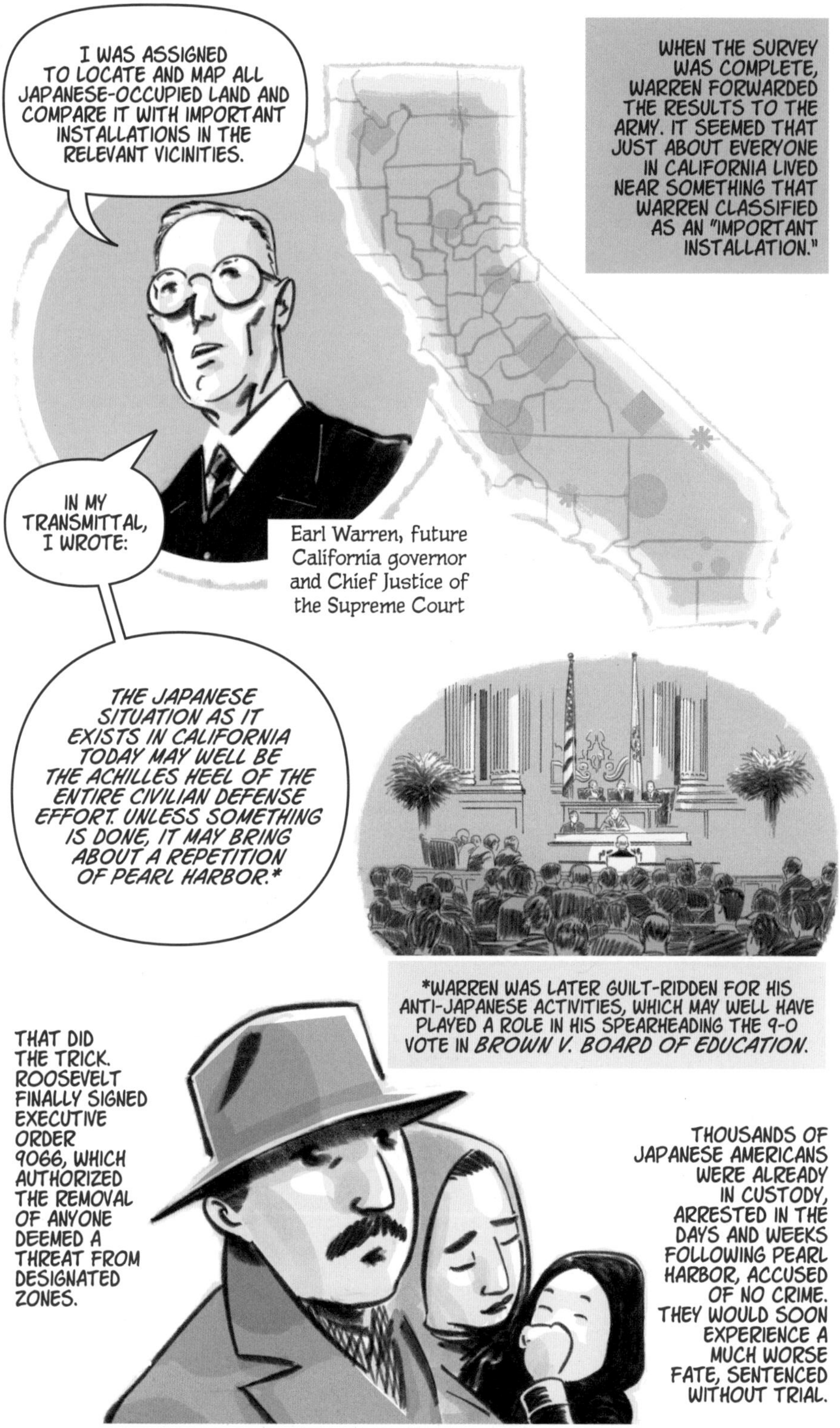
I WAS ASSIGNED TO LOCATE AND MAP ALL JAPANESE-OCCUPIED LAND AND COMPARE IT WITH IMPORTANT INSTALLATIONS IN THE RELEVANT VICINITIES.
WHEN THE SURVEY WAS COMPLETE, WARREN FORWARDED THE RESULTS TO THE ARMY. IT SEEMED THAT JUST ABOUT EVERYONE IN CALIFORNIA LIVED NEAR SOMETHING THAT WARREN CLASSIFIED AS AN "IMPORTANT INSTALLATION."
IN MY TRANSMITTAL, I WROTE:
Earl Warren, future California governor and Chief Justice of the Supreme Court
THE JAPANESE SITUATION AS IT EXISTS IN CALIFORNIA TODAY MAY WELL BE THE ACHILLES HEEL OF THE ENTIRE CIVILIAN DEFENSE EFFORT. UNLESS SOMETHING IS DONE, IT MAY BRING ABOUT A REPETITION OF PEARL HARBOR.*
*WARREN WAS LATER GUILT-RIDDEN FOR HIS ANTI-JAPANESE ACTIVITIES, WHICH MAY WELL HAVE PLAYED A ROLE IN HIS SPEARHEADING THE 9-0 VOTE IN BROWN V. BOARD OF EDUCATION.
THAT DID THE TRICK. ROOSEVELT FINALLY SIGNED EXECUTIVE ORDER 9066, WHICH AUTHORIZED THE REMOVAL OF ANYONE DEEMED A THREAT FROM DESIGNATED ZONES.
THOUSANDS OF JAPANESE AMERICANS WERE ALREADY IN CUSTODY, ARRESTED IN THE DAYS AND WEEKS FOLLOWING PEARL HARBOR, ACCUSED OF NO CRIME. THEY WOULD SOON EXPERIENCE A MUCH WORSE FATE, SENTENCED WITHOUT TRIAL.

IN ONE OF THE MOST SHAMEFUL EPISODES IN THE NATION'S HISTORY, MORE THAN 110,000 JAPANESE, TWO THIRDS OF THEM UNITED STATES CITIZENS, WERE REMOVED FROM THEIR HOMES AND SHIPPED TO WHAT AMERICAN AUTHORITIES THEMSELVES CALLED "CONCENTRATION CAMPS." MOST WOULD REMAIN THERE FOR ALMOST THREE YEARS. DURING THAT TIME, NOT ONE AMERICAN OF JAPANESE ORIGIN WAS ACCUSED OF ANY ACT AGAINST THE UNITED STATES.

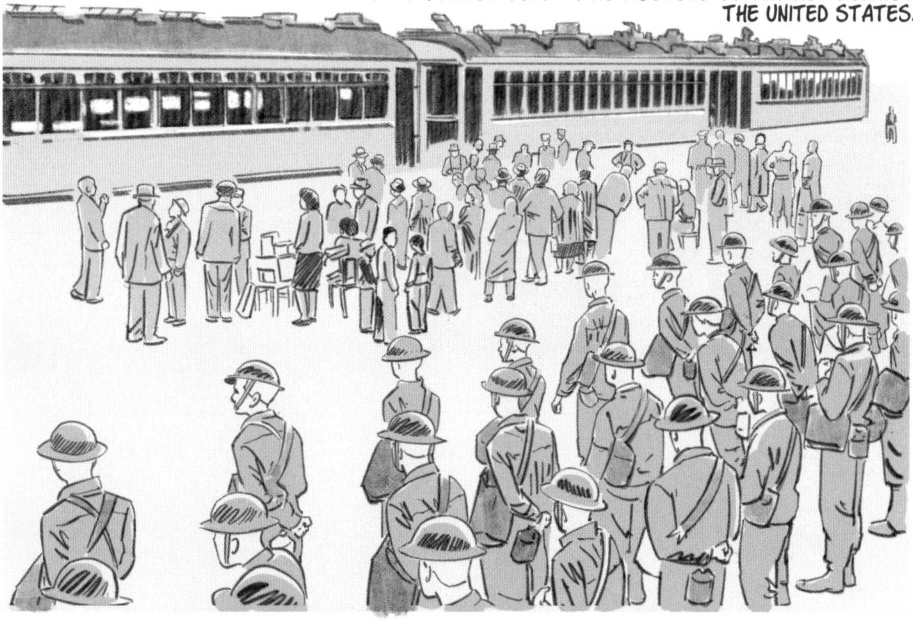

ALL JAPANESE WERE ORDERED TO REPORT TO DEPOTS WITH ONLY WHAT THEY WERE ABLE TO CARRY. THEY WERE HERDED ONTO BUSES OR RAILROAD CARS AND TAKEN TO BARBED-WIRE-ENCLOSED COMPOUNDS IN PARTS OF THE WEST FEW WHITE PEOPLE THOUGHT FIT TO LIVE.

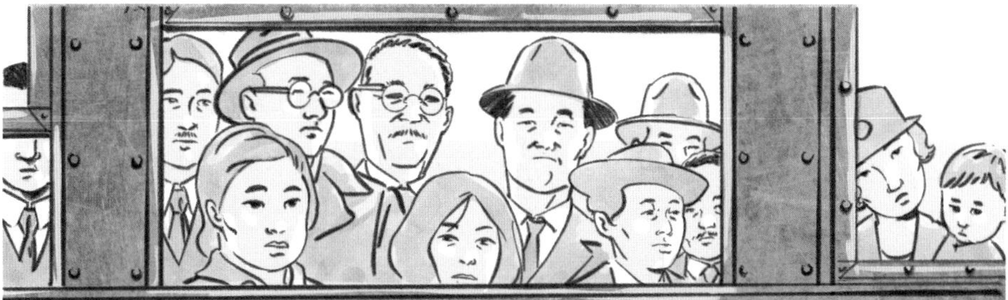

MANY WOULD HAVE THEIR HOMES DESTROYED, THEIR BUSINESSES RANSACKED, AND THEIR FARMS TAKEN OVER BY WHITES.

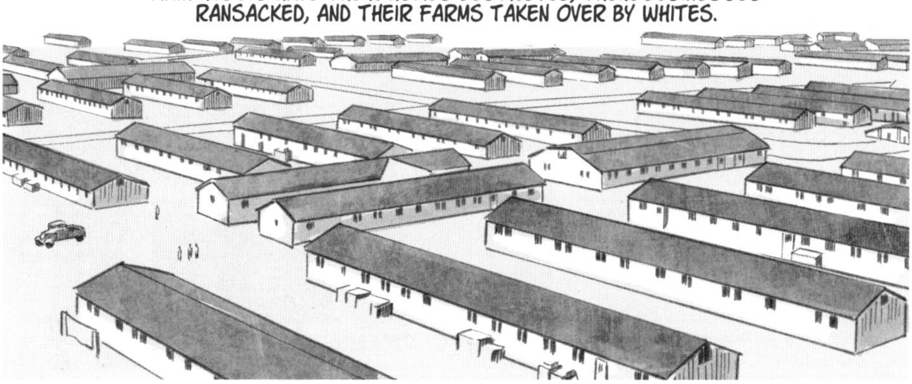

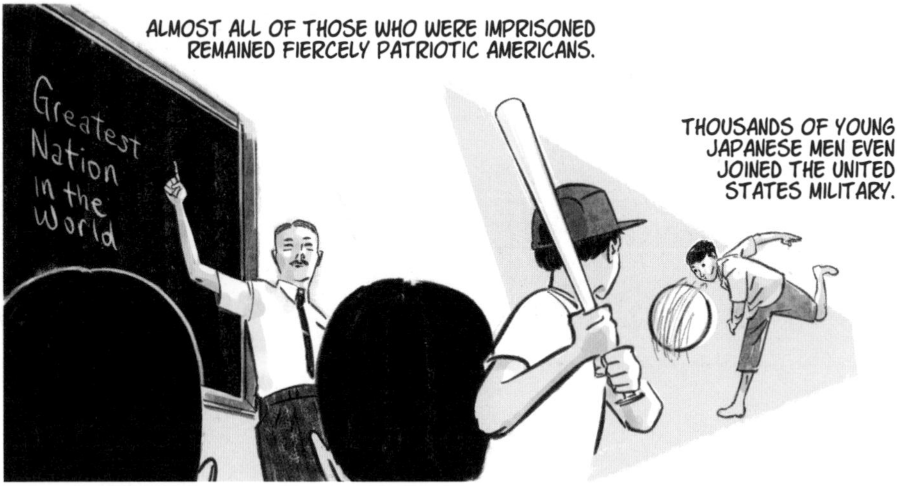
ALMOST ALL OF THOSE WHO WERE IMPRISONED REMAINED FIERCELY PATRIOTIC AMERICANS.
Greatest Nation in the World
THOUSANDS OF YOUNG JAPANESE MEN EVEN JOINED THE UNITED STATES MILITARY.

THEY WERE NOT ALLOWED TO FIGHT IN THE PACIFIC, BUT IN EUROPE, THE 442ND BECAME ONE OF THE MOST HIGHLY DECORATED UNITS IN THE AMERICAN MILITARY, INCLUDING TWENTY-ONE MEN WHO WERE AWARDED THE CONGRESSIONAL MEDAL OF HONOR...

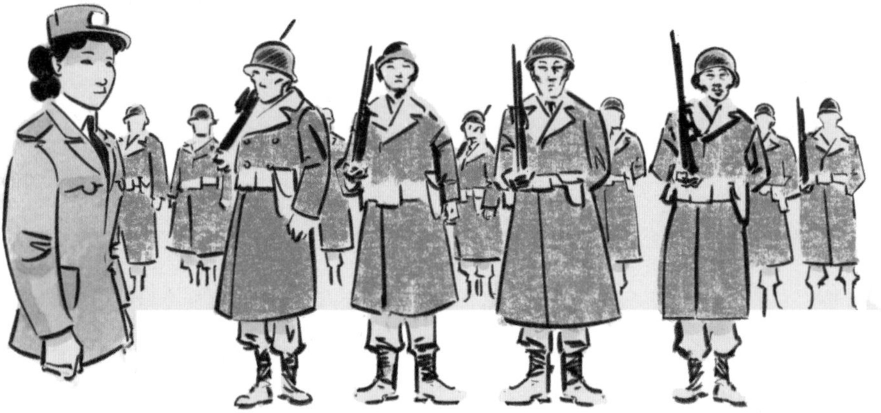

...EVEN THOUGH THEIR FAMILIES WERE FORCED TO REMAIN IN CONCENTRATION CAMPS.

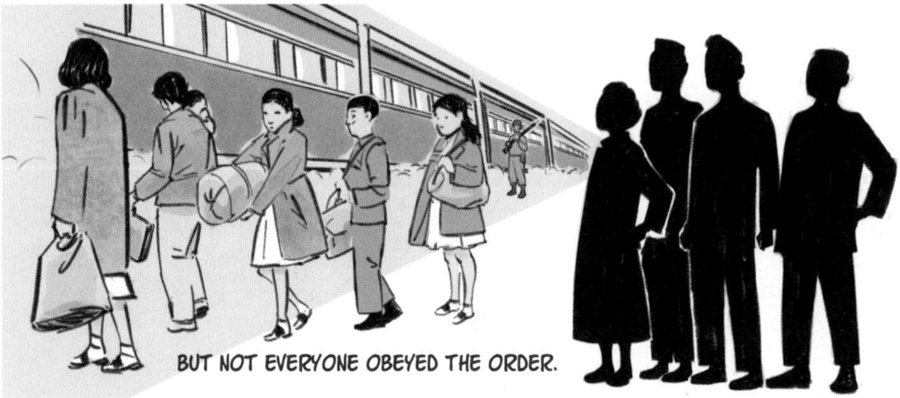
BUT NOT EVERYONE OBEYED THE ORDER.

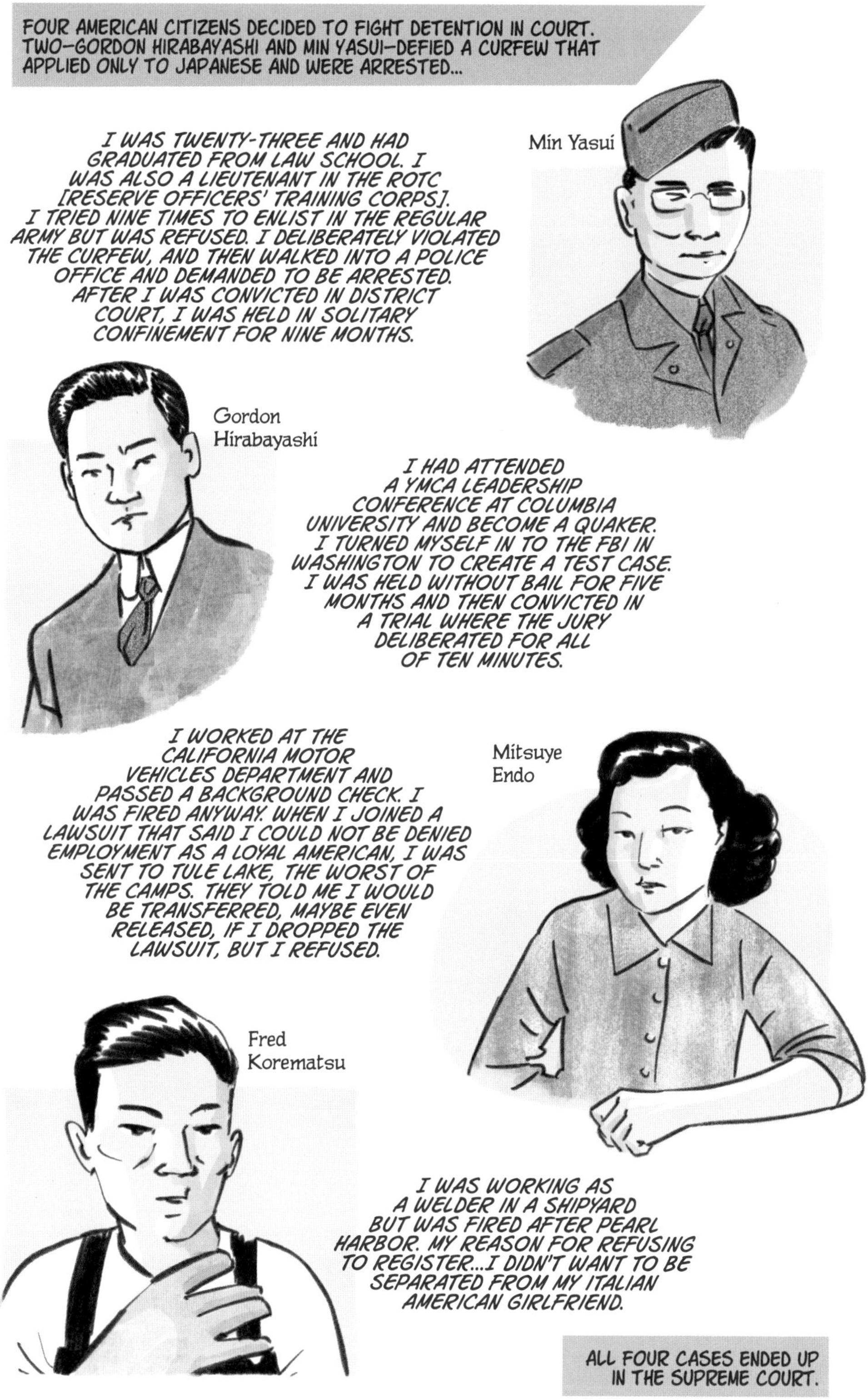
FOUR AMERICAN CITIZENS DECIDED TO FIGHT DETENTION IN COURT. TWO—GORDON HIRABAYASHI AND MIN YASUI—DEFIED A CURFEW THAT APPLIED ONLY TO JAPANESE AND WERE ARRESTED...
I WAS TWENTY-THREE AND HAD GRADUATED FROM LAW SCHOOL. I WAS ALSO A LIEUTENANT IN THE ROTC [RESERVE OFFICERS' TRAINING CORPS]. I TRIED NINE TIMES TO ENLIST IN THE REGULAR ARMY BUT WAS REFUSED. I DELIBERATELY VIOLATED THE CURFEW, AND THEN WALKED INTO A POLICE OFFICE AND DEMANDED TO BE ARRESTED. AFTER I WAS CONVICTED IN DISTRICT COURT, I WAS HELD IN SOLITARY CONFINEMENT FOR NINE MONTHS.
Min Yasui
Gordon Hirabayashi
I HAD ATTENDED A YMCA LEADERSHIP CONFERENCE AT COLUMBIA UNIVERSITY AND BECOME A QUAKER. I TURNED MYSELF IN TO THE FBI IN WASHINGTON TO CREATE A TEST CASE. I WAS HELD WITHOUT BAIL FOR FIVE MONTHS AND THEN CONVICTED IN A TRIAL WHERE THE JURY DELIBERATED FOR ALL OF TEN MINUTES.
I WORKED AT THE CALIFORNIA MOTOR VEHICLES DEPARTMENT AND PASSED A BACKGROUND CHECK. I WAS FIRED ANYWAY. WHEN I JOINED A LAWSUIT THAT SAID I COULD NOT BE DENIED EMPLOYMENT AS A LOYAL AMERICAN, I WAS SENT TO TULE LAKE, THE WORST OF THE CAMPS. THEY TOLD ME I WOULD BE TRANSFERRED, MAYBE EVEN RELEASED, IF I DROPPED THE LAWSUIT, BUT I REFUSED.
Mitsuye Endo
Fred Korematsu
I WAS WORKING AS A WELDER IN A SHIPYARD BUT WAS FIRED AFTER PEARL HARBOR. MY REASON FOR REFUSING TO REGISTER...I DIDN'T WANT TO BE SEPARATED FROM MY ITALIAN AMERICAN GIRLFRIEND.
ALL FOUR CASES ENDED UP IN THE SUPREME COURT.

THE HIRABAYASHI AND YASUI CASES WERE DECIDED IN 1943 BUT ONLY ON WHETHER THE GOVERNMENT HAD THE RIGHT TO SET A CURFEW, NOT WHETHER IT WAS CONSTITUTIONAL TO INTERN AMERICAN CITIZENS WHO HAD NOT BEEN CONVICTED, OR EVEN ACCUSED, OF ANY CRIME.

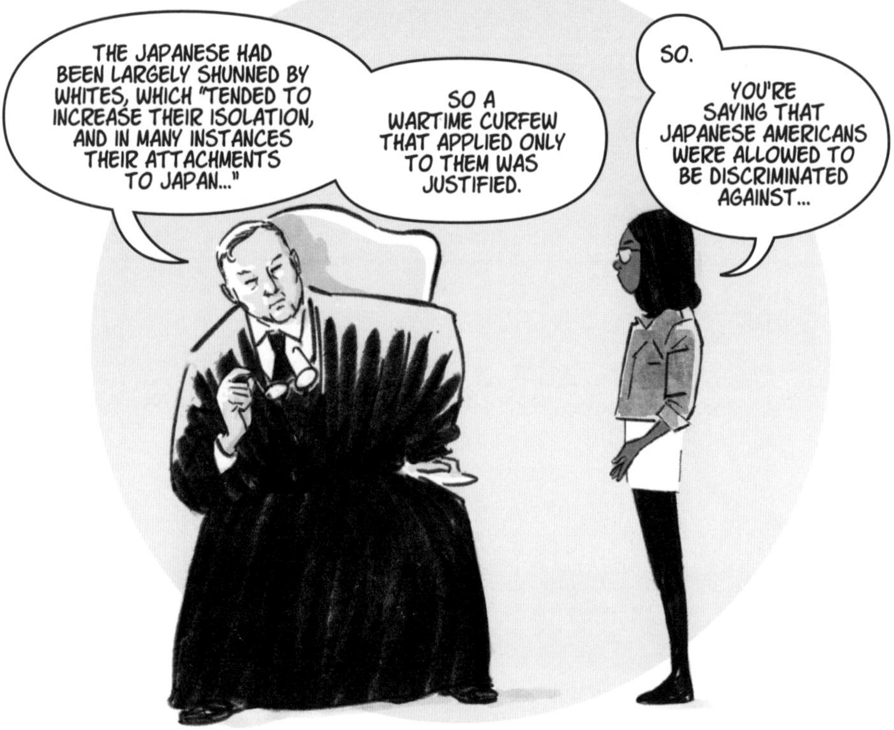
THE JAPANESE HAD BEEN LARGELY SHUNNED BY WHITES, WHICH "TENDED TO INCREASE THEIR ISOLATION, AND IN MANY INSTANCES THEIR ATTACHMENTS TO JAPAN..."
SO A WARTIME CURFEW THAT APPLIED ONLY TO THEM WAS JUSTIFIED.
SO.
YOU'RE SAYING THAT JAPANESE AMERICANS WERE ALLOWED TO BE DISCRIMINATED AGAINST...

Chief Justice Harlan Fiske Stone

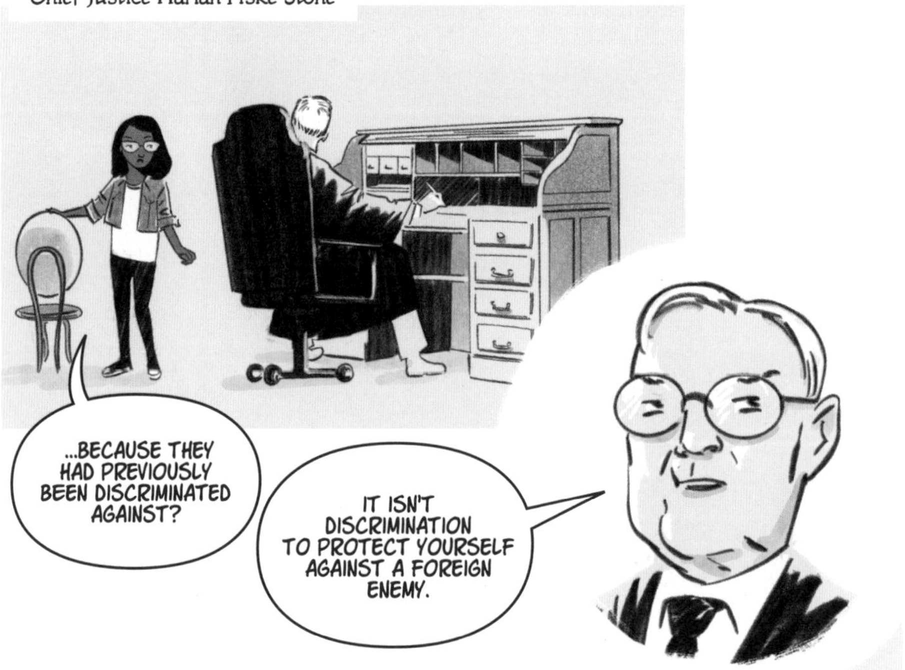
...BECAUSE THEY HAD PREVIOUSLY BEEN DISCRIMINATED AGAINST?
IT ISN'T DISCRIMINATION TO PROTECT YOURSELF AGAINST A FOREIGN ENEMY.

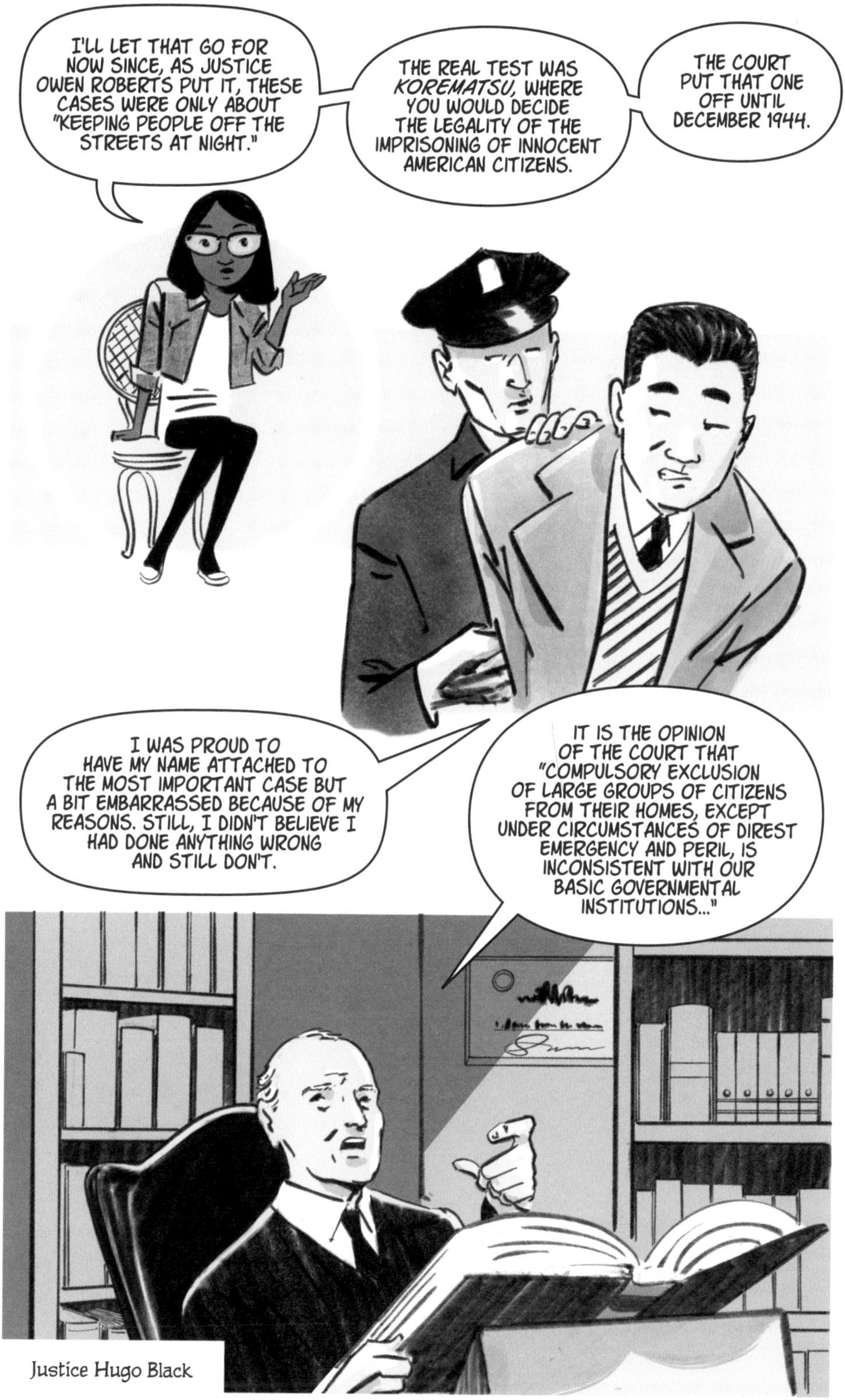
I'LL LET THAT GO FOR NOW SINCE, AS JUSTICE OWEN ROBERTS PUT IT, THESE CASES WERE ONLY ABOUT "KEEPING PEOPLE OFF THE STREETS AT NIGHT."
THE REAL TEST WAS *KOREMATSU*, WHERE YOU WOULD DECIDE THE LEGALITY OF THE IMPRISONING OF INNOCENT AMERICAN CITIZENS.
THE COURT PUT THAT ONE OFF UNTIL DECEMBER 1944.
I WAS PROUD TO HAVE MY NAME ATTACHED TO THE MOST IMPORTANT CASE BUT A BIT EMBARRASSED BECAUSE OF MY REASONS. STILL, I DIDN'T BELIEVE I HAD DONE ANYTHING WRONG AND STILL DON'T.
IT IS THE OPINION OF THE COURT THAT "COMPULSORY EXCLUSION OF LARGE GROUPS OF CITIZENS FROM THEIR HOMES, EXCEPT UNDER CIRCUMSTANCES OF DIREST EMERGENCY AND PERIL, IS INCONSISTENT WITH OUR BASIC GOVERNMENTAL INSTITUTIONS..."
Justice Hugo Black

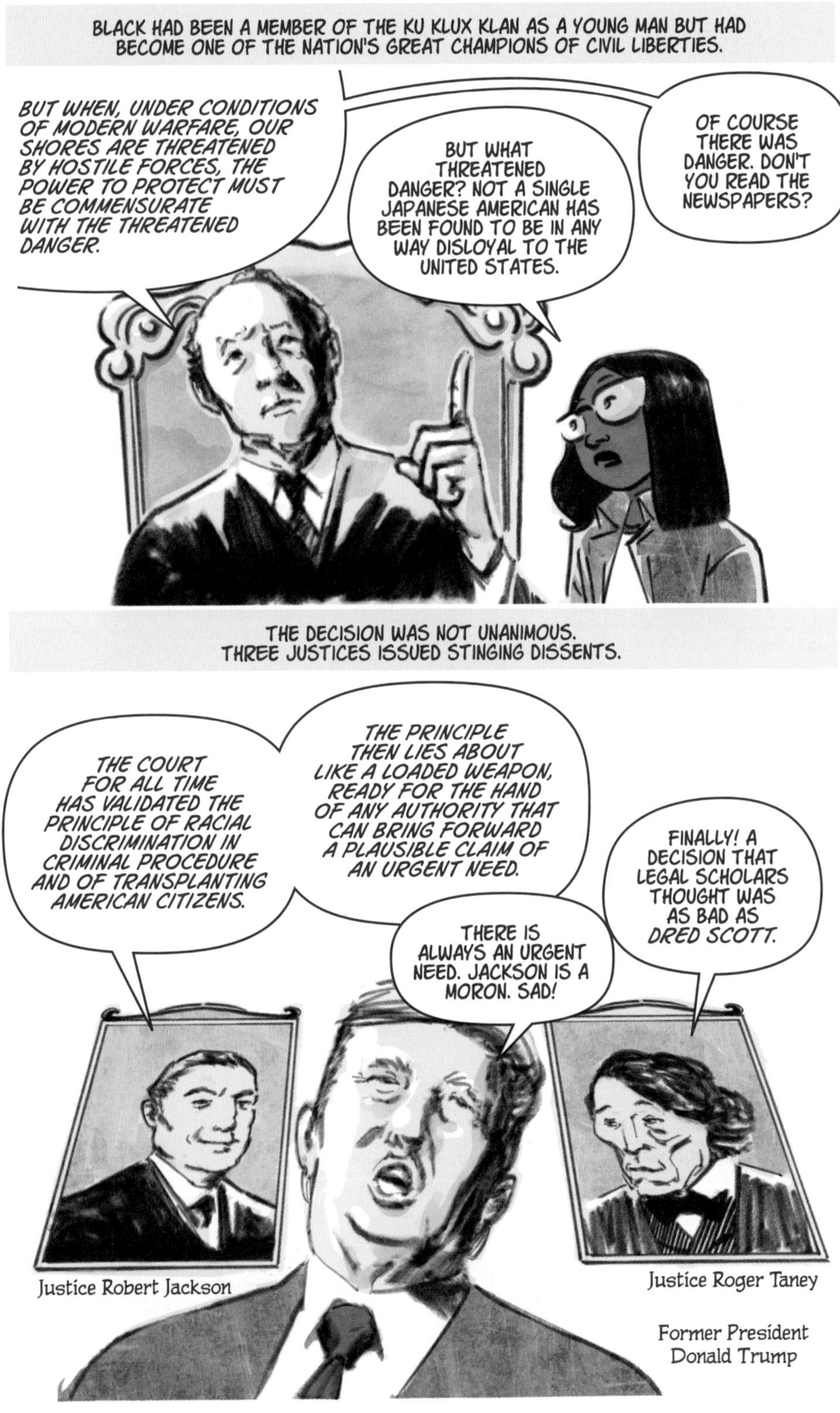
BLACK HAD BEEN A MEMBER OF THE KU KLUX KLAN AS A YOUNG MAN BUT HAD BECOME ONE OF THE NATION'S GREAT CHAMPIONS OF CIVIL LIBERTIES.
BUT WHEN, UNDER CONDITIONS OF MODERN WARFARE, OUR SHORES ARE THREATENED BY HOSTILE FORCES, THE POWER TO PROTECT MUST BE COMMENSURATE WITH THE THREATENED DANGER.
BUT WHAT THREATENED DANGER? NOT A SINGLE JAPANESE AMERICAN HAS BEEN FOUND TO BE IN ANY WAY DISLOYAL TO THE UNITED STATES.
OF COURSE THERE WAS DANGER. DON'T YOU READ THE NEWSPAPERS?
THE DECISION WAS NOT UNANIMOUS. THREE JUSTICES ISSUED STINGING DISSENTS.
THE COURT FOR ALL TIME HAS VALIDATED THE PRINCIPLE OF RACIAL DISCRIMINATION IN CRIMINAL PROCEDURE AND OF TRANSPLANTING AMERICAN CITIZENS.
THE PRINCIPLE THEN LIES ABOUT LIKE A LOADED WEAPON, READY FOR THE HAND OF ANY AUTHORITY THAT CAN BRING FORWARD A PLAUSIBLE CLAIM OF AN URGENT NEED.
THERE IS ALWAYS AN URGENT NEED. JACKSON IS A MORON. SAD!
FINALLY! A DECISION THAT LEGAL SCHOLARS THOUGHT WAS AS BAD AS DRED SCOTT.
Justice Robert Jackson
Justice Roger Taney
Former President Donald Trump

IN DECEMBER 1943, AFTER SIXTY YEARS, THE UNITED STATES FINALLY REPEALED THE 1882 LAW BARRING CHINESE FROM ENTERING THE UNITED STATES. IT ALSO ALLOWED THE CHINESE TO APPLY TO BECOME NATURALIZED CITIZENS.

San Francisco Chronicle

Chinese Exclusion Act Repealed

Wright Firm Ac
Of Defective Pla

IT WAS TO WIPE CLEAN THE STAIN ON AMERICA'S HUMAN RIGHTS RECORD.

Whites Insult Chinese Again

SOME WIPING. DO YOU KNOW HOW MANY CHINESE WERE ALLOWED TO APPLY FOR VISAS EACH YEAR? A HUNDRED AND FIVE. YOU'D HAVE MORE PEOPLE AT A WEDDING.

Congressman
Warren
Magnuson
(D-WA)

EVEN ACCORDING TO THE RACIST 1924 FORMULA, CHINA SHOULD HAVE BEEN ENTITLED TO MORE THAN 2,000 NATURALIZATIONS A YEAR.

Sec. 11. (a) The annual quota of any nationality shall be 2 percent of the number of foreign-born individuals of such nationality resident in the continental United States as determined by the United States census of 1890, but the minimum quota of any nationality shall be 100.

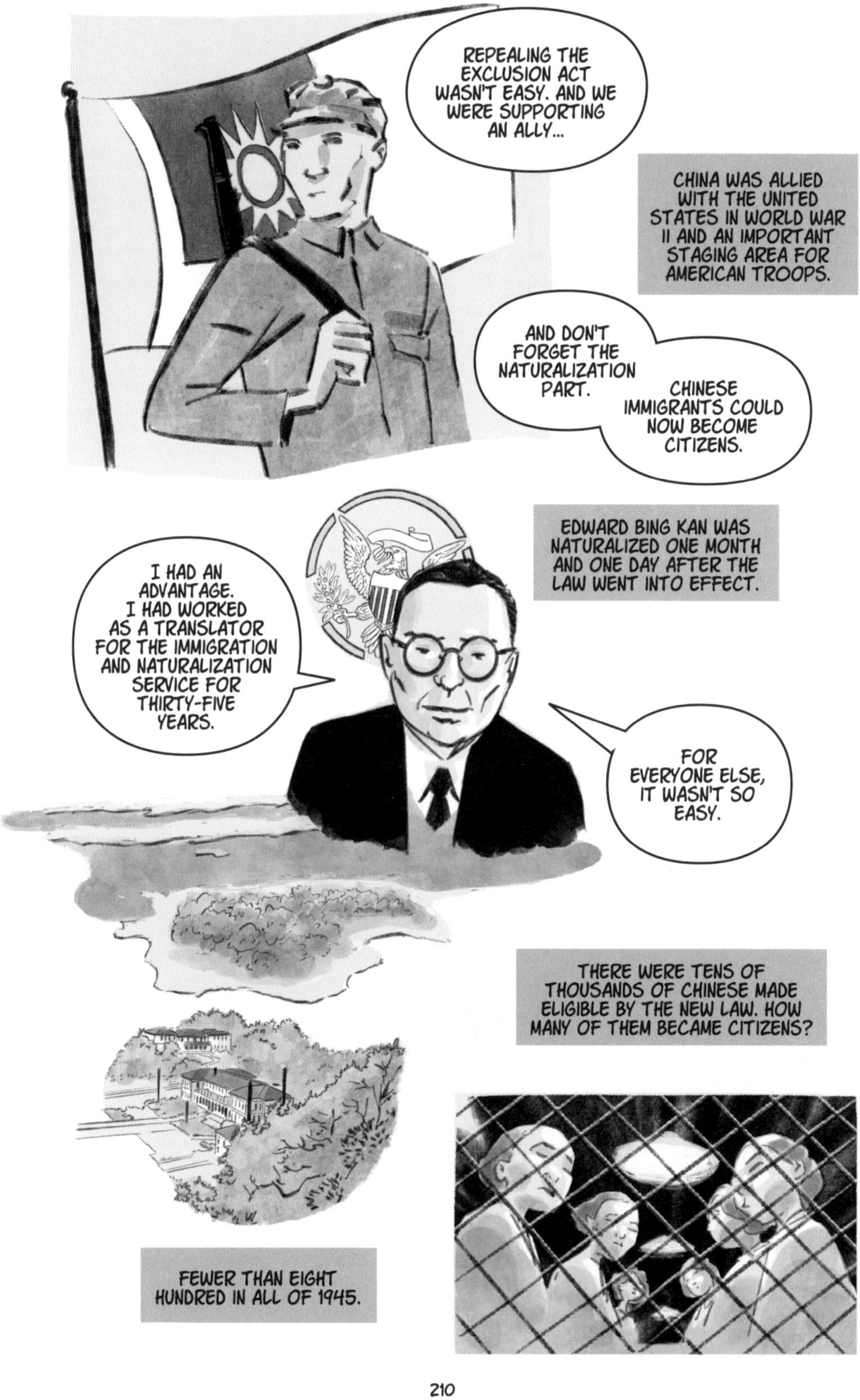

REPEALING THE EXCLUSION ACT WASN'T EASY. AND WE WERE SUPPORTING AN ALLY...
CHINA WAS ALLIED WITH THE UNITED STATES IN WORLD WAR II AND AN IMPORTANT STAGING AREA FOR AMERICAN TROOPS.
AND DON'T FORGET THE NATURALIZATION PART.
CHINESE IMMIGRANTS COULD NOW BECOME CITIZENS.
EDWARD BING KAN WAS NATURALIZED ONE MONTH AND ONE DAY AFTER THE LAW WENT INTO EFFECT.
I HAD AN ADVANTAGE. I HAD WORKED AS A TRANSLATOR FOR THE IMMIGRATION AND NATURALIZATION SERVICE FOR THIRTY-FIVE YEARS.
FOR EVERYONE ELSE, IT WASN'T SO EASY.
THERE WERE TENS OF THOUSANDS OF CHINESE MADE ELIGIBLE BY THE NEW LAW. HOW MANY OF THEM BECAME CITIZENS?
FEWER THAN EIGHT HUNDRED IN ALL OF 1945.

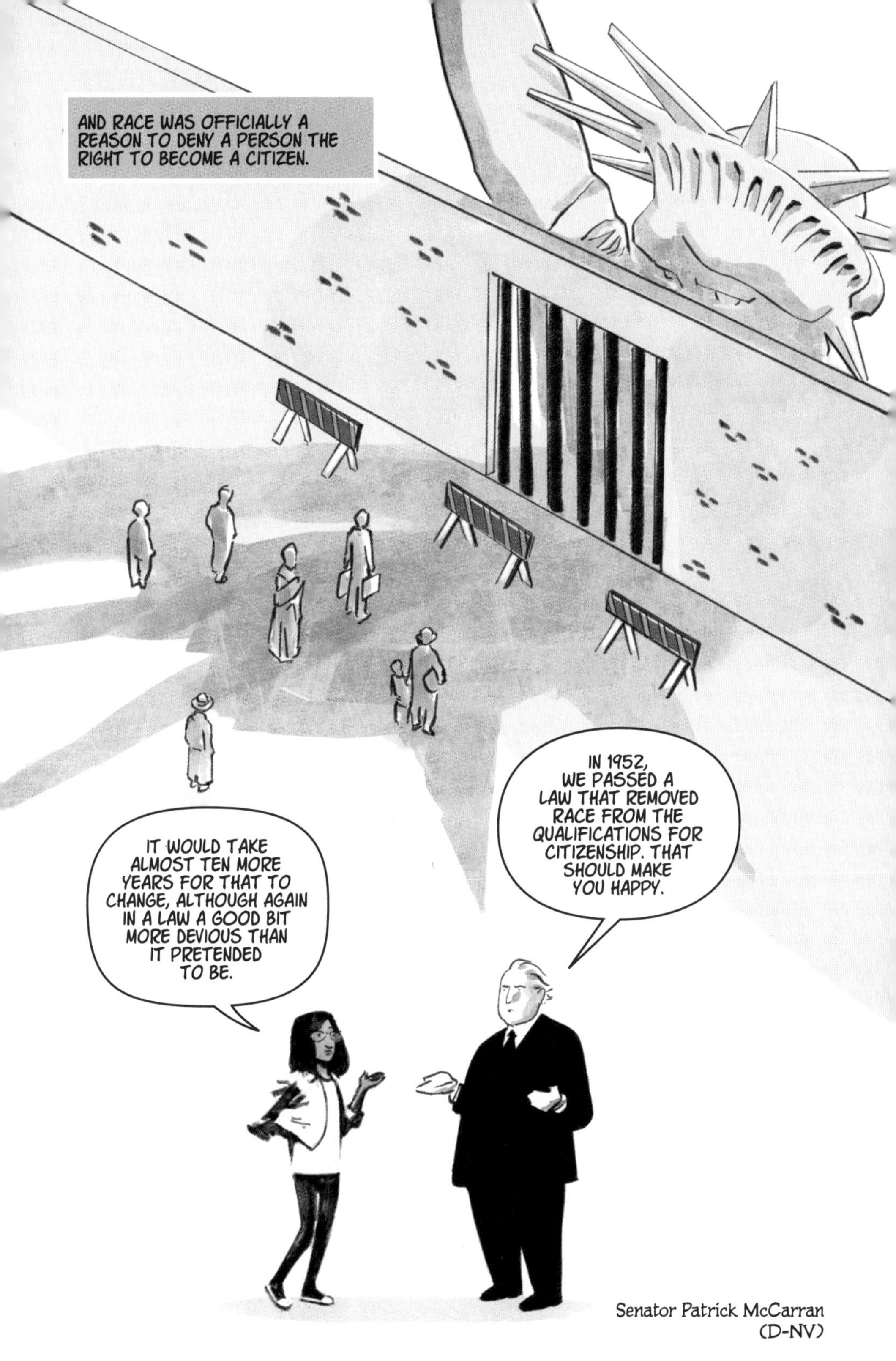
AND RACE WAS OFFICIALLY A REASON TO DENY A PERSON THE RIGHT TO BECOME A CITIZEN.
IN 1952, WE PASSED A LAW THAT REMOVED RACE FROM THE QUALIFICATIONS FOR CITIZENSHIP. THAT SHOULD MAKE YOU HAPPY.
IT WOULD TAKE ALMOST TEN MORE YEARS FOR THAT TO CHANGE, ALTHOUGH AGAIN IN A LAW A GOOD BIT MORE DEVIOUS THAN IT PRETENDED TO BE.
Senator Patrick McCarran (D-NV)

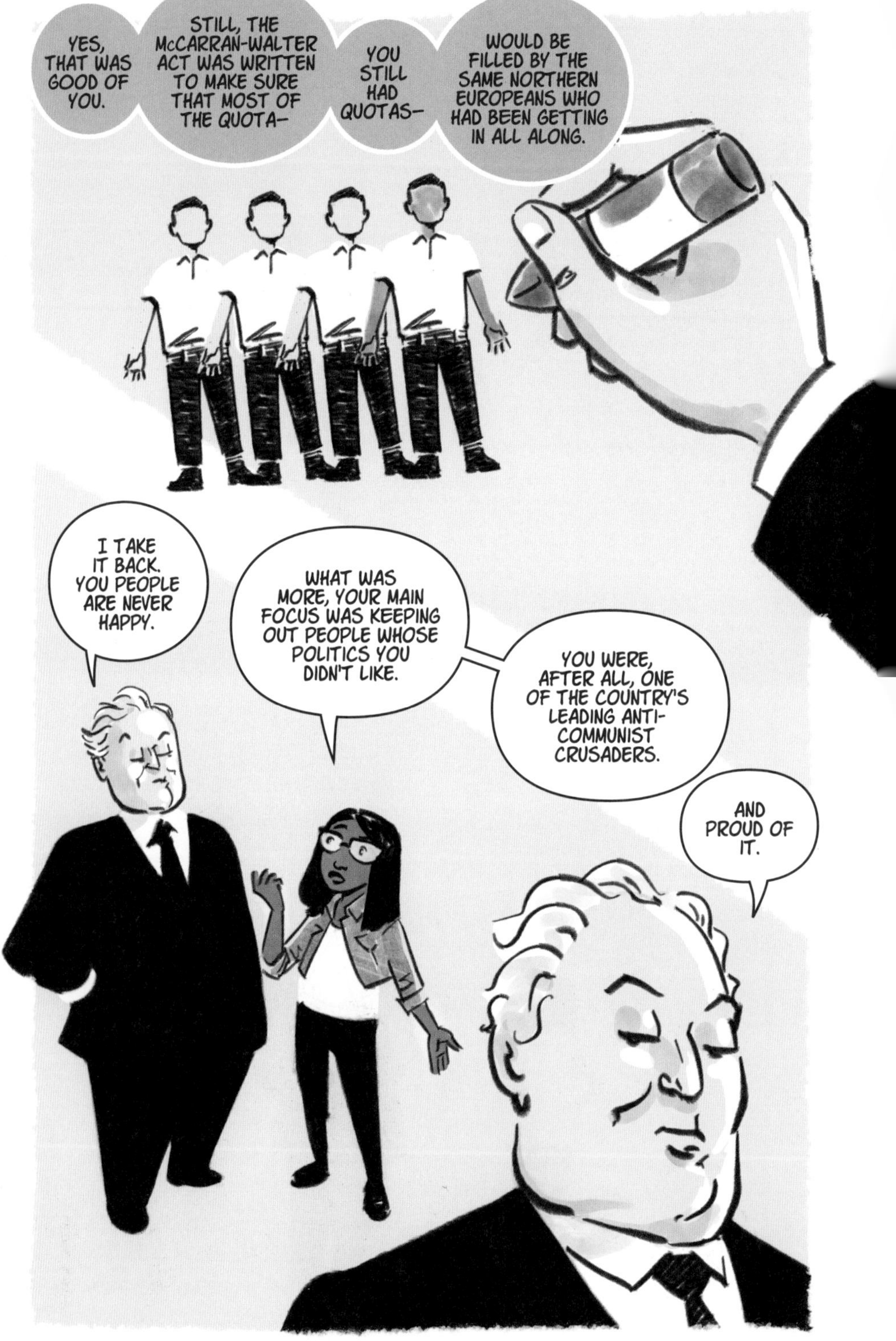
YES, THAT WAS GOOD OF YOU.
STILL, THE McCARRAN-WALTER ACT WAS WRITTEN TO MAKE SURE THAT MOST OF THE QUOTA–
YOU STILL HAD QUOTAS–
WOULD BE FILLED BY THE SAME NORTHERN EUROPEANS WHO HAD BEEN GETTING IN ALL ALONG.
I TAKE IT BACK. YOU PEOPLE ARE NEVER HAPPY.
WHAT WAS MORE, YOUR MAIN FOCUS WAS KEEPING OUT PEOPLE WHOSE POLITICS YOU DIDN'T LIKE.
YOU WERE, AFTER ALL, ONE OF THE COUNTRY'S LEADING ANTI-COMMUNIST CRUSADERS.
AND PROUD OF IT.

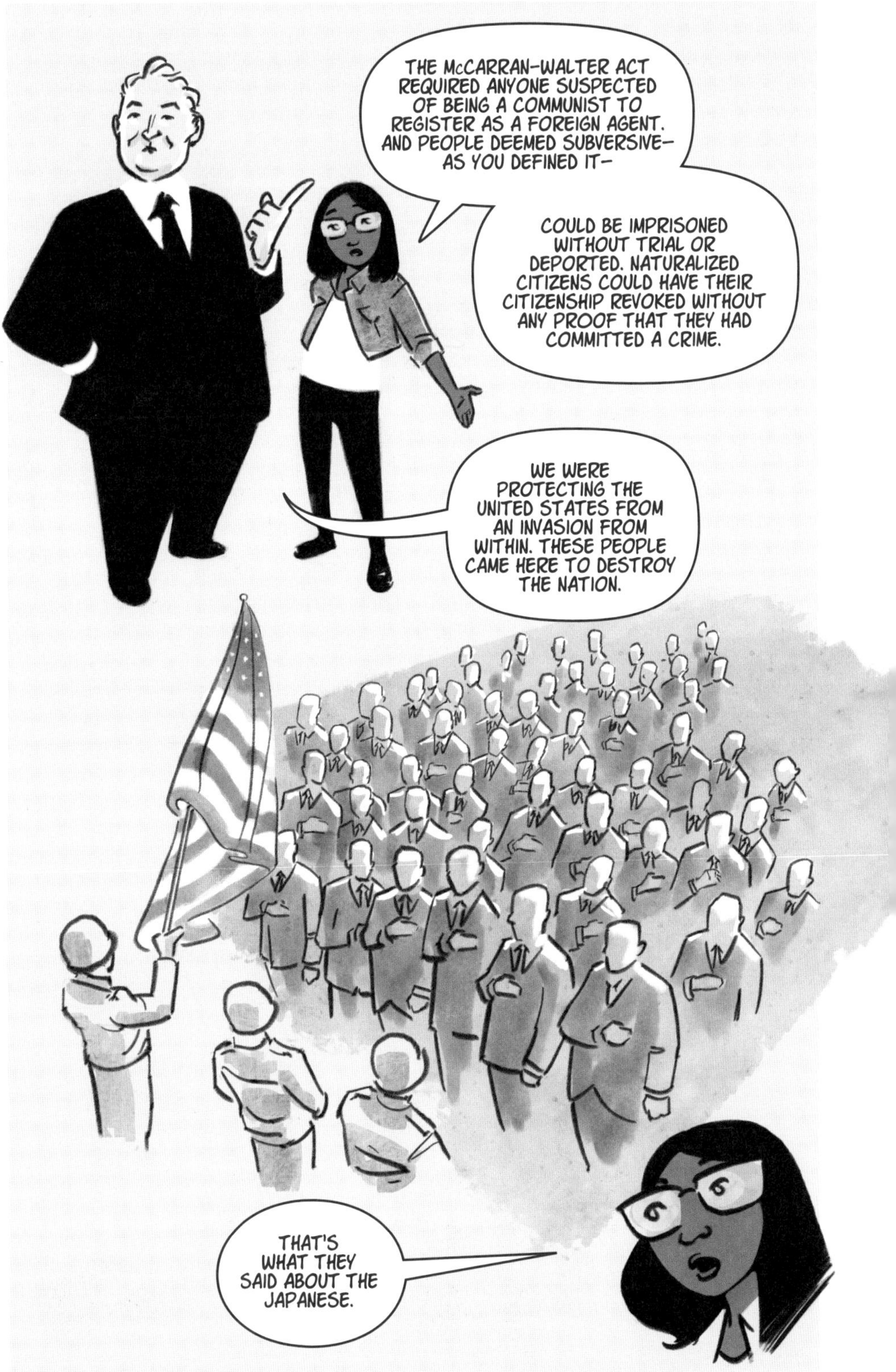
THE McCARRAN-WALTER ACT REQUIRED ANYONE SUSPECTED OF BEING A COMMUNIST TO REGISTER AS A FOREIGN AGENT. AND PEOPLE DEEMED SUBVERSIVE— AS YOU DEFINED IT—
COULD BE IMPRISONED WITHOUT TRIAL OR DEPORTED. NATURALIZED CITIZENS COULD HAVE THEIR CITIZENSHIP REVOKED WITHOUT ANY PROOF THAT THEY HAD COMMITTED A CRIME.
WE WERE PROTECTING THE UNITED STATES FROM AN INVASION FROM WITHIN. THESE PEOPLE CAME HERE TO DESTROY THE NATION.
THAT'S WHAT THEY SAID ABOUT THE JAPANESE.

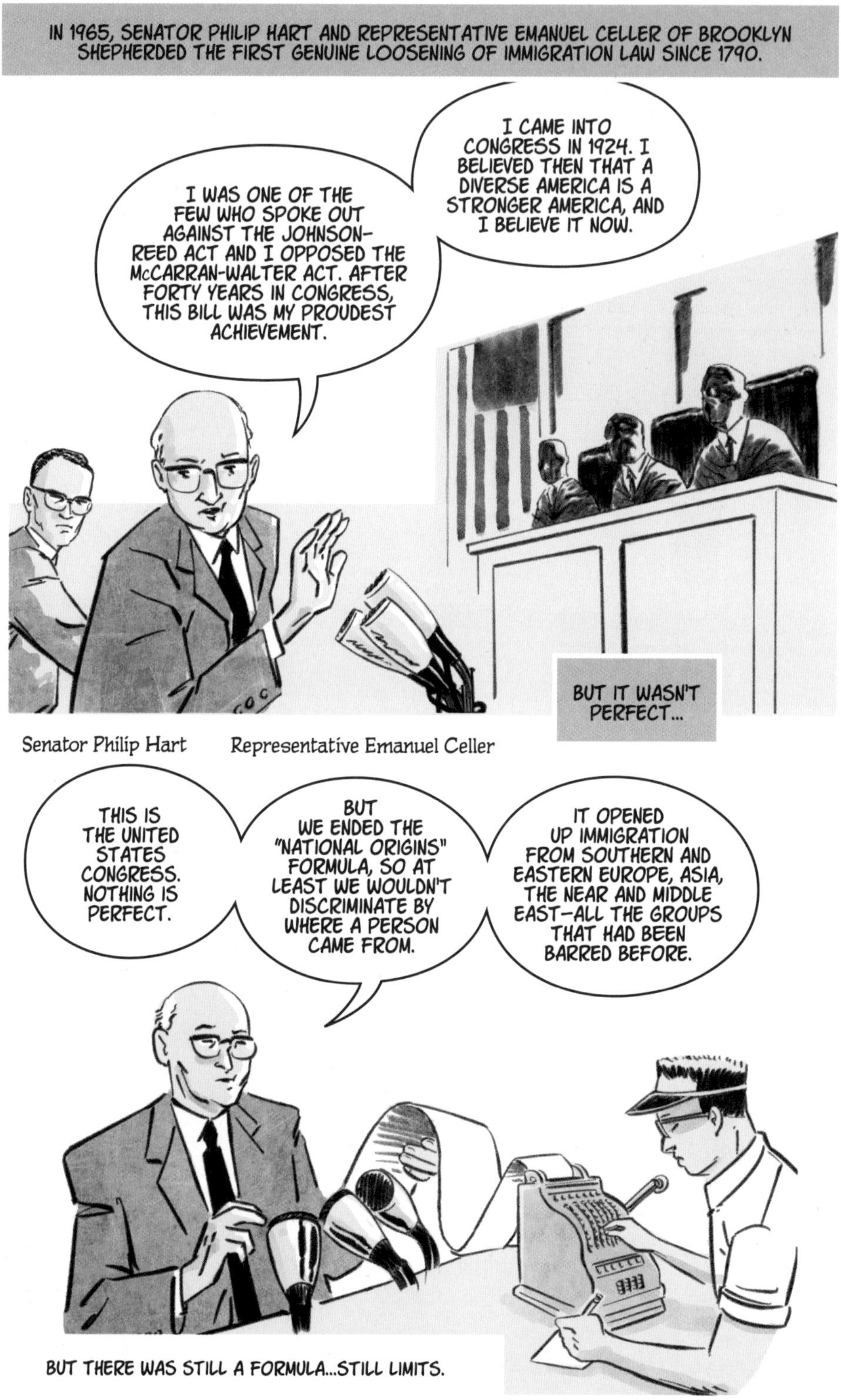
IN 1965, SENATOR PHILIP HART AND REPRESENTATIVE EMANUEL CELLER OF BROOKLYN SHEPHERDED THE FIRST GENUINE LOOSENING OF IMMIGRATION LAW SINCE 1790.
I WAS ONE OF THE FEW WHO SPOKE OUT AGAINST THE JOHNSON-REED ACT AND I OPPOSED THE McCARRAN-WALTER ACT. AFTER FORTY YEARS IN CONGRESS, THIS BILL WAS MY PROUDEST ACHIEVEMENT.
I CAME INTO CONGRESS IN 1924. I BELIEVED THEN THAT A DIVERSE AMERICA IS A STRONGER AMERICA, AND I BELIEVE IT NOW.
BUT IT WASN'T PERFECT...
Senator Philip Hart
Representative Emanuel Celler
THIS IS THE UNITED STATES CONGRESS. NOTHING IS PERFECT.
BUT WE ENDED THE "NATIONAL ORIGINS" FORMULA, SO AT LEAST WE WOULDN'T DISCRIMINATE BY WHERE A PERSON CAME FROM.
IT OPENED UP IMMIGRATION FROM SOUTHERN AND EASTERN EUROPE, ASIA, THE NEAR AND MIDDLE EAST—ALL THE GROUPS THAT HAD BEEN BARRED BEFORE.
BUT THERE WAS STILL A FORMULA...STILL LIMITS.

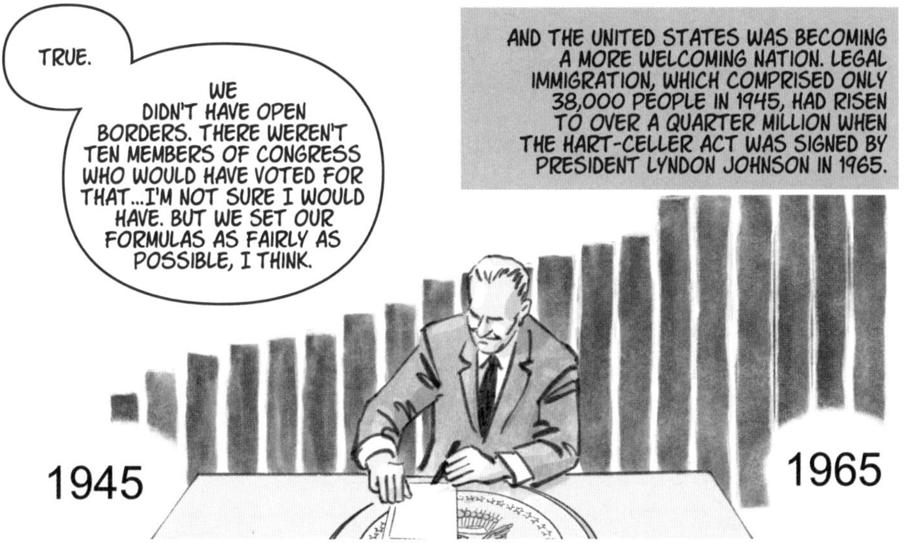
TRUE.
WE DIDN'T HAVE OPEN BORDERS. THERE WEREN'T TEN MEMBERS OF CONGRESS WHO WOULD HAVE VOTED FOR THAT...I'M NOT SURE I WOULD HAVE. BUT WE SET OUR FORMULAS AS FAIRLY AS POSSIBLE, I THINK.
AND THE UNITED STATES WAS BECOMING A MORE WELCOMING NATION. LEGAL IMMIGRATION, WHICH COMPRISED ONLY 38,000 PEOPLE IN 1945, HAD RISEN TO OVER A QUARTER MILLION WHEN THE HART-CELLER ACT WAS SIGNED BY PRESIDENT LYNDON JOHNSON IN 1965.
1945
1965

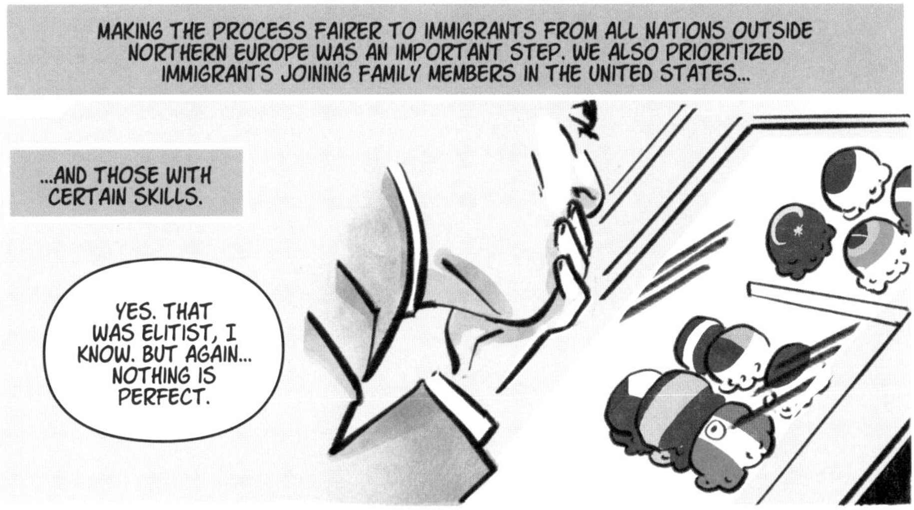
MAKING THE PROCESS FAIRER TO IMMIGRANTS FROM ALL NATIONS OUTSIDE NORTHERN EUROPE WAS AN IMPORTANT STEP. WE ALSO PRIORITIZED IMMIGRANTS JOINING FAMILY MEMBERS IN THE UNITED STATES...
...AND THOSE WITH CERTAIN SKILLS.
YES. THAT WAS ELITIST, I KNOW. BUT AGAIN... NOTHING IS PERFECT.

THE SAME YEAR, A KEY RIGHT OF CITIZENSHIP WAS RESTORED TO A GROUP FROM WHICH IT HAD BEEN STOLEN AWAY.

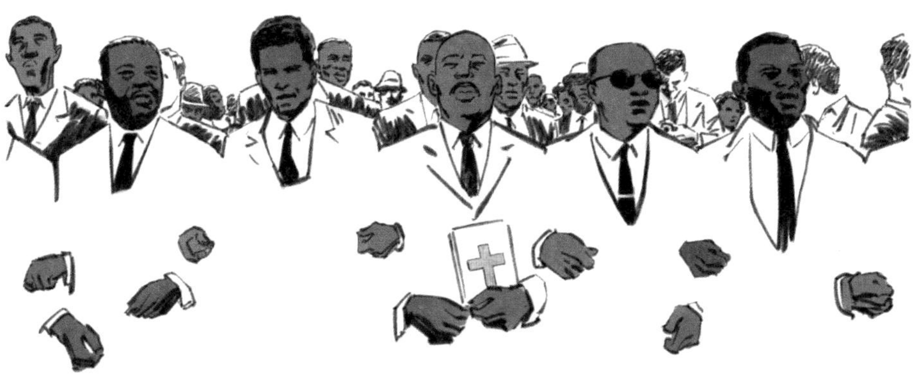

ON MARCH 7, 1965, SIX HUNDRED MEN AND WOMEN SET OUT FROM SELMA, ALABAMA, ON A FIFTY-FOUR-MILE MARCH TO THE STATE CAPITAL IN MONTGOMERY.

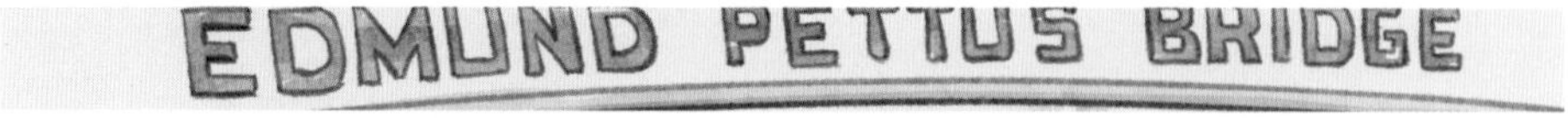
EDMUND PETTUS BRIDGE

THEY WERE LED BY JOHN LEWIS, THE TWENTY-FIVE-YEAR-OLD SON OF AN ALABAMA SHARECROPPER, AND HOSEA WILLIAMS, WHO HAD A MASTER'S DEGREE IN CHEMISTRY AND HAD BEEN WOUNDED IN ACTION IN WORLD WAR II WHILE SERVING IN GENERAL GEORGE S. PATTON'S THIRD ARMY.

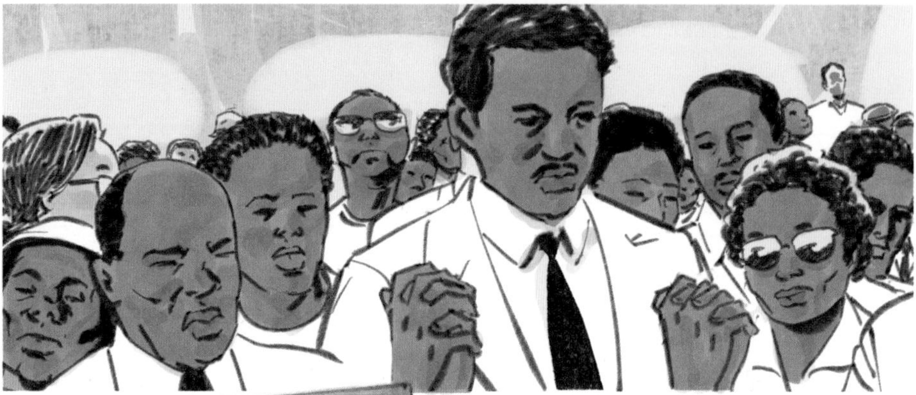

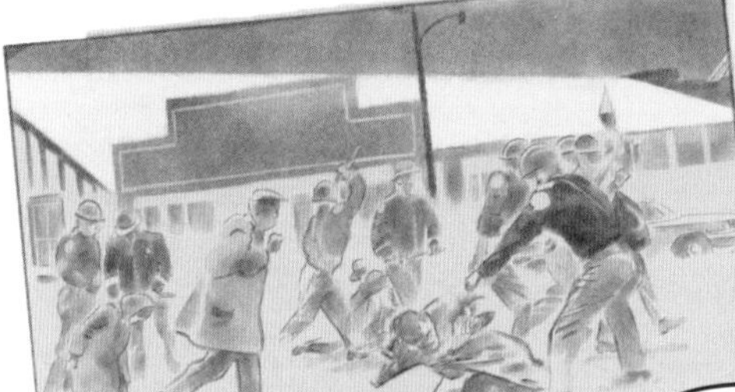

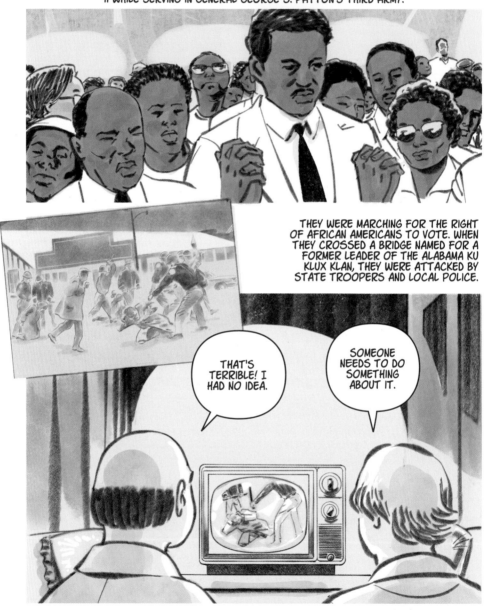

THEY WERE MARCHING FOR THE RIGHT OF AFRICAN AMERICANS TO VOTE. WHEN THEY CROSSED A BRIDGE NAMED FOR A FORMER LEADER OF THE ALABAMA KU KLUX KLAN, THEY WERE ATTACKED BY STATE TROOPERS AND LOCAL POLICE.

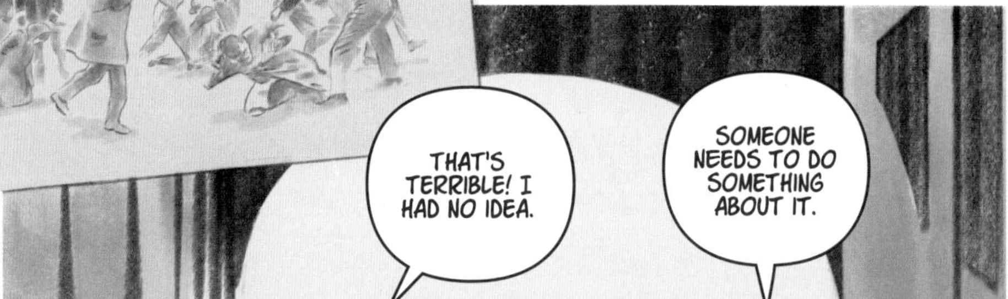
THAT'S TERRIBLE! I HAD NO IDEA.
SOMEONE NEEDS TO DO SOMETHING ABOUT IT.

THE HORRIFIC IMAGES ON TELEVISION IN PRIME TIME SPURRED OUTRAGE ACROSS AMERICA. THE FOLLOWING WEEK, PRESIDENT LYNDON JOHNSON ADDRESSED A JOINT SESSION OF CONGRESS AND DEMANDED CHANGE.

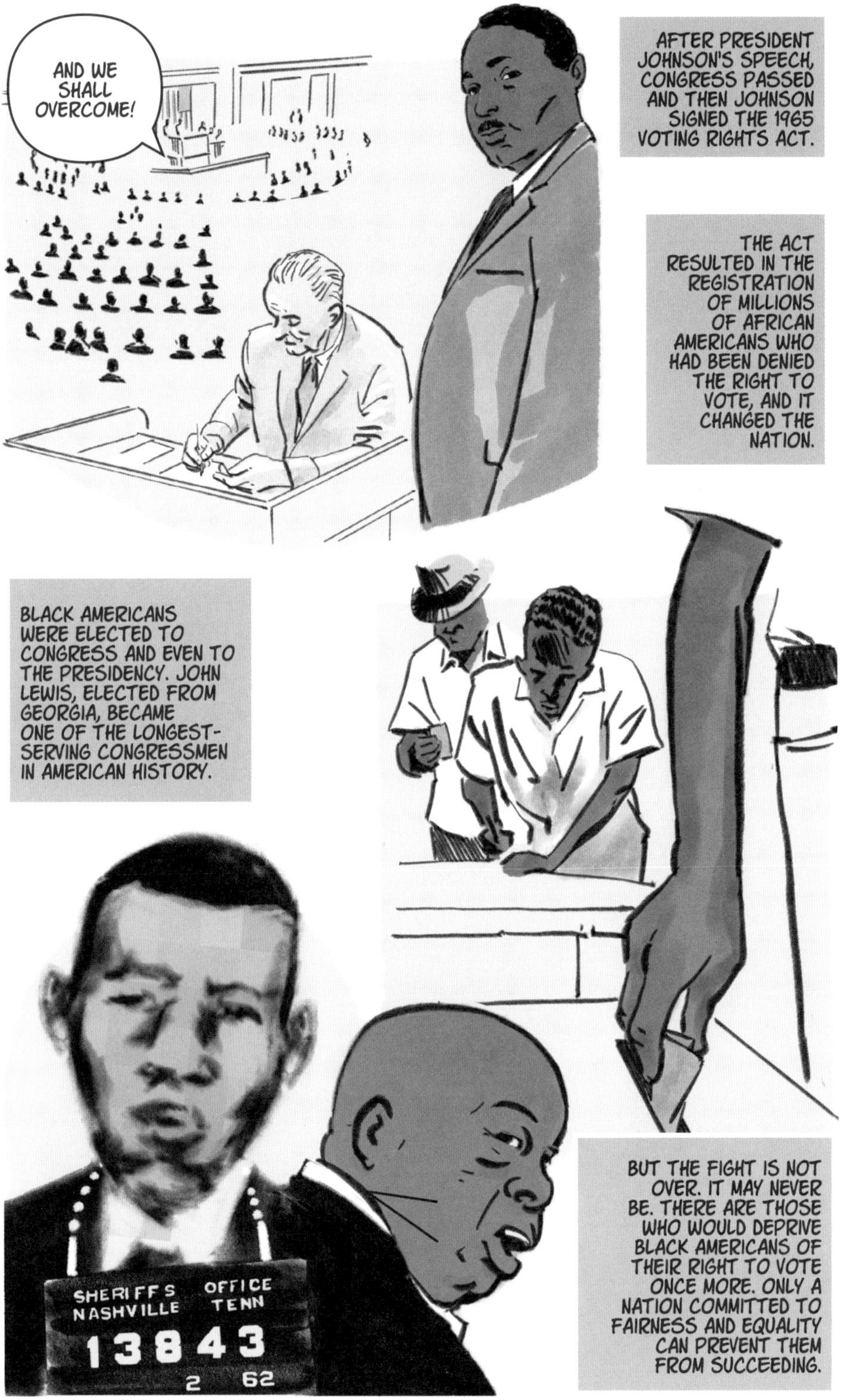
AND WE SHALL OVERCOME!
AFTER PRESIDENT JOHNSON'S SPEECH, CONGRESS PASSED AND THEN JOHNSON SIGNED THE 1965 VOTING RIGHTS ACT.
THE ACT RESULTED IN THE REGISTRATION OF MILLIONS OF AFRICAN AMERICANS WHO HAD BEEN DENIED THE RIGHT TO VOTE, AND IT CHANGED THE NATION.
BLACK AMERICANS WERE ELECTED TO CONGRESS AND EVEN TO THE PRESIDENCY. JOHN LEWIS, ELECTED FROM GEORGIA, BECAME ONE OF THE LONGEST-SERVING CONGRESSMEN IN AMERICAN HISTORY.
SHERIFFS OFFICE
NASHVILLE TENN
13843
2 62
BUT THE FIGHT IS NOT OVER. IT MAY NEVER BE. THERE ARE THOSE WHO WOULD DEPRIVE BLACK AMERICANS OF THEIR RIGHT TO VOTE ONCE MORE. ONLY A NATION COMMITTED TO FAIRNESS AND EQUALITY CAN PREVENT THEM FROM SUCCEEDING.

AFTER TWO CENTURIES OF RESISTING DIVERSITY, THE UNITED STATES OPENLY EMBRACED IT. THEN, IN 1990, PRESIDENT GEORGE H. W. BUSH SIGNED AN IMMIGRATION LAW THAT ESTABLISHED THE DIVERSITY IMMIGRANT VISA.

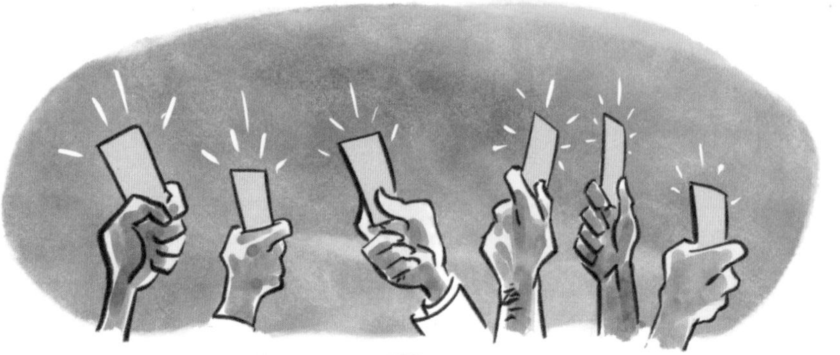

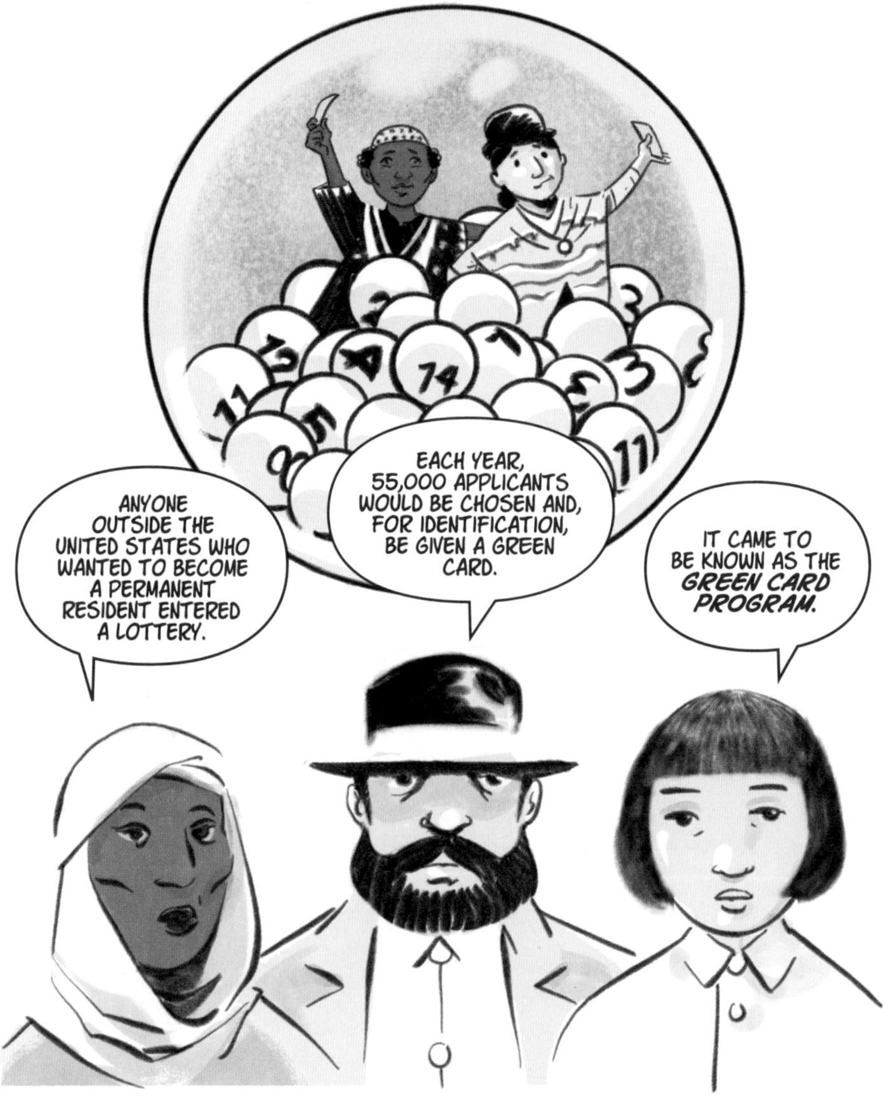
ANYONE OUTSIDE THE UNITED STATES WHO WANTED TO BECOME A PERMANENT RESIDENT ENTERED A LOTTERY.
EACH YEAR, 55,000 APPLICANTS WOULD BE CHOSEN AND, FOR IDENTIFICATION, BE GIVEN A GREEN CARD.
IT CAME TO BE KNOWN AS THE *GREEN CARD PROGRAM.*

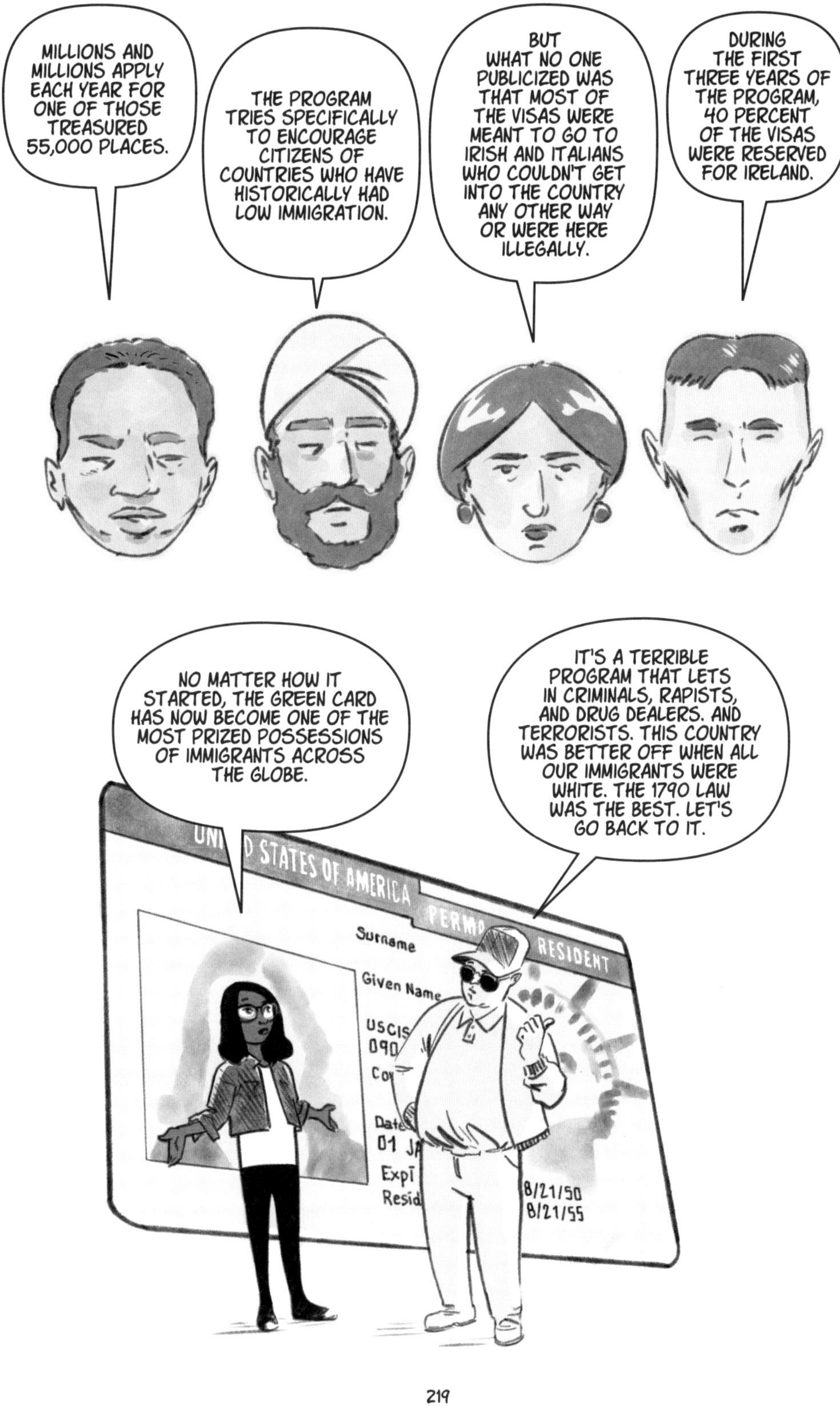
MILLIONS AND MILLIONS APPLY EACH YEAR FOR ONE OF THOSE TREASURED 55,000 PLACES.
THE PROGRAM TRIES SPECIFICALLY TO ENCOURAGE CITIZENS OF COUNTRIES WHO HAVE HISTORICALLY HAD LOW IMMIGRATION.
BUT WHAT NO ONE PUBLICIZED WAS THAT MOST OF THE VISAS WERE MEANT TO GO TO IRISH AND ITALIANS WHO COULDN'T GET INTO THE COUNTRY ANY OTHER WAY OR WERE HERE ILLEGALLY.
DURING THE FIRST THREE YEARS OF THE PROGRAM, 40 PERCENT OF THE VISAS WERE RESERVED FOR IRELAND.
NO MATTER HOW IT STARTED, THE GREEN CARD HAS NOW BECOME ONE OF THE MOST PRIZED POSSESSIONS OF IMMIGRANTS ACROSS THE GLOBE.
IT'S A TERRIBLE PROGRAM THAT LETS IN CRIMINALS, RAPISTS, AND DRUG DEALERS. AND TERRORISTS. THIS COUNTRY WAS BETTER OFF WHEN ALL OUR IMMIGRANTS WERE WHITE. THE 1790 LAW WAS THE BEST. LET'S GO BACK TO IT.
STATES OF AMERICA
RESIDENT
Surname
Given Name
8/21/50
8/21/55

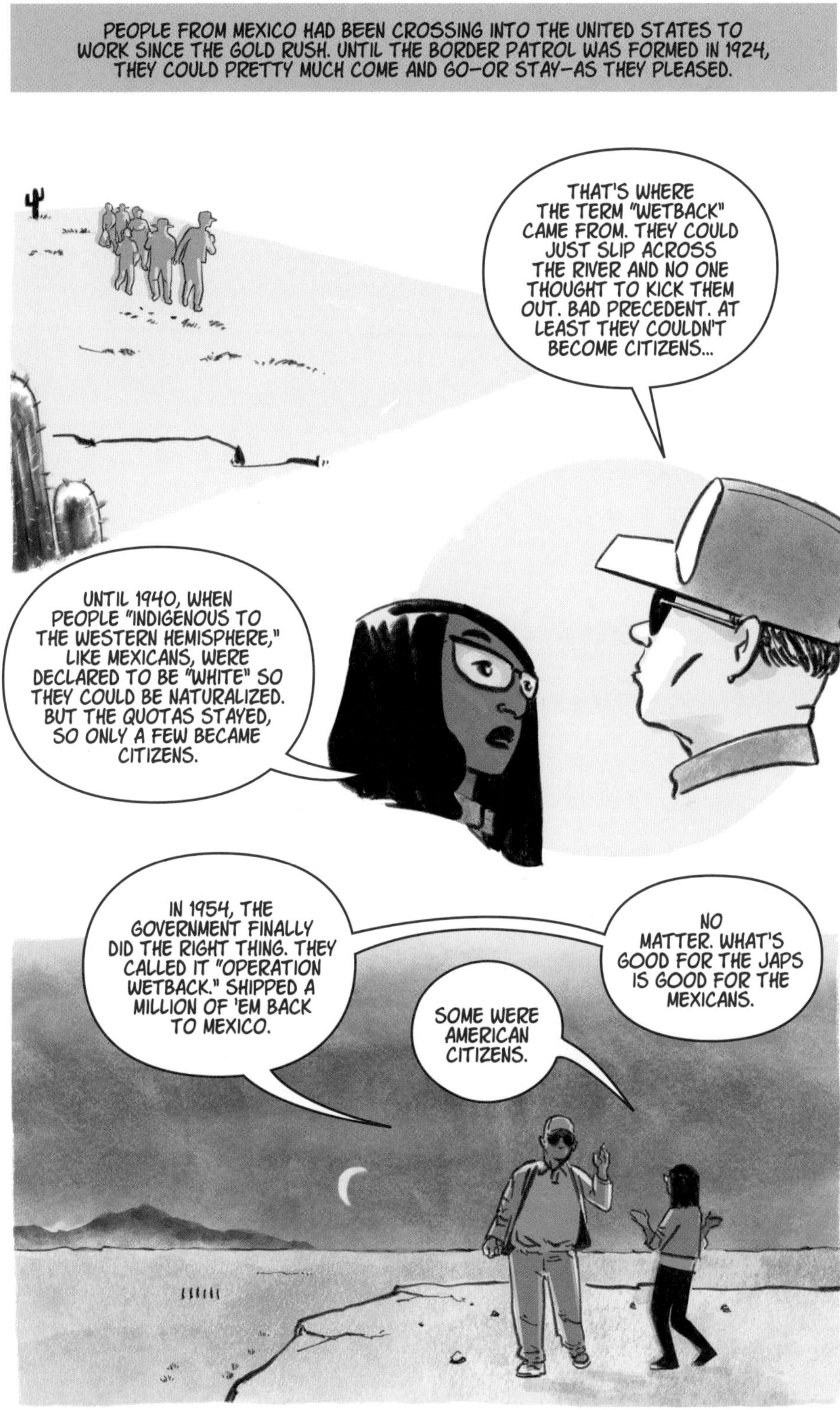
PEOPLE FROM MEXICO HAD BEEN CROSSING INTO THE UNITED STATES TO WORK SINCE THE GOLD RUSH. UNTIL THE BORDER PATROL WAS FORMED IN 1924, THEY COULD PRETTY MUCH COME AND GO—OR STAY—AS THEY PLEASED.
THAT'S WHERE THE TERM "WETBACK" CAME FROM. THEY COULD JUST SLIP ACROSS THE RIVER AND NO ONE THOUGHT TO KICK THEM OUT. BAD PRECEDENT. AT LEAST THEY COULDN'T BECOME CITIZENS...
UNTIL 1940, WHEN PEOPLE "INDIGENOUS TO THE WESTERN HEMISPHERE," LIKE MEXICANS, WERE DECLARED TO BE "WHITE" SO THEY COULD BE NATURALIZED. BUT THE QUOTAS STAYED, SO ONLY A FEW BECAME CITIZENS.
IN 1954, THE GOVERNMENT FINALLY DID THE RIGHT THING. THEY CALLED IT "OPERATION WETBACK." SHIPPED A MILLION OF 'EM BACK TO MEXICO.
SOME WERE AMERICAN CITIZENS.
NO MATTER. WHAT'S GOOD FOR THE JAPS IS GOOD FOR THE MEXICANS.

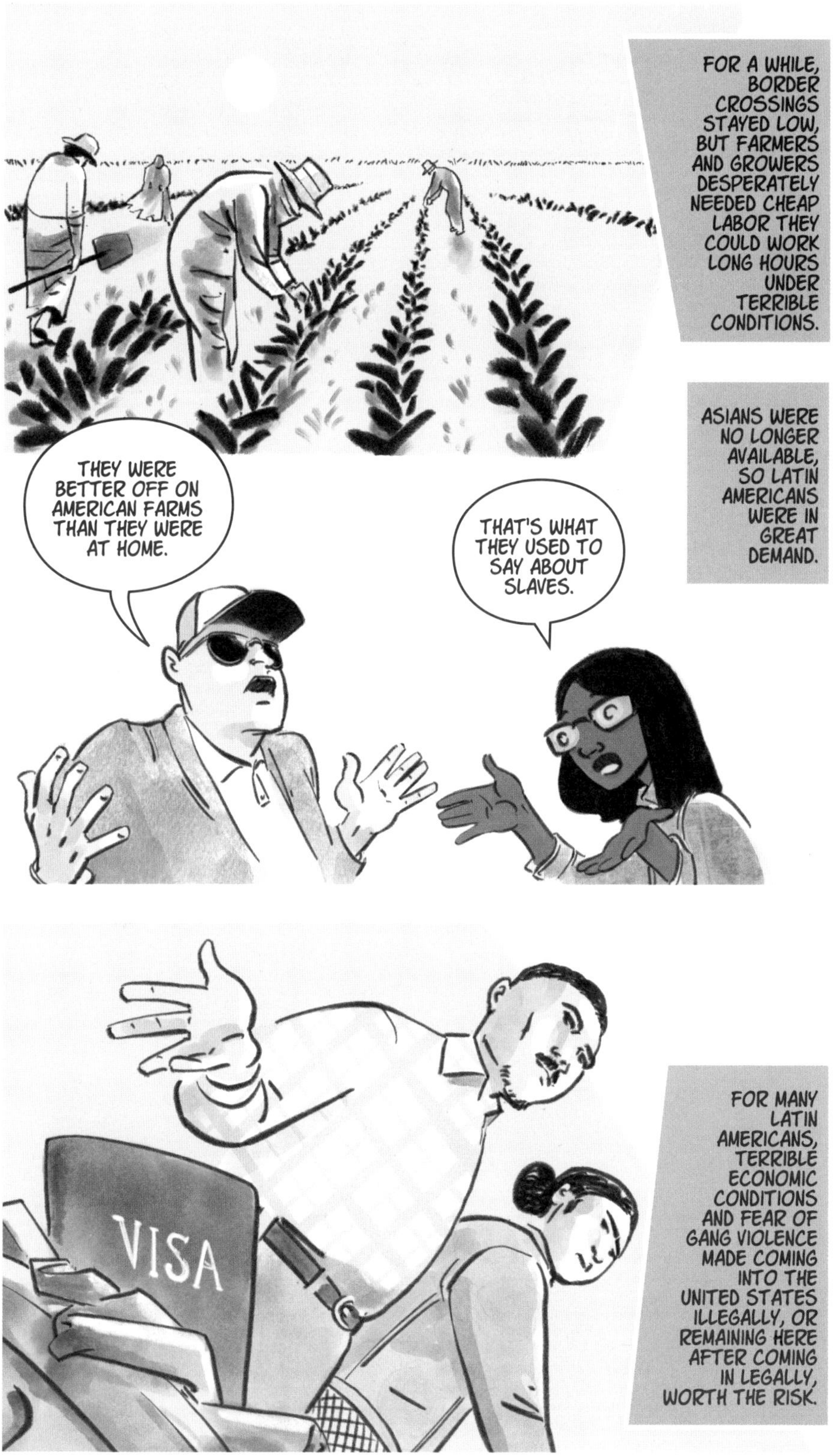
FOR A WHILE, BORDER CROSSINGS STAYED LOW, BUT FARMERS AND GROWERS DESPERATELY NEEDED CHEAP LABOR THEY COULD WORK LONG HOURS UNDER TERRIBLE CONDITIONS.
ASIANS WERE NO LONGER AVAILABLE, SO LATIN AMERICANS WERE IN GREAT DEMAND.
THEY WERE BETTER OFF ON AMERICAN FARMS THAN THEY WERE AT HOME.
THAT'S WHAT THEY USED TO SAY ABOUT SLAVES.
VISA
FOR MANY LATIN AMERICANS, TERRIBLE ECONOMIC CONDITIONS AND FEAR OF GANG VIOLENCE MADE COMING INTO THE UNITED STATES ILLEGALLY, OR REMAINING HERE AFTER COMING IN LEGALLY, WORTH THE RISK.

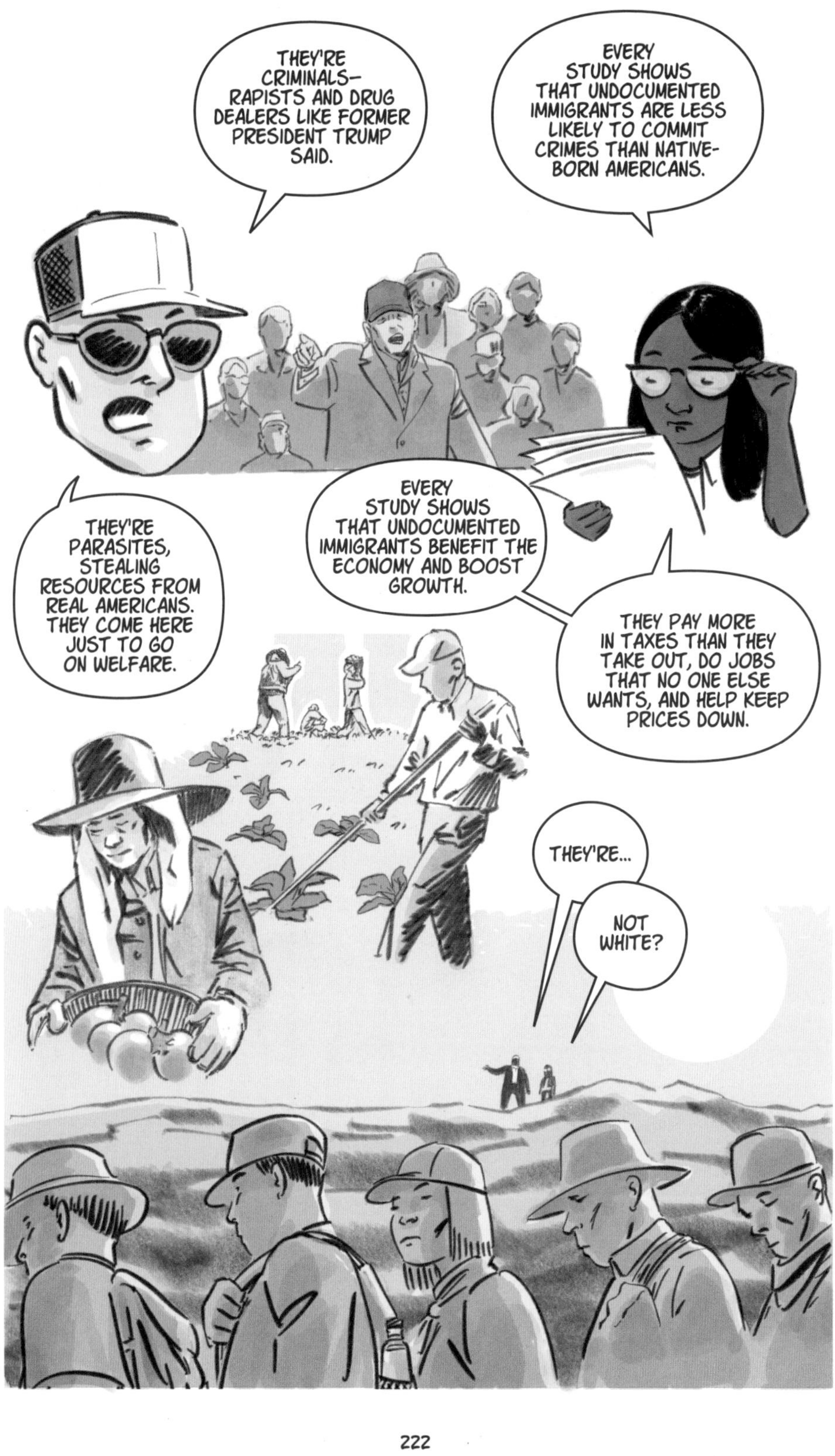
THEY'RE CRIMINALS— RAPISTS AND DRUG DEALERS LIKE FORMER PRESIDENT TRUMP SAID.
EVERY STUDY SHOWS THAT UNDOCUMENTED IMMIGRANTS ARE LESS LIKELY TO COMMIT CRIMES THAN NATIVE-BORN AMERICANS.
THEY'RE PARASITES, STEALING RESOURCES FROM REAL AMERICANS. THEY COME HERE JUST TO GO ON WELFARE.
EVERY STUDY SHOWS THAT UNDOCUMENTED IMMIGRANTS BENEFIT THE ECONOMY AND BOOST GROWTH.
THEY PAY MORE IN TAXES THAN THEY TAKE OUT, DO JOBS THAT NO ONE ELSE WANTS, AND HELP KEEP PRICES DOWN.
THEY'RE...
NOT WHITE?

IN 2012, THE DEFERRED ACTION FOR CHILDHOOD ARRIVALS PROGRAM (DACA) ALLOWED THOSE WHO HAD ENTERED THE COUNTRY ILLEGALLY AS CHILDREN AND WERE NOW BETWEEN FIFTEEN AND THIRTY YEARS OLD TO AVOID DEPORTATION FOR TWO YEARS—RENEWABLE—AND GET A WORK PERMIT FOR THAT TIME...

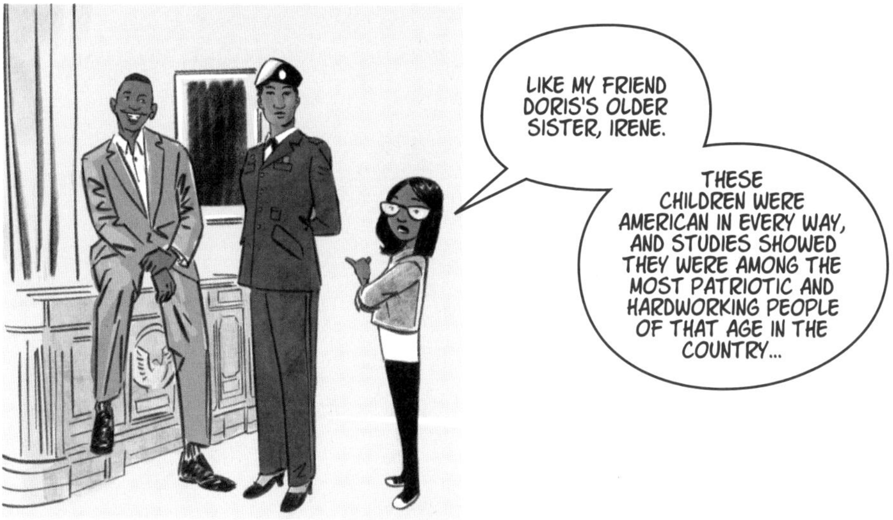
LIKE MY FRIEND DORIS'S OLDER SISTER, IRENE.
THESE CHILDREN WERE AMERICAN IN EVERY WAY, AND STUDIES SHOWED THEY WERE AMONG THE MOST PATRIOTIC AND HARDWORKING PEOPLE OF THAT AGE IN THE COUNTRY...

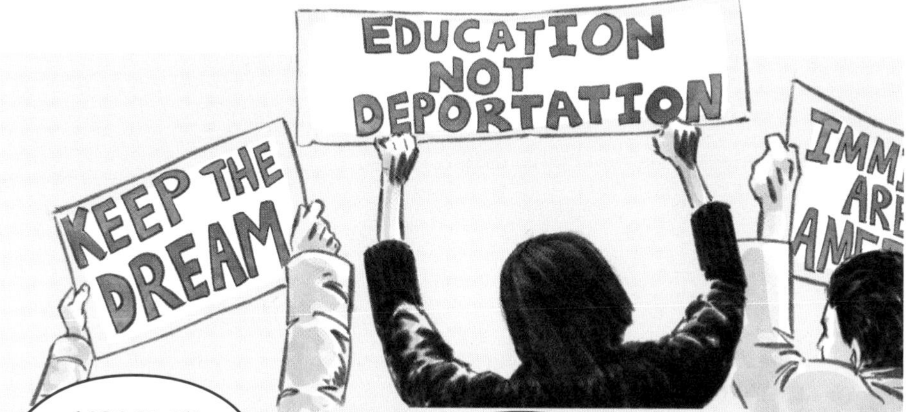
EDUCATION NOT DEPORTATION
KEEP THE DREAM

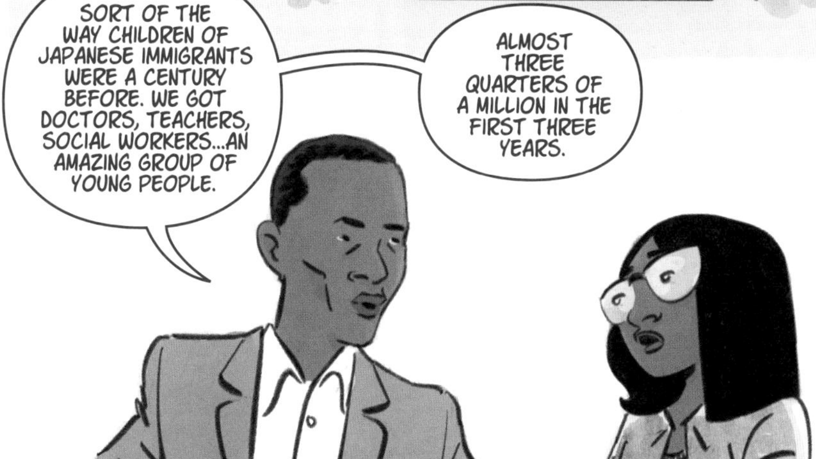
SORT OF THE WAY CHILDREN OF JAPANESE IMMIGRANTS WERE A CENTURY BEFORE. WE GOT DOCTORS, TEACHERS, SOCIAL WORKERS...AN AMAZING GROUP OF YOUNG PEOPLE.
ALMOST THREE QUARTERS OF A MILLION IN THE FIRST THREE YEARS.

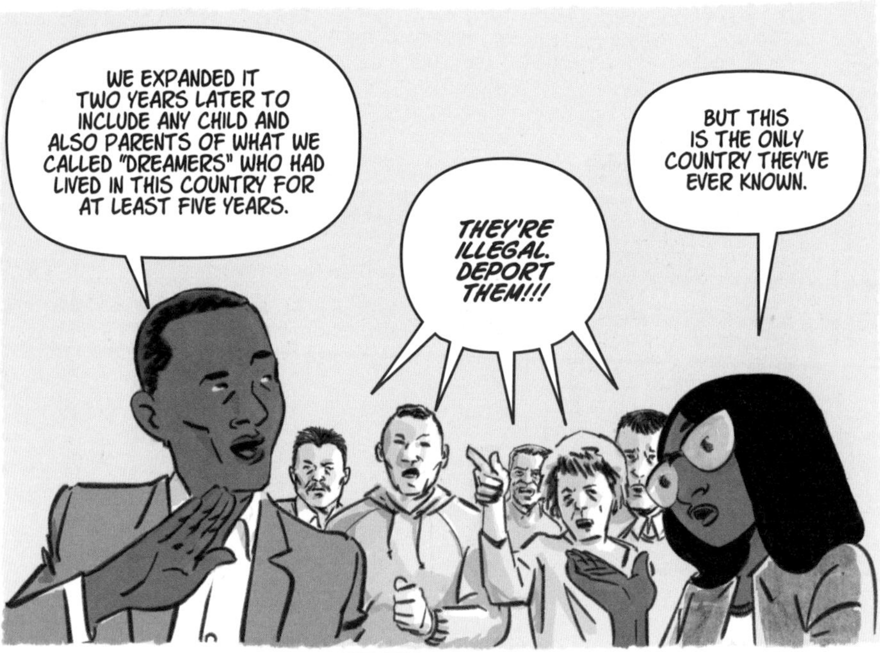
WE EXPANDED IT TWO YEARS LATER TO INCLUDE ANY CHILD AND ALSO PARENTS OF WHAT WE CALLED "DREAMERS" WHO HAD LIVED IN THIS COUNTRY FOR AT LEAST FIVE YEARS.
THEY'RE ILLEGAL. DEPORT THEM!!!
BUT THIS IS THE ONLY COUNTRY THEY'VE EVER KNOWN.

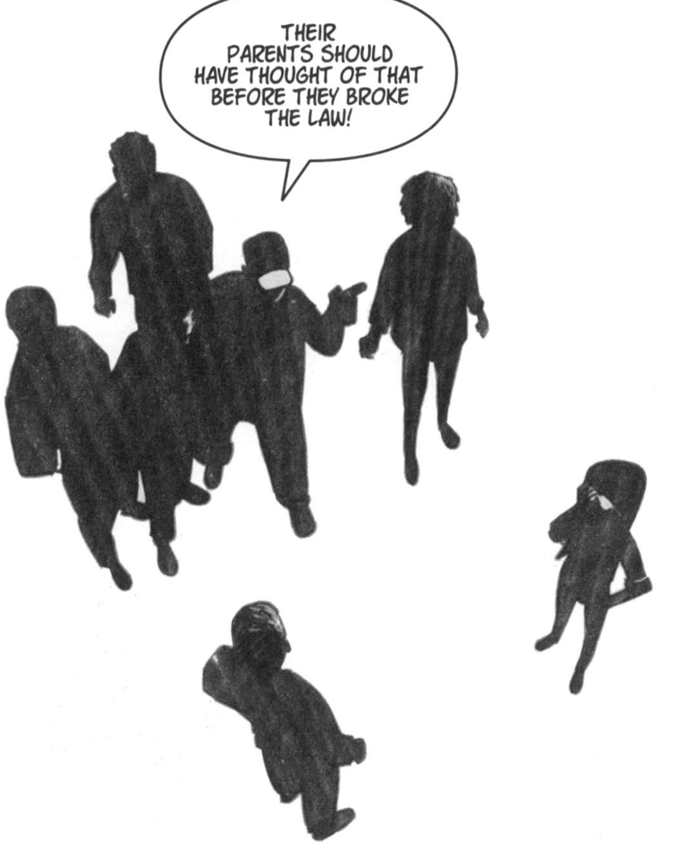
THEIR PARENTS SHOULD HAVE THOUGHT OF THAT BEFORE THEY BROKE THE LAW!

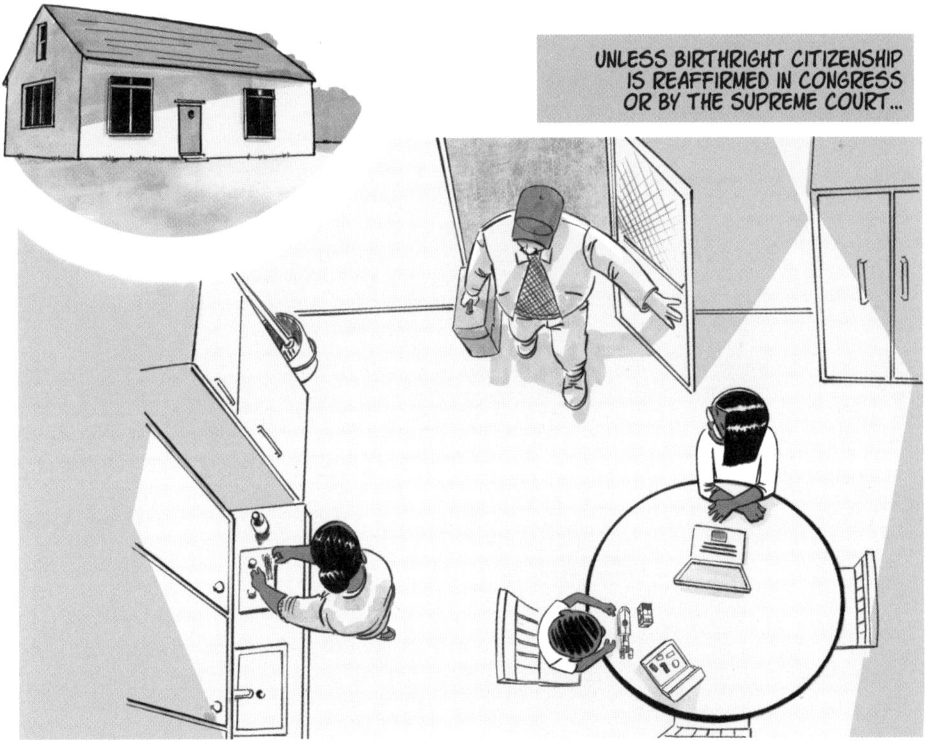
UNLESS BIRTHRIGHT CITIZENSHIP IS REAFFIRMED IN CONGRESS OR BY THE SUPREME COURT...

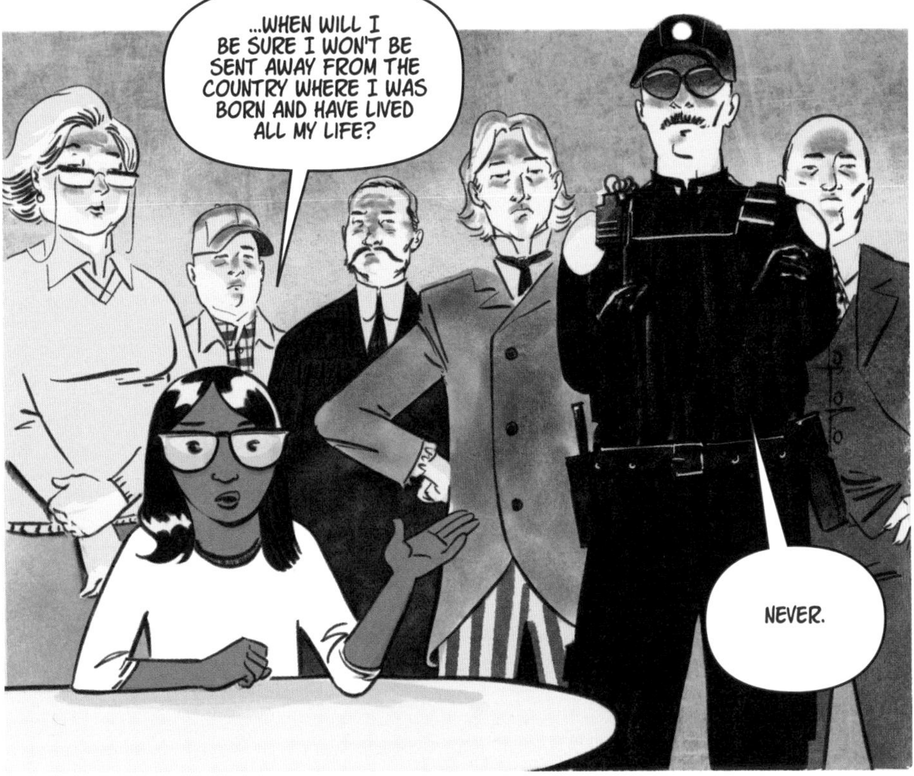
...WHEN WILL I BE SURE I WON'T BE SENT AWAY FROM THE COUNTRY WHERE I WAS BORN AND HAVE LIVED ALL MY LIFE?
NEVER.

In creating this book, the author referenced the Congressional Globe, records and briefs of the United States Supreme Court, United States Statutes at Large (available to browse at govinfo.gov/app/collection/statute), United States Reports, many primary sources collected at Newspapers.com (an online archive created by Ancestry), the Densho Encyclopedia (encyclopedia.densho.org), and the Brennan Center (brennancenter.org). He recommends all of the above for further reading!

Selected Bibliography

"Alexander Hamilton on the Naturalization of Foreigners." *Population and Development Review* 36, no. 1 (March 2010).

"An Immigrant Nation: United States Regulation of Immigration, 1798–1991," U.S. Dept. of Justice, Immigration & Naturalization Service, 1991.

Berger, Bethany R. "Birthright Citizenship on Trial: Elk v. Wilkins and United States v. Wong Kim Ark." *Cardozo Law Review* 37, no. 4 (April 2016): 1185–1258.

Bradburn, Douglas. *The Citizenship Revolution: Politics and the Creation of the American Union, 1774–1804.* Charlottesville, VA: University of Virginia Press, 2009.

Carbado, Devon. "Yellow by Law." *California Law Review* 97 (June 2009): 633–692.

Carpenter, A. H. "Naturalization in England and the American Colonies." *The American Historical Review* 9, no. 2 (January 1904).

Chambers, John S. "The Japanese Invasion." *The Annals of the American Academy of Political and Social Science* 93 (January 1921): 23–29.

Chin, Gabriel, and Daniel K. Tu. "Comprehensive Immigration Reform in the Jim Crow Era: Chinese Exclusion and the McCreary Act of 1893." *Asian American Law Journal* 23, no. 1 (2016): 39–67.

Conmy, Peter T. "The History of California's Japanese Problem and the Part Played by the Native Sons of the Golden West in Its Solution." Privately printed, 1942.

Conn, Stetson et al. *Guarding the United States and Its Outposts*. Washington, DC: U.S. Government Printing Office, 1964.

Coulson, Doug. "British Imperialism, the Indian Independence Movement, and the Racial Eligibility Provisions of the Naturalization Act: *United States v. Thind* Revisited." *Georgetown Journal of Law & Modern Critical Race Perspectives* 7 (2015): 1–42.

Cray, Ed. *Chief Justice: A Biography of Earl Warren*. New York: Simon & Schuster, 1997.

Daniels, Roger. *The Politics of Prejudice: The Anti-Japanese Movement in California and the Struggle for Japanese Exclusion*. Berkeley: University of California Press, 1977.

Fix, Michael. "Repealing Birthright Citizenship: The Unintended Consequences." Migration Policy Institute. https://www.migrationpolicy.org/news/repealing-birthright-citizenship-unintended-consequences.

Goldstone, Lawrence. *Not White Enough: The Long, Shameful Road to Japanese American Internment*. Lawrence, KS: University Press of Kansas, 2023.

Haney-Lopez, Ian. *White by Law: The Legal Construction of Race*. New York: NYU Press, 1996.

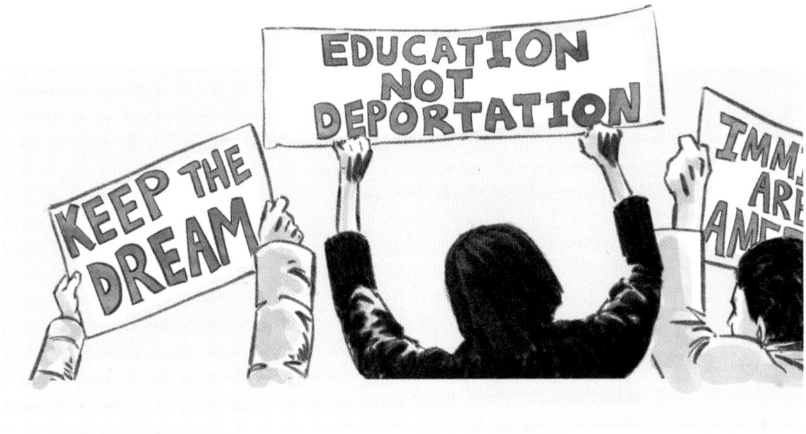
EDUCATION NOT DEPORTATION
KEEP THE DREAM

Hasian, Marouf A., Jr. "Conserving the Nation's Germplasm: Nativist Discourse and the Passage of the 1924 Immigration Restriction Act." *Legal Studies Forum* 24, no. 1 (2000): 157–174.

Hennings, Robert E. "James D. Phelan and the Woodrow Wilson Anti-Oriental Statement of May 3, 1912." *California Historical Society Quarterly* 42, no. 4 (December 1963): 291–300.

Hesson, Ted. "Can Trump Revoke Birthright Citizenship? Nearly All on Left and Right Say No," *Politico*, October 30, 2018. https://www.politico.com/story/2018/10/30/trump-birthright-citizenship-plan-900891.

Hoyt, Edward A. "Naturalization Under the American Colonies: Signs of a New Community." *Political Science Quarterly* 67, no. 2 (June 1952): 248–266.

Ichioka, Yuji. "Amerika Nadeshiko: Japanese Immigrant Women in the United States, 1900–1924." *Pacific Historical Review* 49, no. 2 (May 1980): 339–357.

Kahlan, Anil. "*Trump v. Hawaii* and Chief Justice Roberts's 'Korematsu Overruled' Parlor Trick." *American Constitution Society*. June 29, 2018. https://www.acslaw.org/expertforum/trump-v-hawaii-and-chief-justice-robertss-korematsu-overruled-parlor-trick/

Kettner, James H. *The Making of American Citizenship*. Chapel Hill: UNC Press, 1978.

Lee, Erika. *At America's Gates: Chinese Immigration During the Exclusion Era, 1882–1943*. Chapel Hill: UNC Press, 2003.

Lew-Williams, Beth. *The Chinese Must Go: Violence, Exclusion, and the Making of the Alien in America*. Cambridge: Harvard University Press, 2018.

Maclay, William. *The Journal of William Maclay*, edited by Kenneth R. Bowling and Helen E. Veit. Baltimore: Johns Hopkins University Press, 1988.

Manzella, Abigail G. H. *Migrating Fictions: Gender, Race, and Citizenship in U.S. Internal Displacements*. Columbus: The Ohio State University Press, 2018.

McClain, Charles J. "Tortuous Path, Elusive Goal: The Asian Quest for American Citizenship." *Asian Law Journal* 2 (1995): 33–60.

Nackenoff, Carol, and Julie Novkov. *American by Birth: Wong Kim Ark and the Battle for Citizenship*. Lawrence, KS: University Press of Kansas, 2021.

Ngai, Mae M. *Impossible Subjects: Illegal Aliens and the Making of Modern America*. Princeton: Princeton University Press, 2004.

Okrent, Daniel. *The Guarded Gate*. New York: Scribner, 2018.

Phelan, James D. "Why California Objects to the Japanese Invasion." *The Annals of the American Academy of Political and Social Science* 93 (January 1921): 16–17.

Salyer, Lucy. *Laws Harsh As Tigers: Chinese Immigrants and the Shaping of Modern Immigration Law*. Chapel Hill: UNC Press, 1995.

Sullivan, Casey C. "13 Worst Supreme Court Decisions of All Time." FindLaw, March 21, 2019. https://www.findlaw.com/legalblogs/supreme-court/13-worst-supreme-court-decisions-of-all-time/.

Takaki, Ronald. *Strangers from a Distant Shore*. New York: Little Brown, 1989.

Vialet, Joyce C. "A Brief History of U.S. Immigration Policy." Congressional Research Service, Library of Congress, 1991.

von Spakovsky, Hans A. "Birthright Citizenship: A Fundamental Misunderstanding of the 14th Amendment." The Heritage Foundation, October 30, 2018. https://www.heritage. org/immigration/commentary/birthright-citizenship-fundamental-misunderstanding-the-14th-amendment.

Woodworth, Marshall B. "Who are Citizens of the United States? Wong Kim Ark Case—Interpretation of Citizenship Clause of Fourteenth Amendment." *American Law Review* 32, no. 4 (July–August 1898): 554–561.

Lawrence Goldstone has written extensively on constitutional law and equal rights. His young adult book *Days of Infamy: How a Century of Bigotry Led to Japanese American Internment* won a 2023 Carter G. Woodson Book Award, and his book *On Account of Race: The Supreme Court, White Supremacy, and the Ravaging of African American Voting Rights* won a 2021 Lillian Smith Book Award. His articles, reviews, and opinion pieces have appeared in *The Atlantic*, *Salon*, *Slate*, *New Republic*, the *Boston Globe*, *Los Angeles Times*, the *Wall Street Journal*, the *Chicago Tribune*, and *Miami Herald*. Goldstone holds a PhD in constitutional history from the New School. He has also been a teacher, lecturer, senior member of a Wall Street trading firm, taxi driver, actor, quiz show contestant, and policy analyst at Hudson Institute.

James O. Smith is a writer, illustrator, graphic designer, video editor, and amateur musician. He is the artist behind *Showtime at the Apollo: The Epic Tale of Harlem's Legendary Theater*, and he is the creator of the comics *Gang of Fools* and *Black Heroes of the Wild West*. His clients have included HarperCollins and Abrams ComicArts. Born and raised in Washington, DC, he currently lives in Brooklyn, NY, where his neighbors agree that he is, indeed, an amateur musician. You can find his work at Jamesmith.org.

GRAPHIC NOVELS THAT BELONG ON EVERYONE'S BOOKSHELF

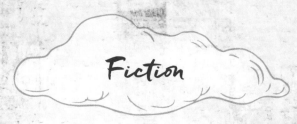

Fiction

"The best graphic novel I've read in years." —NEIL GAIMAN
SCOTT McCLOUD
THE SCULPTOR

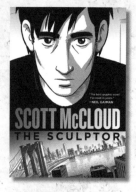

THE SCULPTOR
by Scott McCloud

HAYAO MIYAZAKI
Shuna's Journey
TRANSLATED BY
ALEX DUDOK DE WIT

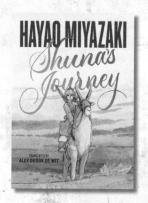

SHUNA'S JOURNEY
by Hayao Miyazaki

SH AD OW LI FE
HIROMI GOTO x ANN XU
WHEN DEATH COMES TOO SOON, FIGHT DIRTY.

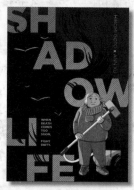

SHADOW LIFE
by Hiromi Goto & Ann Xu

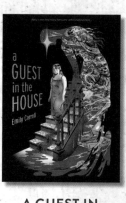

a GUEST in the HOUSE
Emily Carroll

A GUEST IN THE HOUSE
by Emily Carroll

BASED ON THE SMASH HIT PODCAST
bubble
MORRIS • MORGAN • CLIFF • RIESS

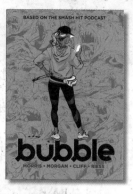

BUBBLE
by Jordan Morris, Sarah Morgan, Tony Cliff & Natalie Riess

BROADWAY
ONE
ONE WAY

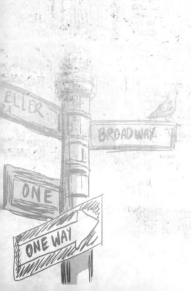

Nonfiction

**DICTATORSHIP:
IT'S EASIER THAN
YOU THINK!**
by Sarah Kendzior,
Andrea Chalupa &
Kasia Babis

ACCIDENTAL CZAR
by Andrew S. Weiss
& Brian "Box" Brown

DRAGON HOOPS
by Gene Luen Yang

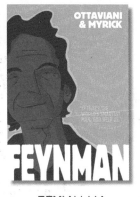

FEYNMAN
by Jim Ottaviani
& Leland Myrick

HAWKING
by Jim Ottaviani
& Leland Myrick

EINSTEIN
by Jim Ottaviani
& Jerel Dye

:01
First Second
New York
FIRSTSECONDBOOKS.COM

First Second

Published by First Second
First Second is an imprint of Roaring Brook Press,
a division of Holtzbrinck Publishing Holdings Limited Partnership
120 Broadway, New York, NY 10271
firstsecondbooks.com

Library of Congress Control Number: 2023948977

Our books may be purchased in bulk for promotional, educational, or business use.
Please contact your local bookseller or the Macmillan Corporate and Premium Sales Department
at (800) 221-7945 ext. 5442 or by email at MacmillanSpecialMarkets@macmillan.com.

First edition, 2024
Edited by Mark Siegel, Alex Lu, and Ally Shwed
Cover design by Kirk Benshoff
Interior book design by Sunny Lee and Angela Boyle
Production editing by Sarah Gompper

Penciled, toned and colored in Clip Studio Paint and Procreate.
Lettered with the Joe Mad font from Comicraft.

Printed in Malaysia

ISBN 978-1-250-79653-0 (hardcover)
1 3 5 7 9 10 8 6 4 2

Don't miss your next favorite book from First Second!
For the latest updates go to firstsecondnewsletter.com and sign up for our enewsletter.